Inside Macintosh™
Volume I

Addison-Wesley Publishing Company, Inc.
Reading, Massachusetts   Menlo Park, California   Don Mills, Ontario   Wokingham, England
Amsterdam   Sydney   Singapore   Tokyo   Mexico City   Bogotá   Santiago   San Juan

Copyright © 1985 by Apple Computer, Inc.

All rights reserved. No part of this publication may be reproduced, stored in a retrieval system, or transmitted, in any form or by any means, electronic, mechanical, photocopying, recording, or otherwise, without prior written permission of Apple Computer, Inc. Printed in the United States of America.

Apple, the Apple logo, the Macintosh logo, MacWrite, MacPaint, MacDraw, Lisa, and MacWorks are trademarks of Apple Computer, Inc.

Macintosh is a trademark of McIntosh Laboratory, Inc., and is being used with express permission of its owner.

Simultaneously published in the United States and Canada.

Written by Caroline Rose with Bradley Hacker, Robert Anders, Katie Withey, Mark Metzler, Steve Chernicoff, Chris Espinosa, Andy Averill, Brent Davis, and Brian Howard, assisted by Sandy Tompkins-Leffler and Louella Pizzuti. Special thanks to Cary Clark and Scott Knaster.

This book was produced using the Apple Macintosh computer and the LaserWriter printer.

ISBN 0-201-17731-5

BCDEFGHIJ-MU-89876
Second Printing, January 1986

Inside Macintosh
Volume I

Warranty Information

ALL IMPLIED WARRANTIES ON THIS MANUAL, INCLUDING IMPLIED WARRANTIES OF MERCHANTABILITY AND FITNESS FOR A PARTICULAR PURPOSE, ARE LIMITED IN DURATION TO NINETY (90) DAYS FROM THE DATE OF THE ORIGINAL RETAIL PURCHASE OF THIS PRODUCT.

Even though Apple has reviewed this manual, **APPLE MAKES NO WARRANTY OR REPRESENTATION, EITHER EXPRESS OR IMPLIED, WITH RESPECT TO THIS MANUAL, ITS QUALITY, ACCURACY, MERCHANTABILITY, OR FITNESS FOR A PARTICULAR PURPOSE. AS A RESULT, THIS MANUAL IS SOLD "AS IS," AND YOU, THE PURCHASER, ARE ASSUMING THE ENTIRE RISK AS TO ITS QUALITY AND ACCURACY.**

IN NO EVENT WILL APPLE BE LIABLE FOR DIRECT, INDIRECT, SPECIAL, INCIDENTAL, OR CONSEQUENTIAL DAMAGES RESULTING FROM ANY DEFECT OR INACCURACY IN THIS MANUAL, even if advised of the possibility of such damages.

THE WARRANTY AND REMEDIES SET FORTH ABOVE ARE EXCLUSIVE AND IN LIEU OF ALL OTHERS, ORAL OR WRITTEN, EXPRESS OR IMPLIED. No Apple dealer, agent, or employee is authorized to make any modification, extension, or addition to this warranty.

Some states do not allow the exclusion or limitation of implied warranties or liability for incidental or consequential damages, so the above limitation or exclusion may not apply to you. This warranty gives you specific legal rights, and you may also have other rights which vary from state to state.

Contents

1	**Preface**
3	About *Inside Macintosh*
4	A Horse of a Different Color
5	The Structure of a Typical Chapter
5	Conventions
7	**1 A Road Map**
9	About This Chapter
9	Overview of the Software
13	A Simple Example Program
21	Where to Go From Here
23	**2 The Macintosh User Interface Guidelines**
27	About This Chapter
27	Introduction
29	Types of Applications
31	Using Graphics
32	Components of the Macintosh System
33	The Keyboard
36	The Mouse
38	Selecting
44	Windows
51	Commands
54	Standard Menus
62	Text Editing
64	Dialogs and Alerts
70	Do's and Don'ts of a Friendly User Interface
71	**3 Macintosh Memory Management: An Introduction**
73	About This Chapter
73	The Stack and the Heap
75	Pointers and Handles
78	General-Purpose Data Types
81	Summary
83	**4 Using Assembly Language**
85	About This Chapter
85	Definition Files
86	Pascal Data Types

Inside Macintosh

87	The Trap Dispatch Table
88	The Trap Mechanism
90	Calling Conventions
95	Pascal Interface to the Toolbox and Operating System
95	Mixing Pascal and Assembly Language
99	Summary
101	**5 The Resource Manager**
103	About This Chapter
103	About the Resource Manager
105	Overview of Resource Files
107	Resource Specification
110	Resource References
112	Using the Resource Manager
113	Resource Manager Routines
127	Resources Within Resources
128	Format of a Resource File
132	Summary of the Resource Manager
135	**6 QuickDraw**
137	About This Chapter
137	About QuickDraw
138	The Mathematical Foundation of QuickDraw
142	Graphic Entities
147	The Drawing Environment: GrafPort
153	Coordinates in GrafPorts
155	General Discussion of Drawing
158	Pictures and Polygons
160	Using QuickDraw
162	QuickDraw Routines
197	Customizing QuickDraw Operations
201	Summary of QuickDraw
215	**7 The Font Manager**
217	About This Chapter
217	About the Font Manager
219	Font Numbers
220	Characters in a Font
220	Font Scaling
222	Using the Font Manager
222	Font Manager Routines

224	Communication Between QuickDraw and the Font Manager
227	Format of a Font
234	Fonts in a Resource File
236	Summary of the Font Manager |//

241	**8 The Toolbox Event Manager**
243	About This Chapter
243	About the Toolbox Event Manager
244	Event Types
245	Priority of Events
246	Keyboard Events
249	Event Records
253	Event Masks
255	Using the Toolbox Event Manager
257	Toolbox Event Manager Routines
261	The Journaling Mechanism
263	Summary of the Toolbox Event Manager

267	**9 The Window Manager**
269	About This Chapter
269	About the Window Manager
271	Windows and GrafPorts
271	Window Regions
272	Windows and Resources
274	Window Records
278	How a Window is Drawn
279	Making a Window Active: Activate Events
280	Using the Window Manager
281	Window Manager Routines
297	Defining Your Own Windows
302	Formats of Resources for Windows
303	Summary of the Window Manager

309	**10 The Control Manager**
311	About This Chapter
311	About the Control Manager
314	Controls and Windows
314	Controls and Resources
315	Part Codes
316	Control Records
318	Using the Control Manager

Inside Macintosh

319	Control Manager Routines
328	Defining Your Own Controls
332	Formats of Resources for Controls
334	Summary of the Control Manager |//
339	**11 The Menu Manager**
341	About This Chapter
341	About the Menu Manager
344	Menus and Resources
344	Menu Records
345	Menu Lists
346	Creating a Menu in Your Program
349	Using the Menu Manager
351	Menu Manager Routines
362	Defining Your Own Menus
363	Formats of Resources for Menus
366	Summary of the Menu Manager
371	**12 TextEdit**
373	About This Chapter
373	About TextEdit
374	Edit Records
381	Using TextEdit
383	TextEdit Routines
392	Summary of TextEdit
397	**13 The Dialog Manager**
399	About This Chapter
399	About the Dialog Manager
401	Dialog and Alert Windows
402	Dialogs, Alerts, and Resources
403	Item Lists in Memory
407	Dialog Records
409	Alerts
410	Using the Dialog Manager
411	Dialog Manager Routines
423	Modifying Templates in Memory
425	Formats of Resources for Dialogs and Alerts
429	Summary of the Dialog Manager

435	**14 The Desk Manager**
437	About This Chapter
437	About the Desk Manager
439	Using the Desk Manager
440	Desk Manager Routines
443	Writing Your Own Desk Accessories
448	Summary of the Desk Manager
451	**15 The Scrap Manager**
453	About This Chapter
453	About the Scrap Manager
454	Memory and the Desk Scrap
454	Desk Scrap Data Types
456	Using the Scrap Manager
457	Scrap Manager Routines
461	Private Scraps
462	Format of the Desk Scrap
463	Summary of the Scrap Manager
465	**16 Toolbox Utilities**
467	About This Chapter
467	Toolbox Utility Routines
476	Formats of Miscellaneous Resources
477	Summary of the Toolbox Utilities
481	**17 The Package Manager**
483	About This Chapter
483	About Packages
484	Package Manager Routines
485	Summary of the Package Manager
487	**18 The Binary-Decimal Conversion Package**
489	About This Chapter
489	Binary-Decimal Conversion Package Routines
491	Summary of the Binary-Decimal Conversion Package
493	**19 The International Utilities Package**
495	About This Chapter
495	International Resources
501	International String Comparison
503	Using the International Utilities Package

504	International Utilities Package Routines
508	Summary of the International Utilities Package

515   20 The Standard File Package

517	About This Chapter
517	About the Standard File Package
518	Using the Standard File Package
519	Standard File Package Routines
527	Summary of the Standard File Package

531   Index

PREFACE

3   About *Inside Macintosh*
3   The Language
4   What's in Each Volume
4   Version Numbers
4   A Horse of a Different Color
5   The Structure of a Typical Chapter
5   Conventions

Inside Macintosh

ABOUT INSIDE MACINTOSH

Inside Macintosh is a three-volume set of manuals that tells you what you need to know to write software for the Apple® Macintosh™ 128K, 512K, or XL (or a Lisa® running MacWorks™ XL). Although directed mainly toward programmers writing standard Macintosh applications, *Inside Macintosh* also contains the information needed to write simple utility programs, desk accessories, device drivers, or any other Macintosh software. It includes:

- the user interface guidelines for applications on the Macintosh
- a complete description of the routines available for your program to call (both those built into the Macintosh and others on disk), along with related concepts and background information
- a description of the Macintosh 128K and 512K hardware

It does *not* include information about:

- Programming in general.
- Getting started as a developer. For this, write to:

    Developer Relations
    Mail Stop 27-S
    Apple Computer, Inc.
    20525 Mariani Avenue
    Cupertino, CA 95014

- Any specific development system, except where indicated. You'll need to have additional documentation for the development system you're using.
- The Standard Apple Numeric Environment (SANE), which your program can access to perform extended-precision floating-point arithmetic and transcendental functions. This environment is described in the *Apple Numerics Manual*.

You should already be familiar with the basic information that's in *Macintosh*, the owner's guide, and have some experience using a standard Macintosh application (such as MacWrite™).

The Language

The routines you'll need to call are written in assembly language, but (with a few exceptions) they're also accessible from high-level languages, such as Pascal on the Lisa Workshop development system. *Inside Macintosh* documents the Lisa Pascal interfaces to the routines and the symbolic names defined for assembly-language programmers using the Lisa Workshop; if you're using a different development system, its documentation should tell you how to apply the information presented here to that system.

Inside Macintosh is intended to serve the needs of both high-level language and assembly-language programmers. Every routine is shown in its Pascal form (if it has one), but assembly-language programmers are told how they can access the routines. Information of interest only to assembly-language programmers is isolated and labeled so that other programmers can conveniently skip it.

Inside Macintosh

Familiarity with Lisa Pascal (or a similar high-level language) is recommended for all readers, since it's used for most examples. Lisa Pascal is described in the documentation for the Lisa Pascal Workshop.

What's in Each Volume

Inside Macintosh consists of three volumes. Volume I begins with the following information of general interest:

- a "road map" to the software and the rest of the documentation
- the user interface guidelines
- an introduction to memory management (the least you need to know, with a complete discussion following in Volume II)
- some general information for assembly-language programmers

It then describes the various parts of the **User Interface Toolbox**, the software in ROM that helps you implement the standard Macintosh user interface in your application. This is followed by descriptions of other, RAM-based software that's similar in function to the User Interface Toolbox. (The software overview in the Road Map chapter gives further details.)

Volume II describes the **Operating System**, the software in ROM that does basic tasks such as input and output, memory management, and interrupt handling. As in Volume I, some functionally similar RAM-based software is then described.

Volume III discusses your program's interface with the Finder and then describes the Macintosh 128K and 512K hardware. A comprehensive summary of all the software is provided, followed by some useful appendices and a glossary of all terms defined in *Inside Macintosh*.

Version Numbers

This edition of *Inside Macintosh* describes the following versions of the software:

- version 105 of the ROM in the Macintosh 128K or 512K
- version 112 of the ROM image installed by MacWorks in the Macintosh XL
- version 1.1 of the Lisa Pascal interfaces and the assembly-language definitions

Some of the RAM-based software is read from the file named System (usually kept in the System Folder). This manual describes the software in the System file whose creation date is May 2, 1984.

A HORSE OF A DIFFERENT COLOR

On an innovative system like the Macintosh, programs don't look quite the way they do on other systems. For example, instead of carrying out a sequence of steps in a predetermined order, your program is driven primarily by user actions (such as clicking and typing) whose order cannot be predicted.

Preface

You'll probably find that many of your preconceptions about how to write applications don't apply here. Because of this, and because of the sheer volume of information in *Inside Macintosh*, it's essential that you read the Road Map chapter. It will help you get oriented and figure out where to go next.

THE STRUCTURE OF A TYPICAL CHAPTER

Most chapters of *Inside Macintosh* have the same structure, as described below. Reading through this now will save you a lot of time and effort later on. It contains important hints on how to find what you're looking for within this vast amount of technical documentation.

Every chapter begins with a very brief description of its subject and a list of what you should already know before reading that chapter. Then there's a section called, for example, "About the Window Manager", which gives you more information about the subject, telling you what you can do with it in general, elaborating on related user interface guidelines, and introducing terminology that will be used in the chapter. This is followed by a series of sections describing important related concepts and background information; unless they're noted to be for advanced programmers only, you'll have to read them in order to understand how to use the routines described later.

Before the routine descriptions themselves, there's a section called, for example, "Using the Window Manager". It introduces you to the routines, telling you how they fit into the general flow of an application program and, most important, giving you an idea of which ones you'll need to use. Often you'll need only a few routines out of many to do basic operations; by reading this section, you can save yourself the trouble of learning routines you'll never use.

Then, for the details about the routines, read on to the next section. It gives the calling sequence for each routine and describes all the parameters, effects, side effects, and so on.

Following the routine descriptions, there may be some sections that won't be of interest to all readers. Usually these contain information about advanced techniques, or behind the scenes details for the curious.

For review and quick reference, each chapter ends with a summary of the subject matter, including the entire Pascal interface and a separate section for assembly-language programmers.

CONVENTIONS

The following notations are used in *Inside Macintosh* to draw your attention to particular items of information:

> **Note:** A note that may be interesting or useful

> **Warning:** A point you need to be cautious about

> **Assembly-language note:** A note of interest to assembly-language programmers only

Inside Macintosh

[Not in ROM]

    Routines marked with this notation are not part of the Macintosh ROM. Depending on how the interfaces have been set up on the development system you're using, these routines may or may not be available. They're available to users of Lisa Pascal; other users should check the documentation for their development system for more information. (For related information of interest to assembly-language programmers, see chapter 4.)

1 A ROAD MAP

9   About This Chapter
9   Overview of the Software
9   The Toolbox and Other High-Level Software
12   The Operating System and Other Low-Level Software
13   A Simple Example Program
21   Where to Go From Here

A Road Map

ABOUT THIS CHAPTER

This chapter introduces you to the "inside" of Macintosh: the Operating System and User Interface Toolbox routines that your application program will call. It will help you figure out which software you need to learn more about and how to proceed with the rest of the *Inside Macintosh* documentation. To orient you to the software, it presents a simple example program.

OVERVIEW OF THE SOFTWARE

The routines available for use in Macintosh programs are divided according to function, into what are in most cases called "managers" of the feature that they support. As shown in Figure 1, most are part of either the Operating System or the User Interface Toolbox and are in the Macintosh ROM.

The **Operating System** is at the lowest level; it does basic tasks such as input and output, memory management, and interrupt handling. The **User Interface Toolbox** is a level above the Operating System; it helps you implement the standard Macintosh user interface in your application. The Toolbox calls the Operating System to do low-level operations, and you'll also call the Operating System directly yourself.

RAM-based software is available as well. In most cases this software performs specialized operations (such as floating-point arithmetic) that aren't integral to the user interface but may be useful to some applications.

The Toolbox and Other High-Level Software

The Macintosh User Interface Toolbox provides a simple means of constructing application programs that conform to the standard Macintosh user interface. By offering a common set of routines that every application calls to implement the user interface, the Toolbox not only ensures familiarity and consistency for the user but also helps reduce the application's code size and development time. At the same time, it allows a great deal of flexibility: An application can use its own code instead of a Toolbox call wherever appropriate, and can define its own types of windows, menus, controls, and desk accessories.

Figure 2 shows the various parts of the Toolbox in rough order of their relative level. There are many interconnections between these parts; the higher ones often call those at the lower levels. A brief description of each part is given below, to help you figure out which ones you'll need to learn more about. Details are given in the *Inside Macintosh* chapter on that part of the Toolbox. The basic Macintosh terms used below are explained in *Macintosh,* the owner's guide.

To keep the data of an application separate from its code, making the data easier to modify and easier to share among applications, the Toolbox includes the **Resource Manager**. The Resource Manager lets you, for example, store menus separately from your code so that they can be edited or translated without requiring recompilation of the code. It also allows you to get standard data, such as the I-beam pointer for inserting text, from a shared system file. When you call other parts of the Toolbox that need access to the data, they call the Resource Manager. Although most applications never need to call the Resource Manager directly, an understanding of the concepts behind it is essential because they're basic to so many other operations.

Inside Macintosh

```
┌─────────────────────────────────────────┐
│      A MACINTOSH APPLICATION PROGRAM     │
└─────────────────────────────────────────┘
                    │
┌───────────────────────────────────────────────────┐
│  ┌─────────────────────────────┐                   │
│  │   THE USER INTERFACE TOOLBOX │                  │
│  │         (in ROM)             │                  │
│  │                              │                  │
│  │   Resource Manager           │                  │
│  │   QuickDraw                  │                  │
│  │   Font Manager               │  ┌────────────────────────────────┐
│  │   Toolbox Event Manager      │  │  OTHER HIGH-LEVEL SOFTWARE     │
│  │   Window Manager             │  │          (in RAM)              │
│  │   Control Manager            │  │                                │
│  │   Menu Manager               │  │  Binary-Decimal Conversion Package │
│  │   TextEdit                   │  │  International Utilities Package   │
│  │   Dialog Manager             │  │  Standard File Package             │
│  │   Desk Manager               │  └────────────────────────────────┘
│  │   Scrap Manager              │                  │
│  │   Toolbox Utilities          │                  │
│  │   Package Manager            │                  │
│  └─────────────────────────────┘                   │
└───────────────────────────────────────────────────┘
                    │
┌───────────────────────────────────────────────────┐
│  ┌─────────────────────────────┐                   │
│  │      THE OPERATING SYSTEM    │                  │
│  │          (in ROM)            │                  │
│  │                              │                  │
│  │   Memory Manager             │  ┌────────────────────────────────┐
│  │   Segment Loader             │  │   OTHER LOW-LEVEL SOFTWARE     │
│  │   Operating System Event Manager │         (in RAM)              │
│  │   File Manager               │  │                                │
│  │   Device Manager             │  │  RAM Serial Driver             │
│  │   Disk Driver                │  │  Printing Manager              │
│  │   Sound Driver               │  │  Printer Driver                │
│  │   ROM Serial Driver          │  │  AppleTalk Manager             │
│  │   Vertical Retrace Manager   │  │  Disk Initialization Package   │
│  │   System Error Handler       │  │  Floating-Point Arithmetic Package │
│  │   Operating System Utilities │  │  Transcendental Functions Package  │
│  └─────────────────────────────┘  └────────────────────────────────┘
└───────────────────────────────────────────────────┘
                    │
┌─────────────────────────────────────────┐
│          THE MACINTOSH HARDWARE          │
└─────────────────────────────────────────┘
```

Figure 1. Overview

A Road Map

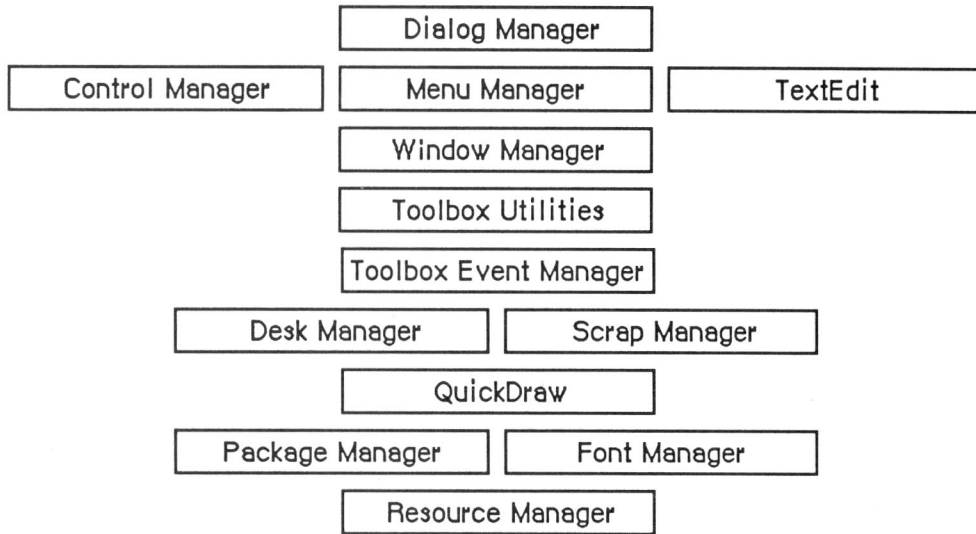

Figure 2. Parts of the Toolbox

Graphics are an important part of every Macintosh application. All graphic operations on the Macintosh are performed by **QuickDraw**. To draw something on the screen, you'll often call one of the other parts of the Toolbox, but it will in turn call QuickDraw. You'll also call QuickDraw directly, usually to draw inside a window, or just to set up constructs like rectangles that you'll need when making other Toolbox calls. QuickDraw's underlying concepts, like those of the Resource Manager, are important for you to understand.

Graphics include text as well as pictures. To draw text, QuickDraw calls the **Font Manager**, which does the background work necessary to make a variety of character fonts available in various sizes and styles. Unless your application includes a font menu, you need to know only a minimal amount about the Font Manager.

An application decides what to do from moment to moment by examining input from the user in the form of mouse and keyboard actions. It learns of such actions by repeatedly calling the **Toolbox Event Manager** (which in turn calls another, lower-level Event Manager in the Operating System). The Toolbox Event Manager also reports occurrences within the application that may require a response, such as when a window that was overlapped becomes exposed and needs to be redrawn.

All information presented by a standard Macintosh application appears in windows. To create windows, activate them, move them, resize them, or close them, you'll call the **Window Manager**. It keeps track of overlapping windows, so you can manipulate windows without concern for how they overlap. For example, the Window Manager tells the Toolbox Event Manager when to inform your application that a window has to be redrawn. Also, when the user presses the mouse button, you call the Window Manager to learn which part of which window it was pressed in, or whether it was pressed in the menu bar or a desk accessory.

Any window may contain controls, such as buttons, check boxes, and scroll bars. You can create and manipulate controls with the **Control Manager**. When you learn from the Window Manager that the user pressed the mouse button inside a window containing controls, you call the Control Manager to find out which control it was pressed in, if any.

Overview of the Software   I-11

Inside Macintosh

A common place for the user to press the mouse button is, of course, in the menu bar. You set up menus in the menu bar by calling the **Menu Manager**. When the user gives a command, either from a menu with the mouse or from the keyboard with the Command key, you call the Menu Manager to find out which command was given.

To accept text typed by the user and allow the standard editing capabilities, including cutting and pasting text within a document via the Clipboard, your application can call **TextEdit**. TextEdit also handles basic formatting such as word wraparound and justification. You can use it just to display text if you like.

When an application needs more information from the user about a command, it presents a dialog box. In case of errors or potentially dangerous situations, it alerts the user with a box containing a message or with sound from the Macintosh's speaker (or both). To create and present dialogs and alerts, and find out the user's responses to them, you call the **Dialog Manager**.

Every Macintosh application should support the use of desk accessories. The user opens desk accessories through the Apple menu, which you set up by calling the Menu Manager. When you learn that the user has pressed the mouse button in a desk accessory, you pass that information on to the accessory by calling the **Desk Manager**. The Desk Manager also includes routines that you must call to ensure that desk accessories work properly.

As mentioned above, you can use TextEdit to implement the standard text editing capability of cutting and pasting via the Clipboard in your application. To allow the use of the Clipboard for cutting and pasting text or graphics between your application and another application or a desk accessory, you need to call the **Scrap Manager**.

Some generally useful operations such as fixed-point arithmetic, string manipulation, and logical operations on bits may be performed with the **Toolbox Utilities**.

The final part of the Toolbox, the **Package Manager**, lets you use RAM-based software called **packages**. The **Standard File Package** will be called by every application whose File menu includes the standard commands for saving and opening documents; it presents the standard user interface for specifying the document. Two of the Macintosh packages can be seen as extensions to the Toolbox Utilities: The **Binary-Decimal Conversion Package** converts integers to decimal strings and vice versa, and the **International Utilities Package** gives you access to country-dependent information such as the formats for numbers, currency, dates, and times.

The Operating System and Other Low-Level Software

The Macintosh Operating System provides the low-level support that applications need in order to use the Macintosh hardware. As the Toolbox is your program's interface to the user, the Operating System is its interface to the Macintosh.

The **Memory Manager** dynamically allocates and releases memory for use by applications and by the other parts of the Operating System. Most of the memory that your program uses is in an area called the **heap**; the code of the program itself occupies space in the heap. Memory space in the heap must be obtained through the Memory Manager.

The **Segment Loader** is the part of the Operating System that loads application code into memory to be executed. Your application can be loaded all at once, or you can divide it up into dynamically loaded segments to economize on memory usage. The Segment Loader also serves as a bridge between the Finder and your application, letting you know whether the application has to open or print a document on the desktop when it starts up.

A Road Map

Low-level, hardware-related events such as mouse-button presses and keystrokes are reported by the **Operating System Event Manager**. (The Toolbox Event Manager then passes them to the application, along with higher-level, software-generated events added at the Toolbox level.) Your program will ordinarily deal only with the Toolbox Event Manager and will rarely call the Operating System Event Manager directly.

File I/O is supported by the **File Manager**, and device I/O by the **Device Manager**. The task of making the various types of devices present the same interface to the application is performed by specialized **device drivers**. The Operating System includes three built-in drivers:

- The **Disk Driver** controls data storage and retrieval on 3 1/2-inch disks.
- The **Sound Driver** controls sound generation, including music composed of up to four simultaneous tones.
- The **Serial Driver** reads and writes asynchronous data through the two serial ports, providing communication between applications and serial peripheral devices such as a modem or printer.

The above drivers are all in ROM; other drivers are RAM-based. There's a Serial Driver in RAM as well as the one in ROM, and there's a **Printer Driver** in RAM that enables applications to print information on any variety of printer via the same interface (called the **Printing Manager**). The **AppleTalk Manager** is an interface to a pair of RAM drivers that enable programs to send and receive information via an AppleTalk network. More RAM drivers can be added independently or built on the existing drivers (by calling the routines in those drivers). For example, the Printer Driver was built on the Serial Driver, and a music driver could be built on the Sound Driver.

The Macintosh video circuitry generates a **vertical retrace interrupt** 60 times a second. An application can schedule routines to be executed at regular intervals based on this "heartbeat" of the system. The **Vertical Retrace Manager** handles the scheduling and execution of tasks during the vertical retrace interrupt.

If a fatal system error occurs while your application is running, the **System Error Handler** assumes control. The System Error Handler displays a box containing an error message and provides a mechanism for the user to start up the system again or resume execution of the application.

The **Operating System Utilities** perform miscellaneous operations such as getting the date and time, finding out the user's preferred speaker volume and other preferences, and doing simple string comparison. (More sophisticated string comparison routines are available in the International Utilities Package.)

Finally, there are three Macintosh packages that perform low-level operations: the **Disk Initialization Package**, which the Standard File Package calls to initialize and name disks; the **Floating-Point Arithmetic Package**, which supports extended-precision arithmetic according to IEEE Standard 754; and the **Transcendental Functions Package**, which contains trigonometric, logarithmic, exponential, and financial functions, as well as a random number generator.

A SIMPLE EXAMPLE PROGRAM

To illustrate various commonly used parts of the software, this section presents an extremely simple example of a Macintosh application program. Though too simple to be practical, this

A Simple Example Program   I-13

Inside Macintosh

example shows the overall structure that every application program will have, and it does many of the basic things every application will do. By looking it over, you can become more familiar with the software and see how your own program code will be structured.

The example program's source code is shown in Figure 4, which begins at the end of this section. A lot of comments are included so that you can see which part of the Toolbox or Operating System is being called and what operation is being performed. These comments, and those that follow below, may contain terms that are unfamiliar to you, but for now just read along to get the general idea. All the terms are explained at length within *Inside Macintosh*. If you want more information right away, you can look up the terms in the Glossary (Volume III) or the Index.

The application, called Sample, displays a single, fixed-size window in which the user can enter and edit text (see Figure 3). It has three menus: the standard Apple menu, from which desk accessories can be chosen; a File menu, containing only a Quit command; and an Edit menu, containing the standard editing commands Undo, Cut, Copy, Paste, and Clear. The Edit menu also includes the standard keyboard equivalents for Undo, Cut, Copy, and Paste: Command-Z, X, C, and V, respectively. The Backspace key may be used to delete, and Shift-clicking will extend or shorten a selection. The user can move the document window around the desktop by dragging it by its title bar.

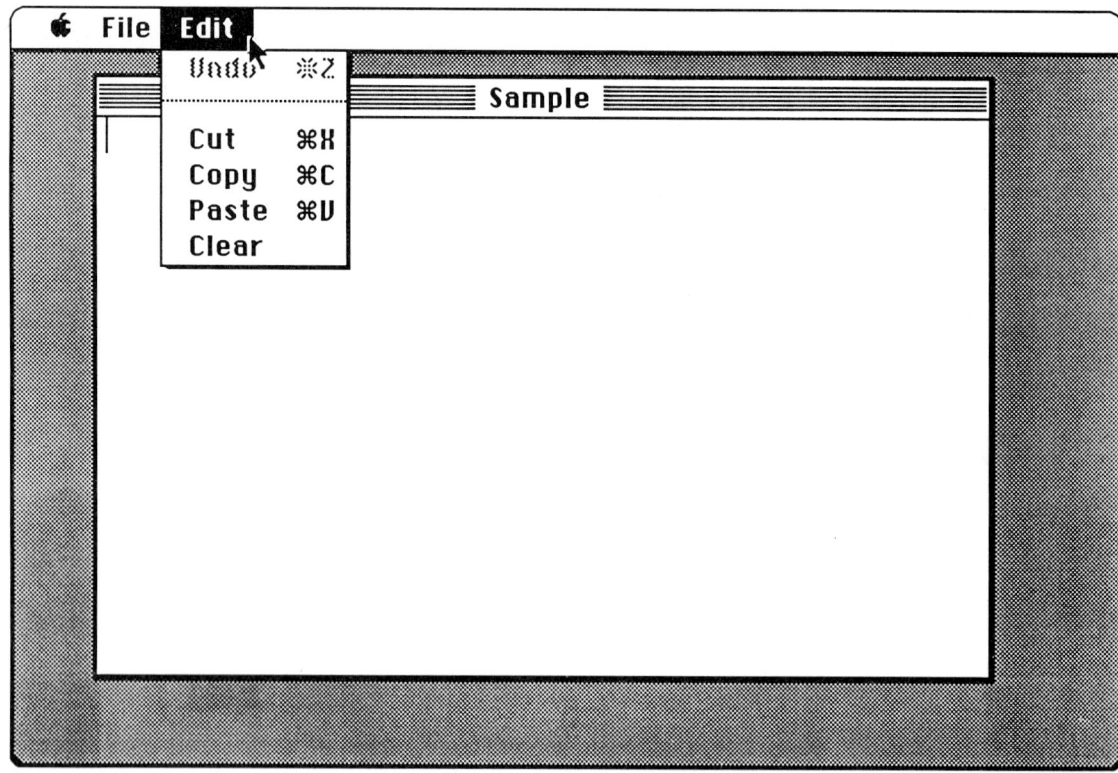

Figure 3. The Sample Application

The Undo command doesn't work in the application's document window, but it and all the other editing commands do work in any desk accessories that allow them (the Note Pad, for example). Some standard features this simple example doesn't support are as follows:

I-14 A Simple Example Program

- Text cannot be cut (or copied) and pasted between the document and a desk accessory.
- The pointer remains an arrow rather than changing to an I-beam within the document.
- Except for Undo, editing commands aren't dimmed when they don't apply (for example, Cut or Copy when there's no text selection).

The document window can't be closed, scrolled, or resized. Because the File menu contains only a Quit command, the document can't be saved or printed. Also, the application doesn't have "About Sample..." as the first command in its Apple menu, or a Hide/Show Clipboard command in its Edit menu (for displaying cut or copied text).

In addition to the code shown in Figure 4, the Sample application has a resource file that includes the data listed below. The program uses the numbers in the second column to identify the resources; for example, it makes a Menu Manager call to get menu number 128 from the resource file.

Resource	Resource ID	Description
Menu	128	Menu with the apple symbol as its title and no commands in it
Menu	129	File menu with one command, Quit, with keyboard equivalent Command-Q
Menu	130	Edit menu with the commands Undo (dimmed), Cut, Copy, Paste, and Clear, in that order, with the standard keyboard equivalents and with a dividing line between Undo and Cut
Window template	128	Document window without a size box; top left corner of (50,40) on QuickDraw's coordinate plane, bottom right corner of (300,450); title "Sample"; no close box

Each menu resource also contains a "menu ID" that's used to identify the menu when the user chooses a command from it; for all three menus, this ID is the same as the resource ID.

Note: To create a resource file with the above contents, you can use the Resource Editor or any similar program that may be available on the development system you're using.

The program starts with a USES clause that specifies all the necessary Pascal interface files. (The names shown are for the Lisa Workshop development system, and may be different for other systems.) This is followed by declarations of some useful constants, to make the source code more readable. Then there are a number of variable declarations, some having simple Pascal data types and others with data types defined in the interface files (like Rect and WindowPtr). Variables used in the program that aren't declared here are global variables defined in the interface to QuickDraw.

The variable declarations are followed by two procedure declarations: SetUpMenus and DoCommand. You can understand them better after looking at the main program and seeing where they're called.

The program begins with a standard initialization sequence. Every application will need to do this same initialization (in the order shown), or something close to it.

Additional initialization needed by the program follows. This includes setting up the menus and the menu bar (by calling SetUpMenus) and creating the application's document window (reading its description from the resource file and displaying it on the screen).

The heart of every application program is its **main event loop,** which repeatedly calls the Toolbox Event Manager to get events and then responds to them as appropriate. The most common event is a press of the mouse button; depending on where it was pressed, as reported by the Window Manager, the sample program may execute a command, move the document window, make the window active, or pass the event on to a desk accessory. The DoCommand procedure takes care of executing a command; it looks at information received by the Menu Manager to determine which command to execute.

Besides events resulting directly from user actions such as pressing the mouse button or a key on the keyboard, events are detected by the Window Manager as a side effect of those actions. For example, when a window changes from active to inactive or vice versa, the Window Manager tells the Toolbox Event Manager to report it to the application program. A similar process happens when all or part of a window needs to be updated (redrawn). The internal mechanism in each case is invisible to the program, which simply responds to the event when notified.

The main event loop terminates when the user takes some action to leave the program—in this case, when the Quit command is chosen.

That's it! Of course, the program structure and level of detail will get more complicated as the application becomes more complex, and every actual application will be more complex than this one. But each will be based on the structure illustrated here.

A Road Map

```
PROGRAM Sample;

{ Sample -- A small sample application written by Macintosh User Education }
{ It displays a single, fixed-size window in which the user can enter and edit text. }


{ The following two compiler commands are required for the Lisa Workshop. }
{$X-}   {turn off automatic stack expansion}
{$U-}   {turn off Lisa libraries}


{ The USES clause brings in the units containing the Pascal interfaces. }
{ The $U expression tells the compiler what file to look in for the specified unit. }
USES {$U Obj/MemTypes } MemTypes,    {basic Memory Manager data types}
     {$U Obj/QuickDraw} QuickDraw,   {interface to QuickDraw}
     {$U Obj/OSIntf   } OSIntf,      {interface to the Operating System}
     {$U Obj/ToolIntf } ToolIntf;    {interface to the Toolbox}


CONST appleID = 128;        {resource IDs/menu IDs for Apple, File, and Edit menus}
      fileID  = 129;
      editID  = 130;

      appleM = 1;           {index for each menu in myMenus (array of menu handles)}
      fileM  = 2;
      editM  = 3;

      menuCount = 3;        {total number of menus}

      windowID = 128;       {resource ID for application's window}

      undoCommand  = 1;     {menu item numbers identifying commands in Edit menu}
      cutCommand   = 3;
      copyCommand  = 4;
      pasteCommand = 5;
      clearCommand = 6;


VAR myMenus: ARRAY[1..menuCount] OF MenuHandle; {array of handles to the menus}
    dragRect: Rect;         {rectangle used to mark boundaries for dragging window}
    txRect: Rect;           {rectangle for text in application window}
    textH: TEHandle;        {handle to information about the text}
    theChar: CHAR;          {character typed on the keyboard or keypad}
    extended: BOOLEAN;      {TRUE if user is Shift-clicking}
    doneFlag: BOOLEAN;      {TRUE if user has chosen Quit command}
    myEvent: EventRecord;   {information about an event}
    wRecord: WindowRecord;  {information about the application window}
    myWindow: WindowPtr;    {pointer to wRecord}
    whichWindow: WindowPtr; {pointer to window in which mouse button was pressed}


PROCEDURE SetUpMenus;
{ Set up menus and menu bar }

  VAR i: INTEGER;
```

Figure 4. Example Program

A Simple Example Program I-17

```pascal
  BEGIN
  { Read menu descriptions from resource file into memory and store handles }
  { in myMenus array }
  myMenus[appleM] := GetMenu(appleID);    {read Apple menu from resource file}
  AddResMenu(myMenus[appleM],'DRVR');     {add desk accessory names to Apple menu}
  myMenus[fileM] := GetMenu(fileID);      {read File menu from resource file}
  myMenus[editM] := GetMenu(editID);      {read Edit menu from resource file}

  FOR i:=1 TO menuCount DO InsertMenu(myMenus[i],0);   {install menus in menu bar }
  DrawMenuBar;                                         { and draw menu bar}
  END;    {of SetUpMenus}

PROCEDURE DoCommand (mResult: LONGINT);
{ Execute command specified by mResult, the result of MenuSelect }

  VAR theItem: INTEGER;       {menu item number from mResult low-order word}
      theMenu: INTEGER;       {menu number from mResult high-order word}
      name: Str255;           {desk accessory name}
      temp: INTEGER;

  BEGIN
    theItem := LoWord(mResult);             {call Toolbox Utility routines to set }
    theMenu := HiWord(mResult);             { menu item number and menu number}

    CASE theMenu OF                         {case on menu ID}

    appleID:
      BEGIN                                 {call Menu Manager to get desk accessory }
        GetItem(myMenus[appleM],theItem,name);  { name, and call Desk Manager to open }
        temp := OpenDeskAcc(name);          { accessory (OpenDeskAcc result not used)}
        SetPort(myWindow);                  {call QuickDraw to restore application }
      END;    {of appleID}                  { window as grafPort to draw in (may have }
                                            { been changed during OpenDeskAcc)}
    fileID:
      doneFlag := TRUE;                     {quit (main loop repeats until doneFlag is TRUE)}

    editID:
      BEGIN                                 {call Desk Manager to handle editing command if }
      IF NOT SystemEdit(theItem-1)          { desk accessory window is the active window}
        THEN                                {application window is the active window}
          CASE theItem OF                   {case on menu item (command) number}

            cutCommand:    TECut(textH);    {call TextEdit to handle command}
            copyCommand:   TECopy(textH);
            pasteCommand:  TEPaste(textH);
            clearCommand:  TEDelete(textH);

          END;    {of item case}
      END;    {of editID}

    END;    {of menu case}                  {to indicate completion of command, call }
    HiliteMenu(0);                          { Menu Manager to unhighlight menu title }
                                            { (highlighted by MenuSelect)}
    END;    {of DoCommand}
```

Figure 4. Example Program (continued)

```
BEGIN    {main program}
{ Initialization }
InitGraf(@thePort);            {initialize QuickDraw}
InitFonts;                     {initialize Font Manager}
FlushEvents(everyEvent,0);     {call OS Event Manager to discard any previous events}
InitWindows;                   {initialize Window Manager}
InitMenus;                     {initialize Menu Manager}
TEInit;                        {initialize TextEdit}
InitDialogs(NIL);              {initialize Dialog Manager}
InitCursor;                    {call QuickDraw to make cursor (pointer) an arrow}

SetUpMenus;                    {set up menus and menu bar}
WITH screenBits.bounds DO      {call QuickDraw to set dragging boundaries; ensure at }
   SetRect(dragRect,4,24,right-4,bottom-4); { least 4 by 4 pixels will remain visible}
doneFlag := FALSE;             {flag to detect when Quit command is chosen}
myWindow := GetNewWindow(windowID,@wRecord,POINTER(-1)); {put up application window}
SetPort(myWindow);             {call QuickDraw to set current grafPort to this window}
txRect := thePort^.portRect;   {rectangle for text in window; call QuickDraw to bring }
InsetRect(txRect,4,0);         { it in 4 pixels from left and right edges of window}
textH := TENew(txRect,txRect); {call TextEdit to prepare for receiving text}

{ Main event loop }
REPEAT                         {call Desk Manager to perform any periodic }
  SystemTask;                  { actions defined for desk accessories}
  TEIdle(textH);               {call TextEdit to make vertical bar blink}

  IF GetNextEvent(everyEvent,myEvent) {call Toolbox Event Manager to get the next }
    THEN                       { event that the application should handle}
      CASE myEvent.what OF     {case on event type}

      mouseDown:               {mouse button down: call Window Manager to learn where}
        CASE FindWindow(myEvent.where,whichWindow) OF

          inSysWindow:         {desk accessory window: call Desk Manager to handle it}
            SystemClick(myEvent,whichWindow);

          inMenuBar:           {menu bar:  call Menu Manager to learn which command, }
            DoCommand(MenuSelect(myEvent.where)); { then execute it}

          inDrag:              {title bar:  call Window Manager to drag}
            DragWindow(whichWindow,myEvent.where,dragRect);

          inContent:                        {body of application window: }
            BEGIN                           { call Window Manager to check whether }
            IF whichWindow <> FrontWindow   { it's the active window and make it }
              THEN SelectWindow(whichWindow) { active if not}
              ELSE
                BEGIN                       {it's already active:  call QuickDraw to }
                GlobalToLocal(myEvent.where); { convert to window coordinates for }
                                            { TEClick, use Toolbox Utility BitAnd to }
                extended := BitAnd(myEvent.modifiers,shiftKey) <> 0; { test for Shift }
                TEClick(myEvent.where,extended,textH);  { key down, and call TextEdit }
                END;                        { to process the event}
            END;    {of inContent}
        END;    {of mouseDown}
```

Figure 4. Example Program (continued)

```
    keyDown, autoKey:                          {key pressed once or held down to repeat}
      BEGIN
        theChar := CHR(BitAnd(myEvent.message,charCodeMask));   {get the character}
        IF BitAnd(myEvent.modifiers,cmdKey) <> 0   {if Command key down, call Menu }
          THEN DoCommand(MenuKey(theChar))         { Manager to learn which command,}
          ELSE TEKey(theChar,textH);               { then execute it; else pass }
        END;                                       { character to TextEdit}

    activateEvt:
      BEGIN
      IF BitAnd(myEvent.modifiers,activeFlag) <> 0
        THEN                       {application window is becoming active: }
          BEGIN                    { call TextEdit to highlight selection }
            TEActivate(textH);     { or display blinking vertical bar, and call }
            DisableItem(myMenus[editM],undoCommand); { Menu Manager to disable }
            END                    { Undo (since application doesn't support Undo)}
        ELSE
          BEGIN                    {application window is becoming inactive: }
            TEDeactivate(textH);   { unhighlight selection or remove blinking }
            EnableItem(myMenus[editM],undoCommand);  { vertical bar, and enable }
            END;                   { Undo (since desk accessory may support it)}
        END;    {of activateEvt}

    updateEvt:                                     {window appearance needs updating}
      BEGIN
      BeginUpdate(WindowPtr(myEvent.message));  {call Window Manager to begin update}
      EraseRect(thePort^.portRect);             {call QuickDraw to erase text area}
      TEUpdate(thePort^.portRect,textH);        {call TextEdit to update the text}
      EndUpdate(WindowPtr(myEvent.message));    {call Window Manager to end update}
      END;    {of updateEvt}

    END;    {of event case}

UNTIL doneFlag;
END.
```

Figure 4. Example Program (continued)

A Road Map

WHERE TO GO FROM HERE

This section contains important directions for every reader of *Inside Macintosh*. It will help you figure out which chapters to read next.

The *Inside Macintosh* chapters are ordered in such a way that you can follow it if you read through it sequentially. Forward references are given wherever necessary to any additional information that you'll need in order to fully understand what's being discussed. Special-purpose information that can possibly be skipped is indicated as such. Most likely you won't need to read everything in each chapter and can even skip entire chapters.

You should begin by reading the following:

1. Chapter 2, The Macintosh User Interface Guidelines. All Macintosh applications should follow these guidelines to ensure that the end user is presented with a consistent, familiar interface.

2. Chapter 3, Macintosh Memory Management: An Introduction.

3. Chapter 4, Using Assembly Language, if you're programming in assembly language. Depending on the debugging tools available on the development system you're using, it may also be helpful or necessary for high-level language programmers to read this chapter. You'll also have to read it if you're creating your own development system and want to know how to write interfaces to the routines.

4. The chapters describing the parts of the Toolbox that deal with the fundamental aspects of the user interface: the Resource Manager, QuickDraw, the Toolbox Event Manager, the Window Manager, and the Menu Manager.

Read the other chapters if you're interested in what they discuss, which you should be able to tell from the overviews in this "road map" and from the introductions to the chapters themselves. Each chapter's introduction will also tell you what you should already know before reading that chapter.

When you're ready to try something out, refer to the appropriate documentation for the development system you'll be using.

2 THE MACINTOSH USER INTERFACE GUIDELINES

- 27 About This Chapter
- 27 Introduction
- 28   Avoiding Modes
- 29   Avoiding Program Dependencies
- 29 Types of Applications
- 31 Using Graphics
- 32   Icons
- 32   Palettes
- 32 Components of the Macintosh System
- 33 The Keyboard
- 33   Character Keys
- 34   Modifier Keys: Shift, Caps Lock, Option, and Command
- 34   Typeahead and Auto-Repeat
- 35   Versions of the Keyboard
- 35   The Numeric Keypad
- 36 The Mouse
- 36   Mouse Actions
- 37   Multiple-Clicking
- 37   Changing Pointer Shapes
- 38 Selecting
- 38   Selection by Clicking
- 39   Range Selection
- 39   Extending a Selection
- 40   Making a Discontinuous Selection
- 40   Selecting Text
- 41   Insertion Point
- 42   Selecting Words
- 43   Selecting a Range of Text
- 43   Graphics Selections
- 44   Selections in Arrays
- 44 Windows
- 45   Multiple Windows
- 45   Opening and Closing Windows
- 46   The Active Window
- 46   Moving a Window
- 47   Changing the Size of a Window
- 47   Scroll Bars
- 48   Automatic Scrolling

49	Splitting a Window
50	Panels
51	Commands
51	The Menu Bar
51	Choosing a Menu Command
52	Appearance of Menu Commands
52	Command Groups
53	Toggled Commands
53	Special Visual Features
54	Standard Menus
54	The Apple Menu
55	The File Menu
56	New
56	Open
56	Close
57	Save
57	Save As
57	Revert to Saved
57	Page Setup
57	Print
57	Quit
58	The Edit Menu
58	The Clipboard
59	Undo
59	Cut
59	Copy
60	Paste
60	Clear
60	Select All
60	Show Clipboard
60	Font-Related Menus
60	Font Menu
61	FontSize Menu
61	Style Menu
62	Text Editing
62	Inserting Text
62	Backspace
62	Replacing Text
63	Intelligent Cut and Paste
63	Editing Fields

64	Dialogs and Alerts
65	Controls
65	Buttons
66	Check Boxes and Radio Buttons
66	Dials
66	Dialogs
67	Modal Dialog Boxes
67	Modeless Dialog Boxes
68	Alerts
70	Do's and Don'ts of a Friendly User Interface

The Macintosh User Interface Guidelines

ABOUT THIS CHAPTER

This chapter describes the Macintosh user interface, for the benefit of people who want to develop Macintosh applications. More details about many of these features can be found in the "About" sections of the other chapters of *Inside Macintosh* (for example, "About the Window Manager").

Unlike the rest of *Inside Macintosh*, this chapter describes applications from the outside, not the inside. The terminology used is the terminology users are familiar with, which is not necessarily the same as that used elsewhere in *Inside Macintosh*.

The Macintosh user interface consists of those features that are generally applicable to a variety of applications. Not all of the features are found in every application. In fact, some features are hypothetical, and may not be found in any current applications.

The best time to familiarize yourself with the user interface is before beginning to design an application. Good application design on the Macintosh happens when a developer has absorbed the spirit as well as the details of the user interface.

Before reading this chapter, you should have some experience using one or more applications, preferably one each of a word processor, spreadsheet or data base, and graphics application. You should also have read *Macintosh*, the owner's guide, or at least be familiar with the terminology used in that manual.

INTRODUCTION

The Macintosh is designed to appeal to an audience of nonprogrammers, including people who have previously feared and distrusted computers. To achieve this goal, Macintosh applications should be easy to learn and to use. To help people feel more comfortable with the applications, the applications should build on skills that people already have, not force them to learn new ones. The user should feel in control of the computer, not the other way around. This is achieved in applications that embody three qualities: responsiveness, permissiveness, and consistency.

Responsiveness means that the user's actions tend to have direct results. The user should be able to accomplish what needs to be done spontaneously and intuitively, rather than having to think: "Let's see; to do C, first I have to do A and B and then...". For example, with pull-down menus, the user can choose the desired command directly and instantaneously.

Permissiveness means that the application tends to allow the user to do anything reasonable. The user, not the system, decides what to do next. Also, error messages tend to come up infrequently. If the user is constantly subjected to a barrage of error messages, something is wrong somewhere.

The most important way in which an application is permissive is in avoiding modes. This idea is so important that it's dealt with in a separate section, "Avoiding Modes", below.

The third and most important principle is consistency. Since Macintosh users usually divide their time among several applications, they would be confused and irritated if they had to learn a completely new interface for each application. The main purpose of this chapter is to describe the shared interface ideas of Macintosh applications, so that developers of new applications can gain leverage from the time spent developing and testing existing applications.

Consistency is easier to achieve on the Macintosh than on many other computers. This is because many of the routines used to implement the user interface are supplied in the Macintosh Operating System and User Interface Toolbox. However, you should be aware that implementing the user interface guidelines in their full glory often requires writing additional code that isn't supplied.

Of course, you shouldn't feel that you're restricted to using existing features. The Macintosh is a growing system, and new ideas are essential. But the bread-and-butter features, the kind that every application has, should certainly work the same way so that the user can easily move back and forth between applications. The best rule to follow is that if your application has a feature that's described in these guidelines, you should implement the feature exactly as the guidelines describe it. It's better to do something completely different than to half-agree with the guidelines.

Illustrations of most of the features described in this chapter can be found in various existing applications. However, there's probably no one application that illustrates these guidelines in every particular. Although it's useful and important for you to get the feeling of the Macintosh user interface by looking at existing applications, the guidelines in this chapter are the ultimate authority. Wherever an application disagrees with the guidelines, follow the guidelines.

Avoiding Modes

"But, gentlemen, you overdo the mode."

— John Dryden, *The Assignation, or Love in a Nunnery*, 1672

A mode is a part of an application that the user has to formally enter and leave, and that restricts the operations that can be performed while it's in effect. Since people don't usually operate modally in real life, having to deal with modes in computer software reinforces the idea that computers are unnatural and unfriendly.

Modes are most confusing when you're in the wrong one. Being in a mode makes future actions contingent upon past ones, restricts the behavior of familiar objects and commands, and may make habitual actions cause unexpected results.

It's tempting to use modes in a Macintosh application, since most existing software leans on them heavily. If you yield to the temptation too frequently, however, users will consider spending time with your application a chore rather than a satisfying experience.

This is not to say that modes are never used in Macintosh applications. Sometimes a mode is the best way out of a particular problem. Most of these modes fall into one of the following categories:

- Long-term modes with a procedural basis, such as doing word processing as opposed to graphics editing. Each application program is a mode in this sense.

- Short-term "spring-loaded" modes, in which the user is constantly doing something to perpetuate the mode. Holding down the mouse button or a key is the most common example of this kind of mode.

- Alert modes, where the user must rectify an unusual situation before proceeding. These modes should be kept to a minimum.

Other modes are acceptable if they meet one of the following requirements:

- They emulate a familiar real-life model that is itself modal, like picking up different-sized paintbrushes in a graphics editor. MacPaint™ and other palette-based applications are examples of this use of modes.

- They change only the attributes of something, and not its behavior, like the boldface and underline modes of text entry.
- They block most other normal operations of the system to emphasize the modality, as in error conditions incurable through software ("There's no disk in the disk drive", for example).

If an application uses modes, there must be a clear visual indication of the current mode, and the indication should be near the object being most affected by the mode. It should also be very easy to get into or out of the mode (such as by clicking on a palette symbol).

Avoiding Program Dependencies

Another important general concept to keep in mind is that your application program should be as country-independent and hardware-independent as possible.

No words that the user sees should be in the program code itself; storing all these words in resources will make it much easier for the application to be translated to other languages. Similarly, there's a mechanism for reading country-dependent information from resources, such as the currency and date formats, so the application will automatically work right in countries where those resources have been properly set up. You should always use mechanisms like this instead of coding such information directly into your program.

The system software provides many variables and routines whose use will ensure independence from the version of the Macintosh being used—whether a Macintosh 128K, 512K, XL, or even a future version. Though you may know a more direct way of getting the information, or a faster way of doing the operation, it's best to use the system-provided features that will ensure hardware independence. You should, for example, access the variable that gives you the current size of the screen rather than use the numbers that match the screen you're using. You can also write your program so that it will print on any printer, regardless of which type of printer happens to be installed on the Macintosh being used.

TYPES OF APPLICATIONS

Everything on a Macintosh screen is displayed graphically; the Macintosh has no text mode. Nevertheless, it's useful to make a distinction among three types of objects that an application deals with: text, graphics, and arrays. Examples of each of these are shown in Figure 1.

Text can be arranged in a variety of ways on the screen. Some applications, such as word processors, might consist of nothing but text, while others, such as graphics-oriented applications, use text almost incidentally. It's useful to consider all the text appearing together in a particular context as a block of text. The size of the block can range from a single field, as in a dialog box, to the whole document, as in a word processor. Regardless of its size or arrangement, the application sees each block as a one-dimensional string of characters. Text is edited the same way regardless of where it appears.

Graphics are pictures, drawn either by the user or by the application. Graphics in a document tend to consist of discrete objects, which can be selected individually. Graphics are discussed further below, under "Using Graphics".

Inside Macintosh

```
The rest to some faint meaning make pretence
But Shadwell never deviates into sense.
Some beams of wit on other souls may fall,
Strike through and make a lucid interval;
But Shadwell's genuine night admits no ray,
His rising fogs prevail upon the day.

MacFlecknoe                              Page 1
```

Text

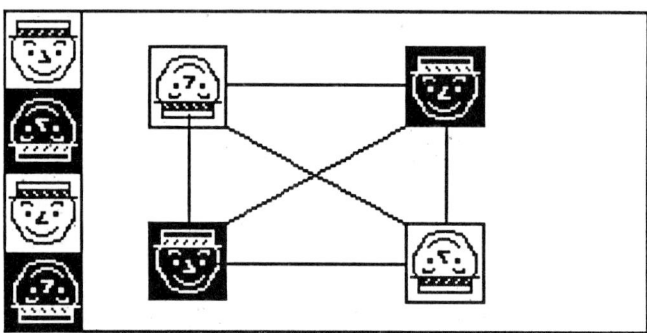

Graphics

Advertising	132.9	
Manufacturing	121.3	
R & D	18.7	
Interest	12.2	
Total	285.1	

Array

Figure 1. Ways of Structuring Information

Arrays are one- or two-dimensional arrangements of fields. If the array is one-dimensional, it's called a form; if it's two-dimensional it's called a table. Each field, in turn, contains a collection of information, usually text, but conceivably graphics. A table can be readily identified on the screen, since it consists of rows and columns of fields (often called cells), separated by horizontal and vertical lines. A form is something you fill out, like a credit-card application. The fields in a form can be arranged in any appropriate way; nevertheless, the application regards the fields as in a definite linear order.

Each of these three ways of presenting information retains its integrity, regardless of the context in which it appears. For example, a field in an array can contain text. When the user is

I-30 Types of Applications

manipulating the field as a whole, the field is treated as part of the array. When the user wants to change the contents of the field, the contents are edited in the same way as any other text.

USING GRAPHICS

A key feature of the Macintosh is its high-resolution graphics screen. To use this screen to its best advantage, Macintosh applications use graphics copiously, even in places where other applications use text. As much as possible, all commands, features, and parameters of an application, and all the user's data, appear as graphic objects on the screen. Figure 2 shows some of the ways that applications can use graphics to communicate with the user.

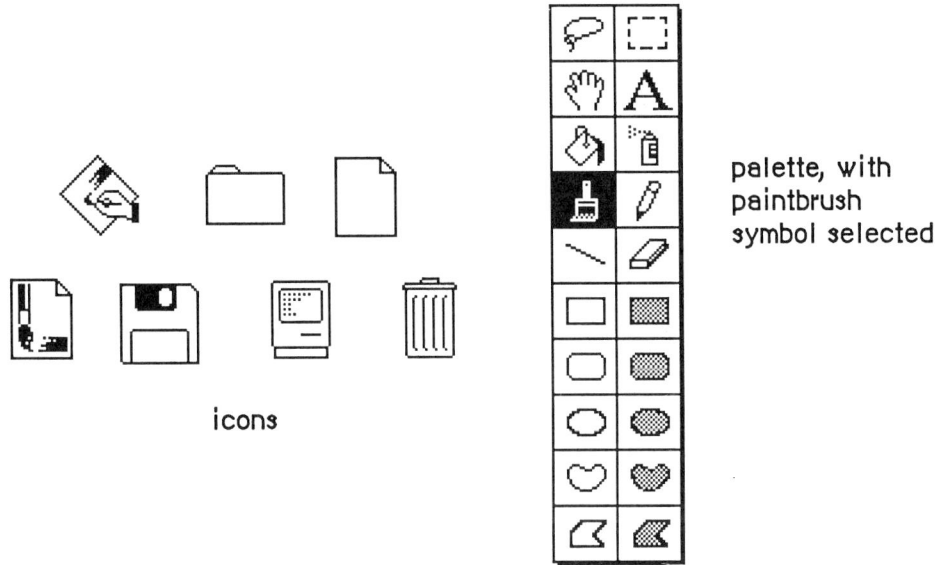

Figure 2. Objects on the Screen

Objects, whenever applicable, resemble the familiar material objects whose functions they emulate. Objects that act like pushbuttons "light up" when pressed; the Trash icon looks like a trash can.

Objects are designed to look good on the screen. Predefined graphics patterns can give objects a shape and texture beyond simple line graphics. Placing a drop-shadow slightly below and to the right of an object can give it a three-dimensional appearance.

Generally, when the user clicks on an object, it's **highlighted** to distinguish it from its peers. The most common way to show this highlighting is by inverting the object: changing black to white and vice versa. In some situations, other forms of highlighting may be more appropriate. The important thing is that there should always be some sort of feedback, so that the user knows that the click had an effect.

One special aspect of the appearance of a document on the screen is visual fidelity. This principle is also known as "what you see is what you get". It primarily refers to printing: The version of a document shown on the screen should be as close as possible to its printed version, taking into account inevitable differences due to different media.

Inside Macintosh

Icons

A fundamental object in Macintosh software is the **icon**, a small graphic object that's usually symbolic of an operation or of a larger entity such as a document.

Icons can contribute greatly to the clarity and attractiveness of an application. The use of icons also makes it much easier to translate programs into other languages. Wherever an explanation or label is needed, consider using an icon instead of text.

Palettes

Some applications use **palettes** as a quick way for the user to change from one operation to another. A palette is a collection of small symbols, usually enclosed in rectangles. A symbol can be an icon, a pattern, a character, or just a drawing, that stands for an operation. When the user clicks on one of the symbols (or in its rectangle), it's distinguished from the other symbols, such as by highlighting, and the previous symbol goes back to its normal state.

Typically, the symbol that's selected determines what operations the user can perform. Selecting a palette symbol puts the user into a mode. This use of modes can be justified because changing from one mode to another is almost instantaneous, and the user can always see at a glance which mode is in effect. Like all modal features, palettes should be used only when they're the most natural way to structure an application.

A palette can either be part of a window (as in MacDraw™), or a separate window (as in MacPaint). Each system has its disadvantages. If the palette is part of the window, then parts of the palette might be concealed if the user makes the window smaller. On the other hand, if it's not part of the window, then it takes up extra space on the desktop. If an application supports multiple documents open at the same time, it might be better to put a separate palette in each window, so that a different palette symbol can be in effect in each document.

COMPONENTS OF THE MACINTOSH SYSTEM

This section explains the relationship among the principal large-scale components of the Macintosh system (from an external point of view).

The main vehicle for the interaction of the user and the system is the application. Only one application is active at a time. When an application is active, it's in control of all communications between the user and the system. The application's menus are in the menu bar, and the application is in charge of all windows as well as the desktop.

To the user, the main unit of information is the document. Each document is a unified collection of information—a single business letter or spreadsheet or chart. A complex application, such as a data base, might require several related documents. Some documents can be processed by more than one application, but each document has a principal application, which is usually the one that created it. The other applications that process the document are called secondary applications.

The only way the user can actually see the document (except by printing it) is through a window. The application puts one or more windows on the screen; each window shows a view of a document or of auxiliary information used in processing the document. The part of the screen underlying all the windows is called the **desktop**.

The user returns to the Finder to change applications. When the Finder is active, if the user opens either an application a document belonging to an application, the application becomes active and displays the document window.

Internally, applications and documents are both kept in files. However, the user never sees files as such, so they don't really enter into the user interface.

THE KEYBOARD

The Macintosh keyboard is used primarily for entering text. Since commands are chosen from menus or by clicking somewhere on the screen, the keyboard isn't needed for this function, although it can be used for alternative ways to enter commands.

The keys on the keyboard are arranged in familiar typewriter fashion. The U.S. keyboard on the Macintosh 128K and 512K is shown in Figure 3. The Macintosh XL keyboard looks the same except that the key to the left of the space bar is labeled with an apple symbol.

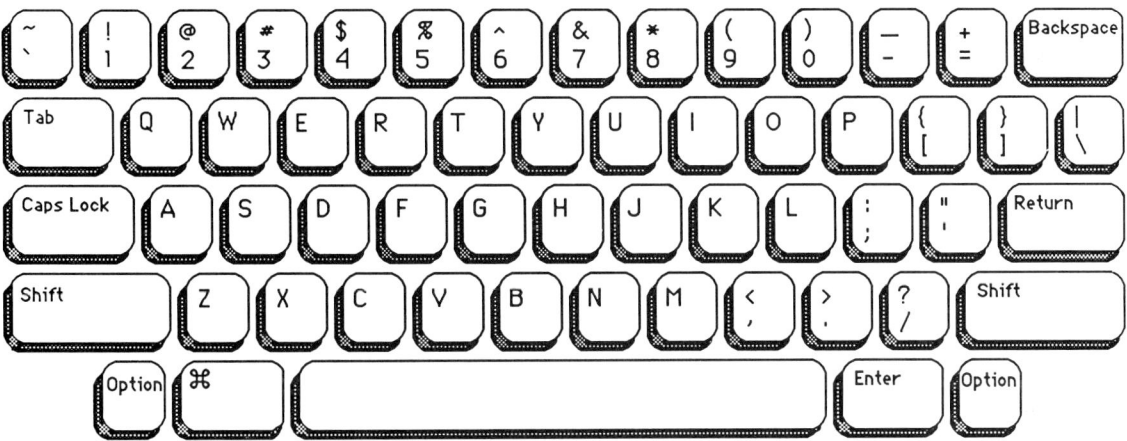

Figure 3. The Macintosh U.S. Keyboard

There are two kinds of keys: **character keys** and **modifier keys**. A character key sends characters to the computer; a modifier key alters the meaning of a character key if it's held down while the character key is pressed.

Character Keys

Character keys include keys for letters, numbers, and symbols, as well as the space bar. If the user presses one of these keys while entering text, the corresponding character is added to the text. Other keys, such as the Enter, Tab, Return, Backspace, and Clear keys, are also considered character keys. However, the result of pressing one of these keys depends on the application and the context.

The Enter key tells the application that the user is through entering information in a particular area of the document, such as a field in an array. Most applications add information to a document as soon as the user types or draws it. However, the application may need to wait until a whole collection of information is available before processing it. In this case, the user presses the Enter key to signal that the information is complete.

The Tab key is a signal to proceed: It signals movement to the next item in a sequence. Tab often implies an Enter operation before the Tab motion is performed.

The Return key is another signal to proceed, but it defines a different type of motion than Tab. A press of the Return key signals movement to the leftmost field one step down (just like a carriage return on a typewriter). Return can also imply an Enter operation before the Return operation.

> **Note:** Return and Enter also dismiss dialog and alert boxes (see "Dialogs and Alerts").

During entry of text into a document, Tab moves to the next tab stop, Return moves to the beginning of the next line, and Enter is ignored.

Backspace is used to delete text or graphics. The exact use of Backspace in text is described in the "Text Editing" section.

The Clear key on the numeric keypad has the same effect as the Clear command in the Edit menu; that is, it removes the selection from the document without putting it in the Clipboard. This is also explained in the "Text Editing" section. Because the keypad is optional equipment on the Macintosh 128K and 512K, no application should ever require use of the Clear key or any other key on the pad.

Modifier Keys: Shift, Caps Lock, Option, and Command

There are six keys on the keyboard that change the interpretation of keystrokes: two Shift keys, two Option keys, one Caps Lock key, and one Command key (the key to the left of the space bar). These keys change the interpretation of keystrokes, and sometimes mouse actions. When one of these keys is held down, the effect of the other keys (or the mouse button) may change.

The Shift and Option keys choose among the characters on each character key. Shift gives the upper character on two-character keys, or the uppercase letter on alphabetic keys. The Shift key is also used in conjunction with the mouse for extending a selection; see "Selecting". Option gives an alternate character set interpretation, including international characters, special symbols, and so on. Shift and Option can be used in combination.

Caps Lock latches in the down position when pressed, and releases when pressed again. When down it gives the uppercase letter on alphabetic keys. The operation of Caps Lock on alphabetic keys is parallel to that of the Shift key, but the Caps Lock key has no effect whatsoever on any of the other keys. Caps Lock and Option can be used in combination on alphabetic keys.

Pressing a character key while holding down the Command key usually tells the application to interpret the key as a command, not as a character (see "Commands").

Typeahead and Auto-Repeat

If the user types when the Macintosh is unable to process the keystrokes immediately, or types more quickly than the Macintosh can handle, the extra keystrokes are queued, to be processed later. This queuing is called typeahead. There's a limit to the number of keystrokes that can be queued, but the limit is usually not a problem unless the user types while the application is performing a lengthy operation.

When a character key is held down for a certain amount of time, it starts repeating automatically. The user can set the delay and the rate of repetition with the Control Panel desk accessory. An application can tell whether a series of n keystrokes was generated by auto-repeat or by pressing the same key n times. It can choose to disregard keystrokes generated by auto-repeat; this is usually a good idea for menu commands chosen with the Command key.

Holding down a modifier key has the same effect as pressing it once. However, if the user holds down a modifier key and a character key at the same time, the effect is the same as if the user held down the modifier key while pressing the character key repeatedly.

Auto-repeat does not function during typeahead; it operates only when the application is ready to accept keyboard input.

Versions of the Keyboard

There are two physical versions of the keyboard: U.S. and international. The international version has one more key than the U.S. version. The standard layout on the international version is designed to conform to the International Standards Organization (ISO) standard; the U.S. key layout mimics that of common American office typewriters. International keyboards have different labels on the keys in different countries, but the overall layout is the same.

> **Note:** An illustration of the international keyboard (with Great Britain key caps) is given in chapter 8.

The Numeric Keypad

An optional numeric keypad can be hooked up between the main unit and the standard keyboard on a Macintosh 128K or 512K; on the Macintosh XL, the numeric keypad is built in, next to the keyboard. Figure 4 shows the U.S. keypad. In other countries, the keys may have different labels.

Figure 4. Numeric Keypad

Inside Macintosh

The keypad contains 18 keys, some of which duplicate keys on the main keyboard, and some of which are unique to the keypad. The application can tell whether the keystrokes have come from the main keyboard or the numeric keypad. The keys on the keypad follow the same rules for typeahead and auto-repeat as the keyboard.

Four keys on the keypad are labeled with "field-motion" symbols: small rectangles with arrows pointing in various directions. Some applications may use these keys to select objects in the direction indicated by the key; the most likely use for this feature is in tables. To obtain the characters (+ * / ,) available on these keys, the user must also hold down the Shift key on the keyboard.

Since the numeric keypad is optional equipment on the Macintosh 128K and 512K, no application should require it or any keys available on it in order to perform standard functions. Specifically, since the Clear key isn't available on the main keyboard, a Clear function may be implemented with this key only as the equivalent of the Clear command in the Edit menu.

THE MOUSE

The mouse is a small device the size of a deck of playing cards, connected to the computer by a long, flexible cable. There's a button on the top of the mouse. The user holds the mouse and rolls it on a flat, smooth surface. A pointer on the screen follows the motion of the mouse.

Simply moving the mouse results only in a corresponding movement of the pointer and no other action. Most actions take place when the user positions the "hot spot" of the pointer over an object on the screen and presses and releases the mouse button. The hot spot should be intuitive, like the point of an arrow or the center of a crossbar.

Mouse Actions

The three basic mouse actions are:

- clicking: positioning the pointer with the mouse, and briefly pressing and releasing the mouse button without moving the mouse
- pressing: positioning the pointer with the mouse, and holding down the mouse button without moving the mouse
- dragging: positioning the pointer with the mouse, holding down the mouse button, moving the mouse to a new position, and releasing the button

The system provides "mouse-ahead"; that is, any mouse actions the user performs when the application isn't ready to process them are saved in a buffer and can be processed at the application's convenience. Alternatively, the application can choose to ignore saved-up mouse actions, but should do so only to protect the user from possibly damaging consequences.

Clicking something with the mouse performs an instantaneous action, such as selecting a location within a document or activating an object.

For certain kinds of objects, pressing on the object has the same effect as clicking it repeatedly. For example, clicking a scroll arrow causes a document to scroll one line; pressing on a scroll arrow causes the document to scroll repeatedly until the mouse button is released or the end of the document is reached.

Dragging can have different effects, depending on what's under the pointer when the mouse button is pressed. The uses of dragging include choosing a menu item, selecting a range of objects, moving an object from one place to another, and shrinking or expanding an object.

Some objects, especially graphic objects, can be moved by dragging. In this case, the application attaches a dotted outline of the object to the pointer and moves the outline as the user moves the pointer. When the user releases the mouse button, the application redraws the complete object at the new location.

An object being moved can be restricted to certain boundaries, such as the edges of a window. If the user moves the pointer outside of the boundaries, the application stops drawing the dotted outline of the object. If the user releases the mouse button while the pointer is outside of the boundaries, the object isn't moved. If, on the other hand, the user moves the pointer back within the boundaries again before releasing the mouse button, the outline is drawn again.

In general, moving the mouse changes nothing except the location, and possibly the shape, of the pointer. Pressing the mouse button indicates the intention to do something, and releasing the button completes the action. Pressing by itself should have no effect except in well-defined areas, such as scroll arrows, where it has the same effect as repeated clicking.

Multiple-Clicking

A variant of clicking involves performing a second click shortly after the end of an initial click. If the downstroke of the second click follows the upstroke of the first by a short amount of time (as set by the user in the Control Panel), and if the locations of the two clicks are reasonably close together, the two clicks constitute a double-click. Its most common use is as a faster or easier way to perform an action that can also be performed in another way. For example, clicking twice on an icon is a faster way to open it than selecting it and choosing Open; clicking twice on a word to select it is faster than dragging through it.

To allow the software to distinguish efficiently between single clicks and double-clicks on objects that respond to both, an operation invoked by double-clicking an object must be an enhancement, superset, or extension of the feature invoked by single-clicking that object.

Triple-clicking is also possible; it should similarly represent an extension of a double-click.

Changing Pointer Shapes

The pointer may change shape to give feedback on the range of activities that make sense in a particular area of the screen, in a current mode, or both:

- The result of any mouse action depends on the item under the pointer when the mouse button is pressed. To emphasize the differences among mouse actions, the pointer may assume different appearances in different areas to indicate the actions possible in each area. This can be distracting, however, and should be kept to a minimum.

- Where an application uses modes for different functions, the pointer can be a different shape in each mode. For example, in MacPaint, the pointer shape always reflects the active palette symbol.

During a particularly lengthy operation, when the user can do nothing but wait until the operation is completed, the pointer may change to indicate this. The standard pointer used for this purpose is a wristwatch.

Inside Macintosh

Figure 5 shows some examples of pointers and their effect. An application can design additional pointers for other contexts.

Pointer	Used for
▸	Scroll bar and other controls, size box title bar, menu bar, desktop, and so on
 I	Selecting text
+	Drawing, shrinking, or stretching graphic objects
✥	Selecting fields in an array
 ⌚	Showing that a lengthy operation is in progress

Figure 5. Pointers

SELECTING

The user selects an object to distinguish it from other objects, just before performing an operation on it. Selecting the object of an operation before identifying the operation is a fundamental characteristic of the Macintosh user interface, since it allows the application to avoid modes.

Selecting an object has no effect on the contents of a document. Making a selection shouldn't commit the user to anything; there should never be a penalty for making an incorrect selection. The user fixes an incorrect selection by making the correct selection.

Although there's a variety of ways to select objects, they fall into easily recognizable groups. Users get used to doing specific things to select objects, and applications that use these methods are therefore easier to learn. Some of these methods apply to every type of application, and some only to particular types of applications.

This section discusses first the general methods, and then the specific methods that apply to text applications, graphics applications, and arrays. Figure 6 shows a comparison of some of the general methods.

Selection by Clicking

The most straightforward method of selecting an object is by clicking on it once. Most things that can be selected in Macintosh applications can be selected this way.

The Macintosh User Interface Guidelines

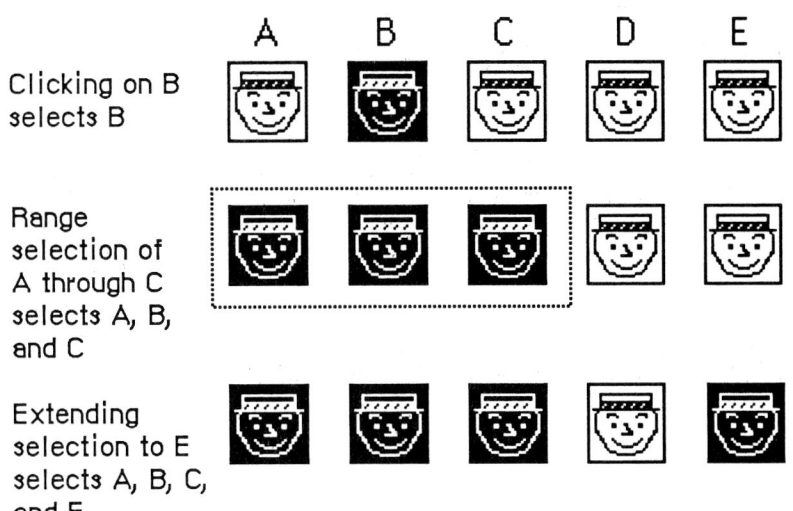

Figure 6. Selection Methods

Some applications support selection by double-clicking and triple-clicking. As always with multiple clicks, the second click extends the effect of the first click, and the third click extends the effect of the second click. In the case of selection, this means that the second click selects the same sort of thing as the first click, only more of them. The same holds true for the third click.

For example, in text, the first click selects an insertion point, whereas the second click selects a whole word. The third click might select a whole block or paragraph of text. In graphics, the first click selects a single object, and double- and triple-clicks might select increasingly larger groups of objects.

Range Selection

The user selects a range of objects by dragging through them. Although the exact meaning of the selection depends on the type of application, the procedure is always the same:

1. The user positions the pointer at one corner of the range and presses the mouse button. This position is called the anchor point of the range.

2. The user moves the pointer in any direction. As the pointer is moved, visual feedback indicates the objects that would be selected if the mouse button were released. For text and arrays, the selected area is continually highlighted. For graphics, a dotted rectangle expands or contracts to show the range that will be selected.

3. When the feedback shows the desired range, the user releases the mouse button. The point at which the button is released is called the endpoint of the range.

Extending a Selection

A user can change the extent of an existing selection by holding down the Shift key and clicking the mouse button. Exactly what happens next depends on the context.

Selecting I-39

Inside Macintosh

In text or an array, the result of a Shift-click is always a range. The position where the button is clicked becomes the new endpoint or anchor point of the range; the selection can be extended in any direction. If the user clicks within the current range, the new range will be smaller than the old range.

In graphics, a selection is extended by adding objects to it; the added objects do not have to be adjacent to the objects already selected. The user can add either an individual object or a range of objects to the selection by holding down the Shift key before making the additional selection. If the user holds down the Shift key and selects one or more objects that are already highlighted, the objects are deselected.

Extended selections can be made across the panes of a split window. (See "Splitting Windows".)

Making a Discontinuous Selection

In graphics applications, objects aren't usually considered to be in any particular sequence. Therefore, the user can use Shift-click to extend a selection by a single object, even if that object is nowhere near the current selection. When this happens, the objects between the current selection and the new object are not automatically included in the selection. This kind of selection is called a discontinuous selection. In the case of graphics, all selections are discontinuous selections.

This is not the case with arrays and text, however. In these two kinds of applications, an extended selection made by a Shift-click always includes everything between the old selection and the new endpoint. To provide the possibility of a discontinuous selection in these applications, Command-click is included in the user interface.

To make a discontinuous selection in a text or array application, the user selects the first piece in the normal way, then holds down the Command key before selecting the remaining pieces. Each piece is selected in the same way as if it were the whole selection, but because the Command key is held down, the new pieces are added to the existing selection instead of supplanting it.

If one of the pieces selected is already within an existing part of the selection, then instead of being added to the selection it's removed from the selection. Figure 7 shows a sequence in which several pieces are selected and deselected.

Not all applications support discontinuous selections, and those that do might restrict the operations that a user can perform on them. For example, a word processor might allow the user to choose a font after making a discontinuous selection, but not to choose Cut.

Selecting Text

Text is used in most applications; it's selected and edited in a consistent way, regardless of where it appears.

A block of text is a string of characters. A text selection is a substring of this string, which can have any length from zero characters to the whole block. Each of the text selection methods selects a different kind of substring. Figure 8 shows different kinds of text selections.

The Macintosh User Interface Guidelines

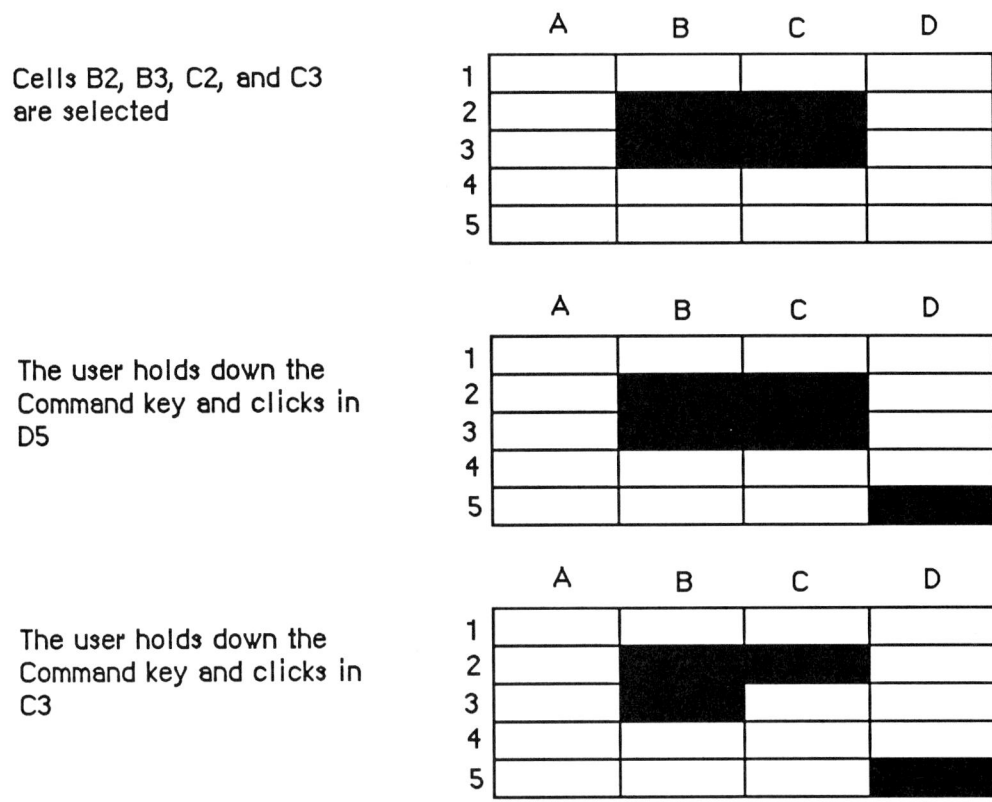

Figure 7. Discontinuous Selection

Insertion point	And|springth the wude nu.
Range of characters	A**nd spr**ingth the wude nu.
Word	**And** springth the wude nu.
Range of words	**And springth** the wude nu.
Discontinuous selection	A**nd spr**ingth the **wude** nu.

Figure 8. Text Selections

Insertion Point

The insertion point is a zero-length text selection. The user establishes the location of the insertion point by clicking between two characters. The insertion point then appears at the nearest character boundary. If the user clicks to the right of the last character on a line, the insertion point

Selecting I-41

Inside Macintosh

appears immediately after the last character. The converse is true if the user clicks to the left of the first character in the line.

The insertion point shows where text will be inserted when the user begins typing, or where cut or copied data (the contents of the Clipboard) will be pasted. After each character is typed, the insertion point is relocated to the right of the insertion.

If, between the mouse-down and the mouse-up, the user moves the pointer more than about half the width of a character, the selection is a range selection rather than an insertion point.

Selecting Words

The user selects a whole word by double-clicking somewhere within that word. If the user begins a double-click sequence, but then drags the mouse between the mouse-down and the mouse-up of the second click, the selection becomes a range of words rather than a single word. As the pointer moves, the application highlights or unhighlights a whole word at a time.

A word, or range of words, can also be selected in the same way as any other range; whether this type of selection is treated as a range of characters or as a range of words depends on the operation. For example, in MacWrite, a range of individual characters that happens to coincide with a range of words is treated like characters for purposes of extending a selection, but is treated like words for purposes of "intelligent" cut and paste (described later in the "Text Editing" section).

A word is defined as any continuous string that contains only the following characters:

- a letter (including letters with diacritical marks)
- a digit
- a nonbreaking space (Option-space)
- a dollar sign, cent sign, English pound symbol, or yen symbol
- a percent sign
- a comma between digits
- a period before a digit
- an apostrophe between letters or digits
- a hyphen, but not a minus sign (Option-hyphen) or a dash (Option-Shift-hyphen)

This is the definition in the United States and Canada; in other countries, it would have to be changed to reflect local formats for numbers, dates, and currency.

If the user double-clicks over any character not on the list above, that character is selected, but it is not considered a word.

Examples of words:

$123,456.78

shouldn't

3 1/2 [with a nonbreaking space]

.5%

Examples of nonwords:

7/10/6

blue cheese   [with a breaking space]

"Yoicks!"   [the quotation marks and exclamation point aren't part of the word]

Selecting a Range of Text

The user selects a range of text by dragging through the range. A range is either a range of words or a range of individual characters, as described under "Selecting Words", above.

If the user extends the range, the way the range is extended depends on what kind of range it is. If it's a range of individual characters, it can be extended one character at a time. If it's a range of words (including a single word), it's extended only by whole words.

Graphics Selections

There are several different ways to select graphic objects and to show selection feedback in existing Macintosh applications. MacDraw, MacPaint, and the Finder all illustrate different possibilities. This section describes the MacDraw paradigm, which is the most extensible to other kinds of applications.

A MacDraw document is a collection of individual graphic objects. To select one of these objects, the user clicks once on the object, which is then shown with knobs. (The knobs are used to stretch or shrink the object, and won't be discussed in these guidelines.) Figure 9 shows some examples of selection in MacDraw.

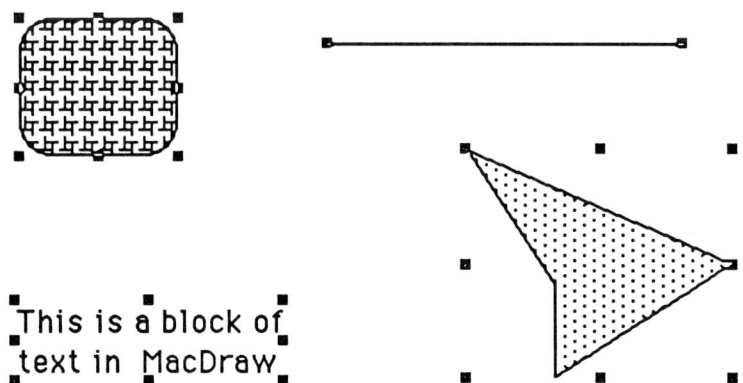

Figure 9. Graphics Selections in MacDraw

To select more than one object, the user can select either a range or a multiple selection. A range selection includes every object completely contained within the dotted rectangle that encloses the range, while an extended selection includes only those objects explicitly selected.

Selections in Arrays

As described above under "Types of Applications", an array is a one- or two-dimensional arrangement of fields. If the array is one-dimensional, it's called a form; if it's two-dimensional, it's called a table. The user can select one or more fields, or part of the contents of a field.

To select a single field, the user clicks in the field. The user can also implicitly select a field by moving into it with the Tab or Return key.

The Tab key cycles through the fields in an order determined by the application. From each field, the Tab key selects the "next" field. Typically, the sequence of fields is first from left to right, and then from top to bottom. When the last field in a form is selected, pressing the Tab key selects the first field in the form. In a form, an application might prefer to select the fields in logical, rather than physical, order.

The Return key selects the first field in the next row. If the idea of rows doesn't make sense in a particular context, then the Return key should have the same effect as the Tab key.

Tables are more likely than forms to support range selections and extended selections. A table can also support selection of rows and columns. The most convenient way for the user to select a column is to click in the column header. To select more than one column, the user drags through several column headers. The same applies to rows.

To select part of the contents of a field, the user must first select the field. The user then clicks again to select the desired part of the field. Since the contents of a field are either text or graphics, this type of selection follows the rules outlined above. Figure 10 shows some selections in an array.

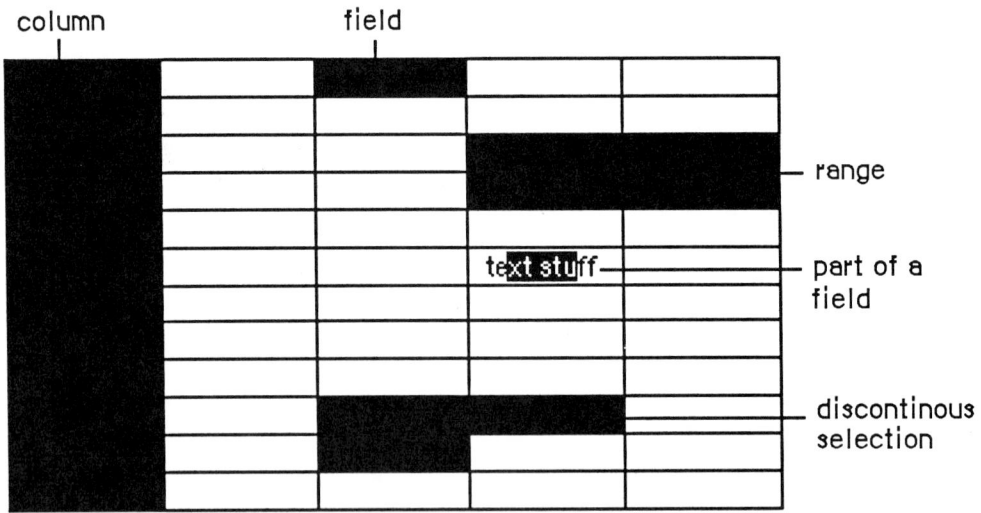

Figure 10. Array Selections

WINDOWS

The rectangles on the desktop that display information are windows. The most commmon types of windows are document windows, desk accessories, dialog boxes, and alert boxes. (Dialog and alert boxes are discussed under "Dialogs and Alerts".) Some of the features described in this section are applicable only to document windows. Figure 11 shows a typical active document window and some of its components.

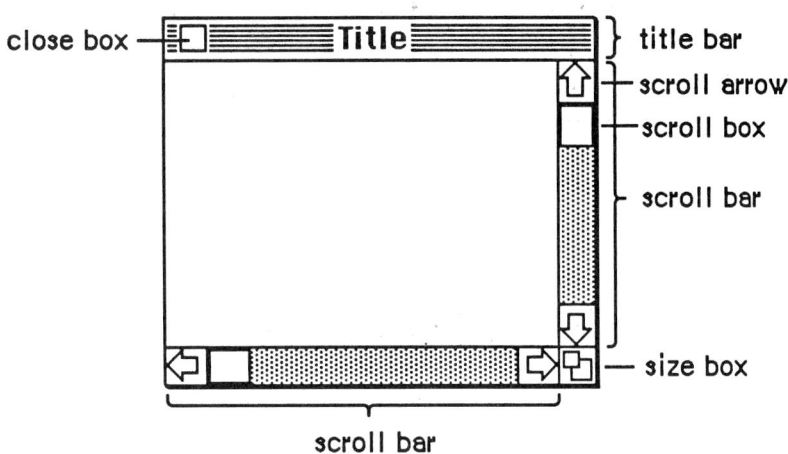

Figure 11. An Active Window

Multiple Windows

Some applications may be able to keep several windows on the desktop at the same time. Each window is in a different plane. Windows can be moved around on the Macintosh's desktop much like pieces of paper can be moved around on a real desktop. Each window can overlap those behind it, and can be overlapped by those in front of it. Even when windows don't overlap, they retain their front-to-back ordering.

Different windows can represent separate documents being viewed or edited simultaneously, or related parts of a logical whole, like the listing, execution, and debugging of a program. Each application may deal with the meaning and creation of multiple windows in its own way.

The advantage of multiple windows is that the user can isolate unrelated chunks of information from each other. The disadvantage is that the desktop can become cluttered, especially if some of the windows can't be moved. Figure 12 shows multiple windows.

Opening and Closing Windows

Windows come up onto the screen in different ways as appropriate to the purpose of the window. The application controls at least the initial size and placement of its windows.

Most windows have a close box that, when clicked, makes the window go away. The application in control of the window determines what's done with the window visually and logically when the close box is clicked. Visually, the window can either shrink to a smaller object such as an icon, or leave no trace behind when it closes. Logically, the information in the window is either retained and then restored when the window is reopened (which is the usual case), or else the window is reinitialized each time it's opened. When a document is closed, the user is given the choice whether to save any changes made to the document since the last time it was saved.

Inside Macintosh

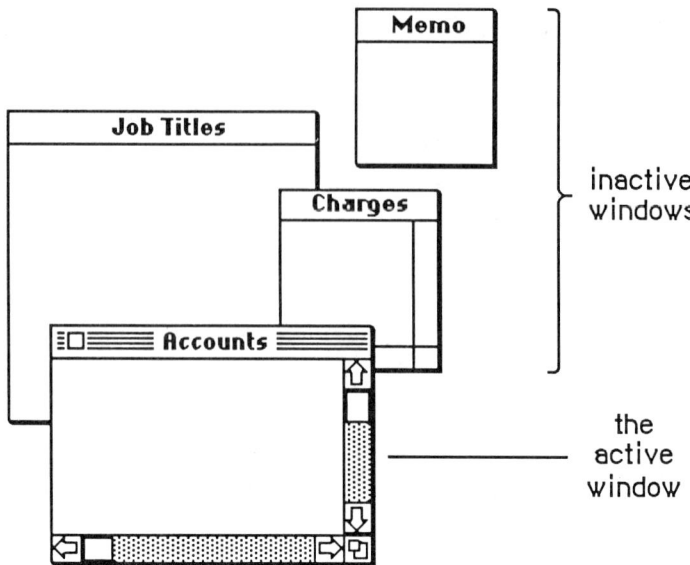

Figure 12. Multiple Windows

If an application doesn't support closing a window with a close box, it shouldn't include a close box on the window.

The Active Window

Of all the windows that are open on the desktop, the user can work in only one window at a time. This window is called the **active** window. All other open windows are **inactive**. To make a window active, the user clicks in it. Making a window active has two immediate consequences:

- The window changes its appearance: Its title bar is highlighted and the scroll bars and size box are shown. If the window is being reactivated, the selection that was in effect when it was deactivated is rehighlighted.
- The window is moved to the frontmost plane, so that it's shown in front of any windows that it overlaps.

Clicking in a window does nothing except activate it. To make a selection in the window, the user must click again. When the user clicks in a window that has been deactivated, the window should be reinstated just the way it was when it was deactivated, with the same position of the scroll box, and the same selection highlighted.

When a window becomes inactive, all the visual changes that took place when it was activated are reversed. The title bar becomes unhighlighted, the scroll bars and size box aren't shown, and no selection is shown in the window.

Moving a Window

Each application initially places windows on the screen wherever it wants them. The user can move a window—to make more room on the desktop or to uncover a window it's overlapping

The Macintosh User Interface Guidelines

—by dragging it by its title bar. As soon as the user presses in the title bar, that window becomes the active window. A dotted outline of the window follows the pointer until the user releases the mouse button. At the release of the button the full window is drawn in its new location. Moving a window doesn't affect the appearance of the document within the window.

If the user holds down the Command key while moving the window, the window isn't made active; it moves in the same plane.

The application should ensure that a window can never be moved completely off the screen.

Changing the Size of a Window

If a window has a size box in its bottom right corner, where the scroll bars come together, the user can change the size of the window—enlarging or reducing it to the desired size.

Dragging the size box attaches a dotted outline of the window to the pointer. The outline's top left corner stays fixed, while the bottom right corner follows the pointer. When the mouse button is released, the entire window is redrawn in the shape of the dotted outline.

Moving windows and sizing them go hand in hand. If a window can be moved, but not sized, then the user ends up constantly moving windows on and off the screen. The reason for this is that if the user moves the window off the right or bottom edge of the screen, the scroll bars are the first thing to disappear. To scroll the window, the user must move the window back onto the screen again. If, on the other hand, the window can be resized, then the user can change its size instead of moving it off the screen, and will still be able to scroll.

Sizing a window doesn't change the position of the top left corner of the window over the document or the appearance of the part of the view that's still showing; it changes only how much of the view is visible inside the window. One exception to this rule is a command such as Reduce to Fit in MacDraw, which changes the scaling of the view to fit the size of the window. If, after choosing this command, the user resizes the window, the application changes the scaling of the view.

The application can define a minimum window size. Any attempt to shrink the window below this size is ignored.

Scroll Bars

Scroll bars are used to change which part of a document view is shown in a window. Only the active window can be scrolled.

A scroll bar (see Figure 11 above) is a light gray shaft, capped on each end with square boxes labeled with arrows; inside the shaft is a white rectangle. The shaft represents one dimension of the entire document; the white rectangle (called the scroll box) represents the location of the portion of the document currently visible inside the window. As the user moves the document under the window, the position of the rectangle in the scroll bar moves correspondingly. If the document is no larger than the window, the scroll bars are inactive (the scrolling apparatus isn't shown in them). If the document window is inactive, the scroll bars aren't shown at all.

There are three ways to move the document under the window: by sequential scrolling, by "paging" windowful by windowful through the document, and by directly positioning the scroll box.

Inside Macintosh

Clicking a scroll arrow lets the user see more of the document in the direction of the scroll arrow, so it moves the document in the *opposite* direction from the arrow. For example, when the user clicks the top scroll arrow, the document moves down, bringing the view closer to the top of the document. The scroll box moves towards the arrow being clicked.

Each click in a scroll arrow causes movement a distance of one unit in the chosen direction, with the unit of distance being appropriate to the application: one line for a word processor, one row or column for a spreadsheet, and so on. Within a document, units should always be the same size, for smooth scrolling. Pressing the scroll arrow causes continuous movement in its direction.

Clicking the mouse anywhere in the gray area of the scroll bar advances the document by windowfuls. The scroll box, and the document view, move toward the place where the user clicked. Clicking below the scroll box, for example, brings the user the next windowful towards the bottom of the document. Pressing in the gray area keeps windowfuls flipping by until the user releases the mouse button, or until the location of the scroll box catches up to the location of the pointer. Each windowful is the height or width of the window, minus one unit overlap (where a unit is the distance the view scrolls when the scroll arrow is clicked once).

In both the above schemes, the user moves the document incrementally until it's in the proper position under the window; as the document moves, the scroll box moves accordingly. The user can also move the document directly to any position simply by moving the scroll box to the corresponding position in the scroll bar. To move the scroll box, the user drags it along the scroll bar; an outline of the scroll box follows the pointer. When the mouse button is released, the scroll box jumps to the position last held by the outline, and the document jumps to the position corresponding to the new position of the scroll box.

If the user starts dragging the scroll box, and then moves the pointer a certain distance outside the scroll bar, the scroll box detaches itself from the pointer and stops following it; if the user releases the mouse button, the scroll box stays in its original position and the document remains unmoved. But if the user still holds the mouse button and drags the pointer back into the scroll bar, the scroll box reattaches itself to the pointer and can be dragged as usual.

If a document has a fixed size, and the user scrolls to the right or bottom edge of the document, the application displays a gray background between the edge of the document and the window frame.

Automatic Scrolling

There are several instances when the application, rather than the user, scrolls the document. These instances involve some potentially sticky problems about how to position the document within the window after scrolling.

The first case is when the user moves the pointer out of the window while selecting by dragging. The window keeps up with the selection by scrolling automatically in the direction the pointer has been moved. The rate of scrolling is the same as if the user were pressing on the corresponding scroll arrow or arrows.

The second case is when the selection isn't currently showing in the window, and the user performs an operation on it. When this happens, it's usually because the user has scrolled the document after making a selection. In this case, the application scrolls the window so that the selection is showing before performing the operation.

The Macintosh User Interface Guidelines

The third case is when the application performs an operation whose side effect is to make a new selection. An example is a search operation, after which the object of the search is selected. If this object isn't showing in the window, the application must scroll the document so as to show it.

The second and third cases present the same problem: Where should the selection be positioned within the window after scrolling? The primary rule is that the application should avoid unnecessary scrolling; users prefer to retain control over the positioning of a document. The following guidelines should be helpful:

- If part of the new selection is already showing in the window, don't scroll at all. An exception to this rule is when the part of the selection that isn't showing is more important than the part that is showing.
- If scrolling in one orientation (horizontal or vertical) is sufficient to reveal the selection, don't scroll in both orientations.
- If the selection is smaller than the window, position the selection so that some of its context is showing on each side. It's better to put the selection somewhere near the middle of the window than right up against the corner.
- Even if the selection is too large to show in the window, it might be preferable to show some context rather than to try to fit as much as possible of the selection in the window.

Splitting a Window

Sometimes it's desirable to be able to see disjoint parts of a document simultaneously. Applications that accommodate such a capability allow the window to be split into independently scrollable **panes**.

Applications that support splitting a window into panes place split bars at the top of the vertical scroll bar and to the left of the horizontal one. Pressing a split bar attaches it to the pointer. Dragging the split bar positions it anywhere along the scroll bar; releasing the mouse button moves the split bar to a new position, splits the window at that location, and divides the appropriate scroll bar into separate scroll bars for each pane. Figure 13 shows the ways a window can be split.

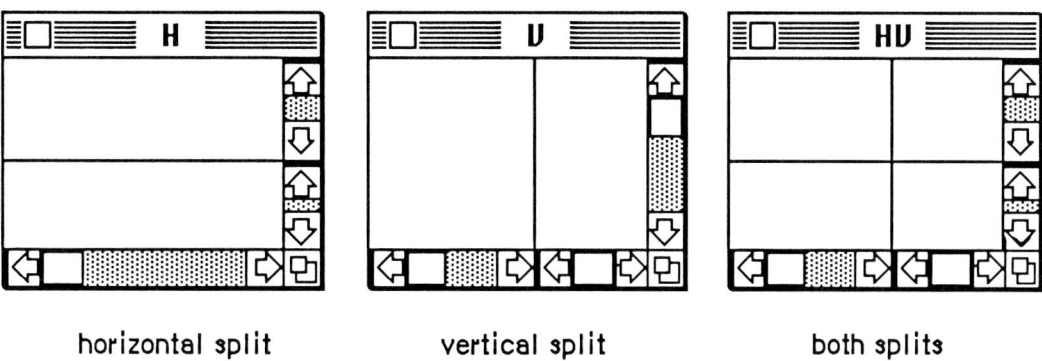

horizontal split   vertical split   both splits

Figure 13. Types of Split Windows

Inside Macintosh

After a split, the document appears the same, except for the split line lying across it. But there are now separate scroll bars for each pane. The panes are still scrolled together in the orientation of the split, but can be scrolled independently in the other orientation. For example, if the split is vertical, then vertical scrolling (using the scroll bar along the right of the window) is still synchronous; horizontal scrolling is controlled separately for each pane, using the two scroll bars along the bottom of the window. This is shown in Figure 14.

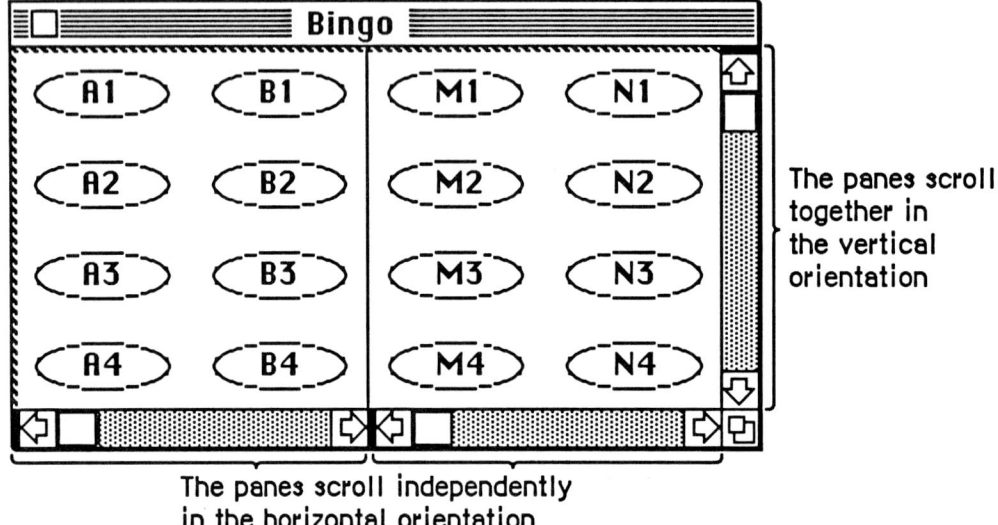

Figure 14. Scrolling a Split Window

To remove a split, the user drags the split bar to either end of the scroll bar.

The number of views in a document doesn't alter the number of selections per document: that is, one. The selection appears highlighted in all views that show it. If the application has to scroll automatically to show the selection, the pane that should be scrolled is the last one that the user clicked in. If the selection is already showing in one of the panes, no automatic scrolling takes place.

Panels

If a document window is more or less permanently divided into different areas, each of which has different content, these areas are called **panels**. Unlike panes, which show different parts of the same document but are functionally identical, panels are functionally different from each other but might show different interpretations of the same part of the document. For example, one panel might show a graphic version of the document while another panel shows a textual version.

Panels can behave much like windows; they can have scroll bars, and can even be split into more than one pane. An example of a panel with scroll bars is the list of files in the Open command's dialog box.

Whether to use panels instead of separate windows is up to the application. Multiple panels in the same window are more compact than separate windows, but they have to be moved, opened, and closed as a unit.

COMMANDS

Once information that's to be operated on has been selected, a command to operate on the information can be chosen from lists of commands called **menus**.

Macintosh's pull-down menus have the advantage that they're not visible until the user wants to see them; at the same time they're easy for the user to see and choose items from.

Most commands either do something, in which case they're verbs or verb phrases, or else they specify an attribute of an object, in which case they're adjectives. They usually apply to the current selection, although some commands apply to the whole document or window.

When you're designing your application, don't assume that everything has to be done through menu commands. Sometimes it's more appropriate for an operation to take place as a result of direct user manipulation of a graphic object on the screen, such as a control or icon. Alternatively, a single command can execute complicated instructions if it brings up a dialog box for the user to fill in.

The Menu Bar

The **menu bar** is displayed at the top of the screen. It contains a number of words and phrases: These are the titles of the menus associated with the current application. Each application has its own menu bar. The names of the menus do not change, except when the user accesses a desk accessory that uses different menus.

Only menu titles appear in the menu bar. If all of the commands in a menu are currently disabled (that is, the user can't choose them), the menu title should be dimmed (drawn in gray). The user can pull down the menu to see the commands, but can't choose any of them.

Choosing a Menu Command

To choose a command, the user positions the pointer over the menu title and presses the mouse button. The application highlights the title and displays the menu, as shown in Figure 15.

While holding down the mouse button, the user moves the pointer down the menu. As the pointer moves to each command, the command is highlighted. The command that's highlighted when the user releases the mouse button is chosen. As soon as the mouse button is released, the command blinks briefly, the menu disappears, and the command is executed. (The user can set the number of times the command blinks in the Control Panel desk accessory.) The menu title in the menu bar remains highlighted until the command has completed execution.

Nothing actually happens until the user chooses the command; the user can look at any of the menus without making a commitment to do anything.

The most frequently used commands should be at the top of a menu; research shows that the easiest item for the user to choose is the second item from the top. The most dangerous commands should be at the bottom of the menu, preferably isolated from the frequently used commands.

Inside Macintosh

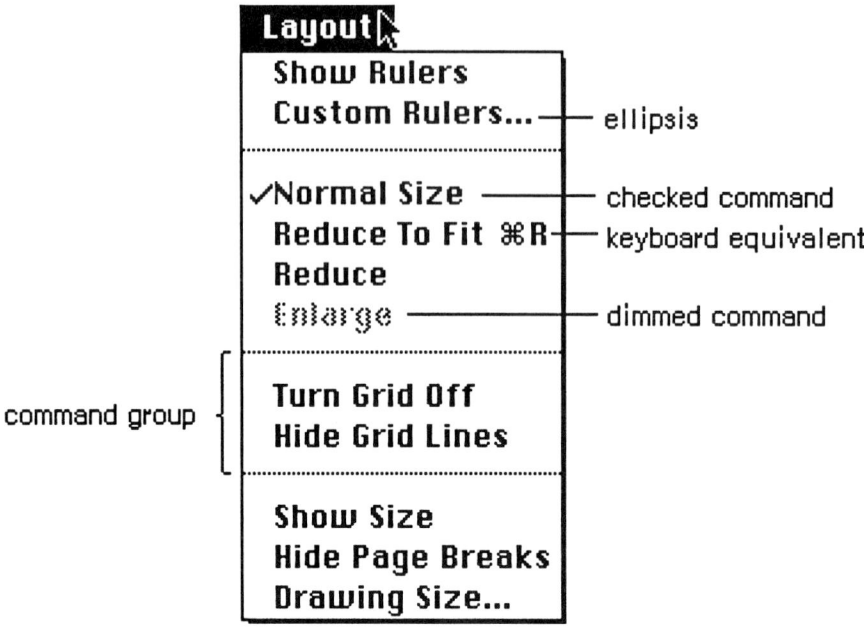

Figure 15. Menu

Appearance of Menu Commands

The commands in a particular menu should be logically related to the title of the menu. In addition to command names, three features of menus help the user understand what each command does: command groups, toggles, and special visual features.

Command Groups

As mentioned above, menu commands can be divided into two kinds: verbs and adjectives, or actions and attributes. An important difference between the two kinds of commands is that an attribute stays in effect until it's canceled, while an action ceases to be relevant after it has been performed. Each of these two kinds can be grouped within a menu. Groups are separated by dotted lines, which are implemented as disabled commands.

The most basic reason to group commands is to break up a menu so it's easier to read. Commands grouped for this reason are logically related, but independent. Commands that are actions are usually grouped this way, such as Cut, Copy, Paste, and Clear in the Edit menu.

Attribute commands that are interdependent are grouped to show this interdependence. Two kinds of attribute command groups are mutually exclusive groups and accumulating groups.

In a mutually exclusive attribute group, only one command in the group is in effect at any time. The command that's in effect is preceded by a check mark. If the user chooses a different command in the group, the check mark is moved to the new command. An example is the Font menu in MacWrite; no more than one font can be in effect at a time.

In an accumulating attribute group, any number of attributes can be in effect at the same time. One special command in the group cancels all the other commands. An example is the Style menu in MacWrite: The user can choose any combination of Bold, Italic, Underline, Outline, or Shadow, but Plain Text cancels all the other commands.

Toggled Commands

Another way to show the presence or absence of an attribute is by a toggled command. In this case, the attribute has two states, and a single command allows the user to toggle between the states. For example, when rulers are showing in MacWrite, a command in the Format menu reads "Hide Rulers". If the user chooses this command, the rulers are hidden, and the command is changed to read "Show Rulers". This kind of group should be used only when the wording of the commands makes it obvious that they're opposites.

Special Visual Features

In addition to the command names and how they're grouped, several other features of commands communicate information to the user:

- A check mark indicates whether an attribute command is currently in effect.

- An ellipsis (...) after a command name means that choosing that command brings up a dialog box. The command isn't actually executed until the user has finished filling in the dialog box and has clicked the OK button or its equivalent.

- The application dims a command when the user can't choose it. If the user moves the pointer over a dimmed item, it isn't highlighted.

- If a command can be chosen from the keyboard, it's followed by the Command key symbol and the character used to choose it. To choose a command this way, the user holds down the Command key and then presses the character key.

Some characters that can be typed along with the Command key are reserved for special purposes, but there are different degrees of stringency. Since almost every application has an Edit menu and a File menu, the keyboard equivalents in those menus are strongly reserved, and should never be used for any other purpose:

Character	Command
C	Copy (Edit menu)
Q	Quit (File menu)
V	Paste (Edit menu)
X	Cut (Edit menu)
Z	Undo (Edit menu)

Note: The keyboard equivalent for the Quit command is useful in case there's a mouse malfunction, so the user will still be able to leave the application in an orderly way (with the opportunity to save any changes to documents that haven't yet been saved).

Inside Macintosh

The keyboard equivalents in the Style menu are conditionally reserved. If an application has this menu, it shouldn't use these characters for any other purpose, but if it doesn't, it can use them however it likes:

Character	Command
B	Bold
I	Italic
O	Outline
P	Plain text
S	Shadow
U	Underline

One keyboard command doesn't have a menu equivalent:

Character	Command
.	Stop current operation

Several other menu features are also supported:

- A command can be shown in Bold, Italic, Outline, Underline, or Shadow character style.
- A command can be preceded by an icon.
- The application can draw its own type of menu. An example of this is the Fill menu in MacDraw.

STANDARD MENUS

One of the strongest ways in which Macintosh applications can take advantage of the consistency of the user interface is by using standard menus. The operations controlled by these menus occur so frequently that it saves considerable time for users if they always match exactly. Three of these menus, the Apple, File, and Edit menus, appear in almost every application. The Font, FontSize, and Style menus affect the appearance of text, and appear only in applications where they're relevant.

The Apple Menu

Macintosh doesn't allow two applications to be running at once. Desk accessories, however, are mini-applications that are available while using any application.

At any time the user can issue a command to call up one of several desk accessories; the available accessories are listed in the Apple menu, as shown in Figure 16.

Accessories are disk-based: Only those accessories on an available disk can be used. The list of accessories is expanded or reduced according to what's available. More than one accessory can be on the desktop at a time.

The Macintosh User Interface Guidelines

Figure 16. Apple Menu

The Apple menu also contains the "About xxx" menu item, where "xxx" is the name of the application. Choosing this item brings up a dialog box with the name and copyright information for the application, as well as any other information the application wants to display.

The File Menu

The File menu lets the user perform certain simple filing operations without leaving the application and returning to the Finder. It also contains the commands for printing and for leaving the application. The standard File menu includes the commands shown in Figure 17. All of these commands are described below.

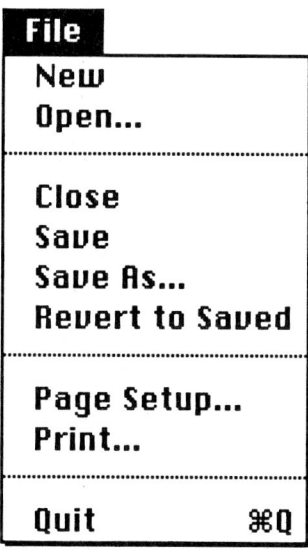

Figure 17. File Menu

Inside Macintosh

New

New opens a new, untitled document. The user names the document the first time it's saved. The New command is disabled when the maximum number of documents allowed by the application is already open; however, an application that allows only one document to be open at a time may make an exception to this, as described below for Open.

Open

Open opens an existing document. To select the document, the user is presented with a dialog box (Figure 18). This dialog box shows a list of all the documents, on the disk whose name is displayed, that can be handled by the current application. The user can scroll this list forward and backward. The dialog box also gives the user the chance to look at documents on another disk, or to eject a disk.

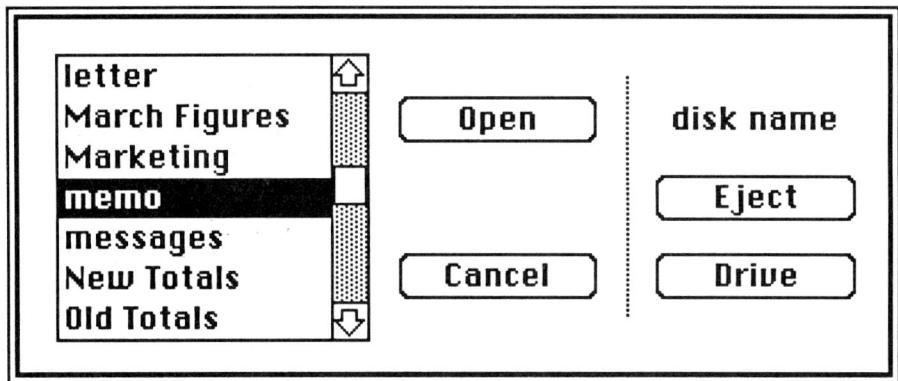

Figure 18. Open Dialog Box

Using the Open command, the user can only open a document that can be processed by the current application. Opening a document that can only be processed by a different application requires leaving the application and returning to the Finder.

The Open command is disabled when the maximum number of documents allowed by the application is already open. An application that allows only one document to be open at a time may make an exception to this, by first closing the open document before opening the new document. In this case, if the user has changed the open document since the last time it was saved, an alert box is presented as when an explicit Close command is given (see below); then the Open dialog box appears. Clicking Cancel in either the Close alert box or the Open dialog box cancels the entire operation.

Close

Close closes the active window, which may be a document window, a desk accessory, or any other type of window. If it's a document window and the user has changed the document since the last time it was saved, the command presents an alert box giving the user the opportunity to save the changes.

The Macintosh User Interface Guidelines

Clicking in the close box of a window is the same as choosing Close.

Save

Save makes permanent any changes to the active document since the last time it was saved. It leaves the document open.

If the user chooses Save for a new document that hasn't been named yet, the application presents the Save As dialog box (see below) to name the document, and then continues with the save. The active document remains active.

If there's not enough room on the disk to save the document, the application asks if the user wants to save the document on another disk. If the answer is yes, the application goes through the Save As dialog to find out which disk.

Save As

Save As saves a copy of the active document under a file name provided by the user.

If the document already has a name, Save As closes the old version of the document, creates a copy with the new name, and displays the copy in the window.

If the document is untitled, Save As saves the original document under the specified name. The active document remains active.

Revert to Saved

Revert to Saved returns the active document to the state it was in the last time it was saved. Before doing so, it puts up an alert box to confirm that this is what the user wants.

Page Setup

Page Setup lets the user specify printing parameters such as the paper size and printing orientation. These parameters remain with the document.

Print

Print lets the user specify various parameters such as print quality and number of copies, and then prints the document. The parameters apply only to the current printing operation.

Quit

Quit leaves the application and returns to the Finder. If any open documents have been changed since the last time they were saved, the application presents the same alert box as for Close, once for each document.

Inside Macintosh

The Edit Menu

The Edit menu contains the commands that delete, move, and copy objects, as well as commands such as Undo, Select All, and Show Clipboard. This section also discusses the Clipboard, which is controlled by the Edit menu commands. Text editing methods that don't use menu commands are discussed under "Text Editing".

If the application supports desk accessories, the order of commands in the Edit menu should be exactly as shown here. This is because, by default, the application passes the numbers, not the names, of the menu commands to the desk accessories. (For details, see chapter 14.) In particular, your application must provide an Undo command for the benefit of the desk accessories, even if it doesn't support the command (in which case it can disable the command until a desk accessory is opened).

The standard order of commands in the Edit menu is shown in Figure 19.

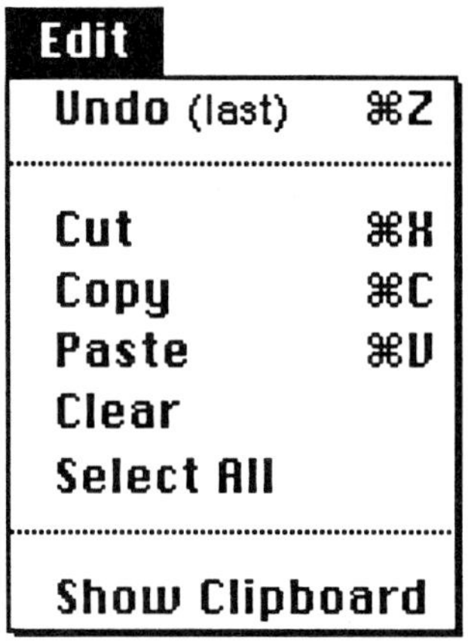

```
┌─────────────────────┐
│ Edit                │
├─────────────────────┤
│ Undo (last)    ⌘Z   │
├─────────────────────┤
│ Cut            ⌘X   │
│ Copy           ⌘C   │
│ Paste          ⌘V   │
│ Clear               │
│ Select All          │
├─────────────────────┤
│ Show Clipboard      │
└─────────────────────┘
```

Figure 19. Edit Menu

The Clipboard

The Clipboard holds whatever is cut or copied from a document. Its contents stay intact when the user changes documents, opens a desk accessory, or leaves the application. An application can show the contents of the Clipboard in a window, and can choose whether to have the Clipboard window open or closed when the application starts up.

The Clipboard window looks like a document window, with a close box but usually without scroll bars or a size box. The user can see its contents but cannot edit them. In most other ways the Clipboard window behaves just like any other window.

Every time the user performs a Cut or Copy on the current selection, a copy of the selection replaces the previous contents of the Clipboard. The previous contents are kept around in case the user chooses Undo.

There's only one Clipboard, which is present for all applications that support Cut, Copy, and Paste. The user can see the Clipboard window by choosing Show Clipboard from the Edit menu. If the window is already showing, it's hidden by choosing Hide Clipboard. (Show Clipboard and Hide Clipboard are a single toggled command.)

Because the contents of the Clipboard remain unchanged when applications begin and end, or when the user opens a desk accessory, the Clipboard can be used for transferring data among mutually compatible applications and desk accessories.

Undo

Undo reverses the effect of the previous operation. Not all operations can be undone; the definition of an undoable operation is somewhat application-dependent. The general rule is that operations that change the contents of the document are undoable, and operations that don't are not. Most menu items are undoable, and so are typing sequences.

A typing sequence is any sequence of characters typed from the keyboard or numeric keypad, including Backspace, Return, and Tab, but not including keyboard equivalents of commands.

Operations that aren't undoable include selecting, scrolling, and splitting the window or changing its size or location. None of these operations interrupts a typing sequence. For example, if the user types a few characters and then scrolls the document, the Undo command still undoes the typing. Whenever the location affected by the Undo operation isn't currently showing on the screen, the application should scroll the document so the user can see the effect of the Undo.

An application should also allow the user to undo any operations that are initiated directly on the screen, without a menu command. This includes operations controlled by setting dials, clicking check boxes, and so on, as well as drawing graphic objects with the mouse.

The actual wording of the Undo command as it appears in the Edit menu is "Undo xxx", where xxx is the name of the last operation. If the last operation isn't a menu command, use some suitable term after the word Undo. If the last operation can't be undone, the command reads "Undo", but is disabled.

If the last operation was Undo, the menu command is "Redo xxx", where xxx is the operation that was undone. If this command is chosen, the Undo is undone.

Cut

The user chooses Cut either to delete the current selection or to move it. A move is eventually completed by choosing Paste.

When the user chooses Cut, the application removes the current selection from the document and puts it in the Clipboard, replacing the Clipboard's previous contents. The place where the selection used to be becomes the new selection; the visual implications of this vary among applications. For example, in text, the new selection is an insertion point, while in an array, it's an empty but highlighted cell. If the user chooses Paste immediately after choosing Cut, the document should be just as it was before the cut.

Copy

Copy is the first stage of a copy operation. Copy puts a copy of the selection in the Clipboard, but the selection also remains in the document. The user completes the copy operation by choosing Paste.

Inside Macintosh

Paste

Paste is the last stage of a move or copy operation. It pastes the contents of the Clipboard into the document, replacing the current selection. The user can choose Paste several times in a row to paste multiple copies. After a paste, the new selection is the object that was pasted, except in text, where it's an insertion point immediately after the pasted text. The Clipboard remains unchanged.

Clear

When the user chooses Clear, or presses the Clear key on the numeric keypad, the application removes the selection, but doesn't put it in the Clipboard. The new selection is the same as it would be after a Cut.

Select All

Select All selects every object in the document.

Show Clipboard

Show Clipboard is a toggled command. When the Clipboard isn't displayed, the command is "Show Clipboard". If the user chooses this command, the Clipboard is displayed and the command changes to "Hide Clipboard".

Font-Related Menus

Three standard menus affect the appearance of text: Font, which determines the font of a text selection; FontSize, which determines the size of the characters; and Style, which determines aspects of its appearance such as boldface, italics, and so on.

A **font** is a set of typographical characters created with a consistent design. Things that relate characters in a font include the thickness of vertical and horizontal lines, the degree and position of curves and swirls, and the use of serifs. A font has the same general appearance, regardless of the size of the characters. Most Macintosh fonts are proportional rather than fixed-width; an application can't make assumptions about exactly how many characters will fit in a given area when these fonts are used.

Font Menu

The Font menu always lists the fonts that are currently available. Figure 20 shows a Font menu with some of the most common fonts.

Figure 20. Font Menu

FontSize Menu

Font sizes are measured in **points**; a point is about 1/72 of an inch. Each font is available in predefined sizes. The numbers of these sizes for each font are shown outlined in the FontSize menu. The font can also be scaled to other sizes, but it may not look as good. Figure 21 shows a FontSize menu with the standard font sizes.

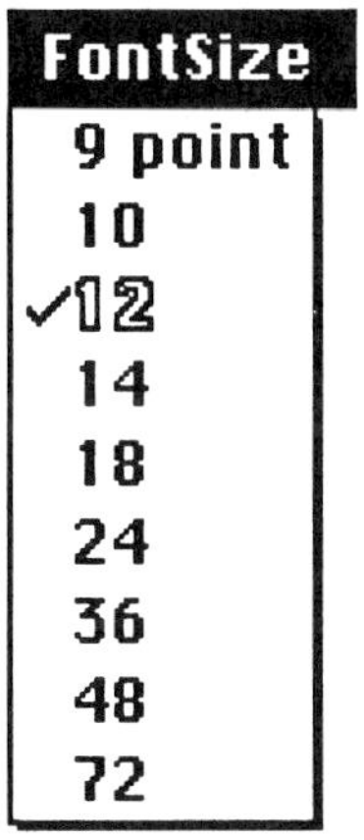

Figure 21. FontSize Menu

If there's insufficient room in the menu bar for the word FontSize, it can be abbreviated to Size. If there's insufficient room for both a Font menu and a Size menu, the sizes can be put at the end of the Font or Style menu.

Style Menu

The commands in the standard Style menu are Plain Text, Bold, Italic, Underline, Outline, and Shadow. All the commands except Plain Text are accumulating attributes; the user can choose any combination. A command that's in effect for the current selection is preceded by a check mark. Plain Text cancels all the other choices. Figure 22 shows these styles.

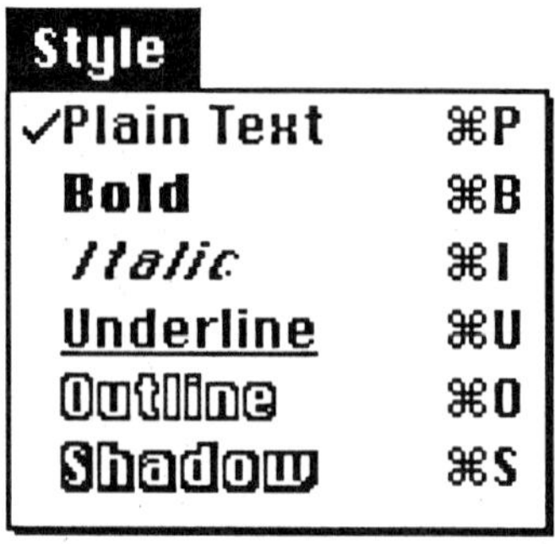

Inside Macintosh

Figure 22. Style Menu

TEXT EDITING

In addition to the operations described under "The Edit Menu" above, there are other ways to edit text that don't use menu items.

Inserting Text

To insert text, the user selects an insertion point by clicking where the text is to go, and then starts typing it. As the user types, the application continually moves the insertion point to the right of each new character.

Applications with multiline text blocks should support **word wraparound**; that is, no word should be broken between lines. The definition of a word is given under "Selecting Words" above.

Backspace

When the user presses the Backspace key, one of two things happens:
- If the current selection is one or more characters, it's deleted.
- If the current selection is an insertion point, the previous character is deleted.

In either case, the insertion point replaces the deleted characters in the document. The deleted characters don't go into the Clipboard, but the deletion can be undone by immediately choosing Undo.

Replacing Text

If the user starts typing when the selection is one or more characters, the characters that are typed replace the selection. The deleted characters don't go into the Clipboard, but the replacement can be undone by immediately choosing Undo.

The Macintosh User Interface Guidelines

Intelligent Cut and Paste

An application that lets the user select a word by double-clicking should also see to it that the user doesn't regret using this feature. The only way to do this is by providing "intelligent" cut and paste.

To understand why this feature is necessary, consider the following sequence of events in an application that doesn't provide it:

1. A sentence in the user's document reads:

    Returns are only accepted if the merchandise is damaged.

    The user wants to change this to:

    Returns are accepted only if the merchandise is damaged.

2. The user selects the word "only" by double-clicking. The letters are highlighted, but not either of the adjacent spaces.

3. The user chooses Cut, clicks just before the word "if", and chooses Paste.

4. The sentence now reads:

    Returns are accepted onlyif the merchandise is damaged.

    To correct the sentence, the user has to remove a space between "are" and "accepted", and add one between "only" and "if". At this point he or she may be wondering why the Macintosh is supposed to be easier to use than other computers.

If an application supports intelligent cut and paste, the rules to follow are:

- If the user selects a word or a range of words, highlight the selection, but not any adjacent spaces.
- When the user chooses Cut, if the character to the left of the selection is a space, discard it. Otherwise, if the character to the right of the selection is a space, discard it.
- When the user chooses Paste, if the character to the left or right of the current selection is part of a word, insert a space before pasting.

If the left or right end of a text selection is a word, follow these rules at that end, regardless of whether there's a word at the other end.

This feature makes more sense if the application supports the full definition of a word (as detailed above under "Selecting Words"), rather than the definition of a word as anything between two spaces.

These rules apply to any selection that's one or more whole words, whether it was chosen with a double click or as a range selection.

Figure 23 shows some examples of intelligent cut and paste.

Editing Fields

If an application isn't primarily a text application, but does use text in fields (such as in a dialog box), it may not be able to provide the full text editing capabilities described so far. It's important, however, that whatever editing capabilities the application provides under these circumstances be upward-compatible with the full text editing capabilities. The following list

Text Editing I-63

Example 1:

1. Select a word.   Drink to me **only** with thine eyes.

2. Choose Cut.   Drink to me| with thine eyes.

3. Select an insertion point. Drink to me with |thine eyes.

4. Choose Paste.   Drink to me with only|thine eyes.

Example 2:

1. Select a word.   How, **now** brown cow

2. Choose Cut.   How,| brown cow

3. Select an insertion point   How|, brown cow

4. Choose Paste.   How now|, brown cow

Figure 23. Intelligent Cut and Paste

shows the capabilities that can be provided, from the minimal to the most sophisticated:

- The user can select the whole field and type in a new value.
- The user can backspace.
- The user can select a substring of the field and replace it.
- The user can select a word by double-clicking.
- The user can choose Undo, Cut, Copy, Paste, and Clear, as described above under "The Edit Menu". In the most sophisticated version, the application implements intelligent cut and paste.

An application should also perform appropriate edit checks. For example, if the only legitimate value for a field is a string of digits, the application might issue an alert if the user typed any nondigits. Alternatively, the application could wait until the user is through typing before checking the validity of the field's contents. In this case, the appropriate time to check the field is when the user clicks anywhere other than within the field.

DIALOGS AND ALERTS

The "select-then-choose" paradigm is sufficient whenever operations are simple and act on only one object. But occasionally a command will require more than one object, or will need additional parameters before it can be executed. And sometimes a command won't be able to carry out its normal function, or will be unsure of the user's real intent. For these special circumstances the Macintosh user interface includes two additional features:

The Macintosh User Interface Guidelines

- dialogs, to allow the user to provide additional information before a command is executed
- alerts, to notify the user whenever an unusual situation occurs

Since both of these features lean heavily on controls, controls are described in this section, even though controls are also used in other places.

Controls

Friendly systems act by direct cause-and-effect; they do what they're told. Performing actions on a system in an indirect fashion reduces the sense of direct manipulation. To give Macintosh users the feeling that they're in control of their machines, many of an application's features are implemented with **controls**: graphic objects that, when manipulated with the mouse, cause instant action with visible results. Controls can also change settings to modify future actions.

There are four main types of controls: buttons, check boxes, radio buttons, and dials (see Figure 24). You can also design your own controls, such as a ruler on which tabs can be set.

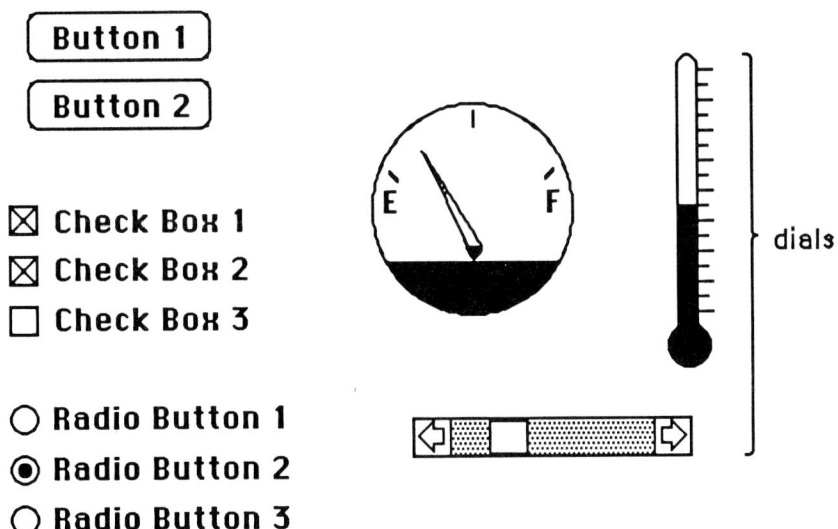

Figure 24. Controls

Buttons

Buttons are small objects labeled with text. Clicking or pressing a button performs the action described by the button's label.

Buttons usually perform instantaneous actions, such as completing operations defined by a dialog box or acknowledging error messages. They can also perform continuous actions, in which case the effect of pressing on the button would be the same as the effect of clicking it repeatedly.

Two particular buttons, OK and Cancel, are especially important in dialogs and alerts; they're discussed under those headings below.

Dialogs and Alerts   I-65

Inside Macintosh

Check Boxes and Radio Buttons

Whereas buttons perform instantaneous or continuous actions, check boxes and radio buttons let the user choose among alternative values for a parameter.

Check boxes act like toggle switches; they're used to indicate the state of a parameter that must be either off or on. The parameter is on if the box is checked, otherwise it's off. The check boxes appearing together in a given context are independent of each other; any number of them can be off or on.

Radio buttons typically occur in groups; they're round and are filled in with a black circle when on. They're called radio buttons because they act like the buttons on a car radio. At any given time, exactly one button in the group is on. Clicking one button in a group turns off the button that's currently on.

Both check boxes and radio buttons are accompanied by text that identifies what each button does.

Dials

Dials display the value, magnitude, or position of something in the application or system, and optionally allow the user to alter that value. Dials are predominantly analog devices, displaying their values graphically and allowing the user to change the value by dragging an **indicator**; dials may also have a digital display.

The most common example of a dial is the scroll bar. The indicator of the scroll bar is the scroll box; it represents the position of the window over the length of the document. The user can drag the scroll box to change that position. (See "Scroll Bars" above.)

Dialogs

Commands in menus normally act on only one object. If a command needs more information before it can be performed, it presents a **dialog box** to gather the additional information from the user. The user can tell which commands bring up dialog boxes because they're followed by an ellipsis (...) in the menu.

A dialog box is a rectangle that may contain text, controls, and icons. There should be some text in the box that indicates which command brought up the dialog box.

The user sets controls and text fields in the dialog box to provide the needed information. When the application puts up the dialog box, it should set the controls to some default setting and fill in the text fields with default values, if possible. One of the text fields (the "first" field) should be highlighted, so that the user can change its value just by typing in the new value. If all the text fields are blank, there should be an insertion point in the first field.

Editing text fields in a dialog box should conform to the guidelines detailed above under "Text Editing".

When the user is through editing an item:

- Pressing Tab accepts the changes made to the item, and selects the next item in sequence.
- Clicking in another item accepts the changes made to the previous item and selects the newly clicked item.

Dialog boxes are either modal or modeless, as described below.

Modal Dialog Boxes

A **modal** dialog box is one that the user must explicitly dismiss before doing anything else, such as making a selection outside the dialog box or choosing a command. Figure 25 shows a modal dialog box.

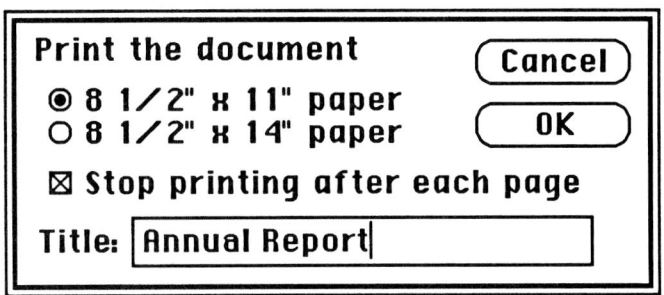

Figure 25. A Modal Dialog Box

Because it restricts the user's freedom of action, this type of dialog box should be used sparingly. In particular, the user can't choose a menu item while a modal dialog box is up, and therefore can only do the simplest kinds of text editing. For these reasons, the main use of a modal dialog box is when it's important for the user to complete an operation before doing anything else.

A modal dialog box usually has at least two buttons: OK and Cancel. OK dismisses the dialog box and performs the original command according to the information provided; it can be given a more descriptive name than "OK". Cancel dismisses the dialog box and cancels the original command; it should always be called "Cancel".

A dialog box can have other kinds of buttons as well; these may or may not dismiss the dialog box. One of the buttons in the dialog box may be outlined boldly. The outlined button is the **default button**; if no button is outlined, then the OK button is the default button. The default button should be the safest button in the current situation. Pressing the Return or Enter key has the same effect as clicking the default button. If there's no default button, Return and Enter have no effect.

A special type of modal dialog box is one with no buttons. This type of box just informs the user of a situation without eliciting any response. Usually, it would describe the progress of an ongoing operation. Since it has no buttons, the user has no way to dismiss it. Therefore, the application must leave it up long enough for the user to read it before taking it down.

Modeless Dialog Boxes

A **modeless** dialog box allows the user to perform other operations without dismissing the dialog box. Figure 26 shows a modeless dialog box.

A modeless dialog box is dismissed by clicking in the close box or by choosing Close when the dialog is active. The dialog box is also dismissed implicitly when the user chooses Quit. It's

Inside Macintosh

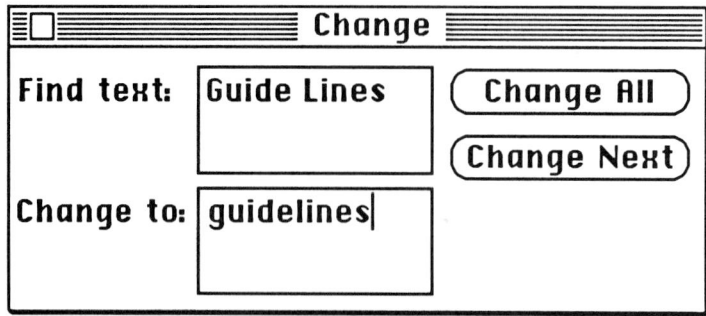

Figure 26. A Modeless Dialog Box

usually a good idea for the application to remember the contents of the dialog box after it's dismissed, so that when it's opened again, it can be restored exactly as it was.

Controls work the same way in modeless dialog boxes as in modal dialog boxes, except that buttons never dismiss the dialog box. In this context, the OK button means "go ahead and perform the operation, but leave the dialog box up", while Cancel usually terminates an ongoing operation.

A modeless dialog box can also have text fields; since the user can choose menu commands, the full range of editing capabilities can be made available.

Alerts

Every user of every application is liable to do something that the application won't understand or can't cope with in a normal manner. **Alerts** give applications a way to respond to errors not only in a consistent manner, but in stages according to the severity of the error, the user's level of expertise, and the particular history of the error. The two kinds of alerts are beeps and alert boxes.

Beeps are used for errors that are both minor and immediately obvious. For example, if the user tries to backspace past the left boundary of a text field, the application could choose to beep instead of putting up an alert box. A beep can also be part of a staged alert, as described below.

An alert box looks like a modal dialog box, except that it's somewhat narrower and appears lower on the screen. An alert box is primarily a one way communication from the system to the user; the only way the user can respond is by clicking buttons. Therefore alert boxes might contain dials and buttons, but usually not text fields, radio buttons, or check boxes. Figure 27 shows a typical alert box.

There are three types of alert boxes:

- Note: A minor mistake that wouldn't have any disastrous consequences if left as is.
- Caution: An operation that may or may not have undesirable results if it's allowed to continue. The user is given the choice whether or not to continue.
- Stop: A serious problem or other situation that requires remedial action by the user.

The Macintosh User Interface Guidelines

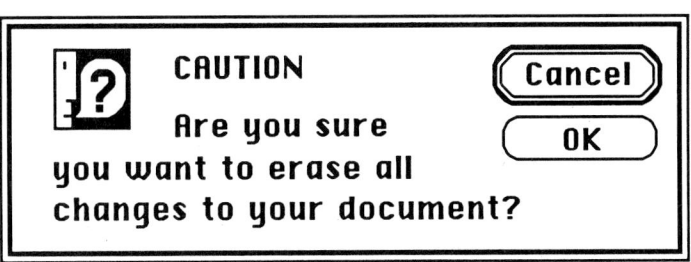

Figure 27. An Alert Box

An application can define different responses for each of several stages of an alert, so that if the user persists in the same mistake, the application can issue increasingly more helpful (or sterner) messages. A typical sequence is for the first two occurrences of the mistake to result in a beep, and for subsequent occurrences to result in an alert box. This type of sequence is especially appropriate when the mistake is one that has a high probability of being accidental (for example, when the user chooses Cut when there's no text selection).

How the buttons in an alert box are labeled depends on the nature of the box. If the box presents the user with a situation in which no alternative actions are available, the box has a single button that's labeled OK. Clicking this button means "I've read the alert." If the user is given alternatives, then typically the alert is phrased as a question that can be answered "yes" or "no". In this case, buttons labeled Yes and No are appropriate, although some variation such as Save and Don't Save is also acceptable. OK and Cancel can be used, as long as their meanings aren't ambiguous.

The preferred (safest) button to use in the current situation is boldly outlined. This is the alert's default button; its effect occurs if the user presses Return or Enter.

It's important to phrase messages in alert boxes so that users aren't left guessing the real meaning. Avoid computer jargon.

Use icons whenever possible. Graphics can better describe some error situations than words, and familiar icons help users distinguish their alternatives better. Icons should be internationally comprehensible; they shouldn't contain any words, or any symbols that are unique to a particular country.

Generally, it's better to be polite than abrupt, even if it means lengthening the message. The role of the alert box is to be helpful and make constructive suggestions, not to give orders. But its focus is to help the user solve the problem, not to give an interesting but academic description of the problem itself.

Under no circumstances should an alert message refer the user to external documentation for further clarification. It should provide an adequate description of the information needed by the user to take appropriate action.

The best way to make an alert message understandable is to think carefully through the error condition itself. Can the application handle this without an error? Is the error specific enough so that the user can fix the situation? What are the recommended solutions? Can the exact item causing the error be displayed in the alert message?

DO'S AND DON'TS OF A FRIENDLY USER INTERFACE

Do:

- Let the user have as much control as possible over the appearance of objects on the screen—their arrangement, size, and visibility.
- Use verbs for menu commands that perform actions.
- Make alert messages self-explanatory.
- Use controls and other graphics instead of just menu commands.
- Take the time to use good graphic design; it really helps.

Don't:

- Overuse modes, including modal dialog boxes.
- Require using the keyboard for an operation that would be easier with the mouse, or require using the mouse for an operation that would be easier with the keyboard.
- Change the way the screen looks unexpectedly, especially by scrolling automatically more than necessary.
- Redraw objects unnecessarily; it causes the screen to flicker annoyingly.
- Make up your own menus and then give them the same names as standard menus.
- Take an old-fashioned prompt-based application originally developed for another machine and pass it off as a Macintosh application.

3 MACINTOSH MEMORY MANAGEMENT: AN INTRODUCTION

- 73 About This Chapter
- 73 The Stack and the Heap
- 75 Pointers and Handles
- 78 General-Purpose Data Types
- 79   Type Coercion
- 81 Summary

Macintosh Memory Management: An Introduction

ABOUT THIS CHAPTER

This chapter contains the minimum information you'll need about memory management on the Macintosh. Memory management is covered in greater detail in chapter 1 of Volume II.

THE STACK AND THE HEAP

A running program can dynamically **allocate** and **release** memory in two places: the stack or the heap. The **stack** is an area of memory that can grow or shrink at one end while the other end remains fixed, as shown in Figure 1. This means that space on the stack is always allocated and released in LIFO (last-in-first-out) order: The last item allocated is always the first to be released. It also means that the allocated area of the stack is always contiguous. Space is released only at the top of the stack, never in the middle, so there can never be any unallocated "holes" in the stack.

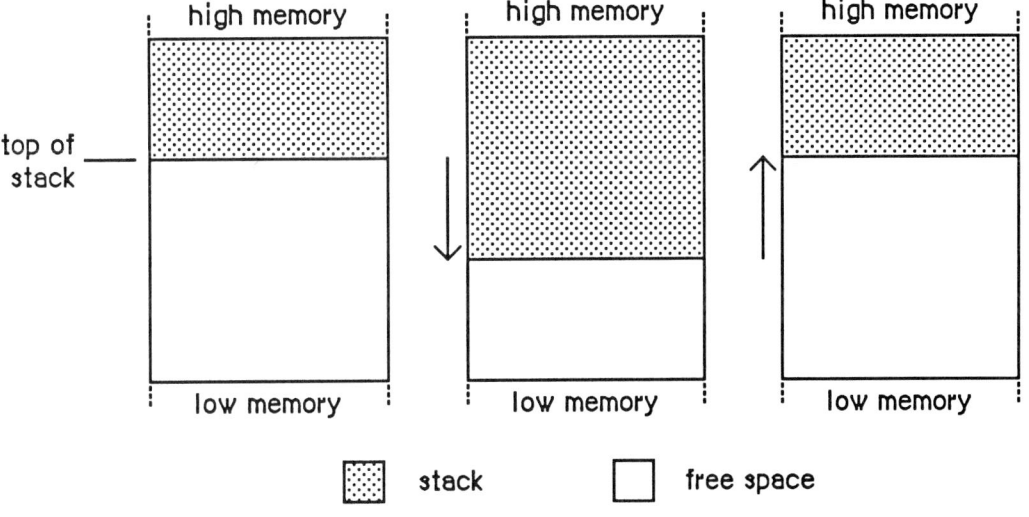

Figure 1. The Stack

By convention, the stack grows from high toward low memory addresses. The end of the stack that grows and shrinks is usually referred to as the "top" of the stack, even though it's actually at the lower end of the stack in memory.

When programs in high-level languages declare static variables (such as with the Pascal VAR declaration), those variables are allocated on the stack.

The other method of dynamic memory allocation is from the **heap**. Heap space is allocated and released only at the program's explicit request, through calls to the Memory Manager.

Space in the heap is allocated in **blocks**, which may be of any size needed for a particular object. The Memory Manager does all the necessary "housekeeping" to keep track of the blocks as they're allocated and released. Because these operations can occur in any order, the heap doesn't

The Stack and the Heap I-73

grow and shrink in an orderly way like the stack. After a program has been running for a while, the heap tends to become fragmented into a patchwork of allocated and free blocks, as shown in Figure 2.

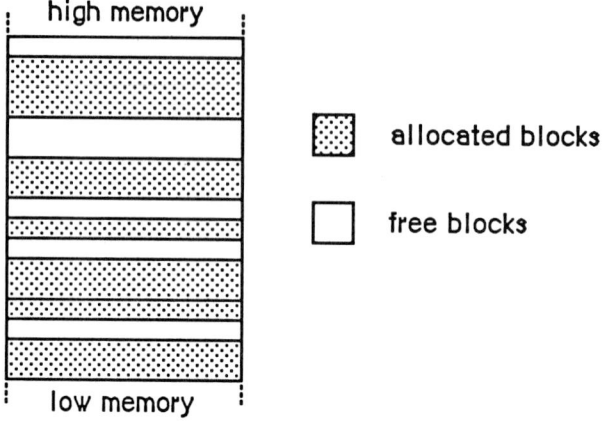

Figure 2. A Fragmented Heap

As a result of heap fragmentation, when the program asks to allocate a new block of a certain size, it may be impossible to satisfy the request even though there's enough free space available, because the space is broken up into blocks smaller than the requested size. When this happens, the Memory Manager will try to create the needed space by **compacting** the heap: moving allocated blocks together in order to collect the free space into a single larger block (see Figure 3).

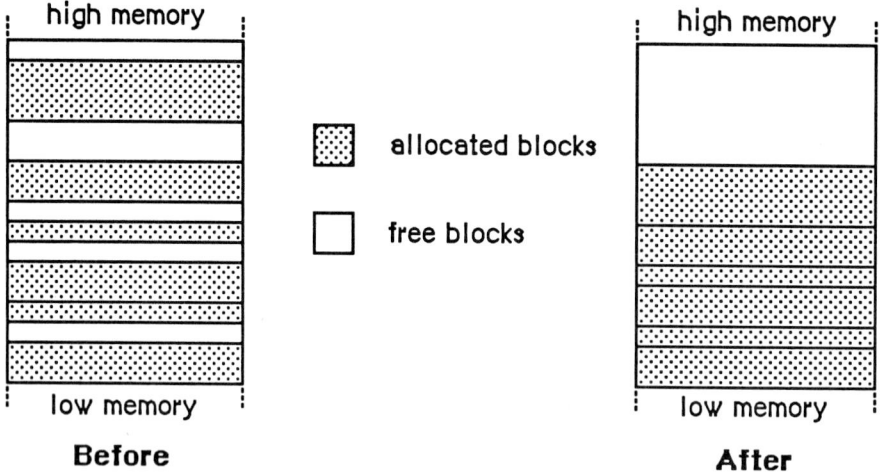

Figure 3. Heap Compaction

There's a **system heap** that's used by the Operating System and an **application heap** that's used by the Toolbox and the application program.

POINTERS AND HANDLES

The Memory Manager contains a few fundamental routines for allocating and releasing heap space. The NewPtr function allocates a block in the heap of a requested size and returns a pointer to the block. You can then make as many copies of the pointer as you need and use them in any way your program requires. When you're finished with the block, you can release the memory it occupies (returning it to available free space) with the DisposPtr procedure.

Once you've called DisposPtr, any pointers you may have to the block become invalid, since the block they're supposed to point to no longer exists. You have to be careful not to use such "dangling" pointers. This type of bug can be very difficult to diagnose and correct, since its effects typically aren't discovered until long after the pointer is left dangling.

Another way a pointer can be left dangling is for its underlying block to be moved to a different location within the heap. To avoid this problem, blocks that are referred to through simple pointers, as in Figure 4, are **nonrelocatable**. The Memory Manager will never move a nonrelocatable block, so you can rely on all pointers to it to remain correct for as long as the block remains allocated.

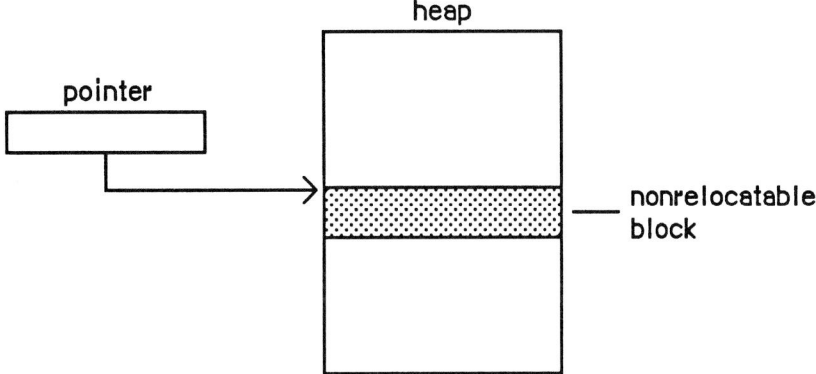

Figure 4. A Pointer to a Nonrelocatable Block

If all blocks in the heap were nonrelocatable, there would be no way to prevent the heap's free space from becoming fragmented. Since the Memory Manager needs to be able to move blocks around in order to compact the heap, it also uses **relocatable** blocks. (All the allocated blocks shown above in Figure 3, the illustration of heap compaction, are relocatable.) To keep from creating dangling pointers, the Memory Manager maintains a single **master pointer** to each relocatable block. Whenever a relocatable block is created, a master pointer is allocated from the heap at the same time and set to point to the block. All references to the block are then made by double indirection, through a pointer to the master pointer, called a **handle** to the block (see Figure 5). If the Memory Manager needs to move the block during compaction, it has only to update the master pointer to point to the block's new location; the master pointer itself is never moved. Since all copies of the handle point to this same master pointer, they can be relied on not to dangle, even after the block has been moved.

Inside Macintosh

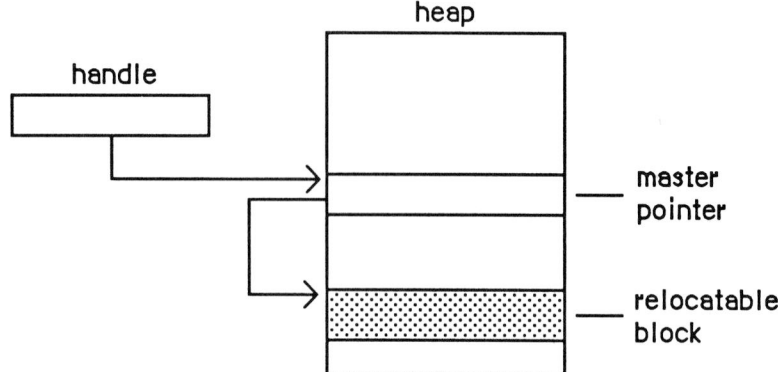

Figure 5. A Handle to a Relocatable Block

Relocatable blocks are moved only by the Memory Manager, and only at well-defined, predictable times. In particular, only the routines listed in Appendix B (Volume III) can cause blocks to move, and these routines can never be called from within an interrupt. If your program doesn't call these routines, you can rely on blocks not being moved.

The NewHandle function allocates a block in the heap of a requested size and returns a handle to the block. You can then make as many copies of the handle as you need and use them in any way your program requires. When you're finished with the block, you can free the space it occupies with the DisposHandle procedure.

> **Note:** Toolbox routines that create new objects of various kinds, such as NewWindow and NewControl, implicitly call the NewPtr and NewHandle routines to allocate the space they need. There are also analogous routines for releasing these objects, such as DisposeWindow and DisposeControl.

If the Memory Manager can't allocate a block of a requested size even after compacting the entire heap, it can try to free some space by **purging** blocks from the heap. Purging a block removes it from the heap and frees the space it occupies. The block's master pointer is set to NIL, but the space occupied by the master pointer itself remains allocated. Any handles to the block now point to a NIL master pointer, and are said to be **empty**. If your program later needs to refer to the purged block, it can detect that the handle has become empty and ask the Memory Manager to **reallocate** the block. This operation updates the original master pointer, so that all handles to the block are left referring correctly to its new location (see Figure 6).

> **Warning:** Reallocating a block recovers only the space it occupies, not its contents. Any information the block contains is lost when the block is purged. It's up to your program to reconstitute the block's contents after reallocating it.

Relocatable and nonrelocatable are permanent properties of a block that can never be changed once the block is allocated. A relocatable block can also be **locked** or **unlocked**, **purgeable** or **unpurgeable**; your program can set and change these attributes as necessary. Locking a block temporarily prevents it from being moved, even if the heap is compacted. The block can later be unlocked, again allowing the Memory Manager to move it during compaction. A block can be purged only if it's relocatable, unlocked, and purgeable. A newly allocated relocatable block is initially unlocked and unpurgeable.

Macintosh Memory Management: An Introduction

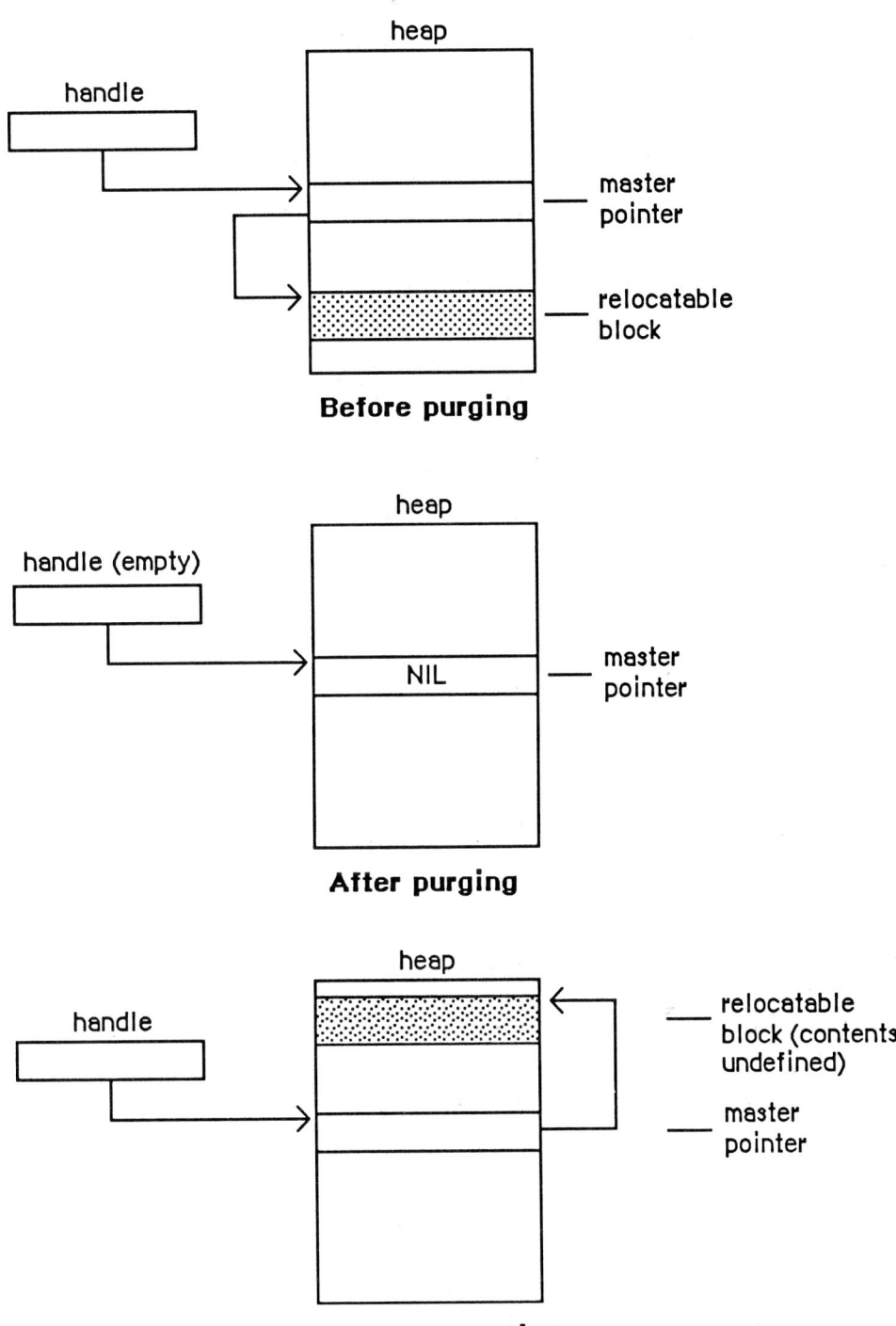

Figure 6. Purging and Reallocating a Block

GENERAL-PURPOSE DATA TYPES

The Memory Manager includes a number of type definitions for general-purpose use. For working with pointers and handles, there are the following definitions:

```
TYPE  SignedByte  = -128..127;
      Byte        = 0..255;
      Ptr         = ^SignedByte;
      Handle      = ^Ptr;
```

SignedByte stands for an arbitrary byte in memory, just to give Ptr and Handle something to point to. You can define a buffer of, say, bufSize untyped memory bytes as a PACKED ARRAY[1..bufSize] OF SignedByte. Byte is an alternative definition that treats byte-length data as unsigned rather than signed quantities.

For working with strings, pointers to strings, and handles to strings, the Memory Manager includes the following definitions:

```
TYPE  Str255       = STRING[255];
      StringPtr    = ^Str255;
      StringHandle = ^StringPtr;
```

For treating procedures and functions as data objects, there's the ProcPtr data type:

```
TYPE  ProcPtr = Ptr;
```

For example, after the declarations

```
VAR aProcPtr: ProcPtr;
    . . .

PROCEDURE MyProc;
  BEGIN
    . . .
  END;
```

you can make aProcPtr point to MyProc by using Lisa Pascal's @ operator, as follows:

```
aProcPtr := @MyProc
```

With the @ operator, you can assign procedures and functions to variables of type ProcPtr, embed them in data structures, and pass them as arguments to other routines. Notice, however, that the data type ProcPtr technically points to an arbitrary byte (SignedByte), not an actual routine. As a result, there's no way in Pascal to access the underlying routine via this pointer in order to call it. Only routines written in assembly language (such as those in the Operating System and the Toolbox) can actually call the routine designated by a pointer of type ProcPtr.

   Warning: You can't use the @ operator with procedures or functions whose declarations are nested within other routines.

Finally, for treating long integers as fixed-point numbers, there's the following data type:

Macintosh Memory Management: An Introduction

```
TYPE Fixed = LONGINT;
```

As illustrated in Figure 7, a **fixed-point number** is a 32-bit signed quantity containing an integer part in the high-order word and a fractional part in the low-order word. Negative numbers are the two's complement; they're formed by treating the fixed-point number as a long integer, inverting each bit, and adding 1 to the least significant bit.

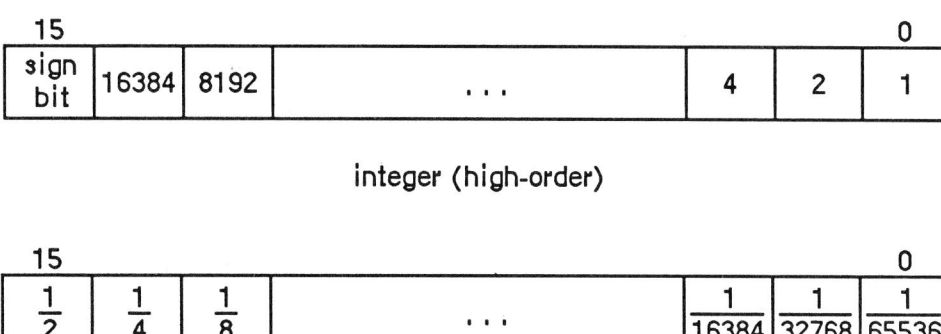

Figure 7. Fixed-Point Number

Type Coercion

Because of Pascal's strong typing rules, you can't directly assign a value of type Ptr to a variable of some other pointer type, or pass it as a parameter of some other pointer type. Instead, you have to coerce the pointer from one type to another. For example, assume the following declarations have been made:

```
TYPE  Thing       =  RECORD
                        . . .
                     END;

      ThingPtr    =  ^Thing;
      ThingHandle =  ^ThingPtr;

VAR   aPtr: Ptr;
      aThingPtr: ThingPtr;
      aThingHandle: ThingHandle;
```

In the Lisa Pascal statement

```
aThingPtr := ThingPtr(NewPtr(SIZEOF(Thing)))
```

NewPtr allocates heap space for a new record of type Thing and returns a pointer of type Ptr, which is then coerced to type ThingPtr so it can be assigned to aThingPtr. The statement

```
DisposPtr(Ptr(aThingPtr))
```

General-Purpose Data Types I-79

disposes of the record pointed to by aThingPtr, first coercing the pointer to type Ptr (as required by the DisposPtr procedure). Similar calls to NewHandle and DisposHandle would require coercion between the data types Handle and ThingHandle. Given a pointer aPtr of type Ptr, you can make aThingPtr point to the same object as aPtr with the assignment

```
aThingPtr := ThingPtr(aPtr)
```

or you can refer to a field of a record of type Thing with the expression

```
ThingPtr(aPtr)^.field
```

In fact, you can use this same syntax to equate any two variables of the same length. For example:

```
VAR aChar: CHAR;
    aByte: Byte;
    . . .

aByte := Byte(aChar)
```

You can also use the Lisa Pascal functions ORD, ORD4, and POINTER, to coerce variables of different length from one type to another. For example:

```
VAR anInteger: INTEGER;
    aLongInt: LONGINT;
    aPointer: Ptr;
    . . .

anInteger := ORD(aLongInt);       {two low-order bytes only}
anInteger := ORD(aPointer);       {two low-order bytes only}
aLongInt  := ORD(anInteger);      {packed into high-order bytes}
aLongInt  := ORD4(anInteger);     {packed into low-order bytes}
aLongInt  := ORD(aPointer);
aPointer  := POINTER(anInteger);
aPointer  := POINTER(aLongInt)
```

Assembly-language note: Of course, assembly-language programmers needn't bother with type coercion.

SUMMARY

```
TYPE SignedByte  = -128..127;
     Byte        = 0..255;
     Ptr         = ^SignedByte;
     Handle      = ^Ptr;

     Str255      = STRING[255];
     StringPtr   = ^Str255;
     StringHandle = ^StringPtr;

     ProcPtr  = Ptr;

     Fixed = LONGINT;
```

4 USING ASSEMBLY LANGUAGE

85   About This Chapter
85   Definition Files
86   Pascal Data Types
87   The Trap Dispatch Table
88   The Trap Mechanism
89   Format of Trap Words
90   Trap Macros
90   Calling Conventions
90   Stack-Based Routines
93   Register-Based Routines
93   Macro Arguments
94   Result Codes
94   Register-Saving Conventions
95   Pascal Interface to the Toolbox and Operating System
95   Mixing Pascal and Assembly Language
99   Summary

Using Assembly Language

ABOUT THIS CHAPTER

This chapter gives you general information that you'll need to write all or part of your Macintosh application program in assembly language. It assumes you already know how to write assembly-language programs for the Motorola MC68000, the microprocessor in the Macintosh.

DEFINITION FILES

The primary aids to assembly-language programmers are a set of definition files for symbolic names used in assembly-language programs. The definition files include equate files, which equate symbolic names with values, and macro files, which define the macros used to call Toolbox and Operating System routines from assembly language. The equate files define a variety of symbolic names for various purposes, such as:

- useful numeric quantities
- masks and bit numbers
- offsets into data structures
- addresses of global variables (which in turn often contain addresses)

It's a good idea to always use the symbolic names defined in an equate file in place of the corresponding numeric values (even if you know them), since some of these values may change. Note that the names of the offsets for a data structure don't always match the field names in the corresponding Pascal definition. In the documentation, the definitions are normally shown in their Pascal form; the corresponding offset constants for assembly-language use are listed in the summary at the end of each chapter.

Some generally useful global variables defined in the equate files are as follows:

Name	Contents
OneOne	$00010001
MinusOne	$FFFFFFFF
Lo3Bytes	$00FFFFFF
Scratch20	20-byte scratch area
Scratch8	8-byte scratch area
ToolScratch	8-byte scratch area
ApplScratch	12-byte scratch area reserved for use by applications

Scratch20, Scratch8, and ToolScratch will not be preserved across calls to the routines in the Macintosh ROM. ApplScratch will be preserved; it should be used only by application programs and not by desk accessories or other drivers.

Other global variables are described where relevant in *Inside Macintosh*. A list of all the variables described is given in Appendix D (Volume III).

Inside Macintosh

PASCAL DATA TYPES

Pascal's strong typing ability lets Pascal programmers write programs without really considering the size of variables. But assembly-language programmers must keep track of the size of every variable. The sizes of the standard Pascal data types, and some of the basic types defined in the Memory Manager, are listed below. (See the *Apple Numerics Manual* for more information about SINGLE, DOUBLE, EXTENDED, and COMP.)

Type	Size	Contents
INTEGER	2 bytes	Two's complement integer
LONGINT	4 bytes	Two's complement integer
BOOLEAN	1 byte	Boolean value in bit 0
CHAR	2 bytes	Extended ASCII code in low-order byte
SINGLE (or REAL)	4 bytes	IEEE standard single format
DOUBLE	8 bytes	IEEE standard double format
EXTENDED	10 bytes	IEEE standard extended format
COMP (or COMPUTATIONAL)	8 bytes	Two's complement integer with reserved value
STRING[n]	n+1 bytes	Byte containing string length (not counting length byte) followed by bytes containing ASCII codes of characters in string
SignedByte	1 byte	Two's complement integer
Byte	2 bytes	Value in low-order byte
Ptr	4 bytes	Address of data
Handle	4 bytes	Address of master pointer

Other data types are constructed from these. For some commonly used data types, the size in bytes is available as a predefined constant.

Before allocating space for any variable whose size is greater than one byte, Pascal adds "padding" to the next word boundary, if it isn't already at a word boundary. It does this not only when allocating variables declared successively in VAR statements, but also within arrays and records. As you would expect, the size of a Pascal array or record is the sum of the sizes of all its elements or fields (which are stored with the first one at the lowest address). For example, the size of the data type

```
TYPE TestRecord =   RECORD
                        testHandle: Handle;
                        testBoolA:  BOOLEAN;
                        testBoolB:  BOOLEAN;
                        testChar:   CHAR
                    END;
```

is eight bytes: four for the handle, one each for the Booleans, and two for the character. If the testBoolB field weren't there, the size would be the same, because of the byte of padding Pascal would add to make the character begin on a word boundary.

In a packed record or array, type BOOLEAN is stored as a bit, and types CHAR and Byte are stored as bytes. The padding rule described above still applies. For example, if the TestRecord data type shown above were declared as PACKED RECORD, it would occupy only six bytes: four for the handle, one for the Booleans (each stored in a bit), and one for the character. If the last field were INTEGER rather than CHAR, padding before the two-byte integer field would cause the size to be eight bytes.

> **Note:** The packing algorithm may not be what you expect. If you need to know exactly how data is packed, or if you have questions about the size of a particular data type, the best thing to do is write a test program in Pascal and look at the results. (You can use the SIZEOF function to get the size.)

THE TRAP DISPATCH TABLE

The Toolbox and Operating System reside in ROM. However, to allow flexibility for future development, application code must be kept free of any specific ROM addresses. So all references to Toolbox and Operating System routines are made indirectly through the **trap dispatch table** in RAM, which contains the addresses of the routines. As long as the location of the trap dispatch table is known, the routines themselves can be moved to different locations in ROM without disturbing the operation of programs that depend on them.

Information about the locations of the various Toolbox and Operating System routines is encoded in compressed form in the ROM itself. When the system starts up, this encoded information is expanded to form the trap dispatch table. Because the trap dispatch table resides in RAM, individual entries can be "patched" to point to addresses other than the original ROM address. This allows changes to be made in the ROM code by loading corrected versions of individual routines into RAM at system startup and patching the trap dispatch table to point to them. It also allows an application program to replace specific Toolbox and Operating System routines with its own "custom" versions. A pair of utility routines for manipulating the trap dispatch table, GetTrapAddress and SetTrapAddress, are described in chapter 13 of Volume II.

For compactness, entries in the trap dispatch table are encoded into one word each, instead of a full long-word address. Since the trap dispatch table is 1024 bytes long, it has room for 512 word-length entries. The high-order bit of each entry tells whether the routine resides in ROM (0) or RAM (1). The remaining 15 bits give the offset of the routine relative to a base address. For routines in ROM, this base address is the beginning of the ROM; for routines in RAM, it's the beginning of the system heap. The two base addresses are kept in a pair of global variables named ROMBase and RAMBase.

The offset in a trap dispatch table entry is expressed in words instead of bytes, taking advantage of the fact that instructions must always fall on word boundaries (even byte addresses). As illustrated in Figure 1, the system does the following to find the absolute address of the routine:

1. checks the high-order bit of the trap dispatch table entry to find out which base address to use
2. doubles the offset to convert it from words to bytes (by left-shifting one bit)
3. adds the result to the designated base address

Inside Macintosh

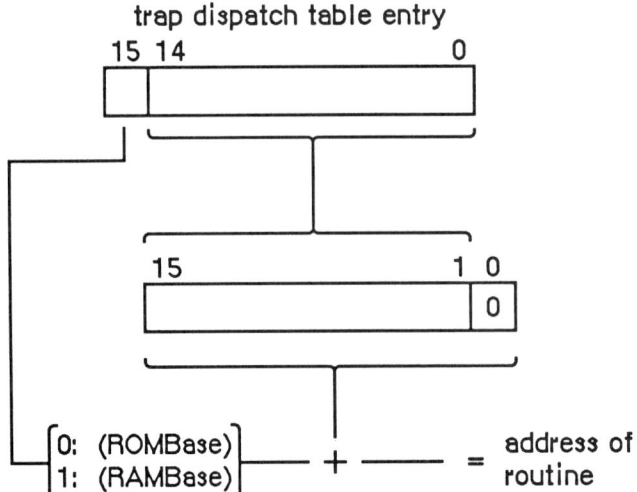

Figure 1. Trap Dispatch Table Entry

Using 15-bit word offsets, the trap dispatch table can address locations within a range of 32K words, or 64K bytes, from the base address. Starting from ROMBase, this range is big enough to cover the entire ROM; but only slightly more than half of the 128K RAM lies within range of RAMBase. RAMBase is set to the beginning of the system heap to maximize the amount of useful space within range; locations below the start of the heap are used to hold global system data and can never contain executable code. If the heap is big enough, however, it's possible for some of the application's code to lie beyond the upper end of the trap dispatch table's range. Any such code is inaccessible through the trap dispatch table.

Note: This problem is particularly acute on the Macintosh 512K and Macintosh XL. To make sure they lie within range of RAMBase, patches to Toolbox and Operating System routines are typically placed in the system heap rather than the application heap.

THE TRAP MECHANISM

Calls to the Toolbox and Operating System via the trap dispatch table are implemented by means of the MC68000's "1010 emulator" trap. To issue such a call in assembly language, you use one of the **trap macros** defined in the macro files. When you assemble your program, the macro generates a **trap word** in the machine-language code. A trap word always begins with the hexadecimal digit $A (binary 1010); the rest of the word identifies the routine you're calling, along with some additional information pertaining to the call.

Note: A list of all Macintosh trap words is given in Appendix C (Volume III).

Instruction words beginning with $A or $F ("A-line" or "F-line" instructions) don't correspond to any valid machine-language instruction, and are known as **unimplemented instructions**. They're used to augment the processor's native instruction set with additional operations that are "emulated" in software instead of being executed directly by the hardware. A-line instructions are

Using Assembly Language

reserved for use by Apple; on a Macintosh, they provide access to the Toolbox and Operating System routines. Attempting to execute such an instruction causes a trap to the **trap dispatcher**, which examines the bit pattern of the trap word to determine what operation it stands for, looks up the address of the corresponding routine in the trap dispatch table, and jumps to the routine.

Note: F-line instructions are reserved by Motorola for use in future processors.

Format of Trap Words

As noted above, a trap word always contains $A in bits 12-15. Bit 11 determines how the remainder of the word will be interpreted; usually it's 0 for Operating System calls and 1 for Toolbox calls, though there are some exceptions.

Figure 2 shows the Toolbox trap word format. Bits 0-8 form the **trap number** (an index into the trap dispatch table), identifying the particular routine being called. Bit 9 is reserved for future use. Bit 10 is the "auto-pop" bit; this bit is used by language systems that, rather than directly invoking the trap like Lisa Pascal, do a JSR to the trap word followed immediately by a return to the calling routine. In this case, the return addresses for the both the JSR and the trap get pushed onto the stack, in that order. The auto-pop bit causes the trap dispatcher to pop the trap's return address from the stack and return directly to the calling program.

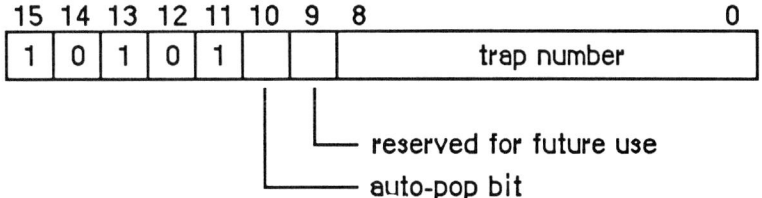

Figure 2. Toolbox Trap Word (Bit 11=1)

For Operating System calls, only the low-order eight bits (bits 0-7) are used for the trap number (see Figure 3). Thus of the 512 entries in the trap dispatch table, only the first 256 can be used for Operating System traps. Bit 8 of an Operating System trap has to do with register usage and is discussed below under "Register-Saving Conventions". Bits 9 and 10 have specialized meanings depending on which routine you're calling, and are covered where relevant in other chapters.

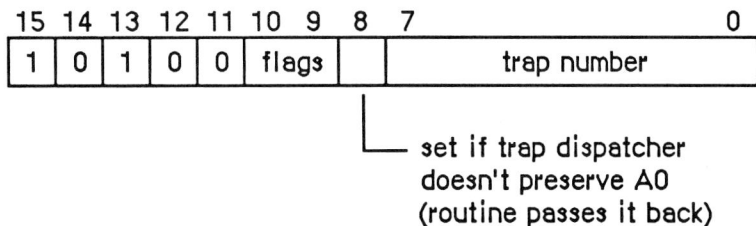

Figure 3. Operating System Trap Word (Bit 11=0)

Inside Macintosh

Trap Macros

The names of all trap macros begin with the underscore character (_), followed by the name of the corresponding routine. As a rule, the macro name is the same as the name used to call the routine from Pascal, as given in the Toolbox and Operating System documentation. For example, to call the Window Manager routine NewWindow, you would use an instruction with the macro name _NewWindow in the opcode field. There are some exceptions, however, in which the spelling of the macro name differs from the name of the Pascal routine itself; these are noted in the documentation for the individual routines.

> **Note:** The reason for the exceptions is that assembler names must be unique to eight characters. Since one character is taken up by the underscore, special macro names must be used for Pascal routines whose names aren't unique to seven characters.

Trap macros for Toolbox calls take no arguments; those for Operating System calls may have as many as three optional arguments. The first argument, if present, is used to load a register with a parameter value for the routine you're calling, and is discussed below under "Register-Based Routines". The remaining arguments control the settings of the various flag bits in the trap word. The form of these arguments varies with the meanings of the flag bits, and is described in the chapters on the relevant parts of the Operating System.

CALLING CONVENTIONS

The calling conventions for Toolbox and Operating System routines fall into two categories: **stack-based** and **register-based**. As the terms imply, stack-based routines communicate via the stack, following the same conventions used by the Pascal Compiler for routines written in Lisa Pascal, while register-based routines receive their parameters and return their results in registers. Before calling any Toolbox or Operating System routine, you have to set up the parameters in the way the routine expects.

> **Note:** As a general rule, Toolbox routines are stack-based and Operating System routines register-based, but there are exceptions on both sides. Throughout *Inside Macintosh*, register-based calling conventions are given for all routines that have them; if none is shown, then the routine is stack-based.

Stack-Based Routines

To call a stack-based routine from assembly language, you have to set up the parameters on the stack in the same way the compiled object code would if your program were written in Pascal. If the routine you're calling is a function, its result is returned on the stack. The number and types of parameters, and the type of result returned by a function, depend on the routine being called. The number of bytes each parameter or result occupies on the stack depends on its type:

Using Assembly Language

Type of parameter or function result	Size	Contents
INTEGER	2 bytes	Two's complement integer
LONGINT	4 bytes	Two's complement integer
BOOLEAN	2 bytes	Boolean value in bit 0 of high-order byte
CHAR	2 bytes	Extended ASCII code in low-order byte
SINGLE (or REAL), DOUBLE, COMP (or COMPUTATIONAL)	4 bytes	Pointer to value converted to EXTENDED
EXTENDED	4 bytes	Pointer to value
STRING[n]	4 bytes	Pointer to string (first byte pointed to is length byte)
SignedByte	2 bytes	Value in low-order byte
Byte	2 bytes	Value in low-order byte
Ptr	4 bytes	Address of data
Handle	4 bytes	Address of master pointer
Record or array	2 or 4 bytes	Contents of structure (padded to word boundary) if <= 4 bytes, otherwise pointer to structure
VAR parameter	4 bytes	Address of variable, regardless of type

The steps to take to call the routine are as follows:

1. If it's a function, reserve space on the stack for the result.
2. Push the parameters onto the stack in the order they occur in the routine's Pascal definition.
3. Call the routine by executing the corresponding trap macro.

The trap pushes the return address onto the stack, along with an extra word of processor status information. The trap dispatcher removes this extra status word, leaving the stack in the state shown in Figure 4 on entry to the routine. The routine itself is responsible for removing its own parameters from the stack before returning. If it's a function, it leaves its result on top of the stack in the space reserved for it; if it's a procedure, it restores the stack to the same state it was in before the call.

For example, the Window Manager function GrowWindow is defined in Pascal as follows:

```
FUNCTION GrowWindow (theWindow: WindowPtr; startPt: Point; sizeRect: Rect)
                : LONGINT;
```

Inside Macintosh

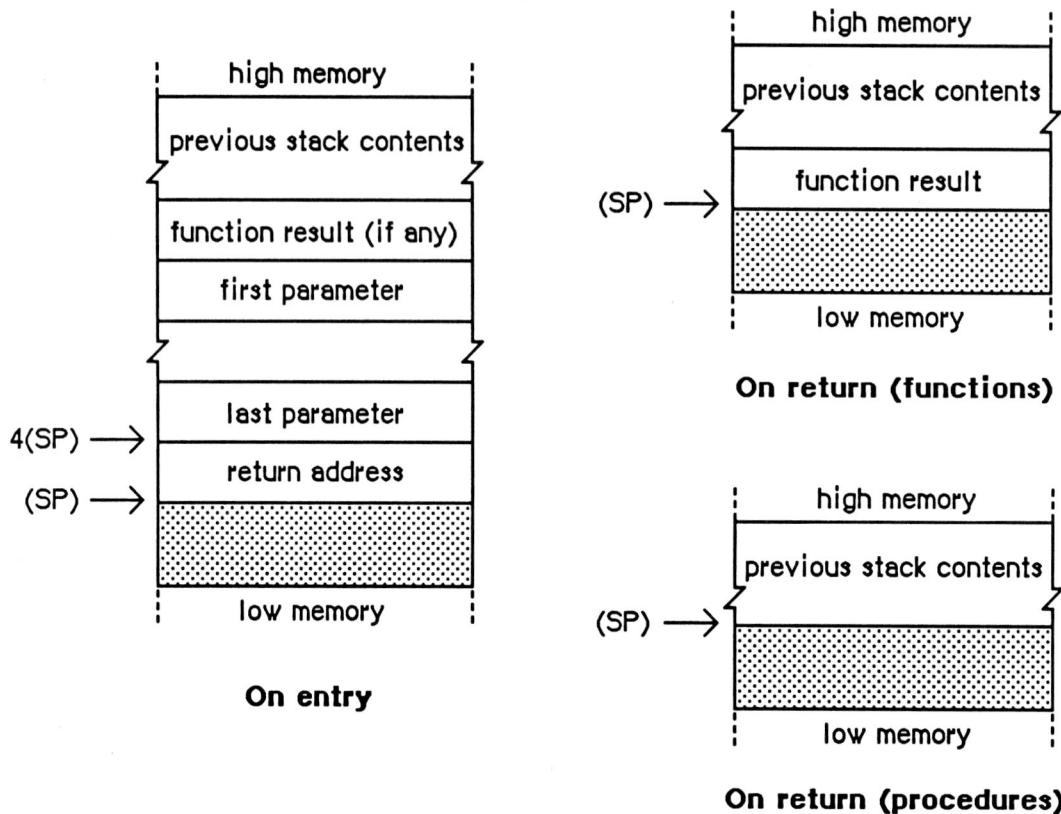

Figure 4. Stack Format for Stack-Based Routines

To call this function from assembly language, you'd write something like the following:

```
SUBQ.L      #4,SP               ;make room for LONGINT result
MOVE.L      theWindow,-(SP)     ;push window pointer
MOVE.L      startPt,-(SP)       ;a Point is a 4-byte record,
                                ; so push actual contents
PEA         sizeRect            ;a Rect is an 8-byte record,
                                ; so push a pointer to it
_GrowWindow                     ;trap to routine
MOVE.L      (SP)+,D3            ;pop result from stack
```

Although the MC68000 hardware provides for separate user and supervisor stacks, each with its own stack pointer, the Macintosh maintains only one stack. All application programs run in supervisor mode and share the same stack with the system; the user stack pointer isn't used.

Warning: For compatibility with future versions of the Macintosh, your program should not rely on capabilities available *only* in supervisor mode (such as the instruction RTE).

Remember that the stack pointer must always be aligned on a word boundary. This is why, for example, a Boolean parameter occupies two bytes; it's actually the Boolean value followed by a byte of padding. Because all Macintosh application code runs in the MC68000's supervisor

I-92 Calling Conventions

Using Assembly Language

mode, an odd stack pointer will cause a "double bus fault": an unrecoverable system failure that causes the system to restart.

To keep the stack pointer properly aligned, the MC68000 automatically adjusts the pointer by 2 instead of 1 when you move a byte-length value to or from the stack. This happens only when all of the following three conditions are met:

- A one-byte value is being transferred.
- Either the source or the destination is specified by predecrement or postincrement addressing.
- The register being decremented or incremented is the stack pointer (A7).

An extra, unused byte will automatically be added in the low-order byte to keep the stack pointer even. (Note that if you need to move a character to or from the stack, you must explicitly use a full word of data, with the character in the low-order byte.)

Warning: If you use any other method to manipulate the stack pointer, it's your responsibility to make sure the pointer stays properly aligned.

Note: Some Toolbox and Operating System routines accept the address of one of your own routines as a parameter, and call that routine under certain circumstances. In these cases, you must set up your routine to be stack-based.

Register-Based Routines

By convention, register-based routines normally use register A0 for passing addresses (such as pointers to data objects) and D0 for other data values (such as integers). Depending on the routine, these registers may be used to pass parameters to the routine, result values back to the calling program, or both. For routines that take more than two parameters (one address and one data value), the parameters are normally collected in a **parameter block** in memory and a pointer to the parameter block is passed in A0. However, not all routines obey these conventions; for example, some expect parameters in other registers, such as A1. See the description of each individual routine for details.

Whatever the conventions may be for a particular routine, it's up to you to set up the parameters in the appropriate registers before calling the routine. For instance, the Memory Manager procedure BlockMove, which copies a block of consecutive bytes from one place to another in memory, expects to find the address of the first source byte in register A0, the address of the first destination location in A1, and the number of bytes to be copied in D0. So you might write something like

```
        LEA       src(A5),A0        ;source address in A0
        LEA       dest(A5),A1       ;destination address in A1
        MOVEQ     #20,D0            ;byte count in D0
        _BlockMove                  ;trap to routine
```

Macro Arguments

The following information applies to the Lisa Workshop Assembler. If you're using some other assembler, you should check its documentation to find out whether this information applies.

Calling Conventions I-93

Inside Macintosh

Many register-based routines expect to find an address of some sort in register A0. You can specify the contents of that register as an argument to the macro instead of explicitly setting up the register yourself. The first argument you supply to the macro, if any, represents an address to be passed in A0. The macro will load the register with an LEA (Load Effective Address) instruction before trapping to the routine. So, for instance, to perform a Read operation on a file, you could set up the parameter block for the operation and then use the instruction

```
    _Read       paramBlock      ;trap to routine with pointer to
                                ; parameter block in A0
```

This feature is purely a convenience, and is optional: If you don't supply any arguments to a trap macro, or if the first argument is null, the LEA to A0 will be omitted from the macro expansion. Notice that A0 is loaded with the address denoted by the argument, not the contents of that address.

> **Note:** You can use any of the MC68000's addressing modes to specify this address, with one exception: You can't use the two-register indexing mode ("address register indirect with index and displacement"). An instruction such as
>
> ```
>     _Read       offset(A3,D5)
> ```
>
> won't work properly, because the comma separating the two registers will be taken as a delimiter marking the end of the macro argument.

Result Codes

Many register-based routines return a result code in the low-order word of register D0 to report successful completion or failure due to some error condition. A result code of 0 indicates that the routine was completed successfully. Just before returning from a register-based call, the trap dispatcher tests the low-order word of D0 with a TST.W instruction to set the processor's condition codes. You can then check for an error by branching directly on the condition codes, without any explicit test of your own. For example:

```
    _PurgeMem                   ;trap to routine
    BEQ         NoError         ;branch if no error
    . . .                       ;handle error
```

> **Warning:** Not all register-based routines return a result code. Some leave the contents of D0 unchanged; others use the full 32 bits of the register to return a long-word result. See the descriptions of individual routines for details.

Register-Saving Conventions

All Toolbox and Operating System routines preserve the contents of all registers except A0, A1, and D0-D2 (and of course A7, which is the stack pointer). In addition, for register-based routines, the trap dispatcher saves registers A1, D1, and D2 before dispatching to the routine and restores them before returning to the calling program. A7 and D0 are never restored; whatever the routine leaves in these registers is passed back unchanged to the calling program, allowing the routine to manipulate the stack pointer as appropriate and to return a result code.

Using Assembly Language

Whether the trap dispatcher preserves register A0 for a register-based trap depends on the setting of bit 8 of the trap word: If this bit is 0, the trap dispatcher saves and restores A0; if it's 1, the routine passes back A0 unchanged. Thus bit 8 of the trap word should be set to 1 only for those routines that return a result in A0, and to 0 for all other routines. The trap macros automatically set this bit correctly for each routine, so you never have to worry about it yourself.

Stack-based traps preserve only registers A2-A6 and D3-D7. If you want to preserve any of the other registers, you have to save them yourself before trapping to the routine—typically on the stack with a MOVEM (Move Multiple) instruction—and restore them afterward.

> **Warning:** When an application starts up, register A5 is set to point to the boundary between the application globals and the application parameters (see the memory map in chapter 1 of Volume II for details). Certain parts of the system rely on finding A5 set up properly (for instance, the first application parameter is a pointer to the first QuickDraw global variable), so you have to be a bit more careful about preserving this register. The safest policy is never to touch A5 at all. If you must use it for your own purposes, just saving its contents at the beginning of a routine and restoring them before returning isn't enough: You have to be sure to restore it before any call that might depend on it. The correct setting of A5 is always available in the global variable CurrentA5.

> **Note:** Any routine in your application that may be called as the result of a Toolbox or Operating System call shouldn't rely on the value of any register except A5, which shouldn't change.

Pascal Interface to the Toolbox and Operating System

When you call a register-based Toolbox or Operating System routine from Pascal, you're actually calling an **interface routine** that fetches the parameters from the stack where the Pascal calling program left them, puts them in the registers where the routine expects them, and then traps to the routine. On return, it moves the routine's result, if any, from a register to the stack and then returns to the calling program. (For routines that return a result code, the interface routine may also move the result code to a global variable, where it can later be accessed.)

For stack-based calls, there's no interface routine; the trap word is inserted directly into the compiled code.

MIXING PASCAL AND ASSEMBLY LANGUAGE

You can mix Pascal and assembly language freely in your own programs, calling routines written in either language from the other. The Pascal and assembly-language portions of the program have to be compiled and assembled separately, then combined with a program such as the Lisa Workshop Linker. For convenience in this discussion, such separately compiled or assembled portions of a program will be called "modules". You can divide a program into any number of modules, each of which may be written in either Pascal or assembly language.

References in one module to routines defined in another are called **external references**, and must be resolved by a program like the Linker that matches them up with their definitions in other modules. You have to identify all the external references in each module so they can be resolved properly. For more information, and for details about the actual process of linking the modules together, see the documentation for the development system you're using.

In addition to being able to call your own Pascal routines from assembly language, you can call certain routines in the Toolbox and Operating System that were created expressly for Lisa Pascal programmers and aren't part of the Macintosh ROM. (These routines may also be available to users of other development systems, depending on how the interfaces have been set up on those systems.) They're marked with the notation

[Not in ROM]

in *Inside Macintosh*. There are no trap macros for these routines (though they may call other routines for which there are trap macros). Some of them were created just to allow Pascal programmers access to assembly-language information, and so won't be useful to assembly-language programmers. Others, however, contain code that's executed before a trap macro is invoked, and you may want to perform the operations they provide.

All calls from one language to the other, in either direction, must obey Pascal's stack-based calling conventions (see "Stack-Based Routines", above). To call your own Pascal routine from assembly language, or one of the Toolbox or Operating System routines that aren't in ROM, push the parameters onto the stack before the call and (if the routine is a function) look for the result on the stack on return. In an assembly-language routine to be called from Pascal, look for the parameters on the stack on entry and leave the result (if any) on the stack before returning.

Under stack-based calling conventions, a convenient way to access a routine's parameters on the stack is with a **frame pointer**, using the MC68000's LINK and UNLK (Unlink) instructions. You can use any address register for the frame pointer (except A7, which is reserved for the stack pointer), but register A6 is conventionally used for this purpose on the Macintosh. The instruction

```
LINK       A6,#-12
```

at the beginning of a routine saves the previous contents of A6 on the stack and sets A6 to point to it. The second operand specifies the number of bytes of stack space to be reserved for the routine's local variables: in this case, 12 bytes. The LINK instruction offsets the stack pointer by this amount after copying it into A6.

> **Warning:** The offset is *added* to the stack pointer, not subtracted from it. So to allocate stack space for local variables, you have to give a *negative* offset; the instruction won't work properly if the offset is positive. Also, to keep the stack pointer correctly aligned, be sure the offset is even. For a routine with no local variables on the stack, use an offset of #0.

Register A6 now points within the routine's **stack frame**; the routine can locate its parameters and local variables by indexing with respect to this register (see Figure 5). The register itself points to its own saved contents, which are often (but needn't necessarily be) the frame pointer of the calling routine. The parameters and return address are found at positive offsets from the frame pointer.

Since the saved contents of the frame pointer register occupy a long word (four bytes) on the stack, the return address is located at 4(A6) and the last parameter at 8(A6). This is followed by the rest of the parameters in reverse order, and finally by the space reserved for the function result, if any. The proper offsets for these remaining parameters and for the function result

Using Assembly Language

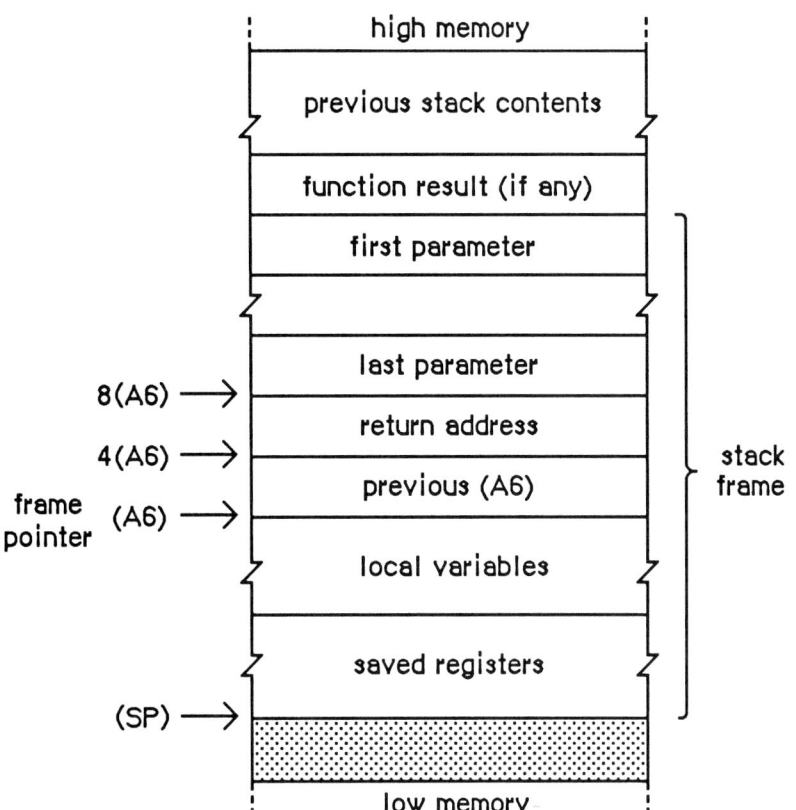

Figure 5. Frame Pointer

depend on the number and types of the parameters, according to the table above under "Stack-Based Routines". If the LINK instruction allocated stack space for any local variables, they can be accessed at negative offsets from the frame pointer, again depending on their number and types.

At the end of the routine, the instruction

    UNLK   A6

reverses the process: First it releases the local variables by setting the stack pointer equal to the frame pointer (A6), then it pops the saved contents back into register A6. This restores the register to its original state and leaves the stack pointer pointing to the routine's return address.

A routine with no parameters can now just return to the caller with an RTS instruction. But if there are any parameters, it's the routine's responsibility to pop them from the stack before returning. The usual way of doing this is to pop the return address into an address register, increment the stack pointer to remove the parameters, and then exit with an indirect jump through the register.

Remember that any routine called from Pascal must preserve registers A2-A6 and D3-D7. This is usually done by saving the registers that the routine will be using on the stack with a MOVEM instruction, and then restoring them before returning. Any routine you write that will be accessed via the trap mechanism—for instance, your own version of a Toolbox or Operating System routine that you've patched into the trap dispatch table—should observe the same conventions.

Mixing Pascal and Assembly Language I-97

Inside Macintosh

Putting all this together, the routine should begin with a sequence like

```
MyRoutine    LINK      A6,#-dd              ;set up frame pointer--
                                            ; dd = number of bytes
                                            ; of local variables

             MOVEM.L   A2-A4/D3-D7,-(SP)    ;...or whatever registers
                                            ; you use
```

and end with something like

```
             MOVEM.L   (SP)+,A2-A4/D3-D7    ;restore registers
             UNLK      A6                   ;restore frame pointer
             MOVE.L    (SP)+,A1             ;save return address in an
                                            ; available register
             ADD.W     #pp,SP               ;pop parameters--
                                            ; pp = number of bytes
                                            ; of parameters
             JMP       (A1)                 ;return to caller
```

Notice that A6 doesn't have to be included in the MOVEM instructions, since it's saved and restored by the LINK and UNLK.

SUMMARY

Variables

OneOne	$00010001
MinusOne	$FFFFFFFF
Lo3Bytes	$00FFFFFF
Scratch20	20-byte scratch area
Scratch8	8-byte scratch area
ToolScratch	8-byte scratch area
ApplScratch	12-byte scratch area reserved for use by applications
ROMBase	Base address of ROM
RAMBase	Trap dispatch table's base address for routines in RAM
CurrentA5	Address of boundary between application globals and application parameters

5 THE RESOURCE MANAGER

103	About This Chapter
103	About the Resource Manager
105	Overview of Resource Files
107	Resource Specification
107	Resource Types
108	Resource ID Numbers
109	Resource IDs of Owned Resources
110	Resource Names
110	Resource References
112	Using the Resource Manager
113	Resource Manager Routines
114	Initialization
114	Opening and Closing Resource Files
116	Checking for Errors
116	Setting the Current Resource File
117	Getting Resource Types
118	Getting and Disposing of Resources
121	Getting Resource Information
122	Modifying Resources
126	Advanced Routines
127	Resources Within Resources
128	Format of a Resource File
132	Summary of the Resource Manager

The Resource Manager

ABOUT THIS CHAPTER

This chapter describes the Resource Manager, the part of the Toolbox through which an application accesses various resources that it uses, such as menus, fonts, and icons. It discusses resource files, where resources are stored. Resources form the foundation of every Macintosh application; even the application's code is a resource. In a resource file, the resources used by the application are stored separately from the code for flexibility and ease of maintenance.

You can use an existing program for creating and editing resource files, or write one of your own; these programs will call Resource Manager routines. Usually you'll access resources indirectly through other parts of the Toolbox, such as the Menu Manager and the Font Manager, which in turn call the Resource Manager to do the low-level resource operations. In some cases, you may need to call a Resource Manager routine directly.

Familiarity with Macintosh files, as described in chapter 4 of Volume II, is useful if you want a complete understanding of the internal structure of a resource file; however, you don't need it to be able to use the Resource Manager.

If you're going to write your own program to create and edit resource files, you also need to know the exact format of each type of resource. The chapter describing the part of the Toolbox that deals with a particular type of resource will tell you what you need to know for that resource.

ABOUT THE RESOURCE MANAGER

Macintosh applications make use of many **resources**, such as menus, fonts, and icons, which are stored in **resource files**. For example, an icon resides in a resource file as a 32-by-32 bit image, and a font as a large bit image containing the characters of the font. In some cases the resource consists of descriptive information (such as, for a menu, the menu title, the text of each command in the menu, whether the command is checked with a check mark, and so on). The Resource Manager keeps track of resources in resource files and provides routines that allow applications and other parts of the Toolbox to access them.

There's a resource file associated with each application, containing the resources specific to that application; these resources include the application code itself. There's also a **system resource file**, which contains standard resources shared by all applications (called **system resources**).

The resources used by an application are created and changed separately from the application's code. This separation is the main advantage to having resource files. A change in the title of a menu, for example, won't require any recompilation of code, nor will translation to another language.

The Resource Manager is initialized by the system when it starts up, and the system resource file is opened as part of the initialization. Your application's resource file is opened when the application starts up. When instructed to get a certain resource, the Resource Manager normally looks first in the application's resource file and then, if the search isn't successful, in the system resource file. This makes it easy to share resources among applications and also to override a system resource with one of your own (if you want to use something other than a standard icon in an alert box, for example).

Resources are grouped logically by function into **resource types**. You refer to a resource by passing the Resource Manager a **resource specification**, which consists of the resource type

Inside Macintosh

and either an ID number or a name. Any resource type is valid, whether one of those recognized by the Toolbox as referring to standard Macintosh resources (such as menus and fonts), or a type created for use by your application. Given a resource specification, the Resource Manager will read the resource into memory and return a handle to it.

> **Note:** The Resource Manager knows nothing about the formats of the individual types of resources. Only the routines in the other parts of the Toolbox that call the Resource Manager have this knowledge.

While most access to resources is read-only, certain applications may want to modify resources. You can change the content of a resource or its ID number, name, or other attributes— everything except its type. For example, you can designate whether the resource should be kept in memory or whether, as is normal for large resources, it can be removed from memory and read in again when needed. You can change existing resources, remove resources from the resource file altogether, or add new resources to the file.

Resource files aren't limited to applications; anything stored in a file can have its own resources. For instance, an unusual font used in only one document can be included in the resource file for that document rather than in the system resource file.

> **Note:** Although shared resources are usually stored in the system resource file, you can have other resource files that contain resources shared by two or more applications (or documents, or whatever).

A number of resource files may be open at one time; the Resource Manager searches the files in the reverse of the order that they were opened. Since the system resource file is opened when the Resource Manager is initialized, it's always searched last. The search starts with the most recently opened resource file, but you can change it to start with a file that was opened earlier. (See Figure 1.)

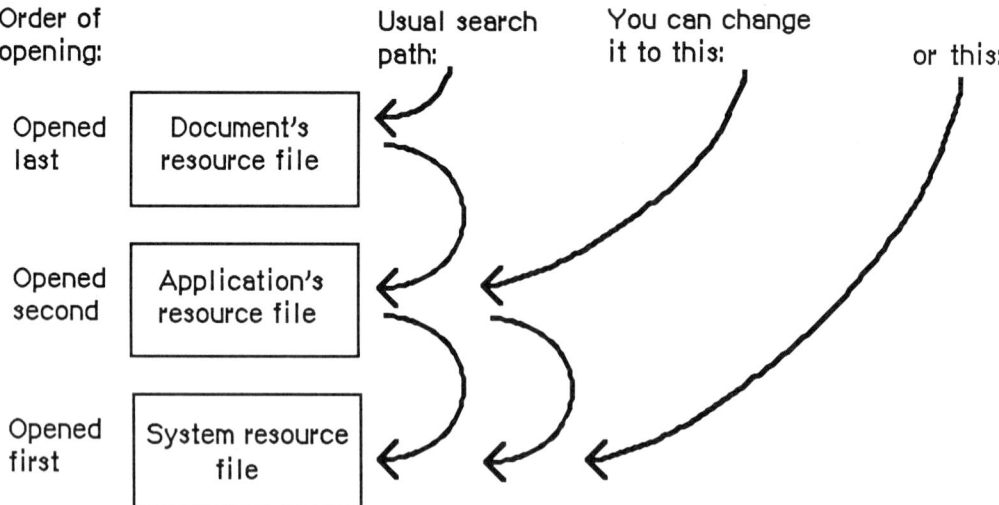

Figure 1. Resource File Searching

The Resource Manager

OVERVIEW OF RESOURCE FILES

Resources may be put in a resource file with the aid of the Resource Editor, or with whatever tools are provided by the development system you're using.

A resource file is not a file in the strictest sense. Although it's functionally like a file in many ways, it's actually just one of two parts, or **forks**, of a file (see Figure 2). Every file has a **resource fork** and a **data fork** (either of which may be empty). The resource fork of an application file contains not only the resources used by the application but also the application code itself. The code may be divided into different segments, each of which is a resource; this allows various parts of the program to be loaded and purged dynamically. Information is stored in the resource fork via the Resource Manager. The data fork of an application file can contain anything an application wants to store there. Information is stored in the data fork via the File Manager.

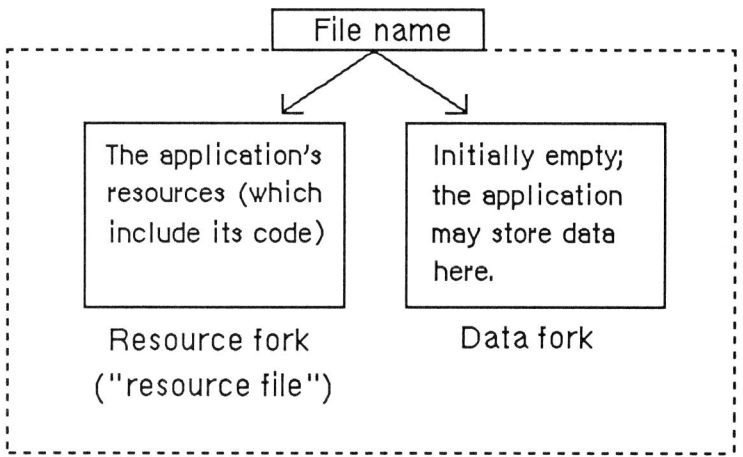

Figure 2. An Application File

As shown in Figure 3, the system resource file has this same structure. The resource fork contains the system resources and the data fork contains "patches" to the routines in the Macintosh ROM. Figure 3 also shows the structure of a file containing a document; the resource fork contains the document's resources and the data fork contains the data that comprises the document.

To open a resource file, the Resource Manager calls the appropriate File Manager routine and returns the **reference number** it gets from the File Manager. This is a number greater than 0 by which you can refer to the file when calling other Resource Manager routines.

   Note: This reference number is actually the path reference number, as described in chapter 4 of Volume II.

Most of the Resource Manager routines don't require the resource file's reference number as a parameter. Rather, they assume that the **current resource file** is where they should perform their operation (or begin it, in the case of a search for a resource). The current resource file is the last one that was opened unless you specify otherwise.

Overview of Resource Files I-105

Inside Macintosh

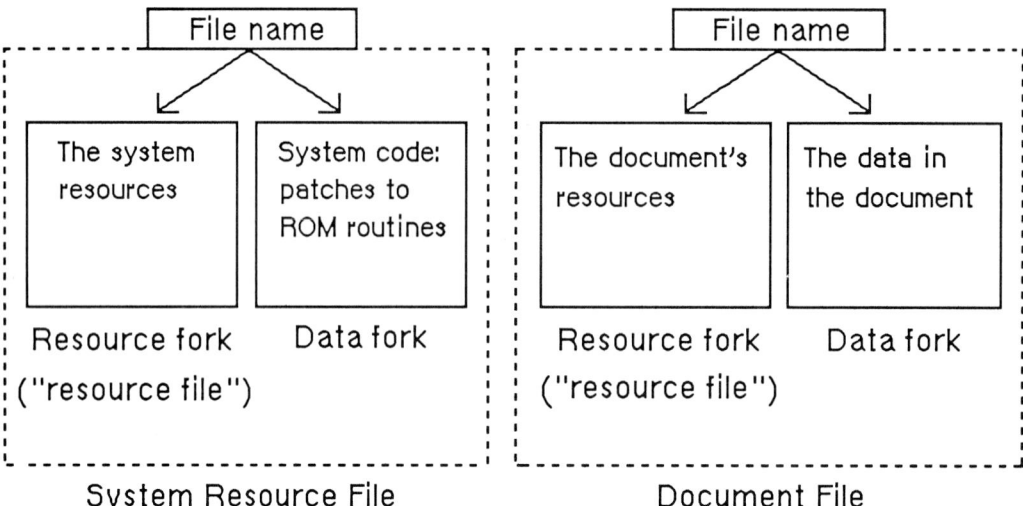

Figure 3. Other Files

A resource file consists primarily of **resource data** and a **resource map**. The resource data consists of the resources themselves (for example, the bit image for an icon or the title and commands for a menu). The resource map contains an entry for each resource that provides the location of its resource data. Each entry in the map either gives the offset of the resource data in the file or contains a handle to the data if it's in memory. The resource map is like the index of a book; the Resource Manager looks in it for the resource you specify and determines where its resource data is located.

The resource map is read into memory when the file is opened and remains there until the file is closed. Although for simplicity we say that the Resource Manager searches resource files, it actually searches the resource maps that were read into memory, and not the resource files on the disk.

Resource data is normally read into memory when needed, though you can specify that it be read in as soon as the resource file is opened. When read in, resource data is stored in a relocatable block in the heap. Resources are designated in the resource map as being either purgeable or unpurgeable; if purgeable, they may be removed from the heap when space is required by the Memory Manager. Resources consisting of a relatively large amount of data are usually designated as purgeable. Before accessing such a resource through its handle, you ask the Resource Manager to read the resource into memory again if it has been purged.

> **Note:** Programmers concerned about the amount of available memory should be aware that there's a 12-byte overhead in the resource map for every resource and an additional 12-byte overhead for memory management if the resource is read into memory.

To modify a resource, you change the resource data or resource map in memory. The change becomes permanent only at your explicit request, and then only when the application terminates or when you call a routine specifically for updating or closing the resource file.

Each resource file also may contain up to 128 bytes of any data the application wants to store there.

RESOURCE SPECIFICATION

In a resource file, every resource is assigned a type, an ID number, and optionally a name. When calling a Resource Manager routine to access a resource, you specify the resource by passing its type and either its ID number or its name. This section gives some general information about resource specification.

Resource Types

The resource type is a sequence of any four characters (printing or nonprinting). Its Pascal data type is:

```
TYPE ResType = PACKED ARRAY[1..4] OF CHAR;
```

The standard Macintosh resource types are as follows:

Resource type	Meaning
'ALRT'	Alert template
'BNDL'	Bundle
'CDEF'	Control definition function
'CNTL'	Control template
'CODE'	Application code segment
'CURS'	Cursor
'DITL'	Item list in a dialog or alert
'DLOG'	Dialog template
'DRVR'	Desk accessory or other device driver
'DSAT'	System startup alert table
'FKEY'	Command-Shift-number routine
'FONT'	Font
'FREF'	File reference
'FRSV'	IDs of fonts reserved for system use
'FWID'	Font widths
'ICN#'	Icon list
'ICON'	Icon
'INIT'	Initialization resource
'INTL'	International resource
'MBAR'	Menu bar
'MDEF'	Menu definition procedure

Resource type	Meaning
'MENU'	Menu
'PACK'	Package
'PAT '	Pattern (The space is required.)
'PAT#'	Pattern list
'PDEF'	Printing code
'PICT'	Picture
'PREC'	Print record
'SERD'	RAM Serial Driver
'STR '	String (The space is required.)
'STR#'	String list
'WDEF'	Window definition function
'WIND'	Window template

> **Warning:** Uppercase and lowercase letters *are* distinguished in resource types. For example, 'Menu' will not be recognized as the resource type for menus.

Notice that some of the resources listed above are "templates". A template is a list of parameters used to build a Toolbox object; it is not the object itself. For example, a window template contains information specifying the size and location of the window, its title, whether it's visible, and so on. After the Window Manager has used this information to build the window in memory, the template isn't needed again until the next window using that template is created.

You can use any four-character sequence (except those listed above) for resource types specific to your application.

Resource ID Numbers

Every resource has an ID number, or **resource ID**. The resource ID should be unique within each resource type, but resources of different types may have the same ID. If you assign the same resource ID to two resources of the same type, the second assignment of the ID will override the first, thereby making the first resource inaccessible by ID.

> **Warning:** Certain resources contain the resource IDs of other resources; for instance, a dialog template contains the resource ID of its item list. In order not to duplicate an existing resource ID, a program that copies resources may need to change the resource ID of a resource; such a program may not, however, change the ID where it is referred to by other resources. For instance, an item list's resource ID contained in a dialog template may not be changed, even though the actual resource ID of the item list was changed to avoid duplication; this would make it impossible for the template to access the item list. Be sure to verify, and if necessary correct, the IDs contained within such resources. (For related information, see the section "Resource IDs of Owned Resources" below.)

By convention, the ID numbers are divided into the following ranges:

Range	Description
–32768 through –16385	Reserved; do not use
–16384 through –1	Used for system resources owned by other system resources (explained below)
0 through 127	Used for other system resources
128 through 32767	Available for your use in whatever way you wish

Note: The chapters that describe the different types of resources in detail give information about resource types that may be more restrictive about the allowable range for their resource IDs. A device driver, for instance, can't have a resource ID greater than 31.

Resource IDs of Owned Resources

This section is intended for advanced programmers who are writing their own desk accessories (or other drivers), or special types of windows, controls, and menus. It's also useful in understanding the way that resource-copying programs recognize resources that are associated with each other.

Certain types of system resources may have resources of their own in the system resource file; the "owning" resource consists of code that reads the "owned" resource into memory. For example, a desk accessory might have its own pattern and string resources. A special numbering convention is used to associate owned system resources with the resources they belong to. This enables resource-copying programs to recognize which additional resources need to be copied along with an owning resource. An owned system resource has the ID illustrated in Figure 4.

```
 15 14 13    11 10              5 4            0
| 1 | 1 | type bits | ID of owning resource | variable |
```

Figure 4. Resource ID of an Owned System Resource

Bits 14 and 15 are always 1. Bits 11-13 specify the type of the owning resource, as follows:

Type bits	Type
000	'DRVR'
001	'WDEF'
010	'MDEF'
011	'CDEF'
100	'PDEF'
101	'PACK'
110	Reserved for future use
111	Reserved for future use

Bits 5-10 contain the resource ID of the owning resource (limited to 0 through 63). Bits 0-4 contain any desired value (0 through 31).

Inside Macintosh

Certain types of resources can't be owned, because their IDs don't conform to the special numbering convention described above. For instance, while a resource of type 'WDEF' can own other resources, it cannot itself be owned since its resource ID can't be more than 12 bits long (as described in chapter 9). Fonts are also an exception because their IDs include the font size. The chapters describing the different types of resources provide detailed information about such restrictions.

An owned resource may itself contain the ID of a resource associated with it. For instance, a dialog template owned by a desk accessory contains the resource ID of its item list. Though the item list is associated with the dialog template, it's actually owned (indirectly) by the desk accessory. The resource ID of the item list should conform to the same special convention as the ID of the template. For example, if the resource ID of the desk accessory is 17, the IDs of both the template and the item list should contain the value 17 in bits 5-10.

As mentioned above, a program that copies resources may need to change the resource ID of a resource in order not to duplicate an existing resource ID. Bits 5-10 of resources owned, directly or indirectly, by the copied resource will also be changed when those resources are copied. For instance, in the above example, if the desk accessory must be given a new ID, bits 5-10 of both the template and the item list will also be changed.

Warning: Remember that while the ID of an owned resource may be changed by a resource-copying program, the ID may not be changed where it appears in other resources (such as an item list's ID contained in a dialog template).

Resource Names

A resource may optionally have a **resource name**. Like the resource ID, the resource name should be unique within each type; if you assign the same resource name to two resources of the same type, the second assignment of the name will override the first, thereby making the first resource inaccessible by name. When comparing resource names, the Resource Manager ignores case (but does not ignore diacritical marks).

RESOURCE REFERENCES

The entries in the resource map that identify and locate the resources in a resource file are known as **resource references**. Using the analogy of an index of a book, resource references are like the individual entries in the index (see Figure 5).

Every resource reference includes the type, ID number, and optional name of the resource. Suppose you're accessing a resource for the first time. You pass a resource specification to the Resource Manager, which looks for a match among all the references in the resource map of the current resource file. If none is found, it looks at the references in the resource map of the next resource file to be searched. (Remember, it looks in the resource map in memory, not in the file.) Eventually it finds a reference matching the specification, which tells it where the resource data is in the file. After reading the resource data into memory, the Resource Manager stores a handle to that data in the reference (again, in the resource map in memory) and returns the handle so you can use it to refer to the resource in subsequent routine calls.

The Resource Manager

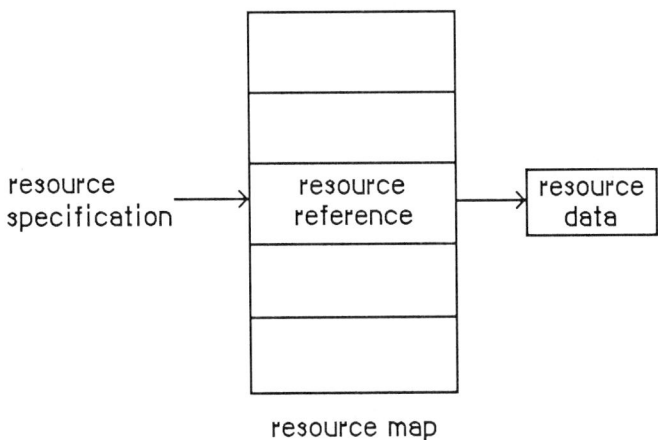

Figure 5. Resource References in Resource Maps

Every resource reference also contains certain **resource attributes** that determine how the resource should be dealt with. In the routine calls for setting or reading them, each attribute is specified by a bit in the low-order byte of a word, as illustrated in Figure 6.

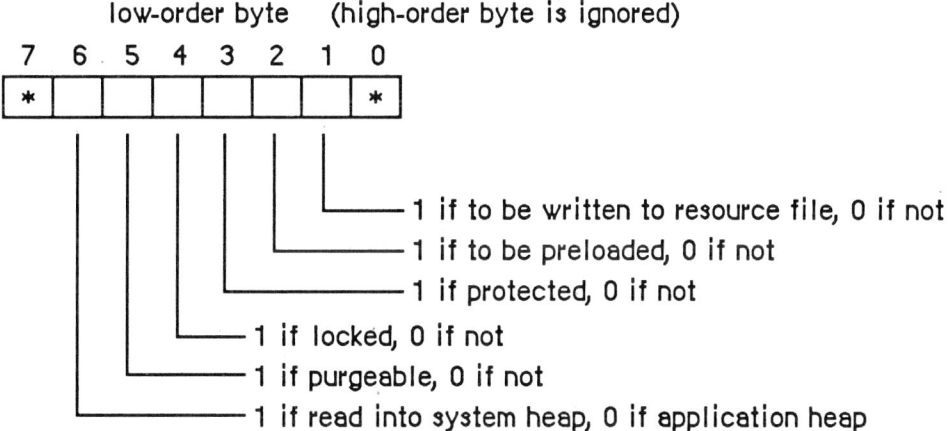

* reserved for use by the Resource Manager

Figure 6. Resource Attributes

The Resource Manager provides a predefined constant for each attribute, in which the bit corresponding to that attribute is set.

```
CONST  resSysHeap    = 64;    {set if read into system heap}
       resPurgeable  = 32;    {set if purgeable}
       resLocked     = 16;    {set if locked}
       resProtected  = 8;     {set if protected}
       resPreload    = 4;     {set if to be preloaded}
       resChanged    = 2;     {set if to be written to resource file}
```

Inside Macintosh

> **Warning:** Your application should not change the setting of bit 0 or 7, nor should it set the resChanged attribute directly. (ResChanged is set as a side effect of the procedure you call to tell the Resource Manager that you've changed a resource.)

The resSysHeap attribute should not be set for your application's resources. If a resource with this attribute set is too large for the system heap, the bit will be cleared, and the resource will be read into the application heap.

Since a locked resource is neither relocatable nor purgeable, the resLocked attribute overrides the resPurgeable attribute; when resLocked is set, the resource will not be purgeable regardless of whether resPurgeable is set.

If the resProtected attribute is set, the application can't use Resource Manager routines to change the ID number or name of the resource, modify its contents, or remove the resource from the resource file. The routine that sets the resource attributes may be called, however, to remove the protection or just change some of the other attributes.

The resPreload attribute tells the Resource Manager to read this resource into memory immediately after opening the resource file. This is useful, for example, if you immediately want to draw ten icons stored in the file; rather than read and draw each one individually in turn, you can have all of them read in when the file is opened and just draw all ten.

The resChanged attribute is used only while the resource map is in memory; it must be 0 in the resource file. It tells the Resource Manager whether this resource has been changed.

USING THE RESOURCE MANAGER

The Resource Manager is initialized automatically when the system starts up: The system resource file is opened and its resource map is read into memory. Your application's resource file is opened when the application starts up; you can call CurResFile to get its reference number. You can also call OpenResFile to open any resource file that you specify by name, and CloseResFile to close any resource file. A function named ResError lets you check for errors that may occur during execution of Resource Manager routines.

> **Note:** These are the only routines you need to know about to use the Resource Manager indirectly through other parts of the Toolbox.

Normally when you want to access a resource for the first time, you'll specify it by type and ID number (or type and name) in a call to GetResource (or GetNamedResource). In special situations, you may want to get every resource of each type. There are two routines which, used together, will tell you all the resource types that are in all open resource files: CountTypes and GetIndType. Similarly, CountResources and GetIndResource may be used to get all resources of a particular type.

If you don't specify otherwise, GetResource, GetNamedResource, and GetIndResource read the resource data into memory and return a handle to it. Sometimes, however, you may not need the data to be in memory. You can use a procedure named SetResLoad to tell the Resource Manager not to read the resource data into memory when you get a resource; in this case, the handle returned for the resource will be an empty handle (a pointer to a NIL master pointer). You can pass the empty handle to routines that operate only on the resource map (such as the routine that sets resource attributes), since the handle is enough for the Resource Manager to tell what resource you're referring to. Should you later want to access the resource data, you can read it

The Resource Manager

into memory with the LoadResource procedure. Before calling any of the above routines that read the resource data into memory, it's a good idea to call SizeResource to see how much space is needed.

Normally the Resource Manager starts looking for a resource in the most recently opened resource file, and searches other open resource files in the reverse of the order that they were opened. In some situations, you may want to change which file is searched first. You can do this with the UseResFile procedure. One such situation might be when you want a resource to be read from the same file as another resource; in this case, you can find out which resource file the other resource was read from by calling the HomeResFile function.

Once you have a handle to a resource, you can call GetResInfo or GetResAttrs to get the information that's stored for that resource in the resource map, or you can access the resource data through the handle. (If the resource was designated as purgeable, first call LoadResource to ensure that the data is in memory.)

Usually you'll just read resources from previously created resource files with the routines described above. You may, however, want to modify existing resources or even create your own resource file. To create your own resource file, call CreateResFile (followed by OpenResFile to open it). The AddResource procedure lets you add resources to a resource file; to be sure a new resource won't override an existing one, you can call the UniqueID function to get an ID number for it. To make a copy of an existing resource, call DetachResource followed by AddResource (with a new resource ID). There are a number of procedures for modifying existing resources:

- To remove a resource, call RmveResource.
- If you've changed the resource data for a resource and want the changed data to be written to the resource file, call ChangedResource; it signals the Resource Manager to write the data out when the resource file is later updated.
- To change the information stored for a resource in the resource map, call SetResInfo or SetResAttrs. If you want the change to be written to the resource file, call ChangedResource. (Remember that ChangedResource will also cause the resource data itself to be written out.)

These procedures for adding and modifying resources change only the resource map in memory. The changes are written to the resource file when the application terminates (at which time all resource files other than the system resource file are updated and closed) or when one of the following routines is called:

- CloseResFile, which updates the resource file before closing it
- UpdateResFile, which simply updates the resource file
- WriteResource, which writes the resource data for a specified resource to the resource file

RESOURCE MANAGER ROUTINES

Assembly-language note: Except for LoadResource, all Resource Manager routines preserve all registers except A0 and D0. LoadResource preserves A0 and D0 as well.

Inside Macintosh

Initialization

Although you don't call these initialization routines (because they're executed automatically for you), it's a good idea to familiarize yourself with what they do.

```
FUNCTION InitResources : INTEGER;
```

InitResources is called by the system when it starts up, and should not be called by the application. It initializes the Resource Manager, opens the system resource file, reads the resource map from the file into memory, and returns a reference number for the file.

Assembly-language note: The name of the system resource file is stored in the global variable SysResName; the reference number for the file is stored in the global variable SysMap. A handle to the resource map of the system resource file is stored in the variable SysMapHndl.

Note: The application doesn't need the reference number for the system resource file, because every Resource Manager routine that has a reference number as a parameter interprets 0 to mean the system resource file.

```
PROCEDURE RsrcZoneInit;
```

RsrcZoneInit is called automatically when your application starts up, to initialize the resource map read from the system resource file; normally you'll have no need to call it directly. It "cleans up" after any resource access that may have been done by a previous application. First it closes all open resource files except the system resource file. Then, for every system resource that was read into the application heap (that is, whose resSysHeap attribute is 0), it replaces the handle to that resource in the resource map with NIL. This lets the Resource Manager know that the resource will have to be read in again (since the previous application heap is no longer around).

Opening and Closing Resource Files

When calling the CreateResFile or OpenResFile routine, described below, you specify a resource file by its file name; the routine assumes that the file has a version number of 0 and is on the default volume. (Version numbers and volumes are described in chapter 4 of Volume II.) If you want the routine to apply to a file on another volume, just set the default volume to that volume.

```
PROCEDURE CreateResFile (fileName: Str255);
```

CreateResFile creates a resource file containing no resource data. If there's no file at all with the given name, it also creates an empty data fork for the file. If there's already a resource file with the given name (that is, a resource fork that isn't empty), CreateResFile will do nothing and the ResError function will return an appropriate Operating System result code.

The Resource Manager

Note: Before you can work with the resource file, you need to open it with OpenResFile.

```
FUNCTION OpenResFile (fileName: Str255) : INTEGER;
```

OpenResFile opens the resource file having the given name and makes it the current resource file. It reads the resource map from the file into memory and returns a reference number for the file. It also reads in every resource whose resPreload attribute is set. If the resource file is already open, it doesn't make it the current resource file; it simply returns the reference number.

Note: You don't have to call OpenResFile to open the system resource file or the application's resource file, because they're opened when the system and the application start up, respectively. To get the reference number of the application's resource file, you can call CurResFile after the application starts up (before you open any other resource file).

If the file can't be opened, OpenResFile will return –1 and the ResError function will return an appropriate Operating System result code. For example, an error occurs if there's no resource file with the given name.

Note: To open a resource file simply for block-level operations such as copying files (without reading the resource map into memory), you can call the File Manager function OpenRF.

Assembly-language note: A handle to the resource map of the most recently opened resource file is stored in the global variable TopMapHndl.

```
PROCEDURE CloseResFile (refNum: INTEGER);
```

Given the reference number of a resource file, CloseResFile does the following:

- updates the resource file by calling the UpdateResFile procedure
- for each resource in the resource file, releases the memory it occupies by calling the ReleaseResource procedure
- releases the memory occupied by the resource map
- closes the resource file

If there's no resource file open with the given reference number, CloseResFile will do nothing and the ResError function will return the result code resFNotFound. A refNum of 0 represents the system resource file, but if you ask to close this file, CloseResFile first closes all other open resource files.

A CloseResFile of every open resource file (except the system resource file) is done automatically when the application terminates. So you only need to call CloseResFile if you want to close a resource file before the application terminates.

Inside Macintosh

Checking for Errors

```
FUNCTION ResError : INTEGER;
```

Called after one of the various Resource Manager routines that may result in an error condition, ResError returns a result code identifying the error, if any. If no error occurred, it returns the result code

```
CONST noErr = 0;    {no error}
```

If an error occurred at the Operating System level, it returns an Operating System result code, such as the File Manager "disk I/O" error or the Memory Manager "out of memory" error. (See Appendix A in Volume III for a list of all result codes.) If an error happened at the Resource Manager level, ResError returns one of the following result codes:

```
CONST  resNotFound  = -192;    {resource not found}
       resFNotFound = -193;    {resource file not found}
       addResFailed = -194;    {AddResource failed}
       rmvResFailed = -196;    {RmveResource failed}
```

Each routine description tells which errors may occur for that routine. You can also check for an error after system startup, which calls InitResources, and application startup, which opens the application's resource file.

> **Warning:** In certain cases, the ResError function will return noError even though a Resource Manager routine was unable to perform the requested operation; the routine descriptions give details about the circumstances under which this will happen.

> **Assembly-language note:** The current value of ResError is stored in the global variable ResErr. In addition, you can specify a procedure to be called whenever there's an error by storing the address of the procedure in the global variable ResErrProc (which is normally 0). Before returning a result code other than noErr, the ResError function places that result code in register D0 and calls your procedure.

Setting the Current Resource File

When calling the CurResFile and HomeResFile routines, described below, be aware that for the system resource file the actual reference number is returned. You needn't worry about this number being used (instead of 0) in the routines that require a reference number; those routines recognize both 0 and the actual reference number as referring to the system resource file.

```
FUNCTION CurResFile : INTEGER;
```

CurResFile returns the reference number of the current resource file. You can call it when the application starts up to get the reference number of its resource file.

The Resource Manager

> **Assembly-language note:** The reference number of the current resource file is stored in the global variable CurMap.

```
FUNCTION HomeResFile (theResource: Handle) : INTEGER;
```

Given a handle to a resource, HomeResFile returns the reference number of the resource file containing that resource. If the given handle isn't a handle to a resource, HomeResFile will return −1 and the ResError function will return the result code resNotFound.

```
PROCEDURE UseResFile (refNum: INTEGER);
```

Given the reference number of a resource file, UseResFile sets the current resource file to that file. If there's no resource file open with the given reference number, UseResFile will do nothing and the ResError function will return the result code resFNotFound. A refNum of 0 represents the system resource file.

Open resource files are arranged as a linked list; the most recently opened file is at the end of the list and is the first one the Resource Manager searches when looking for a resource. UseResFile lets you start the search with a file opened earlier; the file(s) following it in the list are then left out of the search process. Whenever a new resource file is opened, it's added to the end of the list; this overrides any previous calls to UseResFile, causing the entire list of open resource files to be searched. For example, assume there are four open resource files (R0 through R3); the search order is R3, R2, R1, R0. If you call UseResFile(R2), the search order becomes R2, R1, R0; R3 is no longer searched. If you then open a fifth resource file (R4), it's added to the end of the list and the search order becomes R4, R3, R2, R1, R0.

This procedure is useful if you no longer want to override a system resource with one by the same name in your application's resource file. You can call UseResFile(0) to leave the application resource file out of the search, causing only the system resource file to be searched.

> **Warning:** Early versions of some desk accessories may, upon closing, always set the current resource file to the one opened just before the accessory, ignoring any additional resource files that may have been opened while the accessory was open. To be safe, whenever a desk accessory may have been in use, call UseResFile to ensure access to resource files opened while the accessory was open.

Getting Resource Types

```
FUNCTION CountTypes : INTEGER;
```

CountTypes returns the number of resource types in all open resource files.

```
PROCEDURE GetIndType (VAR theType: ResType; index: INTEGER);
```

Given an index ranging from 1 to CountTypes (above), GetIndType returns a resource type in theType. Called repeatedly over the entire range for the index, it returns all the resource types in

Inside Macintosh

all open resource files. If the given index isn't in the range from 1 to CountTypes, GetIndType returns four NUL characters (ASCII code 0).

Getting and Disposing of Resources

```
PROCEDURE SetResLoad (load: BOOLEAN);
```

Normally, the routines that return handles to resources read the resource data into memory if it's not already in memory. SetResLoad(FALSE) affects all those routines so that they will not read the resource data into memory and will return an empty handle. Furthermore, resources whose resPreload attribute is set will not be read into memory when a resource file is opened.

> **Warning:** If you call SetResLoad(FALSE), be sure to restore the normal state as soon as possible, because other parts of the Toolbox that call the Resource Manager rely on it.

> **Assembly-language note:** The current SetResLoad state is stored in the global variable ResLoad.

```
FUNCTION CountResources (theType: ResType) : INTEGER;
```

CountResources returns the total number of resources of the given type in all open resource files.

```
FUNCTION GetIndResource (theType: ResType; index: INTEGER) :
         Handle;
```

Given an index ranging from 1 to CountResources(theType), GetIndResource returns a handle to a resource of the given type (see CountResources, above). Called repeatedly over the entire range for the index, it returns handles to all resources of the given type in all open resource files. GetIndResource reads the resource data into memory if it's not already in memory, unless you've called SetResLoad(FALSE).

> **Warning:** The handle returned will be an empty handle if you've called SetResLoad(FALSE) (and the data isn't already in memory). The handle will become empty if the resource data for a purgeable resource is read in but later purged. (You can test for an empty handle with, for example, myHndl^ = NIL.) To read in the data and make the handle no longer be empty, you can call LoadResource.

GetIndResource returns handles for all resources in the most recently opened resource file first, and then for those in the resource files opened before it, in the reverse of the order that they were opened.

> **Note:** The UseResFile procedure affects which file the Resource Manager searches first when looking for a particular resource but not when getting indexed resources with GetIndResource.

I-118 Resource Manager Routines

The Resource Manager

If you want to find out how many resources of a given type are in a particular resource file, you can do so as follows: Call GetIndResource repeatedly with the index ranging from 1 to the number of resources of that type (CountResources(theType)). Pass each handle returned by GetIndResource to HomeResFile and count all occurrences where the reference number returned is that of the desired file. Be sure to start the index from 1, and to call SetResLoad(FALSE) so the resources won't be read in.

If the given index is 0 or negative, GetIndResource returns NIL, but the ResError function will return the result code noErr. If the given index is larger than the value CountResources(theType), GetIndResource returns NIL and the ResError function will return the result code resNotFound. GetIndResource also returns NIL if the resource is to be read into memory but won't fit; in this case, ResError will return an appropriate Operating System result code.

```
FUNCTION GetResource (theType: ResType; theID: INTEGER) : Handle;
```

GetResource returns a handle to the resource having the given type and ID number, reading the resource data into memory if it's not already in memory and if you haven't called SetResLoad(FALSE) (see the warning above for GetIndResource). If the resource data is already in memory, GetResource just returns the handle to the resource.

GetResource looks in the current resource file and all resource files opened before it, in the reverse of the order that they were opened; the system resource file is searched last. If it doesn't find the resource, GetResource returns NIL and the ResError function will return the result code resNotFound. GetResource also returns NIL if the resource is to be read into memory but won't fit; in this case, ResError will return an appropriate Operating System result code.

Note: If you call GetResource with a resource type that isn't in any open resource file, it returns NIL but the ResError function will return the result code noErr.

```
FUNCTION GetNamedResource (theType: ResType; name: Str255) :
        Handle;
```

GetNamedResource is the same as GetResource (above) except that you pass a resource name instead of an ID number.

```
PROCEDURE LoadResource (theResource: Handle);
```

Given a handle to a resource (returned by GetIndResource, GetResource, or GetNamedResource), LoadResource reads that resource into memory. It does nothing if the resource is already in memory or if the given handle isn't a handle to a resource; in the latter case, the ResError function will return the result code resNotFound. Call this procedure if you want to access the data for a resource through its handle and either you've called SetResLoad(FALSE) or the resource is purgeable.

If you've changed the resource data for a purgeable resource and the resource is purged before being written to the resource file, the changes will be lost; LoadResource will reread the original resource from the resource file. See the descriptions of ChangedResource and SetResPurge for information about how to ensure that changes made to purgeable resources will be written to the resource file.

Inside Macintosh

Assembly-language note: LoadResource preserves *all* registers.

```
PROCEDURE ReleaseResource (theResource: Handle);
```

Given a handle to a resource, ReleaseResource releases the memory occupied by the resource data, if any, and replaces the handle to that resource in the resource map with NIL (see Figure 7). The given handle will no longer be recognized as a handle to a resource; if the Resource Manager is subsequently called to get the released resource, a new handle will be allocated. Use this procedure only after you're completely through with a resource.

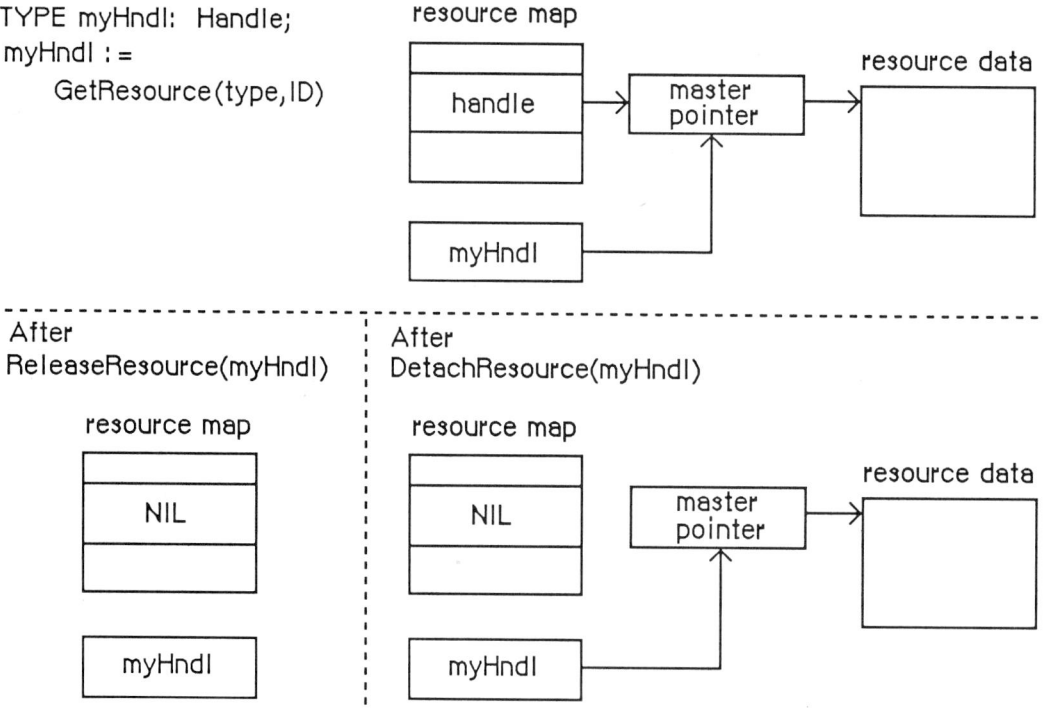

Figure 7. ReleaseResource and DetachResource

If the given handle isn't a handle to a resource, ReleaseResource will do nothing and the ResError function will return the result code resNotFound. ReleaseResource won't let you release a resource whose resChanged attribute has been set; however, ResError will still return noErr.

```
PROCEDURE DetachResource (theResource: Handle);
```

Given a handle to a resource, DetachResource replaces the handle to that resource in the resource map with NIL (see Figure 7 above). The given handle will no longer be recognized as a handle to a resource; if the Resource Manager is subsequently called to get the detached resource, a new handle will be allocated.

The Resource Manager

DetachResource is useful if you want the resource data to be accessed only by yourself through the given handle and not by the Resource Manager. DetachResource is also useful in the unusual case that you don't want a resource to be released when a resource file is closed. To copy a resource, you can call DetachResource followed by AddResource (with a new resource ID).

If the given handle isn't a handle to a resource, DetachResource will do nothing and the ResError function will return the result code resNotFound. DetachResource won't let you detach a resource whose resChanged attribute has been set; however, ResError will still return noErr.

Getting Resource Information

```
FUNCTION UniqueID (theType: ResType) : INTEGER;
```

UniqueID returns an ID number greater than 0 that isn't currently assigned to any resource of the given type in any open resource file. Using this number when you add a new resource to a resource file ensures that you won't duplicate a resource ID and override an existing resource.

Warning: It's possible that UniqueID will return an ID in the range reserved for system resources (0 to 127). You should check that the ID returned is greater than 127; if it isn't, call UniqueID again.

```
PROCEDURE GetResInfo (theResource: Handle; VAR theID: INTEGER;
        VAR theType: ResType; VAR name: Str255);
```

Given a handle to a resource, GetResInfo returns the ID number, type, and name of the resource. If the given handle isn't a handle to a resource, GetResInfo will do nothing and the ResError function will return the result code resNotFound.

```
FUNCTION GetResAttrs (theResource: Handle) : INTEGER;
```

Given a handle to a resource, GetResAttrs returns the resource attributes for the resource. (Resource attributes are described above under "Resource References".) If the given handle isn't a handle to a resource, GetResAttrs will do nothing and the ResError function will return the result code resNotFound.

```
FUNCTION SizeResource (theResource: Handle) : LONGINT;
```

Assembly-language note: The macro you invoke to call SizeResource from assembly language is named _SizeRsrc.

Given a handle to a resource, SizeResource returns the size in bytes of the resource in the resource file. If the given handle isn't a handle to a resource, SizeResource will return –1 and the ResError function will return the result code resNotFound. It's a good idea to call SizeResource and ensure that sufficient space is available before reading a resource into memory.

Resource Manager Routines I-121

Inside Macintosh

Modifying Resources

Except for UpdateResFile and WriteResource, all the routines described below change the resource map in memory and not the resource file itself.

```
PROCEDURE SetResInfo (theResource: Handle; theID: INTEGER; name:
        Str255);
```

Given a handle to a resource, SetResInfo changes the ID number and name of the resource to the given ID number and name.

Assembly-language note: If you pass 0 for the name parameter, the name will not be changed.

Warning: It's a dangerous practice to change the ID number and name of a system resource, because other applications may already access the resource and may no longer work properly.

The change will be written to the resource file when the file is updated if you follow SetResInfo with a call to ChangedResource.

Warning: Even if you don't call ChangedResource for this resource, the change may be written to the resource file when the file is updated. If you've *ever* called ChangedResource for *any* resource in the file, or if you've added or removed a resource, the Resource Manager will write out the entire resource map when it updates the file, so all changes made to resource information in the map will become permanent. If you want any of the changes to be temporary, you'll have to restore the original information before the file is updated.

SetResInfo does nothing in the following cases:

- The given handle isn't a handle to a resource. The ResError function will return the result code resNotFound.

- The resource map becomes too large to fit in memory (which can happen if a name is passed) or the modified resource file can't be written out to the disk. ResError will return an appropriate Operating System result code.

- The resProtected attribute for the resource is set. ResError will, however, return the result code noErr.


```
PROCEDURE SetResAttrs (theResource: Handle; attrs: INTEGER);
```

Given a handle to a resource, SetResAttrs sets the resource attributes for the resource to attrs. (Resource attributes are described above under "Resource References".) The resProtected attribute takes effect immediately; the others take effect the next time the resource is read in.

Warning: Do not use SetResAttrs to set the resChanged attribute; you must call ChangedResource instead. Be sure that the attrs parameter passed to SetResAttrs doesn't change the current setting of this attribute; to determine the current setting, first call GetResAttrs.

The attributes set with SetResAttrs will be written to the resource file when the file is updated if you follow SetResAttrs with a call to ChangedResource. However, even if you don't call ChangedResource for this resource, the change may be written to the resource file when the file is updated. See the last warning for SetResInfo (above).

If the given handle isn't a handle to a resource, SetResAttrs will do nothing and the ResError function will return the result code resNotFound.

```
PROCEDURE ChangedResource (theResource: Handle);
```

Call ChangedResource after changing either the information about a resource in the resource map (as described above under SetResInfo and SetResAttrs) or the resource data for a resource, if you want the change to be permanent. Given a handle to a resource, ChangedResource sets the resChanged attribute for the resource. This attribute tells the Resource Manager to do *both* of the following:

- write the resource data for the resource to the resource file when the file is updated or when WriteResource is called
- write the entire resource map to the resource file when the file is updated

Warning: If you change information in the resource map with SetResInfo or SetResAttrs and then call ChangedResource, remember that not only the resource map but also the resource data will be written out when the resource file is updated.

To change the resource data for a purgeable resource and make the change permanent, you have to take special precautions to ensure that the resource won't be purged while you're changing it. You can make the resource temporarily unpurgeable and then write it out with WriteResource before making it purgeable again. You have to use the Memory Manager procedures HNoPurge and HPurge to make the resource unpurgeable and purgeable; SetResAttrs can't be used because it won't take effect immediately. For example:

```
myHndl := GetResource(type,ID);        {or LoadResource(myHndl) if }
                                       { you've gotten it previously}
HNoPurge(myHndl);                      {make it unpurgeable}
...                                    {make the changes here}
ChangedResource(myHndl);               {mark it changed}
WriteResource(myHndl);                 {write it out}
HPurge(myHndl)                         {make it purgeable again}
```

Or, instead of calling WriteResource to write the data out immediately, you can call SetResPurge(TRUE) before making any changes to purgeable resource data.

ChangedResource does nothing in the following cases:

- The given handle isn't a handle to a resource. The ResError function will return the result code resNotFound.
- The modified resource file can't be written out to the disk. ResError will return an appropriate Operating System result code.

- The resProtected attribute for the modified resource is set. ResError will, however, return the result code noErr.

Warning: Be aware that if the modified file can't be written out to the disk, the resChanged attribute won't be set. This means that when WriteResource is called, it won't know that the resource file has been changed; it won't write out the modified file and no error will be returned. For this reason, always check to see that ChangedResource returns noErr.

```
PROCEDURE AddResource (theData: Handle; theType: ResType; theID:
        INTEGER; name: Str255);
```

Given a handle to data in memory (not a handle to an existing resource), AddResource adds to the current resource file a resource reference that points to the data. It sets the resChanged attribute for the resource, so the data will be written to the resource file when the file is updated or when WriteResource is called. If the given handle is empty, zero-length resource data will be written.

Note: To make a copy of an existing resource, call DetachResource before calling AddResource. To add the same data to several different resource files, call the Operating System Utility function HandToHand to duplicate the handle for each resource reference.

AddResource does nothing in the following cases:

- The given handle is NIL or is already a handle to an existing resource. The ResError function will return the result code addResFailed.
- The resource map becomes too large to fit in memory or the modified resource file can't be written out to the disk. ResError will return an appropriate Operating System result code. (The warning under ChangedResource above concerning the resChanged attribute also applies to AddResource.)

Warning: AddResource doesn't verify whether the resource ID you pass is already assigned to another resource of the same type; be sure to call UniqueID before adding a resource.

```
PROCEDURE RmveResource (theResource: Handle);
```

Given a handle to a resource in the current resource file, RmveResource removes its resource reference. The resource data will be removed from the resource file when the file is updated.

Note: RmveResource doesn't release the memory occupied by the resource data; to do that, call the Memory Manager procedure DisposHandle after calling RmveResource.

If the resProtected attribute for the resource is set or if the given handle isn't a handle to a resource in the current resource file, RmveResource will do nothing and the ResError function will return the result code rmvResFailed.

The Resource Manager

```
PROCEDURE UpdateResFile (refNum: INTEGER);
```

Given the reference number of a resource file, UpdateResFile does the following:

- Changes, adds, or removes resource data in the file as appropriate to match the map. Remember that changed resource data is written out only if you called ChangedResource (and the call was successful). UpdateResFile calls WriteResource to write out changed or added resources.

- Compacts the resource file, closing up any empty space created when a resource was removed, made smaller, or made larger. (If the size of a changed resource is greater than its original size in the resource file, it's written at the end of the file rather than at its original location; the space occupied by the original is then compacted.) The actual size of the resource file will be adjusted when a resource is removed or made larger, but not when a resource is made smaller.

- Writes out the resource map of the resource file, if you ever called ChangedResource for any resource in the file or if you added or removed a resource. All changes to resource information in the map will become permanent as a result of this, so if you want any such changes to be temporary, you must restore the original information before calling UpdateResFile.

If there's no open resource file with the given reference number, UpdateResFile will do nothing and the ResError function will return the result code resFNotFound. A refNum of 0 represents the system resource file.

The CloseResFile procedure calls UpdateResFile before it closes the resource file, so you only need to call UpdateResFile yourself if you want to update the file without closing it.

```
PROCEDURE WriteResource (theResource: Handle);
```

Given a handle to a resource, WriteResource checks the resChanged attribute for that resource and, if it's set (which it will be if you called ChangedResource or AddResource successfully), writes its resource data to the resource file and clears its resChanged attribute.

Warning: Be aware that ChangedResource and AddResource determine whether the modified file can be written out to the disk; if it can't, the resChanged attribute won't be set and WriteResource will be unaware of the modifications. For this reason, always verify that ChangedResource and AddResource return noErr.

If the resource is purgeable and has been purged, zero-length resource data will be written. WriteResource does nothing if the resProtected attribute for the resource is set or if the resChanged attribute isn't set; in both cases, however, the ResError function will return the result code noErr. If the given handle isn't a handle to a resource, WriteResource will do nothing and the ResError function will return the result code resNotFound.

Since the resource file is updated when the application terminates or when you call UpdateResFile (or CloseResFile, which calls UpdateResFile), you only need to call WriteResource if you want to write out just one or a few resources immediately.

Warning: The maximum size for a resource to be written to a resource file is 32K bytes.

Inside Macintosh

```
PROCEDURE SetResPurge (install: BOOLEAN);
```

SetResPurge(TRUE) sets a "hook" in the Memory Manager such that before purging data specified by a handle, the Memory Manager will first pass the handle to the Resource Manager. The Resource Manager will determine whether the handle is that of a resource in the application heap and, if so, will call WriteResource to write the resource data for that resource to the resource file if its resChanged attribute is set (see ChangedResource and WriteResource). SetResPurge(FALSE) restores the normal state, clearing the hook so that the Memory Manager will once again purge without checking with the Resource Manager.

SetResPurge(TRUE) is useful in applications that modify purgeable resources. You still have to make the resources temporarily unpurgeable while making the changes, as shown in the description of ChangedResource, but you can set the purge hook instead of writing the data out immediately with WriteResource. Notice that you won't know exactly when the resources are being written out; most applications will want more control than this. If you wish, you can set your own such hook; for details, refer to the section "Memory Manager Data Structures" in chapter 1 of Volume II.

Advanced Routines

The routines described in this section allow advanced programmers to have even greater control over resource file operations. Just as individual resources have attributes, an entire resource file also has attributes, which these routines manipulate. Like the attributes of individual resources, resource file attributes are specified by bits in the low-order byte of a word. The Resource Manager provides the following masks for setting or testing these bits:

```
CONST   mapReadOnly = 128;      {set if file is read-only}
        mapCompact  = 64;       {set to compact file on update}
        mapChanged  = 32;       {set to write map on update}
```

When the mapReadOnly attribute is set, the Resource Manager will neither write anything to the resource file nor check whether the file can be written out to the disk when the resource map is modified. When this attribute is set, UpdateResFile and WriteResource will do nothing, but the ResError function will return the result code noErr.

Warning: If you set mapReadOnly but then later clear it, the resource file will be written even if there's no room for it on the disk. This would destroy the file.

The mapCompact attribute causes the resource file to be compacted when the file is updated. It's set by the Resource Manager when a resource is removed, or when a resource is made larger and thus has to be written at the end of the resource file. You may want to set mapCompact to force compaction when you've only made resources smaller.

The mapChanged attribute causes the resource map to be written to the resource file when the file is updated. It's set by the Resource Manager when you call ChangedResource or when you add or remove a resource. You can set mapChanged if, for example, you've changed resource attributes only and don't want to call ChangedResource because you don't want the resource data to be written out.

The Resource Manager

```
FUNCTION GetResFileAttrs (refNum: INTEGER) : INTEGER;
```

Given the reference number of a resource file, GetResFileAttrs returns the resource file attributes for the file. If there's no resource file with the given reference number, GetResFileAttrs will do nothing and the ResError function will return the result code resFNotFound. A refNum of 0 represents the system resource file.

```
PROCEDURE SetResFileAttrs (refNum: INTEGER; attrs: INTEGER);
```

Given the reference number of a resource file, SetResFileAttrs sets the resource file attributes of the file to attrs. If there's no resource file with the given reference number, SetResFileAttrs will do nothing but the ResError function will return the result code noErr. A refNum of 0 represents the system resource file, but you shouldn't change its resource file attributes.

RESOURCES WITHIN RESOURCES

Resources may point to other resources; this section discusses how this is normally done, for programmers who are interested in background information about resources or who are defining their own resource types.

In a resource file, one resource points to another with the ID number of the other resource. For example, the resource data for a menu includes the ID number of the menu's definition procedure (a separate resource that determines how the menu looks and behaves). To work with the resource data in memory, however, it's faster and more convenient to have a handle to the other resource rather than its ID number. Since a handle occupies two words, the ID number in the resource file is followed by a word containing 0; these two words together serve as a placeholder for the handle. Once the other resource has been read into memory, these two words can be replaced by a handle to it. (See Figure 8.)

> **Note:** The practice of using the ID number followed by 0 as a placeholder is simply a convention. If you like, you can set up your own resources to have the ID number followed by a dummy word, or even a word of useful information, or you can put the ID in the second rather than the first word of the placeholder.

In the case of menus, the Menu Manager function GetMenu calls the Resource Manager to read the menu and the menu definition procedure into memory, and then replaces the placeholder in the menu with the handle to the procedure. There may be other cases where you call the Resource Manager directly and store the handle in the placeholder yourself. It might be useful in these cases to call HomeResFile to learn which resource file the original resource is located in, and then, before getting the resource it points to, call UseResFile to set the current resource file to that file. This will ensure that the resource pointed to is read from that same file (rather than one that was opened after it).

> **Warning:** If you modify a resource that points to another resource and you make the change permanent by calling ChangedResource, be sure you reverse the process described here, restoring the other resource's ID number in the placeholder.

Inside Macintosh

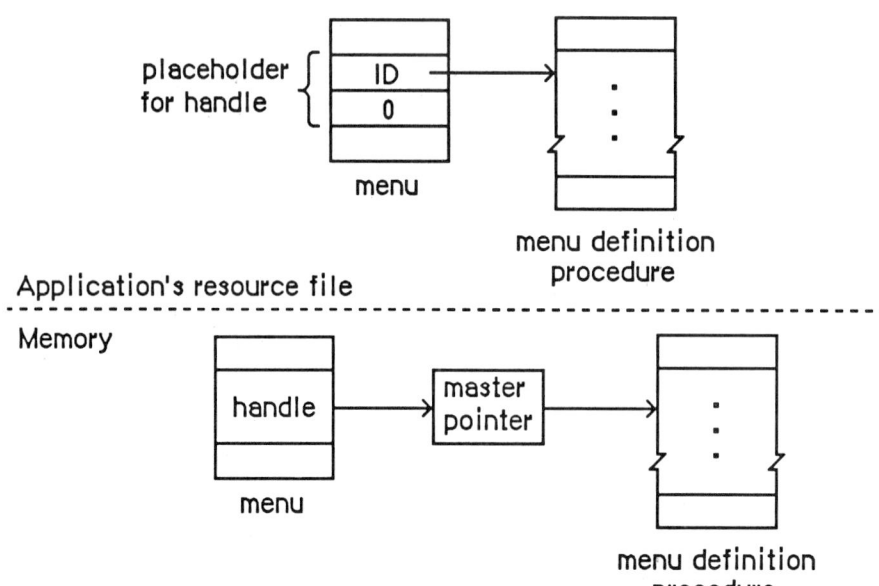

Figure 8. How Resources Point to Resources

FORMAT OF A RESOURCE FILE

You need to know the exact format of a resource file, described below, only if you're writing a program that will create or modify resource files directly; you don't have to know it to be able to use the Resource Manager routines.

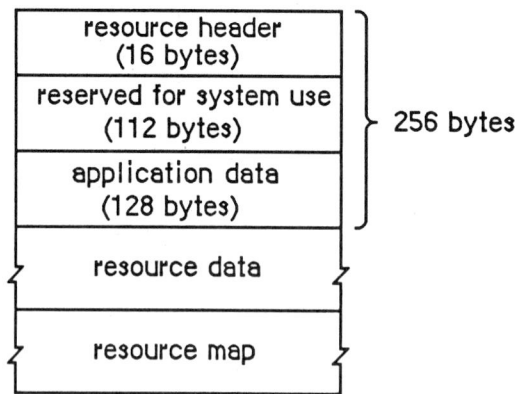

Figure 9. Format of a Resource File

As illustrated in Figure 9, every resource file begins with a **resource header**. The resource header gives the offsets to and lengths of the resource data and resource map parts of the file, as follows:

I-128 Resources Within Resources

Number of bytes	Contents
4 bytes	Offset from beginning of resource file to resource data
4 bytes	Offset from beginning of resource file to resource map
4 bytes	Length of resource data
4 bytes	Length of resource map

Note: All offsets and lengths in the resource file are given in bytes.

This is what immediately follows the resource header:

Number of bytes	Contents
112 bytes	Reserved for system use
128 bytes	Available for application data

The application data may be whatever you want.

The resource data follows the space reserved for the application data. It consists of the following for each resource in the file:

Number of bytes	Contents
For each resource:	
4 bytes	Length of following resource data
n bytes	Resource data for this resource

To learn exactly what the resource data is for a standard type of resource, see the chapter describing the part of the Toolbox that deals with that resource type.

After the resource data, the resource map begins as follows:

Number of bytes	Contents
16 bytes	0 (reserved for copy of resource header)
4 bytes	0 (reserved for handle to next resource map to be searched)
2 bytes	0 (reserved for file reference number)
2 bytes	Resource file attributes
2 bytes	Offset from beginning of resource map to type list (see below)
2 bytes	Offset from beginning of resource map to resource name list (see below)

After reading the resource map into memory, the Resource Manager stores the indicated information in the reserved areas at the beginning of the map.

The resource map continues with a type list, reference lists, and a resource name list. The type list contains the following:

Inside Macintosh

Number of bytes	Contents
2 bytes	Number of resource types in the map minus 1
For each type:	
4 bytes	Resource type
2 bytes	Number of resources of this type in the map minus 1
2 bytes	Offset from beginning of type list to reference list for resources of this type

This is followed by the reference list for each type of resource, which contains the resource references for all resources of that type. The reference lists are contiguous and in the same order as the types in the type list. The format of a reference list is as follows:

Number of bytes	Contents
For each reference of this type:	
2 bytes	Resource ID
2 bytes	Offset from beginning of resource name list to length of resource name, or −1 if none
1 byte	Resource attributes
3 bytes	Offset from beginning of resource data to length of data for this resource
4 bytes	0 (reserved for handle to resource)

The resource name list follows the reference list and has this format:

Number of bytes	Contents
For each name:	
1 byte	Length of following resource name
n bytes	Characters of resource name

Figure 10 shows where the various offsets lead to in a resource file, in general and also specifically for a resource reference.

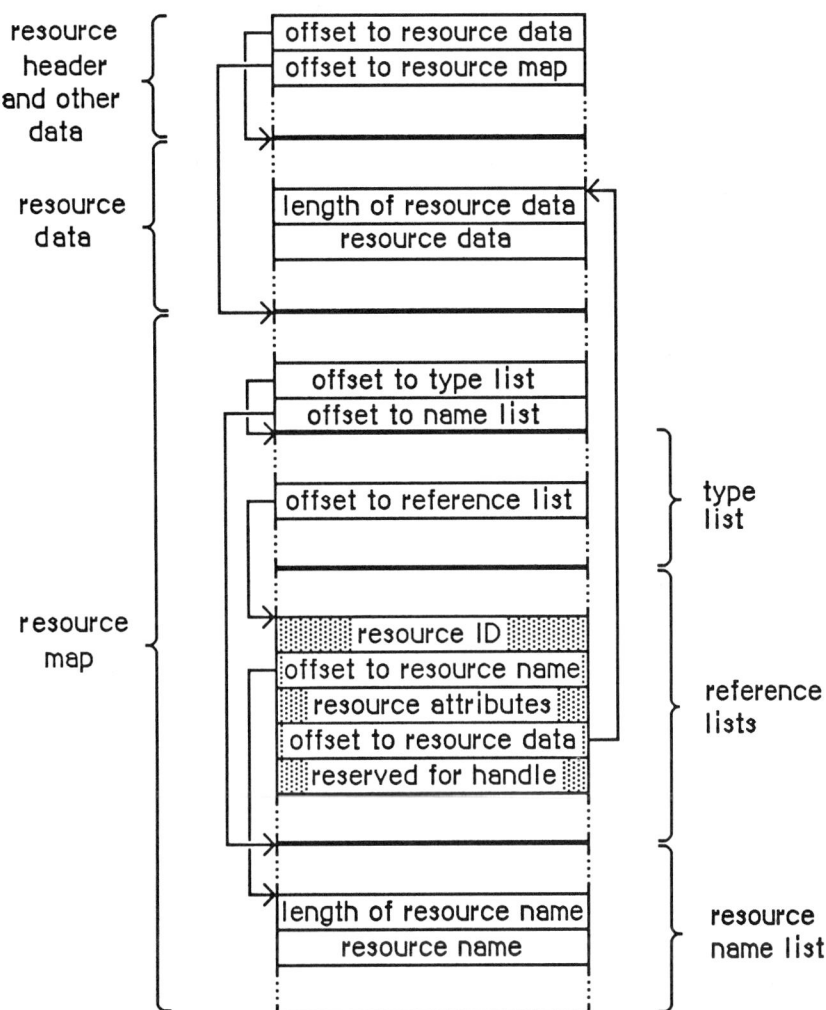

Figure 10. Resource Reference in a Resource File

SUMMARY OF THE RESOURCE MANAGER

Constants

```
CONST    { Masks for resource attributes }

         resSysHeap    = 64;      {set if read into system heap}
         resPurgeable  = 32;      {set if purgeable}
         resLocked     = 16;      {set if locked}
         resProtected  = 8;       {set if protected}
         resPreload    = 4;       {set if to be preloaded}
         resChanged    = 2;       {set if to be written to resource file}

         { Resource Manager result codes }

         resNotFound   = -192;    {resource not found}
         resFNotFound  = -193;    {resource file not found}
         addResFailed  = -194;    {AddResource failed}
         rmvResFailed  = -196;    {RmveResource failed}

         { Masks for resource file attributes }

         mapReadOnly = 128;       {set if file is read-only}
         mapCompact  = 64;        {set to compact file on update}
         mapChanged  = 32;        {set to write map on update}
```

Data Types

```
TYPE ResType = PACKED ARRAY[1..4] OF CHAR;
```

Routines

Initialization

```
FUNCTION  InitResources : INTEGER;
PROCEDURE RsrcZoneInit;
```

Opening and Closing Resource Files

```
PROCEDURE CreateResFile (fileName: Str255);
FUNCTION  OpenResFile   (fileName: Str255) : INTEGER;
PROCEDURE CloseResFile  (refNum: INTEGER);
```

Checking for Errors

```
FUNCTION ResError : INTEGER;
```

Setting the Current Resource File

```
FUNCTION    CurResFile : INTEGER;
FUNCTION    HomeResFile (theResource: Handle) : INTEGER;
PROCEDURE   UseResFile  (refNum: INTEGER);
```

Getting Resource Types

```
FUNCTION    CountTypes : INTEGER;
PROCEDURE   GetIndType  (VAR theType: ResType; index: INTEGER);
```

Getting and Disposing of Resources

```
PROCEDURE   SetResLoad       (load: BOOLEAN);
FUNCTION    CountResources   (theType: ResType) : INTEGER;
FUNCTION    GetIndResource   (theType: ResType; index: INTEGER) : Handle;
FUNCTION    GetResource      (theType: ResType; theID: INTEGER) : Handle;
FUNCTION    GetNamedResource (theType: ResType; name: Str255) : Handle;
PROCEDURE   LoadResource     (theResource: Handle);
PROCEDURE   ReleaseResource  (theResource: Handle);
PROCEDURE   DetachResource   (theResource: Handle);
```

Getting Resource Information

```
FUNCTION    UniqueID    (theType: ResType) : INTEGER;
PROCEDURE   GetResInfo  (theResource: Handle; VAR theID: INTEGER; VAR
                          theType: ResType; VAR name: Str255);
FUNCTION    GetResAttrs (theResource: Handle) : INTEGER;
FUNCTION    SizeResource (theResource: Handle) : LONGINT;
```

Modifying Resources

```
PROCEDURE   SetResInfo       (theResource: Handle; theID: INTEGER; name:
                               Str255);
PROCEDURE   SetResAttrs      (theResource: Handle; attrs: INTEGER);
PROCEDURE   ChangedResource  (theResource: Handle);
PROCEDURE   AddResource      (theData: Handle; theType: ResType; theID:
                               INTEGER; name: Str255);
PROCEDURE   RmveResource     (theResource: Handle);
PROCEDURE   UpdateResFile    (refNum: INTEGER);
PROCEDURE   WriteResource    (theResource: Handle);
PROCEDURE   SetResPurge      (install: BOOLEAN);
```

Inside Macintosh

Advanced Routines

```
FUNCTION GetResFileAttrs (refNum: INTEGER) : INTEGER;
PROCEDURE SetResFileAttrs (refNum: INTEGER; attrs: INTEGER);
```

Assembly-Language Information

Constants

```
; Resource attributes

resSysHeap      .EQU    6       ;set if read into system heap
resPurgeable    .EQU    5       ;set if purgeable
resLocked       .EQU    4       ;set if locked
resProtected    .EQU    3       ;set if protected
resPreload      .EQU    2       ;set if to be preloaded
resChanged      .EQU    1       ;set if to be written to resource file

; Resource Manager result codes

resNotFound     .EQU    -192    ;resource not found
resFNotFound    .EQU    -193    ;resource file not found
addResFailed    .EQU    -194    ;AddResource failed
rmvResFailed    .EQU    -196    ;RmveResource failed

; Resource file attributes

mapReadOnly     .EQU    7       ;set if file is read-only
mapCompact      .EQU    6       ;set to compact file on update
mapChanged      .EQU    5       ;set to write map on update
```

Special Macro Names

Pascal name	Macro name
SizeResource	_SizeRsrc

Variables

TopMapHndl	Handle to resource map of most recently opened resource file
SysMapHndl	Handle to map of system resource file
SysMap	Reference number of system resource file (word)
CurMap	Reference number of current resource file (word)
ResLoad	Current SetResLoad state (word)
ResErr	Current value of ResError (word)
ResErrProc	Address of resource error procedure
SysResName	Name of system resource file (length byte followed by up to 19 characters)

6 QUICKDRAW

137	About This Chapter
137	About QuickDraw
138	The Mathematical Foundation of QuickDraw
138	The Coordinate Plane
139	Points
140	Rectangles
141	Regions
142	Graphic Entities
143	Bit Images
144	Bit Maps
145	Patterns
146	Cursors
147	Graphic Entities as Resources
147	The Drawing Environment: GrafPort
150	Pen Characteristics
151	Text Characteristics
153	Coordinates in GrafPorts
155	General Discussion of Drawing
156	Transfer Modes
158	Drawing in Color
158	Pictures and Polygons
158	Pictures
159	Polygons
160	Using QuickDraw
162	QuickDraw Routines
162	GrafPort Routines
167	Cursor-Handling Routines
168	Pen and Line-Drawing Routines
171	Text-Drawing Routines
173	Drawing in Color
174	Calculations with Rectangles
176	Graphic Operations on Rectangles
177	Graphic Operations on Ovals
178	Graphic Operations on Rounded-Corner Rectangles
179	Graphic Operations on Arcs and Wedges
181	Calculations with Regions
186	Graphic Operations on Regions
187	Bit Transfer Operations

Inside Macintosh

189	Pictures
190	Calculations with Polygons
191	Graphic Operations on Polygons
193	Calculations with Points
194	Miscellaneous Routines
197	Customizing QuickDraw Operations
201	Summary of QuickDraw

ABOUT THIS CHAPTER

This chapter describes QuickDraw, the part of the Toolbox that allows Macintosh programmers to perform highly complex graphic operations very easily and very quickly. It describes the data types used by QuickDraw and gives details of the procedures and functions available in QuickDraw.

ABOUT QUICKDRAW

QuickDraw allows you to draw many different things on the Macintosh screen; some of these are illustrated in Figure 1.

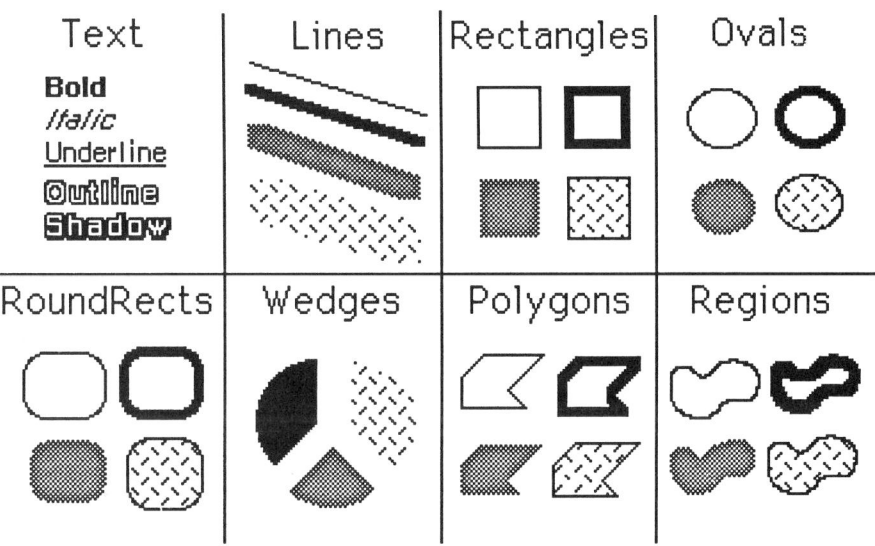

Figure 1. Samples of QuickDraw's Abilities

You can draw:

- text characters in a number of proportionally-spaced fonts, with variations that include boldfacing, italicizing, underlining, and outlining
- straight lines of any length, width, and pattern
- a variety of shapes, including rectangles, rounded-corner rectangles, circles and ovals, and polygons, all either outlined and hollow or filled in with a pattern
- arcs of ovals, or wedge-shaped sections filled in with a pattern
- any other arbitrary shape or collection of shapes
- a picture composed of any combination of the above, drawn with just a single procedure call

Inside Macintosh

QuickDraw also has some other abilities that you won't find in many other graphics packages. These abilities take care of most of the "housekeeping"—the trivial but time-consuming overhead that's necessary to keep things in order. They include:

- The ability to define many distinct "ports" on the screen. Each port has its own complete drawing environment—its own coordinate system, drawing location, character set, location on the screen, and so on. You can easily switch from one drawing port to another.

- Full and complete "clipping" to arbitrary areas, so that drawing will occur only where you want. It's like an electronic coloring book that won't let you color outside the lines. You don't have to worry about accidentally drawing over something else on the screen, or drawing off the screen and destroying memory.

- Off-screen drawing. Anything you can draw on the screen, you can also draw into an off-screen buffer, so you can prepare an image for an output device without disturbing the screen, or you can prepare a picture and move it onto the screen very quickly.

And QuickDraw lives up to its name: It's very fast. The speed and responsiveness of the Macintosh user interface are due primarily to the speed of QuickDraw. You can do good-quality animation, fast interactive graphics, and complex yet speedy text displays using the full features of QuickDraw. This means you don't have to bypass the general-purpose QuickDraw routines by writing a lot of special routines to improve speed.

In addition to its routines and data types, QuickDraw provides global variables that you can use from your Pascal program. For example, there's a variable named thePort that points to the current drawing port.

Assembly-language note: See the discussion of InitGraf in the "QuickDraw Routines" section for details on how to access the QuickDraw global variables from assembly language.

THE MATHEMATICAL FOUNDATION OF QUICKDRAW

To create graphics that are both precise and pretty requires not supercharged features but a firm mathematical foundation for the features you have. If the mathematics that underlie a graphics package are imprecise or fuzzy, the graphics will be, too. QuickDraw defines some clear mathematical constructs that are widely used in its procedures, functions, and data types: the coordinate plane, the point, the rectangle, and the region.

The Coordinate Plane

All information about location or movement is given to QuickDraw in terms of coordinates on a plane. The **coordinate plane** is a two-dimensional grid, as illustrated in Figure 2.

Note the following features of the QuickDraw coordinate plane:

- All grid coordinates are integers (in the range –32767 to 32767).
- All grid lines are infinitely thin.

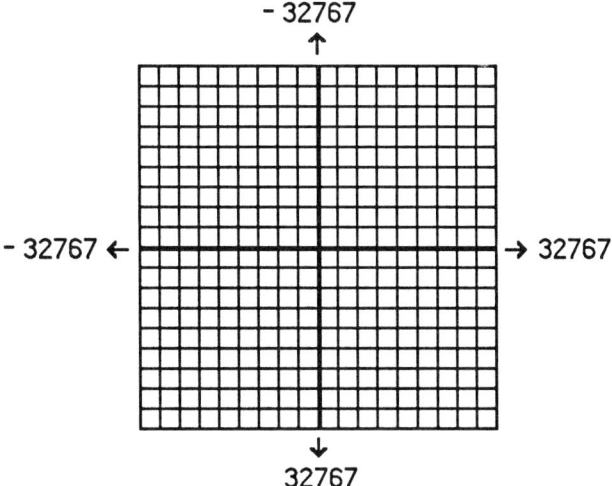

Figure 2. The Coordinate Plane

These concepts are important. First, they mean that the QuickDraw plane is finite, not infinite (although it's very large). Second, they mean that all elements represented on the coordinate plane are mathematically pure. Mathematical calculations using integer arithmetic will produce intuitively correct results. If you keep in mind that grid lines are infinitely thin, you'll never have "endpoint paranoia"—the confusion that results from not knowing whether that last dot is included in the line.

Points

There are 4,294,836,224 unique **points** on the coordinate plane. Each point is at the intersection of a horizontal grid line and a vertical grid line. As the grid lines are infinitely thin, so a point is infinitely small. Of course, there are many more points on this grid than there are dots on the Macintosh screen: When using QuickDraw you associate small parts of the grid with areas on the screen, so that you aren't bound into an arbitrary, limited coordinate system.

The coordinate origin (0,0) is in the middle of the grid. Horizontal coordinates increase as you move from left to right, and vertical coordinates increase as you move from top to bottom. This is the way both a TV screen and a page of English text are scanned: from the top left to the bottom right.

Figure 3 shows the relationship between points, grid lines, and **pixels**, the physical dots on the screen. (Pixels correspond to bits in memory, as described in the next section.)

You can store the coordinates of a point into a Pascal variable of type Point, defined by QuickDraw as a record of two integers:

```
TYPE  VHSelect = (v,h);
      Point    = RECORD CASE INTEGER OF
                    0: (v: INTEGER:     {vertical coordinate}
                        h: INTEGER);    {horizontal coordinate}
                    1: (vh: ARRAY[VHSelect] OF INTEGER)
                 END;
```

Inside Macintosh

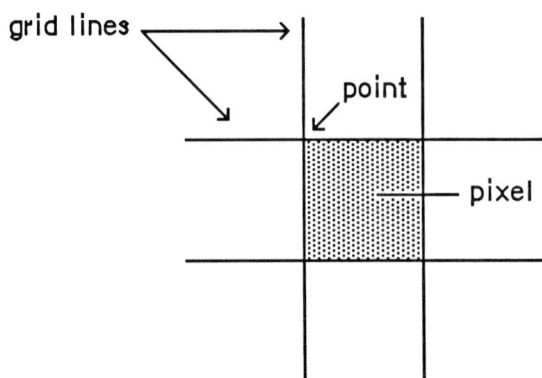

Figure 3. Points and Pixels

The variant part of this record lets you access the vertical and horizontal coordinates of a point either individually or as an array. For example, if the variable goodPt is declared to be of type Point, the following will all refer to the coordinates of the point:

```
goodPt.v            goodPt.h
goodPt.vh[v]        goodPt.vh[h]
```

Rectangles

Any two points can define the top left and bottom right corners of a rectangle. As these points are infinitely small, the borders of the rectangle are infinitely thin (see Figure 4).

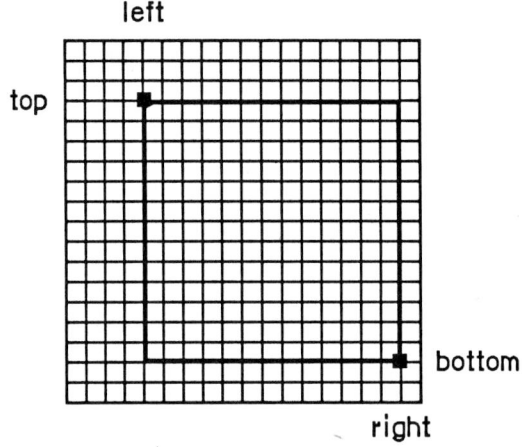

Figure 4. A Rectangle

Rectangles are used to define active areas on the screen, to assign coordinate systems to graphic entities, and to specify the locations and sizes for various drawing commands. QuickDraw also allows you to perform many mathematical calculations on rectangles—changing their sizes, shifting them around, and so on.

Note: Remember that rectangles, like points, are mathematical concepts that have no direct representation on the screen. The association between these conceptual elements and their physical representations is made by the BitMap data type, described in the following section.

The data type for rectangles is called Rect, and consists of four integers or two points:

```
TYPE Rect = RECORD CASE INTEGER OF
            0: (top:     INTEGER;
                left:    INTEGER;
                bottom:  INTEGER;
                right:   INTEGER);
            1: (topLeft: Point;
                botRight: Point)
            END;
```

Again, the record variant allows you to access a variable of type Rect either as four boundary coordinates or as two diagonally opposite corner points. Combined with the record variant for points, all of the following references to the rectangle named aRect are legal:

```
aRect                                              {type Rect}

aRect.topLeft           aRect.botRight             {type Point}

aRect.top               aRect.left                 {type INTEGER}
aRect.topLeft.v         aRect.topLeft.h            {type INTEGER}
aRect.topLeft.vh[v]     aRect.topLeft.vh[h]        {type INTEGER}

aRect.bottom            aRect.right                {type INTEGER}
aRect.botRight.v        aRect.botRight.h           {type INTEGER}
aRect.botRight.vh[v]    aRect.botRight.vh[h]       {type INTEGER}
```

Note: If the bottom coordinate of a rectangle is equal to or less than the top, or the right coordinate is equal to or less than the left, the rectangle is an **empty** rectangle (that is, one that contains no bits).

Regions

Unlike most graphics packages that can manipulate only simple geometric structures (usually rectilinear, at that), QuickDraw has the ability to gather an arbitrary set of spatially coherent points into a structure called a **region**, and perform complex yet rapid manipulations and calculations on such structures. Regions not only make your programs simpler and faster, but will let you perform operations that would otherwise be nearly impossible.

You define a region by calling routines that draw lines and shapes (even other regions). The outline of a region should be one or more closed loops. A region can be concave or convex, can consist of one area or many disjoint areas, and can even have "holes" in the middle. In Figure 5, the region on the left has a hole in the middle, and the region on the right consists of two disjoint areas.

The Mathematical Foundation of QuickDraw

Inside Macintosh

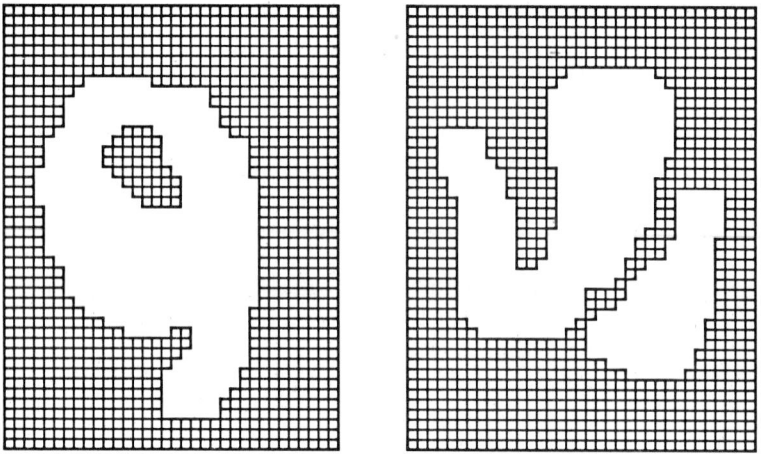

Figure 5. Regions

The data structure for a region consists of two fixed-length fields followed by a variable-length field:

```
TYPE Region =   RECORD
                    rgnSize: INTEGER;   {size in bytes}
                    rgnBBox: Rect;      {enclosing rectangle}
                    {more data if not rectangular}
                END;
```

The rgnSize field contains the size, in bytes, of the region variable. The maximum size of a region is 32K bytes. The rgnBBox field is a rectangle that completely encloses the region.

The simplest region is a rectangle. In this case, the rgnBBox field defines the entire region, and there's no optional region data. For rectangular regions (or empty regions), the rgnSize field contains 10.

The region definition data for nonrectangular regions is stored in a compact way that allows for highly efficient access by QuickDraw routines.

All regions are accessed through handles:

```
TYPE RgnPtr    = ^Region;
     RgnHandle = ^RgnPtr;
```

Many calculations can be performed on regions. A region can be "expanded" or "shrunk" and, given any two regions, QuickDraw can find their union, intersection, difference, and exclusive-OR; it can also determine whether a given point intersects a region, and so on.

GRAPHIC ENTITIES

Points, rectangles, and regions are all mathematical models rather than actual graphic elements—they're data types that QuickDraw uses for drawing, but they don't actually appear on the screen. Some entities that do have a direct graphic interpretation are the bit image, bit map, pattern, and cursor. This section describes these graphic entities and relates them to the mathematical constructs described above.

Bit Images

A **bit image** is a collection of bits in memory that have a rectilinear representation. Take a collection of words in memory and lay them end to end so that bit 15 of the lowest-numbered word is on the left and bit 0 of the highest-numbered word is on the far right. Then take this array of bits and divide it, on word boundaries, into a number of equal-size rows. Stack these rows vertically so that the first row is on the top and the last row is on the bottom. The result is a matrix like the one shown in Figure 6—rows and columns of bits, with each row containing the same number of bytes. The number of bytes in each row of the bit image is called the **row width** of that image. A bit image can be any length that's a multiple of the row width.

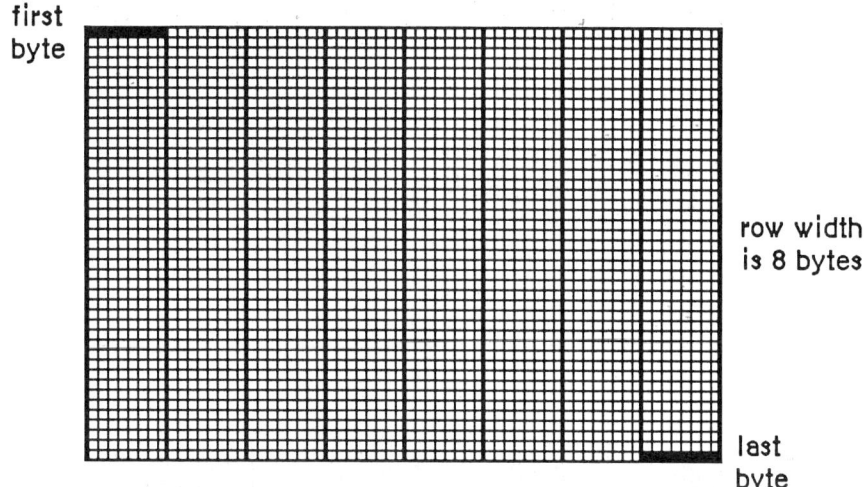

Figure 6. A Bit Image

The screen itself is one large visible bit image. On a Macintosh 128K or 512K, for example, the screen is a 342-by-512 bit image, with a row width of 64 bytes. These 21,888 bytes of memory are displayed as a matrix of 175,104 pixels on the screen, each bit corresponding to one pixel. If a bit's value is 0, its pixel is white; if the bit's value is 1, the pixel is black.

Warning: The numbers given here apply *only* to the Macintosh 128K and 512K systems. To allow for your application running on any version of the Macintosh, you should never use explicit numbers for screen dimensions. The QuickDraw global variable screenBits (a bit map, described below) gives you access to a rectangle whose dimensions are those of the screen, whatever version of the Macintosh is being used.

On a Macintosh 128K or 512K, each pixel on the screen is square, and there are 72 pixels per inch in each direction. On an unmodified Macintosh XL, each pixel is one and a half times taller than it is wide, meaning a rectangle 30 pixels wide by 20 tall looks square; there are 90 pixels per inch horizontally, and 60 per inch vertically. A Macintosh XL may be modified to have square pixels. You can get the the screen resolution by calling the Toolbox Utility procedure ScreenRes.

Inside Macintosh

Note: The values given for pixels per inch may not be exactly the measurement on the screen, but they're the values you should use when calculating the size of printed output.

Note: Since each pixel on the screen represents one bit in a bit image, wherever this chapter says "bit", you can substitute "pixel" if the bit image is the screen. Likewise, this chapter often refers to pixels on the screen where the discussion applies equally to bits in an off-screen bit image.

Bit Maps

A **bit map** in QuickDraw is a data structure that defines a physical bit image in terms of the coordinate plane. A bit map has three parts: a pointer to a bit image, the row width of that image, and a boundary rectangle that gives the bit map both its dimensions and a coordinate system.

There can be several bit maps pointing to the same bit image, each imposing a different coordinate system on it. This important feature is explained in "Coordinates in GrafPorts", below.

As shown in Figure 7, the structure of a bit map is as follows:

```
TYPE BitMap =   RECORD
                    baseAddr:   Ptr;        {pointer to bit image}
                    rowBytes:   INTEGER;    {row width}
                    bounds:     Rect        {boundary rectangle}
                END;
```

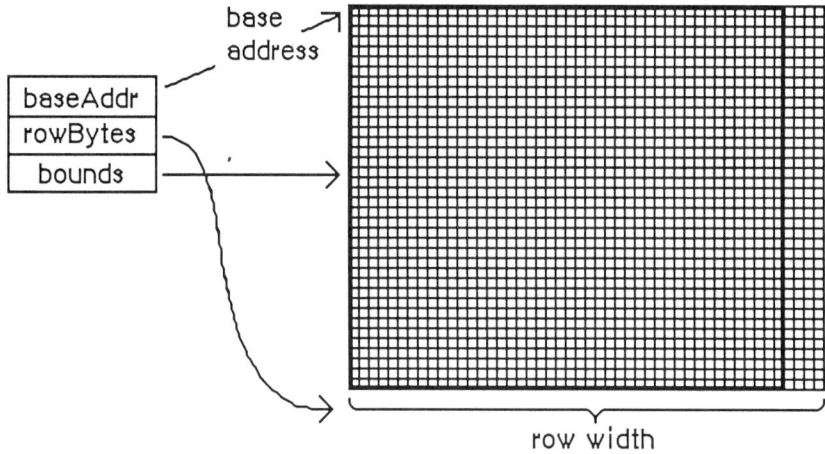

Figure 7. A Bit Map

BaseAddr is a pointer to the beginning of the bit image in memory. RowBytes is the row width in bytes. Both of these must always be even: A bit map must always begin on a word boundary and contain an integral number of words in each row.

The bounds field is the bit map's **boundary rectangle**, which both encloses the active area of the bit image and imposes a coordinate system on it. The top left corner of the boundary rectangle is aligned around the first bit in the bit image.

The relationship between the boundary rectangle and the bit image in a bit map is simple yet very important. First, some general rules:

- Bits in a bit image fall between points on the coordinate plane.
- A rectangle that is H points wide and V points tall encloses exactly (H–1)*(V–1) bits.

The coordinate system assigns integer values to the lines that border and separate bits, not to the bit positions themselves. For example, if a bit map is assigned the boundary rectangle with corners (10,–8) and (34,8), the bottom right bit in the image will be *between* horizontal coordinates 33 and 34, and *between* vertical coordinates 7 and 8 (see Figure 8).

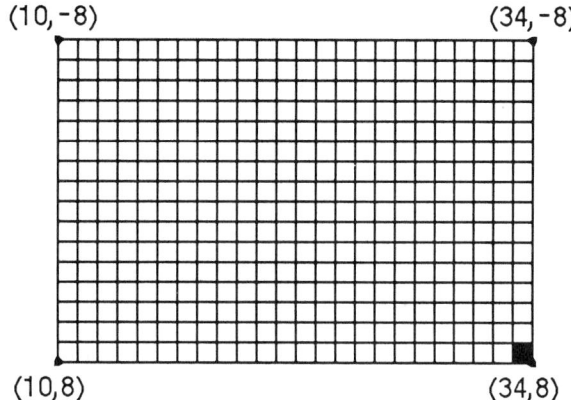

Figure 8. Coordinates and Bit Maps

The width of the boundary rectangle determines how many bits of one row are logically owned by the bit map. This width must not exceed the number of bits in each row of the bit image. The height of the boundary rectangle determines how many rows of the image are logically owned by the bit map. The number of rows enclosed by the boundary rectangle must not exceed the number of rows in the bit image.

Normally, the boundary rectangle completely encloses the bit image. If the rectangle is smaller than the dimensions of the image, the least significant bits in each row, as well as the last rows in the image, aren't affected by any operations on the bit map.

There's a QuickDraw global variable, named screenBits, that contains a bit map corresponding to the screen of the Macintosh being used. Wherever your program needs the exact dimensions of the screen, it should get them from the boundary rectangle of this variable.

Patterns

A **pattern** is a 64-bit image, organized as an 8-by-8-bit square, that's used to define a repeating design (such as stripes) or tone (such as gray). Patterns can be used to draw lines and shapes or to fill areas on the screen.

When a pattern is drawn, it's aligned so that adjacent areas of the same pattern in the same graphics port will blend with it into a continuous, coordinated pattern. QuickDraw provides predefined patterns in global variables named white, black, gray, ltGray, and dkGray. Any other 64-bit variable or constant can also be used as a pattern. The data type definition for a pattern is as follows:

Inside Macintosh

```
TYPE Pattern = PACKED ARRAY[0..7] OF 0..255;
```

The row width of a pattern is one byte.

Cursors

A **cursor** is a small image that appears on the screen and is controlled by the mouse. (It appears only on the screen, and never in an off-screen bit image.)

> **Note:** Macintosh user manuals call this image a "pointer", since it points to a location on the screen. To avoid confusion with other meanings of "pointer" in *Inside Macintosh*, we use the alternate term "cursor".

A cursor is defined as a 256-bit image, a 16-by-16-bit square. The row width of a cursor is two bytes. Figure 9 illustrates four cursors.

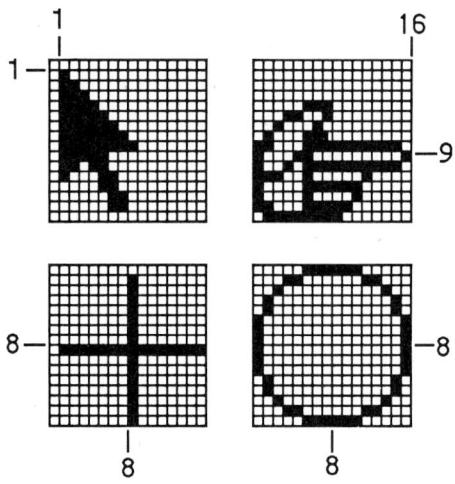

Figure 9. Cursors

A cursor has three fields: a 16-word data field that contains the image itself, a 16-word mask field that contains information about the screen appearance of each bit of the cursor, and a **hotSpot** point that aligns the cursor with the mouse location.

```
TYPE Bits16 = ARRAY[0..15] OF INTEGER;

     Cursor = RECORD
                data:    Bits16;  {cursor image}
                mask:    Bits16;  {cursor mask}
                hotSpot: Point    {point aligned with mouse}
              END;
```

The data for the cursor must begin on a word boundary.

The cursor appears on the screen as a 16-by-16-bit square. The appearance of each bit of the square is determined by the corresponding bits in the data and mask and, if the mask bit is 0, by the pixel "under" the cursor (the pixel already on the screen in the same position as this bit of the cursor):

Data	Mask	Resulting pixel on screen
0	1	White
1	1	Black
0	0	Same as pixel under cursor
1	0	Inverse of pixel under cursor

Notice that if all mask bits are 0, the cursor is completely transparent, in that the image under the cursor can still be viewed: Pixels under the white part of the cursor appear unchanged, while under the black part of the cursor, black pixels show through as white.

The hotSpot aligns a point (*not* a bit) in the image with the mouse location. Imagine the rectangle with corners (0,0) and (16,16) framing the image, as in each of the examples in Figure 9; the hotSpot is defined in this coordinate system. A hotSpot of (0,0) is at the top left of the image. For the arrow in Figure 9 to point to the mouse location, (1,1) would be its hotSpot. A hotSpot of (8,8) is in the exact center of the image; the center of the plus sign or circle in Figure 9 would coincide with the mouse location if (8,8) were the hotSpot for that cursor. Similarly, the hotSpot for the pointing hand would be (16,9).

Whenever you move the mouse, the low-level interrupt-driven mouse routines move the cursor's hotSpot to be aligned with the new mouse location.

QuickDraw supplies a predefined cursor in the global variable named arrow; this is the standard arrow cursor (illustrated in Figure 9).

Graphic Entities as Resources

You can create cursors and patterns in your program code, but it's usually simpler and more convenient to store them in a resource file and read them in when you need them. Standard cursors and patterns are available not only through the global variables provided by QuickDraw, but also as system resources stored in the system resource file. QuickDraw itself operates independently of the Resource Manager, so it doesn't contain routines for accessing graphics-related resources; instead, these routines are included in the Toolbox Utilities (see chapter 16 for more information).

Besides patterns and cursors, two other graphic entities that may be stored in resource files (and accessed via Toolbox Utility routines) are a QuickDraw picture, described later in this chapter, and an **icon**, a 32-by-32 bit image that's used to graphically represent an object, concept, or message.

THE DRAWING ENVIRONMENT: GRAFPORT

A **grafPort** is a complete drawing environment that defines where and how graphic operations will take place. You can have many grafPorts open at once, and each one will have its own coordinate system, drawing pattern, background pattern, pen size and location, character font and style, and bit map in which drawing takes place. You can instantly switch from one port to another. GrafPorts are the structures upon which a program builds windows, which are fundamental to the Macintosh "overlapping windows" user interface. Besides being used for windows on the screen, grafPorts are used for printing and for off-screen drawing.

A grafPort is defined as follows:

```
TYPE GrafPtr   = ^GrafPort;
     GrafPort  = RECORD
                   device:     INTEGER;    {device-specific information}
                   portBits:   BitMap;     {grafPort's bit map}
                   portRect:   Rect;       {grafPort's rectangle}
                   visRgn:     RgnHandle;  {visible region}
                   clipRgn:    RgnHandle;  {clipping region}
                   bkPat:      Pattern;    {background pattern}
                   fillPat:    Pattern;    {fill pattern}
                   pnLoc:      Point;      {pen location}
                   pnSize:     Point;      {pen size}
                   pnMode:     INTEGER;    {pen's transfer mode}
                   pnPat:      Pattern;    {pen pattern}
                   pnVis:      INTEGER;    {pen visibility}
                   txFont:     INTEGER;    {font number for text}
                   txFace:     Style;      {text's character style}
                   txMode:     INTEGER;    {text's transfer mode}
                   txSize:     INTEGER;    {font size for text}
                   spExtra:    Fixed;      {extra space}
                   fgColor:    LONGINT;    {foreground color}
                   bkColor:    LONGINT;    {background color}
                   colrBit:    INTEGER;    {color bit}
                   patStretch: INTEGER;    {used internally}
                   picSave:    Handle;     {picture being saved}
                   rgnSave:    Handle;     {region being saved}
                   polySave:   Handle;     {polygon being saved}
                   grafProcs:  QDProcsPtr  {low-level drawing routines}
                 END;
```

All QuickDraw operations refer to grafPorts via grafPtrs. (For historical reasons, grafPort is one of the few objects in the Macintosh system software that's referred to by a pointer rather than a handle.)

> **Warning:** You can access all fields and subfields of a grafPort normally, but you should not store new values directly into them. QuickDraw has routines for altering all fields of a grafPort, and using these routines ensures that changing a grafPort produces no unusual side effects.

The device field of a grafPort contains device-specific information that's used by the Font Manager to achieve the best possible results when drawing text in the grafPort. There may be physical differences in the same logical font for different output devices, to ensure the highest-quality printing on the device being used. The default value of the device field is 0, for best results on output to the screen. For more information, see chapter 7.

The portBits field is the bit map that points to the bit image to be used by the grafPort. The default bit map uses the entire screen as its bit image. The bit map may be changed to indicate a different structure in memory: All graphics routines work in exactly the same way regardless of whether their effects are visible on the screen. A program can, for example, prepare an image to be printed on a printer without ever displaying the image on the screen, or develop a picture in an off-screen bit map before transferring it to the screen. The portBits.bounds rectangle determines the coordinate system of the grafPort; all other coordinates in the grafPort are expressed in this system.

The portRect field is a rectangle that defines a subset of the bit map that will be used for drawing: All drawing done by the application occurs inside the portRect. Its coordinates are in the coordinate system defined by the portBits.bounds rectangle. The portRect usually falls within the portBits.bounds rectangle, but it's not required to do so. The portRect usually defines the "writable" interior area of a window, document, or other object on the screen.

The visRgn field is manipulated by the Window Manager; you will normally never change a grafPort's visRgn. It indicates the region of the grafPort that's actually visible on the screen, that is, the part of the window that's not covered by other windows. For example, if you move one window in front of another, the Window Manager logically removes the area of overlap from the visRgn of the window in back. When you draw into the back window, whatever's being drawn is clipped to the visRgn so that it doesn't run over onto the front window. The default visRgn is set to the portRect. The visRgn has no effect on images that aren't displayed on the screen.

The clipRgn is the grafPort's **clipping region**, an arbitrary region that you can use to limit drawing to any region within the portRect. If, for example, you want to draw a half circle on the screen, you can set the clipRgn to half the square that would enclose the whole circle, and then draw the whole circle. Only the half within the clipRgn will actually be drawn in the grafPort. The default clipRgn is set arbitrarily large; you have full control over its setting. Unlike the visRgn, the clipRgn affects the image even if it isn't displayed on the screen.

Figure 10 illustrates a typical bit map (as defined by portBits), portRect, visRgn, and clipRgn.

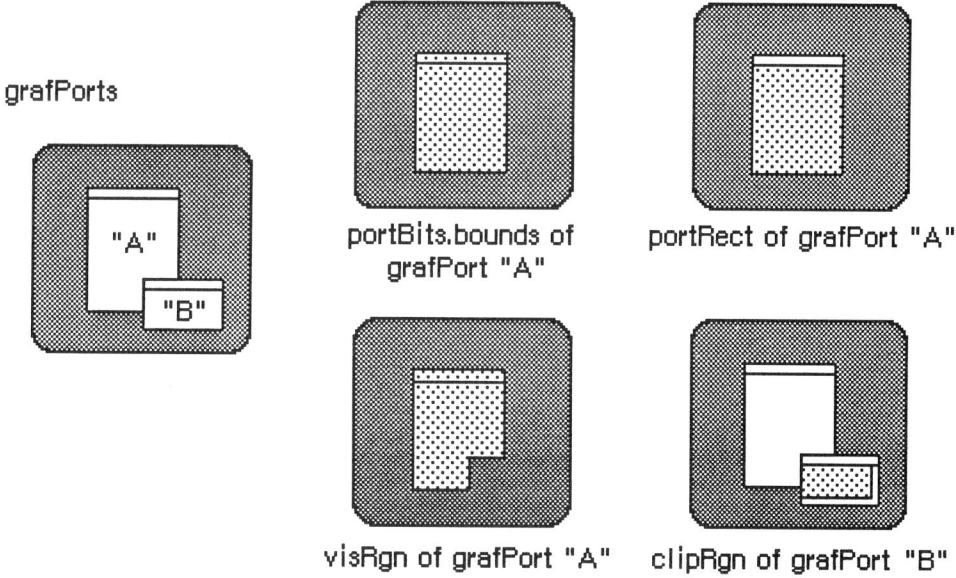

Figure 10. GrafPort Regions

The bkPat and fillPat fields of a grafPort contain patterns used by certain QuickDraw routines. BkPat is the "background" pattern that's used when an area is erased or when bits are scrolled out of it. When asked to fill an area with a specified pattern, QuickDraw stores the given pattern in

Inside Macintosh

the fillPat field and then calls a low-level drawing routine that gets the pattern from that field. The various graphic operations are discussed in detail later in the descriptions of individual QuickDraw routines.

Of the next ten fields, the first five determine characteristics of the graphics pen and the last five determine characteristics of any text that may be drawn; these are described in separate sections below.

The fgColor, bkColor, and colrBit fields contain values related to drawing in color. FgColor is the grafPort's foreground color and bkColor is its background color. ColrBit tells the color imaging software which plane of the color picture to draw into. For more information, see "Drawing in Color" in the section "General Discussion of Drawing".

The patStretch field is used during output to a printer to expand patterns if necessary. The application should not change its value.

The picSave, rgnSave, and polySave fields reflect the state of picture, region, and polygon definition, respectively. To define a region, for example, you "open" it, call routines that draw it, and then "close" it. If no region is open, rgnSave contains NIL; otherwise, it contains a handle to information related to the region definition. The application shouldn't be concerned about exactly what information the handle leads to; you may, however, save the current value of rgnSave, set the field to NIL to disable the region definition, and later restore it to the saved value to resume the region definition. The picSave and polySave fields work similarly for pictures and polygons.

Finally, the grafProcs field may point to a special data structure that the application stores into if it wants to customize QuickDraw drawing routines or use QuickDraw in other advanced, highly specialized ways (see "Customizing QuickDraw Operations"). If grafProcs is NIL, QuickDraw responds in the standard ways described in this chapter.

Pen Characteristics

The pnLoc, pnSize, pnMode, pnPat, and pnVis fields of a grafPort deal with the graphics "pen". Each grafPort has one and only one such pen, which is used for drawing lines, shapes, and text. The pen has four characteristics: a location, a size (height and width), a drawing mode, and a drawing pattern (see Figure 11).

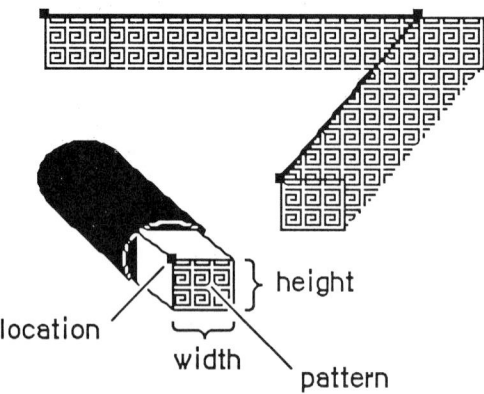

Figure 11. A Graphics Pen

The pnLoc field specifies the point where QuickDraw will begin drawing the next line, shape, or character. It can be anywhere on the coordinate plane: There are no restrictions on the movement or placement of the pen. Remember that the pen location is a point in the grafPort's coordinate system, not a pixel in a bit image. The top left corner of the pen is at the pen location; the pen hangs below and to the right of this point.

The pen is rectangular in shape, and its width and height are specified by pnSize. The default size is a 1-by-1-bit square; the width and height can range from (0,0) to (30000,30000). If either the pen width or the pen height is less than 1, the pen will not draw.

The pnMode and pnPat fields of a grafPort determine how the bits under the pen are affected when lines or shapes are drawn. The pnPat is a pattern that's used like the "ink" in the pen. This pattern, like all other patterns drawn in the grafPort, is always aligned with the port's coordinate system: The top left corner of the pattern is aligned with the top left corner of the portRect, so that adjacent areas of the same pattern will blend into a continuous, coordinated pattern.

The pnMode field determines how the pen pattern is to affect what's already in the bit image when lines or shapes are drawn. When the pen draws, QuickDraw first determines what bits in the bit image will be affected and finds their corresponding bits in the pattern. It then does a bit-by-bit comparison based on the pen mode, which specifies one of eight Boolean operations to perform. The resulting bit is stored into its proper place in the bit image. The pen modes are described under "Transfer Modes" in the section "General Discussion of Drawing".

The pnVis field determines the pen's visibility, that is, whether it draws on the screen. For more information, see the descriptions of HidePen and ShowPen under "Pen and Line-Drawing Routines" in the "QuickDraw Routines" section.

Text Characteristics

The txFont, txFace, txMode, txSize, and spExtra fields of a grafPort determine how text will be drawn—the font, style, and size of characters and how they will be placed in the bit image. QuickDraw can draw characters as quickly and easily as it draws lines and shapes, and in many prepared fonts. **Font** means the complete set of characters of one typeface. The characters may be drawn in any size and **character style** (that is, with stylistic variations such as bold, italic, and underline). Figure 12 shows two characters drawn by QuickDraw and some terms associated with drawing text.

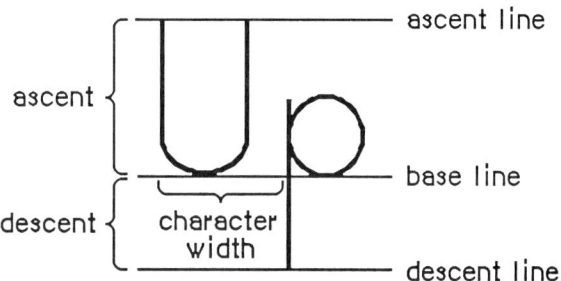

Figure 12. QuickDraw Characters

Text is drawn with the base line positioned at the pen location.

The txFont field is a font number that identifies the character font to be used in the grafPort. The font number 0 represents the system font. For more information about the system font, the other font numbers recognized by the Font Manager, and the construction, layout, and loading of fonts, see chapter 7.

Inside Macintosh

A character font is defined as a collection of images that make up the individual characters of the font. The characters can be of unequal widths, and they're not restricted to their "cells": The lower curl of a lowercase j, for example, can stretch back under the previous character (typographers call this **kerning**). A font can consist of up to 255 distinct characters, yet not all characters need to be defined in a single font. In addition, each font contains a **missing symbol** to be drawn in case of a request to draw a character that's missing from the font.

The txFace field controls the character style of the text with values from the set defined by the Style data type:

```
TYPE StyleItem = (bold,italic,underline,outline,shadow,condense,
                  extend);
     Style     = SET OF StyleItem;
```

Assembly-language note: In assembly language, this set is stored as a word whose low-order byte contains bits representing the style. The bit numbers are specified by the following global constants:

```
boldBit      .EQU    0
italicBit    .EQU    1
ulineBit     .EQU    2
outlineBit   .EQU    3
shadowBit    .EQU    5
extendBit    .EQU    6
```

If all bits are 0, it represents the plain character style.

You can apply stylistic variations either alone or in combination; Figure 13 illustrates some as applied to the Geneva font. Most combinations usually look good only for large font sizes.

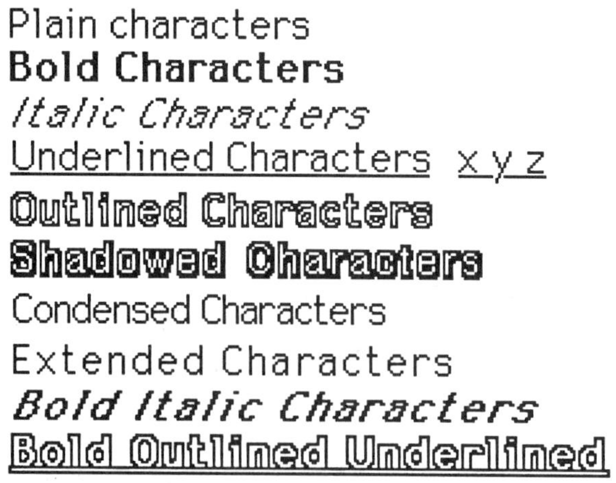

Plain characters
Bold Characters
Italic Characters
Underlined Characters x y z
Outlined Characters
Shadowed Characters
Condensed Characters
Extended Characters
Bold Italic Characters
Bold Outlined Underlined

Figure 13. Stylistic Variations

If you specify bold, each character is repeatedly drawn one bit to the right an appropriate number of times for extra thickness.

Italic adds an italic slant to the characters. Character bits above the base line are skewed right; bits below the base line are skewed left.

Underline draws a line below the base line of the characters. If part of a character descends below the base line (as "y" in Figure 13), the underline isn't drawn through the pixel on either side of the descending part.

Outline makes a hollow, outlined character rather than a solid one. Shadow also makes an outlined character, but the outline is thickened below and to the right of the character to achieve the effect of a shadow. If you specify bold along with outline or shadow, the hollow part of the character is widened.

Condense and extend affect the horizontal distance between all characters, including spaces. Condense decreases the distance between characters and extend increases it, by an amount that the Font Manager determines is appropriate.

The txMode field controls the way characters are placed in the bit image. It functions much like a pnMode: When a character is drawn, QuickDraw determines which bits in the bit image will be affected, does a bit-by-bit comparison based on the mode, and stores the resulting bits into the bit image. These modes are described under "Transfer Modes" in the section "General Discussion of Drawing". Only three of them—srcOr, srcXor, and srcBic—should be used for drawing text.

Note: If you use scrCopy, some extra blank space will be appended at the end of the text.

The txSize field specifies the **font size** in points (where "point" is a typographical term meaning approximately 1/72 inch). Any size from 1 to 127 points may be specified. If the Font Manager doesn't have the font in a specified size, it will scale a size it does have as necessary to produce the size desired. A value of 0 in this field represents the system font size (12 points).

Finally, the spExtra field is useful when a line of characters is to be drawn justified such that it's aligned with both a left and a right margin (sometimes called "full justification"). SpExtra contains a fixed-point number equal to the average number of pixels by which each space character should be widened to fill out the line. The Fixed data type is described in chapter 3.

COORDINATES IN GRAFPORTS

Each grafPort has its own **local coordinate system.** All fields in the grafPort are expressed in these coordinates, and all calculations and actions performed in QuickDraw use the local coordinate system of the currently selected port.

Two things are important to remember:

- Each grafPort maps a portion of the coordinate plane into a similarly-sized portion of a bit image.
- The portBits.bounds rectangle defines the local coordinates for a grafPort.

The top left corner of portBits.bounds is always aligned around the first bit in the bit image; the coordinates of that corner "anchor" a point on the grid to that bit in the bit image. This forms a common reference point for multiple grafPorts that use the same bit image (such as the screen); given a portBits.bounds rectangle for each port, you know that their top left corners coincide.

The relationship between the portBits.bounds and portRect rectangles is very important: The portBits.bounds rectangle establishes a coordinate system for the port, and the portRect rectangle

Inside Macintosh

indicates the section of the coordinate plane (and thus the bit image) that will be used for drawing. The portRect usually falls inside the portBits.bounds rectangle, but it's not required to do so.

When a new grafPort is created, its bit map is set to point to the entire screen, and both the portBits.bounds and the portRect are set to rectangles enclosing the screen. The point (0,0) corresponds to the screen's top left corner.

You can redefine the local coordinates of the top left corner of the grafPort's portRect, using the SetOrigin procedure. This offsets the coordinates of the grafPort's portBits.bounds rectangle, recalculating the coordinates of all points in the grafPort to be relative to the new corner coordinates. For example, consider these procedure calls:

```
SetPort(gamePort);
SetOrigin(90,80)
```

The call to SetPort sets the current grafPort to gamePort; the call to SetOrigin changes the local coordinates of the top left corner of that port's portRect to (90,80) (see Figure 14).

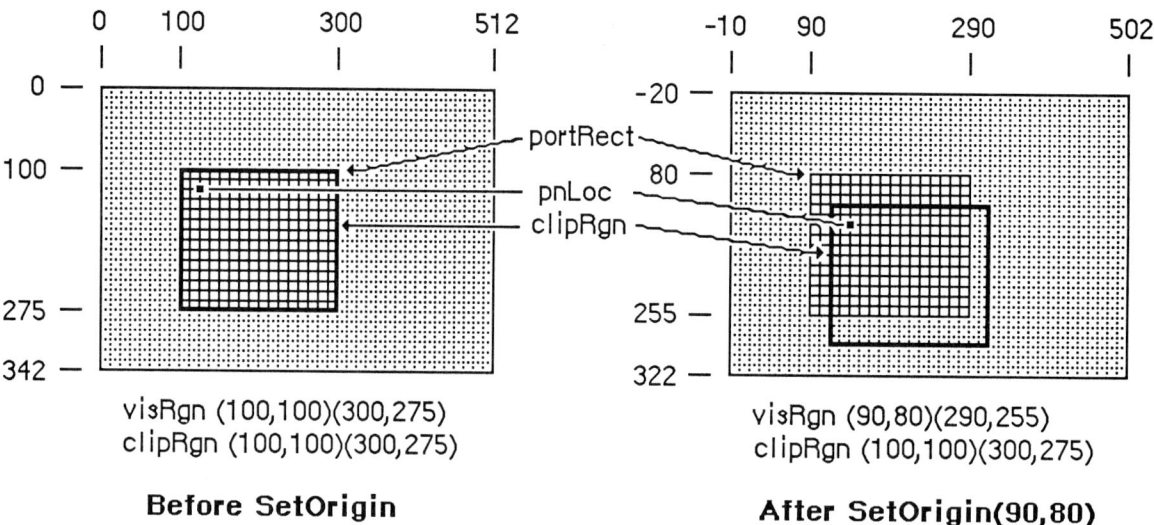

Figure 14. Changing Local Coordinates

This offsets the coordinates of the following elements:

```
gamePort^.portBits.bounds
gamePort^.portRect
gamePort^.visRgn
```

These three elements are always kept "in sync".

Notice that when the local coordinates of a grafPort are offset, the grafPort's clipRgn and pen location are *not* offset. A good way to think of it is that the port's structure "sticks" to the screen, while the document in the grafPort (along with the pen and clipRgn) "sticks" to the coordinate system. For example, in Figure 14, before SetOrigin, the visRgn and clipRgn are the same as the portRect. After the SetOrigin call, the locations of portBits.bounds, portRect, and visRgn do not change on the screen; their coordinates are simply offset. As always, the top left corner of portBits.bounds remains "anchored" around the first bit in the bit image (the first pixel on the screen); the image on the screen doesn't move as a result of SetOrigin. However, the pen location and clipRgn do move on the screen; the top left corner of the clipRgn is still (100,100), but this location has moved down and to the right, and the pen has similarly moved.

If you're moving, comparing, or otherwise dealing with mathematical items in different grafPorts (for example, finding the intersection of two regions in two different grafPorts), you must adjust to a common coordinate system before you perform the operation. A QuickDraw procedure, LocalToGlobal, lets you convert a point's local coordinates to a **global coordinate system** where the top left corner of the bit image is (0,0); by converting the various local coordinates to global coordinates, you can compare and mix them with confidence. For more information, see the description of LocalToGlobal under "Calculations with Points" in the "QuickDraw Routines" section.

GENERAL DISCUSSION OF DRAWING

Drawing occurs:

- always inside a grafPort, in the bit image and coordinate system defined by the grafPort's bit map
- always within the intersection of the grafPort's portBits.bounds and portRect, and clipped to its visRgn and clipRgn
- always at the grafPort's pen location
- usually with the grafPort's pen size, pattern, and mode

With QuickDraw routines, you can draw lines, shapes, and text. Shapes include rectangles, ovals, rounded-corner rectangles, wedge-shaped sections of ovals, regions, and polygons.

Lines are defined by two points: the current pen location and a destination location. When drawing a line, QuickDraw moves the top left corner of the pen along the mathematical trajectory from the current location to the destination. The pen hangs below and to the right of the trajectory (see Figure 15).

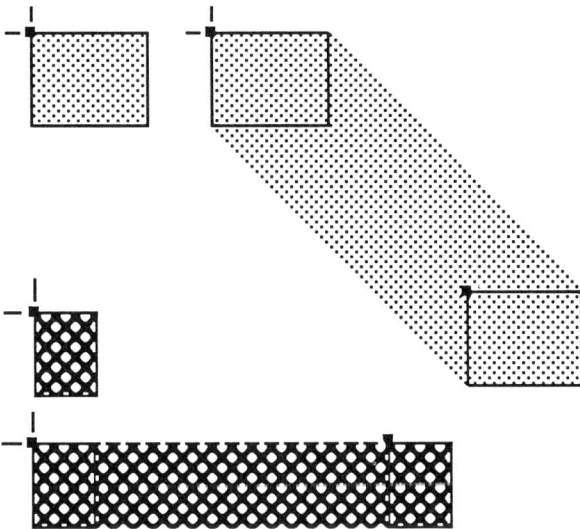

Figure 15. Drawing Lines

Inside Macintosh

Note: No mathematical element (such as the pen location) is ever affected by clipping; clipping only determines what appears where in the bit image. If you draw a line to a location outside the intersection of the portRect, visRgn and clipRgn, the pen location will move there, but only the portion of the line that's inside that area will actually be drawn. This is true for all drawing routines.

Rectangles, ovals, and rounded-corner rectangles are defined by two corner points. The shapes always appear inside the mathematical rectangle defined by the two points. A region is defined in a more complex manner, but also appears only within the rectangle enclosing it. Remember, these enclosing rectangles have infinitely thin borders and are not visible on the screen.

As illustrated in Figure 16, shapes may be drawn either **solid** (filled in with a pattern) or **framed** (outlined and hollow).

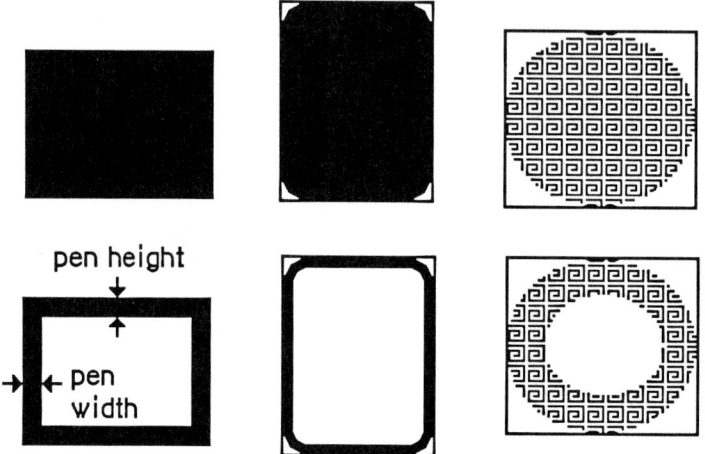

Figure 16. Solid Shapes and Framed Shapes

In the case of framed shapes, the outline appears completely within the enclosing rectangle—with one exception—and the vertical and horizontal thickness of the outline is determined by the pen size. The exception is polygons, as discussed in the section "Pictures and Polygons" below.

The pen pattern is used to fill in the bits that are affected by the drawing operation. The pen mode defines how those bits are to be affected by directing QuickDraw to apply one of eight Boolean operations to the bits in the shape and the corresponding pixels on the screen.

Text drawing doesn't use the pnSize, pnPat, or pnMode, but it does use the pnLoc. QuickDraw starts drawing each character from the current pen location, with the character's base line at the pen location. After a character is drawn, the pen moves to the right to the location where it will draw the next character. No wraparound or carriage return is performed automatically. Clipping of text is performed in exactly the same manner as all other clipping in QuickDraw.

Transfer Modes

When lines or shapes are drawn, the pnMode field of the grafPort determines how the drawing is to appear in the port's bit image; similarly, the txMode field determines how text is to appear. There's also a QuickDraw procedure that transfers a bit image from one bit map to another, and this procedure has a mode parameter that determines the appearance of the result. In all these cases, the mode, called a **transfer mode**, specifies one of eight Boolean operations: For each bit in the item to be drawn, QuickDraw finds the corresponding bit in the destination bit map, performs the Boolean operation on the pair of bits, and stores the resulting bit into the bit image.

There are two types of transfer mode:

- **pattern transfer modes**, for drawing lines or shapes with a pattern
- **source transfer modes**, for drawing text or transferring any bit image between two bit maps

For each type of mode, there are four basic operations—Copy, Or, Xor, and Bic ("bit clear"). The Copy operation simply replaces the pixels in the destination with the pixels in the pattern or source, "painting" over the destination without regard for what's already there. The Or, Xor, and Bic operations leave the destination pixels under the white part of the pattern or source unchanged, and differ in how they affect the pixels under the black part: Or replaces those pixels with black pixels, thus "overlaying" the destination with the black part of the pattern or source; Xor inverts the pixels under the black part; and Bic erases them to white.

Each of the basic operations has a variant in which every pixel in the pattern or source is inverted before the operation is performed, giving eight operations in all. Each mode is defined by name as a constant in QuickDraw (see Figure 17).

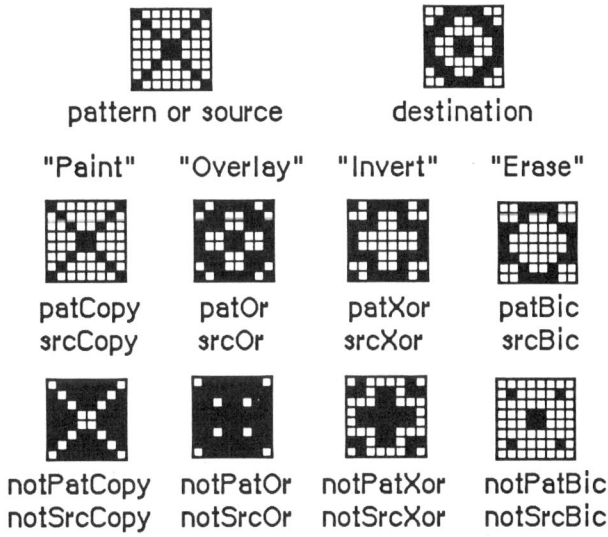

Figure 17. Transfer Modes

Pattern transfer mode	Source transfer mode	Action on each pixel in destination:	
		If black pixel in pattern or source	If white pixel in pattern or source
patCopy	srcCopy	Force black	Force white
patOr	srcOr	Force black	Leave alone
patXor	srcXor	Invert	Leave alone
patBic	srcBic	Force white	Leave alone
notPatCopy	notSrcCopy	Force white	Force black
notPatOr	notSrcOr	Leave alone	Force black
notPatXor	notSrcXor	Leave alone	Invert
notPatBic	notSrcBic	Leave alone	Force white

Drawing in Color

Your application can draw on color output devices by using QuickDraw procedures to set the foreground color and the background color. Eight standard colors may be specified with the following predefined constants:

```
CONST  blackColor    = 33;
       whiteColor    = 30;
       redColor      = 205;
       greenColor    = 341;
       blueColor     = 409;
       cyanColor     = 273;
       magentaColor  = 137;
       yellowColor   = 69;
```

Initially, the foreground color is blackColor and the background color is whiteColor. If you specify a color other than whiteColor, it will appear as black on a black-and-white output device.

To apply the table in the "Transfer Modes" section above to drawing in color, make the following translation: Where the table shows "Force black", read "Force foreground color", and where it shows "Force white", read "Force background color". The effect of inverting a color depends on the device being used.

Note: QuickDraw can support output devices that have up to 32 bits of color information per pixel. A color picture may be thought of, then, as having up to 32 planes. At any one time, QuickDraw draws into only one of these planes. A QuickDraw routine called by the color-imaging software specifies which plane.

PICTURES AND POLYGONS

QuickDraw lets you save a sequence of drawing commands and "play them back" later with a single procedure call. There are two such mechanisms: one for drawing any picture to scale in a destination rectangle that you specify, and another for drawing polygons in all the ways you can draw other shapes in QuickDraw.

Pictures

A **picture** in QuickDraw is a transcript of calls to routines that draw something—anything—in a bit image. Pictures make it easy for one program to draw something defined in another program, with great flexibility and without knowing the details about what's being drawn.

For each picture you define, you specify a rectangle that surrounds it; this rectangle is called the **picture frame**. When you later call the procedure that plays back the saved picture, you supply a destination rectangle, and QuickDraw scales the picture so that its frame is completely aligned with the destination rectangle. Thus, the picture may be expanded or shrunk to fit its destination rectangle. For example, if the picture is a circle inside a square picture frame, and the destination rectangle is not square, the picture will be drawn as an oval.

Since a picture may include any sequence of drawing commands, its data structure is a variable-length entity. It consists of two fixed-length fields followed by a variable-length field:

```
TYPE Picture =    RECORD
                     picSize:  INTEGER;  {size in bytes}
                     picFrame: Rect;     {picture frame}
                     {picture definition data}
                  END;
```

The picSize field contains the size, in bytes, of the picture variable. The maximum size of a picture is 32K bytes. The picFrame field is the picture frame that surrounds the picture and gives a frame of reference for scaling when the picture is played back. The rest of the structure contains a compact representation of the drawing commands that define the picture.

All pictures are accessed through handles:

```
TYPE PicPtr    = ^Picture;
     PicHandlle = ^PicPtr;
```

To define a picture, you call a QuickDraw function that returns a picHandle, and then call the drawing routines that define the picture.

QuickDraw also allows you to intersperse **picture comments** with the definition of a picture. These comments, which do not affect the picture's appearance, may be used to provide additional information about the picture when it's played back. This is especially valuable when pictures are transmitted from one application to another. There are two standard types of comments which, like parentheses, serve to group drawing commands together (such as all the commands that draw a particular part of a picture):

```
CONST picLParen = 0;
      picRParen = 1;
```

The application defining the picture can use these standard comments as well as comments of its own design.

Polygons

Polygons are similar to pictures in that you define them by a sequence of calls to QuickDraw routines. They're also similar to other shapes that QuickDraw knows about, since there's a set of procedures for performing graphic operations and calculations on them.

A **polygon** is simply any sequence of connected lines (see Figure 18). You define a polygon by moving to the starting point of the polygon and drawing lines from there to the next point, from that point to the next, and so on.

The data structure for a polygon consists of two fixed-length fields followed by a variable-length array:

```
TYPE Polygon =    RECORD
                     polySize:   INTEGER;   {size in bytes}
                     polyBBox:   Rect;      {enclosing rectangle}
                     polyPoints: ARRAY[0..0] OF Point
                  END;
```

Inside Macintosh

Figure 18. Polygons

The polySize field contains the size, in bytes, of the polygon variable. The maximum size of a polygon is 32K bytes. The polyBBox field is a rectangle that just encloses the entire polygon. The polyPoints array expands as necessary to contain the points of the polygon—the starting point followed by each successive point to which a line is drawn.

Like pictures and regions, polygons are accessed through handles:

```
TYPE  PolyPtr    = ^Polygon;
      PolyHandle = ^PolyPtr;
```

To define a polygon, you call a routine that returns a polyHandle, and then call the line-drawing routines that define the polygon.

Just as for other shapes that QuickDraw knows about, there's a set of graphic operations to draw polygons on the screen. QuickDraw draws a polygon by moving to the starting point and then drawing lines to the remaining points in succession, just as when the routines were called to define the polygon. In this sense it "plays back" those routine calls. As a result, polygons are not treated exactly the same as other QuickDraw shapes. For example, the procedure that frames a polygon draws outside the actual boundary of the polygon, because QuickDraw line-drawing routines draw below and to the right of the pen location. The procedures that fill a polygon with a pattern, however, stay within the boundary of the polygon; if the polygon's ending point isn't the same as its starting point, these procedures add a line between them to complete the shape.

QuickDraw also scales a polygon differently from a similarly-shaped region if it's being drawn as part of a picture: When stretched, a slanted line is drawn more smoothly if it's part of a polygon rather than a region. You may find it helpful to keep in mind the conceptual difference between polygons and regions: A polygon is treated more as a continuous shape, a region more as a set of bits.

USING QUICKDRAW

Call the InitGraf procedure to initialize QuickDraw at the beginning of your program, before initializing any other parts of the Toolbox.

When your application starts up, the cursor will be a wristwatch; the Finder sets it to this to indicate that a lengthy operation is in progress. Call the InitCursor procedure when the application is ready to respond to user input, to change the cursor to the standard arrow. Each time through the main event loop, you should call SetCursor to change the cursor as appropriate for its screen location.

All graphic operations are performed in grafPorts. Before a grafPort can be used, it must be allocated and initialized with the OpenPort procedure. Normally, you don't call OpenPort yourself—in most cases your application will draw into a window you've created with Window Manager routines, and these routines call OpenPort to create the window's grafPort. Likewise, a grafPort's regions are disposed of with ClosePort, and the grafPort itself is disposed of with the Memory Manager procedure DisposPtr—but when you call the Window Manager to close or dispose of a window, it calls these routines for you.

In an application that uses multiple windows, each is a separate grafPort. If your application draws into more than one grafPort, you can call SetPort to set the grafPort that you want to draw in. At times you may need to preserve the current grafPort; you can do this by calling GetPort to save the current port, SetPort to set the port you want to draw in, and then SetPort again when you need to restore the previous port.

Each grafPort has its own local coordinate system. Some Toolbox routines return or expect points that are expressed in a common, global coordinate system, while others use local coordinates. For example, when the Event Manager reports an event, it gives the mouse location in global coordinates; but when you call the Control Manager to find out whether the user clicked in a control in one of your windows, you pass the mouse location in local coordinates. The GlobalToLocal procedure lets you convert global coordinates to local coordinates, and the LocalToGlobal procedure lets you do the reverse.

The SetOrigin procedure will adjust a grafPort's local coordinate system. If your application performs scrolling, you'll use ScrollRect to shift the bits of the image, and then SetOrigin to readjust the coordinate system after this shift.

You can redefine a grafPort's clipping region with the SetClip or ClipRect procedure. Just as GetPort and SetPort are used to preserve the current grafPort, GetClip and SetClip are useful for saving the grafPort's clipRgn while you temporarily perform other clipping functions. This is useful, for example, when you want to reset the clipRgn to redraw the newly displayed portion of a document that's been scrolled.

When drawing text in a grafPort, you can set the font characteristics with TextFont, TextFace, TextMode, and TextSize. CharWidth, StringWidth, or TextWidth will tell you how much horizontal space the text will require, and GetFontInfo will tell you how much vertical space. You can draw text with DrawChar, DrawString, and DrawText.

The LineTo procedure draws a line from the current pen location to a given point, and the Line procedure draws a line between two given points. You can set the pen location with the MoveTo or Move procedure, and set other pen characteristics with PenSize, PenMode, and PenPat.

In addition to drawing text and lines, you can use QuickDraw to draw a variety of shapes. Most of them are defined simply by a rectangle that encloses the shape. Others require you to call a series of routines to define them:

- To define a region, call the NewRgn function to allocate space for it, then call OpenRgn, and then specify the outline of the region by calling routines that draw lines and shapes. End the region definition by calling routines that draw lines and shapes. End the region definition by calling CloseRgn. When you're completely done with the region, call DisposeRgn to release the memory it occupies.

- To define a polygon, call the OpenPoly function and then form the polygon by calling procedures that draw lines. Call ClosePoly when you're finished defining the polygon, and KillPoly when you're completely done with it.

You can perform the following graphic operations on rectangles, rounded-corner rectangles, ovals, arcs/wedges, regions, and polygons:

- frame, to outline the shape using the current pen pattern and size
- paint, to fill the shape using the current pen pattern
- erase, to paint the shape using the current background pattern
- invert, to invert the pixels in the shape
- fill, to fill the shape with a specified pattern

QuickDraw pictures let you record and play back complex drawing sequences. To define a picture, call the OpenPicture function and then the drawing routines that form the picture. Call ClosePicture when you're finished defining the picture. To draw a picture, call DrawPicture. When you're completely done with a picture, call KillPicture (or the Resource Manager procedure ReleaseResource, if the picture's a resource).

You'll use points, rectangles, and regions not only when drawing with QuickDraw, but also when using other parts of the Toolbox and Operating System. At times, you may find it useful to perform calculations on these entities. You can, for example, add and subtract points, and perform a number of calculations on rectangles and regions, such as offsetting them, rescaling them, calculating their union or intersection, and so on.

> **Note:** When performing a calculation on entities in different grafPorts, you need to adjust to a common coordinate system first, by calling LocalToGlobal to convert to global coordinates.

To transfer a bit image from one bit map to another, you can use the CopyBits procedure. For example, you can call SetPortBits to change the bit map of the current grafPort to an off-screen buffer, draw into that grafPort, and then call CopyBits to transfer the image from the off-screen buffer onto the screen.

QUICKDRAW ROUTINES

GrafPort Routines

```
PROCEDURE InitGraf (globalPtr: Ptr);
```

Call InitGraf once and only once at the beginning of your program to initialize QuickDraw. It initializes the global variables listed below (as well as some private global variables for its own internal use).

Variable	Type	Initial setting
thePort	GrafPtr	NIL
white	Pattern	An all-white pattern
black	Pattern	An all-black pattern
gray	Pattern	A 50% gray pattern
ltGray	Pattern	A 25% gray pattern
dkGray	Pattern	A 75% gray pattern

QuickDraw

Variable	Type	Initial setting
arrow	Cursor	The standard arrow cursor
screenBits	BitMap	The entire screen
randSeed	LONGINT	1

You must pass, in the globalPtr parameter, a pointer to the first QuickDraw global variable, thePort. From Pascal programs, you should always pass @thePort for globalPtr.

Assembly-language note: The QuickDraw global variables are stored in reverse order, from high to low memory, and require the number of bytes specified by the global constant grafSize. Most development systems (including the Lisa Workshop) preallocate space for these globals immediately below the location pointed to by register A5. Since thePort is four bytes, you would pass the globalPtr parameter as follows:

```
PEA        -4(A5)
_InitGraf
```

InitGraf stores this pointer to thePort in the location pointed to by A5. This value is used as a base address when accessing the other QuickDraw global variables, which are accessed using negative offsets (the offsets have the same names as the Pascal global variables). For example:

```
MOVE.L   (A5),A0           ;point to first QuickDraw global
MOVE.L   randSeed(A0),A1   ;get global variable randSeed
```

Note: To initialize the cursor, call InitCursor (described under "Cursor-Handling Routines" below).

```
PROCEDURE OpenPort (port: GrafPtr);
```

OpenPort allocates space for the given grafPort's visRgn and clipRgn, initializes the fields of the grafPort as indicated below, and makes the grafPort the current port (by calling SetPort). OpenPort is called by the Window Manager when you create a window, and you normally won't call it yourself. If you do call OpenPort, you can create the grafPtr with the Memory Manager procedure NewPtr or reserve the space on the stack (with a variable of type GrafPort).

Field	Type	Initial setting
device	INTEGER	0 (the screen)
portBits	BitMap	screenBits
portRect	Rect	screenBits.bounds
visRgn	RgnHandle	handle to a rectangular region coincident with screenBits.bounds
clipRgn	RgnHandle	handle to the rectangular region (–32767,–32767) (32767,32767)
bkPat	Pattern	white

Field	Type	Initial setting
fillPat	Pattern	black
pnLoc	Point	(0,0)
pnSize	Point	(1,1)
pnMode	INTEGER	patCopy
pnPat	Pattern	black
pnVis	INTEGER	0 (visible)
txFont	INTEGER	0 (system font)
txFace	Style	plain
txMode	INTEGER	srcOr
txSize	INTEGER	0 (system font size)
spExtra	Fixed	0
fgColor	LONGINT	blackColor
bkColor	LONGINT	whiteColor
colrBit	INTEGER	0
patStretch	INTEGER	0
picSave	Handle	NIL
rgnSave	Handle	NIL
polySave	Handle	NIL
grafProcs	QDProcsPtr	NIL

```
PROCEDURE InitPort (port: GrafPtr);
```

Given a pointer to a grafPort that's been opened with OpenPort, InitPort reinitializes the fields of the grafPort and makes it the current port. It's unlikely that you'll ever have a reason to call this procedure.

Note: InitPort does everything OpenPort does except allocate space for the visRgn and clipRgn.

```
PROCEDURE ClosePort (port: GrafPtr);
```

ClosePort releases the memory occupied by the given grafPort's visRgn and clipRgn. When you're completely through with a grafPort, call this procedure and then dispose of the grafPort with the Memory Manager procedure DisposPtr (if it was allocated with NewPtr). This is normally done for you when you call the Window Manager to close or dispose of a window.

Warning: If ClosePort isn't called before a grafPort is disposed of, the memory used by the visRgn and clipRgn will be unrecoverable.

QuickDraw

```
PROCEDURE SetPort (port: GrafPtr);
```

SetPort makes the specified grafPort the current port.

> **Note:** Only SetPort (and OpenPort and InitPort, which call it) changes the current port. All the other routines in the Toolbox and Operating System (even those that call SetPort, OpenPort, or InitPort) leave the current port set to what it was when they were called.

The global variable thePort always points to the current port. All QuickDraw drawing routines affect the bit map thePort^.portBits and use the local coordinate system of thePort^.

Each port has its own pen and text characteristics, which remain unchanged when the port isn't selected as the current port.

```
PROCEDURE GetPort (VAR port: GrafPtr);
```

GetPort returns a pointer to the current grafPort. This pointer is also available through the global variable thePort, but you may prefer to use GetPort for better readability of your program text. For example, a procedure could do a GetPort(savePort) before setting its own grafPort and a SetPort(savePort) afterwards to restore the previous port.

```
PROCEDURE GrafDevice (device: INTEGER);
```

GrafDevice sets the device field of the current grafPort to the given value, which consists of device-specific information that's used by the Font Manager to achieve the best possible results when drawing text in the grafPort. The initial value of the device field is 0, for best results on output to the screen. For more information, see chapter 7.

> **Note:** This field is used for communication between QuickDraw and the Font Manager; normally you won't set it yourself.

```
PROCEDURE SetPortBits (bm: BitMap);
```

Assembly-language note: The macro you invoke to call SetPortBits from assembly language is named _SetPBits.

SetPortBits sets the portBits field of the current grafPort to any previously defined bit map. This allows you to perform all normal drawing and calculations on a buffer other than the screen—for example, a small off-screen image for later "stamping" onto the screen (with the CopyBits procedure, described under "Bit Transfer Operations" below).

Remember to prepare all fields of the bit map before you call SetPortBits.

```
PROCEDURE PortSize (width,height: INTEGER);
```

PortSize changes the size of the current grafPort's portRect. This does *not* affect the screen; it merely changes the size of the "active area" of the grafPort.

> **Note:** This procedure is normally called only by the Window Manager.

The top left corner of the portRect remains at its same location; the width and height of the portRect are set to the given width and height. In other words, PortSize moves the bottom right corner of the portRect to a position relative to the top left corner.

PortSize doesn't change the clipRgn or the visRgn, nor does it affect the local coordinate system of the grafPort: It changes only the portRect's width and height. Remember that all drawing occurs only in the intersection of the portBits.bounds and the portRect, clipped to the visRgn and the clipRgn.

```
PROCEDURE MovePortTo (leftGlobal,topGlobal: INTEGER);
```

MovePortTo changes the position of the current grafPort's portRect. This does *not* affect the screen; it merely changes the location at which subsequent drawing inside the port will appear.

> **Note:** This procedure is normally called only by the Window Manager and the System Error Handler.

The leftGlobal and topGlobal parameters set the distance between the top left corner of portBits.bounds and the top left corner of the new portRect.

Like PortSize, MovePortTo doesn't change the clipRgn or the visRgn, nor does it affect the local coordinate system of the grafPort.

```
PROCEDURE SetOrigin (h,v: INTEGER);
```

SetOrigin changes the local coordinate system of the current grafPort. This does *not* affect the screen; it does, however, affect where subsequent drawing inside the port will appear.

The h and v parameters set the coordinates of the top left corner of the portRect. All other coordinates are calculated from this point; SetOrigin also offsets the coordinates of the portBits.bounds rectangle and the visRgn. Relative distances among elements in the port remain the same; only their absolute local coordinates change. All subsequent drawing and calculation routines use the new coordinate system.

> **Note:** SetOrigin does not offset the coordinates of the clipRgn or the pen; the pen and clipRgn "stick" to the coordinate system, and therefore change position on the screen (unlike the portBits.bounds, portRect, and visRgn, which "stick" to the screen, and don't change position). See the "Coordinates in GrafPorts" section for an illustration.

SetOrigin is useful for readjusting the coordinate system after a scrolling operation. (See ScrollRect under "Bit Transfer Operations" below.)

> **Note:** All other routines in the Toolbox and Operating System preserve the local coordinate system of the current grafPort.

```
PROCEDURE SetClip (rgn: RgnHandle);
```

SetClip changes the clipping region of the current grafPort to a region that's equivalent to the given region. Note that this doesn't change the region handle, but affects the clipping region

QuickDraw

itself. Since SetClip makes a copy of the given region, any subsequent changes you make to that region will not affect the clipping region of the port.

You can set the clipping region to any arbitrary region, to aid you in drawing inside the grafPort. The initial clipRgn is an arbitrarily large rectangle.

> **Note:** All routines in the Toolbox and Operating System preserve the current clipRgn.

```
PROCEDURE GetClip (rgn: RgnHandle);
```

GetClip changes the given region to a region that's equivalent to the clipping region of the current grafPort. This is the reverse of what SetClip does. Like SetClip, it doesn't change the region handle. GetClip and SetClip are used to preserve the current clipRgn (they're analogous to GetPort and SetPort).

```
PROCEDURE ClipRect (r: Rect);
```

ClipRect changes the clipping region of the current grafPort to a rectangle that's equivalent to the given rectangle. Note that this doesn't change the region handle, but affects the clipping region itself.

```
PROCEDURE BackPat (pat: Pattern);
```

BackPat sets the background pattern of the current grafPort to the given pattern. The background pattern is used in ScrollRect and in all QuickDraw routines that perform an "erase" operation.

Cursor-Handling Routines

```
PROCEDURE InitCursor;
```

InitCursor sets the current cursor to the standard arrow and sets the **cursor level** to 0, making the cursor visible. The cursor level keeps track of the number of times the cursor has been hidden to compensate for nested calls to HideCursor and ShowCursor, explained below.

```
PROCEDURE SetCursor (crsr: Cursor);
```

SetCursor sets the current cursor to the given cursor. If the cursor is hidden, it remains hidden and will attain the new appearance when it's uncovered; if the cursor is already visible, it changes to the new appearance immediately.

The cursor image is initialized by InitCursor to the standard arrow, visible on the screen.

> **Note:** You'll normally get a cursor from a resource file, by calling the Toolbox Utility function GetCursor, and then doubly dereference the handle it returns.

QuickDraw Routines I-167

Inside Macintosh

PROCEDURE HideCursor;

HideCursor removes the cursor from the screen, restoring the bits under it, and decrements the cursor level (which InitCursor initialized to 0). Every call to HideCursor should be balanced by a subsequent call to ShowCursor.

> **Note:** See also the description of the Toolbox Utility procedure ShieldCursor.

PROCEDURE ShowCursor;

ShowCursor increments the cursor level, which may have been decremented by HideCursor, and displays the cursor on the screen if the level becomes 0. A call to ShowCursor should balance each previous call to HideCursor. The level isn't incremented beyond 0, so extra calls to ShowCursor have no effect.

The low-level interrupt-driven routines link the cursor with the mouse position, so that if the cursor level is 0 (visible), the cursor automatically follows the mouse. You don't need to do anything but a ShowCursor to have the cursor track the mouse.

If the cursor has been changed (with SetCursor) while hidden, ShowCursor presents the new cursor.

PROCEDURE ObscureCursor;

ObscureCursor hides the cursor until the next time the mouse is moved. It's normally called when the user begins to type. Unlike HideCursor, it has no effect on the cursor level and must not be balanced by a call to ShowCursor.

Pen and Line-Drawing Routines

The pen and line-drawing routines all depend on the coordinate system of the current grafPort. Remember that each grafPort has its own pen; if you draw in one grafPort, change to another, and return to the first, the pen will remain in the same location.

PROCEDURE HidePen;

HidePen decrements the current grafPort's pnVis field, which is initialized to 0 by OpenPort; whenever pnVis is negative, the pen doesn't draw on the screen. PnVis keeps track of the number of times the pen has been hidden to compensate for nested calls to HidePen and ShowPen (below). Every call to HidePen should be balanced by a subsequent call to ShowPen. HidePen is called by OpenRgn, OpenPicture, and OpenPoly so that you can define regions, pictures, and polygons without drawing on the screen.

PROCEDURE ShowPen;

ShowPen increments the current grafPort's pnVis field, which may have been decremented by HidePen; if pnVis becomes 0, QuickDraw resumes drawing on the screen. Extra calls to

ShowPen will increment pnVis beyond 0, so every call to ShowPen should be balanced by a call to HidePen. ShowPen is called by CloseRgn, ClosePicture, and ClosePoly.

```
PROCEDURE GetPen  (VAR pt: Point);
```

GetPen returns the current pen location, in the local coordinates of the current grafPort.

```
PROCEDURE GetPenState  (VAR pnState: PenState);
```

GetPenState saves the pen location, size, pattern, and mode in pnState, to be restored later with SetPenState. This is useful when calling subroutines that operate in the current port but must change the graphics pen: Each such procedure can save the pen's state when it's called, do whatever it needs to do, and restore the previous pen state immediately before returning. The PenState data type is defined as follows:

```
TYPE PenState =  RECORD
                    pnLoc:   Point;    {pen location}
                    pnSize:  Point;    {pen size}
                    pnMode:  INTEGER;  {pen's transfer mode}
                    pnPat:   Pattern   {pen pattern}
                 END;
```

```
PROCEDURE SetPenState  (pnState: PenState);
```

SetPenState sets the pen location, size, pattern, and mode in the current grafPort to the values stored in pnState. This is usually called at the end of a procedure that has altered the pen parameters and wants to restore them to their state at the beginning of the procedure. (See GetPenState, above.)

```
PROCEDURE PenSize  (width,height: INTEGER);
```

PenSize sets the dimensions of the graphics pen in the current grafPort. All subsequent calls to Line, LineTo, and the procedures that draw framed shapes in the current grafPort will use the new pen dimensions.

The pen dimensions can be accessed in the variable thePort^.pnSize, which is of type Point. If either of the pen dimensions is set to a negative value, the pen assumes the dimensions (0,0) and no drawing is performed. For a discussion of how the pen draws, see the "General Discussion of Drawing" section.

```
PROCEDURE PenMode  (mode: INTEGER);
```

PenMode sets the transfer mode through which the pen pattern is transferred onto the bit map when lines or shapes are drawn in the current grafPort. The mode may be any one of the pattern transfer modes:

```
patCopy             notPatCopy
patOr               notPatOr
patXor              notPatXor
patBic              notPatBic
```

If the mode is one of the source transfer modes (or negative), no drawing is performed. The current pen mode can be accessed in the variable thePort^.pnMode. The initial pen mode is patCopy, in which the pen pattern is copied directly to the bit map.

```
PROCEDURE PenPat (pat: Pattern);
```

PenPat sets the pattern that's used by the pen in the current grafPort. The standard patterns white, black, gray, ltGray, and dkGray are predefined; the initial pen pattern is black. The current pen pattern can be accessed in the variable thePort^.pnPat, and this value can be assigned to any other variable of type Pattern.

```
PROCEDURE PenNormal;
```

PenNormal resets the initial state of the pen in the current grafPort, as follows:

Field	**Setting**
pnSize	(1,1)
pnMode	patCopy
pnPat	black

The pen location is not changed.

```
PROCEDURE MoveTo (h,v: INTEGER);
```

MoveTo moves the pen to location (h,v) in the local coordinates of the current grafPort. No drawing is performed.

```
PROCEDURE Move (dh,dv: INTEGER);
```

This procedure moves the pen a distance of dh horizontally and dv vertically from its current location; it calls MoveTo(h+dh,v+dv), where (h,v) is the current location. The positive directions are to the right and down. No drawing is performed.

```
PROCEDURE LineTo (h,v: INTEGER);
```

LineTo draws a line from the current pen location to the location specified (in local coordinates) by h and v. The new pen location is (h,v) after the line is drawn. See the "General Discussion of Drawing" section.

If a region or polygon is open and being formed, its outline is infinitely thin and is not affected by the pnSize, pnMode, or pnPat. (See OpenRgn and OpenPoly.)

```
PROCEDURE Line (dh,dv: INTEGER);
```

This procedure draws a line to the location that's a distance of dh horizontally and dv vertically from the current pen location; it calls LineTo(h+dh,v+dv), where (h,v) is the current location. The positive directions are to the right and down. The pen location becomes the coordinates of the end of the line after the line is drawn. See the "General Discussion of Drawing" section.

If a region or polygon is open and being formed, its outline is infinitely thin and is not affected by the pnSize, pnMode, or pnPat. (See OpenRgn and OpenPoly.)

Text-Drawing Routines

Each grafPort has its own text characteristics, and all these procedures deal with those of the current port.

```
PROCEDURE TextFont (font: INTEGER);
```

TextFont sets the current grafPort's font (thePort^.txFont) to the given font number. The initial font number is 0, which represents the system font.

```
PROCEDURE TextFace (face: Style);
```

TextFace sets the current grafPort's character style (thePort^.txFace). The Style data type allows you to specify a set of one or more of the following predefined constants: bold, italic, underline, outline, shadow, condense, and extend. For example:

```
TextFace([bold]);                      {bold}
TextFace([bold,italic]);               {bold and italic}
TextFace(thePort^.txFace+[bold]);      {whatever it was plus bold}
TextFace(thePort^.txFace-[bold]);      {whatever it was but not bold}
TextFace([]);                          {plain text}
```

```
PROCEDURE TextMode (mode: INTEGER);
```

TextMode sets the current grafPort's transfer mode for drawing text (thePort^.txMode). The mode should be srcOr, srcXor, or srcBic. The initial transfer mode for drawing text is srcOr.

```
PROCEDURE TextSize (size: INTEGER);
```

TextSize sets the current grafPort's font size (thePort^.txSize) to the given number of points. Any size may be specified, but the result will look best if the Font Manager has the font in that size (otherwise it will scale a size it does have). The next best result will occur if the given size is an even multiple of a size available for the font. If 0 is specified, the system font size (12 points) will be used. The initial txSize setting is 0.

```
PROCEDURE SpaceExtra (extra: Fixed);
```

SpaceExtra sets the current grafPort's spExtra field, which specifies the average number of pixels by which to widen each space in a line of text. This is useful when text is being fully justified (that is, aligned with both a left and a right margin). The initial spExtra setting is 0.

SpaceExtra will also accept a negative parameter, but be careful not to narrow spaces so much that the text is unreadable.

```
PROCEDURE DrawChar (ch: CHAR);
```

DrawChar places the given character to the right of the pen location, with the left end of its base line at the pen's location, and advances the pen accordingly. If the character isn't in the font, the font's missing symbol is drawn.

> **Note:** If you're drawing a series of characters, it's faster to make one DrawString or DrawText call rather than a series of DrawChar calls.

```
PROCEDURE DrawString (s: Str255);
```

DrawString calls DrawChar for each character in the given string. The string is placed beginning at the current pen location and extending right. No formatting (such as carriage returns and line feeds) is performed by QuickDraw. The pen location ends up to the right of the last character in the string.

> **Warning:** QuickDraw temporarily stores on the stack *all* of the text you ask it to draw, even if the text will be clipped. When drawing large font sizes or complex style variations, it's best to draw only what will be visible on the screen. You can determine how many characters will actually fit on the screen by calling the StringWidth function before calling DrawString.

```
PROCEDURE DrawText (textBuf: Ptr; firstByte,byteCount: INTEGER);
```

DrawText calls DrawChar for each character in the arbitrary structure in memory specified by textBuf, starting firstByte bytes into the structure and continuing for byteCount bytes (firstByte starts at 0). The text is placed beginning at the current pen location and extending right. No formatting (such as carriage returns and line feeds) is performed by QuickDraw. The pen location ends up to the right of the last character in the string.

> **Warning:** Inside a picture definition, DrawText can't have a byteCount greater than 255.

> **Note:** You can determine how many characters will actually fit on the screen by calling the TextWidth function before calling DrawText. (See the warning under DrawString above.)

```
FUNCTION CharWidth (ch: CHAR) : INTEGER;
```

CharWidth returns the character width of the specified character, that is, the value that will be added to the pen horizontal coordinate if the specified character is drawn. CharWidth includes the effects of the stylistic variations set with TextFace; if you change these after determining the character width but before actually drawing the character, the predetermined width may not be correct. If the character is a space, CharWidth also includes the effect of SpaceExtra.

```
FUNCTION StringWidth (s: Str255) : INTEGER;
```

StringWidth returns the width of the given text string, which it calculates by adding the CharWidths of all the characters in the string (see above).

```
FUNCTION TextWidth (textBuf: Ptr; firstByte,byteCount: INTEGER) :
        INTEGER;
```

TextWidth returns the width of the text stored in the arbitrary structure in memory specified by textBuf, starting firstByte bytes into the structure and continuing for byteCount bytes (firstByte starts at 0). TextWidth calculates the width by adding the CharWidths of all the characters in the text. (See CharWidth, above.)

```
PROCEDURE GetFontInfo (VAR info: FontInfo);
```

GetFontInfo returns the following information about the current grafPort's character font, taking into consideration the style and size in which the characters will be drawn: the ascent, descent, maximum character width (the greatest distance the pen will move when a character is drawn), and leading (the vertical distance between the descent line and the ascent line below it), all in pixels. The FontInfo data type is defined as follows:

```
TYPE FontInfo = RECORD
                  ascent:   INTEGER;   {ascent}
                  descent:  INTEGER;   {descent}
                  widMax:   INTEGER;   {maximum character width}
                  leading:  INTEGER    {leading}
                END;
```

The line height (in pixels) can be determined by adding the ascent, descent, and leading.

Drawing in Color

These routines enable applications to do color drawing on color output devices. All nonwhite colors will appear as black on black-and-white output devices.

```
PROCEDURE ForeColor (color: LONGINT);
```

ForeColor sets the foreground color for all drawing in the current grafPort (thePort^.fgColor) to the given color. The following standard colors are predefined: blackColor, whiteColor,

Inside Macintosh

redColor, greenColor, blueColor, cyanColor, magentaColor, and yellowColor. The initial foreground color is blackColor.

```
PROCEDURE BackColor (color: LONGINT);
```

BackColor sets the background color for all drawing in the current grafPort (thePort^.bkColor) to the given color. Eight standard colors are predefined (see ForeColor above). The initial background color is whiteColor.

```
PROCEDURE ColorBit (whichBit: INTEGER);
```

ColorBit is called by printing software for a color printer, or other color-imaging software, to set the current grafPort's colrBit field to whichBit; this tells QuickDraw which plane of the color picture to draw into. QuickDraw will draw into the plane corresponding to bit number whichBit. Since QuickDraw can support output devices that have up to 32 bits of color information per pixel, the possible range of values for whichBit is 0 through 31. The initial value of the colrBit field is 0.

Calculations with Rectangles

Calculation routines are independent of the current coordinate system; a calculation will operate the same regardless of which grafPort is active.

Remember that if the parameters to a calculation procedure were defined in different grafPorts, you must first adjust them to global coordinates.

```
PROCEDURE SetRect (VAR r: Rect; left,top,right,bottom: INTEGER);
```

SetRect assigns the four boundary coordinates to the given rectangle. The result is a rectangle with coordinates (left,top) (right,bottom).

This procedure is supplied as a utility to help you shorten your program text. If you want a more readable text at the expense of length, you can assign integers (or points) directly into the rectangle's fields. There's no significant code size or execution speed advantage to either method.

```
PROCEDURE OffsetRect (VAR r: Rect; dh,dv: INTEGER);
```

OffsetRect moves the given rectangle by adding dh to each horizontal coordinate and dv to each vertical coordinate. If dh and dv are positive, the movement is to the right and down; if either is negative, the corresponding movement is in the opposite direction. The rectangle retains its shape and size; it's merely moved on the coordinate plane. This doesn't affect the screen unless you subsequently call a routine to draw within the rectangle.

```
PROCEDURE InsetRect (VAR r: Rect; dh,dv: INTEGER);
```

InsetRect shrinks or expands the given rectangle. The left and right sides are moved in by the amount specified by dh; the top and bottom are moved toward the center by the amount specified by dv. If dh or dv is negative, the appropriate pair of sides is moved outward instead of inward. The effect is to alter the size by 2*dh horizontally and 2*dv vertically, with the rectangle remaining centered in the same place on the coordinate plane.

If the resulting width or height becomes less than 1, the rectangle is set to the empty rectangle (0,0)(0,0).

```
FUNCTION SectRect (src1,src2: Rect; VAR dstRect: Rect) : BOOLEAN;
```

SectRect calculates the rectangle that's the intersection of the two given rectangles, and returns TRUE if they indeed intersect or FALSE if they don't. Rectangles that "touch" at a line or a point are not considered intersecting, because their intersection rectangle (actually, in this case, an intersection line or point) doesn't enclose any bits in the bit image.

If the rectangles don't intersect, the destination rectangle is set to (0,0)(0,0). SectRect works correctly even if one of the source rectangles is also the destination.

```
PROCEDURE UnionRect (src1,src2: Rect; VAR dstRect: Rect);
```

UnionRect calculates the smallest rectangle that encloses both of the given rectangles. It works correctly even if one of the source rectangles is also the destination.

```
FUNCTION PtInRect (pt: Point; r: Rect) : BOOLEAN;
```

PtInRect determines whether the pixel below and to the right of the given coordinate point is enclosed in the specified rectangle, and returns TRUE if so or FALSE if not.

```
PROCEDURE Pt2Rect (pt1,pt2: Point; VAR dstRect: Rect);
```

Pt2Rect returns the smallest rectangle that encloses the two given points.

```
PROCEDURE PtToAngle (r: Rect; pt: Point; VAR angle: INTEGER);
```

PtToAngle calculates an integer angle between a line from the center of the rectangle to the given point and a line from the center of the rectangle pointing straight up (12 o'clock high). The angle is in degrees from 0 to 359, measured clockwise from 12 o'clock, with 90 degrees at 3 o'clock, 180 at 6 o'clock, and 270 at 9 o'clock. Other angles are measured relative to the rectangle: If the line to the given point goes through the top right corner of the rectangle, the angle returned is 45 degrees, even if the rectangle isn't square; if it goes through the bottom right corner, the angle is 135 degrees, and so on (see Figure 19).

Inside Macintosh

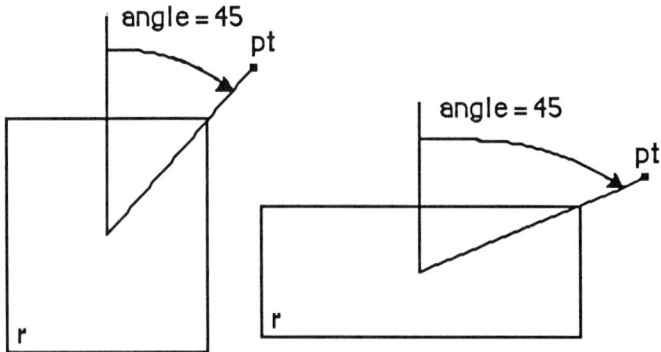

Figure 19. PtToAngle

The angle returned might be used as input to one of the procedures that manipulate arcs and wedges, as described below under "Graphic Operations on Arcs and Wedges".

```
FUNCTION EqualRect (rect1,rect2: Rect) : BOOLEAN;
```

EqualRect compares the two given rectangles and returns TRUE if they're equal or FALSE if not The two rectangles must have identical boundary coordinates to be considered equal.

```
FUNCTION EmptyRect (r: Rect) : BOOLEAN;
```

EmptyRect returns TRUE if the given rectangle is an empty rectangle or FALSE if not. A rectangle is considered empty if the bottom coordinate is less than or equal to the top or the right coordinate is less than or equal to the left.

Graphic Operations on Rectangles

See also the ScrollRect procedure under "Bit Transfer Operations".

```
PROCEDURE FrameRect (r: Rect);
```

FrameRect draws an outline just inside the specified rectangle, using the current grafPort's pen pattern, mode, and size. The outline is as wide as the pen width and as tall as the pen height. It's drawn with the pnPat, according to the pattern transfer mode specified by pnMode. The pen location is not changed by this procedure.

If a region is open and being formed, the outside outline of the new rectangle is mathematically added to the region's boundary.

```
PROCEDURE PaintRect (r: Rect);
```

PaintRect paints the specified rectangle with the current grafPort's pen pattern and mode. The rectangle is filled with the pnPat, according to the pattern transfer mode specified by pnMode. The pen location is not changed by this procedure.

```
PROCEDURE EraseRect (r: Rect);
```

EraseRect paints the specified rectangle with the current grafPort's background pattern bkPat (in patCopy mode). The grafPort's pnPat and pnMode are ignored; the pen location is not changed.

```
PROCEDURE InvertRect (r: Rect);
```

Assembly-language note: The macro you invoke to call InvertRect from assembly language is named _InverRect.

InvertRect inverts the pixels enclosed by the specified rectangle: Every white pixel becomes black and every black pixel becomes white. The grafPort's pnPat, pnMode, and bkPat are all ignored; the pen location is not changed.

```
PROCEDURE FillRect (r: Rect; pat: Pattern);
```

FillRect fills the specified rectangle with the given pattern (in patCopy mode). The grafPort's pnPat, pnMode, and bkPat are all ignored; the pen location is not changed.

Graphic Operations on Ovals

Ovals are drawn inside rectangles that you specify. If you specify a square rectangle, QuickDraw draws a circle.

```
PROCEDURE FrameOval (r: Rect);
```

FrameOval draws an outline just inside the oval that fits inside the specified rectangle, using the current grafPort's pen pattern, mode, and size. The outline is as wide as the pen width and as tall as the pen height. It's drawn with the pnPat, according to the pattern transfer mode specified by pnMode. The pen location is not changed by this procedure.

If a region is open and being formed, the outside outline of the new oval is mathematically added to the region's boundary.

Inside Macintosh

```
PROCEDURE PaintOval (r: Rect);
```

PaintOval paints an oval just inside the specified rectangle with the current grafPort's pen pattern and mode. The oval is filled with the pnPat, according to the pattern transfer mode specified by pnMode. The pen location is not changed by this procedure.

```
PROCEDURE EraseOval (r: Rect);
```

EraseOval paints an oval just inside the specified rectangle with the current grafPort's background pattern bkPat (in patCopy mode). The grafPort's pnPat and pnMode are ignored; the pen location is not changed.

```
PROCEDURE InvertOval (r: Rect);
```

InvertOval inverts the pixels enclosed by an oval just inside the specified rectangle: Every white pixel becomes black and every black pixel becomes white. The grafPort's pnPat, pnMode, and bkPat are all ignored; the pen location is not changed.

```
PROCEDURE FillOval (r: Rect; pat: Pattern);
```

FillOval fills an oval just inside the specified rectangle with the given pattern (in patCopy mode). The grafPort's pnPat, pnMode, and bkPat are all ignored; the pen location is not changed.

Graphic Operations on Rounded-Corner Rectangles

```
PROCEDURE FrameRoundRect (r: Rect; ovalWidth,ovalHeight:
        INTEGER);
```

FrameRoundRect draws an outline just inside the specified rounded-corner rectangle, using the current grafPort's pen pattern, mode, and size. OvalWidth and ovalHeight specify the diameters of curvature for the corners (see Figure 20). The outline is as wide as the pen width and as tall as the pen height. It's drawn with the pnPat, according to the pattern transfer mode specified by pnMode. The pen location is not changed by this procedure.

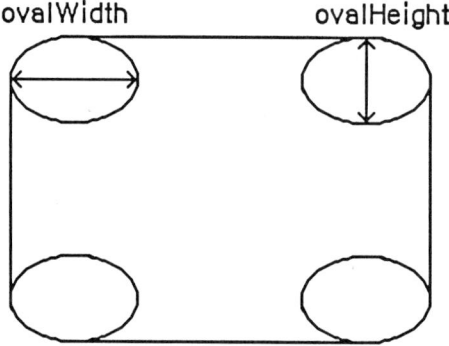

Figure 20. Rounded-Corner Rectangle

QuickDraw

If a region is open and being formed, the outside outline of the new rounded-corner rectangle is mathematically added to the region's boundary.

```
PROCEDURE PaintRoundRect (r: Rect; ovalWidth,ovalHeight:
        INTEGER);
```

PaintRoundRect paints the specified rounded-corner rectangle with the current grafPort's pen pattern and mode. OvalWidth and ovalHeight specify the diameters of curvature for the corners.

The rounded-corner rectangle is filled with the pnPat, according to the pattern transfer mode specified by pnMode. The pen location is not changed by this procedure.

```
PROCEDURE EraseRoundRect (r: Rect; ovalWidth,ovalHeight:
        INTEGER);
```

EraseRoundRect paints the specified rounded-corner rectangle with the current grafPort's background pattern bkPat (in patCopy mode).

OvalWidth and ovalHeight specify the diameters of curvature for the corners. The grafPort's pnPat and pnMode are ignored; the pen location is not changed.

```
PROCEDURE InvertRoundRect (r: Rect; ovalWidth,ovalHeight:
        INTEGER);
```

Assembly-language note: The macro you invoke to call InvertRoundRect from assembly language is named _InverRoundRect.

InvertRoundRect inverts the pixels enclosed by the specified rounded-corner rectangle: Every white pixel becomes black and every black pixel becomes white. OvalWidth and ovalHeight specify the diameters of curvature for the corners. The grafPort's pnPat, pnMode, and bkPat are all ignored; the pen location is not changed.

```
PROCEDURE FillRoundRect (r: Rect; ovalWidth,ovalHeight: INTEGER;
        pat: Pattern);
```

FillRoundRect fills the specified rounded-corner rectangle with the given pattern (in patCopy mode). OvalWidth and ovalHeight specify the diameters of curvature for the corners. The grafPort's pnPat, pnMode, and bkPat are all ignored; the pen location is not changed.

Graphic Operations on Arcs and Wedges

These procedures perform graphic operations on arcs and wedge-shaped sections of ovals. See also PtToAngle under "Calculations with Rectangles".

Inside Macintosh

```
PROCEDURE FrameArc (r: Rect; startAngle,arcAngle: INTEGER);
```

FrameArc draws an arc of the oval that fits inside the specified rectangle, using the current grafPort's pen pattern, mode, and size. StartAngle indicates where the arc begins and is treated MOD 360. ArcAngle defines the extent of the arc. The angles are given in positive or negative degrees; a positive angle goes clockwise, while a negative angle goes counterclockwise. Zero degrees is at 12 o'clock high, 90 (or –270) is at 3 o'clock, 180 (or –180) is at 6 o'clock, and 270 (or –90) is at 9 o'clock. Other angles are measured relative to the enclosing rectangle: A line from the center of the rectangle through its top right corner is at 45 degrees, even if the rectangle isn't square; a line through the bottom right corner is at 135 degrees, and so on (see Figure 21).

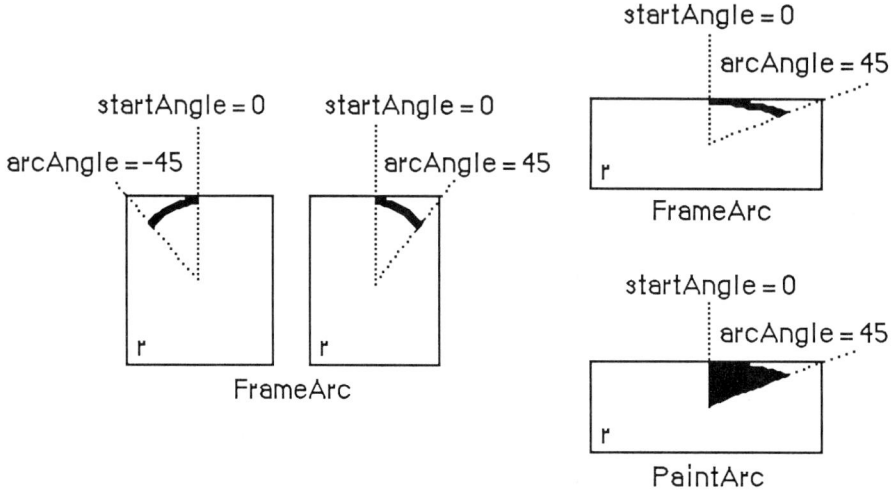

Figure 21. Operations on Arcs and Wedges

The arc is as wide as the pen width and as tall as the pen height. It's drawn with the pnPat, according to the pattern transfer mode specified by pnMode. The pen location is not changed by this procedure.

Warning: FrameArc differs from other QuickDraw routines that frame shapes in that the arc is not mathematically added to the boundary of a region that's open and being formed.

Note: QuickDraw doesn't provide a routine for drawing an outlined wedge of an oval.

```
PROCEDURE PaintArc (r: Rect; startAngle,arcAngle: INTEGER);
```

PaintArc paints a wedge of the oval just inside the specified rectangle with the current grafPort's pen pattern and mode. StartAngle and arcAngle define the arc of the wedge as in FrameArc. The wedge is filled with the pnPat, according to the pattern transfer mode specified by pnMode. The pen location is not changed by this procedure.

```
PROCEDURE EraseArc (r: Rect; startAngle,arcAngle: INTEGER);
```

EraseArc paints a wedge of the oval just inside the specified rectangle with the current grafPort's background pattern bkPat (in patCopy mode). StartAngle and arcAngle define the arc of the

QuickDraw

wedge as in FrameArc. The grafPort's pnPat and pnMode are ignored; the pen location is not changed.

```
PROCEDURE InvertArc (r: Rect; startAngle,arcAngle: INTEGER);
```

InvertArc inverts the pixels enclosed by a wedge of the oval just inside the specified rectangle: Every white pixel becomes black and every black pixel becomes white. StartAngle and arcAngle define the arc of the wedge as in FrameArc. The grafPort's pnPat, pnMode, and bkPat are all ignored; the pen location is not changed.

```
PROCEDURE FillArc (r: Rect; startAngle,arcAngle: INTEGER; pat:
          Pattern);
```

FillArc fills a wedge of the oval just inside the specified rectangle with the given pattern (in patCopy mode). StartAngle and arcAngle define the arc of the wedge as in FrameArc. The grafPort's pnPat, pnMode, and bkPat are all ignored; the pen location is not changed.

Calculations with Regions

Remember that if the parameters to a calculation procedure were defined in different grafPorts, you must first adjust them to global coordinates.

```
FUNCTION NewRgn : RgnHandle;
```

NewRgn allocates space for a new, variable-size region, initializes it to the empty region defined by the rectangle (0,0)(0,0), and returns a handle to the new region.

> **Warning:** Only this function creates new regions; all other routines just alter the size and shape of existing regions. Before a region's handle can be passed to any drawing or calculation routine, space must already have been allocated for the region.

```
PROCEDURE OpenRgn;
```

OpenRgn tells QuickDraw to allocate temporary space and start saving lines and framed shapes for later processing as a region definition. While a region is open, all calls to Line, LineTo, and the procedures that draw framed shapes (except arcs) affect the outline of the region. Only the line endpoints and shape boundaries affect the region definition; the pen mode, pattern, and size do not affect it. In fact, OpenRgn calls HidePen, so no drawing occurs on the screen while the region is open (unless you called ShowPen just after OpenRgn, or you called ShowPen previously without balancing it by a call to HidePen). Since the pen hangs below and to the right of the pen location, drawing lines with even the smallest pen will change bits that lie outside the region you define.

The outline of a region is mathematically defined and infinitely thin, and separates the bit image into two groups of bits: Those within the region and those outside it. A region should consist of one or more closed loops. Each framed shape itself constitutes a loop. Any lines drawn with Line or LineTo should connect with each other or with a framed shape. Even though the on-screen presentation of a region is clipped, the definition of a region is not; you can define a region anywhere on the coordinate plane with complete disregard for the location of various grafPort entities on that plane.

When a region is open, the current grafPort's rgnSave field contains a handle to information related to the region definition. If you want to temporarily disable the collection of lines and shapes, you can save the current value of this field, set the field to NIL, and later restore the saved value to resume the region definition. Also, calling SetPort while a region is being formed will discontinue formation of the region until another call to SetPort resets the region's original grafPort.

Warning: Do not call OpenRgn while another region or polygon is already open. All open regions but the most recent will behave strangely.

Note: Regions are limited to 32K bytes. You can determine the current size of a region by calling the Memory Manager function GetHandleSize.

```
PROCEDURE CloseRgn (dstRgn: RgnHandle);
```

CloseRgn stops the collection of lines and framed shapes, organizes them into a region definition, and saves the resulting region in the region indicated by dstRgn. CloseRgn does *not* create the destination region; space must already have been allocated for it. You should perform one and only one CloseRgn for every OpenRgn. CloseRgn calls ShowPen, balancing the HidePen call made by OpenRgn.

Here's an example of how to create and open a region, define a barbell shape, close the region, draw it, and dispose of it:

```
   barbell := NewRgn;                       {create a new region}
   OpenRgn;                                 {begin collecting stuff}
      SetRect(tempRect,20,20,30,50);        {form the left weight}
      FrameOval(tempRect);
      SetRect(tempRect,25,30,85,40);        {form the bar}
      FrameRect(tempRect);
      SetRect(tempRect,80,20,90,50);        {form the right weight}
      FrameOval(tempRect);
   CloseRgn(barbell);                       {we're done; save in barbell}
   FillRgn(barbell,black);                  {draw it on the screen}
   DisposeRgn(barbell)                      {dispose of the region}
```

```
PROCEDURE DisposeRgn (rgn: RgnHandle);
```

Assembly-language note: The macro you invoke to call DisposeRgn from assembly language is named _DisposRgn.

DisposeRgn releases the memory occupied by the given region. Use this only after you're completely through with a temporary region.

```
PROCEDURE CopyRgn (srcRgn,dstRgn: RgnHandle);
```

CopyRgn copies the mathematical structure of srcRgn into dstRgn; that is, it makes a duplicate copy of srcRgn. Once this is done, srcRgn may be altered (or even disposed of) without affecting dstRgn. CopyRgn does *not* create the destination region; space must already have been allocated for it.

```
PROCEDURE SetEmptyRgn (rgn: RgnHandle);
```

SetEmptyRgn destroys the previous structure of the given region, then sets the new structure to the empty region defined by the rectangle (0,0)(0,0).

```
PROCEDURE SetRectRgn (rgn: RgnHandle; left,top,right,bottom:
          INTEGER);
```

Assembly-language note: The macro you invoke to call SetRectRgn from assembly language is named _SetRecRgn.

SetRectRgn destroys the previous structure of the given region, and then sets the new structure to the rectangle specified by left, top, right, and bottom.

If the specified rectangle is empty (that is, right<=left or bottom<=top), the region is set to the empty region defined by the rectangle (0,0)(0,0).

```
PROCEDURE RectRgn (rgn: RgnHandle; r: Rect);
```

RectRgn destroys the previous structure of the given region, and then sets the new structure to the rectangle specified by r. This is the same as SetRectRgn, except the given rectangle is defined by a rectangle rather than by four boundary coordinates.

```
PROCEDURE OffsetRgn (rgn: RgnHandle; dh,dv: INTEGER);
```

Assembly-language note: The macro you invoke to call OffsetRgn from assembly language is named _OfsetRgn.

OffsetRgn moves the region on the coordinate plane, a distance of dh horizontally and dv vertically. This doesn't affect the screen unless you subsequently call a routine to draw the region. If dh and dv are positive, the movement is to the right and down; if either is negative, the corresponding movement is in the opposite direction. The region retains its size and shape.

Note: OffsetRgn is an especially efficient operation, because most of the data defining a region is stored relative to rgnBBox and so isn't actually changed by OffsetRgn.

Inside Macintosh

```
PROCEDURE InsetRgn (rgn: RgnHandle; dh,dv: INTEGER);
```

InsetRgn shrinks or expands the region. All points on the region boundary are moved inwards a distance of dv vertically and dh horizontally; if dh or dv is negative, the points are moved outwards in that direction. InsetRgn leaves the region "centered" at the same position, but moves the outline in (for positive values of dh and dv) or out (for negative values of dh and dv). InsetRgn of a rectangular region works just like InsetRect.

Note: InsetRgn temporarily uses heap space that's twice the size of the original region.

```
PROCEDURE SectRgn (srcRgnA,srcRgnB,dstRgn: RgnHandle);
```

SectRgn calculates the intersection of two regions and places the intersection in a third region. This does *not* create the destination region; space must already have been allocated for it. The destination region can be one of the source regions, if desired.

If the regions do not intersect, or one of the regions is empty, the destination is set to the empty region defined by the rectangle (0,0)(0,0).

Note: SectRgn may temporarily use heap space that's twice the size of the two input regions.

```
PROCEDURE UnionRgn (srcRgnA,srcRgnB,dstRgn: RgnHandle);
```

UnionRgn calculates the union of two regions and places the union in a third region. This does *not* create the destination region; space must already have been allocated for it. The destination region can be one of the source regions, if desired.

If both regions are empty, the destination is set to the empty region defined by the rectangle (0,0)(0,0).

Note: UnionRgn may temporarily use heap space that's twice the size of the two input regions.

```
PROCEDURE DiffRgn (srcRgnA,srcRgnB,dstRgn: RgnHandle);
```

DiffRgn subtracts srcRgnB from srcRgnA and places the difference in a third region. This does *not* create the destination region; space must already have been allocated for it. The destination region can be one of the source regions, if desired.

If the first source region is empty, the destination is set to the empty region defined by the rectangle (0,0)(0,0).

Note: DiffRgn may temporarily use heap space that's twice the size of the two input regions.

```
PROCEDURE XorRgn  (srcRgnA,srcRgnB,dstRgn: RgnHandle);
```

XorRgn calculates the difference between the union and the intersection of srcRgnA and srcRgnB and places the result in dstRgn. This does *not* create the destination region; space must already have been allocated for it. The destination region can be one of the source regions, if desired.

If the regions are coincident, the destination is set to the empty region defined by the rectangle (0,0)(0,0).

Note: XorRgn may temporarily use heap space that's twice the size of the two input regions.

```
FUNCTION PtInRgn  (pt: Point; rgn: RgnHandle)  : BOOLEAN;
```

PtInRgn checks whether the pixel below and to the right of the given coordinate point is within the specified region, and returns TRUE if so or FALSE if not.

```
FUNCTION RectInRgn  (r: Rect; rgn: RgnHandle)  : BOOLEAN;
```

RectInRgn checks whether the given rectangle intersects the specified region, and returns TRUE if the intersection encloses at least one bit or FALSE if not.

Note: RectInRgn will sometimes return TRUE when the rectangle merely intersects the region's enclosing rectangle. If you need to know exactly whether a given rectangle intersects the actual region, you can use RectRgn to set the rectangle to a region, and call SectRgn to see whether the two regions intersect: If the result of SectRgn is an empty region, then the rectangle doesn't intersect the region.

```
FUNCTION EqualRgn  (rgnA,rgnB: RgnHandle)  : BOOLEAN;
```

EqualRgn compares the two given regions and returns TRUE if they're equal or FALSE if not. The two regions must have identical sizes, shapes, and locations to be considered equal. Any two empty regions are always equal.

```
FUNCTION EmptyRgn  (rgn: RgnHandle)  : BOOLEAN;
```

EmptyRgn returns TRUE if the region is an empty region or FALSE if not. Some of the circumstances in which an empty region can be created are: a NewRgn call; a CopyRgn of an empty region; a SetRectRgn or RectRgn with an empty rectangle as an argument; CloseRgn without a previous OpenRgn or with no drawing after an OpenRgn; OffsetRgn of an empty region; InsetRgn with an empty region or too large an inset; SectRgn of nonintersecting regions; UnionRgn of two empty regions; and DiffRgn or XorRgn of two identical or nonintersecting regions.

Inside Macintosh

Graphic Operations on Regions

These routines all depend on the coordinate system of the current grafPort. If a region is drawn in a different grafPort than the one in which it was defined, it may not appear in the proper position in the port.

> **Warning:** If any horizontal or vertical line drawn through the region would intersect the region's outline more than 50 times, the results of these graphic operations are undefined. The FrameRgn procedure in particular requires that there would be no more than 25 such intersections.

```
PROCEDURE FrameRgn (rgn: RgnHandle);
```

FrameRgn draws an outline just inside the specified region, using the current grafPort's pen pattern, mode, and size. The outline is as wide as the pen width and as tall as the pen height. It's drawn with the pnPat, according to the pattern transfer mode specified by pnMode. The outline will never go outside the region boundary. The pen location is not changed by this procedure.

If a region is open and being formed, the outside outline of the region being framed is mathematically added to that region's boundary.

> **Note:** FrameRgn actually does a CopyRgn, an InsetRgn, and a DiffRgn; it may temporarily use heap space that's three times the size of the original region.

```
PROCEDURE PaintRgn (rgn: RgnHandle);
```

PaintRgn paints the specified region with the current grafPort's pen pattern and pen mode. The region is filled with the pnPat, according to the pattern transfer mode specified by pnMode. The pen location is not changed by this procedure.

```
PROCEDURE EraseRgn (rgn: RgnHandle);
```

EraseRgn paints the specified region with the current grafPort's background pattern bkPat (in patCopy mode). The grafPort's pnPat and pnMode are ignored; the pen location is not changed.

```
PROCEDURE InvertRgn (rgn: RgnHandle);
```

> **Assembly-language note:** The macro you invoke to call InvertRgn from assembly language is named _InverRgn.

InvertRgn inverts the pixels enclosed by the specified region: Every white pixel becomes black and every black pixel becomes white. The grafPort's pnPat, pnMode, and bkPat are all ignored; the pen location is not changed.

```
PROCEDURE FillRgn (rgn: RgnHandle; pat: Pattern);
```

FillRgn fills the specified region with the given pattern (in patCopy mode). The grafPort's pnPat, pnMode, and bkPat are all ignored; the pen location is not changed.

Bit Transfer Operations

```
PROCEDURE ScrollRect (r: Rect; dh,dv: INTEGER; updateRgn:
        RgnHandle);
```

ScrollRect shifts ("scrolls") the bits that are inside the intersection of the specified rectangle and the visRgn, clipRgn, portRect, and portBits.bounds of the current grafPort. No other bits are affected. The bits are shifted a distance of dh horizontally and dv vertically. The positive directions are to the right and down. Bits that are shifted out of the scroll area are lost—they're neither placed outside the area nor saved. The space created by the scroll is filled with the grafPort's background pattern (thePort^.bkPat), and the updateRgn is changed to this filled area (see Figure 22).

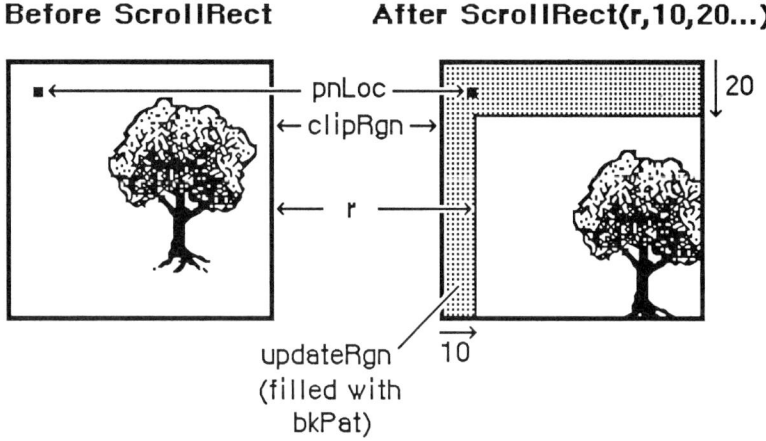

Figure 22. Scrolling

ScrollRect doesn't change the coordinate system of the grafPort, it simply moves the entire document to *different* coordinates. Notice that ScrollRect doesn't move the pen and the clipRgn. However, since the document has moved, they're in a different position relative to the document.

To restore the coordinates of the document to what they were before the ScrollRect, you can use the SetOrigin procedure. In Figure 22, suppose that before the ScrollRect the top left corner of the document was at coordinates (100,100). After ScrollRect(r,10,20...), the coordinates of the document are offset by the specified values. You could call SetOrigin(90,80) to offset the coordinate system to compensate for the scroll (see Figure 14 in the "Coordinates in GrafPorts" section for an illustration). The document itself doesn't move as a result of SetOrigin, but the pen and clipRgn move down and to the right, and are restored to their original position relative to the document. Notice that updateRgn will still need to be redrawn.

Inside Macintosh

```
PROCEDURE CopyBits (srcBits,dstBits: BitMap; srcRect,dstRect:
        Rect; mode: INTEGER; maskRgn: RgnHandle);
```

CopyBits transfers a bit image between any two bit maps and clips the result to the area specified by the maskRgn parameter. The transfer may be performed in any of the eight source transfer modes. The result is always clipped to the maskRgn and the boundary rectangle of the destination bit map; if the destination bit map is the current grafPort's portBits, it's also clipped to the intersection of the grafPort's clipRgn and visRgn. If you don't want to clip to a maskRgn, just pass NIL for the maskRgn parameter. The dstRect and maskRgn coordinates are in terms of the dstBits.bounds coordinate system, and the srcRect coordinates are in terms of the srcBits.bounds coordinates.

> **Warning:** The source bit map must not occupy more memory than half the available stack space. A good rule of thumb is not to copy more than 3K bytes.

> **Warning:** If you perform a CopyBits between two grafPorts that overlap, you must first convert to global coordinates, and then specify screenBits for both srcBits and dstBits.

The bits enclosed by the source rectangle are transferred into the destination rectangle according to the rules of the chosen mode. The source transfer modes are as follows:

```
srcCopy         notSrcCopy
srcOr           notSrcXor
srcXor          notSrcOr
srcBic          notSrcBic
```

The source rectangle is completely aligned with the destination rectangle; if the rectangles are of different sizes, the bit image is expanded or shrunk as necessary to fit the destination rectangle. For example, if the bit image is a circle in a square source rectangle, and the destination rectangle is not square, the bit image appears as an oval in the destination (see Figure 23).

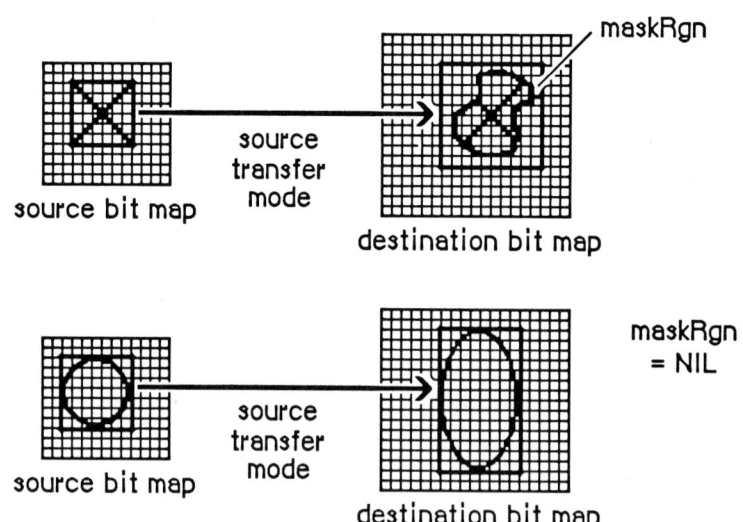

Figure 23. Operation of CopyBits

Pictures

```
FUNCTION OpenPicture (picFrame: Rect) : PicHandle;
```

OpenPicture returns a handle to a new picture that has the given rectangle as its picture frame, and tells QuickDraw to start saving as the picture definition all calls to drawing routines and all picture comments (if any).

OpenPicture calls HidePen, so no drawing occurs on the screen while the picture is open (unless you call ShowPen just after OpenPicture, or you called ShowPen previously without balancing it by a call to HidePen).

When a picture is open, the current grafPort's picSave field contains a handle to information related to the picture definition. If you want to temporarily disable the collection of routine calls and picture comments, you can save the current value of this field, set the field to NIL, and later restore the saved value to resume the picture definition.

> **Warning:** Do not call OpenPicture while another picture is already open.

> **Warning:** A grafPort's clipRgn is initialized to an arbitrarily large region. You should always change the clipRgn to a smaller region *before* calling OpenPicture, or no drawing may occur when you call DrawPicture.

> **Note:** Pictures are limited to 32K bytes; you can determine the picture size while it's being formed by calling the Memory Manager function GetHandleSize.

```
PROCEDURE ClosePicture;
```

ClosePicture tells QuickDraw to stop saving routine calls and picture comments as the definition of the currently open picture. You should perform one and only one ClosePicture for every OpenPicture. ClosePicture calls ShowPen, balancing the HidePen call made by OpenPicture.

```
PROCEDURE PicComment (kind,dataSize: INTEGER; dataHandle:
         Handle);
```

PicComment inserts the specified comment into the definition of the currently open picture. The kind parameter identifies the type of comment. DataHandle is a handle to additional data if desired, and dataSize is the size of that data in bytes. If there's no additional data for the comment, dataHandle should be NIL and dataSize should be 0. An application that processes the comments must include a procedure to do the processing and store a pointer to it in the data structure pointed to by the grafProcs field of the grafPort (see "Customizing QuickDraw Operations").

> **Note:** The standard low-level procedure for processing picture comments simply ignores all comments.

```
PROCEDURE DrawPicture (myPicture: PicHandle; dstRect: Rect);
```

DrawPicture takes the part of the given picture that's inside the picture frame and draws it in dstRect, expanding or shrinking it as necessary to align the borders of the picture frame with dstRect. DrawPicture passes any picture comments to a low-level procedure accessed indirectly through the grafProcs field of the grafPort (see PicComment above).

Warning: If you call DrawPicture with the initial, arbitrarily large clipRgn and the destination rectangle is offset from the picture frame, you may end up with an empty clipRgn, and no drawing will take place.

Note: Because of a convention not to copy more than 3K bytes with CopyBits, a buffer of approximately 3.5K bytes on the stack should suffice when "playing back" a picture.

```
PROCEDURE KillPicture (myPicture: PicHandle);
```

KillPicture releases the memory occupied by the given picture. Use this only when you're completely through with a picture (unless the picture is a resource, in which case use the Resource Manager procedure ReleaseResource).

Calculations with Polygons

```
FUNCTION OpenPoly : PolyHandle;
```

OpenPoly returns a handle to a new polygon and tells QuickDraw to start saving the polygon definition as specified by calls to line-drawing routines. While a polygon is open, all calls to Line and LineTo affect the outline of the polygon. Only the line endpoints affect the polygon definition; the pen mode, pattern, and size do not affect it. In fact, OpenPoly calls HidePen, so no drawing occurs on the screen while the polygon is open (unless you call ShowPen just after OpenPoly, or you called ShowPen previously without balancing it by a call to HidePen).

A polygon should consist of a sequence of connected lines. Even though the on-screen presentation of a polygon is clipped, the definition of a polygon is not; you can define a polygon anywhere on the coordinate plane.

When a polygon is open, the current grafPort's polySave field contains a handle to information related to the polygon definition. If you want to temporarily disable the polygon definition, you can save the current value of this field, set the field to NIL, and later restore the saved value to resume the polygon definition.

Warning: Do not call OpenPoly while a region or another polygon is already open.

Note: Polygons are limited to 32K bytes; you can determine the polygon size while it's being formed by calling the Memory Manager function GetHandleSize.

```
PROCEDURE ClosePoly;
```

Assembly-language note: The macro you invoke to call ClosePoly from assembly language is named _ClosePgon.

ClosePoly tells QuickDraw to stop saving the definition of the currently open polygon and computes the polyBBox rectangle. You should perform one and only one ClosePoly for every OpenPoly. ClosePoly calls ShowPen, balancing the HidePen call made by OpenPoly.

Here's an example of how to open a polygon, define it as a triangle, close it, and draw it:

```
triPoly := OpenPoly;              {save handle and begin collecting stuff}
   MoveTo(300,100);               {move to first point and }
   LineTo(400,200);               {            form         }
   LineTo(200,200);               {            the          }
   LineTo(300,100);               {          triangle       }
ClosePoly;                        {stop collecting stuff}
FillPoly(triPoly,gray);           {draw it on the screen}
KillPoly(triPoly)                 {we're all done}
```

```
PROCEDURE KillPoly (poly: PolyHandle);
```

KillPoly releases the memory occupied by the given polygon. Use this only when you're completely through with a polygon.

```
PROCEDURE OffsetPoly (poly: PolyHandle; dh,dv: INTEGER);
```

OffsetPoly moves the polygon on the coordinate plane, a distance of dh horizontally and dv vertically. This doesn't affect the screen unless you subsequently call a routine to draw the polygon. If dh and dv are positive, the movement is to the right and down; if either is negative, the corresponding movement is in the opposite direction. The polygon retains its shape and size.

> **Note:** OffsetPoly is an especially efficient operation, because the data defining a polygon is stored relative to the first point of the polygon and so isn't actually changed by OffsetPoly.

Graphic Operations on Polygons

Four of the operations described here—PaintPoly, ErasePoly, InvertPoly, and FillPoly—temporarily convert the polygon into a region to perform their operations. The amount of memory required for this temporary region may be far greater than the amount required by the polygon alone. You can estimate the size of this region by scaling down the polygon with MapPoly, converting it into a region, checking the region's size with the Memory Manager function GetHandleSize, and multiplying that value by the factor by which you scaled down the polygon.

> **Warning:** If any horizontal or vertical line drawn through the polygon would intersect the polygon's outline more than 50 times, the results of these graphic operations are undefined.

Inside Macintosh

```
PROCEDURE FramePoly (poly: PolyHandle);
```

FramePoly plays back the line-drawing routine calls that define the given polygon, using the current grafPort's pen pattern, mode, and size. The pen will hang below and to the right of each point on the boundary of the polygon; thus, the polygon drawn will extend beyond the right and bottom edges of poly^^.polyBBox by the pen width and pen height, respectively. All other graphic operations occur strictly within the boundary of the polygon, as for other shapes. You can see this difference in Figure 24, where each of the polygons is shown with its polyBBox.

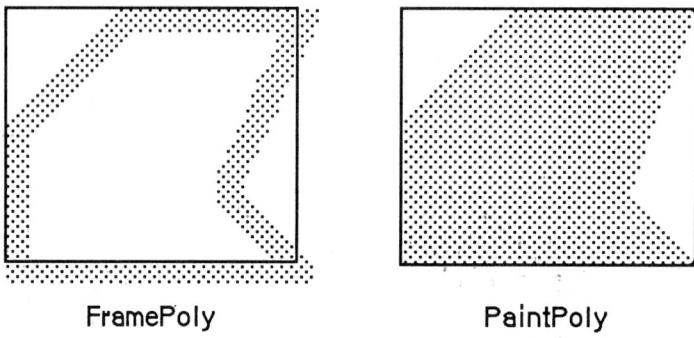

Figure 24. Drawing Polygons

If a polygon is open and being formed, FramePoly affects the outline of the polygon just as if the line-drawing routines themselves had been called. If a region is open and being formed, the outside outline of the polygon being framed is mathematically added to the region's boundary.

```
PROCEDURE PaintPoly (poly: PolyHandle);
```

PaintPoly paints the specified polygon with the current grafPort's pen pattern and pen mode. The polygon is filled with the pnPat, according to the pattern transfer mode specified by pnMode. The pen location is not changed by this procedure.

```
PROCEDURE ErasePoly (poly: PolyHandle);
```

ErasePoly paints the specified polygon with the current grafPort's background pattern bkPat (in patCopy mode). The pnPat and pnMode are ignored; the pen location is not changed.

```
PROCEDURE InvertPoly (poly: PolyHandle);
```

InvertPoly inverts the pixels enclosed by the specified polygon: Every white pixel becomes black and every black pixel becomes white. The grafPort's pnPat, pnMode, and bkPat are all ignored; the pen location is not changed.

```
PROCEDURE FillPoly (poly: PolyHandle; pat: Pattern);
```

FillPoly fills the specified polygon with the given pattern (in patCopy mode). The grafPort's pnPat, pnMode, and bkPat are all ignored; the pen location is not changed.

Calculations with Points

```
PROCEDURE AddPt (srcPt: Point; VAR dstPt: Point);
```

AddPt adds the coordinates of srcPt to the coordinates of dstPt, and returns the result in dstPt.

```
PROCEDURE SubPt (srcPt: Point; VAR dstPt: Point);
```

SubPt subtracts the coordinates of srcPt from the coordinates of dstPt, and returns the result in dstPt.

> **Note:** To get the results of coordinate subtraction returned as a function result, you can use the Toolbox Utility function DeltaPoint.

```
PROCEDURE SetPt (VAR pt: Point; h,v: INTEGER);
```

SetPt assigns the two given coordinates to the point pt.

```
FUNCTION EqualPt (pt1,pt2: Point) : BOOLEAN;
```

EqualPt compares the two given points and returns TRUE if they're equal or FALSE if not.

```
PROCEDURE LocalToGlobal (VAR pt: Point);
```

LocalToGlobal converts the given point from the current grafPort's local coordinate system into a global coordinate system with the origin (0,0) at the top left corner of the port's bit image (such as the screen). This global point can then be compared to other global points, or be changed into the local coordinates of another grafPort.

Since a rectangle is defined by two points, you can convert a rectangle into global coordinates by performing two LocalToGlobal calls. You can also convert a rectangle, region, or polygon into global coordinates by calling OffsetRect, OffsetRgn, or OffsetPoly. For examples, see GlobalToLocal below.

```
PROCEDURE GlobalToLocal (VAR pt: Point);
```

GlobalToLocal takes a point expressed in global coordinates (with the top left corner of the bit image as coordinate (0,0)) and converts it into the local coordinates of the current grafPort. The global point can be obtained with the LocalToGlobal call (see above). For example, suppose a game draws a "ball" within a rectangle named ballRect, defined in the grafPort named gamePort (as illustrated in Figure 25). If you want to draw that ball in the grafPort named selectPort, you can calculate the ball's selectPort coordinates like this:

```
SetPort(gamePort);                    {start in origin port}
selectBall := ballRect;               {make a copy to be moved}
LocalToGlobal(selectBall.topLeft);    {put both corners into }
LocalToGlobal(selectBall.botRight);   { global coordinates}

SetPort(selectPort);                  {switch to destination port}
GlobalToLocal(selectBall.topLeft);    {put both corners into }
GlobalToLocal(selectBall.botRight);   { these local coordinates}
FillOval(selectBall,ballColor)        {draw the ball}
```

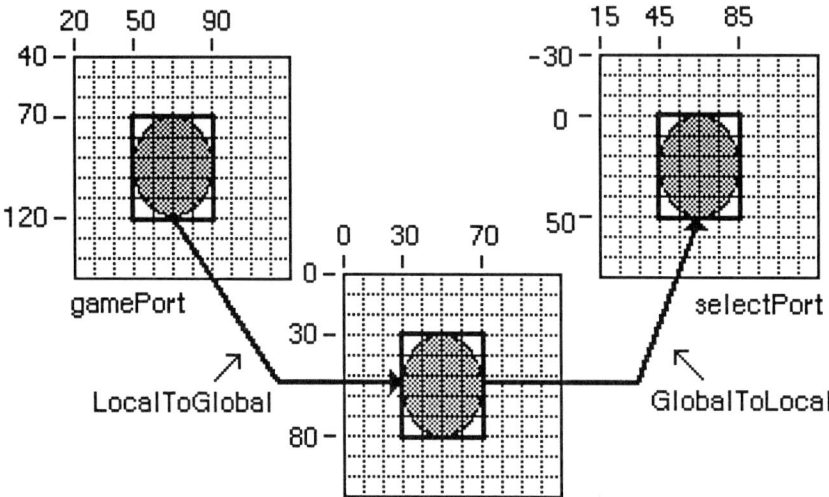

Figure 25. Converting between Coordinate Systems

You can see from Figure 25 that LocalToGlobal and GlobalToLocal simply offset the coordinates of the rectangle by the coordinates of the top left corner of the local grafPort's portBits.bounds rectangle. You could also do this with OffsetRect. In fact, the way to convert regions and polygons from one coordinate system to another is with OffsetRgn or OffsetPoly rather than LocalToGlobal and GlobalToLocal. For example, if myRgn were a region enclosed by a rectangle having the same coordinates as ballRect in gamePort, you could convert the region to global coordinates with

```
OffsetRgn(myRgn,-20,-40)
```

and then convert it to the coordinates of the selectPort grafPort with

```
OffsetRgn(myRgn,15,-30)
```

Miscellaneous Routines

```
FUNCTION Random : INTEGER;
```

This function returns a pseudo-random integer, uniformly distributed in the range –32767 through 32767. The value the sequence starts from depends on the global variable randSeed, which InitGraf initializes to 1. To start the sequence over again from where it began, reset randSeed to 1. To start a new sequence each time, you must reset randSeed to a random number.

Note: You can start a new sequence by storing the current date and time in randSeed; see GetDateTime in chapter 13 of Volume II.

Assembly-language note: From assembly language, it's better to start a new sequence by storing the value of the system global variable RndSeed in randSeed.

```
FUNCTION GetPixel (h,v: INTEGER) : BOOLEAN;
```

GetPixel looks at the pixel associated with the given coordinate point and returns TRUE if it's black or FALSE if it's white. The selected pixel is immediately below and to the right of the point whose coordinates are given in h and v, in the local coordinates of the current grafPort. There's no guarantee that the specified pixel actually belongs to the port, however; it may have been drawn by a port overlapping the current one. To see if the point indeed belongs to the current port, you could call PtInRgn(pt, thePort^.visRgn).

Note: To find out which window's grafPort a point lies in, you call the Window Manager function FindWindow, as described in chapter 9.

```
PROCEDURE StuffHex (thingPtr: Ptr; s: Str255);
```

StuffHex stores bits (expressed as a string of hexadecimal digits) into any data structure. You can easily create a pattern in your program with StuffHex (though more likely, you'll store patterns in a resource file). For example,

```
StuffHex(@stripes,'0102040810204080')
```

places a striped pattern into the pattern variable named stripes.

Warning: There's no range checking on the size of the destination variable. It's easy to overrun the variable and destroy something if you don't know what you're doing.

```
PROCEDURE ScalePt (VAR pt: Point; srcRect,dstRect: Rect);
```

A width and height are passed in pt; the horizontal component of pt is the width, and its vertical component is the height. ScalePt scales these measurements as follows and returns the result in pt: It multiplies the given width by the ratio of dstRect's width to srcRect's width, and multiplies the given height by the ratio of dstRect's height to srcRect's height.

ScalePt can be used, for example, for scaling the pen dimensions. In Figure 26, where dstRect's width is twice srcRect's width and its height is three times srcRect's height, the pen width is scaled from 3 to 6 and the pen height is scaled from 2 to 6.

Note: The minimum value ScalePt will return is (1,1).

Inside Macintosh

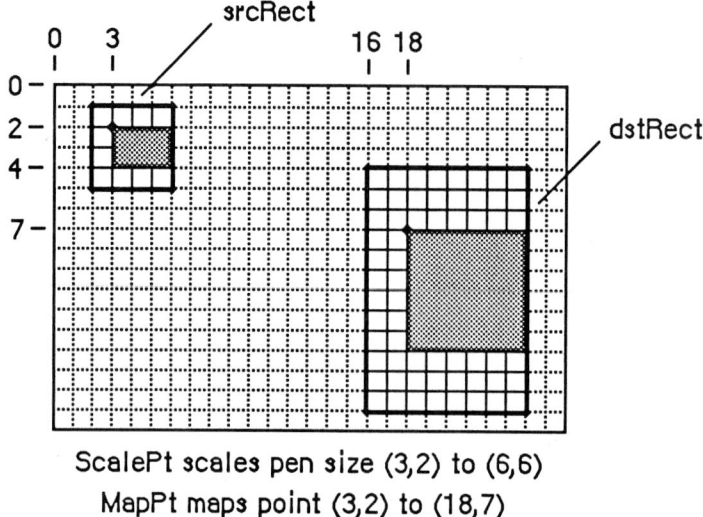

Figure 26. ScalePt and MapPt

```
PROCEDURE MapPt (VAR pt: Point; srcRect,dstRect: Rect);
```

Given a point within srcRect, MapPt maps it to a similarly located point within dstRect (that is, to where it would fall if it were part of a drawing being expanded or shrunk to fit dstRect). The result is returned in pt. A corner point of srcRect would be mapped to the corresponding corner point of dstRect, and the center of srcRect to the center of dstRect. In Figure 26, the point (3,2) in srcRect is mapped to (18,7) in dstRect. SrcRect and dstRect may overlap, and pt need not actually be within srcRect.

Note: Remember, if you're going to draw inside the destination rectangle, you'll probably also want to scale the pen size accordingly with ScalePt.

```
PROCEDURE MapRect (VAR r: Rect; srcRect,dstRect: Rect);
```

Given a rectangle within srcRect, MapRect maps it to a similarly located rectangle within dstRect by calling MapPt to map the top left and bottom right corners of the rectangle. The result is returned in r.

```
PROCEDURE MapRgn (rgn: RgnHandle; srcRect,dstRect: Rect);
```

Given a region within srcRect, MapRgn maps it to a similarly located region within dstRect by calling MapPt to map all the points in the region.

Note: MapRgn is useful for determining whether a region operation will exceed available memory: By mapping a large region into a smaller one and performing the operation (without actually drawing), you can estimate how much memory will be required by the anticipated operation.

```
PROCEDURE MapPoly (poly: PolyHandle; srcRect,dstRect: Rect);
```

Given a polygon within srcRect, MapPoly maps it to a similarly located polygon within dstRect by calling MapPt to map all the points that define the polygon.

> **Note:** Like MapRgn, MapPoly is useful for determining whether a polygon operation will succeed.

CUSTOMIZING QUICKDRAW OPERATIONS

For each shape that QuickDraw knows how to draw, there are procedures that perform these basic graphic operations on the shape: frame, paint, erase, invert, and fill. Those procedures in turn call a low-level drawing routine for the shape. For example, the FrameOval, PaintOval, EraseOval, InvertOval, and FillOval procedures all call a low-level routine that draws the oval. For each type of object QuickDraw can draw, including text and lines, there's a pointer to such a routine. By changing these pointers, you can install your own routines, and either completely override the standard ones or call them after your routines have modified parameters as necessary.

Other low-level routines that you can install in this way are:

- The procedure that does bit transfer and is called by CopyBits.
- The function that measures the width of text and is called by CharWidth, StringWidth, and TextWidth.
- The procedure that processes picture comments and is called by DrawPicture. The standard such procedure ignores picture comments.
- The procedure that saves drawing commands as the definition of a picture, and the one that retrieves them. This enables the application to draw on remote devices, print to the disk, get picture input from the disk, and support large pictures.

The grafProcs field of a grafPort determines which low-level routines are called; if it contains NIL, the standard routines are called, so that all operations in that grafPort are done in the standard ways described in this chapter. You can set the grafProcs field to point to a record of pointers to routines. The data type of grafProcs is QDProcsPtr:

```
TYPE QDProcsPtr = ^QDProcs;
     QDProcs    = RECORD
                    textProc:    Ptr;  {text drawing}
                    lineProc:    Ptr;  {line drawing}
                    rectProc:    Ptr;  {rectangle drawing}
                    rRectProc:   Ptr;  {roundRect drawing}
                    ovalProc:    Ptr;  {oval drawing}
                    arcProc:     Ptr;  {arc/wedge drawing}
                    polyProc:    Ptr;  {polygon drawing}
                    rgnProc:     Ptr;  {region drawing}
                    bitsProc:    Ptr;  {bit transfer}
                    commentProc: Ptr;  {picture comment processing}
                    txMeasProc:  Ptr;  {text width measurement}
                    getPicProc:  Ptr;  {picture retrieval}
                    putPicProc:  Ptr   {picture saving}
                  END;
```

Inside Macintosh

To assist you in setting up a QDProcs record, QuickDraw provides the following procedure:

```
PROCEDURE SetStdProcs (VAR procs: QDProcs);
```

This procedure sets all the fields of the given QDProcs record to point to the standard low-level routines. You can then change the ones you wish to point to your own routines. For example, if your procedure that processes picture comments is named MyComments, you'll store @MyComments in the commentProc field of the QDProcs record.

You can either write your own routines to completely replace the standard ones, or do preprocessing and then call the standard routines. The routines you install must of course have the same calling sequences as the standard routines, which are described below.

Note: These low-level routines should be called only from your customized routines.

The standard drawing routines tell which graphic operation to perform from a parameter of type GrafVerb:

```
TYPE GrafVerb = (frame,paint,erase,invert,fill);
```

When the grafVerb is fill, the pattern to use during filling is passed in the fillPat field of the grafPort.

```
PROCEDURE StdText (byteCount: INTEGER; textBuf: Ptr; numer,denom:
           Point);
```

StdText is the standard low-level routine for drawing text. It draws text from the arbitrary structure in memory specified by textBuf, starting from the first byte and continuing for byteCount bytes. Numer and denom specify the scaling factor: numer.v over denom.v gives the vertical scaling, and numer.h over denom.h gives the horizontal scaling.

```
PROCEDURE StdLine (newPt: Point);
```

StdLine is the standard low-level routine for drawing a line. It draws a line from the current pen location to the location specified (in local coordinates) by newPt.

```
PROCEDURE StdRect (verb: GrafVerb; r: Rect);
```

StdRect is the standard low-level routine for drawing a rectangle. It draws the given rectangle according to the specified grafVerb.

```
PROCEDURE StdRRect (verb: GrafVerb; r: Rect; ovalwidth,
            ovalHeight: INTEGER)
```

StdRRect is the standard low-level routine for drawing a rounded-corner rectangle. It draws the given rounded-corner rectangle according to the specified grafVerb. OvalWidth and ovalHeight specify the diameters of curvature for the corners.

```
PROCEDURE StdOval (verb: GrafVerb; r: Rect);
```

StdOval is the standard low-level routine for drawing an oval. It draws an oval inside the given rectangle according to the specified grafVerb.

```
PROCEDURE StdArc (verb: GrafVerb; r: Rect; startAngle,arcAngle:
          INTEGER);
```

StdArc is the standard low-level routine for drawing an arc or a wedge. It draws an arc or wedge of the oval that fits inside the given rectangle, beginning at startAngle and extending to arcAngle. The grafVerb specifies the graphic operation; if it's the frame operation, an arc is drawn; otherwise, a wedge is drawn.

```
PROCEDURE StdPoly (verb: GrafVerb; poly: PolyHandle);
```

StdPoly is the standard low-level routine for drawing a polygon. It draws the given polygon according to the specified grafVerb.

```
PROCEDURE StdRgn (verb: GrafVerb; rgn: RgnHandle);
```

StdRgn is the standard low-level routine for drawing a region. It draws the given region according to the specified grafVerb.

```
PROCEDURE StdBits (VAR srcBits: BitMap; VAR srcRect,dstRect: Rect;
          mode: INTEGER; maskRgn: RgnHandle);
```

StdBits is the standard low-level routine for doing bit transfer. It transfers a bit image between the given bit map and thePort^.portBits, just as if CopyBits were called with the same parameters and with a destination bit map equal to thePort^.portBits.

```
PROCEDURE StdComment (kind,dataSize: INTEGER; dataHandle:
          Handle);
```

StdComment is the standard low-level routine for processing a picture comment. The kind parameter identifies the type of comment. DataHandle is a handle to additional data, and dataSize is the size of that data in bytes. If there's no additional data for the comment, dataHandle will be NIL and dataSize will be 0. StdComment simply ignores the comment.

```
FUNCTION StdTxMeas (byteCount: INTEGER; textAddr: Ptr; VAR numer,
          denom: Point; VAR info: FontInfo) : INTEGER;
```

StdTxMeas is the standard low-level routine for measuring text width. It returns the width of the text stored in the arbitrary structure in memory specified by textAddr, starting with the first byte and continuing for byteCount bytes. Numer and denom specify the scaling as in the StdText procedure; note that StdTxMeas may change them.

```
PROCEDURE StdGetPic (dataPtr: Ptr; byteCount: INTEGER);
```

StdGetPic is the standard low-level routine for retrieving information from the definition of a picture. It retrieves the next byteCount bytes from the definition of the currently open picture and stores them in the data structure pointed to by dataPtr.

```
PROCEDURE StdPutPic (dataPtr: Ptr; byteCount: INTEGER);
```

StdPutPic is the standard low-level routine for saving information as the definition of a picture. It saves as the definition of the currently open picture the drawing commands stored in the data structure pointed to by dataPtr, starting with the first byte and continuing for the next byteCount bytes.

SUMMARY OF QUICKDRAW

Constants

```
CONST  { Source transfer modes }

       srcCopy    = 0;
       srcOr      = 1;
       srcXor     = 2;
       srcBic     = 3;
       notSrcCopy = 4;
       notSrcOr   = 5;
       notSrcXor  = 6;
       notSrcBic  = 7;

       { Pattern transfer modes }

       patCopy    = 8;
       patOr      = 9;
       patXor     = 10;
       patBic     = 11;
       notPatCopy = 12;
       notPatOr   = 13;
       notPatXor  = 14;
       notPatBic  = 15;

       { Standard colors for ForeColor and BackColor }

       blackColor   = 33;
       whiteColor   = 30;
       redColor     = 205;
       greenColor   = 341;
       blueColor    = 409;
       cyanColor    = 273;
       magentaColor = 137;
       yellowColor  = 69;

       { Standard picture comments }

       picLParen = 0;
       picRParen = 1;
```

Data Types

```
TYPE  StyleItem = (bold,italic,underline,outline,shadow,condense,extend);
      Style     = SET OF StyleItem;
```

```
VHSelect = (v,h);
Point    = RECORD CASE INTEGER OF
              0: (v: INTEGER;   {vertical coordinate}
                  h: INTEGER);  {horizontal coordinate}
              1: (vh: ARRAY[VHSelect] OF INTEGER)
           END;

Rect = RECORD CASE INTEGER OF
          0: (top:    INTEGER;
              left:   INTEGER;
              bottom: INTEGER;
              right:  INTEGER);
          1: (topLeft:  Point;
              botRight: Point)
       END;

RgnHandle = ^RgnPtr;
RgnPtr    = ^Region;
Region    = RECORD
               rgnSize: INTEGER;  {size in bytes}
               rgnBBox: Rect;     {enclosing rectangle}
               {more data if not rectangular}
            END;

BitMap = RECORD
            baseAddr: Ptr;      {pointer to bit image}
            rowBytes: INTEGER;  {row width}
            bounds:   Rect      {boundary rectangle}
         END;

Pattern = PACKED ARRAY[0..7] OF 0..255;

Bits16 = ARRAY[0..15] OF INTEGER;

Cursor = RECORD
            data:    Bits16;  {cursor image}
            mask:    Bits16;  {cursor mask}
            hotSpot: Point    {point aligned with mouse}
         END;
```

```
QDProcsPtr = ^QDProcs;
QDProcs    = RECORD
                textProc:    Ptr;        {text drawing}
                lineProc:    Ptr;        {line drawing}
                rectProc:    Ptr;        {rectangle drawing}
                rRectProc:   Ptr;        {roundRect drawing}
                ovalProc:    Ptr;        {oval drawing}
                arcProc:     Ptr;        {arc/wedge drawing}
                rgnProc:     Ptr;        {region drawing}
                bitsProc:    Ptr;        {bit transfer}
                commentProc: Ptr;        {picture comment processing}
                txMeasProc:  Ptr;        {text width measurement}
                getPicProc:  Ptr;        {picture retrieval}
                putPicProc:  Ptr         {picture saving}
             END;

GrafPtr  = ^GrafPort;
GrafPort = RECORD
                device:      INTEGER;    {device-specific information}
                portBits:    BitMap;     {grafPort's bit map}
                portRect:    Rect;       {grafPort's rectangle}
                visRgn:      RgnHandle;  {visible region}
                clipRgn:     RgnHandle;  {clipping region}
                bkPat:       Pattern;    {background pattern}
                fillPat:     Pattern;    {fill pattern}
                pnLoc:       Point;      {pen location}
                pnSize:      Point;      {pen size}
                pnMode:      INTEGER;    {pen's transfer mode}
                pnPat:       Pattern;    {pen pattern}
                pnVis:       INTEGER;    {pen visibility}
                txFont:      INTEGER;    {font number for text}
                txFace:      Style;      {text's character style}
                txMode:      INTEGER;    {text's transfer mode}
                txSize:      INTEGER;    {font size for text}
                spExtra:     Fixed;      {extra space}
                fgColor:     LONGINT;    {foreground color}
                bkColor:     LONGINT;    {background color}
                colrBit:     INTEGER;    {color bit}
                patStretch:  INTEGER;    {used internally}
                picSave:     Handle;     {picture being saved}
                rgnSave:     Handle;     {region being saved}
                polySave:    Handle;     {polygon being saved}
                grafProcs:   QDProcsPtr  {low-level drawing routines}
             END;

PicHandle = ^PicPtr;
PicPtr    = ^Picture;
Picture   = RECORD
                picSize:  INTEGER;   {size in bytes}
                picFrame: Rect;      {picture frame}
                {picture definition data}
             END;
```

Summary of QuickDraw I-203

```
PolyHandle = ^PolyPtr;
PolyPtr    = ^Polygon;
Polygon    = RECORD
                polySize:   INTEGER;    {size in bytes}
                polyBBox:   Rect;       {enclosing rectangle}
                polyPoints: ARRAY[0..0] OF Point
             END;

PenState = RECORD
              pnLoc:  Point;    {pen location}
              pnSize: Point;    {pen size}
              pnMode: INTEGER;  {pen's transfer mode}
              pnPat:  Pattern   {pen pattern}
           END;

FontInfo = RECORD
              ascent:  INTEGER;  {ascent}
              descent: INTEGER;  {descent}
              widMax:  INTEGER;  {maximum character width}
              leading: INTEGER   {leading}
           END;

GrafVerb = (frame,paint,erase,invert,fill);
```

Variables

```
VAR thePort:    GrafPtr;   {pointer to current grafPort}
    white:      Pattern;   {all-white pattern}
    black:      Pattern;   {all-black pattern}
    gray:       Pattern;   {50% gray pattern}
    ltGray:     Pattern;   {25% gray pattern}
    dkGray:     Pattern;   {75% gray pattern}
    arrow:      Cursor;    {standard arrow cursor}
    screenBits: BitMap;    {the entire screen}
    randSeed:   LONGINT;   {determines where Random sequence begins}
```

Routines

GrafPort Routines

```
PROCEDURE InitGraf     (globalPtr: Ptr);
PROCEDURE OpenPort     (port: GrafPtr);
PROCEDURE InitPort     (port: GrafPtr);
PROCEDURE ClosePort    (port: GrafPtr);
PROCEDURE SetPort      (port: GrafPtr);
PROCEDURE GetPort      (VAR port: GrafPtr);
PROCEDURE GrafDevice   (device: INTEGER);
PROCEDURE SetPortBits  (bm: BitMap);
PROCEDURE PortSize     (width,height: INTEGER);
```

```
PROCEDURE MovePortTo     (leftGlobal,topGlobal: INTEGER);
PROCEDURE SetOrigin      (h,v: INTEGER);
PROCEDURE SetClip        (rgn: RgnHandle);
PROCEDURE GetClip        (rgn: RgnHandle);
PROCEDURE ClipRect       (r: Rect);
PROCEDURE BackPat        (pat: Pattern);
```

Cursor Handling

```
PROCEDURE InitCursor;
PROCEDURE SetCursor (crsr: Cursor);
PROCEDURE HideCursor;
PROCEDURE ShowCursor;
PROCEDURE ObscureCursor;
```

Pen and Line Drawing

```
PROCEDURE HidePen;
PROCEDURE ShowPen;
PROCEDURE GetPen         (VAR pt: Point);
PROCEDURE GetPenState    (VAR pnState: PenState);
PROCEDURE SetPenState    (pnState: PenState);
PROCEDURE PenSize        (width,height: INTEGER);
PROCEDURE PenMode        (mode: INTEGER);
PROCEDURE PenPat         (pat: Pattern);
PROCEDURE PenNormal;
PROCEDURE MoveTo         (h,v: INTEGER);
PROCEDURE Move           (dh,dv: INTEGER);
PROCEDURE LineTo         (h,v: INTEGER);
PROCEDURE Line           (dh,dv: INTEGER);
```

Text Drawing

```
PROCEDURE TextFont       (font: INTEGER);
PROCEDURE TextFace       (face: Style);
PROCEDURE TextMode       (mode: INTEGER);
PROCEDURE TextSize       (size: INTEGER);
PROCEDURE SpaceExtra     (extra: Fixed);
PROCEDURE DrawChar       (ch: CHAR);
PROCEDURE DrawString     (s: Str255);
PROCEDURE DrawText       (textBuf: Ptr; firstByte,byteCount: INTEGER);
FUNCTION  CharWidth      (ch: CHAR) : INTEGER;
FUNCTION  StringWidth    (s: Str255) : INTEGER;
FUNCTION  TextWidth      (textBuf: Ptr; firstByte,byteCount: INTEGER) :
                            INTEGER;
PROCEDURE GetFontInfo    (VAR info: FontInfo);
```

Drawing in Color

```
PROCEDURE ForeColor   (color: LONGINT);
PROCEDURE BackColor   (color: LONGINT);
PROCEDURE ColorBit    (whichBit: INTEGER);
```

Calculations with Rectangles

```
PROCEDURE SetRect     (VAR r: Rect; left,top,right,bottom: INTEGER);
PROCEDURE OffsetRect  (VAR r: Rect; dh,dv: INTEGER);
PROCEDURE InsetRect   (VAR r: Rect; dh,dv: INTEGER);
FUNCTION  SectRect    (src1,src2: Rect; VAR dstRect: Rect) : BOOLEAN;
PROCEDURE UnionRect   (src1,src2: Rect; VAR dstRect: Rect);
FUNCTION  PtInRect    (pt: Point; r: Rect) : BOOLEAN;
PROCEDURE Pt2Rect     (pt1,pt2: Point; VAR dstRect: Rect);
PROCEDURE PtToAngle   (r: Rect; pt: Point; VAR angle: INTEGER);
FUNCTION  EqualRect   (rect1,rect2: Rect) : BOOLEAN;
FUNCTION  EmptyRect   (r: Rect) : BOOLEAN;
```

Graphic Operations on Rectangles

```
PROCEDURE FrameRect   (r: Rect);
PROCEDURE PaintRect   (r: Rect);
PROCEDURE EraseRect   (r: Rect);
PROCEDURE InvertRect  (r: Rect);
PROCEDURE FillRect    (r: Rect; pat: Pattern);
```

Graphic Operations on Ovals

```
PROCEDURE FrameOval   (r: Rect);
PROCEDURE PaintOval   (r: Rect);
PROCEDURE EraseOval   (r: Rect);
PROCEDURE InvertOval  (r: Rect);
PROCEDURE FillOval    (r: Rect; pat: Pattern);
```

Graphic Operations on Rounded-Corner Rectangles

```
PROCEDURE FrameRoundRect   (r: Rect; ovalWidth,ovalHeight: INTEGER);
PROCEDURE PaintRoundRect   (r: Rect; ovalWidth,ovalHeight: INTEGER);
PROCEDURE EraseRoundRect   (r: Rect; ovalWidth,ovalHeight: INTEGER);
PROCEDURE InvertRoundRect  (r: Rect; ovalWidth,ovalHeight: INTEGER);
PROCEDURE FillRoundRect    (r: Rect; ovalWidth,ovalHeight: INTEGER; pat:
                            Pattern);
```

QuickDraw

Graphic Operations on Arcs and Wedges

```
PROCEDURE FrameArc    (r: Rect; startAngle,arcAngle: INTEGER);
PROCEDURE PaintArc    (r: Rect; startAngle,arcAngle: INTEGER);
PROCEDURE EraseArc    (r: Rect; startAngle,arcAngle: INTEGER);
PROCEDURE InvertArc   (r: Rect; startAngle,arcAngle: INTEGER);
PROCEDURE FillArc     (r: Rect; startAngle,arcAngle: INTEGER; pat:
                       Pattern);
```

Calculations with Regions

```
FUNCTION  NewRgn :        RgnHandle;
PROCEDURE OpenRgn;
PROCEDURE CloseRgn       (dstRgn: RgnHandle);
PROCEDURE DisposeRgn     (rgn: RgnHandle);
PROCEDURE CopyRgn        (srcRgn,dstRgn: RgnHandle);
PROCEDURE SetEmptyRgn    (rgn: RgnHandle);
PROCEDURE SetRectRgn     (rgn: RgnHandle; left,top,right,bottom: INTEGER);
PROCEDURE RectRgn        (rgn: RgnHandle; r: Rect);
PROCEDURE OffsetRgn      (rgn: RgnHandle; dh,dv: INTEGER);
PROCEDURE InsetRgn       (rgn: RgnHandle; dh,dv: INTEGER);
PROCEDURE SectRgn        (srcRgnA,srcRgnB,dstRgn: RgnHandle);
PROCEDURE UnionRgn       (srcRgnA,srcRgnB,dstRgn: RgnHandle);
PROCEDURE DiffRgn        (srcRgnA,srcRgnB,dstRgn: RgnHandle);
PROCEDURE XorRgn         (srcRgnA,srcRgnB,dstRgn: RgnHandle);
FUNCTION  PtInRgn        (pt: Point; rgn: RgnHandle) : BOOLEAN;
FUNCTION  RectInRgn      (r: Rect; rgn: RgnHandle) : BOOLEAN;
FUNCTION  EqualRgn       (rgnA,rgnB: RgnHandle) : BOOLEAN;
FUNCTION  EmptyRgn       (rgn: RgnHandle) : BOOLEAN;
```

Graphic Operations on Regions

```
PROCEDURE FrameRgn       (rgn: RgnHandle);
PROCEDURE PaintRgn       (rgn: RgnHandle);
PROCEDURE EraseRgn       (rgn: RgnHandle);
PROCEDURE InvertRgn      (rgn: RgnHandle);
PROCEDURE FillRgn        (rgn: RgnHandle; pat: Pattern);
```

Bit Transfer Operations

```
PROCEDURE ScrollRect     (r: Rect; dh,dv: INTEGER; updateRgn: RgnHandle);
PROCEDURE CopyBits       (srcBits,dstBits: BitMap; srcRect,dstRect: Rect;
                          mode: INTEGER; maskRgn: RgnHandle);
```

Summary of QuickDraw

Pictures

```
FUNCTION  OpenPicture   (picFrame: Rect) : PicHandle;
PROCEDURE PicComment    (kind,dataSize: INTEGER; dataHandle: Handle);
PROCEDURE ClosePicture;
PROCEDURE DrawPicture   (myPicture: PicHandle; dstRect: Rect);
PROCEDURE KillPicture   (myPicture: PicHandle);
```

Calculations with Polygons

```
FUNCTION  OpenPoly  :   PolyHandle;
PROCEDURE ClosePoly;
PROCEDURE KillPoly      (poly: PolyHandle);
PROCEDURE OffsetPoly    (poly: PolyHandle; dh,dv: INTEGER);
```

Graphic Operations on Polygons

```
PROCEDURE FramePoly     (poly: PolyHandle);
PROCEDURE PaintPoly     (poly: PolyHandle);
PROCEDURE ErasePoly     (poly: PolyHandle);
PROCEDURE InvertPoly    (poly: PolyHandle);
PROCEDURE FillPoly      (poly: PolyHandle; pat: Pattern);
```

Calculations with Points

```
PROCEDURE AddPt         (srcPt: Point; VAR dstPt: Point);
PROCEDURE SubPt         (srcPt: Point; VAR dstPt: Point);
PROCEDURE SetPt         (VAR pt: Point; h,v: INTEGER);
FUNCTION  EqualPt       (pt1,pt2: Point) : BOOLEAN;
PROCEDURE LocalToGlobal (VAR pt: Point);
PROCEDURE GlobalToLocal (VAR pt: Point);
```

Miscellaneous Routines

```
FUNCTION  Random   :    INTEGER;
FUNCTION  GetPixel      (h,v: INTEGER) : BOOLEAN;
PROCEDURE StuffHex      (thingPtr: Ptr; s: Str255);
PROCEDURE ScalePt       (VAR pt: Point; srcRect,dstRect: Rect);
PROCEDURE MapPt         (VAR pt: Point; srcRect,dstRect: Rect);
PROCEDURE MapRect       (VAR r: Rect; srcRect,dstRect: Rect);
PROCEDURE MapRgn        (rgn: RgnHandle; srcRect,dstRect: Rect);
PROCEDURE MapPoly       (poly: PolyHandle; srcRect,dstRect: Rect);
```

Customizing QuickDraw Operations

```
PROCEDURE SetStdProcs   (VAR procs: QDProcs);
PROCEDURE StdText       (byteCount: INTEGER; textBuf: Ptr; numer,denom:
                         Point);
PROCEDURE StdLine       (newPt: Point);
PROCEDURE StdRect       (verb: GrafVerb; r: Rect);
PROCEDURE StdRRect      (verb: GrafVerb; r: Rect; ovalwidth,ovalHeight:
                         INTEGER);
PROCEDURE StdOval       (verb: GrafVerb; r: Rect);
PROCEDURE StdArc        (verb: GrafVerb; r: Rect; startAngle,arcAngle:
                         INTEGER);
PROCEDURE StdPoly       (verb: GrafVerb; poly: PolyHandle);
PROCEDURE StdRgn        (verb: GrafVerb; rgn: RgnHandle);
PROCEDURE StdBits       (VAR srcBits: BitMap; VAR srcRect,dstRect: Rect;
                         mode: INTEGER; maskRgn: RgnHandle);
PROCEDURE StdComment    (kind,dataSize: INTEGER; dataHandle: Handle);
FUNCTION  StdTxMeas     (byteCount: INTEGER; textAddr: Ptr; VAR numer,
                         denom: Point; VAR info: FontInfo) : INTEGER;
PROCEDURE StdGetPic     (dataPtr: Ptr; byteCount: INTEGER);
PROCEDURE StdPutPic     (dataPtr: Ptr; byteCount: INTEGER);
```

Assembly-Language Information

Constants

```
; Size in bytes of QuickDraw global variables

grafSize        .EQU    206

; Source transfer modes

srcCopy         .EQU    0
srcOr           .EQU    1
srcXor          .EQU    2
srcBic          .EQU    3
notSrcCopy      .EQU    4
notSrcOr        .EQU    5
notSrcXor       .EQU    6
notSrcBic       .EQU    7

; Pattern transfer modes

patCopy         .EQU    8
patOr           .EQU    9
patXor          .EQU    10
patBic          .EQU    11
notPatCopy      .EQU    12
notPatOr        .EQU    13
notPatXor       .EQU    14
notPatBic       .EQU    15
```

Summary of QuickDraw I-209

```
; Standard colors for ForeColor and BackColor

blackColor      .EQU    33
whiteColor      .EQU    30
redColor        .EQU    205
greenColor      .EQU    341
blueColor       .EQU    409
cyanColor       .EQU    273
magentaColor    .EQU    137
yellowColor     .EQU    69

; Standard picture comments

picLParen       .EQU    0
picRParen       .EQU    1

; Character style

boldBit         .EQU    0
italicBit       .EQU    1
ulineBit        .EQU    2
outlineBit      .EQU    3
shadowBit       .EQU    4
condenseBit     .EQU    5
extendBit       .EQU    6

; Graphic operations

frame           .EQU    0
paint           .EQU    1
erase           .EQU    2
invert          .EQU    3
fill            .EQU    4
```

Point Data Structure

v	Vertical coordinate (word)
h	Horizontal coordinate (word)

Rectangle Data Structure

top	Vertical coordinate of top left corner (word)
left	Horizontal coordinate of top left corner (word)
bottom	Vertical coordinate of bottom right corner (word)
right	Horizontal coordinate of bottom right corner (word)
topLeft	Top left corner (point; long)
botRight	Bottom right corner (point; long)

Region Data Structure

rgnSize	Size in bytes (word)
rgnBBox	Enclosing rectangle (8 bytes)
rgnData	More data if not rectangular

Bit Map Data Structure

baseAddr	Pointer to bit image
rowBytes	Row width (word)
bounds	Boundary rectangle (8 bytes)
bitMapRec	Size in bytes of bit map data structure

Cursor Data Structure

data	Cursor image (32 bytes)
mask	Cursor mask (32 bytes)
hotSpot	Point aligned with mouse (long)
cursRec	Size in bytes of cursor data structure

Structure of QDProcs Record

textProc	Address of text-drawing routine
lineProc	Address of line-drawing routine
rectProc	Address of rectangle-drawing routine
rRectProc	Address of roundRect-drawing routine
ovalProc	Address of oval-drawing routine
arcProc	Address of arc/wedge-drawing routine
polyProc	Address of polygon-drawing routine
rgnProc	Address of region-drawing routine
bitsProc	Address of bit-transfer routine
commentProc	Address of routine for processing picture comments
txMeasProc	Address of routine for measuring text width
getPicProc	Address of picture-retrieval routine
putPicProc	Address of picture-saving routine
qdProcsRec	Size in bytes of QDProcs record

GrafPort Data Structure

device	Font-specific information (word)
portBits	GrafPort's bit map (bitMapRec bytes)
portBounds	Boundary rectangle of grafPort's bit map (8 bytes)
portRect	GrafPort's rectangle (8 bytes)
visRgn	Handle to visible region
clipRgn	Handle to clipping region
bkPat	Background pattern (8 bytes)
fillPat	Fill pattern (8 bytes)
pnLoc	Pen location (point; long)

Inside Macintosh

pnSize	Pen size (point; long)
pnMode	Pen's transfer mode (word)
pnPat	Pen pattern (8 bytes)
pnVis	Pen visibility (word)
txFont	Font number for text (word)
txFace	Text's character style (word)
txMode	Text's transfer mode (word)
txSize	Font size for text (word)
spExtra	Extra space (long)
fgColor	Foreground color (long)
bkColor	Background color (long)
colrBit	Color bit (word)
picSave	Handle to picture being saved
rgnSave	Handle to region being saved
polySave	Handle to polygon being saved
grafProcs	Pointer to QDProcs record
portRec	Size in bytes of grafPort

Picture Data Structure

picSize	Size in bytes (word)
picFrame	Picture frame (rectangle; 8 bytes)
picData	Picture definition data

Polygon Data Structure

polySize	Size in bytes (word)
polyBBox	Enclosing rectangle (8 bytes)
polyPoints	Polygon points

Pen State Data Structure

psLoc	Pen location (point; long)
psSize	Pen size (point; long)
psMode	Pen's transfer mode (word)
psPat	Pen pattern (8 bytes)
psRec	Size in bytes of pen state data structure

Font Information Data Structure

ascent	Ascent (word)
descent	Descent (word)
widMax	Maximum character width (word)
leading	Leading (word)

Special Macro Names

Pascal name	Macro name
SetPortBits	_SetPBits
InvertRect	_InverRect
InvertRoundRect	_InverRoundRect
DisposeRgn	_DisposRgn
SetRectRgn	_SetRecRgn
OffsetRgn	_OfSetRgn
InvertRgn	_InverRgn
ClosePoly	_ClosePgon

Variables

RndSeed   Random number seed (long)

Inside Macintosh

7 THE FONT MANAGER

- 217 About This Chapter
- 217 About the Font Manager
- 219 Font Numbers
- 220 Characters in a Font
- 220 Font Scaling
- 222 Using the Font Manager
- 222 Font Manager Routines
- 222   Initializing the Font Manager
- 222   Getting Font Information
- 223   Keeping Fonts in Memory
- 223   Advanced Routine
- 224 Communication Between QuickDraw and the Font Manager
- 227 Format of a Font
- 230   Font Records
- 233   Font Widths
- 233   How QuickDraw Draws Text
- 234 Fonts in a Resource File
- 236 Summary of the Font Manager

Inside Macintosh

The Font Manager

ABOUT THIS CHAPTER

The Font Manager is the part of the Toolbox that supports the use of various character fonts when you draw text with QuickDraw. This chapter introduces you to the Font Manager and describes the routines your application can call to get font information. It also describes the data structures of fonts and discusses how the Font Manager communicates with QuickDraw.

You should already be familiar with:

- the Resource Manager
- the basic concepts and structures behind QuickDraw, particularly bit images and how to draw text

ABOUT THE FONT MANAGER

The main function of the Font Manager is to provide font support for QuickDraw. To the Macintosh user, **font** means the complete set of characters of one typeface; it doesn't include the size of the characters, and usually doesn't include any stylistic variations (such as bold and italic).

> **Note:** Usually fonts are defined in the plain style and stylistic variations are applied to them; for example, the italic style simply slants the plain characters. However, fonts may be designed to include stylistic variations in the first place.

The way you identify a font to QuickDraw or the Font Manager is with a **font number**. Every font also has a name (such as "New York") that's appropriate to include in a menu of available fonts.

The size of the characters, called the **font size**, is given in **points**. Here this term doesn't have the same meaning as the "point" that's an intersection of lines on the QuickDraw coordinate plane, but instead is a typographical term that stands for approximately 1/72 inch. The font size measures the distance between the ascent line of one line of text and the ascent line of the next line of single-spaced text (see Figure 1).

> **Note:** Because measurements cannot be exact on a bit-mapped output device, the actual font size may be slightly different from what it would be in normal typography. Also be aware that two fonts with the same font size may not actually appear to be the same size; the font size is more useful for distinguishing different sizes of the same font (this is true even in typography).

Whenever you call a QuickDraw routine that does anything with text, QuickDraw passes the following information to the Font Manager:

- The font number.
- The character style, which is a set of stylistic variations. The empty set indicates plain text. (See chapter 6 for details.)
- The font size. The size may range from 1 point to 127 points, but for readability should be at least 6 points.

Inside Macintosh

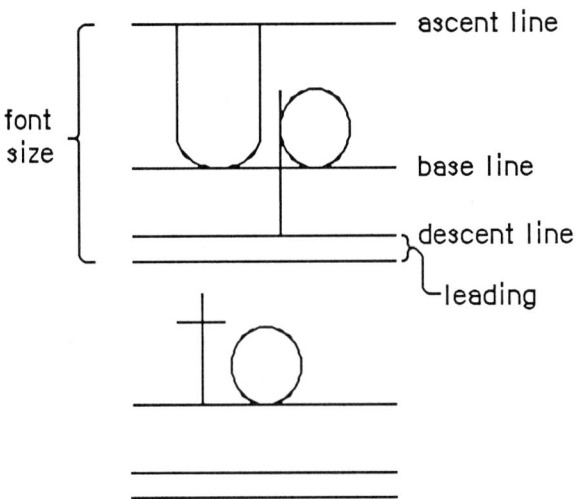

Figure 1. Font Size

- The horizontal and vertical **scaling factors**, each of which is represented by a numerator and a denominator (for example, a numerator of 2 and a denominator of 1 indicates 2-to-1 scaling in that direction).

- A Boolean value indicating whether the characters will actually be drawn or not. They will not be drawn, for example, when the QuickDraw function CharWidth is called (since it only measures characters) or when text is drawn after the pen has been hidden (such as by the HidePen procedure or the OpenPicture function, which calls HidePen).

- Device specific information that enables the Font Manager to achieve the best possible results when drawing text on a particular device. For details, see the section "Communication between QuickDraw and the Font Manager" below.

Given this information, the Font Manager provides QuickDraw with information describing the font and—if the characters will actually be drawn—the bits comprising the characters.

Fonts are stored as resources in resource files; the Font Manager calls the Resource Manager to read them into memory. System-defined fonts are stored in the system resource file. You may define your own fonts and include them in the system resource file so they can be shared among applications. In special cases, you may want to store a font in an application's resource file or even in the resource file for a document. It's also possible to store only the character widths and general font information, and not the bits comprising the characters, for those cases where the characters won't actually be drawn.

A font may be stored in any number of sizes in a resource file. If a size is needed that's not available as a resource, the Font Manager scales an available size.

Fonts occupy a large amount of storage: A 12-point font typically occupies about 3K bytes, and a 24-point font, about 10K bytes; fonts for use on a high resolution output device can take up four times as much space as that (up to 32K bytes). Fonts are normally purgeable, which means they may be removed from the heap when space is required by the Memory Manager. If you wish, you can call a Font Manager routine to make a font temporarily unpurgeable.

The Font Manager

There are also routines that provide information about a font. You can find out the name of a font having a particular font number, or the font number for a font having a particular name. You can also learn whether a font is available in a certain size or will have to be scaled to that size.

FONT NUMBERS

The Font Manager includes the following font numbers for identifying system-defined fonts:

```
CONST  systemFont  = 0;     {system font}
       applFont    = 1;     {application font}
       newYork     = 2;
       geneva      = 3;
       monaco      = 4;
       venice      = 5;
       london      = 6;
       athens      = 7;
       sanFran     = 8;
       toronto     = 9;
       cairo       = 11;
       losAngeles  = 12;
       times       = 20;
       helvetica   = 21;
       courier     = 22;
       symbol      = 23;
       taliesin    = 24;
```

The **system font** is so called because it's the font used by the system (for drawing menu titles and commands in menus, for example). The name of the system font is Chicago. The size of text drawn by the system in this font is fixed at 12 points (called the **system font size**).

The **application font** is the font your application will use unless you specify otherwise. Unlike the system font, the application font isn't a separate font, but is essentially a reference to another font—Geneva, by default. (The application font number is determined by a value that you can set in parameter RAM; see chapter 13 in Volume II for more information.)

Assembly-language note: You can get the application font number from the global variable ApFontID.

Font numbers range from 0 to 255. Font numbers 0 through 127 are reserved for fonts provided by Apple. Font numbers 128 through 255 are assigned by Apple to fonts created by software vendors. To obtain a font number for your font and register its name (which must be unique), write to:

Macintosh Technical Support
Mail Stop 3-T
Apple Computer, Inc.
20525 Mariani Avenue
Cupertino, CA 95014

CHARACTERS IN A FONT

A font can consist of up to 255 distinct characters; not all characters need to be defined in a single font. Figure 2 shows the standard printing characters on the Macintosh and their ASCII codes (for example, the ASCII code for "A" is 41 hexadecimal, or 65 decimal).

Note: Codes $00 through $1F and code $7F are normally nonprinting characters (see chapter 8 for details).

The special characters in the system font with codes $11 through $14 can't normally be typed from the keyboard or keypad. The Font Manager defines constants for these characters:

```
CONST   commandMark  = $11;   {Command key symbol}
        checkMark    = $12;   {check mark}
        diamondMark  = $13;   {diamond symbol}
        appleMark    = $14;   {apple symbol}
```

In addition to its maximum of 255 characters, every font contains a **missing symbol** that's drawn in case of a request to draw a character that's missing from the font.

FONT SCALING

The information QuickDraw passes to the Font Manager includes the font size and the scaling factors QuickDraw wants to use. The Font Manager determines the font information it will return to QuickDraw by looking for the exact size needed among the sizes stored for the font. If the exact size requested isn't available, it then looks for a nearby size that it can scale, as follows:

1. It looks first for a font that's twice the size, and scales down that size if there is one.
2. If there's no font that's twice the size, it looks for a font that's half the size, and scales up that size if there is one.
3. If there's no font that's half the size, it looks for a larger size of the font, and scales down the next larger size if there is one.
4. If there's no larger size, it looks for a smaller size of the font, and scales up the closest smaller size if there is one.
5. If the font isn't available in any size at all, it uses the application font instead, scaling the font to the size requested.
6. If the application font isn't available in any size at all, it uses the system font instead, scaling the font to the size requested.

Scaling looks best when the scaled size is an even multiple of an available size.

First digit

Second digit ↓	0	1	2	3	4	5	6	7	8	9	A	B	C	D	E	F
0			space	0	@	P	`	p	Ä	ê	†	∞	¿	–		
1		⌘	!	1	A	Q	a	q	Å	ë	°	±	¡	—		
2		✓	"	2	B	R	b	r	Ç	í	¢	≤	¬	“		
3		◆	#	3	C	S	c	s	É	ì	£	≥	√	”		
4			$	4	D	T	d	t	Ñ	î	§	¥	ƒ	‘		
5			%	5	E	U	e	u	Ö	ï	●	µ	≈	’		
6			&	6	F	V	f	v	Ü	ñ	¶	∂	∆	÷		
7			'	7	G	W	g	w	á	ó	ß	Σ	«	◊		
8			(	8	H	X	h	x	à	ò	®	∏	»	ÿ		
9			)	9	I	Y	i	y	â	ô	©	π	…			
A			*	:	J	Z	j	z	ä	ö	™	∫	␣			
B			+	;	K	[	k	{	ã	õ	´	ª	À			
C			,	<	L	\	l	|	å	ú	¨	º	Ã			
D			-	=	M	]	m	}	ç	ù	≠	Ω	Õ			
E			.	>	N	^	n	~	é	û	Æ	æ	Œ			
F			/	?	O	_	o		è	ü	Ø	ø	œ			

␣ stands for a nonbreaking space, the same width as a digit.
The first four characters are only in the system font (Chicago).
The shaded characters are not in all fonts.
Codes $D9 through $FF are reserved for future expansion.

Figure 2. Font Characters

7 Font Manager

Inside Macintosh

> **Assembly-language note:** You can use the global variable FScaleDisable to disable scaling, if desired. Normally, FScaleDisable is 0. If you set it to a nonzero value, the Font Manager will look for the size as described above but will return the font unscaled.

USING THE FONT MANAGER

The InitFonts procedure initializes the Font Manager; you should call it after initializing QuickDraw but before initializing the Window Manager.

You can set up a menu of fonts in your application by using the Menu Manager procedure AddResMenu (see chapter 11 for details). When the user chooses a menu item from the font menu, call the Menu Manager procedure GetItem to get the name of the corresponding font, and then the Font Manager function GetFNum to get the font number. The GetFontName function does the reverse of GetFNum: Given a font number, it returns the font name.

In a menu of font sizes in your application, you may want to let the user know which sizes the current font is available in and therefore will not require scaling (this is usually done by showing those font sizes outlined in the menu). You can call the RealFont function to find out whether a font is available in a given size.

If you know you'll be using a font a lot and don't want it to be purged, you can use the SetFontLock procedure to make the font unpurgeable during that time.

Advanced programmers who want to write their own font editors or otherwise manipulate fonts can access fonts directly with the FMSwapFont function.

FONT MANAGER ROUTINES

Initializing the Font Manager

```
PROCEDURE InitFonts;
```

InitFonts initializes the Font Manager. If the system font isn't already in memory, InitFonts reads it into memory. Call this procedure once before all other Font Manager routines or any Toolbox routine that will call the Font Manager.

Getting Font Information

> **Warning:** Before returning, the routines in this section issue the Resource Manager call SetResLoad(TRUE). If your program previously called SetResLoad(FALSE) and you still want that to be in effect after calling one of these Font Manager routines, you'll have to call SetResLoad(FALSE) again.

The Font Manager

```
PROCEDURE GetFontName (fontNum: INTEGER; VAR theName: Str255);
```

Assembly-language note: The macro you invoke to call GetFontName from assembly language is named _GetFName.

GetFontName returns in theName the name of the font having the font number fontNum. If there's no such font, GetFontName returns the empty string.

```
PROCEDURE GetFNum (fontName: Str255; VAR theNum: INTEGER);
```

GetFNum returns in theNum the font number for the font having the given fontName. If there's no such font, GetFNum returns 0.

```
FUNCTION RealFont (fontNum: INTEGER; size: INTEGER) : BOOLEAN;
```

RealFont returns TRUE if the font having the font number fontNum is available in the given size in a resource file, or FALSE if the font has to be scaled to that size.

Note: RealFont will always return FALSE if you pass applFont in fontNum. To find out if the application font is available in a particular size, call GetFontName and then GetFNum to get the actual font number for the application font, and then call RealFont with that number.

Keeping Fonts in Memory

```
PROCEDURE SetFontLock (lockFlag: BOOLEAN);
```

SetFontLock applies to the font in which text was most recently drawn. If lockFlag is TRUE, SetFontLock makes the font unpurgeable (reading it into memory if it isn't already there). If lockFlag is FALSE, it releases the memory occupied by the font (by calling the Resource Manager procedure ReleaseResource). Since fonts are normally purgeable, this procedure is useful for making a font temporarily unpurgeable.

Advanced Routine

The following low-level routine is called by QuickDraw and won't normally be used by an application directly, but it may be of interest to advanced programmers who want to bypass the QuickDraw routines that deal with text.

```
FUNCTION FMSwapFont (inRec: FMInput) : FMOutPtr;
```

FMSwapFont returns a pointer to a font output record containing the size, style, and other information about an adapted version of the font requested in the given font input record. (Font

Inside Macintosh

input and output records are explained in the following section.) FMSwapFont is called by QuickDraw every time a QuickDraw routine that does anything with text is used. If you want to call FMSwapFont yourself, you must build a font input record and then use the pointer returned by FMSwapFont to access the resulting font output record.

COMMUNICATION BETWEEN QUICKDRAW AND THE FONT MANAGER

This section describes the data structures that allow QuickDraw and the Font Manager to exchange information. It also discusses the communication that may occur between the Font Manager and the driver of the device on which the characters are being drawn or printed. You can skip this section if you want to change fonts, character style, and font sizes by calling QuickDraw and aren't interested in the lower-level data structures and routines of the Font Manager. To understand this section fully, you'll have to be familiar with device drivers and the Device Manager.

Whenever you call a QuickDraw routine that does anything with text, QuickDraw requests information from the Font Manager about the characters. The Font Manager performs any necessary calculations and returns the requested information to QuickDraw. As illustrated in Figure 3, this information exchange occurs via two data structures, a font input record (type FMInput) and a font output record (type FMOutput).

First, QuickDraw passes the Font Manager a font input record:

```
TYPE FMInput = PACKED RECORD
        family:   INTEGER;   {font number}
        size:     INTEGER;   {font size}
        face:     Style;     {character style}
        needBits: BOOLEAN;   {TRUE if drawing}
        device:   INTEGER;   {device-specific information}
        numer:    Point;     {numerators of scaling factors}
        denom:    Point      {denominators of scaling factors}
    END;
```

The first three fields contain the font number, size, and character style that QuickDraw wants to use.

The needBits field indicates whether the characters actually will be drawn or not. If the characters are being drawn, all of the information describing the font, including the bit image comprising the characters, will be read into memory. If the characters aren't being drawn and there's a resource consisting of only the character widths and general font information, that resource will be read instead.

The high-order byte of the device field contains a device driver reference number. From the driver reference number, the Font Manager can determine the optimum stylistic variations on the font to produce the highest-quality printing or drawing available on a device (as explained below). The low-order byte of the device field is ignored by the Font Manager but may contain information used by the device driver.

The Font Manager

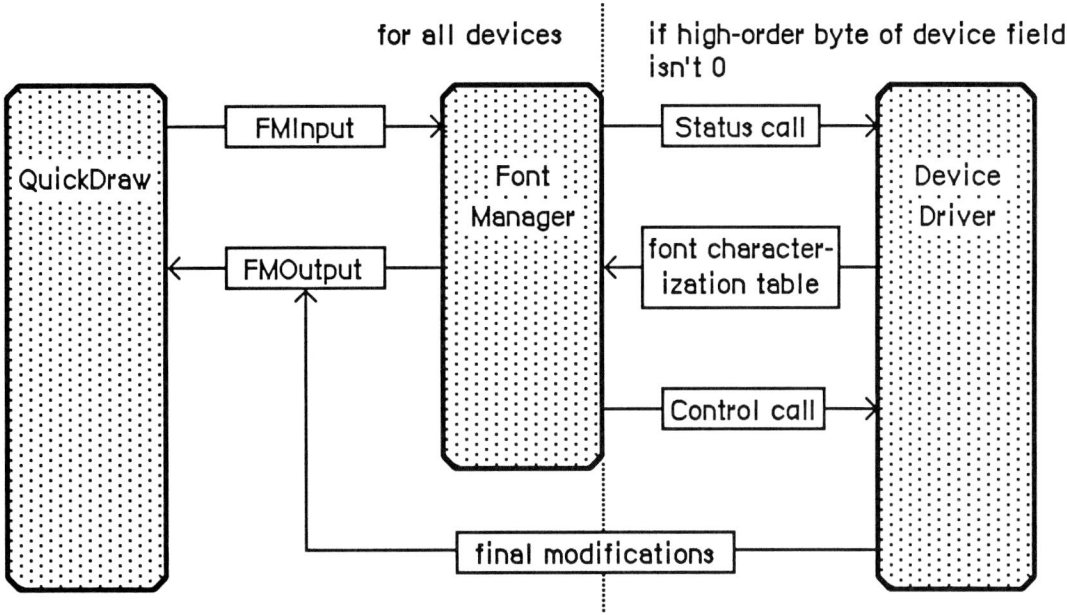

Figure 3. Communication About Fonts

The numer and denom fields contain the scaling factors to be used; numer.v divided by denom.v gives the vertical scaling, and numer.h divided by denom.h gives the horizontal scaling.

The Font Manager takes the font input record and asks the Resource Manager for the font. If the requested size isn't available, the Font Manager scales another size to match (as described under "Font Scaling" above).

Then the Font Manager gets the **font characterization table** via the device field. If the high-order byte of the device field is 0, the Font Manager gets the screen's font characterization table (which is stored in the Font Manager). If the high-order byte of the device field is nonzero, the Font Manager calls the status routine of the device driver having that reference number, and the status routine returns a font characterization table. The status routine may use the value of the low-order byte of the device field to determine the font characterization table it should return.

Note: If you want to make your own calls to the device driver's Status function, the reference number must be the driver reference number from the font input record's device field, csCode must be 8, csParam must be a pointer to where the device driver should put the font characterization table, and csParam+4 must be an integer containing the value of the font input record's device field.

Figure 4 shows the structure of a font characterization table and, on the right, the values it contains for the Macintosh screen.

Inside Macintosh

byte		screen
0	dots per vertical inch on device	80
2	dots per horizontal inch on device	80
4	bold characteristics	0, 1, 1
7	italic characteristics	1, 8, 0
10	not used	0, 0, 0
13	outline characteristics	5, 1, 1
16	shadow characteristics	5, 2, 2
19	condensed characteristics	0, 0,-1
22	extended characteristics	0, 0, 1
25	underline characteristics	1, 1, 1

Figure 4. Font Characterization Table

The first two words of the font characterization table contain the approximate number of dots per inch on the device. These values are only used for scaling between devices; they don't necessarily correspond to a device's actual resolution.

The remainder of the table consists of three-byte triplets providing information about the different stylistic variations. For all but the triplet defining the underline characteristics:

- The first byte in the triplet indicates which byte beyond the bold field of the font output record (see below) is affected by the triplet.
- The second byte contains the amount to be stored in the affected field.
- The third byte indicates the amount by which the extra field of the font output record is to be incremented (starting from 0).

The triplet defining the underline characteristics indicates the amount by which the font output record's ulOffset, ulShadow, and ulThick fields (respectively) should be incremented.

Based on the information in the font characterization table, the Font Manager determines the optimum ascent, descent, and leading, so that the highest-quality printing or drawing available will be produced. It then stores this information in a font output record:

```
TYPE FMOutput =
    PACKED RECORD
        errNum:     INTEGER;        {not used}
        fontHandle: Handle;         {handle to font record}
        bold:       Byte;           {bold factor}
        italic:     Byte;           {italic factor}
        ulOffset:   Byte;           {underline offset}
        ulShadow:   Byte;           {underline shadow}
        ulThick:    Byte;           {underline thickness}
        shadow:     Byte;           {shadow factor}
        extra:      SignedByte;     {width of style}
        ascent:     Byte;           {ascent}
        descent:    Byte;           {descent}
        widMax:     Byte;           {maximum character width}
        leading:    SignedByte;     {leading}
        unused:     Byte;           {not used}
        numer:      Point;          {numerators of scaling factors}
        denom:      Point           {denominators of scaling factors}
    END;
```

ErrNum is reserved for future use, and is set to 0. FontHandle is a handle to the font record of the font, as described in the next section. Bold, italic, ulOffset, ulShadow, ulThick, and shadow are all fields that modify the way stylistic variations are done; their values are taken from the font characterization table, and are used by QuickDraw. (You'll need to experiment with these values if you want to determine exactly how they're used.) Extra indicates the number of pixels that each character has been widened by stylistic variation. For example, using the screen values shown in Figure 4, the extra field for bold shadowed characters would be 3. Ascent, descent, widMax, and leading are the same as the fields of the FontInfo record returned by the QuickDraw procedure GetFontInfo. Numer and denom contain the scaling factors.

Just before returning this record to QuickDraw, the Font Manager calls the device driver's control routine to allow the driver to make any final modifications to the record. Finally, the font information is returned to QuickDraw via a pointer to the record, defined as follows:

```
TYPE FMOutPtr = ^FMOutput;
```

Note: If you want to make your own calls to the device driver's Control function, the reference number must be the driver reference number from the font input record's device field, csCode must be 8, csParam must be a pointer to the font output record, and csParam+4 must be the value of the font input record's device field.

FORMAT OF A FONT

This section describes the data structure that defines a font; you need to read it only if you're going to define your own fonts or write your own font editor.

Each character in a font is defined by bits arranged in rows and columns. This bit arrangement is called a **character image**; it's the image inside each of the character rectangles shown in Figure 5.

The **base line** is a horizontal line coincident with the bottom of each character, excluding descenders.

Inside Macintosh

The **character origin** is a point on the base line used as a reference location for drawing the character. Conceptually the base line is the line that the pen is on when it starts drawing a character, and the characer origin is the point where the pen starts drawing.

The **character rectangle** is a rectangle enclosing the character image; its sides are defined by the **image width** and the **font height**:

- The image width is simply the width of the character image, which varies among characters in the font. It may or may not include space on either side of the character; to minimize the amount of memory required to store the font, it should not include space.
- The font height is the distance from the ascent line to the descent line (which is the same for all characters in the font).

The image width is different from the **character width**, which is the distance to move the pen from this character's origin to the next character's origin while drawing. The character width may be 0, in which case the following character will be superimposed on this character (useful for accents, underscores, and so on). Characters whose image width is 0 (such as a space) can have a nonzero character width.

Characters in a **proportional font** all have character widths proportional to their image width, whereas characters in a **fixed-width** font all have the same character width.

Characters can **kern**; that is, they can overlap adjacent characters. The first character in Figure 5 below doesn't kern, but the second one kerns left.

In addition to the terms used to describe individual characters, there are terms describing features of the font as a whole (see Figure 6).

The **font rectangle** is related to the character rectangle. Imagine that all the character images in the font are superimposed with their origins coinciding. The smallest rectangle enclosing all the superimposed images is the font rectangle.

The **ascent** is the distance from the base line to the top of the font rectangle, and the **descent** is the distance from the base line to the bottom of the font rectangle.

The height of the font rectangle is the font height, which is the same as the height of each character rectangle. The maximum height is 127 pixels. The maximum width of the font rectangle is 254 pixels.

The **leading** is the amount of blank space to draw between lines of single spaced text—the distance between the descent line of one line of text and the ascent line of the next line of text.

Finally, for each character in a font there's a **character offset**. As illustrated in Figure 7, the character offset is simply the difference in position of the character rectangle for a given character and the font rectangle.

Every font has a bit image that contains a complete sequence of all its character images (see Figure 8). The number of rows in the bit image is equivalent to the font height. The character images in the font are stored in the bit image as though the characters were laid out horizontally (in ASCII order, by convention) along a common base line.

The bit image doesn't have to contain a character image for every character in the font. Instead, any characters marked as being missing from the font are omitted from the bit image. When QuickDraw tries to draw such characters, a missing symbol is drawn instead. The missing symbol is stored in the bit image after all the other character images.

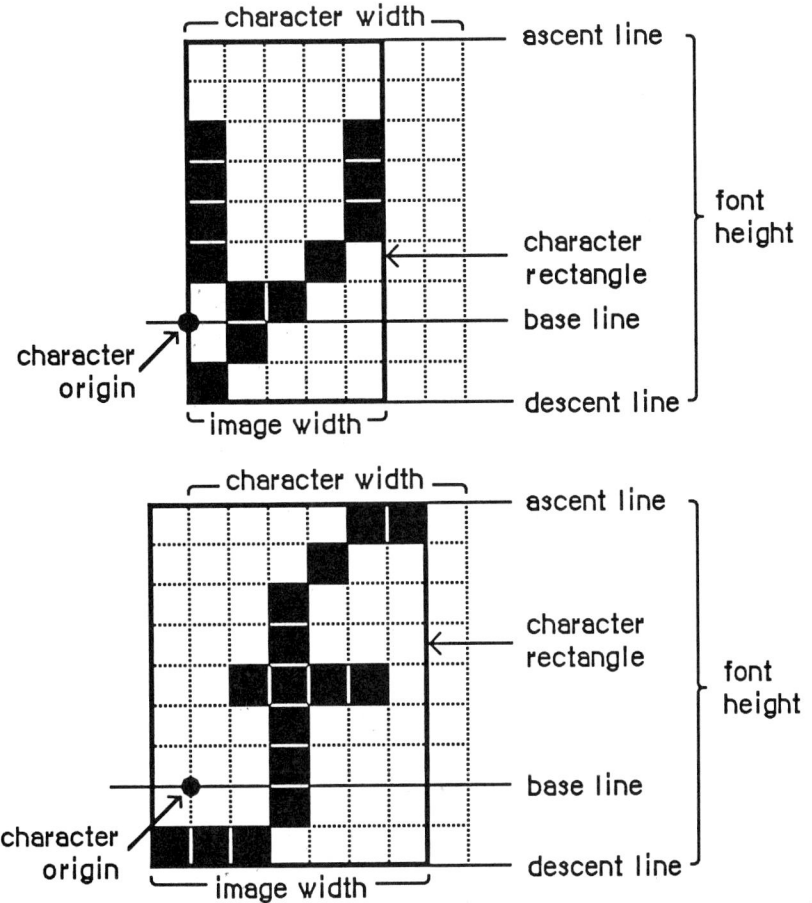

Figure 5. Character Images

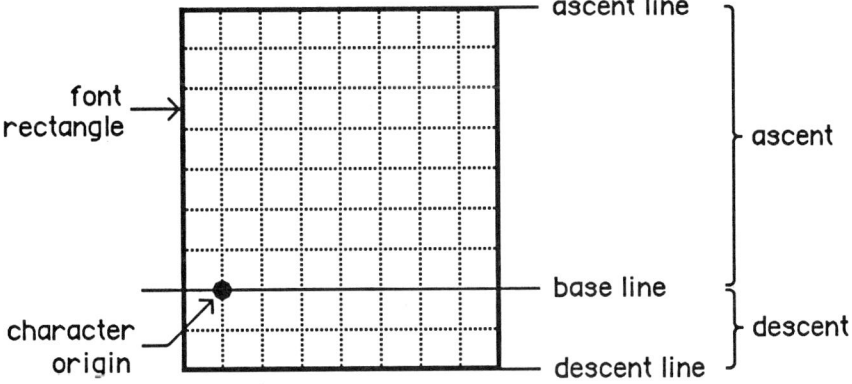

Figure 6. Features of Fonts

Inside Macintosh

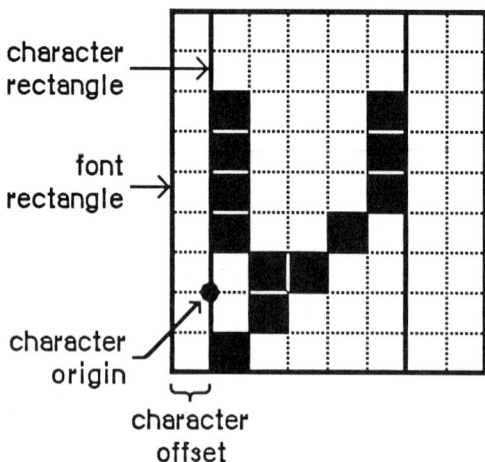

Figure 7. Character Offset

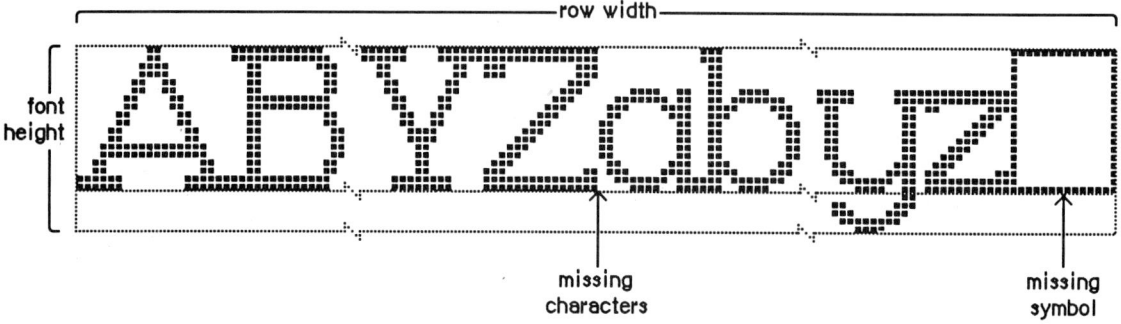

Figure 8. Partial Bit Image for a Font

Warning: Every font *must* have a missing symbol. The characters with ASCII codes 0 (NUL), $09 (horizontal tab), and $0D (Return) must *not* be missing from the font if there's any chance it will ever be used by TextEdit; usually they'll be zero-length, but you may want to store a space for the tab character.

Font Records

The information describing a font is contained in a data structure called a **font record**, which contains the following:

- the font type (fixed-width or proportional)
- the ASCII code of the first character and the last character in the font

- the maximum character width and maximum amount any character kerns
- the font height, ascent, descent, and leading
- the bit image of the font
- a **location table**, which is an array of words specifying the location of each character image within the bit image
- an **offset/width table**, which is an array of words specifying the character offset and character width for each character in the font

For every character, the location table contains a word that specifies the bit offset to the location of that character's image in the bit image. The entry for a character missing from the font contains the same value as the entry for the next character. The last word of the table contains the offset to one bit beyond the end of the bit image (that is, beyond the character image for the missing symbol). The image width of each character is determined from the location table by subtracting the bit offset to that character from the bit offset to the next character in the table.

There's also one word in the offset/width table for every character: The high-order byte specifies the character offset and the low order byte specifies the character width. Missing characters are flagged in this table by a word value of –1. The last word is also –1, indicating the end of the table.

Note: The total space occupied by the bit image, location table, and offset/width table cannot exceed 32K bytes. For this reason, the practical font size limit for a full font is about 40 points.

Figure 9 illustrates a sample location table and offset/width table corresponding to the bit image in Figure 8 above.

A font record is referred to by a handle that you can get by calling the FMSwapFont function or the Resource Manager function GetResource. The data type for a font record is as follows:

```
TYPE FontRec =
        RECORD
            fontType:       INTEGER;    {font type}
            firstChar:      INTEGER;    {ASCII code of first character}
            lastChar:       INTEGER;    {ASCII code of last character}
            widMax:         INTEGER;    {maximum character width}
            kernMax:        INTEGER;    {negative of maximum character kern}
            nDescent:       INTEGER;    {negative of descent}
            fRectWidth:     INTEGER;    {width of font rectangle}
            fRectHeight:    INTEGER;    {height of font rectangle}
            owTLoc:         INTEGER;    {offset to offset/width table}
            ascent:         INTEGER;    {ascent}
            descent:        INTEGER;    {descent}
            leading:        INTEGER;    {leading}
            rowWords:       INTEGER;    {row width of bit image / 2}
        {   bitImage:       ARRAY[1..rowWords,1..fRectHeight] OF INTEGER; }
                                        {bit image}
        {   locTable:       ARRAY[firstChar..lastChar+2] OF INTEGER; }
                                        {location table}
        {   owTable:        ARRAY[firstChar..lastChar+2] OF INTEGER; }
                                        {offset/width table}
        END;
```

Inside Macintosh

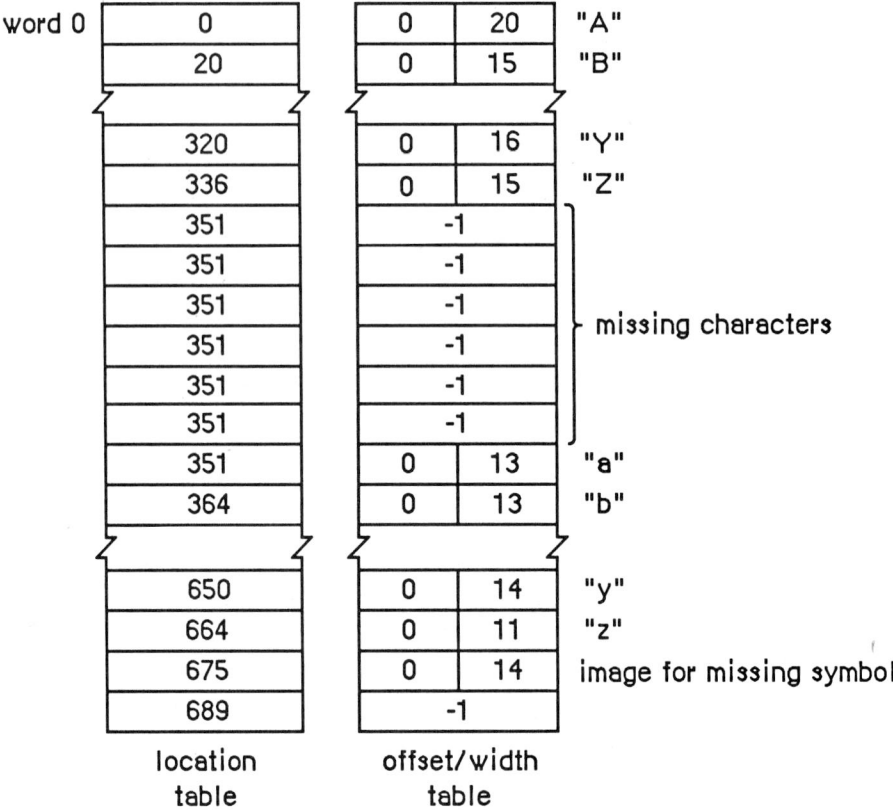

Figure 9. Sample Location Table and Offset/Width Table

Note: The variable-length arrays appear as comments because they're not valid Pascal syntax; they're used only as conceptual aids.

The fontType field must contain one of the following predefined constants:

```
CONST propFont  = $9000;    {proportional font}
      fixedFont = $B000;    {fixed-width font}
```

The values in the widMax, kernMax, nDescent, fRectWidth, fRectHeight, ascent, descent, and leading fields all specify a number of pixels.

KernMax indicates the largest number of pixels any character kerns, that is, the distance from the character origin to the left edge of the font rectangle. It should always be 0 or negative, since the kerned pixels are to the left of the character origin. NDescent is the negative of the descent (the distance from the character origin to the bottom of the font rectangle).

The owTLoc field contains a word offset from itself to the offset/width table; it's equivalent to

4 + (rowWords * fRectHeight) + (lastChar–firstChar+3) + 1

Warning: Remember, the offset and row width in a font record are given in *words*, not bytes.

The Font Manager

> **Assembly-language note:** The global variable ROMFont0 contains a handle to the font record for the system font.

Font Widths

A resource can be defined that consists of only the character widths and general font information —everything but the font's bit image and location table. If there is such a resource, it will be read in whenever QuickDraw doesn't need to draw the text, such as when you call one of the routines CharWidth, HidePen, or OpenPicture (which calls HidePen). The FontRec data type described above, minus the rowWords, bitImage, and locTable fields, reflects the structure of this type of resource. The owTLoc field will contain 4, and the fontType field will contain the following predefined constant:

```
CONST fontWid = $ACB0;   {font width data}
```

How QuickDraw Draws Text

This section provides a conceptual discussion of the steps QuickDraw takes to draw characters (without scaling or stylistic variations such as bold and outline). Basically, QuickDraw simply copies the character image onto the drawing area at a specific location.

1. Take the initial pen location as the character origin for the first character.

2. In the offset/width table, check the word for the character to see if it's –1.

   2a. The character exists if the entry in the offset/width table isn't –1. Determine the character offset and character width from this entry. Find the character image at the location in the bit image specified by the location table. Calculate the image width by subtracting this word from the succeeding word in the location table. Determine the number of pixels the character kerns by adding kernMax to the character offset.

   2b. The character is missing if the entry in the offset/width table is –1; information about the missing symbol is needed. Determine the missing symbol's character offset and character width from the next-to-last word in the offset/width table. Find the missing symbol at the location in the bit image specified by the next-to-last word in the location table. Calculate the image width by subtracting the next-to-last word in the location table from the last word in the table. Determine the number of pixels the missing symbol kerns by adding kernMax to the character offset.

3. If the fontType field is fontWid, return to step 2; otherwise, copy each row of the character image onto the drawing area, one row at a time. The number of bits to copy from each word is given by the image width, and the number of words is given by the fRectHeight field.

4. If the fontType field is propFont, move the pen to the right the number of pixels specified by the character width. If fontType is fixedFont, move the pen to the right the number of pixels specified by the widMax field.

5. Return to step 2.

Inside Macintosh

FONTS IN A RESOURCE FILE

Every size of a font is stored as a separate resource. The resource type for a font is 'FONT'. The resource data for a font is simply a font record:

Number of bytes	Contents
2 bytes	FontType field of font record
2 bytes	FirstChar field of font record
2 bytes	LastChar field of font record
2 bytes	WidMax field of font record
2 bytes	KernMax field of font record
2 bytes	NDescent field of font record
2 bytes	FRectWidth field of font record
2 bytes	FRectHeight field of font record
2 bytes	OWTLoc field of font record
2 bytes	Ascent field of font record
2 bytes	Descent field of font record
2 bytes	Leading field of font record
2 bytes	RowWords field of font record
n bytes	Bit image of font n = 2 * rowWords * fRectHeight
m bytes	Location table of font m = 2 * (lastChar–firstChar+3)
m bytes	Offset/width table of font m = 2 * (lastChar–firstChar+3)

The resource type 'FWID' is used to store only the character widths and general information for a font; its resource data is a font record without the rowWords field, bit image, and location table.

As shown in Figure 10, the resource ID of a font has the following format: Bits 0-6 are the font size, bits 7-14 are the font number, and bit 15 is 0. Thus the resource ID corresponding to a given font number and size is

   (128 * font number) + font size

Since 0 is not a valid font size, the resource ID having 0 in the size field is used to provide only the name of the font: The name of the resource is the font name. For example, for a font named Griffin and numbered 200, the resource naming the font would have a resource ID of 25600 and the resource name 'Griffin'. Size 10 of that font would be stored in a resource numbered 25610.

The Font Manager

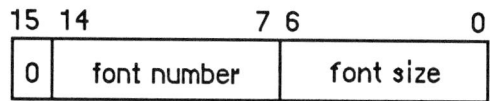

Figure 10. Resource ID for a Font

There's another type of resource related to fonts: 'FRSV', which identifies fonts that are used by the system. Its format is as follows:

Number of bytes	Contents
2 bytes	Number of font resource IDs
n * 2 bytes	n font resource IDs

The Font Mover program looks at the 'FRSV' resource having the resource ID 1, and won't remove the indicated fonts from the system resource file.

Inside Macintosh

SUMMARY OF THE FONT MANAGER

Constants

```
CONST  { Font numbers }

       systemFont  = 0;    {system font}
       applFont    = 1;    {application font}
       newYork     = 2;
       geneva      = 3;
       monaco      = 4;
       venice      = 5;
       london      = 6;
       athens      = 7;
       sanFran     = 8;
       toronto     = 9;
       cairo       = 11;
       losAngeles  = 12;
       times       = 20;
       helvetica   = 21;
       courier     = 22;
       symbol      = 23;
       taliesin    = 24;

       { Special characters }

       commandMark  = $11;    {Command key symbol}
       checkMark    = $12;    {check mark}
       diamondMark  = $13;    {diamond symbol}
       appleMark    = $14;    {apple symbol}

       { Font types }

       propFont   = $9000;   {proportional font}
       fixedFont  = $B000;   {fixed-width font}
       fontWid    = $ACB0;   {font width data}
```

Data Types

```
TYPE FMInput = PACKED RECORD
                 family:   INTEGER;   {font number}
                 size:     INTEGER;   {font size}
                 face:     Style;     {character style}
                 needBits: BOOLEAN;   {TRUE if drawing}
                 device:   INTEGER;   {device-specific information}
                 numer:    Point;     {numerators of scaling factors}
                 denom:    Point      {denominators of scaling factors}
               END;
```

```
FMOutPtr = ^FMOutput;
FMOutput =
    PACKED RECORD
        errNum:     INTEGER;        {not used}
        fontHandle: Handle;         {handle to font record}
        bold:       Byte;           {bold factor}
        italic:     Byte;           {italic factor}
        ulOffset:   Byte;           {underline offset}
        ulShadow:   Byte;           {underline shadow}
        ulThick:    Byte;           {underline thickness}
        shadow:     Byte;           {shadow factor}
        extra:      SignedByte;     {width of style}
        ascent:     Byte;           {ascent}
        descent:    Byte;           {descent}
        widMax:     Byte;           {maximum character width}
        leading:    SignedByte;     {leading}
        unused:     Byte;           {not used}
        numer:      Point;          {numerators of scaling factors}
        denom:      Point           {denominators of scaling factors}
    END;

FontRec =
    RECORD
        fontType:    INTEGER;       {font type}
        firstChar:   INTEGER;       {ASCII code of first character}
        lastChar:    INTEGER;       {ASCII code of last character}
        widMax:      INTEGER;       {maximum character width}
        kernMax:     INTEGER;       {negative of maximum character kern}
        nDescent:    INTEGER;       {negative of descent}
        fRectWidth:  INTEGER;       {width of font rectangle}
        fRectHeight: INTEGER;       {height of font rectangle}
        owTLoc:      INTEGER;       {offset to offset/width table}
        ascent:      INTEGER;       {ascent}
        descent:     INTEGER;       {descent}
        leading:     INTEGER;       {leading}
        rowWords:    INTEGER;       {row width of bit image / 2}
    { bitImage:      ARRAY[1..rowWords,1..fRectHeight] OF INTEGER; }
                                    {bit image}
    { locTable:      ARRAY[firstChar..lastChar+2] OF INTEGER; }
                                    {location table}
    { owTable:       ARRAY[firstChar..lastChar+2] OF INTEGER; }
                                    {offset/width table}
    END;
```

Routines

Initializing the Font Manager

```
PROCEDURE InitFonts;
```

Inside Macintosh

Getting Font Information

```
PROCEDURE GetFontName (fontNum: INTEGER; VAR theName: Str255);
PROCEDURE GetFNum    (fontName: Str255; VAR theNum: INTEGER);
FUNCTION  RealFont   (fontNum: INTEGER; size: INTEGER) : BOOLEAN;
```

Keeping Fonts in Memory

```
PROCEDURE SetFontLock (lockFlag: BOOLEAN);
```

Advanced Routine

```
FUNCTION FMSwapFont (inRec: FMInput) : FMOutPtr;
```

Assembly-Language Information

Constants

```
; Font numbers

sysFont       .EQU   0          ;system font
applFont      .EQU   1          ;application font
newYork       .EQU   2
geneva        .EQU   3
monaco        .EQU   4
venice        .EQU   5
london        .EQU   6
athens        .EQU   7
sanFran       .EQU   8
toronto       .EQU   9
cairo         .EQU   11
losAngeles    .EQU   12
times         .EQU   20
helvetica     .EQU   21
courier       .EQU   22
symbol        .EQU   23
taliesin      .EQU   24

; Special characters

commandMark   .EQU   $11        ;Command key symbol
checkMark     .EQU   $12        ;check mark
diamondMark   .EQU   $13        ;diamond symbol
appleMark     .EQU   $14        ;apple symbol
```

```
; Font types

propFont      .EQU    $9000   ;proportional font
fixedFont     .EQU    $B000   ;fixed-width font
fontWid       .EQU    $ACB0   ;font width data

; Control and Status call code

fMgrCtl1      .EQU    8       ;code used to get and modify font
                              ; characterization table
```

Font Input Record Data Structure

fmInFamily	Font number (word)
fmInSize	Font size (word)
fmInFace	Character style (word)
fmInNeedBits	Nonzero if drawing (byte)
fmInDevice	Device-specific information (byte)
fmInNumer	Numerators of scaling factors (point; long)
fmInDenom	Denominators of scaling factors (point; long)

Font Output Record Data Structure

fmOutFontH	Handle to font record
fmOutBold	Bold factor (byte)
fmOutItalic	Italic factor (byte)
fmOutUlOffset	Underline offset (byte)
fmOutUlShadow	Underline shadow (byte)
fmOutUlThick	Underline thickness (byte)
fmOutShadow	Shadow factor (byte)
fmOutExtra	Width of style (byte)
fmOutAscent	Ascent (byte)
fmOutDescent	Descent (byte)
fmOutWidMax	Maximum character width (byte)
fmOutLeading	Leading (byte)
fmOutNumer	Numerators of scaling factors (point; long)
fmOutDenom	Denominators of scaling factors (point; long)

Font Record Data Structure

fFontType	Font type (word)
fFirstChar	ASCII code of first character (word)
fLastChar	ASCII code of last character (word)
fWidMax	Maximum character width (word)
fKernMax	Negative of maximum character kern (word)
fNDescent	Negative of descent (word)
fFRectWidth	Width of font rectangle (word)
fFRectHeight	Height of font rectangle (word)
fOWTLoc	Offset to offset/width table (word)

fAscent	Ascent (word)
fDescent	Descent (word)
fLeading	Leading (word)
fRowWords	Row width of bit image / 2 (word)

Special Macro Names

Pascal name	Macro name
GetFontName	_GetFName

Variables

ApFontID	Font number of application font (word)
FScaleDisable	Nonzero to disable scaling (byte)
ROMFont0	Handle to font record for system font

8 THE TOOLBOX EVENT MANAGER

- 243 About This Chapter
- 243 About the Toolbox Event Manager
- 244 Event Types
- 245 Priority of Events
- 246 Keyboard Events
- 249 Event Records
- 249   Event Code
- 250   Event Message
- 252   Modifier Flags
- 253 Event Masks
- 255 Using the Toolbox Event Manager
- 255   Responding to Mouse Events
- 256   Responding to Keyboard Events
- 256   Responding to Activate and Update Events
- 257   Responding to Disk-Inserted Events
- 257   Other Operations
- 257 Toolbox Event Manager Routines
- 257   Accessing Events
- 259   Reading the Mouse
- 259   Reading the Keyboard and Keypad
- 260   Miscellaneous Routines
- 261 The Journaling Mechanism
- 261   Writing Your Own Journaling Device Driver
- 263 Summary of the Toolbox Event Manager

The Toolbox Event Manager

ABOUT THIS CHAPTER

This chapter describes the Event Manager, the part of the Toolbox that allows your application to monitor the user's actions, such as those involving the mouse, keyboard, and keypad. The Event Manager is also used by other parts of the Toolbox; for instance, the Window Manager uses events to coordinate the ordering and display of windows on the screen.

There are actually two Event Managers: one in the Operating System and one in the Toolbox. The Toolbox Event Manager calls the Operating System Event Manager and serves as an interface between it and your application; it also adds some features that aren't present at the Operating System level, such as the window management facilities mentioned above. This chapter describes the Toolbox Event Manager, which is the one your application will ordinarily deal with. All references to "the Event Manager" should be understood to refer to the Toolbox Event Manager. For information on the Operating System's Event Manager, see chapter 3 of Volume II.

> **Note:** Most of the constants and data types presented in this chapter are actually defined in the Operating System Event Manager; they're explained here because they're essential to understanding the Toolbox Event Manager.

You should already be familiar with resources and with the basic concepts and structures behind QuickDraw.

ABOUT THE TOOLBOX EVENT MANAGER

The Toolbox Event Manager is your application's link to its user. Whenever the user presses the mouse button, types on the keyboard or keypad, or inserts a disk in a disk drive, your application is notified by means of an **event**. A typical Macintosh application program is event-driven: It decides what to do from moment to moment by asking the Event Manager for events and responding to them one by one in whatever way is appropriate.

Although the Event Manager's primary purpose is to monitor the user's actions and pass them to your application in an orderly way, it also serves as a convenient mechanism for sending signals from one part of your application to another. For instance, the Window Manager uses events to coordinate the ordering and display of windows as the user activates and deactivates them and moves them around on the screen. You can also define your own types of events and use them in any way you wish.

Most events waiting to be processed are kept in the **event queue**, where they're stored (**posted**) by the Operating System Event Manager. The Toolbox Event Manager retrieves events from this queue for your application and also reports other events that aren't kept in the queue, such as those related to windows. In general, events are collected from a variety of sources and reported to your application on demand, one at a time. Events aren't necessarily reported in the order they occurred; some have a higher priority than others.

There are several different types of events. You can restrict some Event Manager routines to apply only to certain event types, in effect disabling the other types.

Other operations your application can perform with Event Manager routines include:

About the Toolbox Event Manager I-243

Inside Macintosh

- directly reading the current state of the keyboard, keypad, and mouse button
- monitoring the location of the mouse
- finding out how much time has elapsed since the system last started up

The Event Manager also provides a **journaling mechanism**, which enables events to be fed to the Event Manager from a source other than the user.

EVENT TYPES

Events are of various types, depending on their origin and meaning. Some report actions by the user; others are generated by the Window Manager, by device drivers, or by your application itself for its own purposes. Some events are handled by the system before your application ever sees them; others are left for your application to handle in its own way.

The most important event types are those that record actions by the user:

- **Mouse-down** and **mouse-up events** occur when the user presses or releases the mouse button.

- **Key-down** and **key-up events** occur when the user presses or releases a key on the keyboard or keypad. **Auto-key events** are generated when the user holds down a repeating key. Together, these three event types are called **keyboard events**.

- **Disk-inserted events** occur when the user inserts a disk into a disk drive or takes any other action that requires a volume to be mounted (as described in chapter 4 in Volume II). For example, a hard disk that contains several volumes may also post a disk-inserted event.

Note: Mere movements of the mouse are not reported as events. If necessary, your application can keep track of them by periodically asking the Event Manager for the current location of the mouse.

The following event types are generated by the Window Manager to coordinate the display of windows on the screen:

- **Activate events** are generated whenever an inactive window becomes active or an active window becomes inactive. They generally occur in pairs (that is, one window is deactivated and then another is activated).

- **Update events** occur when all or part of a window's contents need to be drawn or redrawn, usually as a result of the user's opening, closing, activating, or moving a window.

Another event type (**device driver event**) may be generated by device drivers in certain situations; for example, a driver might be set up to report an event when its transmission of data is interrupted. The chapters describing the individual drivers will tell you about any specific device driver events that may occur.

A **network event** may be generated by the AppleTalk Manager. It contains a handle to a parameter block; for details, see chapter 10 of Volume II.

In addition, your application can define as many as four event types of its own and use them for any desired purpose.

The Toolbox Event Manager

Note: You place application-defined events in the event queue with the Operating System Event Manager procedure PostEvent. See chapter 3 of Volume II for details.

One final type of event is the **null event**, which is what the Event Manager returns if it has no other events to report.

PRIORITY OF EVENTS

The event queue is a FIFO (first-in-first-out) list—that is, events are retrieved from the queue in the order they were originally posted. However, the way that various types of events are generated and detected causes some events to have higher priority than others. (Remember, not all events are kept in the event queue.) Furthermore, when you ask the Event Manager for an event, you can specify particular types that are of interest; doing so can cause some events to be passed over in favor of others that were actually posted later. The following discussion is limited to the event types you've specifically requested in your Event Manager call.

The Event Manager always returns the highest-priority event available of the requested types. The priority ranking is as follows:

1. activate (window becoming inactive before window becoming active)
2. mouse-down, mouse-up, key-down, key-up, disk-inserted, network, device driver, application-defined (all in FIFO order)
3. auto-key
4. update (in front-to-back order of windows)
5. null

Activate events take priority over all others; they're detected in a special way, and are never actually placed in the event queue. The Event Manager checks for pending activate events before looking in the event queue, so it will always return such an event if one is available. Because of the special way activate events are detected, there can never be more than two such events pending at the same time; at most there will be one for a window becoming inactive followed by another for a window becoming active.

Category 2 includes most of the event types. Within this category, events are retrieved from the queue in the order they were posted.

If no event is available in categories 1 and 2, the Event Manager reports an auto-key event if the appropriate conditions hold for one. (These conditions are described in detail in the next section.)

Next in priority are update events. Like activate events, these are not placed in the event queue, but are detected in another way. If no higher-priority event is available, the Event Manager checks for windows whose contents need to be drawn. If it finds one, it returns an update event for that window. Windows are checked in the order in which they're displayed on the screen, from front to back, so if two or more windows need to be updated, an update event will be returned for the frontmost such window.

Finally, if no other event is available, the Event Manager returns a null event.

Note: The event queue normally has a capacity of 20 events. If the queue should become full, the Operating System Event Manager will begin discarding old events to make room for new ones as they're posted. The events discarded are always the oldest ones in the

Inside Macintosh

queue. The capacity of the event queue is determined by the system startup information stored on a volume; for more information, see the section "Data Organization on Volumes" in chapter 4 of Volume II.

KEYBOARD EVENTS

The **character keys** on the Macintosh keyboard and numeric keypad generate key-down and key-up events when pressed and released; this includes all keys except Shift, Caps Lock, Command, and Option, which are called **modifier keys**. (Modifier keys are treated specially, as described below, and generate no keyboard events of their own.) In addition, an auto-key event is posted whenever all of the following conditions apply:

- Auto-key events haven't been disabled. (This is discussed further under "Event Masks" below.)
- No higher-priority event is available.
- The user is currently holding down a character key.
- The appropriate time interval (see below) has elapsed since the last key-down or auto-key event.

Two different time intervals are associated with auto-key events. The first auto-key event is generated after a certain initial delay has elapsed since the original key-down event (that is, since the key was originally pressed); this is called the **auto-key threshold**. Subsequent auto-key events are then generated each time a certain repeat interval has elapsed since the last such event; this is called the **auto-key rate**. The default values are 16 **ticks** (sixtieths of a second) for the auto-key threshold and four ticks for the auto-key rate. The user can change these values with the Control Panel desk accessory, by adjusting the keyboard touch and the rate of repeating keys.

> **Assembly-language note:** The current values for the auto-key threshold and rate are stored in the global variables KeyThresh and KeyRepThresh, respectively.

When the user presses, holds down, or releases a character key, the character generated by that key is identified internally with a **character code**. Character codes are given in the extended version of ASCII (the American Standard Code for Information Interchange) used by the Macintosh. A table showing the character codes for the standard Macintosh character set appears in Figure 1. All character codes are given in hexadecimal in this table. The first digit of a character's hexadecimal value is shown at the top of the table, the second down the left side. For example, character code $47 stands for "G", which appears in the table at the intersection of column 4 and row 7.

Macintosh, the owner's guide, describes the method of generating the printing characters (codes $20 through $D8) shown in Figure 1. Notice that in addition to the regular space character ($20) there's a **nonbreaking space** ($CA), which is generated by pressing the space bar with the Option key down.

The Toolbox Event Manager

Second digit ↓ \ First digit →	0	1	2	3	4	5	6	7	8	9	A	B	C	D	E	F
0	NUL	DLE	space	0	@	P	`	p	Ä	ê	†	∞	¿	–		
1	SOH	DC1	!	1	A	Q	a	q	Å	ë	°	±	¡	—		
2	STX	DC2	"	2	B	R	b	r	Ç	í	¢	≤	¬	"		
3	ETX	DC3	#	3	C	S	c	s	É	ì	£	≥	√	"		
4	EOT	DC4	$	4	D	T	d	t	Ñ	î	§	¥	ƒ	'		
5	ENQ	NAK	%	5	E	U	e	u	Ö	ï	●	µ	≈	'		
6	ACK	SYN	&	6	F	V	f	v	Ü	ñ	¶	∂	∆	÷		
7	BEL	ETB	'	7	G	W	g	w	á	ó	ß	Σ	«	◊		
8	BS	CAN	(	8	H	X	h	x	à	ò	®	∏	»	ÿ		
9	HT	EM	)	9	I	Y	i	y	â	ô	©	π	…			
A	LF	SUB	*	:	J	Z	j	z	ä	ö	™	∫	␣			
B	VT	ESC	+	;	K	[	k	{	ã	õ	´	ª	À			
C	FF	FS	,	<	L	\	l	|	å	ú	¨	º	Ã			
D	CR	GS	–	=	M	]	m	}	ç	ù	≠	Ω	Õ			
E	SO	RS	.	>	N	^	n	~	é	û	Æ	æ	Œ			
F	SI	US	/	?	O	_	o	DEL	è	ü	Ø	ø	œ			

␣ stands for a nonbreaking space, the same width as a digit.
The shaded characters cannot normally be generated from the Macintosh keyboard or keypad.

Figure 1. Macintosh Character Set

Nonprinting or "control" characters ($00 through $1F, as well as $7F) are identified in the table by their traditional ASCII abbreviations; those that are shaded have no special meaning on the Macintosh and cannot normally be generated from the Macintosh keyboard or keypad. Those that can be generated are listed below along with the method of generating them:

Code	Abbreviation	Key
$03	ETX	Enter key on keyboard or keypad
$08	BS	Backspace key on keyboard
$09	HT	Tab key on keyboard
$0D	CR	Return key on keyboard
$1B	ESC	Clear key on keypad
$1C	FS	Left arrow key on keypad
$1D	GS	Right arrow key on keypad
$1E	RS	Up arrow key on keypad
$1F	US	Down arrow key on keypad

The association between characters and keys on the keyboard or the keypad is defined by a **keyboard configuration,** which is a resource stored in a resource file. The particular character that's generated by a character key depends on three things:

- the character key being pressed
- which, if any, of the modifier keys were held down when the character key was pressed
- the keyboard configuration currently in effect

The modifier keys, instead of generating keyboard events themselves, modify the meaning of the character keys by changing the character codes that those keys generate. For example, under the standard U.S. keyboard configuration, the "C" key generates any of the following, depending on which modifier keys are held down:

Key(s) pressed	Character generated
"C" by itself	Lowercase c
"C" with Shift or Caps Lock down	Capital C
"C" with Option down	Lowercase c with a cedilla(ç), used in foreign languages
"C" with Option and Shift down, or with Option and Caps Lock down	Capital C with a cedilla (Ç)

The state of each of the modifier keys is also reported in a field of the event record (see next section), where your application can examine it directly.

Note: As described in the owner's guide, some accented characters are generated by pressing Option along with another key for the accent, and then typing the character to be accented. In these cases, a single key-down event occurs for the accented character; there's no event corresponding to the typing of the accent.

Under the standard keyboard configuration, only the Shift, Caps Lock, and Option keys actually modify the character code generated by a character key on the keyboard; the Command key has no effect on the character code generated. Similarly, character codes for the keypad are affected only by the Shift key. To find out whether the Command key was down at the time of an event (or Caps Lock or Option in the case of one generated from the keypad), you have to examine the event record field containing the state of the modifier keys.

The Toolbox Event Manager

EVENT RECORDS

Every event is represented internally by an **event record** containing all pertinent information about that event. The event record includes the following information:

- the type of event
- the time the event was posted (in ticks since system startup)
- the location of the mouse at the time the event was posted (in global coordinates)
- the state of the mouse button and modifier keys at the time the event was posted
- any additional information required for a particular type of event, such as which key the user pressed or which window is being activated

Every event has an event record containing this information—even null events.

Event records are defined as follows:

```
TYPE EventRecord =  RECORD
                what:       INTEGER;    {event code}
                message:    LONGINT;    {event message}
                when:       LONGINT;    {ticks since startup}
                where:      Point;      {mouse location}
                modifiers:  INTEGER     {modifier flags}
            END;
```

The when field contains the number of ticks since the system last started up, and the where field gives the location of the mouse, in global coordinates, at the time the event was posted. The other three fields are described below.

Event Code

The what field of an event record contains an **event code** identifying the type of the event. The event codes are available as predefined constants:

```
CONST   nullEvent       = 0;    {null}
        mouseDown       = 1;    {mouse-down}
        mouseUp         = 2;    {mouse-up}
        keyDown         = 3;    {key-down}
        keyUp           = 4;    {key-up}
        autoKey         = 5;    {auto-key}
        updateEvt       = 6;    {update}
        diskEvt         = 7;    {disk-inserted}
        activateEvt     = 8;    {activate}
        networkEvt      = 10;   {network}
        driverEvt       = 11;   {device driver}
        app1Evt         = 12;   {application-defined}
        app2Evt         = 13;   {application-defined}
        app3Evt         = 14;   {application-defined}
        app4Evt         = 15;   {application-defined}
```

Inside Macintosh

Event Message

The message field of an event record contains the **event message**, which conveys additional important information about the event. The nature of this information depends on the event type, as summarized in the following table and described below.

Event type	Event message
Keyboard	Character code and key code in low-order word
Activate, update	Pointer to window
Disk-inserted	Drive number in low-order word, File Manager result code in high-order word
Mouse-down, mouse-up, null	Undefined
Network	Handle to parameter block
Device driver	See chapter describing driver
Application-defined	Whatever you wish

For keyboard events, only the low-order word of the event message is used, as shown in Figure 2. The low-order byte of this word contains the ASCII character code generated by the key or combination of keys that was pressed or released; usually this is all you'll need.

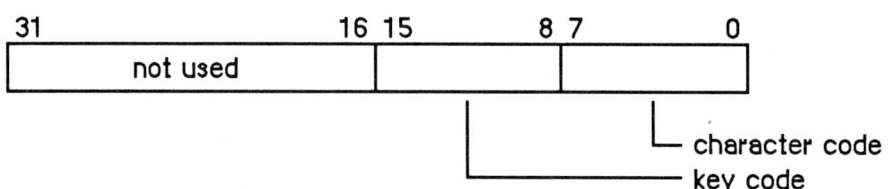

Figure 2. Event Message for Keyboard Events

The **key code** in the event message for a keyboard event represents the character key that was pressed or released; this value is always the same for any given character key, regardless of the modifier keys pressed along with it. Key codes are useful in special cases—in a music generator, for example—where you want to treat the keyboard as a set of keys unrelated to characters. Figure 3 gives the key codes for all the keys on the keyboard and keypad. (Key codes are shown for modifier keys here because they're meaningful in other contexts, as explained later.) Both the U.S. and international keyboards are shown; in some cases the codes are quite different (for example, space and Enter are reversed).

The following predefined constants are available to help you access the character code and key code:

```
CONST charCodeMask = $000000FF;   {character code}
      keyCodeMask  = $0000FF00;   {key code}
```

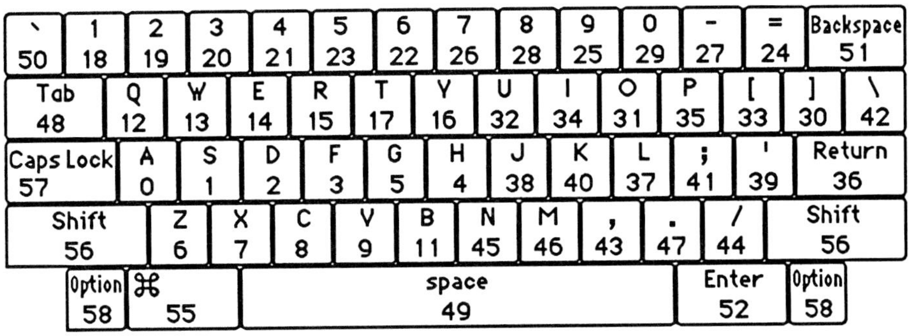

U.S. keyboard

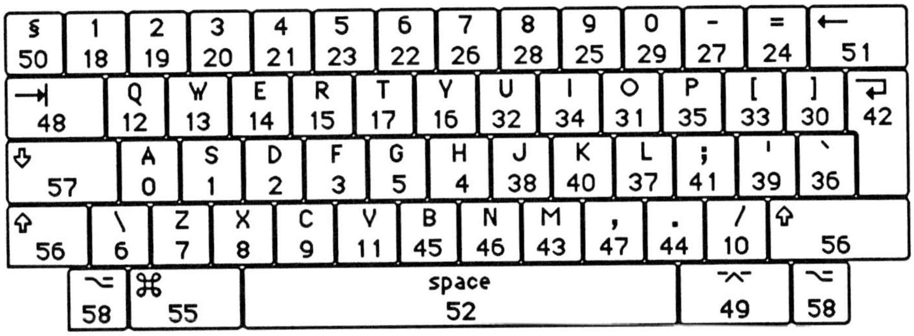

International keyboard (Great Britain key caps shown)

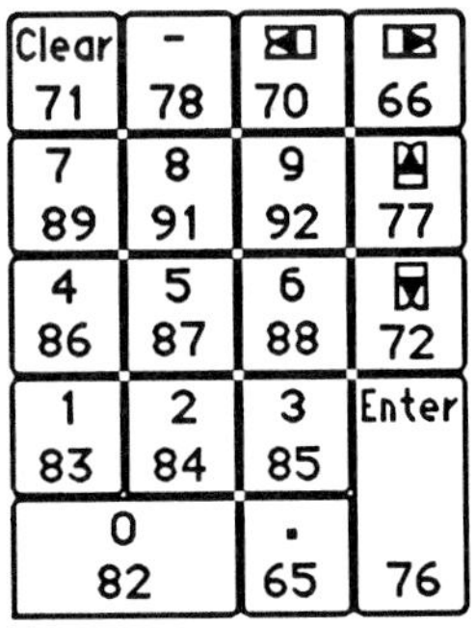

Keypad (U.S. key caps shown)

Figure 3. Key Codes

Note: You can use the Toolbox Utility function BitAnd with these constants; for instance, to access the character code, use

```
charCode := BitAnd(myEvent.message,charCodeMask)
```

Inside Macintosh

For activate and update events, the event message is a pointer to the window affected. (If the event is an activate event, additional important information about the event can be found in the modifiers field of the event record, as described below.)

For disk-inserted events, the low-order word of the event message contains the drive number of the disk drive into which the disk was inserted: 1 for the Macintosh's built-in drive, and 2 for the external drive, if any. Numbers greater than 2 denote additional disk drives connected to the Macintosh. By the time your application receives a disk-inserted event, the system will already have attempted to mount the volume on the disk by calling the File Manager function MountVol; the high-order word of the event message will contain the result code returned by MountVol.

For mouse-down, mouse-up, and null events, the event message is undefined and should be ignored. The event message for a network event contains a handle to a parameter block, as described in chapter 10 of Volume II. For device driver events, the contents of the event message depend on the situation under which the event was generated; the chapters describing those situations will give the details. Finally, you can use the event message however you wish for application-defined event types.

Modifier Flags

As mentioned above, the modifiers field of an event record contains further information about activate events and the state of the modifier keys and mouse button at the time the event was posted (see Figure 4). You might look at this field to find out, for instance, whether the Command key was down when a mouse-down event was posted (which in many applications affects the way objects are selected) or when a key-down event was posted (which could mean the user is choosing a menu item by typing its keyboard equivalent).

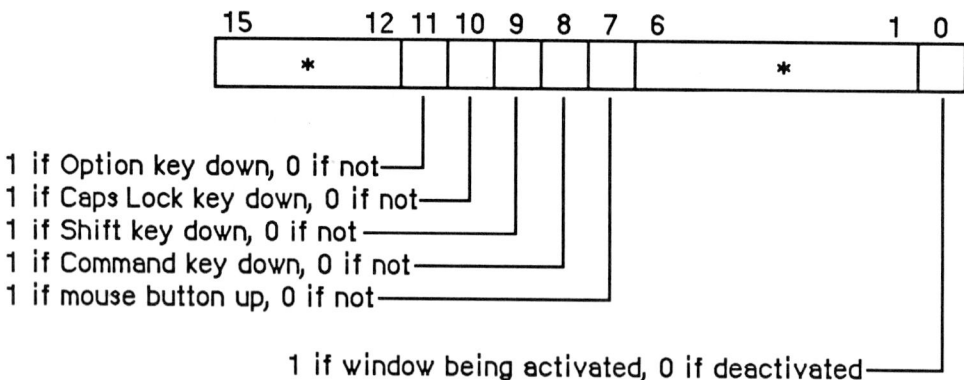

*reserved for future use

Figure 4. Modifier Flags

I-252 *Event Records*

The Toolbox Event Manager

The following predefined constants are useful as masks for reading the flags in the modifiers field:

```
CONST activeFlag = 1;    {set if window being activated}
      btnState   = 128;  {set if mouse button up}
      cmdKey     = 256;  {set if Command key down}
      shiftKey   = 512;  {set if Shift key down}
      alphaLock  = 1024; {set if Caps Lock key down}
      optionKey  = 2048; {set if Option key down}
```

The activeFlag bit gives further information about activate events; it's set if the window pointed to by the event message is being activated, or 0 if the window is being deactivated. The remaining bits indicate the state of the mouse button and modifier keys. Notice that the btnState bit is set if the mouse button is *up*, whereas the bits for the four modifier keys are set if their corresponding keys are *down*.

EVENT MASKS

Some of the Event Manager routines can be restricted to operate on a specific event type or group of types; in other words, the specified event types are enabled while all others are disabled. For instance, instead of just requesting the next available event, you can specifically ask for the next keyboard event.

You specify which event types a particular Event Manager call applies to by supplying an **event mask** as a parameter. This is an integer in which there's one bit position for each event type, as shown in Figure 5. The bit position representing a given type corresponds to the event code for that type—for example, update events (event code 6) are specified by bit 6 of the mask. A 1 in bit 6 means that this Event Manager call applies to update events; a 0 means that it doesn't.

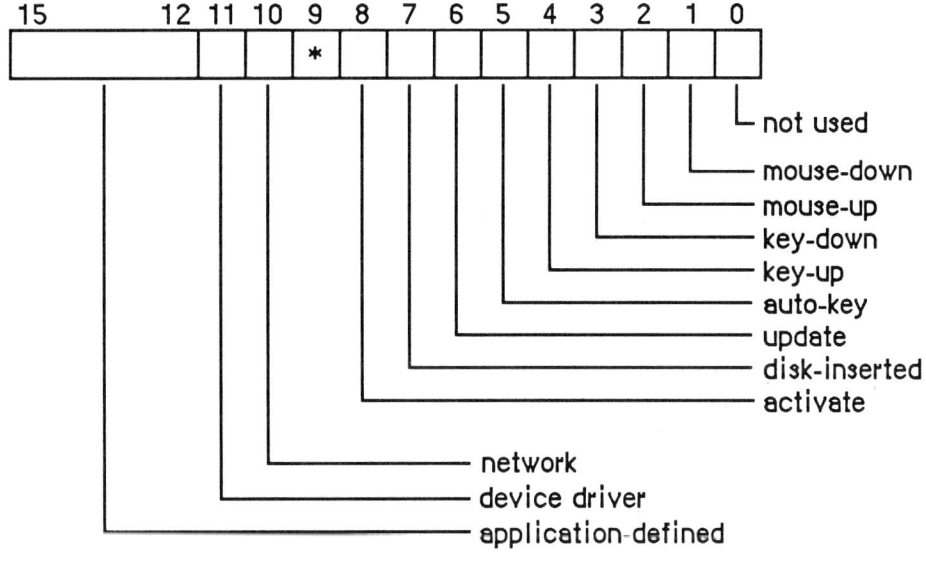

*reserved for future use

Figure 5. Event Mask

Inside Macintosh

Masks for each individual event type are available as predefined constants:

```
CONST mDownMask    =  2;          {mouse-down}
      mUpMask      =  4;          {mouse-up}
      keyDownMask  =  8;          {key-down}
      keyUpMask    =  16;         {key-up}
      autoKeyMask  =  32;         {auto-key}
      updateMask   =  64;         {update}
      diskMask     =  128;        {disk-inserted}
      activMask    =  256;        {activate}
      networkMask  =  1024;       {network}
      driverMask   =  2048;       {device driver}
      app1Mask     =  4096;       {application-defined}
      app2Mask     =  8192;       {application-defined}
      app3Mask     =  16384;      {application-defined}
      app4Mask     = -32768;      {application-defined}
```

Note: Null events can't be disabled; a null event will always be reported when none of the enabled types of events are available.

The following predefined mask designates all event types:

```
CONST everyEvent = -1;    {all event types}
```

You can form any mask you need by adding or subtracting these mask constants. For example, to specify every keyboard event, use

```
keyDownMask + keyUpMask + autoKeyMask
```

For every event except an update, use

```
everyEvent - updateMask
```

Note: It's recommended that you always use the event mask everyEvent unless there's a specific reason not to.

There's also a global **system event mask** that controls which event types get posted into the event queue. Only event types corresponding to bits set in the system event mask are posted; all others are ignored. When the system starts up, the system event mask is set to post all except key-up event—that is, it's initialized to

```
everyEvent - keyUpMask
```

Note: Key-up events are meaningless for most applications. Your application will usually want to ignore them; if not, it can set the system event mask with the Operating System Event Manager procedure SetEventMask.

USING THE TOOLBOX EVENT MANAGER

Before using the Event Manager, you should initialize the Window Manager by calling its procedure InitWindows; parts of the Event Manager rely on the Window Manager's data structures and will not work properly unless those structures have been properly initialized. Initializing the Window Manager requires you to have initialized QuickDraw and the Font Manager.

> **Assembly-language note:** If you want to use events but not windows, set the global variable WindowList (a long word) to 0 instead of calling InitWindows.

It's also usually a good idea to issue the Operating System Event Manager call FlushEvents(everyEvent,0) to empty the event queue of any stray events left over from before your application started up (such as keystrokes typed to the Finder). See chapter 3 of Volume II for a description of FlushEvents.

Most Macintosh application programs are event-driven. Such programs have a main loop that repeatedly calls GetNextEvent to retrieve the next available event, and then uses a CASE statement to take whatever action is appropriate for each type of event; some typical responses to commonly occurring events are described below. Your program is expected to respond only to those events that are directly related to its own operations. After calling GetNextEvent, you should test its Boolean result to find out whether your application needs to respond to the event: TRUE means the event may be of interest to your application; FALSE usually means it will not be of interest.

In some cases, you may simply want to look at a pending event while leaving it available for subsequent retrieval by GetNextEvent. You can do this with the EventAvail function.

Responding to Mouse Events

On receiving a mouse-down event, your application should first call the Window Manager function FindWindow to find out where on the screen the mouse button was pressed, and then respond in whatever way is appropriate. Depending on the part of the screen in which the button was pressed, this may involve calls to Toolbox routines such as the Menu Manager function MenuSelect, the Desk Manager procedure SystemClick, the Window Manager routines SelectWindow, DragWindow, GrowWindow, and TrackGoAway, and the Control Manager routines FindControl, TrackControl, and DragControl. See the relevant chapters for details.

If your application attaches some special significance to pressing a modifier key along with the mouse button, you can discover the state of that modifier key while the mouse button is down by examining the appropriate flag in the modifiers field.

If you're using the TextEdit part of the Toolbox to handle text editing, mouse double-clicks will work automatically as a means of selecting a word; to respond to double-clicks in any other context, however, you'll have to detect them yourself. You can do so by comparing the time and location of a mouse-up event with those of the immediately following mouse-down event. You should assume a double-click has occurred if both of the following are true:

- The times of the mouse-up event and the mouse-down event differ by a number of ticks less than or equal to the value returned by the Event Manager function GetDblTime.

- The locations of the two mouse-down events separated by the mouse-up event are sufficiently close to each other. Exactly what this means depends on the particular application. For instance, in a word-processing application, you might consider the two locations essentially the same if they fall on the same character, whereas in a graphics application you might consider them essentially the same if the sum of the horizontal and vertical changes in position is no more than five pixels.

Mouse-up events may be significant in other ways; for example, they might signal the end of dragging to select more than one object. Most simple applications, however, will ignore mouse-up events.

Responding to Keyboard Events

For a key-down event, you should first check the modifiers field to see whether the character was typed with the Command key held down; if so, the user may have been choosing a menu item by typing its keyboard equivalent. To find out, pass the character that was typed to the Menu Manager function MenuKey. (See chapter 11 for details.)

If the key-down event was not a menu command, you should then respond to the event in whatever way is appropriate for your application. For example, if one of your windows is active, you might want to insert the typed character into the active document; if none of your windows is active, you might want to ignore the event.

Usually your application can handle auto-key events the same as key-down events. You may, however, want to ignore auto-key events that invoke commands that shouldn't be continually repeated.

Note: Remember that most applications will want to ignore key-up events; with the standard system event mask you won't get any.

If you wish to periodically inspect the state of the keyboard or keypad—say, while the mouse button is being held down—use the procedure GetKeys; this procedure is also the only way to tell whether a modifier key is being pressed alone.

Responding to Activate and Update Events

When your application receives an activate event for one of its own windows, the Window Manager will already have done all of the normal "housekeeping" associated with the event, such as highlighting or unhighlighting the window. You can then take any further action that your application may require, such as showing or hiding a scroll bar or highlighting or unhighlighting a selection.

On receiving an update event for one of its own windows, your application should usually call the Window Manager procedure BeginUpdate, draw the window's contents, and then call EndUpdate. See chapter 9 for important additional information on activate and update events.

Responding to Disk-Inserted Events

Most applications will use the Standard File Package, which responds to disk-inserted events for you during standard file saving and opening; you'll usually want to ignore any other disk-inserted events, such as the user's inserting a disk when not expected. If, however, you do want to respond to other disk-inserted events, or if you plan not to use the Standard File Package, then you'll have to handle such events yourself.

When you receive a disk-inserted event, the system will already have attempted to mount the volume on the disk by calling the File Manager function MountVol. You should examine the result code returned by the File Manager in the high-order word of the event message. If the result code indicates that the attempt to mount the volume was unsuccessful, you might want to take some special action, such as calling the Disk Initialization Package function DIBadMount. See chapters 4 and 14 of Volume II for further details.

Other Operations

In addition to receiving the user's mouse and keyboard actions in the form of events, you can directly read the keyboard (and keypad), mouse location, and state of the mouse button by calling GetKeys, GetMouse, and Button, respectively. To follow the mouse when the user moves it with the button down, use StillDown or WaitMouseUp.

The function TickCount returns the number of ticks since the last system startup; you might, for example, compare this value to the when field of an event record to discover the delay since that event was posted.

Finally, the function GetCaretTime returns the number of ticks between blinks of the "caret" (usually a vertical bar) marking the insertion point in editable text. You should call GetCaretTime if you aren't using TextEdit and therefore need to cause the caret to blink yourself. You would check this value each time through your program's main event loop, to ensure a constant frequency of blinking.

TOOLBOX EVENT MANAGER ROUTINES

Accessing Events

```
FUNCTION GetNextEvent (eventMask: INTEGER; VAR theEvent:
        EventRecord) : BOOLEAN;
```

GetNextEvent returns the next available event of a specified type or types and, if the event is in the event queue, removes it from the queue. The event is returned in the parameter theEvent. The eventMask parameter specifies which event types are of interest. GetNextEvent returns the next available event of any type designated by the mask, subject to the priority rules discussed above under "Priority of Events". If no event of any of the designated types is available, GetNextEvent returns a null event.

Inside Macintosh

Note: Events in the queue that aren't designated in the mask are kept in the queue; if you want to remove them, you can do so by calling the Operating System Event Manager procedure FlushEvents.

Before reporting an event to your application, GetNextEvent first calls the Desk Manager function SystemEvent to see whether the system wants to intercept and respond to the event. If so, or if the event being reported is a null event, GetNextEvent returns a function result of FALSE; a function result of TRUE means that your application should handle the event itself. The Desk Manager intercepts the following events:

- activate and update events directed to a desk accessory
- mouse-up and keyboard events, if the currently active window belongs to a desk accessory

Note: In each case, the event is intercepted by the Desk Manager only if the desk accessory can handle that type of event; however, as a rule all desk accessories should be set up to handle activate, update, and keyboard events and should not handle mouse-up events.

The Desk Manager also intercepts disk-inserted events: It attempts to mount the volume on the disk by calling the File Manager function MountVol. GetNextEvent will always return TRUE in this case, though, so that your application can take any further appropriate action after examining the result code returned by MountVol in the event message. (See chapter 14 of Volume I and chapter 4 of Volume II for further details.) GetNextEvent returns TRUE for all other non-null events (including all mouse-down events, regardless of which window is active), leaving them for your application to handle.

GetNextEvent also makes the following processing happen, invisible to your program:

- If the "alarm" is set and the current time is the alarm time, the alarm goes off (a beep followed by blinking the apple symbol in the menu bar). The user can set the alarm with the Alarm Clock desk accessory.
- If the user holds down the Command and Shift keys while pressing a numeric key that has a special effect, that effect occurs. The standard such keys are 1 and 2 for ejecting the disk in the internal or external drive, and 3 and 4 for writing a snapshot of the screen to a MacPaint document or to the printer.

Note: Advanced programmers can implement their own code to be executed in response to Command-Shift-number combinations (except for Command-Shift-1 and 2, which can't be changed). The code corresponding to a particular number must be a routine having no parameters, stored in a resource whose type is 'FKEY' and whose ID is the number. The system resource file contains code for the numbers 3 and 4.

Assembly-language note: You can disable GetNextEvent's processing of Command-Shift-number combinations by setting the global variable ScrDmpEnb (a byte) to 0.

The Toolbox Event Manager

```
FUNCTION EventAvail (eventMask: INTEGER; VAR theEvent:
            EventRecord) : BOOLEAN;
```

EventAvail works exactly the same as GetNextEvent except that if the event is in the event queue, it's left there.

Note: An event returned by EventAvail will not be accessible later if in the meantime the queue becomes full and the event is discarded from it; since the events discarded are always the oldest ones in the queue, however, this will happen only in an unusually busy environment.

Reading the Mouse

```
PROCEDURE GetMouse (VAR mouseLoc: Point);
```

GetMouse returns the current mouse location in the mouseLoc parameter. The location is given in the local coordinate system of the current grafPort (which might be, for example, the currently active window). Notice that this differs from the mouse location stored in the where field of an event record; that location is always in global coordinates.

```
FUNCTION Button : BOOLEAN;
```

The Button function returns TRUE if the mouse button is currently down, and FALSE if it isn't.

```
FUNCTION StillDown : BOOLEAN;
```

Usually called after a mouse-down event, StillDown tests whether the mouse button is still down. It returns TRUE if the button is currently down and there are no more mouse events pending in the event queue. This is a true test of whether the button is still down from the original press—unlike Button (above), which returns TRUE whenever the button is currently down, even if it has been released and pressed again since the original mouse-down event.

```
FUNCTION WaitMouseUp : BOOLEAN;
```

WaitMouseUp works exactly the same as StillDown (above), except that if the button is not still down from the original press, WaitMouseUp removes the preceding mouse-up event before returning FALSE. If, for instance, your application attaches some special significance both to mouse double-clicks and to mouse-up events, this function would allow your application to recognize a double-click without being confused by the intervening mouse-up.

Reading the Keyboard and Keypad

```
PROCEDURE GetKeys (VAR theKeys: KeyMap);
```

GetKeys reads the current state of the keyboard (and keypad, if any) and returns it in the form of a keyMap:

Inside Macintosh

```
TYPE KeyMap = PACKED ARRAY[0..127] OF BOOLEAN;
```

Each key on the keyboard or keypad corresponds to an element in the keyMap. The index into the keyMap for a particular key is the same as the key code for that key. (The key codes are shown in Figure 3 above.) The keyMap element is TRUE if the corresponding key is down and FALSE if it isn't. The maximum number of keys that can be down simultaneously is two character keys plus any combination of the four modifier keys.

Miscellaneous Routines

```
FUNCTION TickCount : LONGINT;
```

TickCount returns the current number of ticks (sixtieths of a second) since the system last started up.

> **Warning:** Don't rely on the tick count being exact; it will usually be accurate to within one tick, but may be off by more than that. The tick count is incremented during the vertical retrace interrupt, but it's possible for this interrupt to be disabled. Furthermore, don't rely on the tick count being incremented to a certain value, such as testing whether it has become equal to its old value plus 1; check instead for "greater than or equal to" (since an interrupt task may keep control for more than one tick).

> **Assembly-language note:** The value returned by this function is also contained in the global variable Ticks.

```
FUNCTION GetDblTime : LONGINT;    [Not in ROM]
```

GetDblTime returns the suggested maximum difference (in ticks) that should exist between the times of a mouse-up event and a mouse-down event for those two mouse clicks to be considered a double-click. The user can adjust this value by means of the Control Panel desk accessory.

> **Assembly-language note:** This value is available to assembly-language programmers in the global variable DoubleTime.

```
FUNCTION GetCaretTime : LONGINT;    [Not in ROM]
```

GetCaretTime returns the time (in ticks) between blinks of the "caret" (usually a vertical bar) marking the insertion point in editable text. If you aren't using TextEdit, you'll need to cause the caret to blink yourself; on every pass through your program's main event loop, you should check this value against the elapsed time since the last blink of the caret. The user can adjust this value by means of the Control Panel desk accessory.

> **Assembly-language note:** This value is available to assembly-language programmers in the global variable CaretTime.

THE JOURNALING MECHANISM

So far, this chapter has described the Event Manager as responding to events generated by users—keypresses, mouse clicks, disk insertions, and so on. By using the Event Manager's journaling mechanism, though, you can "decouple" the Event Manager from the user and feed it events from some other source. Such a source might be a file into which have been recorded all the events that occurred during some portion of a user's session with the Macintosh. This section briefly describes the journaling mechanism and some examples of its use, and then gives the technical information you'll need if you want to use this mechanism yourself.

Note: The journaling mechanism can be accessed only through assembly language; Pascal programmers may want to skip this discussion.

In the usual sense, "journaling" means the recording of a sequence of user-generated events into a file; specifically, this file is a recording of all calls to the Event Manager routines GetNextEvent, EventAvail, GetMouse, Button, GetKeys, and TickCount. When a journal is being recorded, every call to any of these routines is sent to a journaling device driver, which records the call (and the results of the call) in a file. When the journal is played back, these recorded Event Manager calls are taken from the journal file and sent directly to the Event Manager. The result is that the recorded sequence of user-generated events is reproduced when the journal is played back. The Macintosh Guided Tour is an example of such a journal.

Using the journaling mechanism need not involve a file. Before Macintosh was introduced, Macintosh Software Engineering created a special desk accessory of its own for testing Macintosh software. This desk accessory, which was based on the journaling mechanism, didn't use a file—it generated events randomly, putting Macintosh "through its paces" for long periods of time without requiring a user's attention.

So, the Event Manager's journaling mechanism has a much broader utility than a mechanism simply for "journaling" as it's normally defined. With the journaling mechanism, you can decouple the Event Manager from the user and feed it events from a journaling device driver of your own design. Figure 6 illustrates what happens when the journaling mechanism is off, in recording mode, and in playback mode.

Writing Your Own Journaling Device Driver

If you want to implement journaling in a new way, you'll need to write your own journaling device driver. Details about how to do this are given below; however, you must already have read about writing your own device driver in chapter 6 of Volume II. Furthermore, if you want to implement your journaling device driver as a desk accessory, you'll have to be familiar with details given in chapter 14.

Whenever a call is made to any of the Event Manager routines GetNextEvent, EventAvail, GetMouse, Button, GetKeys, and TickCount, the information returned by the routine is passed to the journaling device driver by means of a Control call. The routine makes the Control call to the journaling device driver with the reference number stored in the global variable JournalRef; the journaling device driver should put its reference number in this variable when it's opened.

You control whether the journaling mechanism is playing or recording by setting the global variable JournalFlag to a negative or positive value. Before the Event Manager routine makes the

Inside Macintosh

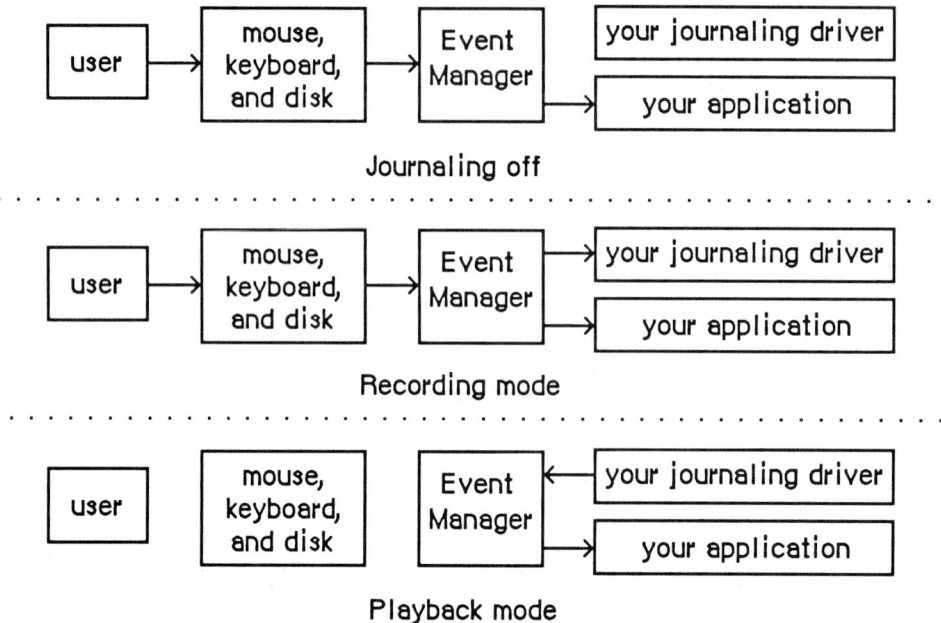

Figure 6. The Journaling Mechanism

Control call, it copies one of the following global constants into the csCode parameter of the Control call, depending on the value of JournalFlag:

JournalFlag	Value of csCode	Meaning
Negative	jPlayCtl .EQU 16	Journal in playback mode
Positive	jRecordCtl .EQU 17	Journal in recording mode

If you set the value of JournalFlag to 0, the Control call won't be made at all.

Before the Event Manager routine makes the Control call, it copies into csParam a pointer to the actual data being polled by the routine (for example, a pointer to a keyMap for GetKeys, or a pointer to an event record for GetNextEvent). It also copies, into csParam+4, a **journal code** designating which routine is making the call:

Control call made during:	csParam contains pointer to:	Journal code at csParam+4:		
TickCount	Long word	jcTickCount	.EQU	0
GetMouse	Point	jcGetMouse	.EQU	1
Button	Boolean	jcButton	.EQU	2
GetKeys	KeyMap	jcGetKeys	.EQU	3
GetNextEvent	Event record	jcEvent	.EQU	4
EventAvail	Event record	jcEvent	.EQU	4

SUMMARY OF THE TOOLBOX EVENT MANAGER

Constants

```
CONST { Event codes }

    nullEvent    = 0;      {null}
    mouseDown    = 1;      {mouse-down}
    mouseUp      = 2;      {mouse-up}
    keyDown      = 3;      {key-down}
    keyUp        = 4;      {key-up}
    autoKey      = 5;      {auto-key}
    updateEvt    = 6;      {update}
    diskEvt      = 7;      {disk-inserted}
    activateEvt  = 8;      {activate}
    networkEvt   = 10;     {network}
    driverEvt    = 11;     {device driver}
    app1Evt      = 12;     {application-defined}
    app2Evt      = 13;     {application-defined}
    app3Evt      = 14;     {application-defined}
    app4Evt      = 15;     {application-defined}

    { Masks for keyboard event message }

    charCodeMask = $000000FF;  {character code}
    keyCodeMask  = $0000FF00;  {key code}

    { Masks for forming event mask }

    mDownMask    = 2;      {mouse-down}
    mUpMask      = 4;      {mouse-up}
    keyDownMask  = 8;      {key-down}
    keyUpMask    = 16;     {key-up}
    autoKeyMask  = 32;     {auto-key}
    updateMask   = 64;     {update}
    diskMask     = 128;    {disk-inserted}
    activMask    = 256;    {activate}
    networkMask  = 1024;   {network}
    driverMask   = 2048;   {device driver}
    app1Mask     = 4096;   {application-defined}
    app2Mask     = 8192;   {application-defined}
    app3Mask     = 16384;  {application-defined}
    app4Mask     = -32768; {application-defined}
    everyEvent   = -1;     {all event types}
```

Inside Macintosh

```
{ Modifier flags in event record }

activeFlag  = 1;     {set if window being activated}
btnState    = 128;   {set if mouse button up}
cmdKey      = 256;   {set if Command key down}
shiftKey    = 512;   {set if Shift key down}
alphaLock   = 1024;  {set if Caps Lock key down}
optionKey   = 2048;  {set if Option key down}
```

Data Types

```
TYPE EventRecord =  RECORD
                      what:       INTEGER;    {event code}
                      message:    LONGINT;    {event message}
                      where:      Point;      {mouse location}
                      modifiers:  INTEGER     {modifier flags}
                    END;

     KeyMap = PACKED ARRAY[0..127] OF BOOLEAN;
```

Routines

Accessing Events

```
FUNCTION GetNextEvent (eventMask: INTEGER; VAR theEvent: EventRecord) :
                      BOOLEAN;
FUNCTION EventAvail   (eventMask: INTEGER; VAR theEvent: EventRecord) :
                      BOOLEAN;
```

Reading the Mouse

```
PROCEDURE GetMouse      (VAR mouseLoc: Point);
FUNCTION  Button :      BOOLEAN;
FUNCTION  StillDown :   BOOLEAN;
FUNCTION  WaitMouseUp : BOOLEAN;
```

Reading the Keyboard and Keypad

```
PROCEDURE GetKeys (VAR theKeys: KeyMap);
```

Miscellaneous Routines

```
FUNCTION TickCount     : LONGINT;
FUNCTION GetDblTime    : LONGINT;   [Not in ROM]
FUNCTION GetCaretTime  : LONGINT;   [Not in ROM]
```

Event Message in Event Record

Event type	Event message
Keyboard	Character code and key code in low-order word
Activate, update	Pointer to window
Disk-inserted	Drive number in low-order word, File Manager result code in high-order word
Mouse-down, mouse-up, null	Undefined
Network	Handle to parameter block
Device driver	See chapter describing driver
Application-defined	Whatever you wish

Assembly-Language Information

Constants

```
; Event codes

nullEvt         .EQU    0       ;null
mButDwnEvt      .EQU    1       ;mouse-down
mButUpEvt       .EQU    2       ;mouse-up
keyDwnEvt       .EQU    3       ;key-down
keyUpEvt        .EQU    4       ;key-up
autoKeyEvt      .EQU    5       ;auto-key
updatEvt        .EQU    6       ;update
diskInsertEvt   .EQU    7       ;disk-inserted
activateEvt     .EQU    8       ;activate
networkEvt      .EQU    10      ;network
ioDrvrEvt       .EQU    11      ;device driver
app1Evt         .EQU    12      ;application-defined
app2Evt         .EQU    13      ;application-defined
app3Evt         .EQU    14      ;application-defined
app4Evt         .EQU    15      ;application-defined

; Modifier flags in event record

activeFlag      .EQU    0       ;set if window being activated
btnState        .EQU    2       ;set if mouse button up
cmdKey          .EQU    3       ;set if Command key down
shiftKey        .EQU    4       ;set if Shift key down
alphaLock       .EQU    5       ;set if Caps Lock key down
optionKey       .EQU    6       ;set if Option key down
```

```
; Journaling mechanism Control call

jPlayCtl      .EQU  16    ;journal in playback mode
jRecordCtl    .EQU  17    ;journal in recording mode
jcTickCount   .EQU  0     ;journal code for TickCount
jcGetMouse    .EQU  1     ;journal code for GetMouse
jcButton      .EQU  2     ;journal code for Button
jcGetKeys     .EQU  3     ;journal code for GetKeys
jcEvent       .EQU  4     ;journal code for GetNextEvent and EventAvail
```

Event Record Data Structure

evtNum	Event code (word)
evtMessage	Event message (long)
evtTicks	Ticks since startup (long)
evtMouse	Mouse location (point; long)
evtMeta	State of modifier keys (byte)
evtMBut	State of mouse button (byte)
evtBlkSize	Size in bytes of event record

Variables

KeyThresh	Auto-key threshold (word)
KeyRepThresh	Auto-key rate (word)
WindowList	0 if using events but not windows (long)
ScrDmpEnb	0 if GetNextEvent shouldn't process Command-Shift-number combinations (byte)
Ticks	Current number of ticks since system startup (long)
DoubleTime	Double-click interval in ticks (long)
CaretTime	Caret-blink interval in ticks (long)
JournalRef	Reference number of journaling device driver (word)
JournalFlag	Journaling mode (word)

9 THE WINDOW MANAGER

269	About This Chapter
269	About the Window Manager
271	Windows and GrafPorts
271	Window Regions
272	Windows and Resources
274	Window Records
275	Window Pointers
276	The WindowRecord Data Type
278	How a Window is Drawn
279	Making a Window Active: Activate Events
280	Using the Window Manager
281	Window Manager Routines
281	Initialization and Allocation
284	Window Display
287	Mouse Location
289	Window Movement and Sizing
291	Update Region Maintenance
293	Miscellaneous Routines
295	Low-Level Routines
297	Defining Your Own Windows
298	The Window Definition Function
299	The Draw Window Frame Routine
300	The Hit Routine
301	The Routine to Calculate Regions
301	The Initialize Routine
301	The Dispose Routine
301	The Grow Routine
302	The Draw Size Box Routine
302	Formats of Resources for Windows
303	Summary of the Window Manager

ABOUT THIS CHAPTER

The Window Manager is the part of the Toolbox that allows you to create, manipulate, and dispose of windows. This chapter describes the Window Manager in detail.

You should already be familiar with:

- Resources, as discussed in chapter 5.
- The basic concepts and structures behind QuickDraw, particularly points, rectangles, regions, grafPorts, and pictures. You don't have to know the QuickDraw routines in order to use the Window Manager, though you'll be using QuickDraw to draw inside a window.
- The Toolbox Event Manager.

ABOUT THE WINDOW MANAGER

The Window Manager is a tool for dealing with windows on the Macintosh screen. The screen represents a working surface or **desktop**; graphic objects appear on the desktop and can be manipulated with the mouse. A **window** is an object on the desktop that presents information, such as a document or a message. Windows can be any size or shape, and there can be one or many of them, depending on the application.

Some standard types of windows are predefined. One of these is the **document window**, as illustrated in Figure 1. Every document window has a 20-pixel-high title bar containing a title that's centered and in the system font and system font size. In addition, a particular document window may or may not have a close box or a size box; you'll learn in this chapter how to implement them. There may also be scroll bars along the bottom and/or right edge of a document window. Scroll bars are controls, and are supported by the Control Manager.

Figure 1. An Active Document Window

Your application can easily create standard types of windows such as document windows, and can also define its own types of windows. Some windows may be created indirectly for you

Inside Macintosh

when you use other parts of the Toolbox; an example is the window the Dialog Manager creates to display an alert box. Windows created either directly or indirectly by an application are collectively called **application windows**. There's also a class of windows called **system windows**; these are the windows in which desk accessories are displayed.

The document window shown in Figure 1 is the **active** (frontmost) window, the one that will be acted on when the user types, gives commands, or whatever is appropriate to the application being used. Its title bar is **highlighted**—displayed in a distinctive visual way—so that the window will stand out from other, **inactive** windows that may be on the screen. Since a close box, size box, and scroll bars will have an effect only in an active window, none of them appear in an inactive window (see Figure 2).

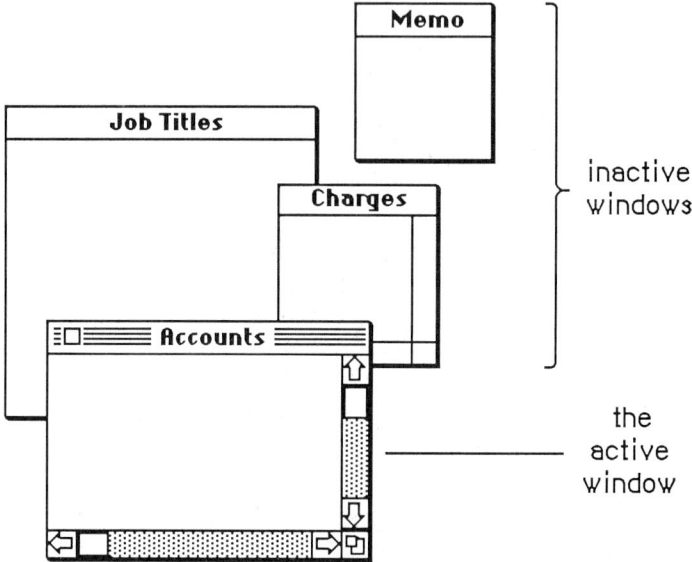

Figure 2. Overlapping Document Windows

Note: If a document window has neither a size box nor scroll bars, the lines delimiting those areas aren't drawn, as in the Memo window in Figure 2.

An important function of the Window Manager is to keep track of overlapping windows. You can draw in any window without running over onto windows in front of it. You can move windows to different places on the screen, change their plane (their front-to-back ordering), or change their size, all without concern for how the various windows overlap. The Window Manager keeps track of any newly exposed areas and provides a convenient mechanism for you to ensure that they're properly redrawn.

Finally, you can easily set up your application so that mouse actions cause these standard responses inside a document window, or similar responses inside other windows:

- Clicking anywhere in an inactive window makes it the active window by bringing it to the front and highlighting its title bar.

- Clicking inside the close box of the active window closes the window. Depending on the application, this may mean that the window disappears altogether, or a representation of the window (such as an icon) may be left on the desktop.

The Window Manager

- Dragging anywhere inside the title bar of a window (except in the close box, if any) pulls an outline of the window across the screen, and releasing the mouse button moves the window to the new location. If the window isn't the active window, it becomes the active window unless the Command key was also held down. A window can never be moved completely off the screen; by convention, it can't be moved such that the visible area of the title bar is less than four pixels square.

- Dragging inside the size box of the active window changes the size of the window.

WINDOWS AND GRAFPORTS

It's easy for applications to use windows: To the application, a window is a grafPort that it can draw into like any other with QuickDraw routines. When you create a window, you specify a rectangle that becomes the portRect of the grafPort in which the window contents will be drawn. The bit map for this grafPort, its pen pattern, and other characteristics are the same as the default values set by QuickDraw, except for the character font, which is set to the application font. These characteristics will apply whenever the application draws in the window, and they can easily be changed with QuickDraw routines (SetPort to make the grafPort the current port, and other routines as appropriate).

There is, however, more to a window than just the grafPort that the application draws in. In a standard document window, for example, the title bar and outline of the window are drawn by the Window Manager, not by the application. The part of a window that the Window Manager draws is called the **window frame**, since it usually surrounds the rest of the window. For drawing window frames, the Window Manager creates a grafPort that has the entire screen as its portRect; this grafPort is called the **Window Manager port**.

WINDOW REGIONS

Every window has the following two regions:

- the **content region**: the area that your application draws in
- the **structure region**: the entire window; its complete "structure" (the content region plus the window frame)

The content region is bounded by the rectangle you specify when you create the window (that is, the portRect of the window's grafPort); for a document window, it's the entire portRect. This is where your application presents information and where the size box and scroll bars of a document window are located.

A window may also have any of the regions listed below. Clicking or dragging in one of these regions causes the indicated action.

- A **go-away region** within the window frame. Clicking in this region of the active window closes the window.
- A **drag region** within the window frame. Dragging in this region pulls an outline of the window across the screen, moves the window to a new location, and makes it the active window (if it isn't already) unless the Command key was held down.

Inside Macintosh

- A **grow region**, usually within the content region. Dragging in this region of the active window changes the size of the window. In a document window, the grow region is in the content region, but in windows of your own design it may be in either the content region or the window frame.

Clicking in any region of an inactive window simply makes it the active window.

Note: The results of clicking and dragging that are discussed here don't happen automatically; you have to make the right Window Manager calls to cause them to happen.

Figure 3 illustrates the various regions of a standard document window and its window frame.

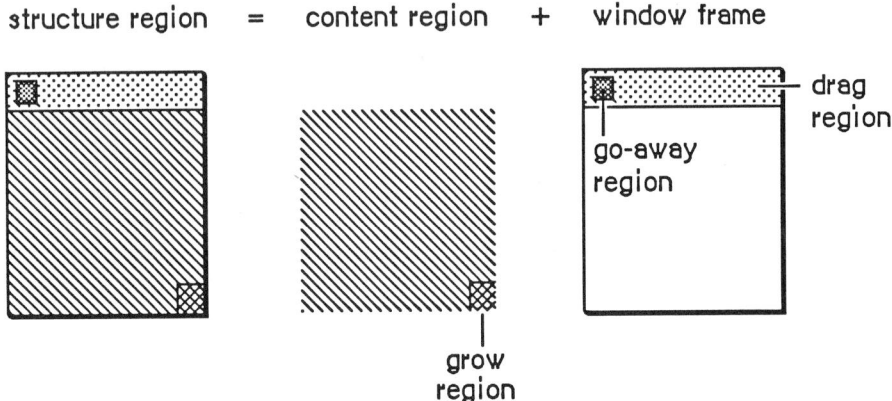

Figure 3. Document Window Regions and Frame

An example of a window that has no drag region is the window that displays an alert box. On the other hand, you could design a window whose drag region is the entire structure region and whose content region is empty; such a window might present a fixed picture rather than information that's to be manipulated.

Another important window region is the **update region**. Unlike the regions described above, the update region is dynamic rather than fixed: The Window Manager keeps track of all areas of the content region that have to be redrawn and accumulates them into the update region. For example, if you bring to the front a window that was overlapped by another window, the Window Manager adds the formerly overlapped (now exposed) area of the front window's content region to its update region. You'll also accumulate areas into the update region yourself; the Window Manager provides update region maintenance routines for this purpose.

WINDOWS AND RESOURCES

The general appearance and behavior of a window is determined by a routine called its **window definition function**, which is stored as a resource in a resource file. The window definition function performs all actions that differ from one window type to another, such as drawing the window frame. The Window Manager calls the window definition function whenever it needs to perform one of these type-dependent actions (passing it a message that tells which action to perform).

The system resource file includes window definition functions for the standard document window and other standard types of windows. If you want to define your own, nonstandard window types, you'll have to write window definition functions for them, as described later in the section "Defining Your Own Windows".

When you create a window, you specify its type with a **window definition ID,** which tells the Window Manager the resource ID of the definition function for that type of window. You can use one of the following constants as a window definition ID to refer to a standard type of window (see Figure 4):

```
CONST  documentProc   = 0;    {standard document window}
       dBoxProc       = 1;    {alert box or modal dialog box}
       plainDBox      = 2;    {plain box}
       altDBoxProc    = 3;    {plain box with shadow}
       noGrowDocProc  = 4;    {document window without size box}
       rDocProc       = 16;   {rounded-corner window}
```

Figure 4. Standard Types of Windows

DocumentProc represents a standard document window that may or may not contain a size box; noGrowDocProc is exactly the same except that the window must *not* contain a size box. If you're working with a number of document windows that need to be treated similarly, but some will have size boxes and some won't, you can use documentProc for all of them. If none of the windows will have size boxes, however, it's more convenient to use noGrowDocProc.

The dBoxProc type of window resembles an alert box or a "modal" dialog box (the kind that requires the user to respond before doing any other work on the desktop). It's a rectangular window with no go-away region, drag region, or grow region and with a two-pixel-thick border two pixels in from the edge. It has no special highlighted state because alerts and modal dialogs are always displayed in the frontmost window. PlainDBox and altDBoxProc are variations of dBoxProc: plainDBox is just a plain box with no inner border, and altDBoxProc has a two-pixel-thick shadow instead of a border.

The rDocProc type of window is like a document window with no grow region, with rounded corners, and with a method of highlighting that inverts the entire title bar (that is, changes white to black and vice versa). It's often used for desk accessories. Rounded-corner windows are drawn by the QuickDraw procedure FrameRoundRect, which requires the diameters of curvature to be passed as parameters. For an rDocProc type of window, the diameters of curvature are both 16. You can add a number from 1 to 7 to rDocProc to get different diameters:

Window definition ID	Diameters of curvature
rDocProc	16, 16
rDocProc + 1	4, 4
rDocProc + 2	6, 6
rDocProc + 3	8, 8
rDocProc + 4	10, 10
rDocProc + 5	12, 12
rDocProc + 6	20, 20
rDocProc + 7	24, 24

To create a window, the Window Manager needs to know not only the window definition ID but also other information specific to this window, such as its title (if any), its location, and its plane. You can supply all the needed information in individual parameters to a Window Manager routine or, better yet, you can store it as a single resource in a resource file and just pass the resource ID. This type of resource is called a **window template**. Using window templates simplifies the process of creating a number of windows of the same type. More important, it allows you to isolate specific window descriptions from your application's code. Translation of window titles to another language, for example, would require only a change to the resource file.

WINDOW RECORDS

The Window Manager keeps all the information it requires for its operations on a particular window in a **window record**. The window record contains the following:

- The grafPort for the window.
- A handle to the window definition function.
- A handle to the window's title, if any.
- The **window class**, which tells whether the window is a system window, a dialog or alert window, or a window created directly by the application.
- A handle to the window's **control list**, which is a list of all the controls, if any, in the window. The Control Manager maintains this list.
- A pointer to the next window in the **window list**, which is a list of all windows on the desktop ordered according to their front-to-back positions.

The window record also contains an indication of whether the window is currently **visible** or **invisible**. These terms refer only to whether the window is drawn in its plane, not necessarily whether you can see it on the screen. If, for example, it's completely overlapped by another window, it's still "visible" even though it can't be seen in its current location.

The 32-bit **reference value** field of the window record is reserved for use by your application. You specify an initial reference value when you create a window, and can then read or change the

The Window Manager

reference value whenever you wish. For example, it might be a handle to data associated with the window, such as a TextEdit edit record.

Finally, a window record may contain a handle to a QuickDraw picture of the window contents. For a window whose contents never change, the application can simply have the Window Manager redraw this picture instead of using the update event mechanism. For more information, see "How a Window is Drawn".

The data type for a window record is called WindowRecord. A window record is referred to by a pointer, as discussed further under "Window Pointers" below. You can store into and access most of the fields of a window record with Window Manager routines, so normally you don't have to know the exact field names. Occasionally—particularly if you define your own type of window—you may need to know the exact structure; it's given below under "The WindowRecord Data Type".

Window Pointers

There are two types of pointer through which you can access windows: WindowPtr and WindowPeek. Most programmers will only need to use WindowPtr.

The Window Manager defines the following type of window pointer:

```
TYPE WindowPtr = GrafPtr;
```

It can do this because the first field of a window record contains the window's grafPort. This type of pointer can be used to access fields of the grafPort or can be passed to QuickDraw routines that expect pointers to grafPorts as parameters. The application might call such routines to draw into the window, and the Window Manager itself calls them to perform many of its operations. The Window Manager gets the additional information it needs from the rest of the window record beyond the grafPort.

In some cases, however, a more direct way of accessing the window record may be necessary or desirable. For this reason, the Window Manager also defines the following type of window pointer:

```
TYPE WindowPeek = ^WindowRecord;
```

Programmers who want to access WindowRecord fields directly must use this type of pointer (which derives its name from the fact that it lets you "peek" at the additional information about the window). A WindowPeek pointer is also used wherever the Window Manager will not be calling QuickDraw routines and will benefit from a more direct means of getting to the data stored in the window record.

Assembly-language note: From assembly language, of course, there's no type checking on pointers, and the two types of pointer are equal.

Inside Macintosh

The WindowRecord Data Type

The exact data structure of a window record is as follows:

```
TYPE WindowRecord =
         RECORD
            port:          GrafPort;         {window's grafPort}
            windowKind:    INTEGER;          {window class}
            visible:       BOOLEAN;          {TRUE if visible}
            hilited:       BOOLEAN;          {TRUE if highlighted}
            goAwayFlag:    BOOLEAN;          {TRUE if has go-away region}
            spareFlag:     BOOLEAN;          {reserved for future use}
            strucRgn:      RgnHandle;        {structure region}
            contRgn:       RgnHandle;        {content region}
            updateRgn:     RgnHandle;        {update region}
            windowDefProc: Handle;           {window definition function}
            dataHandle:    Handle;           {data used by windowDefProc}
            titleHandle:   StringHandle;     {window's title}
            titleWidth:    INTEGER;          {width of title in pixels}
            controlList:   ControlHandle;    {window's control list}
            nextWindow:    WindowPeek;       {next window in window list}
            windowPic:     PicHandle;        {picture for drawing window}
            refCon:        LONGINT           {window's reference value}
         END;
```

The port is the window's grafPort.

WindowKind identifies the window class. If negative, it means the window is a system window (it's the desk accessory's reference number, as described in chapter 14). It may also be one of the following predefined constants:

```
CONST dialogKind = 2;   {dialog or alert window}
      userKind   = 8;   {window created directly by the application}
```

DialogKind is the window class for a dialog or alert window, whether created by the system or indirectly (via the Dialog Manger) by your application. UserKind represents a window created directly by application calls to the Window Manager; for such windows the application can in fact set the window class to any value greater than 8 if desired.

> **Note:** WindowKind values 0, 1, and 3 through 7 are reserved for future use by the system.

When visible is TRUE, the window is currently visible.

Hilited and goAwayFlag are checked by the window definition function when it draws the window frame, to determine whether the window should be highlighted and whether it should have a go-away region. For a document window, this means that if hilited is TRUE, the title bar of the window is highlighted, and if goAwayFlag is also TRUE, a close box appears in the highlighted title bar.

> **Note:** The Window Manager sets the visible and hilited flags to TRUE by storing 255 in them rather than 1. This may cause problems in Lisa Pascal; to be safe, you should check

for the truth or falsity of these flags by comparing ORD of the flag to 0. For example, you would check to see if the flag is TRUE with ORD(myWindow^.visible) <> 0.

StrucRgn, contRgn, and updateRgn are region handles, as defined in QuickDraw, to the structure region, content region, and update region of the window. These regions are all in global coordinates.

WindowDefProc is a handle to the window definition function for this type of window. When you create a window, you identify its type with a window definition ID, which is converted into a handle and stored in the windowDefProc field. Thereafter, the Window Manager uses this handle to access the definition function; you should never need to access this field directly.

> **Note:** The high-order byte of the windowDefProc field contains some additional information that the Window Manager gets from the window definition ID; for details, see the section "Defining Your Own Windows".

DataHandle is reserved for use by the window definition function. If the window is one of your own definition, your window definition function may use this field to store and access any desired information. If no more than four bytes of information are needed, the definition function can store the information directly in the dataHandle field rather than use a handle. For example, the definition function for rounded-corner windows uses this field to store the diameters of curvature.

TitleHandle is a string handle to the window's title, if any.

TitleWidth is the width, in pixels, of the window's title in the system font and system font size. This width is determined by the Window Manager and is normally of no concern to the application.

ControlList is a control handle to the window's control list. The ControlHandle data type is defined in the Control Manager.

NextWindow is a pointer to the next window in the window list, that is, the window behind this window. If this window is the farthest back (with no windows between it and the desktop), nextWindow is NIL.

Assembly-language note: The global variable WindowList contains a pointer to the first window in the window list. Remember that any window in the list may be invisible.

WindowPic is a handle to a QuickDraw picture of the window contents, or NIL if the application will draw the window contents in response to an update event, as described below under "How a Window is Drawn".

RefCon is the window's reference value field, which the application may store into and access for any purpose.

> **Note:** Notice that the go-away, drag, and grow regions are not included in the window record. Although these are conceptually regions, they don't necessarily have the formal data structure for regions as defined in QuickDraw. The window definition function determines where these regions are, and it can do so with great flexibility.

Inside Macintosh

HOW A WINDOW IS DRAWN

When a window is drawn or redrawn, the following two-step process usually takes place: The Window Manager draws the window frame, then the application draws the window contents.

To perform the first step of this process, the Window Manager calls the window definition function with a request that the window frame be drawn. It manipulates regions of the Window Manager port as necessary before calling the window definition function, to ensure that only what should and must be drawn is actually drawn on the screen. Depending on a parameter passed to the routine that created the window, the window definition function may or may not draw a go-away region in the window frame (a close box in the title bar, for a document window).

Usually the second step is that the Window Manager generates an **update event** to get the application to draw the window contents. It does this by accumulating in the update region the areas of the window's content region that need updating. The Toolbox Event Manager periodically checks to see if there's any window whose update region is not empty; if it finds one, it reports (via the GetNextEvent function) that an update event has occurred, and passes along the window pointer in the event message. (If it finds more than one such window, it issues an update event for the frontmost one, so that update events are reported in front-to-back order.) The application should respond as follows:

1. Call BeginUpdate. This procedure temporarily replaces the visRgn of the window's grafPort with the intersection of the visRgn and the update region. It then sets the update region to an empty region; this "clears" the update event so it won't be reported again.

2. Draw the window contents, entirely or in part. Normally it's more convenient to draw the entire content region, but it suffices to draw only the visRgn. In either case, since the visRgn is limited to where it intersects the old update region, only the parts of the window that require updating will actually be drawn on the screen.

3. Call EndUpdate, which restores the normal visRgn.

Figure 5 illustrates the effect of BeginUpdate and EndUpdate on the visRgn and update region of a window that's redrawn after being brought to the front.

If you choose to draw only the visRgn in step 2, there are various ways you can check to see whether what you need to draw falls in that region. With the QuickDraw function PtInRgn, you can check whether a point lies in the visRgn. It may be more convenient to look at the visRgn's enclosing rectangle, which is stored in its rgnBBox field. The QuickDraw functions PtInRect and SectRect let you check for intersection with a rectangle.

To be able to respond to update events for one of its windows, the application has to keep track of the window's contents, usually in a data structure. In most cases, it's best *never* to draw immediately into a window; when you need to draw something, just keep track of it and add the area where it should be drawn to the window's update region (by calling one of the Window Manager's update region maintenance routines, InvalRect and InvalRgn). Do the actual drawing only in response to an update event. Usually this will simplify the structure of your application considerably, but be aware of the following possible problems:

- This method doesn't work if you want to do continuous scrolling while the user presses a scroll arrow; in this case, you would draw directly into the window.

- This method isn't convenient to apply to areas that aren't easily defined by a rectangle or a region; again, just draw directly into the window.

The Window Manager

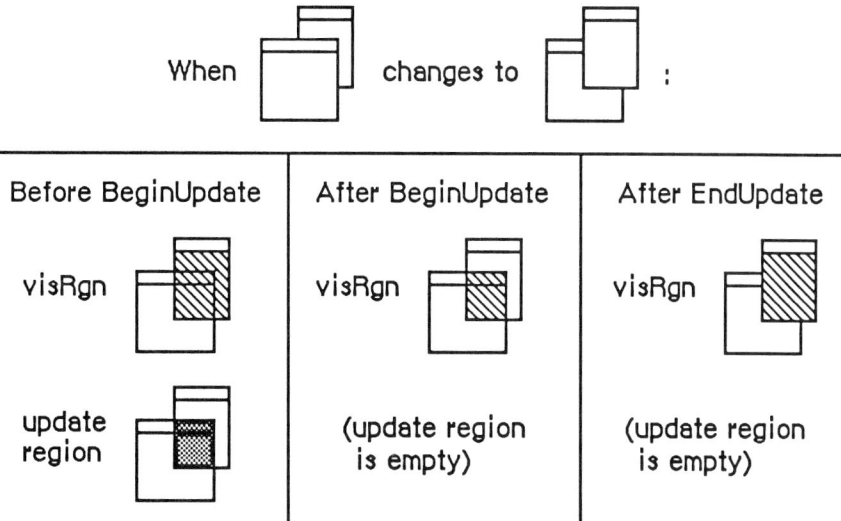

Figure 5. Updating Window Contents

- If you find that sometimes there's too long a delay before an update event happens, you can get update events first when necessary by calling GetNextEvent with a mask that accepts only that type of event.

The Window Manager allows an alternative to the update event mechanism that may be useful for windows whose contents never change: A handle to a QuickDraw picture may be stored in the window record. If this is done, the Window Manager doesn't generate an update event to get the application to draw the window contents; instead, it calls the QuickDraw procedure DrawPicture to draw the picture whose handle is stored in the window record (and it does all the necessary region manipulation).

MAKING A WINDOW ACTIVE: ACTIVATE EVENTS

A number of Window Manager routines change the state of a window from inactive to active or from active to inactive. For each such change, the Window Manager generates an **activate event**, passing along the window pointer in the event message. The activeFlag bit in the modifiers field of the event record is set if the window has become active, or cleared if it has become inactive.

When the Toolbox Event Manager finds out from the Window Manager that an activate event has been generated, it passes the event on to the application (via the GetNextEvent function). Activate events have the highest priority of any type of event.

Usually when one window becomes active another becomes inactive, and vice versa, so activate events are most commonly generated in pairs. When this happens, the Window Manager generates first the event for the window becoming inactive, and then the event for the window becoming active. Sometimes only a single activate event is generated, such as when there's only one window in the window list, or when the active window is permanently disposed of (since it no longer exists).

Inside Macintosh

Activate events for dialog and alert windows are handled by the Dialog Manager. In response to activate events for windows created directly by your application, you might take actions such as the following:

- In a document window containing a size box or scroll bars, erase the size box icon or scroll bars when the window becomes inactive and redraw them when it becomes active.

- In a window that contains text being edited, remove the highlighting or blinking vertical bar from the text when the window becomes inactive and restore it when the window becomes active.

- Enable or disable a menu or certain menu items as appropriate to match what the user can do when the window becomes active or inactive.

Assembly-language note: The global variable CurActivate contains a pointer to a window for which an activate event has been generated; the event, however, may not yet have been reported to the application via GetNextEvent, so you may be able to keep the event from happening by clearing CurActivate. Similarly, you may be able to keep a deactivate event from happening by clearing the global variable CurDeactive.

USING THE WINDOW MANAGER

To use the Window Manager, you must have previously called InitGraf to initialize QuickDraw and InitFonts to initialize the Font Manager. The first Window Manager routine to call is the initialization routine InitWindows, which draws the desktop and the (empty) menu bar.

Where appropriate in your program, use NewWindow or GetNewWindow to create any windows you need; these functions return a window pointer, which you can then use to refer to the window. NewWindow takes descriptive information about the window from its parameters, whereas GetNewWindow gets the information from a window template in a resource file. You can supply a pointer to the storage for the window record or let it be allocated by the routine creating the window; when you no longer need a window, call CloseWindow if you supplied the storage, or DisposeWindow if not.

When the Toolbox Event Manager function GetNextEvent reports that an update event has occurred, call BeginUpdate, draw the visRgn or the entire content region, and call EndUpdate (see "How a Window is Drawn"). You can also use InvalRect or InvalRgn to prepare a window for updating, and ValidRect or ValidRgn to protect portions of the window from updating.

When drawing the contents of a window that contains a size box in its content region, you'll draw the size box if the window is active or just the lines delimiting the size box and scroll bar areas if it's inactive. The FrontWindow function tells you which is the active window; the DrawGrowIcon procedure helps you draw the size box or delimiting lines. You'll also call the latter procedure when an activate event occurs that makes the window active or inactive.

Note: Before drawing in a window or making a call that affects the update region, remember to set the window to be the current grafPort with the QuickDraw procedure SetPort.

When GetNextEvent reports a mouse-down event, call the FindWindow function to find out which part of which window the mouse button was pressed in.

The Window Manager

- If it was pressed in the content region of an inactive window, make that window the active window by calling SelectWindow.

- If it was pressed in the grow region of the active window, call GrowWindow to pull around an image that shows how the window's size will change, and then SizeWindow to actually change the size.

- If it was pressed in the drag region of any window, call DragWindow, which will pull an outline of the window across the screen, move the window to a new location, and, if the window is inactive, make it the active window (unless the Command key was held down).

- If it was pressed in the go-away region of the active window, call TrackGoAway to handle the highlighting of the go-away region and to determine whether the mouse is inside the region when the button is released. Then do whatever is appropriate as a response to this mouse action in the particular application. For example, call CloseWindow or DisposeWindow if you want the window to go away permanently, or HideWindow if you want it to disappear temporarily.

Note: If the mouse button was pressed in the content region of an active window (but not in the grow region), call the Control Manager function FindControl if the window contains controls. If it was pressed in a system window, call the Desk Manager procedure SystemClick. See chapters 10 and 14 for details.

The MoveWindow procedure simply moves a window without pulling around an outline of it. Note, however, that the application shouldn't surprise the user by moving (or sizing) windows unexpectedly. There are other routines that you normally won't need to use that let you change the title of a window, place one window behind another, make a window visible or invisible, and access miscellaneous fields of the window record. There are also low-level routines that may be of interest to advanced programmers.

WINDOW MANAGER ROUTINES

Initialization and Allocation

```
PROCEDURE InitWindows;
```

InitWindows initializes the Window Manager. It creates the Window Manager port; you can get a pointer to this port with the GetWMgrPort procedure. InitWindows draws the desktop (as a rounded-corner rectangle with diameters of curvature 16,16, in the desktop pattern) and the (empty) menu bar. Call this procedure once before all other Window Manager routines.

Note: The desktop pattern is the pattern whose resource ID is:

```
CONST deskPatID = 16;
```

If you store a pattern with resource ID deskPatID in the application's resource file, that pattern will be used whenever the desktop is drawn.

Inside Macintosh

> **Warning:** InitWindows creates the Window Manager port as a nonrelocatable block in the application heap. To prevent heap fragmentation, call InitWindows in the main segment of your program, before any references to routines in other segments.

> **Assembly-language note:** InitWindows initializes the global variable GrayRgn to be a handle to the desktop region (a rounded-corner rectangle occupying the entire screen, minus the menu bar), and draws this region. It initializes the global variable DeskPattern to the pattern whose resource ID is deskPatID, and paints the desktop with this pattern. Any subsequent time that the desktop needs to be drawn, such as when a new area of it is exposed after a window is closed or moved, the Window Manager calls the procedure pointed to by the global variable DeskHook, if any (normally DeskHook is 0). The DeskHook procedure is called with 0 in register D0 to distinguish this use of it from its use in responding to clicks on the desktop (discussed in the description of FindWindow); it should respond by painting thePort^.clipRgn with DeskPattern and then doing anything else it wants.

```
PROCEDURE GetWMgrPort (VAR wPort: GrafPtr);
```

GetWMgrPort returns in wPort a pointer to the Window Manager port.

> **Warning:** Do not change any regions of the Window Manager port, or overlapping windows may not be handled properly.

> **Assembly-language note:** This pointer is stored in the global variable WMgrPort.

```
FUNCTION NewWindow (wStorage: Ptr; boundsRect: Rect; title:
        Str255; visible: BOOLEAN; procID: INTEGER; behind:
        WindowPtr; goAwayFlag: BOOLEAN; refCon: LONGINT) :
        WindowPtr;
```

NewWindow creates a window as specified by its parameters, adds it to the window list, and returns a windowPtr to the new window. It allocates space for the structure and content regions of the window and asks the window definition function to calculate those regions.

WStorage is a pointer to where to store the window record. For example, if you've declared the variable wRecord of type WindowRecord, you can pass @wRecord as the first parameter to NewWindow. If you pass NIL for wStorage, the window record will be allocated as a nonrelocatable object in the heap; in that case, though, you risk ending up with a fragmented heap.

BoundsRect, a rectangle given in global coordinates, determines the window's size and location, and becomes the portRect of the window's grafPort; note, however, that the portRect is in local coordinates. NewWindow sets the top left corner of the portRect to (0,0). For the standard types of windows, the boundsRect defines the content region of the window.

> **Note:** The bit map, pen pattern, and other characteristics of the window's grafPort are the same as the default values set by the OpenPort procedure in QuickDraw, except for the

character font, which is set to the application font rather than the system font. (NewWindow actually calls OpenPort to initialize the window's grafPort.) Note, however, that the coordinates of the grafPort's portBits.bounds and visRgn are changed along with its portRect.

The title parameter is the window's title. If the title of a document window is longer than will fit in the title bar, it's truncated in one of two ways: If the window has a close box, the characters that don't fit are truncated from the end of the title; if there's no close box, the title is centered and truncated at both ends.

If the visible parameter is TRUE, NewWindow draws the window. First it calls the window definition function to draw the window frame; if goAwayFlag is also TRUE and the window is frontmost (as specified by the behind parameter, below), it draws a go-away region in the frame. Then it generates an update event for the entire window contents.

ProcID is the window definition ID, which leads to the window definition function for this type of window. The function is read into memory if it's not already in memory. If it can't be read, NewWindow returns NIL. The window definition IDs for the standard types of windows are listed above under "Windows and Resources". Window definition IDs for windows of your own design are discussed later under "Defining Your Own Windows".

The behind parameter determines the window's plane. The new window is inserted in back of the window pointed to by this parameter. To put the new window behind all other windows, use behind=NIL. To place it in front of all other windows, use behind=POINTER(−1); in this case, NewWindow will unhighlight the previously active window, highlight the window being created, and generate appropriate activate events.

RefCon is the window's reference value, set and used only by your application.

NewWindow also sets the window class in the window record to indicate that the window was created directly by the application.

```
FUNCTION GetNewWindow (windowID: INTEGER; wStorage: Ptr; behind:
        WindowPtr) : WindowPtr;
```

Like NewWindow (above), GetNewWindow creates a window as specified by its parameters, adds it to the window list, and returns a windowPtr to the new window. The only difference between the two functions is that instead of having the parameters boundsRect, title, visible, procID, goAwayFlag, and refCon, GetNewWindow has a single windowID parameter, where windowID is the resource ID of a window template that supplies the same information as those parameters. If the window template can't be read from the resource file, GetNewWindow returns NIL. GetNewWindow releases the memory occupied by the resource before returning. The wStorage and behind parameters have the same meaning as in NewWindow.

```
PROCEDURE CloseWindow (theWindow: WindowPtr);
```

CloseWindow removes the given window from the screen and deletes it from the window list. It releases the memory occupied by all data structures associated with the window, but *not* the memory taken up by the window record itself. Call this procedure when you're done with a window if you supplied NewWindow or GetNewWindow a pointer to the window storage (in the wStorage parameter) when you created the window.

Inside Macintosh

Any update events for the window are discarded. If the window was the frontmost window and there was another window behind it, the latter window is highlighted and an appropriate activate event is generated.

> **Warning:** If you allocated memory yourself and stored a handle to it in the refCon field, CloseWindow won't know about it—you must release the memory before calling CloseWindow. Similarly, if you used the windowPic field to access a picture stored as a resource, you must release the memory it occupies; CloseWindow assumes the picture isn't a resource, and calls the QuickDraw procedure KillPicture to delete it.

```
PROCEDURE DisposeWindow (theWindow: WindowPtr);
```

> **Assembly-language note:** The macro you invoke to call DisposeWindow from assembly language is named _DisposWindow.

DisposeWindow calls CloseWindow (above) and then releases the memory occupied by the window record. Call this procedure when you're done with a window if you let the window record be allocated in the heap when you created the window (by passing NIL as the wStorage parameter to NewWindow or GetNewWindow).

Window Display

These procedures affect the appearance or plane of a window but not its size or location.

```
PROCEDURE SetWTitle (theWindow: WindowPtr; title: Str255);
```

SetWTitle sets theWindow's title to the given string, performing any necessary redrawing of the window frame.

```
PROCEDURE GetWTitle (theWindow: WindowPtr; VAR title: Str255);
```

GetWTitle returns theWindow's title as the value of the title parameter.

```
PROCEDURE SelectWindow (theWindow: WindowPtr);
```

SelectWindow makes theWindow the active window as follows: It unhighlights the previously active window, brings theWindow in front of all other windows, highlights theWindow, and generates the appropriate activate events. Call this procedure if there's a mouse-down event in the content region of an inactive window.

```
PROCEDURE HideWindow (theWindow: WindowPtr);
```

HideWindow makes theWindow invisible. If theWindow is the frontmost window and there's a window behind it, HideWindow also unhighlights theWindow, brings the window behind it to the front, highlights that window, and generates appropriate activate events (see Figure 6). If theWindow is already invisible, HideWindow has no effect.

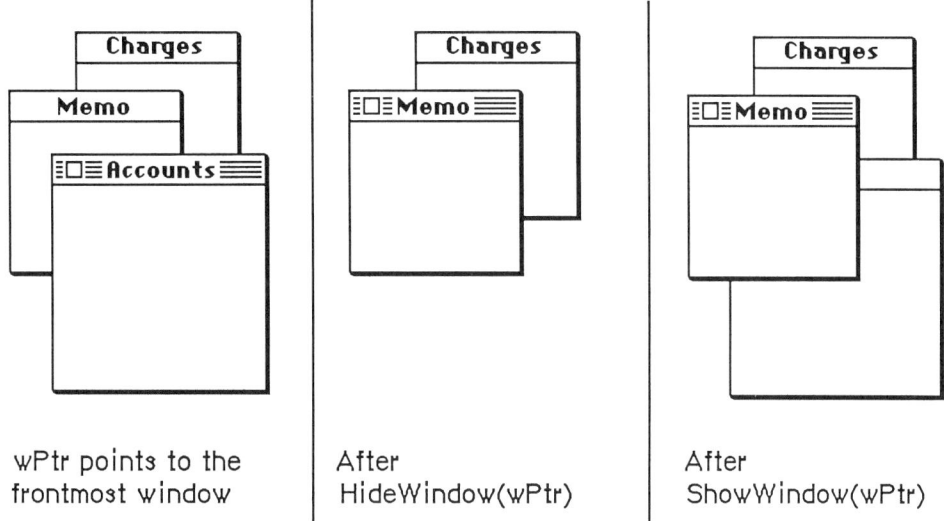

Figure 6. Hiding and Showing Document Windows

```
PROCEDURE ShowWindow (theWindow: WindowPtr);
```

ShowWindow makes theWindow visible. It does not change the front-to-back ordering of the windows. Remember that if you previously hid the frontmost window with HideWindow, HideWindow will have brought the window behind it to the front; so if you then do a ShowWindow of the window you hid, it will no longer be frontmost (see Figure 6). If theWindow is already visible, ShowWindow has no effect.

> **Note:** Although it's inadvisable, you can create a situation where the frontmost window is invisible. If you do a ShowWindow of such a window, it will highlight the window if it's not already highlighted and will generate an activate event to force this window from inactive to active.

```
PROCEDURE ShowHide (theWindow: WindowPtr; showFlag: BOOLEAN);
```

If showFlag is TRUE, ShowHide makes theWindow visible if it's not already visible and has no effect if it is already visible. If showFlag is FALSE, ShowHide makes theWindow invisible if it's not already invisible and has no effect if it is already invisible. Unlike HideWindow and ShowWindow, ShowHide never changes the highlighting or front-to-back ordering of windows or generates activate events.

Inside Macintosh

> **Warning:** Use this procedure carefully, and only in special circumstances where you need more control than allowed by HideWindow and ShowWindow.

```
PROCEDURE HiliteWindow (theWindow: WindowPtr; fHilite: BOOLEAN);
```

If fHilite is TRUE, this procedure highlights theWindow if it's not already highlighted and has no effect if it is highlighted. If fHilite is FALSE, HiliteWindow unhighlights theWindow if it is highlighted and has no effect if it's not highlighted. The exact way a window is highlighted depends on its window definition function.

Normally you won't have to call this procedure, since you should call SelectWindow to make a window active, and SelectWindow takes care of the necessary highlighting changes. Highlighting a window that isn't the active window is contrary to the Macintosh User Interface Guidelines.

```
PROCEDURE BringToFront (theWindow: WindowPtr);
```

BringToFront brings theWindow to the front of all other windows and redraws the window as necessary. Normally you won't have to call this procedure, since you should call SelectWindow to make a window active, and SelectWindow takes care of bringing the window to the front. If you do call BringToFront, however, remember to call HiliteWindow to make the necessary highlighting changes.

```
PROCEDURE SendBehind (theWindow,behindWindow: WindowPtr);
```

SendBehind sends theWindow behind behindWindow, redrawing any exposed windows. If behindWindow is NIL, it sends theWindow behind all other windows. If theWindow is the active window, it unhighlights theWindow, highlights the new active window, and generates the appropriate activate events.

> **Warning:** Do not use SendBehind to deactivate a previously active window. Calling SelectWindow to make a window active takes care of deactivating the previously active window.
>
> **Note:** If you're moving theWindow closer to the front (that is, if it's initially even farther behind behindWindow), you must make the following calls after calling SendBehind:
>
> ```
> wPeek := POINTER(theWindow);
> PaintOne(wPeek, wPeek^.strucRgn);
> CalcVis(wPeek)
> ```
>
> PaintOne and CalcVis are described under "Low-Level Routines".

```
FUNCTION FrontWindow : WindowPtr;
```

FrontWindow returns a pointer to the first visible window in the window list (that is, the active window). If there are no visible windows, it returns NIL.

The Window Manager

Assembly-language note: In the global variable GhostWindow, you can store a pointer to a window that's not to be considered frontmost even if it is (for example, if you want to have a special editing window always present and floating above all the others). If the window pointed to by GhostWindow is the first window in the window list, FrontWindow will return a pointer to the next visible window.

```
PROCEDURE DrawGrowIcon (theWindow: WindowPtr);
```

Call DrawGrowIcon in response to an update or activate event involving a window that contains a size box in its content region. If theWindow is active, DrawGrowIcon draws the size box; otherwise, it draws whatever is appropriate to show that the window temporarily cannot be sized. The exact appearance and location of what's drawn depend on the window definition function. For an active document window, DrawGrowIcon draws the size box icon in the bottom right corner of the portRect of the window's grafPort, along with the lines delimiting the size box and scroll bar areas (15 pixels in from the right edge and bottom of the portRect). It doesn't erase the scroll bar areas, so if the window doesn't contain scroll bars you should erase those areas yourself after the window's size changes. For an inactive document window, DrawGrowIcon draws only the lines delimiting the size box and scroll bar areas, and erases the size box icon.

Mouse Location

```
FUNCTION FindWindow (thePt: Point; VAR whichWindow: WindowPtr) :
         INTEGER;
```

When a mouse-down event occurs, the application should call FindWindow with thePt equal to the point where the mouse button was pressed (in global coordinates, as stored in the where field of the event record). FindWindow tells which part of which window, if any, the mouse button was pressed in. If it was pressed in a window, the whichWindow parameter is set to the window pointer; otherwise, it's set to NIL. The integer returned by FindWindow is one of the following predefined constants:

```
CONST inDesk      = 0;  {none of the following}
      inMenuBar   = 1;  {in menu bar}
      inSysWindow = 2;  {in system window}
      inContent   = 3;  {in content region (except grow, if active)}
      inDrag      = 4;  {in drag region}
      inGrow      = 5;  {in grow region (active window only)}
      inGoAway    = 6;  {in go-away region (active window only)}
```

InDesk usually means that the mouse button was pressed on the desktop, outside the menu bar or any windows; however, it may also mean that the mouse button was pressed inside a window frame but not in the drag region or go-away region of the window. Usually one of the last four values is returned for windows created by the application.

Assembly-language note: If you store a pointer to a procedure in the global variable DeskHook, it will be called when the mouse button is pressed on the desktop. The DeskHook procedure will be called with –1 in register D0 to distinguish this use of it from its use in drawing the desktop (discussed in the description of InitWindows). Register A0 will contain a pointer to the event record for the mouse-down event. When you use DeskHook in this way, FindWindow does not return inDesk when the mouse button is pressed on the desktop; it returns inSysWindow, and the Desk Manager procedure SystemClick calls the DeskHook procedure.

If the window is a documentProc type of window that doesn't contain a size box, the application should treat inGrow the same as inContent; if it's a noGrowDocProc type of window, FindWindow will never return inGrow for that window. If the window is a documentProc, noGrowDocProc, or rDocProc type of window with no close box, FindWindow will never return inGoAway for that window.

```
FUNCTION TrackGoAway (theWindow: WindowPtr; thePt: Point) :
        BOOLEAN;
```

When there's a mouse-down event in the go-away region of theWindow, the application should call TrackGoAway with thePt equal to the point where the mouse button was pressed (in global coordinates, as stored in the where field of the event record). TrackGoAway keeps control until the mouse button is released, highlighting the go-away region as long as the mouse location remains inside it, and unhighlighting it when the mouse moves outside it. The exact way a window's go-away region is highlighted depends on its window definition function; the highlighting of a document window's close box is illustrated in Figure 7. When the mouse button is released, TrackGoAway unhighlights the go-away region and returns TRUE if the mouse is inside the go-away region or FALSE if it's outside the region (in which case the application should do nothing).

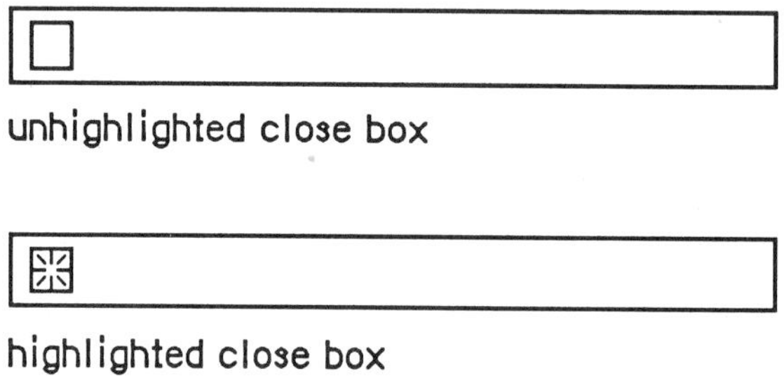

unhighlighted close box

highlighted close box

Figure 7. A Document Window's Close Box

Assembly-language note: If you store a pointer to a procedure in the global variable DragHook, TrackGoAway will call that procedure repeatedly (with no parameters) for as long as the user holds down the mouse button.

The Window Manager

Window Movement and Sizing

```
PROCEDURE MoveWindow (theWindow: WindowPtr; hGlobal,vGlobal:
        INTEGER; front: BOOLEAN);
```

MoveWindow moves theWindow to another part of the screen, without affecting its size or plane. The top left corner of the portRect of the window's grafPort is moved to the screen point indicated by the global coordinates hGlobal and vGlobal. The local coordinates of the top left corner remain the same. If the front parameter is TRUE and theWindow isn't the active window, MoveWindow makes it the active window by calling SelectWindow(theWindow).

```
PROCEDURE DragWindow (theWindow: WindowPtr; startPt: Point;
        boundsRect: Rect);
```

When there's a mouse-down event in the drag region of theWindow, the application should call DragWindow with startPt equal to the point where the mouse button was pressed (in global coordinates, as stored in the where field of the event record). DragWindow pulls a dotted outline of theWindow around, following the movements of the mouse until the button is released. When the mouse button is released, DragWindow calls MoveWindow to move theWindow to the location to which it was dragged. If theWindow isn't the active window (and the Command key wasn't being held down), DragWindow makes it the active window by passing TRUE for the front parameter when calling MoveWindow. If the Command key was being held down, the window is moved without being made the active window.

BoundsRect is also given in global coordinates. If the mouse button is released when the mouse location is outside the limits of boundsRect, DragWindow returns without moving theWindow or making it the active window. For a document window, boundsRect typically will be four pixels in from the menu bar and from the other edges of the screen, to ensure that there won't be less than a four-pixel-square area of the title bar visible on the screen.

Assembly-language note: As for TrackGoAway, if you store a pointer to a procedure in the global variable DragHook, that procedure will be called repeatedly while the user holds down the mouse button. (DragWindow calls DragGrayRgn, which calls the DragHook procedure).

```
FUNCTION GrowWindow (theWindow: WindowPtr; startPt: Point;
        sizeRect: Rect) : LONGINT;
```

When there's a mouse-down event in the grow region of theWindow, the application should call GrowWindow with startPt equal to the point where the mouse button was pressed (in global coordinates, as stored in the where field of the event record). GrowWindow pulls a **grow image** of the window around, following the movements of the mouse until the button is released. The grow image for a document window is a dotted outline of the entire window and also the lines delimiting the title bar, size box, and scroll bar areas; Figure 8 illustrates this for a document window containing both scroll bars, but the grow image would be the same even if the window contained one or no scroll bars. In general, the grow image is defined in the window definition function and is whatever is appropriate to show that the window's size will change.

Inside Macintosh

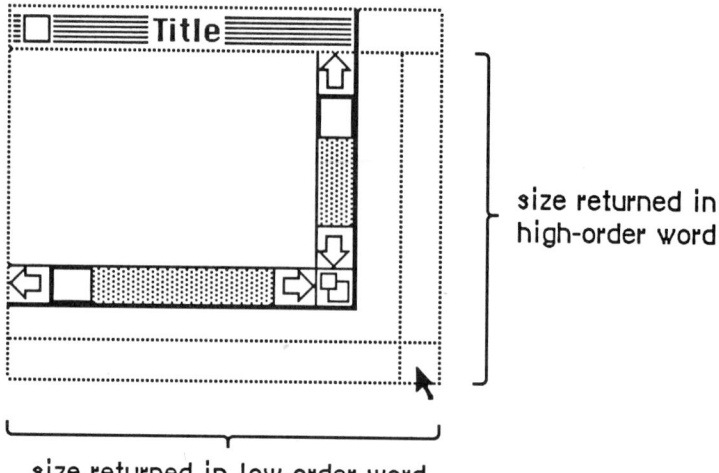

Figure 8. GrowWindow Operation on a Document Window

The application should subsequently call SizeWindow to change the portRect of the window's grafPort to the new one outlined by the grow image. The sizeRect parameter specifies limits, in pixels, on the vertical and horizontal measurements of what will be the new portRect. SizeRect.top is the minimum vertical measurement, sizeRect.left is the minimum horizontal measurement, sizeRect.bottom is the maximum vertical measurement, and sizeRect.right is the maximum horizontal measurement.

GrowWindow returns the actual size for the new portRect as outlined by the grow image when the mouse button is released. The high-order word of the long integer is the vertical measurement in pixels and the low-order word is the horizontal measurement. A return value of 0 indicates that the size is the same as that of the current portRect.

> **Note:** The Toolbox Utility function HiWord takes a long integer as a parameter and returns an integer equal to its high-order word; the function LoWord returns the low-order word.

Assembly-language note: Like TrackGoAway, GrowWindow repeatedly calls the procedure pointed to by the global variable DragHook (if any) as long as the mouse button is held down.

```
PROCEDURE SizeWindow (theWindow: WindowPtr; w,h: INTEGER; fUpdate:
        BOOLEAN);
```

SizeWindow enlarges or shrinks the portRect of theWindow's grafPort to the width and height specified by w and h, or does nothing if w and h are 0. The window's position on the screen does not change. The new window frame is drawn; if the width of a document window changes, the title is again centered in the title bar, or is truncated if it no longer fits. If fUpdate is TRUE, SizeWindow accumulates any newly created area of the content region into the update region (see

Figure 9); normally this is what you'll want. If you pass FALSE for fUpdate, you're responsible for the update region maintenance yourself. For more information, see InvalRect and ValidRect.

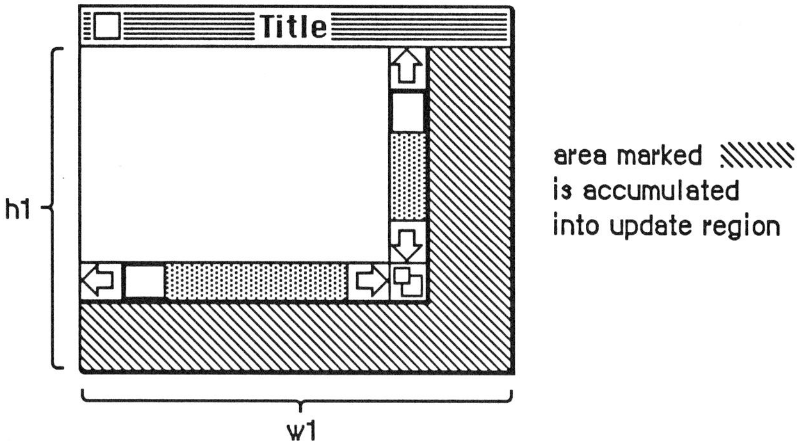

After SizeWindow(wPtr, w1, h1, TRUE)

area marked ▨▨▨ is accumulated into update region

Figure 9. SizeWindow Operation on a Document Window

Update Region Maintenance

PROCEDURE InvalRect (badRect: Rect);

InvalRect accumulates the given rectangle into the update region of the window whose grafPort is the current port. This tells the Window Manager that the rectangle has changed and must be updated. The rectangle is given in local coordinates and is clipped to the window's content region.

For example, this procedure is useful when you're calling SizeWindow for a document window that contains a size box or scroll bars. Suppose you're going to call SizeWindow with fUpdate=TRUE. If the window is enlarged as shown in Figure 8, you'll want not only the newly created part of the content region to be updated, but also the two rectangular areas containing the (former) size box and scroll bars; before calling SizeWindow, you can call InvalRect twice to accumulate those areas into the update region. In case the window is made smaller, you'll want the new size box and scroll bar areas to be updated, and so can similarly call InvalRect for those areas after calling SizeWindow. See Figure 10 for an illustration of this type of update region maintenance.

As another example, suppose your application scrolls up text in a document window and wants to show new text added at the bottom of the window. You can cause the added text to be redrawn by accumulating that area into the update region with InvalRect.

PROCEDURE InvalRgn (badRgn: RgnHandle);

InvalRgn is the same as InvalRect but for a region that has changed rather than a rectangle.

Inside Macintosh

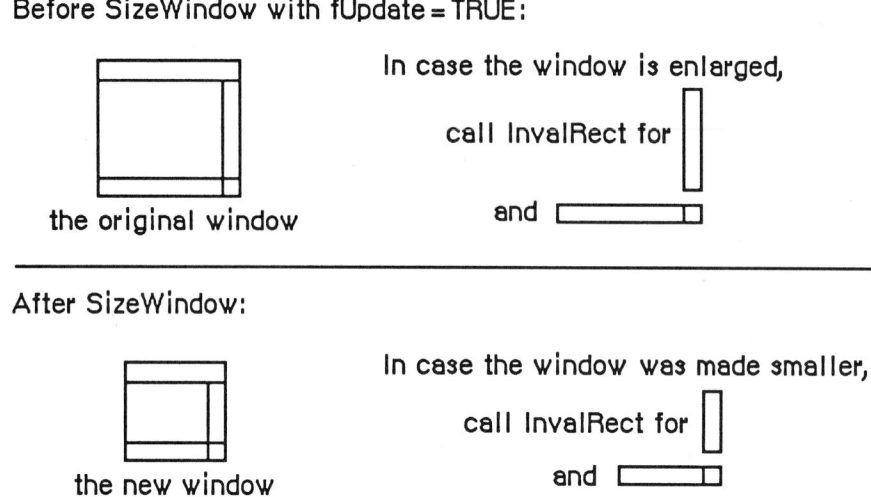

Figure 10. Update Region Maintenance with InvalRect

```
PROCEDURE ValidRect (goodRect: Rect);
```

ValidRect removes goodRect from the update region of the window whose grafPort is the current port. This tells the Window Manager that the application has already drawn the rectangle and to cancel any updates accumulated for that area. The rectangle is clipped to the window's content region and is given in local coordinates. Using ValidRect results in better performance and less redundant redrawing in the window.

For example, suppose you've called SizeWindow with fUpdate=TRUE for a document window that contains a size box or scroll bars. Depending on the dimensions of the newly sized window, the new size box and scroll bar areas may or may not have been accumulated into the window's update region. After calling SizeWindow, you can redraw the size box or scroll bars immediately and then call ValidRect for the areas they occupy in case they were in fact accumulated into the update region; this will avoid redundant drawing.

```
PROCEDURE ValidRgn (goodRgn: RgnHandle);
```

ValidRgn is the same as ValidRect but for a region that has been drawn rather than a rectangle.

```
PROCEDURE BeginUpdate (theWindow: WindowPtr);
```

Call BeginUpdate when an update event occurs for theWindow. BeginUpdate replaces the visRgn of the window's grafPort with the intersection of the visRgn and the update region and then sets the window's update region to an empty region. You would then usually draw the entire content region, though it suffices to draw only the visRgn; in either case, only the parts of the window that require updating will actually be drawn on the screen. Every call to BeginUpdate must be balanced by a call to EndUpdate. (See "How a Window is Drawn".)

The Window Manager

Note: In Pascal, BeginUpdate and EndUpdate calls can't be nested (that is, you must call EndUpdate before the next call to BeginUpdate).

Assembly-language note: A handle to a copy of the original visRgn (in global coordinates) is stored in the global variable SaveVisRgn. You can nest BeginUpdate and EndUpdate calls in assembly language if you save and restore this region.

PROCEDURE EndUpdate (theWindow: WindowPtr);

Call EndUpdate to restore the normal visRgn of theWindow's grafPort, which was changed by BeginUpdate as described above.

Miscellaneous Routines

PROCEDURE SetWRefCon (theWindow: WindowPtr; data: LONGINT);

SetWRefCon sets theWindow's reference value to the given data.

FUNCTION GetWRefCon (theWindow: WindowPtr) : LONGINT;

GetWRefCon returns theWindow's current reference value.

PROCEDURE SetWindowPic (theWindow: WindowPtr; pic: PicHandle);

SetWindowPic stores the given picture handle in the window record for theWindow, so that when theWindow's contents are to be drawn, the Window Manager will draw this picture rather than generate an update event.

FUNCTION GetWindowPic (theWindow: WindowPtr) : PicHandle;

GetWindowPic returns the handle to the picture that draws theWindow's contents, previously stored with SetWindowPic.

FUNCTION PinRect (theRect: Rect; thePt: Point) : LONGINT;

PinRect "pins" thePt inside theRect: If thePt is inside theRect, thePt is returned; otherwise, the point associated with the nearest pixel within theRect is returned. (The high-order word of the long integer returned is the vertical coordinate; the low-order word is the horizontal coordinate.) More precisely, for theRect (left,top) (right,bottom) and thePt (h,v), PinRect does the following:

- If h < left, it returns left.
- If v < top, it returns top.
- If h > right, it returns right–1.

- If v > bottom, it returns bottom–1.

Note: The 1 is subtracted when thePt is below or to the right of theRect so that a pixel drawn at that point will lie within theRect. However, if thePt is exactly on the bottom or right edge of theRect, 1 should be subtracted but isn't.

```
FUNCTION DragGrayRgn (theRgn: RgnHandle; startPt: Point;
          limitRect,slopRect: Rect; axis: INTEGER; actionProc:
          ProcPtr) : LONGINT;
```

Called when the mouse button is down inside theRgn, DragGrayRgn pulls a dotted (gray) outline of the region around, following the movements of the mouse until the button is released. DragWindow calls this function before actually moving the window. You can call it yourself to pull around the outline of any region, and then use the information it returns to determine where to move the region.

Note: DragGrayRgn alters the region; if you don't want the original region changed, pass DragGrayRgn a handle to a copy.

The startPt parameter is assumed to be the point where the mouse button was originally pressed, in the local coordinates of the current grafPort.

LimitRect and slopRect are also in the local coordinates of the current grafPort. To explain these parameters, the concept of "offset point" must be introduced: This is initially the point whose vertical and horizontal offsets from the top left corner of the region's enclosing rectangle are the same as those of startPt. The offset point follows the mouse location, except that DragGrayRgn will never move the offset point outside limitRect; this limits the travel of the region's outline (but not the movements of the mouse). SlopRect, which should completely enclose limitRect, allows the user some "slop" in moving the mouse. DragGrayRgn's behavior while tracking the mouse depends on the location of the mouse with respect to these two rectangles:

- When the mouse is inside limitRect, the region's outline follows it normally. If the mouse button is released there, the region should be moved to the mouse location.
- When the mouse is outside limitRect but inside slopRect, DragGrayRgn "pins" the offset point to the edge of limitRect. If the mouse button is released there, the region should be moved to this pinned location.
- When the mouse is outside slopRect, the outline disappears from the screen, but DragGrayRgn continues to follow the mouse; if it moves back into slopRect, the outline reappears. If the mouse button is released outside slopRect, the region should not be moved from its original position.

Figure 11 illustrates what happens when the mouse is moved outside limitRect but inside slopRect, for a rectangular region. The offset point is pinned as the mouse location moves on.

If the mouse button is released within slopRect, the high-order word of the value returned by DragGrayRgn contains the vertical coordinate of the ending mouse location minus that of startPt and the low-order word contains the difference between the horizontal coordinates. If the mouse button is released outside slopRect, both words contain –32768 ($8000).

The Window Manager

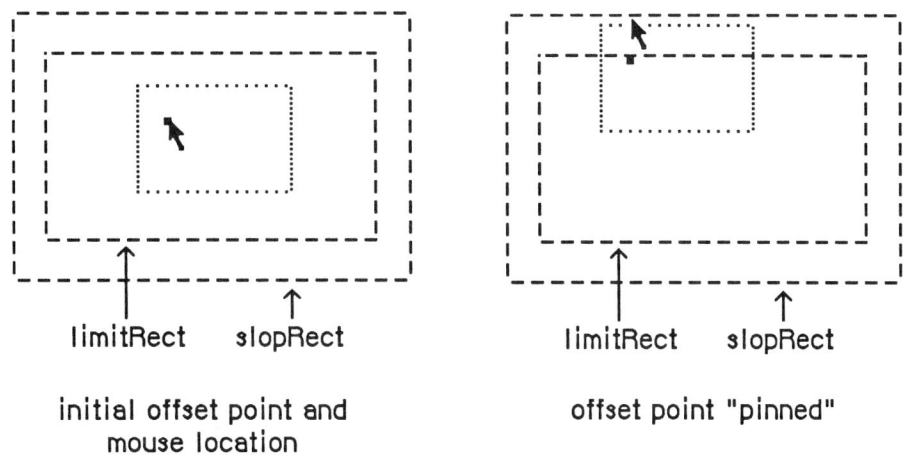

limitRect   slopRect

initial offset point and mouse location

limitRect   slopRect

offset point "pinned"

Figure 11. DragGrayRgn Operation on a Rectangular Region

The axis parameter allows you to constrain the region's motion to only one axis. It has one of the following values:

```
CONST noConstraint = 0;   {no constraint}
      hAxisOnly    = 1;   {horizontal axis only}
      vAxisOnly    = 2;   {vertical axis only}
```

If an axis constraint is in effect, the outline will follow the mouse's movements along the specified axis only, ignoring motion along the other axis. With or without an axis constraint, the mouse must still be inside the slop rectangle for the outline to appear at all.

The actionProc parameter is a pointer to a procedure that defines some action to be performed repeatedly for as long as the user holds down the mouse button; the procedure should have no parameters. If actionProc is NIL, DragGrayRgn simply retains control until the mouse button is released.

Assembly-language note: DragGrayRgn calls the procedure pointed to by the global variable DragHook, if any, as long as the mouse button is held down. (If there's an actionProc procedure, the actionProc procedure is called first.)

If you want the region's outline to be drawn in a pattern other than gray, you can store the pattern in the global variable DragPattern and then invoke the macro _DragTheRgn.

Low-Level Routines

These routines are called by higher-level routines; normally you won't need to call them yourself.

Inside Macintosh

```
FUNCTION CheckUpdate (VAR theEvent: EventRecord) : BOOLEAN;
```

CheckUpdate is called by the Toolbox Event Manager. From the front to the back in the window list, it looks for a visible window that needs updating (that is, whose update region is not empty). If it finds one whose window record contains a picture handle, it draws the picture (doing all the necessary region manipulation) and looks for the next visible window that needs updating. If it ever finds one whose window record doesn't contain a picture handle, it stores an update event for that window in theEvent and returns TRUE. If it never finds such a window, it returns FALSE.

```
PROCEDURE ClipAbove (window: WindowPeek);
```

ClipAbove sets the clipRgn of the Window Manager port to be the desktop intersected with the current clipRgn, minus the structure regions of all the windows in front of the given window.

Assembly-language note: ClipAbove gets the desktop region from the global variable GrayRgn.

```
PROCEDURE SaveOld (window: WindowPeek);
```

SaveOld saves the given window's current structure region and content region for the DrawNew operation (see below). It must be balanced by a subsequent call to DrawNew.

```
PROCEDURE DrawNew (window: WindowPeek; update: BOOLEAN);
```

If the update parameter is TRUE, DrawNew updates the area

(OldStructure XOR NewStructure) UNION (OldContent XOR NewContent)

where OldStructure and OldContent are the structure and content regions saved by the SaveOld procedure, and NewStructure and NewContent are the current structure and content regions. It erases the area and adds it to the window's update region. If update is FALSE, it only erases the area.

Warning: In Pascal, SaveOld and DrawNew are *not* nestable.

Assembly-language note: In assembly language, you can nest SaveOld and DrawNew if you save and restore the values of the global variables OldStructure and OldContent.

```
PROCEDURE PaintOne (window: WindowPeek; clobberedRgn: RgnHandle);
```

PaintOne "paints" the given window, clipped to clobberedRgn and all windows above it: It draws the window frame and, if some content is exposed, erases the exposed area (paints it with the background pattern) and adds it to the window's update region. If the window parameter is NIL, the window is the desktop and so is painted with the desktop pattern.

> **Assembly-language note:** The global variables SaveUpdate and PaintWhite are flags used by PaintOne. Normally both flags are set. Clearing SaveUpdate prevents clobberedRgn from being added to the window's update region. Clearing PaintWhite prevents clobberedRgn from being erased before being added to the update region (this is useful, for example, if the background of the window isn't the background pattern). The Window Manager sets both flags periodically, so you should clear the appropriate flag just before each situation you wish it to apply to.

```
PROCEDURE PaintBehind (startWindow: WindowPeek; clobberedRgn:
            RgnHandle);
```

PaintBehind calls PaintOne for startWindow and all the windows behind startWindow, clipped to clobberedRgn.

> **Assembly-language note:** PaintBehind clears the global variable PaintWhite before calling PaintOne, so clobberedRgn isn't erased. (PaintWhite is reset after the call to PaintOne.)

```
PROCEDURE CalcVis (window: WindowPeek);
```

CalcVis calculates the visRgn of the given window by starting with its content region and subtracting the structure region of each window in front of it.

```
PROCEDURE CalcVisBehind (startWindow: WindowPeek; clobberedRgn:
            RgnHandle);
```

> **Assembly-language note:** The macro you invoke to call CalcVisBehind from assembly language is named _CalcVBehind.

CalcVisBehind calculates the visRgns of startWindow and all windows behind startWindow that intersect clobberedRgn. It should be called after PaintBehind.

DEFINING YOUR OWN WINDOWS

Certain types of windows, such as the standard document window, are predefined for you. However, you may want to define your own type of window—maybe a round or hexagonal

Inside Macintosh

window, or even a window shaped like an apple. QuickDraw and the Window Manager make it possible for you to do this.

> **Note:** For the convenience of your application's user, remember to conform to the Macintosh User Interface Guidelines for windows as much as possible.

To define your own type of window, you write a window definition function and store it in a resource file. When you create a window, you provide a window definition ID, which leads to the window definition function. The window definition ID is an integer that contains the resource ID of the window definition function in its upper 12 bits and a **variation code** in its lower four bits. Thus, for a given resource ID and variation code, the window definition ID is

16 * resource ID + variation code

The variation code allows a single window definition function to implement several related types of window as "variations on a theme". For example, the dBoxProc type of window is a variation of the standard document window; both use the window definition function whose resource ID is 0, but the document window has a variation code of 0 while the dBoxProc window has a variation code of 1.

The Window Manager calls the Resource Manager to access the window definition function with the given resource ID. The Resource Manager reads the window definition function into memory and returns a handle to it. The Window Manager stores this handle in the windowDefProc field of the window record, along with the variation code in the high-order byte of that field. Later, when it needs to perform a type-dependent action on the window, it calls the window definition function and passes it the variation code as a parameter. Figure 12 illustrates this process.

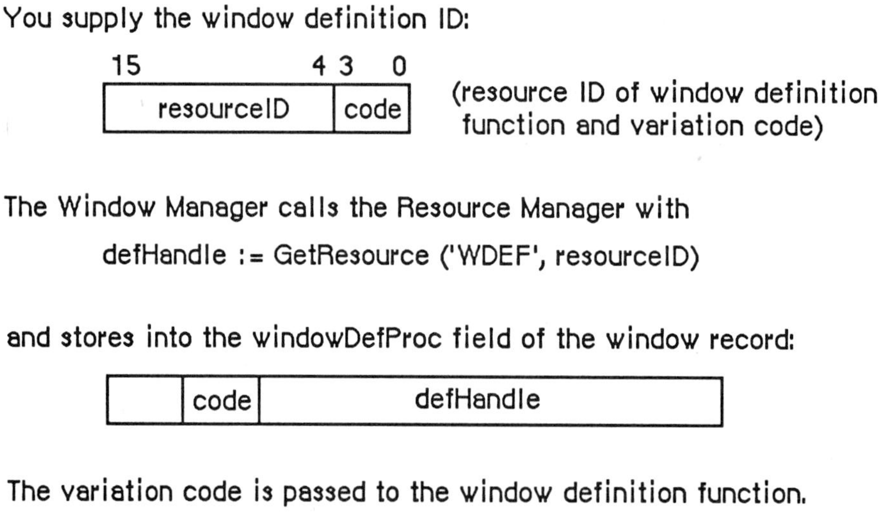

You supply the window definition ID:

```
  15              4 3     0
 ┌──────────────┬─────────┐
 │  resourceID  │  code   │    (resource ID of window definition
 └──────────────┴─────────┘      function and variation code)
```

The Window Manager calls the Resource Manager with

defHandle := GetResource ('WDEF', resourceID)

and stores into the windowDefProc field of the window record:

```
 ┌──────┬─────────────────────┐
 │ code │      defHandle      │
 └──────┴─────────────────────┘
```

The variation code is passed to the window definition function.

Figure 12. Window Definition Handling

The Window Definition Function

The window definition function is usually written in assembly language, but may be written in Pascal.

I-298 Defining Your Own Windows

The Window Manager

Assembly-language note: The function's entry point must be at the beginning.

You may choose any name you wish for your window definition function. Here's how you would declare one named MyWindow:

```
FUNCTION MyWindow (varCode: INTEGER; theWindow: WindowPtr; message:
         INTEGER; param: LONGINT) : LONGINT;
```

VarCode is the variation code, as described above.

TheWindow indicates the window that the operation will affect. If the window definition function needs to use a WindowPeek type of pointer more than a WindowPtr, you can simply specify WindowPeek instead of WindowPtr in the function declaration.

The message parameter identifies the desired operation. It has one of the following values:

```
CONST wDraw      = 0;   {draw window frame}
      wHit       = 1;   {tell what region mouse button was pressed in}
      wCalcRgns  = 2;   {calculate strucRgn and contRgn}
      wNew       = 3;   {do any additional window initialization}
      wDispose   = 4;   {take any additional disposal actions}
      wGrow      = 5;   {draw window's grow image}
      wDrawGIcon = 6;   {draw size box in content region}
```

As described below in the discussions of the routines that perform these operations, the value passed for param, the last parameter of the window definition function, depends on the operation. Where it's not mentioned below, this parameter is ignored. Similarly, the window definition function is expected to return a function result only where indicated; in other cases, the function should return 0.

> **Note:** "Routine" here doesn't necessarily mean a procedure or function. While it's a good idea to set these up as subprograms inside the window definition function, you're not required to do so.

The Draw Window Frame Routine

When the window definition function receives a wDraw message, it should draw the window frame in the current grafPort, which will be the Window Manager port. (For details on drawing, see chapter 6.)

This routine should make certain checks to determine exactly what it should do. If the visible field in the window record is FALSE, the routine should do nothing; otherwise, it should examine the value of param received by the window definition function, as described below.

If param is 0, the routine should draw the entire window frame. If the hilited field in the window record is TRUE, the window frame should be highlighted in whatever way is appropriate to show that this is the active window. If goAwayFlag in the window record is also TRUE, the highlighted window frame should include a go-away region; this is useful when you want to define a window such that a particular window of that type may or may not have a go-away region, depending on the situation.

Special action should be taken if the value of param is wInGoAway (a predefined constant, equal to 4, which is one of those returned by the hit routine described below). If param is wInGoAway, the routine should do nothing but "toggle" the state of the window's go-away region from unhighlighted to highlighted or vice versa. The highlighting should be whatever is appropriate to show that the mouse button has been pressed inside the region. Simple inverse highlighting may be used or, as in document windows, the appearance of the region may change considerably. In the latter case, the routine could use a "mask" consisting of the unhighlighted state of the region XORed with its highlighted state (where XOR stands for the logical operation "exclusive or"). When such a mask is itself XORed with either state of the region, the result is the other state; Figure 13 illustrates this for a document window.

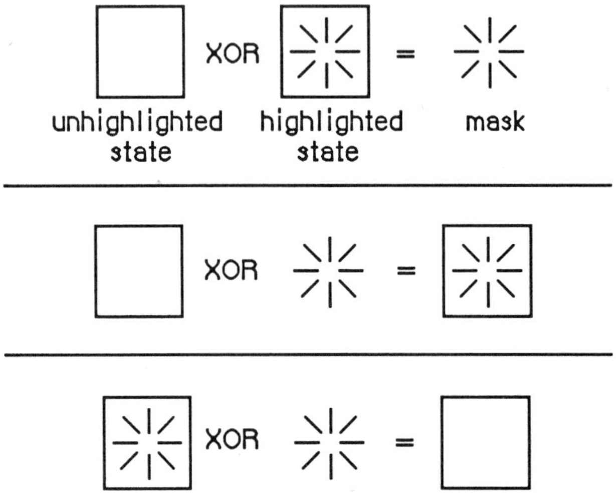

Figure 13. Toggling the Go-Away Region

Typically the window frame will include the window's title, which should be in the system font and system font size. The Window Manager port will already be set to use the system font and system font size.

Note: Nothing drawn outside the window's structure region will be visible.

The Hit Routine

When the window definition function receives a wHit message, it also receives as its param value the point where the mouse button was pressed. This point is given in global coordinates, with the vertical coordinate in the high-order word of the long integer and the horizontal coordinate in the low-order word. The window definition function should determine where the mouse button "hit" and then return one of these predefined constants:

```
CONST  wNoHit     = 0;   {none of the following}
       wInContent = 1;   {in content region (except grow, if active)}
       wInDrag    = 2;   {in drag region}
       wInGrow    = 3;   {in grow region (active window only)}
       wInGoAway  = 4;   {in go-away region (active window only)}
```

The Window Manager

Usually, wNoHit means the given point isn't anywhere within the window, but this is not necessarily so. For example, the document window's hit routine returns wNoHit if the point is in the window frame but not in the title bar.

The constants wInGrow and wInGoAway should be returned only if the window is active, since by convention the size box and go-away region won't be drawn if the window is inactive (or, if drawn, won't be operable). In an inactive document window, if the mouse button is pressed in the title bar where the close box would be if the window were active, the hit routine returns wInDrag.

Of the regions that may have been hit, only the content region necessarily has the structure of a region and is included in the window record. The hit routine can determine in any way it likes whether the drag, grow, or go-away "region" has been hit.

The Routine to Calculate Regions

The routine executed in response to a wCalcRgns message should calculate the window's structure region and content region based on the current grafPort's portRect. These regions, whose handles are in the strucRgn and contRgn fields, are in global coordinates. The Window Manager will request this operation only if the window is visible.

> **Warning:** When you calculate regions for your own type of window, do not alter the clipRgn or the visRgn of the window's grafPort. The Window Manager and QuickDraw take care of this for you. Altering the clipRgn or visRgn may result in damage to other windows.

The Initialize Routine

After initializing fields as appropriate when creating a new window, the Window Manager sends the message wNew to the window definition function. This gives the definition function a chance to perform any type-specific initialization it may require. For example, if the content region is unusually shaped, the initialize routine might allocate space for the region and store the region handle in the dataHandle field of the window record. The initialize routine for a standard document window does nothing.

The Dispose Routine

The Window Manager's CloseWindow and DisposeWindow procedures send the message wDispose to the window definition function, telling it to carry out any additional actions required when disposing of the window. The dispose routine might, for example, release space that was allocated by the initialize routine. The dispose routine for a standard document window does nothing.

The Grow Routine

When the window definition function receives a wGrow message, it also receives a pointer to a rectangle as its param value. The rectangle is in global coordinates and is usually aligned at its top left corner with the portRect of the window's grafPort. The grow routine should draw a grow image of the window to fit the given rectangle (that is, whatever is appropriate to show that the window's size will change, such as an outline of the content region). The Window Manager requests this operation repeatedly as the user drags inside the grow region. The grow routine should draw in the current grafPort, which will be the Window Manager port, and should use the grafPort's current pen pattern and pen mode, which are set up (as gray and notPatXor) to conform to the Macintosh User Interface Guidelines.

The grow routine for a standard document window draws a dotted (gray) outline of the window and also the lines delimiting the title bar, size box, and scroll bar areas.

The Draw Size Box Routine

If the window's grow region is in the content region, the wDrawGIcon message tells the window definition function to draw the size box in the grow region if the window is active (highlighted); if the window is inactive it should draw whatever is appropriate to show that the window temporarily can't be sized. For active document windows, this routine draws the size box icon in the bottom right corner of the portRect of the window's grafPort, along with the lines delimiting the size box and scroll bar areas; for inactive windows, it draws just the delimiting lines, and erases the size box icon.

If the grow region is located in the window frame rather than the content region, this routine should do nothing.

FORMATS OF RESOURCES FOR WINDOWS

The Window Manager function GetNewWindow takes the resource ID of a window template as a parameter, and gets from the template the same information that the NewWindow function gets from six of its parameters. The resource type for a window template is 'WIND', and the resource data has the following format:

Number of bytes	Contents
8 bytes	Same as boundsRect parameter to NewWindow
2 bytes	Same as procID parameter to NewWindow
2 bytes	Same as visible parameter to NewWindow
2 bytes	Same as goAwayFlag parameter to NewWindow
4 bytes	Same as refCon parameter to NewWindow
n bytes	Same as title parameter to NewWindow (1-byte length in bytes, followed by the characters of the title)

The resource type for a window definition function is 'WDEF', and the resource data is simply the compiled or assembled code of the function.

SUMMARY OF THE WINDOW MANAGER

Constants

```
CONST  { Window definition IDs }

    documentProc   = 0;    {standard document window}
    dBoxProc       = 1;    {alert box or modal dialog box}
    plainDBox      = 2;    {plain box}
    altDBoxProc    = 3;    {plain box with shadow}
    noGrowDocProc  = 4;    {document window without size box}
    rDocProc       = 16;   {rounded-corner window}

    { Window class, in windowKind field of window record }

    dialogKind     = 2;    {dialog or alert window}
    userKind       = 8;    {window created directly by the application}

    { Values returned by FindWindow }

    inDesk         = 0;    {none of the following}
    inMenuBar      = 1;    {in menu bar}
    inSysWindow    = 2;    {in system window}
    inContent      = 3;    {in content region (except grow, if active)}
    inDrag         = 4;    {in drag region}
    inGrow         = 5;    {in grow region (active window only)}
    inGoAway       = 6;    {in go-away region (active window only)}

    { Axis constraints for DragGrayRgn }

    noConstraint   = 0;    {no constraint}
    hAxisOnly      = 1;    {horizontal axis only}
    vAxisOnly      = 2;    {vertical axis only}

    { Messages to window definition function }

    wDraw          = 0;    {draw window frame}
    wHit           = 1;    {tell what region mouse button was pressed in}
    wCalcRgns      = 2;    {calculate strucRgn and contRgn}
    wNew           = 3;    {do any additional window initialization}
    wDispose       = 4;    {take any additional disposal actions}
    wGrow          = 5;    {draw window's grow image}
    wDrawGIcon     = 6;    {draw size box in content region}

    { Values returned by window definition function's hit routine }

    wNoHit         = 0;    {none of the following}
    wInContent     = 1;    {in content region (except grow, if active)}
    wInDrag        = 2;    {in drag region}
    wInGrow        = 3;    {in grow region (active window only)}
    wInGoAway      = 4;    {in go-away region (active window only)}
```

```
{ Resource ID of desktop pattern }

deskPatID = 16;
```

Data Types

```
TYPE WindowPtr  = GrafPtr;
     WindowPeek = ^WindowRecord;

     WindowRecord =
          RECORD
               port:          GrafPort;        {window's grafPort}
               windowKind:    INTEGER;         {window class}
               visible:       BOOLEAN;         {TRUE if visible}
               hilited:       BOOLEAN;         {TRUE if highlighted}
               goAwayFlag:    BOOLEAN;         {TRUE if has go-away region}
               spareFlag:     BOOLEAN;         {reserved for future use}
               strucRgn:      RgnHandle;       {structure region}
               contRgn:       RgnHandle;       {content region}
               updateRgn:     RgnHandle;       {update region}
               windowDefProc: Handle;          {window definition function}
               dataHandle:    Handle;          {data used by windowDefProc}
               titleHandle:   StringHandle;    {window's title}
               titleWidth:    INTEGER;         {width of title in pixels}
               controlList:   ControlHandle;   {window's control list}
               nextWindow:    WindowPeek;      {next window in window list}
               windowPic:     PicHandle;       {picture for drawing window}
               refCon:        LONGINT          {window's reference value}
          END;
```

Routines

Initialization and Allocation

```
PROCEDURE InitWindows;
PROCEDURE GetWMgrPort    (VAR wPort: GrafPtr);
FUNCTION  NewWindow      (wStorage: Ptr; boundsRect: Rect; title: Str255;
                          visible: BOOLEAN; procID: INTEGER; behind:
                          WindowPtr; goAwayFlag: BOOLEAN; refCon:
                          LONGINT) : WindowPtr;
FUNCTION  GetNewWindow   (windowID: INTEGER; wStorage: Ptr; behind:
                          WindowPtr) : WindowPtr;
PROCEDURE CloseWindow    (theWindow: WindowPtr);
PROCEDURE DisposeWindow  (theWindow: WindowPtr);
```

The Window Manager

Window Display

```
PROCEDURE SetWTitle      (theWindow: WindowPtr; title: Str255);
PROCEDURE GetWTitle      (theWindow: WindowPtr; VAR title: Str255);
PROCEDURE SelectWindow   (theWindow: WindowPtr);
PROCEDURE HideWindow     (theWindow: WindowPtr);
PROCEDURE ShowWindow     (theWindow: WindowPtr);
PROCEDURE ShowHide       (theWindow: WindowPtr; showFlag: BOOLEAN);
PROCEDURE HiliteWindow   (theWindow: WindowPtr; fHilite: BOOLEAN);
PROCEDURE BringToFront   (theWindow: WindowPtr);
PROCEDURE SendBehind     (theWindow,behindWindow: WindowPtr);
FUNCTION  FrontWindow :  WindowPtr;
PROCEDURE DrawGrowIcon   (theWindow: WindowPtr);
```

Mouse Location

```
FUNCTION FindWindow    (thePt: Point; VAR whichWindow: WindowPtr) :
                          INTEGER;
FUNCTION TrackGoAway   (theWindow: WindowPtr; thePt: Point) : BOOLEAN;
```

Window Movement and Sizing

```
PROCEDURE MoveWindow    (theWindow: WindowPtr; hGlobal,vGlobal: INTEGER;
                          front: BOOLEAN);
PROCEDURE DragWindow    (theWindow: WindowPtr; startPt: Point; boundsRect:
                          Rect);
FUNCTION  GrowWindow    (theWindow: WindowPtr; startPt: Point; sizeRect:
                          Rect) : LONGINT;
PROCEDURE SizeWindow    (theWindow: WindowPtr; w,h: INTEGER; fUpdate:
                          BOOLEAN);
```

Update Region Maintenance

```
PROCEDURE InvalRect      (badRect: Rect);
PROCEDURE InvalRgn       (badRgn: RgnHandle);
PROCEDURE ValidRect      (goodRect: Rect);
PROCEDURE ValidRgn       (goodRgn: RgnHandle);
PROCEDURE BeginUpdate    (theWindow: WindowPtr);
PROCEDURE EndUpdate      (theWindow: WindowPtr);
```

Miscellaneous Routines

```
PROCEDURE SetWRefCon     (theWindow: WindowPtr; data: LONGINT);
FUNCTION  GetWRefCon     (theWindow: WindowPtr) : LONGINT;
PROCEDURE SetWindowPic   (theWindow: WindowPtr; pic: PicHandle);
FUNCTION  GetWindowPic   (theWindow: WindowPtr) : PicHandle;
FUNCTION  PinRect        (theRect: Rect; thePt: Point) : LONGINT;
```

Inside Macintosh

```
FUNCTION  DragGrayRgn    (theRgn: RgnHandle; startPt: Point; limitRect,
                          slopRect: Rect; axis: INTEGER; actionProc:
                          ProcPtr) : LONGINT;
```

Low-Level Routines

```
FUNCTION   CheckUpdate    (VAR theEvent: EventRecord) : BOOLEAN;
PROCEDURE  ClipAbove      (window: WindowPeek);
PROCEDURE  SaveOld        (window: WindowPeek);
PROCEDURE  DrawNew        (window: WindowPeek; update: BOOLEAN);
PROCEDURE  PaintOne       (window: WindowPeek; clobberedRgn: RgnHandle);
PROCEDURE  PaintBehind    (startWindow: WindowPeek; clobberedRgn:
                           RgnHandle);
PROCEDURE  CalcVis        (window: WindowPeek);
PROCEDURE  CalcVisBehind  (startWindow: WindowPeek; clobberedRgn:
                           RgnHandle);
```

Diameters of Curvature for Rounded-Corner Windows

Window definition ID	Diameters of curvature
rDocProc	16, 16
rDocProc + 1	4, 4
rDocProc + 2	6, 6
rDocProc + 3	8, 8
rDocProc + 4	10, 10
rDocProc + 5	12, 12
rDocProc + 6	20, 20
rDocProc + 7	24, 24

Window Definition Function

```
FUNCTION MyWindow (varCode: INTEGER; theWindow: WindowPtr; message:
                   INTEGER; param: LONGINT) : LONGINT;
```

Assembly-Language Information

Constants

```
; Window definition IDs

documentProc    .EQU    0    ;standard document window
dBoxProc        .EQU    1    ;alert box or modal dialog box
```

```
plainDBox         .EQU  2   ;plain box
altDBoxProc       .EQU  3   ;plain box with shadow
noGrowDocProc     .EQU  4   ;document window without size box
rDocProc          .EQU  16  ;rounded-corner window
```

; Window class, in windowKind field of window record

```
dialogKind        .EQU  2   ;dialog or alert window
userKind          .EQU  8   ;window created directly by the application
```

; Values returned by FindWindow

```
inDesk            .EQU  0   ;none of the following
inMenuBar         .EQU  1   ;in menu bar
inSysWindow       .EQU  2   ;in system window
inContent         .EQU  3   ;in content region (except grow, if active)
inDrag            .EQU  4   ;in drag region
inGrow            .EQU  5   ;in grow region (active window only)
inGoAway          .EQU  6   ;in go-away region (active window only)
```

; Axis constraints for DragGrayRgn

```
noConstraint      .EQU  0   ;no constraint
hAxisOnly         .EQU  1   ;horizontal axis only
vAxisOnly         .EQU  2   ;vertical axis only
```

; Messages to window definition function

```
wDrawMsg          .EQU  0   ;draw window frame
wHitMsg           .EQU  1   ;tell what region mouse button was pressed in
wCalcRgnMsg       .EQU  2   ;calculate strucRgn and contRgn
wInitMsg          .EQU  3   ;do any additional window initialization
wDisposeMsg       .EQU  4   ;take any additional disposal actions
wGrowMsg          .EQU  5   ;draw window's grow image
wGIconMsg         .EQU  6   ;draw size box in content region
```

; Value returned by window definition function's hit routine

```
wNoHit            .EQU  0   ;none of the following
wInContent        .EQU  1   ;in content region (except grow, if active)
wInDrag           .EQU  2   ;in drag region
wInGrow           .EQU  3   ;in grow region (active window only)
wInGoAway         .EQU  4   ;in go-away region (active window only)
```

; Resource ID of desktop pattern

```
deskPatID         .EQU  16
```

Window Record Data Structure

windowPort	Window's grafPort (portRec bytes)
windowKind	Window class (word)
wVisible	Nonzero if window is visible (byte)

wHilited	Nonzero if window is highlighted (byte)
wGoAway	Nonzero if window has go-away region (byte)
structRgn	Handle to structure region of window
contRgn	Handle to content region of window
updateRgn	Handle to update region of window
windowDef	Handle to window definition function
wDataHandle	Handle to data used by window definition function
wTitleHandle	Handle to window's title (preceded by length byte)
wTitleWidth	Width of title in pixels (word)
wControlList	Handle to window's control list
nextWindow	Pointer to next window in window list
windowPic	Picture handle for drawing window
wRefCon	Window's reference value (long)
windowSize	Size in bytes of window record

Special Macro Names

Pascal name	Macro name
CalcVisBehind	_CalcVBehind
DisposeWindow	_DisposWindow
DragGrayRgn	_DragGrayRgn or, after setting the global variable DragPattern, _DragTheRgn

Variables

WindowList	Pointer to first window in window list
SaveUpdate	Flag for whether to generate update events (word)
PaintWhite	Flag for whether to paint window white before update event (word)
CurActivate	Pointer to window to receive activate event
CurDeactive	Pointer to window to receive deactivate event
GrayRgn	Handle to region drawn as desktop
DeskPattern	Pattern with which desktop is painted (8 bytes)
DeskHook	Address of procedure for painting desktop or responding to clicks on desktop
WMgrPort	Pointer to Window Manager port
GhostWindow	Pointer to window never to be considered frontmost
DragHook	Address of procedure to execute during TrackGoAway, DragWindow, GrowWindow, and DragGrayRgn
DragPattern	Pattern of dragged region's outline (8 bytes)
OldStructure	Handle to saved structure region
OldContent	Handle to saved content region
SaveVisRgn	Handle to saved visRgn

10 THE CONTROL MANAGER

311	About This Chapter
311	About the Control Manager
314	Controls and Windows
314	Controls and Resources
315	Part Codes
316	Control Records
317	The ControlRecord Data Type
318	Using the Control Manager
319	Control Manager Routines
319	Initialization and Allocation
321	Control Display
323	Mouse Location
325	Control Movement and Sizing
326	Control Setting and Range
327	Miscellaneous Routines
328	Defining Your Own Controls
328	The Control Definition Function
330	The Draw Routine
330	The Test Routine
330	The Routine to Calculate Regions
331	The Initialize Routine
331	The Dispose Routine
331	The Drag Routine
331	The Position Routine
332	The Thumb Routine
332	The Track Routine
332	Formats of Resources for Controls
334	Summary of the Control Manager

The Control Manager

ABOUT THIS CHAPTER

This chapter describes the Control Manager, the part of the Toolbox that deals with controls, such as buttons, check boxes, and scroll bars. Using the Control Manager, your application can create, manipulate, and dispose of controls.

You should already be familiar with:

- resources, as discussed in chapter 5
- the basic concepts and structures behind QuickDraw, particularly points, rectangles, regions, and grafPorts
- the Toolbox Event Manager
- the Window Manager

Note: Except for scroll bars, most controls appear only in dialog or alert boxes. To learn how to implement dialogs and alerts in your application, you'll have to read chapter 13.

ABOUT THE CONTROL MANAGER

The Control Manager is the part of the Toolbox that deals with controls. A **control** is an object on the Macintosh screen with which the user, using the mouse, can cause instant action with visible results or change settings to modify a future action. Using the Control Manager, your application can:

- create and dispose of controls
- display or hide controls
- monitor the user's operation of a control with the mouse and respond accordingly
- read or change the setting or other properties of a control
- change the size, location, or appearance of a control

Your application performs these actions by calling the appropriate Control Manager routines. The Control Manager carries out the actual operations, but it's up to you to decide when, where, and how.

Controls may be of various types (see Figure 1), each with its own characteristic appearance on the screen and responses to the mouse. Each individual control has its own specific properties—such as its location, size, and setting—but controls of the same type behave in the same general way.

Certain standard types of controls are predefined for you. Your application can easily create and use controls of these standard types, and can also define its own "custom" control types. Among the standard control types are the following:

- **Buttons** cause an immediate or continuous action when clicked or pressed with the mouse. They appear on the screen as rounded-corner rectangles with a title centered inside.

Inside Macintosh

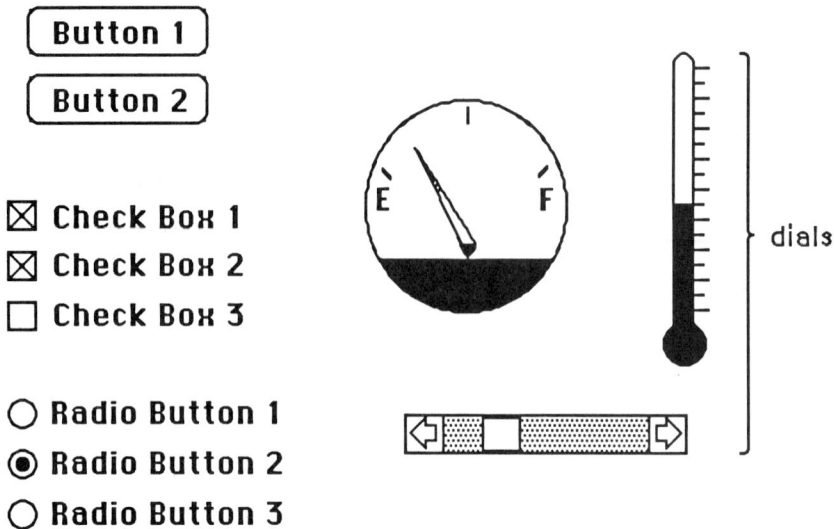

Figure 1. Controls

- **Check boxes** retain and display a setting, either checked (on) or unchecked (off); clicking with the mouse reverses the setting. On the screen, a check box appears as a small square with a title alongside it; the box is either filled in with an "X" (checked) or empty (unchecked). Check boxes are frequently used to control or modify some future action, instead of causing an immediate action of their own.

- **Radio buttons** also retain and display an on-or-off setting. They're organized into groups, with the property that only one button in the group can be on at a time: Clicking one button in a group both turns it on and turns off the button that was on, like the buttons on a car radio. Radio buttons are used to offer a choice among several alternatives. On the screen, they look like round check boxes; the radio button that's on is filled in with a small black circle instead of an "X".

Note: The Control Manager doesn't know how radio buttons are grouped, and doesn't automatically turn one off when the user clicks another one on: It's up to your program to handle this.

Another important category of controls is **dials**. These display the value, magnitude, or position of something, typically in some pseudoanalog form such as the position of a sliding switch, the reading on a thermometer scale, or the angle of a needle on a gauge; the setting may be displayed digitally as well. The control's moving part that displays the current setting is called the **indicator**. The user may be able to change a dial's setting by dragging its indicator with the mouse, or the dial may simply display a value not under the user's direct control (such as the amount of free space remaining on a disk).

One type of dial is predefined for you: The standard Macintosh scroll bars. Figure 2 shows the five parts of a scroll bar and the terms used by the Control Manager (and this chapter) to refer to them. Notice that the part of the scroll bar that Macintosh users know as the "scroll box" is called the "thumb" here. Also, for simplicity, the terms "up" and "down" are used even when referring to horizontal scroll bars (in which case "up" really means "left" and "down" means "right").

The Control Manager

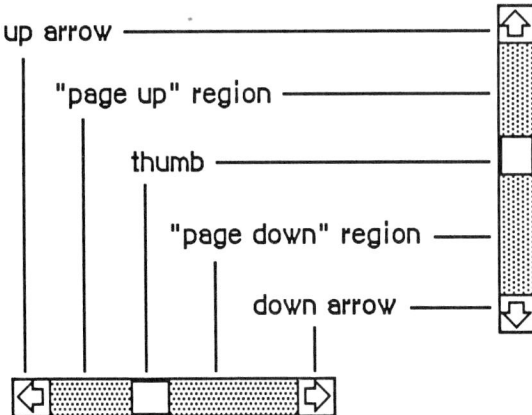

Figure 2. Parts of a Scroll Bar

The up and down arrows scroll the window's contents a line at a time. The two paging regions scroll a "page" (windowful) at a time. The thumb can be dragged to any position in the scroll bar, to scroll to a corresponding position within the document. Although they may seem to behave like individual controls, these are all parts of a single control, the scroll bar type of dial. You can define other dials of any shape or complexity for yourself if your application needs them.

A control may be **active** or **inactive**. Active controls respond to the user's mouse actions; inactive controls don't. When an active control is clicked or pressed, it's usually highlighted (see Figure 3). Standard button controls are inverted, but some control types may use other forms of highlighting, such as making the outline heavier. It's also possible for just a part of a control to be highlighted: For example, when the user presses the mouse button inside a scroll arrow or the thumb in a scroll bar, the arrow or thumb (not the whole scroll bar) becomes highlighted until the button is released.

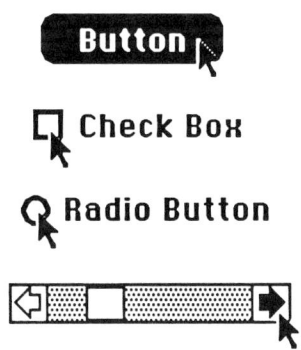

Figure 3. Highlighted Active Controls

A control is made inactive when it has no meaning or effect in the current context, such as an "Open" button when no document has been selected to open, or a scroll bar when there's currently nothing to scroll to. An inactive control remains visible, but is highlighted in some special way, depending on its control type (see Figure 4). For example, the title of an inactive button, check box, or radio button is **dimmed** (drawn in gray rather than black).

Inside Macintosh

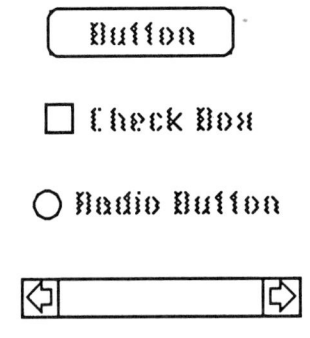

Figure 4. Inactive Controls

CONTROLS AND WINDOWS

Every control "belongs" to a particular window: When displayed, the control appears within that window's content region; when manipulated with the mouse, it acts on that window. All coordinates pertaining to the control (such as those describing its location) are given in its window's local coordinate system.

> **Warning:** In order for the Control Manager to draw a control properly, the control's window must have the top left corner of its grafPort's portRect at coordinates (0,0). If you change a window's local coordinate system for any reason (with the QuickDraw procedure SetOrigin), be sure to change it back—so that the top left corner is again at (0,0)—before drawing any of its controls. Since almost all of the Control Manager routines can (at least potentially) redraw a control, the safest policy is simply to change the coordinate system back before calling *any* Control Manager routine.

Normally you'll include buttons and check boxes in dialog or alert windows only. You create such windows with the Dialog Manager, and the Dialog Manager takes care of drawing the controls and letting you know whether the user clicked one of them. See chapter 13 for details.

CONTROLS AND RESOURCES

The relationship between controls and resources is analogous to the relationship between windows and resources: Just as there are window definition functions and window templates, there are control definition functions and control templates.

Each type of control has a **control definition function** that determines how controls of that type look and behave. The Control Manager calls the control definition function whenever it needs to perform a type-dependent action, such as drawing the control on the screen. Control definition functions are stored as resources and accessed through the Resource Manager. The system resource file includes definition functions for the standard control types (buttons, check boxes, radio buttons, and scroll bars). If you want to define your own, nonstandard control types, you'll have to write control definition functions for them, as described later in the section "Defining Your Own Controls".

The Control Manager

When you create a control, you specify its type with a **control definition ID**, which tells the Control Manager the resource ID of the definition function for that control type. The Control Manager provides the following predefined constants for the definition IDs of the standard control types:

```
CONST  pushButProc   = 0;    {simple button}
       checkBoxProc  = 1;    {check box}
       radioButProc  = 2;    {radio button}
       scrollBarProc = 16;   {scroll bar}
```

Note: The control definition function for scroll bars figures out whether a scroll bar is vertical or horizontal from a rectangle you specify when you create the control.

The title of a button, check box, or radio button normally appears in the system font, but you can add the following constant to the definition ID to specify that you instead want to use the font currently associated with the window's grafPort:

```
CONST  useWFont = 8;   {use window's font}
```

To create a control, the Control Manager needs to know not only the control definition ID but also other information specific to this control, such as its title (if any), the window it belongs to, and its location within the window. You can supply all the needed information in individual parameters to a Control Manager routine, or you can store it in a **control template** in a resource file and just pass the template's resource ID. Using templates is highly recommended, since it simplifies the process of creating controls and isolates the control descriptions from your application's code.

PART CODES

Some controls, such as buttons, are simple and straightforward. Others can be complex objects with many parts: For example, a scroll bar has two scroll arrows, two paging regions, and a thumb (see Figure 2 above). To allow different parts of a control to respond to the mouse in different ways, many of the Control Manager routines accept a **part code** as a parameter or return one as a result.

A part code is an integer between 1 and 253 that stands for a particular part of a control. Each type of control has its own set of part codes, assigned by the control definition function for that type. A simple control such as a button or check box might have just one "part" that encompasses the entire control; a more complex control such as a scroll bar can have as many parts as are needed to define how the control operates.

Note: The values 254 and 255 aren't used for part codes—254 is reserved for future use, and 255 means the entire control is inactive.

The part codes for the standard control types are as follows:

Inside Macintosh

```
CONST  inButton     = 10;   {simple button}
       inCheckBox   = 11;   {check box or radio button}
       inUpButton   = 20;   {up arrow of a scroll bar}
       inDownButton = 21;   {down arrow of a scroll bar}
       inPageUp     = 22;   {"page up" region of a scroll bar}
       inPageDown   = 23;   {"page down" region of a scroll bar}
       inThumb      = 129;  {thumb of a scroll bar}
```

Notice that inCheckBox applies to both check boxes and radio buttons.

Note: For special information about assigning part codes to your own control types, see "Defining Your Own Controls".

CONTROL RECORDS

Every control is represented internally by a **control record** containing all pertinent information about that control. The control record contains the following:

- A pointer to the window the control belongs to.
- A handle to the next control in the window's control list.
- A handle to the control definition function.
- The control's title, if any.
- A rectangle that completely encloses the control, which determines the control's size and location within its window. The entire control, including the title of a check box or radio button, is drawn inside this rectangle.
- An indication of whether the control is currently active and how it's to be highlighted.
- The current setting of the control (if this type of control retains a setting) and the minimum and maximum values the setting can assume. For check boxes and radio buttons, a setting of 0 means the control is off and 1 means it's on.

The control record also contains an indication of whether the control is currently **visible** or **invisible**. These terms refer only to whether the control is drawn in its window, not to whether you can see it on the screen. A control may be "visible" and still not appear on the screen, because it's obscured by overlapping windows or other objects.

There's a field in the control record for a pointer to the control's default **action procedure**. An action procedure defines some action to be performed repeatedly for as long as the user holds down the mouse button inside the control. The default action procedure may be used by the Control Manager function TrackControl if you call it without passing a pointer to an action procedure; this is discussed in detail in the description of TrackControl in the "Control Manager Routines" section.

Finally, the control record includes a 32-bit **reference value** field, which is reserved for use by your application. You specify an initial reference value when you create a control, and can then read or change the reference value whenever you wish.

The data type for a control record is called ControlRecord. A control record is referred to by a handle:

The Control Manager

```
TYPE ControlPtr    = ^ControlRecord;
     ControlHandle = ^ControlPtr;
```

The Control Manager functions for creating a control return a handle to a newly allocated control record; thereafter, your program should normally refer to the control by this handle. Most of the Control Manager routines expect a control handle as their first parameter.

You can store into and access most of a control record's fields with Control Manager routines, so normally you don't have to know the exact field names. However, if you want more information about the exact structure of a control record—if you're defining your own control types, for instance—it's given below.

The ControlRecord Data Type

The ControlRecord data type is defined as follows:

```
TYPE ControlRecord =
    PACKED RECORD
        nextControl:    ControlHandle;  {next control}
        contrlOwner:    WindowPtr;      {control's window}
        contrlRect:     Rect;           {enclosing rectangle}
        contrlVis:      Byte;           {255 if visible}
        contrlHilite:   Byte;           {highlight state}
        contrlValue:    INTEGER;        {control's current setting}
        contrlMin:      INTEGER;        {control's minimum setting}
        contrlMax:      INTEGER;        {control's maximum setting}
        contrlDefProc:  Handle;         {control definition function}
        contrlData:     Handle;         {data used by contrlDefProc}
        contrlAction:   ProcPtr;        {default action procedure}
        contrlRfCon:    LONGINT;        {control's reference value}
        contrlTitle:    Str255          {control's title}
    END;
```

NextControl is a handle to the next control associated with this control's window. All the controls belonging to a given window are kept in a linked list, beginning in the controlList field of the window record and chained together through the nextControl fields of the individual control records. The end of the list is marked by a NIL value; as new controls are created, they're added to the beginning of the list.

ContrlOwner is a pointer to the window that this control belongs to.

ContrlRect is the rectangle that completely encloses the control, in the local coordinates of the control's window.

When contrlVis is 0, the control is currently invisible; when it's 255, the control is visible.

ContrlHilite specifies whether and how the control is to be highlighted, indicating whether it's active or inactive. The HiliteControl procedure lets you set this field; see the description of HiliteControl for more information about the meaning of the field's value.

ContrlValue is the control's current setting. For check boxes and radio buttons, 0 means the control is off and 1 means it's on. For dials, the fields contrlMin and contrlMax define the range of possible settings; contrlValue may take on any value within that range. Other (custom) control types can use these three fields as they see fit.

Inside Macintosh

ContrlDefProc is a handle to the control definition function for this type of control. When you create a control, you identify its type with a control definition ID, which is converted into a handle to the control definition function and stored in the contrlDefProc field. Thereafter, the Control Manager uses this handle to access the definition function; you should never need to refer to this field directly.

> **Note:** The high-order byte of the contrlDefProc field contains some additional information that the Control Manager gets from the control definition ID; for details, see the section "Defining Your Own Controls".

ContrlData is reserved for use by the control definition function, typically to hold additional information specific to a particular control type. For example, the standard definition function for scroll bars uses this field for a handle to the region containing the scroll bar's thumb. If no more than four bytes of additional information are needed, the definition function can store the information directly in the contrlData field rather than use a handle.

ContrlAction is a pointer to the control's default action procedure, if any. The Control Manager function TrackControl may call this procedure to respond to the user's dragging the mouse inside the control.

ContrlRfCon is the control's reference value field, which the application may store into and access for any purpose.

ContrlTitle is the control's title, if any.

USING THE CONTROL MANAGER

To use the Control Manager, you must have previously called InitGraf to initialize QuickDraw, InitFonts to initialize the Font Manager, and InitWindows to initialize the Window Manager.

> **Note:** For controls in dialogs or alerts, the Dialog Manager makes some of the basic Control Manager calls for you; see chapter 13 for more information.

Where appropriate in your program, use NewControl or GetNewControl to create any controls you need. NewControl takes descriptive information about the new control from its parameters; GetNewControl gets the information from a control template in a resource file. When you no longer need a control, call DisposeControl to remove it from its window's control list and release the memory it occupies. To dispose of all of a given window's controls at once, use KillControls.

> **Note:** The Window Manager procedures DisposeWindow and CloseWindow automatically dispose of all the controls associated with the given window.

When the Toolbox Event Manager function GetNextEvent reports that an update event has occurred for a window, the application should call DrawControls to redraw the window's controls as part of the process of updating the window.

After receiving a mouse-down event from GetNextEvent, do the following:

1. First call FindWindow to determine which part of which window the mouse button was pressed in.

2. If it was in the content region of the active window, call FindControl for that window to find out whether it was in an active control, and if so, in which part of which control.

3. Finally, take whatever action is appropriate when the user presses the mouse button in that part of the control, using routines such as TrackControl (to perform some action repeatedly for as long as the mouse button is down, or to allow the user to drag the control's indicator with the mouse), DragControl (to pull an outline of the control across the screen and move the control to a new location), and HiliteControl (to change the way the control is highlighted).

For the standard control types, step 3 involves calling TrackControl. TrackControl handles the highlighting of the control and determines whether the mouse is still in the control when the mouse button is released. It also handles the dragging of the thumb in a scroll bar and, via your action procedure, the response to presses or clicks in the other parts of a scroll bar. When TrackControl returns the part code for a button, check box, or radio button, the application must do whatever is appropriate as a response to a click of that control. When TrackControl returns the part code for the thumb of a scroll bar, the application must scroll to the corresponding relative position in the document.

The application's exact response to mouse activity in a control that retains a setting will depend on the current setting of the control, which is available from the GetCtlValue function. For controls whose values can be set by the user, the SetCtlValue procedure may be called to change the control's setting and redraw the control accordingly. You'll call SetCtlValue, for example, when a check box or radio button is clicked, to change the setting and draw or clear the mark inside the control.

Wherever needed in your program, you can call HideControl to make a control invisible or ShowControl to make it visible. Similarly, MoveControl, which simply changes a control's location without pulling around an outline of it, can be called at any time, as can SizeControl, which changes its size. For example, when the user changes the size of a document window that contains a scroll bar, you'll call HideControl to remove the old scroll bar, MoveControl and SizeControl to change its location and size, and ShowControl to display it as changed.

Whenever necessary, you can read various attributes of a control with GetCTitle, GetCtlMin, GetCtlMax, GetCRefCon, or GetCtlAction; you can change them with SetCTitle, SetCtlMin, SetCtlMax, SetCRefCon, or SetCtlAction.

CONTROL MANAGER ROUTINES

Initialization and Allocation

```
FUNCTION NewControl (theWindow: WindowPtr; boundsRect: Rect;
        title: Str255; visible: BOOLEAN; value: INTEGER;
        min,max: INTEGER; procID: INTEGER; refCon: LONGINT) :
        ControlHandle;
```

NewControl creates a control, adds it to the beginning of theWindow's control list, and returns a handle to the new control. The values passed as parameters are stored in the corresponding fields of the control record, as described below. The field that determines highlighting is set to 0 (no highlighting) and the pointer to the default action procedure is set to NIL (none).

> **Note:** The control definition function may do additional initialization, including changing any of the fields of the control record. The only standard control for which additional initialization is done is the scroll bar; its control definition function allocates space for a region to hold the thumb and stores the region handle in the contrlData field of the control record.

TheWindow is the window the new control will belong to. All coordinates pertaining to the control will be interpreted in this window's local coordinate system.

BoundsRect, given in theWindow's local coordinates, is the rectangle that encloses the control and thus determines its size and location. Note the following about the enclosing rectangle for the standard controls:

- Simple buttons are drawn to fit the rectangle exactly. (The control definition function calls the QuickDraw procedure FrameRoundRect.) To allow for the tallest characters in the system font, there should be at least a 20-point difference between the top and bottom coordinates of the rectangle.

- For check boxes and radio buttons, there should be at least a 16-point difference between the top and bottom coordinates.

- By convention, scroll bars are 16 pixels wide, so there should be a 16-point difference between the left and right (or top and bottom) coordinates. (If there isn't, the scroll bar will be scaled to fit the rectangle.) A standard scroll bar should be at least 48 pixels long, to allow room for the scroll arrows and thumb.

Title is the control's title, if any (if none, you can just pass the empty string as the title). Be sure the title will fit in the control's enclosing rectangle; if it won't it will be truncated on the right for check boxes and radio buttons, or centered and truncated on both ends for simple buttons.

If the visible parameter is TRUE, NewControl draws the control.

> **Note:** It does *not* use the standard window updating mechanism, but instead draws the control immediately in the window.

The min and max parameters define the control's range of possible settings; the value parameter gives the initial setting. For controls that don't retain a setting, such as buttons, the values you supply for these parameters will be stored in the control record but will never be used. So it doesn't matter what values you give for those controls—0 for all three parameters will do. For controls that just retain an on-or-off setting, such as check boxes or radio buttons, min should be 0 (meaning the control is off) and max should be 1 (meaning it's on). For dials, you can specify whatever values are appropriate for min, max, and value.

ProcID is the control definition ID, which leads to the control definition function for this type of control. (The function is read into memory if it isn't already in memory.) The control definition IDs for the standard control types are listed above under "Controls and Resources". Control definition IDs for custom control types are discussed later under "Defining Your Own Controls".

RefCon is the control's reference value, set and used only by your application.

```
FUNCTION GetNewControl (controlID: INTEGER; theWindow:
        WindowPtr) : ControlHandle;
```

GetNewControl creates a control from a control template stored in a resource file, adds it to the beginning of theWindow's control list, and returns a handle to the new control. ControlID is the resource ID of the template. GetNewControl works exactly the same as NewControl (above), except that it gets the initial values for the new control's fields from the specified control template instead of accepting them as parameters. If the control template can't be read from the resource file, GetNewControl returns NIL. It releases the memory occupied by the resource before returning.

```
PROCEDURE DisposeControl (theControl: ControlHandle);
```

Assembly-language note: The macro you invoke to call DisposeControl from assembly language is named _DisposControl.

DisposeControl removes theControl from the screen, deletes it from its window's control list, and releases the memory occupied by the control record and any data structures associated with the control.

```
PROCEDURE KillControls (theWindow: WindowPtr);
```

KillControls disposes of all controls associated with theWindow by calling DisposeControl (above) for each.

Note: Remember that the Window Manager procedures CloseWindow and DisposeWindow automatically dispose of all controls associated with the given window.

Control Display

These procedures affect the appearance of a control but not its size or location.

```
PROCEDURE SetCTitle (theControl: ControlHandle; title: Str255);
```

SetCTitle sets theControl's title to the given string and redraws the control.

```
PROCEDURE GetCTitle (theControl: ControlHandle; VAR title:
        Str255);
```

GetCTitle returns theControl's title as the value of the title parameter.

Inside Macintosh

```
PROCEDURE HideControl (theControl: ControlHandle);
```

HideControl makes theControl invisible. It fills the region the control occupies within its window with the background pattern of the window's grafPort. It also adds the control's enclosing rectangle to the window's update region, so that anything else that was previously obscured by the control will reappear on the screen. If the control is already invisible, HideControl has no effect.

```
PROCEDURE ShowControl (theControl: ControlHandle);
```

ShowControl makes theControl visible. The control is drawn in its window but may be completely or partially obscured by overlapping windows or other objects. If the control is already visible, ShowControl has no effect.

```
PROCEDURE DrawControls (theWindow: WindowPtr);
```

DrawControls draws all controls currently visible in theWindow. The controls are drawn in reverse order of creation; thus in case of overlap the earliest-created controls appear frontmost in the window.

> **Note:** Window Manager routines such as SelectWindow, ShowWindow, and BringToFront do not automatically call DrawControls to display the window's controls. They just add the appropriate regions to the window's update region, generating an update event. Your program should always call DrawControls explicitly upon receiving an update event for a window that contains controls.

```
PROCEDURE HiliteControl (theControl: ControlHandle; hiliteState:
         INTEGER);
```

HiliteControl changes the way theControl is highlighted. HiliteState has one of the following values:

- The value 0 means no highlighting. (The control is active.)
- A value between 1 and 253 is interpreted as a part code designating the part of the (active) control to be highlighted.
- The value 255 means that the control is to be made inactive and highlighted accordingly.

> **Note:** The value 254 should not be used; this value is reserved for future use.

HiliteControl calls the control definition function to redraw the control with its new highlighting.

The Control Manager

Mouse Location

```
FUNCTION FindControl (thePoint: Point; theWindow: WindowPtr; VAR
        whichControl: ControlHandle) : INTEGER;
```

When the Window Manager function FindWindow reports that the mouse button was pressed in the content region of a window, and the window contains controls, the application should call FindControl with theWindow equal to the window pointer and thePoint equal to the point where the mouse button was pressed (in the window's local coordinates). FindControl tells which of the window's controls, if any, the mouse button was pressed in:

- If it was pressed in a visible, active control, FindControl sets the whichControl parameter to the control handle and returns a part code identifying the part of the control that it was pressed in.
- If it was pressed in an invisible or inactive control, or not in any control, FindControl sets whichControl to NIL and returns 0 as its result.

Warning: Notice that FindControl expects the mouse point in the window's local coordinates, whereas FindWindow expects it in global coordinates. Always be sure to convert the point to local coordinates with the QuickDraw procedure GlobalToLocal before calling FindControl.

Note: FindControl also returns NIL for whichControl and 0 as its result if the window is invisible or doesn't contain the given point. In these cases, however, FindWindow wouldn't have returned this window in the first place, so the situation should never arise.

```
FUNCTION TrackControl (theControl: ControlHandle; startPt: Point;
        actionProc: ProcPtr) : INTEGER;
```

When the mouse button is pressed in a visible, active control, the application should call TrackControl with theControl equal to the control handle and startPt equal to the point where the mouse button was pressed (in the local coordinates of the control's window). TrackControl follows the movements of the mouse and responds in whatever way is appropriate until the mouse button is released; the exact response depends on the type of control and the part of the control in which the mouse button was pressed. If highlighting is appropriate, TrackControl does the highlighting, and undoes it before returning. When the mouse button is released, TrackControl returns with the part code if the mouse is in the same part of the control that it was originally in, or with 0 if not (in which case the application should do nothing).

If the mouse button was pressed in an indicator, TrackControl drags a dotted outline of it to follow the mouse. When the mouse button is released, TrackControl calls the control definition function to reposition the control's indicator. The control definition function for scroll bars responds by redrawing the thumb, calculating the control's current setting based on the new relative position of the thumb, and storing the current setting in the control record; for example, if the minimum and maximum settings are 0 and 10, and the thumb is in the middle of the scroll bar, 5 is stored as the current setting. The application must then scroll to the corresponding relative position in the document.

TrackControl may take additional actions beyond highlighting the control or dragging the indicator, depending on the value passed in the actionProc parameter, as described below. The

Inside Macintosh

following tells you what to pass for the standard control types; for a custom control, what you pass will depend on how the control is defined.

- If actionProc is NIL, TrackControl performs no additional actions. This is appropriate for simple buttons, check boxes, radio buttons, and the thumb of a scroll bar.

- ActionProc may be a pointer to an action procedure that defines some action to be performed repeatedly for as long as the user holds down the mouse button. (See below for details.)

- If actionProc is POINTER(–1), TrackControl looks in the control record for a pointer to the control's default action procedure. If that field of the control record contains a procedure pointer, TrackControl uses the action procedure it points to; if the field contains POINTER (–1), TrackControl calls the control definition function to perform the necessary action. (If the field contains NIL, TrackControl does nothing.)

The action procedure in the control definition function is described in the section "Defining Your Own Controls". The following paragraphs describe only the action procedure whose pointer is passed in the actionProc parameter or stored in the control record.

If the mouse button was pressed in an indicator, the action procedure (if any) should have no parameters. This procedure must allow for the fact that the mouse may not be inside the original control part.

If the mouse button was pressed in a control part other than an indicator, the action procedure should be of the form

```
PROCEDURE MyAction (theControl: ControlHandle; partCode: INTEGER);
```

In this case, TrackControl passes the control handle and the part code to the action procedure. (It passes 0 in the partCode parameter if the mouse has moved outside the original control part.) As an example of this type of action procedure, consider what should happen when the mouse button is pressed in a scroll arrow or paging region in a scroll bar. For these cases, your action procedure should examine the part code to determine exactly where the mouse button was pressed, scroll up or down a line or page as appropriate, and call SetCtlValue to change the control's setting and redraw the thumb.

Warning: Since it has a different number of parameters depending on whether the mouse button was pressed in an indicator or elsewhere, the action procedure you pass to TrackControl (or whose pointer you store in the control record) can be set up for only one case or the other. If you store a pointer to a default action procedure in a control record, be sure it will be used only when appropriate for that type of action procedure. The only way to specify actions in response to all mouse-down events in a control, regardless of whether they're in an indicator, is via the control definition function.

Assembly-language note: If you store a pointer to a procedure in the global variable DragHook, that procedure will be called repeatedly (with no parameters) for as long as the user holds down the mouse button. TrackControl invokes the Window Manager macro _DragTheRgn, which calls the DragHook procedure. _DragTheRgn uses the pattern stored in the global variable DragPattern for the dragged outline of the indicator.

The Control Manager

```
FUNCTION TestControl (theControl: ControlHandle; thePoint: Point)
          : INTEGER;
```

If theControl is visible and active, TestControl tests which part of the control contains thePoint (in the local coordinates of the control's window); it returns the corresponding part code, or 0 if the point is outside the control. If the control is invisible or inactive, TestControl returns 0. TestControl is called by FindControl and TrackControl; normally you won't need to call it yourself.

Control Movement and Sizing

```
PROCEDURE MoveControl (theControl: ControlHandle; h,v: INTEGER);
```

MoveControl moves theControl to a new location within its window. The top left corner of the control's enclosing rectangle is moved to the horizontal and vertical coordinates h and v (given in the local coordinates of the control's window); the bottom right corner is adjusted accordingly, to keep the size of the rectangle the same as before. If the control is currently visible, it's hidden and then redrawn at its new location.

```
PROCEDURE DragControl (theControl: ControlHandle; startPt: Point;
          limitRect,slopRect: Rect; axis: INTEGER);
```

Called with the mouse button down inside theControl, DragControl pulls a dotted outline of the control around the screen, following the movements of the mouse until the button is released. When the mouse button is released, DragControl calls MoveControl to move the control to the location to which it was dragged.

> **Note:** Before beginning to follow the mouse, DragControl calls the control definition function to allow it to do its own "custom dragging" if it chooses. If the definition function doesn't choose to do any custom dragging, DragControl uses the default method of dragging described here.

The startPt, limitRect, slopRect, and axis parameters have the same meaning as for the Window Manager function DragGrayRgn. These parameters are reviewed briefly below; see the description of DragGrayRgn in chapter 9 for more details.

- StartPt is assumed to be the point where the mouse button was originally pressed, in the local coordinates of the control's window.
- LimitRect limits the travel of the control's outline, and should normally coincide with or be contained within the window's content region.
- SlopRect allows the user some "slop" in moving the mouse; it should completely enclose limitRect.
- The axis parameter allows you to constrain the control's motion to only one axis. It has one of the following values:

```
CONST noConstraint = 0;  {no constraint}
      hAxisOnly    = 1;  {horizontal axis only}
      vAxisOnly    = 2;  {vertical axis only}
```

Inside Macintosh

Assembly-language note: Like TrackControl, DragControl invokes the macro _DragTheRgn, so you can use the global variables DragHook and DragPattern.

```
PROCEDURE SizeControl (theControl: ControlHandle; w,h: INTEGER);
```

SizeControl changes the size of theControl's enclosing rectangle. The bottom right corner of the rectangle is adjusted to set the rectangle's width and height to the number of pixels specified by w and h; the position of the top left corner is not changed. If the control is currently visible, it's hidden and then redrawn in its new size.

Control Setting and Range

```
PROCEDURE SetCtlValue (theControl: ControlHandle; theValue:
        INTEGER);
```

SetCtlValue sets theControl's current setting to theValue and redraws the control to reflect the new setting. For check boxes and radio buttons, the value 1 fills the control with the appropriate mark, and 0 clears it. For scroll bars, SetCtlValue redraws the thumb where appropriate.

If the specified value is out of range, it's forced to the nearest endpoint of the current range (that is, if theValue is less than the minimum setting, SetCtlValue sets the current setting to the minimum; if theValue is greater than the maximum setting, it sets the current setting to the maximum).

```
FUNCTION GetCtlValue (theControl: ControlHandle) : INTEGER;
```

GetCtlValue returns theControl's current setting.

```
PROCEDURE SetCtlMin (theControl: ControlHandle; minValue:
        INTEGER);
```

Assembly-language note: The macro you invoke to call SetCtlMin from assembly language is named _SetMinCtl.

SetCtlMin sets theControl's minimum setting to minValue and redraws the control to reflect the new range. If the control's current setting is less than minValue, the setting is changed to the new minimum.

```
FUNCTION GetCtlMin (theControl: ControlHandle) : INTEGER;
```

Assembly-language note: The macro you invoke to call GetCtlMin from assembly language is named _GetMinCtl.

GetCtlMin returns theControl's minimum setting.

```
PROCEDURE SetCtlMax (theControl: ControlHandle; maxValue:
        INTEGER);
```

Assembly-language note: The macro you invoke to call SetCtlMax from assembly language is named _SetMaxCtl.

SetCtlMax sets theControl's maximum setting to maxValue and redraws the control to reflect the new range. If the control's current setting is greater than maxValue, the setting is changed to the new maximum.

Note: If you set the maximum setting of a scroll bar equal to its minimum setting, the control definition function will make the scroll bar inactive.

```
FUNCTION GetCtlMax (theControl: ControlHandle) : INTEGER;
```

Assembly-language note: The macro you invoke to call GetCtlMax from assembly language is named _GetMaxCtl.

GetCtlMax returns theControl's maximum setting.

Miscellaneous Routines

```
PROCEDURE SetCRefCon (theControl: ControlHandle; data: LONGINT);
```

SetCRefCon sets theControl's reference value to the given data.

```
FUNCTION GetCRefCon (theControl: ControlHandle) : LONGINT;
```

GetCRefCon returns theControl's current reference value.

Inside Macintosh

```
PROCEDURE SetCtlAction (theControl: ControlHandle; actionProc:
            ProcPtr);
```

SetCtlAction sets theControl's default action procedure to actionProc.

```
FUNCTION GetCtlAction (theControl: ControlHandle) : ProcPtr;
```

GetCtlAction returns a pointer to theControl's default action procedure, if any. (It returns whatever is in that field of the control record.)

DEFINING YOUR OWN CONTROLS

In addition to the standard, built-in control types (buttons, check boxes, radio buttons, and scroll bars), the Control Manager allows you to define "custom" control types of your own. Maybe you need a three-way selector switch, a memory-space indicator that looks like a thermometer, or a thruster control for a spacecraft simulator—whatever your application calls for. Controls and their indicators may occupy regions of any shape, in the full generality permitted by QuickDraw.

To define your own type of control, you write a control definition function and store it in a resource file. When you create a control, you provide a control definition ID, which leads to the control definition function. The control definition ID is an integer that contains the resource ID of the control definition function in its upper 12 bits and a **variation code** in its lower four bits. Thus, for a given resource ID and variation code, the control definition ID is

   16 * resource ID + variation code

For example, buttons, check boxes, and radio buttons all use the standard definition function whose resource ID is 0, but they have variation codes of 0, 1, and 2, respectively.

The Control Manager calls the Resource Manager to access the control definition function with the given resource ID. The Resource Manager reads the control definition function into memory and returns a handle to it. The Control Manager stores this handle in the contrlDefProc field of the control record, along with the variation code in the high-order byte of the field. Later, when it needs to perform a type-dependent action on the control, it calls the control definition function and passes it the variation code as a parameter. Figure 5 illustrates this process.

Keep in mind that the calls your application makes to use a control depend heavily on the control definition function. What you pass to the TrackControl function, for example, depends on whether the definition function contains an action procedure for the control. Just as you need to know how to call TrackControl for the standard controls, each custom control type will have a particular calling protocol that must be followed for the control to work properly.

The Control Definition Function

The control definition function is usually written in assembly language, but may be written in Pascal.

You supply the control definition ID:

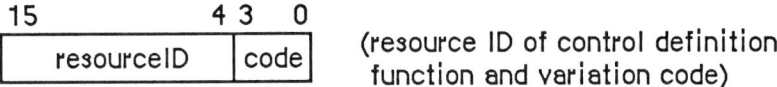

(resource ID of control definition function and variation code)

The Control Manager calls the Resource Manager with

    defHandle := GetResource ('CDEF', resourceID)

and stores into the contrlDefProc field of the control record:

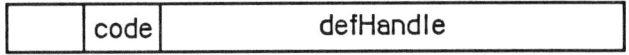

The variation code is passed to the control definition function.

Figure 5. Control Definition Handling

Assembly-language note: The function's entry point must be at the beginning.

You can give your control definition function any name you like. Here's how you would declare one named MyControl:

```
FUNCTION MyControl (varCode: INTEGER; theControl: ControlHandle;
        message: INTEGER; param: LONGINT) : LONGINT;
```

VarCode is the variation code, as described above.

TheControl is a handle to the control that the operation will affect.

The message parameter identifies the desired operation. It has one of the following values:

```
CONST drawCntl   = 0;    {draw the control (or control part)}
      testCntl   = 1;    {test where mouse button was pressed}
      calcCRgns  = 2;    {calculate control's region (or indicator's)}
      initCntl   = 3;    {do any additional control initialization}
      dispCntl   = 4;    {take any additional disposal actions}
      posCntl    = 5;    {reposition control's indicator and update it}
      thumbCntl  = 6;    {calculate parameters for dragging indicator}
      dragCntl   = 7;    {drag control (or its indicator)}
      autoTrack  = 8;    {execute control's action procedure}
```

As described below in the discussions of the routines that perform these operations, the value passed for param, the last parameter of the control definition function, depends on the operation. Where it's not mentioned below, this parameter is ignored. Similarly, the control definition function is expected to return a function result only where indicated; in other cases, the function should return 0.

Defining Your Own Controls I-329

Inside Macintosh

In some cases, the value of param or the function result is a part code. The part code 128 is reserved for future use and shouldn't be used for parts of your controls. Part codes greater than 128 should be used for indicators; however, 129 has special meaning to the control definition function, as described below.

Note: "Routine" here doesn't necessarily mean a procedure or function. While it's a good idea to set these up as subprograms inside the control definition function, you're not required to do so.

The Draw Routine

The message drawCntl asks the control definition function to draw all or part of the control within its enclosing rectangle. The value of param is a part code specifying which part of the control to draw, or 0 for the entire control. If the control is invisible (that is, if its contrlVis field is 0), there's nothing to do; if it's visible, the definition function should draw it (or the requested part), taking into account the current values of its contrlHilite and contrlValue fields. The control may be either scaled or clipped to the enclosing rectangle.

If param is the part code of the control's indicator, the draw routine can assume that the indicator hasn't moved; it might be called, for example, to highlight the indicator. There's a special case, though, in which the draw routine has to allow for the fact that the indicator may have moved: This happens when the Control Manager procedures SetCtlValue, SetCtlMin, and SetCtlMax call the control definition function to redraw the indicator after changing the control setting. Since they have no way of knowing what part code you chose for your indicator, they all pass 129 to mean the indicator. The draw routine must detect this part code as a special case, and remove the indicator from its former location before drawing it.

Note: If your control has more than one indicator, 129 should be interpreted to mean all indicators.

The Test Routine

The Control Manager function FindControl sends the message testCntl to the control definition function when the mouse button is pressed in a visible control. This message asks in which part of the control, if any, a given point lies. The point is passed as the value of param, in the local coordinates of the control's window; the vertical coordinate is in the high-order word of the long integer and the horizontal coordinate is in the low-order word. The control definition function should return the part code for the part of the control that contains the point; it should return 0 if the point is outside the control or if the control is inactive.

The Routine to Calculate Regions

The control definition function should respond to the message calcCRgns by calculating the region the control occupies within its window. Param is a QuickDraw region handle; the definition function should update this region to the region occupied by the control, expressed in the local coordinate system of its window.

I-330 Defining Your Own Controls

If the high-order bit of param is set, the region requested is that of the control's indicator rather than the control as a whole. The definition function should clear the high *byte* (not just the high bit) of the region handle before attempting to update the region.

The Initialize Routine

After initializing fields as appropriate when creating a new control, the Control Manager sends the message initCntl to the control definition function. This gives the definition function a chance to perform any type-specific initialization it may require. For example, if you implement the control's action procedure in its control definition function, you'll set up the initialize routine to store POINTER(–1) in the contrlAction field; TrackControl calls for this control would pass POINTER(–1) in the actionProc parameter.

The control definition function for scroll bars allocates space for a region to hold the scroll bar's thumb and stores the region handle in the contrlData field of the new control record. The initialize routine for standard buttons, check boxes, and radio buttons does nothing.

The Dispose Routine

The Control Manager's DisposeControl procedure sends the message dispCntl to the control definition function, telling it to carry out any additional actions required when disposing of the control. For example, the standard definition function for scroll bars releases the space occupied by the thumb region, whose handle is kept in the control's contrlData field. The dispose routine for standard buttons, check boxes, and radio buttons does nothing.

The Drag Routine

The message dragCntl asks the control definition function to drag the control or its indicator around on the screen to follow the mouse until the user releases the mouse button. Param specifies whether to drag the indicator or the whole control: 0 means drag the whole control, while a nonzero value means drag only the indicator.

The control definition function need not implement any form of "custom dragging"; if it returns a result of 0, the Control Manager will use its own default method of dragging (calling DragControl to drag the control or the Window Manager function DragGrayRgn to drag its indicator). Conversely, if the control definition function chooses to do its own custom dragging, it should signal the Control Manager not to use the default method by returning a nonzero result.

If the whole control is being dragged, the definition function should call MoveControl to reposition the control to its new location after the user releases the mouse button. If just the indicator is being dragged, the definition function should execute its own position routine (see below) to update the control's setting and redraw it in its window.

The Position Routine

For controls that don't use the Control Manager's default method of dragging the control's indicator (as performed by DragGrayRgn), the control definition function must include a position routine. When the mouse button is released inside the indicator of such a control, TrackControl calls the control definition function with the message posCntl to reposition the indicator and update the control's setting accordingly. The value of param is a point giving the vertical and horizontal offset, in pixels, by which the indicator is to be moved relative to its current position. (Typically, this is the offset between the points where the user pressed and released the mouse button while dragging the indicator.) The vertical offset is given in the high-order word of the long integer and the horizontal offset in the low-order word. The definition function should calculate the control's new setting based on the given offset, update the contrlValue field, and redraw the control within its window to reflect the new setting.

> **Note:** The Control Manager procedures SetCtlValue, SetCtlMin, and SetCtlMax do *not* call the control definition function with this message; instead, they pass the drawCntl message to execute the draw routine (see above).

The Thumb Routine

Like the position routine, the thumb routine is required only for controls that don't use the Control Manager's default method of dragging the control's indicator. The control definition function for such a control should respond to the message thumbCntl by calculating the limiting rectangle, slop rectangle, and axis constraint for dragging the control's indicator. Param is a pointer to the following data structure:

```
RECORD
   limitRect,slopRect: Rect;
   axis: INTEGER
END;
```

On entry, param^.limitRect.topLeft contains the point where the mouse button was first pressed. The definition function should store the appropriate values into the fields of the record pointed to by param; they're analogous to the similarly named parameters to DragGrayRgn.

The Track Routine

You can design a control to have its action procedure in the control definition function. To do this, set up the control's initialize routine to store POINTER(–1) in the contrlAction field of the control record, and pass POINTER(–1) in the actionProc parameter to TrackControl. TrackControl will respond by calling the control definition function with the message autoTrack. The definition function should respond like an action procedure, as discussed in detail in the description of TrackControl. It can tell which part of the control the mouse button was pressed in from param, which contains the part code. The track routine for each of the standard control types does nothing.

FORMATS OF RESOURCES FOR CONTROLS

The GetNewControl function takes the resource ID of a control template as a parameter, and gets from that template the same information that the NewControl function gets from eight of its parameters. The resource type for a control template is 'CNTL', and the resource data has the following format:

Number of bytes	Contents
8 bytes	Same as boundsRect parameter to NewControl
2 bytes	Same as value parameter to NewControl
2 bytes	Same as visible parameter to NewControl
2 bytes	Same as max parameter to NewControl
2 bytes	Same as min parameter to NewControl
2 bytes	Same as procID parameter to NewControl
4 bytes	Same as refCon parameter to NewControl
n bytes	Same as title parameter to NewControl (1-byte length in bytes, followed by the characters of the title)

The resource type for a control definition function is 'CDEF'. The resource data is simply the compiled or assembled code of the function.

SUMMARY OF THE CONTROL MANAGER

Constants

```
CONST  { Control definition IDs }

       pushButProc    = 0;    {simple button}
       checkBoxProc   = 1;    {check box}
       radioButProc   = 2;    {radio button}
       useWFont       = 8;    {add to above to use window's font}
       scrollBarProc  = 16;   {scroll bar}

       { Part codes }

       inButton       = 10;   {simple button}
       inCheckBox     = 11;   {check box or radio button}
       inUpButton     = 20;   {up arrow of a scroll bar}
       inDownButton   = 21;   {down arrow of a scroll bar}
       inPageUp       = 22;   {"page up" region of a scroll bar}
       inPageDown     = 23;   {"page down" region of a scroll bar}
       inThumb        = 129;  {thumb of a scroll bar}

       { Axis constraints for DragControl }

       noConstraint   = 0;    {no constraint}
       hAxisOnly      = 1;    {horizontal axis only}
       vAxisOnly      = 2;    {vertical axis only}

       { Messages to control definition function }

       drawCntl   = 0;  {draw the control (or control part)}
       testCntl   = 1;  {test where mouse button was pressed}
       calcCRgns  = 2;  {calculate control's region (or indicator's)}
       initCntl   = 3;  {do any additional control initialization}
       dispCntl   = 4;  {take any additional disposal actions}
       posCntl    = 5;  {reposition control's indicator and update it}
       thumbCntl  = 6;  {calculate parameters for dragging indicator}
       dragCntl   = 7;  {drag control (or its indicator)}
       autoTrack  = 8;  {execute control's action procedure}
```

Data Types

```
TYPE ControlHandle = ^ControlPtr;
     ControlPtr    = ^ControlRecord;
```

The Control Manager

```
ControlRecord =
    PACKED RECORD
        nextControl:    ControlHandle;      {next control}
        contrlOwner:    WindowPtr;          {control's window}
        contrlRect:     Rect;               {enclosing rectangle}
        contrlVis:      Byte;               {255 if visible}
        contrlHilite:   Byte;               {highlight state}
        contrlValue:    INTEGER;            {control's current setting}
        contrlMin:      INTEGER;            {control's minimum setting}
        contrlMax:      INTEGER;            {control's maximum setting}
        contrlDefProc:  Handle;             {control definition function}
        contrlData:     Handle;             {data used by contrlDefProc}
        contrlAction:   ProcPtr;            {default action procedure}
        contrlRfCon:    LONGINT;            {control's reference value}
        contrlTitle:    Str255              {control's title}
    END;
```

Routines

Initialization and Allocation

```
FUNCTION   NewControl      (theWindow: WindowPtr; boundsRect: Rect; title:
                            Str255; visible: BOOLEAN; value: INTEGER;
                            min,max: INTEGER; procID: INTEGER; refCon:
                            LONGINT) : ControlHandle;
FUNCTION   GetNewControl   (controlID: INTEGER; theWindow: WindowPtr) :
                            ControlHandle;
PROCEDURE  DisposeControl  (theControl: ControlHandle);
PROCEDURE  KillControls    (theWindow: WindowPtr);
```

Control Display

```
PROCEDURE  SetCTitle       (theControl: ControlHandle; title: Str255);
PROCEDURE  GetCTitle       (theControl: ControlHandle; VAR title: Str255);
PROCEDURE  HideControl     (theControl: ControlHandle);
PROCEDURE  ShowControl     (theControl: ControlHandle);
PROCEDURE  DrawControls    (theWindow: WindowPtr);
PROCEDURE  HiliteControl   (theControl: ControlHandle; hiliteState:
                            INTEGER);
```

Mouse Location

```
FUNCTION FindControl    (thePoint: Point; theWindow: WindowPtr; VAR
                         whichControl: ControlHandle) : INTEGER;
FUNCTION TrackControl   (theControl: ControlHandle; startPt: Point;
                         actionProc: ProcPtr) : INTEGER;
FUNCTION TestControl    (theControl: ControlHandle; thePoint: Point) :
                         INTEGER;
```

Inside Macintosh

Control Movement and Sizing

```
PROCEDURE MoveControl    (theControl: ControlHandle; h,v: INTEGER);
PROCEDURE DragControl    (theControl: ControlHandle; startPt: Point;
                         limitRect,slopRect: Rect; axis: INTEGER);
PROCEDURE SizeControl    (theControl: ControlHandle; w,h: INTEGER);
```

Control Setting and Range

```
PROCEDURE SetCtlValue    (theControl: ControlHandle; theValue: INTEGER);
FUNCTION  GetCtlValue    (theControl: ControlHandle) : INTEGER;
PROCEDURE SetCtlMin      (theControl: ControlHandle; minValue: INTEGER);
FUNCTION  GetCtlMin      (theControl: ControlHandle) : INTEGER;
PROCEDURE SetCtlMax      (theControl: ControlHandle; maxValue INTEGER);
FUNCTION  GetCtlMax      (theControl: ControlHandle) : INTEGER;
```

Miscellaneous Routines

```
PROCEDURE SetCRefCon     (theControl: ControlHandle; data: LONGINT);
FUNCTION  GetCRefCon     (theControl: ControlHandle) : LONGINT;
PROCEDURE SetCtlAction   (theControl: ControlHandle; actionProc ProcPtr);
FUNCTION  GetCtlAction   (theControl: ControlHandle) : ProcPtr;
```

Action Procedure for TrackControl

```
If an indicator:       PROCEDURE MyAction;
If not an indicator:   PROCEDURE MyAction (theControl: ControlHandle;
                                           partCode: INTEGER);
```

Control Definition Function

```
FUNCTION MyControl  (varCode: INTEGER; theControl: ControlHandle;
                    message: INTEGER; param: LONGINT) : LONGINT;
```

Assembly-Language Information

Constants

```
; Control definition IDs

pushButProc     .EQU  0    ;simple button
checkBoxProc    .EQU  1    ;check box
radioButProc    .EQU  2    ;radio button
useWFont        .EQU  8    ;add to above to use window's font
scrollBarProc   .EQU  16   ;scroll bar
```

```
; Part codes

inButton        .EQU    10      ;simple button
inCheckBox      .EQU    11      ;check box or radio button
inUpButton      .EQU    20      ;up arrow of a scroll bar
inDownButton    .EQU    21      ;down arrow of a scroll bar
inPageUp        .EQU    22      ;"page up" region of a scroll bar
inPageDown      .EQU    23      ;"page down" region of a scroll bar
inThumb         .EQU    129     ;thumb of a scroll bar

; Axis constraints for DragControl

noConstraint    .EQU    0       ;no constraint
hAxisOnly       .EQU    1       ;horizontal axis only
vAxisOnly       .EQU    2       ;vertical axis only

; Messages to control definition function

drawCtlMsg      .EQU    0       ;draw the control (or control part)
hitCtlMsg       .EQU    1       ;test where mouse button was pressed
calcCtlMsg      .EQU    2       ;calculate control's region (or indicator's)
newCtlMsg       .EQU    3       ;do any additional control initialization
dispCtlMsg      .EQU    4       ;take any additional disposal actions
posCtlMsg       .EQU    5       ;reposition control's indicator and update it
thumbCtlMsg     .EQU    6       ;calculate parameters for dragging indicator
dragCtlMsg      .EQU    7       ;drag control (or its indicator)
trackCtlMsg     .EQU    8       ;execute control's action procedure
```

Control Record Data Structure

nextControl	Handle to next control in control list
contrlOwner	Pointer to this control's window
contrlRect	Control's enclosing rectangle (8 bytes)
contrlVis	255 if control is visible (byte)
contrlHilite	Highlight state (byte)
contrlValue	Control's current setting (word)
contrlMin	Control's minimum setting (word)
contrlMax	Control's maximum setting (word)
contrlDefHandle	Handle to control definition function
contrlData	Data used by control definition function (long)
contrlAction	Address of default action procedure
contrlRfCon	Control's reference value (long)
contrlTitle	Handle to control's title (preceded by length byte)
contrlSize	Size in bytes of control record except contrlTitle field

Inside Macintosh

Special Macro Names

Pascal name	Macro name
DisposeControl	_DisposControl
GetCtlMax	_GetMaxCtl
GetCtlMin	_GetMinCtl
SetCtlMax	_SetMaxCtl
SetCtlMin	_SetMinCtl

Variables

DragHook	Address of procedure to execute during TrackControl and DragControl
DragPattern	Pattern of dragged region's outline (8 bytes)

11 THE MENU MANAGER

341 About This Chapter
341 About the Menu Manager
341   The Menu Bar
342   Appearance of Menus
343   Keyboard Equivalents for Commands
344 Menus and Resources
344 Menu Records
345   The MenuInfo Data Type
345 Menu Lists
346 Creating a Menu in Your Program
347   Multiple Items
347   Items with Icons
347   Marked Items
348   Character Style of Items
348   Items with Keyboard Equivalents
349   Disabled Items
349 Using the Menu Manager
351 Menu Manager Routines
351   Initialization and Allocation
352   Forming the Menus
353   Forming the Menu Bar
355   Choosing From a Menu
357   Controlling the Appearance of Items
361   Miscellaneous Routines
362 Defining Your Own Menus
362   The Menu Definition Procedure
363 Formats of Resources for Menus
364   Menus in a Resource File
365   Menu Bars in a Resource File
366 Summary of the Menu Manager

The Menu Manager

ABOUT THIS CHAPTER

This chapter describes the Menu Manager, the part of the Toolbox that allows you to create sets of menus, and allows the user to choose from the commands in those menus.

You should already be familiar with:

- resources, as described in chapter 5
- the basic concepts and structures behind QuickDraw, particularly points, rectangles, and character style
- the Toolbox Event Manager

ABOUT THE MENU MANAGER

The Menu Manager supports the use of **menus**, an integral part of the Macintosh user interface. Menus allow users to examine all choices available to them at any time without being forced to choose one of them, and without having to remember command words or special keys. The Macintosh user simply positions the cursor in the **menu bar** and presses the mouse button over a **menu title**. The application then calls the Menu Manager, which highlights that title (by inverting it) and "pulls down" the menu below it. As long as the mouse button is held down, the menu is displayed. Dragging through the menu causes each of the **menu items** (commands) in it to be highlighted in turn. If the mouse button is released over an item, that item is "chosen". The item blinks briefly to confirm the choice, and the menu disappears.

When the user chooses an item, the Menu Manager tells the application which item was chosen, and the application performs the corresponding action. When the application completes the action, it removes the highlighting from the menu title, indicating to the user that the operation is complete.

If the user moves the cursor out of the menu with the mouse button held down, the menu remains visible, though no menu items are highlighted. If the mouse button is released outside the menu, no choice is made: The menu just disappears and the application takes no action. The user can always look at a menu without causing any changes in the document or on the screen.

The Menu Bar

The menu bar always appears at the top of the Macintosh screen; nothing but the cursor ever appears in front of it. The menu bar is white, 20 pixels high, and as wide as the screen, with a 1-pixel black lower border. The menu titles in it are always in the system font and the system font size (see Figure 1).

In applications that support desk accessories, the first menu should be the standard Apple menu (the menu whose title is an apple symbol). The Apple menu contains the names of all available desk accessories. When the user chooses a desk accessory from the menu, the title of a menu belonging to the desk accessory may appear in the menu bar, for as long as the accessory is active, or the entire menu bar may be replaced by menus belonging to the desk accessory. (Desk accessories are discussed in detail in chapter 14.)

Inside Macintosh

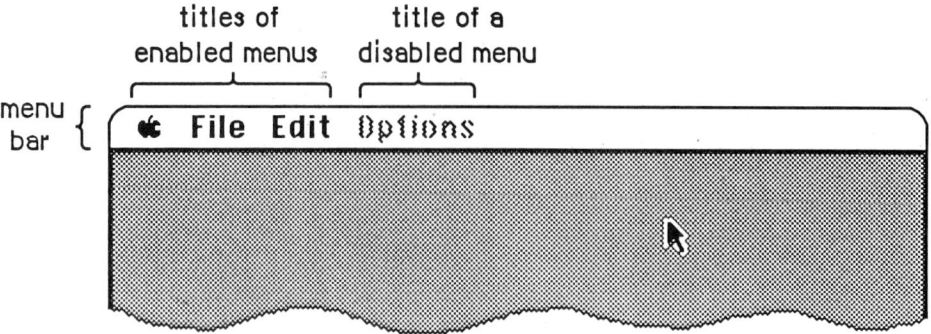

Figure 1. The Menu Bar

A menu may be temporarily **disabled**, so that none of the items in it can be chosen. A disabled menu can still be pulled down, but its title and all the items in it are dimmed.

The maximum number of menu titles in the menu bar is 16; however, ten to twelve titles are usually all that will fit, and you must leave at least enough room in the menu bar for one desk accessory menu. Also keep in mind that if your program is likely to be translated into other languages, the menu titles may take up more space. If you're having trouble fitting your menus into the menu bar, you should review your menu organization and menu titles.

Appearance of Menus

A standard menu consists of a number of menu items listed vertically inside a shadowed rectangle. A menu item may be the text of a command, or just a line dividing groups of choices (see Figure 2). An ellipsis (...) following the text of an item indicates that selecting the item will bring up a dialog box to get further information before the command is executed. Menus always appear in front of everything else (except the cursor); in Figure 2, the menu appears in front of a document window already on the screen.

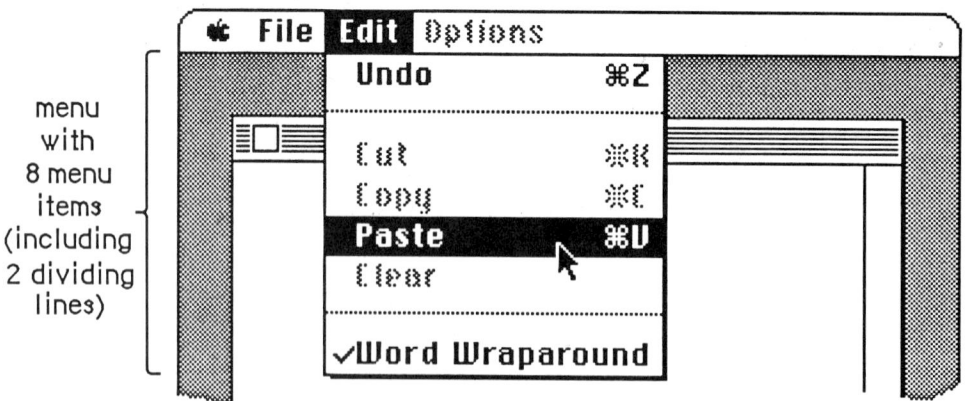

Figure 2. A Standard Menu

The text of a menu item always appears in the system font and the system font size. Each item can have a few visual variations from the standard appearance:

The Menu Manager

- An icon to the left of the item's text, to give a symbolic representation of the item's meaning or effect.
- A check mark or other character to the left of the item's text (or icon, if any), to denote the status of the item or of the mode it controls.
- The Command key symbol and another character to the right of the item's text, to show that the item may be invoked from the keyboard (that is, it has a **keyboard equivalent**). Pressing this key while holding down the Command key invokes the item just as if it had been chosen from the menu (see "Keyboard Equivalents for Commands" below).
- A character style other than the standard, such as bold, italic, underline, or a combination of these. (Chapter 6 gives a full discussion of character style.)
- A dimmed appearance, to indicate that the item is disabled, and can't be chosen. The Cut, Copy, and Clear commands in Figure 2 are disabled; dividing lines are always disabled.

Note: Special symbols or icons may have an unusual appearance when dimmed; notice the dimmed Command symbol in the Cut and Copy menu items in Figure 2.

The maximum number of menu items that will fit in a standard menu is 20 (less 1 for each item that contains an icon). The fewer menu items you have, the simpler and clearer the menu appears to the user.

If the standard menu doesn't suit your needs—for example, if you want more graphics, or perhaps a nonlinear text arrangement—you can define a custom menu that, although visibly different to the user, responds to your application's Menu Manager calls just like a standard menu.

Keyboard Equivalents for Commands

Your program can set up a keyboard equivalent for any of its menu commands so the command can be invoked from the keyboard with the Command key. The character you specify for a keyboard equivalent will usually be a letter. The user can type the letter in either uppercase or lowercase. For example, typing either "C" or "c" while holding down the Command key invokes the command whose equivalent is "C".

Note: For consistency between applications, you should specify the letter in uppercase in the menu.

You can specify characters other than letters for keyboard equivalents. However, the Shift key will be ignored when the equivalent is typed, so you shouldn't specify shifted characters. For example, when the user types Command-+, the system reads it as Command-=.

Command-Shift-number combinations are *not* keyboard equivalents. They're detected and handled by the Toolbox Event Manager function GetNextEvent, and are never returned to your program. (This is how disk ejection with Command-Shift-1 or 2 is implemented.) Although it's possible to use unshifted Command-number combinations as keyboard equivalents, you shouldn't do so, to avoid confusion.

Warning: You must use the standard keyboard equivalents Z, X, C, and V for the editing commands Undo, Cut, Copy, and Paste, or editing won't work correctly in desk accessories.

About the Menu Manager I-343

MENUS AND RESOURCES

The general appearance and behavior of a menu is determined by a routine called its **menu definition procedure,** which is stored as a resource in a resource file. The menu definition procedure performs all actions that differ from one menu type to another, such as drawing the menu. The Menu Manager calls the menu definition procedure whenever it needs to perform one of these basic actions, passing it a message that tells which action to perform.

The standard menu definition procedure is part of the system resource file. It lists the menu items vertically, and each item may have an icon, a check mark or other symbol, a keyboard equivalent, a different character style, or a dimmed appearance. If you want to define your own, nonstandard menu types, you'll have to write menu definition procedures for them, as described later in the section "Defining Your Own Menus".

You can also use a resource file to store the contents of your application's menus. This allows the menus to be edited or translated to another language without affecting the application's source code. The Menu Manager lets you read complete menu bars as well as individual menus from a resource file.

> **Warning:** Menus in a resource file must not be purgeable.

Even if you don't store entire menus in resource files, it's a good idea to store the text strings they contain as resources; you can call the Resource Manager directly to read them in. Icons in menus are read from resource files; the Menu Manager calls the Resource Manager to read in the icons.

There's a Menu Manager procedure that scans all open resource files for resources of a given type and installs the names of all available resources of that type into a given menu. This is how you fill a menu with the names of all available desk accessories or fonts, for example.

> **Note:** If you use a menu of this type, check to make sure that at least one item is in the menu; if not, you should put a disabled item in it that says "None" (or something else indicating the menu is empty).

MENU RECORDS

The Menu Manager keeps all the information it needs for its operations on a particular menu in a **menu record**. The menu record contains the following:

- The **menu ID**, a number that identifies the menu. The menu ID can be the same number as the menu's resource ID, though it doesn't have to be.
- The menu title.
- The contents of the menu—the text and other parts of each item.
- The horizontal and vertical dimensions of the menu, in pixels. The menu items appear inside the rectangle formed by these dimensions; the black border and shadow of the menu appear outside that rectangle.
- A handle to the menu definition procedure.

The Menu Manager

- Flags telling whether each menu item is enabled or disabled, and whether the menu itself is enabled or disabled.

The data type for a menu record is called MenuInfo. A menu record is referred to by a handle:

```
TYPE  MenuPtr     = ^MenuInfo;
      MenuHandle  = ^MenuPtr;
```

You can store into and access all the necessary fields of a menu record with Menu Manager routines, so normally you don't have to know the exact field names. However, if you want more information about the exact structure of a menu record—if you're defining your own menu types, for instance—it's given below.

The MenuInfo Data Type

The type MenuInfo is defined as follows:

```
TYPE MenuInfo =
        RECORD
            menuID:       INTEGER;   {menu ID}
            menuWidth:    INTEGER;   {menu width in pixels}
            menuHeight:   INTEGER;   {menu height in pixels}
            menuProc:     Handle;    {menu definition procedure}
            enableFlags:  LONGINT;   {tells if menu or items are enabled}
            menuData:     Str255     {menu title (and other data)}
        END;
```

The menuID field contains the menu ID. MenuWidth and menuHeight are the menu's horizontal and vertical dimensions in pixels. MenuProc is a handle to the menu definition procedure for this type of menu.

Bit 0 of the enableFlags field is 1 if the menu is enabled, or 0 if it's disabled. Bits 1 to 31 similarly tell whether each item in the menu is enabled or disabled.

The menuData field contains the menu title followed by variable-length data that defines the text and other parts of the menu items. The Str255 data type enables you to access the title from Pascal; there's actually additional data beyond the title that's inaccessible from Pascal and is not reflected in the MenuInfo data structure.

Warning: You can read the menu title directly from the menuData field, but do not change the title directly, or the data defining the menu items may be destroyed.

MENU LISTS

A **menu list** contains handles to one or more menus, along with information about the position of each menu in the menu bar. The current menu list contains handles to all the menus currently in the menu bar; the menu bar shows the titles, in order, of all menus in the menu list. When you initialize the Menu Manager, it allocates space for the maximum-size menu list.

Inside Macintosh

The Menu Manager provides all the necessary routines for manipulating the current menu list, so there's no need to access it directly yourself. As a general rule, routines that deal specifically with menus in the menu list use the menu ID to refer to menus; those that deal with any menus, whether in the menu list or not, use the menu handle to refer to menus. Some routines refer to the menu list as a whole, with a handle.

Assembly-language note: The global variable MenuList contains a handle to the current menu list. The menu list has the format shown below.

Number of bytes	Contents
2 bytes	Offset from beginning of menu list to last menu handle (the number of menus in the list times 6)
2 bytes	Horizontal coordinate of right edge of menu title of last menu in list
2 bytes	Not used
For each menu:	
4 bytes	Menu handle
2 bytes	Horizontal coordinate of left edge of menu

CREATING A MENU IN YOUR PROGRAM

The best way to create your application's menus is to set them up as resources and read them in from a resource file. If you want your application to create the menus itself, though, it must call the NewMenu and AppendMenu routines. NewMenu creates a new menu data structure, returning a handle to it. AppendMenu takes a string and a handle to a menu and adds the items in the string to the end of the menu.

The string passed to AppendMenu consists mainly of the text of the menu items. For a dividing line, use one hyphen (–); AppendMenu ignores any following characters, and draws a dotted line across the width of the menu. For a blank item, use one or more spaces. Other characters interspersed in the string have special meaning to the Menu Manager. These "meta-characters" are used in conjunction with text to separate menu items or alter their appearance (for example, you can use one to disable any dividing line or blank item). The meta-characters aren't displayed in the menu.

Meta-character	Meaning
; or Return	Separates items
^	Item has an icon
!	Item has a check or other mark
<	Item has a special character style
/	Item has a keyboard equivalent
(	Item is disabled

None, any, or all of these meta-characters can appear in the AppendMenu string; they're described in detail below. To add one text-only item to a menu would require a simple string without any meta-characters:

    AppendMenu(thisMenu,'Just Enough')

An extreme example could use many meta-characters:

    AppendMenu(thisMenu,'(Too Much^1<B/T')

This example adds to the menu an item whose text is "Too Much", which is disabled, has icon number 1, is boldfaced, and can be invoked by Command-T. Your menu items should be much simpler than this.

> **Note:** If you want any of the meta-characters to appear in the text of a menu item, you can include them by changing the text with the Menu Manager procedure SetItem.

Multiple Items

Each call to AppendMenu can add one or many items to the menu. To add multiple items in the same call, use a semicolon (;) or a Return character to separate the items. The call

    AppendMenu(thisMenu,'Cut;Copy')

has exactly the same effect as the calls

    AppendMenu(thisMenu,'Cut');
    AppendMenu(thisMenu,'Copy')

Items with Icons

A circumflex (^) followed by a digit from 1 to 9 indicates that an icon should appear to the left of the text in the menu. The digit, called the **icon number**, yields the resource ID of the icon in the resource file. Icon resource IDs 257 through 511 are reserved for menu icons; thus the Menu Manager adds 256 to the icon number to get the proper resource ID.

> **Note:** The Menu Manager gets the icon number by subtracting 48 from the ASCII code of the character following the "^" (since, for example, the ASCII code of "1" is 49). You can actually follow the "^" with any character that has an ASCII code greater than 48.

You can also use the SetItemIcon procedure to install icons in a menu; it accepts any icon number from 1 to 255.

Marked Items

You can use an exclamation point (!) to cause a check mark or any other character to be placed to the left of the text (or icon, if any). Follow the exclamation point with the character of your choice; note, however, that normally you can't type a check mark from the keyboard. To specify

Inside Macintosh

a check mark, you need to take special measures: Declare a string variable to have the length of the desired AppendMenu string, and assign it that string with a space following the exclamation point. Then separately store the check mark in the position of the space.

For example, suppose you want to use AppendMenu to specify a menu item that has the text "Word Wraparound" (15 characters) and a check mark to its left. You can declare the string variable

```
VAR s: STRING[17];
```

and do the following:

```
s := '! Word Wraparound';
s[2] := CHR(checkMark);
AppendMenu(thisMenu,s);
```

The constant checkMark is defined by the Font Manager as the character code for the check mark.

> **Note:** The Font Manager also defines constants for certain other special characters that can't normally be typed from the keyboard: the apple symbol, the Command key symbol, and a diamond symbol. These symbols can be specified in the same way as the check mark.

You can call the SetItemMark or CheckItem procedures to change or clear the mark, and the GetItemMark procedure to find out what mark, if any, is being used.

Character Style of Items

The system font is the only font available for menus; however, you can vary the character style of menu items for clarity and distinction. The meta-character for specifying the character style of an item's text is the less-than symbol (<). With AppendMenu, you can assign one and only one of the stylistic variations listed below.

        <B   Bold
        <I   Italic
        <U   Underline
        <O   Outline
        <S   Shadow

The SetItemStyle procedure allows you to assign any combination of stylistic variations to an item. For a further discussion of character style, see chapter 6.

Items with Keyboard Equivalents

A slash (/) followed by a character associates that character with the item, allowing the item to be invoked from the keyboard with the Command key. The specified character (preceded by the Command key symbol) appears at the right of the item's text in the menu.

> **Note:** Remember to specify the character in uppercase if it's a letter, and not to specify other shifted characters or numbers.

The Menu Manager

Given a keyboard equivalent typed by the user, you call the MenuKey function to find out which menu item was invoked.

Disabled Items

The meta-character that disables an item is the left parenthesis, "(". A disabled item cannot be chosen; it appears dimmed in the menu and is not highlighted when the cursor moves over it.

Menu items that are used to separate groups of items (such as a line or a blank item) should always be disabled. For example, the call

    AppendMenu(thisMenu,'Undo;(-;Cut')

adds two enabled menu items, Undo and Cut, with a disabled item consisting of a line between them.

You can change the enabled or disabled state of a menu item with the DisableItem and EnableItem procedures.

USING THE MENU MANAGER

To use the Menu Manager, you must have previously called InitGraf to initialize QuickDraw, InitFonts to initialize the Font Manager, and InitWindows to initialize the Window Manager. The first Menu Manager routine to call is the initialization procedure InitMenus.

Your application can set up the menus it needs in any number of ways:

- Read an entire prepared menu list from a resource file with GetNewMBar, and place it in the menu bar with SetMenuBar.
- Read the menus individually from a resource file using GetMenu, and place them in the menu bar using InsertMenu.
- Allocate the menus with NewMenu, fill them with items using AppendMenu, and place them in the menu bar using InsertMenu.
- Allocate a menu with NewMenu, fill it with items using AddResMenu to get the names of all available resources of a given type, and place the menu in the menu bar using InsertMenu.

You can use AddResMenu or InsertResMenu to add items from resource files to any menu, regardless of how you created the menu or whether it already contains any items.

When you no longer need a menu, call the Resource Manager procedure ReleaseResource if you read the menu from a resource file, or DisposeMenu if you allocated it with NewMenu.

   Note: If you want to save changes made to a menu that was read from a resource file, write it back to the resource file before calling ReleaseResource.

If you call NewMenu to allocate a menu, it will store a handle to the standard menu definition procedure in the menu record, so if you want the menu to be one you've designed, you must replace that handle with a handle to your own menu definition procedure. For more information, see "Defining Your Own Menus".

After setting up the menu bar, you need to draw it with the DrawMenuBar procedure.

You can use the SetItem and GetItem procedures to change or examine a menu item's text at any time—for example, to change between the two forms of a toggled command. You can set or examine an item's icon, style, or mark with the procedures SetItemIcon, GetItemIcon, SetItemStyle, GetItemStyle, CheckItem, SetItemMark, and GetItemMark. Individual items or whole menus can be enabled or disabled with the EnableItem and DisableItem procedures. You can change the number of menus in the menu list with InsertMenu or DeleteMenu, remove all the menus with ClearMenuBar, or change the entire menu list with GetNewMBar or GetMenuBar followed by SetMenuBar.

When your application receives a mouse-down event, and the Window Manager's FindWindow function returns the predefined constant inMenuBar, your application should call the Menu Manager's MenuSelect function, supplying it with the point where the mouse button was pressed. MenuSelect will pull down the appropriate menu, and retain control—tracking the mouse, highlighting menu items, and pulling down other menus—until the user releases the mouse button. MenuSelect returns a long integer to the application: The high-order word contains the menu ID of the menu that was chosen, and the low-order word contains the **menu item number** of the item that was chosen. The menu item number is the index, starting from 1, of the item in the menu. If no item was chosen, the high-order word of the long integer is 0, and the low-order word is undefined.

- If the high-order word of the long integer returned is 0, the application should just continue to poll for further events.

- If the high-order word is nonzero, the application should invoke the menu item specified by the low-order word, in the menu specified by the high-order word. Only after the action is completely finished (after all dialogs, alerts, or screen actions have been taken care of) should the application remove the highlighting from the menu bar by calling HiliteMenu(0), signaling the completion of the action.

Note: The Menu Manager automatically saves and restores the bits behind the menu; you don't have to worry about it.

Keyboard equivalents are handled in much the same manner. When your application receives a key-down event with the Command key held down, it should call the MenuKey function, supplying it with the character that was typed. MenuKey will return a long integer with the same format as that of MenuSelect, and the application can handle the long integer in the manner described above. Applications should respond the same way to auto-key events as to key-down events when the Command key is held down if the command being invoked is repeatable.

Note: You can use the Toolbox Utility routines LoWord and HiWord to extract the high-order and low-order words of a given long integer, as described in chapter 16.

There are several miscellaneous Menu Manager routines that you normally won't need to use. CalcMenuSize calculates the dimensions of a menu. CountMItems counts the number of items in a menu. GetMHandle returns the handle of a menu in the menu list. FlashMenuBar inverts the menu bar. SetMenuFlash controls the number of times a menu item blinks when it's chosen.

The Menu Manager

MENU MANAGER ROUTINES

Initialization and Allocation

```
PROCEDURE InitMenus;
```

InitMenus initializes the Menu Manager. It allocates space for the menu list (a relocatable block in the heap large enough for the maximum-size menu list), and draws the (empty) menu bar. Call InitMenus once before all other Menu Manager routines. An application should never have to call this procedure more than once; to start afresh with all new menus, use ClearMenuBar.

> **Note:** The Window Manager initialization procedure InitWindows has already drawn the empty menu bar; InitMenus redraws it.

```
FUNCTION NewMenu (menuID: INTEGER; menuTitle: Str255) :
        MenuHandle;
```

NewMenu allocates space for a new menu with the given menu ID and title, and returns a handle to it. It sets up the menu to use the standard menu definition procedure. (The menu definition procedure is read into memory if it isn't already in memory.) The new menu (which is created empty) is not installed in the menu list. To use this menu, you must first call AppendMenu or AddResMenu to fill it with items, InsertMenu to place it in the menu list, and DrawMenuBar to update the menu bar to include the new title.

Application menus should always have positive menu IDs. Negative menu IDs are reserved for menus belonging to desk accessories. No menu should ever have a menu ID of 0.

If you want to set up the title of the Apple menu from your program instead of reading it in from a resource file, you can use the constant appleMark (defined by the Font Manager as the character code for the apple symbol). For example, you can declare the string variable

```
VAR myTitle: STRING[1];
```

and do the following:

```
myTitle := ' ';
myTitle[1] := CHR(appleMark)
```

To release the memory occupied by a menu that you created with NewMenu, call DisposeMenu.

```
FUNCTION GetMenu (resourceID: INTEGER) : MenuHandle;
```

> **Assembly-language note:** The macro you invoke to call GetMenu from assembly language is named _GetRMenu.

Inside Macintosh

GetMenu returns a menu handle for the menu having the given resource ID. It calls the Resource Manager to read the menu from the resource file into a menu record in memory. GetMenu stores the handle to the menu definition procedure in the menu record, reading the procedure from the resource file into memory if necessary. If the menu or the menu definition procedure can't be read from the resource file, GetMenu returns NIL. To use the menu, you must call InsertMenu to place it in the menu list and DrawMenuBar to update the menu bar to include the new title.

Warning: Call GetMenu only once for a particular menu. If you need the menu handle to a menu that's already in memory, use the Resource Manager function GetResource.

To release the memory occupied by a menu that you read from a resource file with GetMenu, use the Resource Manager procedure ReleaseResource.

```
PROCEDURE DisposeMenu (theMenu: MenuHandle);
```

Assembly-language note: The macro you invoke to call DisposeMenu from assembly language is named _DisposMenu.

Call DisposeMenu to release the memory occupied by a menu that you allocated with NewMenu. (For menus read from a resource file with GetMenu, use the Resource Manager procedure ReleaseResource instead.) This is useful if you've created temporary menus that you no longer need.

Warning: Make sure you remove the menu from the menu list (with DeleteMenu) before disposing of it.

Forming the Menus

```
PROCEDURE AppendMenu (theMenu: MenuHandle; data: Str255);
```

AppendMenu adds an item or items to the end of the given menu, which must previously have been allocated by NewMenu or read from a resource file by GetMenu. The data string consists of the text of the menu item; it may be blank but should not be the empty string. If it begins with a hyphen (–), the item will be a dividing line across the width of the menu. As described in the section "Creating a Menu in Your Program", the following meta-characters may be embedded in the data string:

Meta-character	Usage
; or Return	Separates multiple items
^	Followed by an icon number, adds that icon to the item
!	Followed by a character, marks the item with that character
<	Followed by B, I, U, O, or S, sets the character style of the item
/	Followed by a character, associates a keyboard equivalent with the item
(	Disables the item

Once items have been appended to a menu, they cannot be removed or rearranged. AppendMenu works properly whether or not the menu is in the menu list.

```
PROCEDURE AddResMenu (theMenu: MenuHandle; theType: ResType);
```

AddResMenu searches all open resource files for resources of type theType and appends the names of all resources it finds to the given menu. Each resource name appears in the menu as an enabled item, without an icon or mark, and in the plain character style. The standard Menu Manager calls can be used to get the name or change its appearance, as described in the section "Controlling the Appearance of Items".

Note: So that you can have resources of the given type that won't appear in the menu, any resource names that begin with a period (.) or a percent sign (%) aren't appended by AddResMenu.

Use this procedure to fill a menu with the names of all available fonts or desk accessories. For example, if you declare a variable as

```
VAR fontMenu: MenuHandle;
```

you can set up a menu containing all font names as follows:

```
fontMenu := NewMenu(5,'Fonts');
AddResMenu(fontMenu,'FONT')
```

Warning: Before returning, AddResMenu issues the Resource Manager call SetResLoad(TRUE). If your program previously called SetResLoad(FALSE) and you still want that to be in effect after calling AddResMenu, you'll have to call it again.

```
PROCEDURE InsertResMenu (theMenu: MenuHandle; theType: ResType;
        afterItem: INTEGER);
```

InsertResMenu is the same as AddResMenu (above) except that it inserts the resource names in the menu where specified by the afterItem parameter: If afterItem is 0, the names are inserted before the first menu item; if it's the item number of an item in the menu, they're inserted after that item; if it's equal to or greater than the last item number, they're appended to the menu.

Note: InsertResMenu inserts the names in the reverse of the order that AddResMenu appends them. For consistency between applications in the appearance of menus, use AddResMenu instead of InsertResMenu if possible.

Forming the Menu Bar

```
PROCEDURE InsertMenu (theMenu: MenuHandle; beforeID: INTEGER);
```

InsertMenu inserts a menu into the menu list before the menu whose menu ID equals beforeID. If beforeID is 0 (or isn't the ID of any menu in the menu list), the new menu is added after all

Inside Macintosh

others. If the menu is already in the menu list or the menu list is already full, InsertMenu does nothing. Be sure to call DrawMenuBar to update the menu bar.

```
PROCEDURE DrawMenuBar;
```

DrawMenuBar redraws the menu bar according to the menu list, incorporating any changes since the last call to DrawMenuBar. This procedure should always be called after a sequence of InsertMenu or DeleteMenu calls, and after ClearMenuBar, SetMenuBar, or any other routine that changes the menu list.

> **Warning:** Don't call DrawMenuBar while a menu title is highlighted, or the menu bar may be drawn incorrectly.

```
PROCEDURE DeleteMenu (menuID: INTEGER);
```

DeleteMenu deletes a menu from the menu list. If there's no menu with the given menu ID in the menu list, DeleteMenu has no effect. Be sure to call DrawMenuBar to update the menu bar; the menu titles following the deleted menu will move over to fill the vacancy.

> **Note:** DeleteMenu simply removes the menu from the list of currently available menus; it doesn't release the memory occupied by the menu data structure.

```
PROCEDURE ClearMenuBar;
```

Call ClearMenuBar to remove all menus from the menu list when you want to start afresh with all new menus. Be sure to call DrawMenuBar to update the menu bar.

> **Note:** ClearMenuBar, like DeleteMenu, doesn't release the memory occupied by the menu data structures; it merely removes them from the menu list.

You don't have to call ClearMenuBar at the beginning of your program, because InitMenus clears the menu list for you.

```
FUNCTION GetNewMBar (menuBarID: INTEGER) : Handle;
```

GetNewMBar creates a menu list as defined by the menu bar resource having the given resource ID, and returns a handle to it. If the resource isn't already in memory, GetNewMBar reads it into memory from the resource file. If the resource can't be read, GetNewMBar returns NIL. GetNewMBar calls GetMenu to get each of the individual menus.

To make the menu list created by GetNewMBar the current menu list, call SetMenuBar. To release the memory occupied by the menu list, use the Memory Manager procedure DisposHandle.

> **Warning:** You don't have to know the individual menu IDs to use GetNewMBar, but that doesn't mean you don't have to know them at all: To do anything further with a particular menu, you have to know its ID or its handle (which you can get by passing the ID to GetMHandle, as described in the section "Miscellaneous Routines").

The Menu Manager

```
FUNCTION GetMenuBar : Handle;
```

GetMenuBar creates a copy of the current menu list and returns a handle to the copy. You can then add or remove menus from the menu list (with InsertMenu, DeleteMenu, or ClearMenuBar), and later restore the saved menu list with SetMenuBar. To release the memory occupied by the saved menu list, use the Memory Manager procedure DisposHandle.

> **Warning:** GetMenuBar doesn't copy the menus themselves, only a list containing their handles. Do not dispose of any menus that might be in a saved menu list.

```
PROCEDURE SetMenuBar (menuList: Handle);
```

SetMenuBar copies the given menu list to the current menu list. You can use this procedure to restore a menu list previously saved by GetMenuBar, or pass it a handle returned by GetNewMBar. Be sure to call DrawMenuBar to update the menu bar.

Choosing From a Menu

```
FUNCTION MenuSelect (startPt: Point) : LONGINT;
```

When there's a mouse-down event in the menu bar, the application should call MenuSelect with startPt equal to the point (in global coordinates) where the mouse button was pressed. MenuSelect keeps control until the mouse button is released, tracking the mouse, pulling down menus as needed, and highlighting enabled menu items under the cursor. When the mouse button is released over an enabled item in an application menu, MenuSelect returns a long integer whose high-order word is the menu ID of the menu, and whose low-order word is the menu item number for the item chosen (see Figure 3). It leaves the selected menu title highlighted. After performing the chosen task, your application should call HiliteMenu(0) to remove the highlighting from the menu title.

If no choice is made, MenuSelect returns 0 in the high-order word of the long integer, and the low-order word is undefined. This includes the case where the mouse button is released over a disabled menu item (such as Cut, Copy, Clear, or one of the dividing lines in Figure 3), over any menu title, or outside the menu.

If the mouse button is released over an enabled item in a menu belonging to a desk accessory, MenuSelect passes the menu ID and item number to the Desk Manager procedure SystemMenu for processing, and returns 0 to your application in the high-order word of the result.

> **Note:** When a menu is pulled down, the bits behind it are stored as a relocatable object in the application heap. If your application has large menus, this can temporarily use up a lot of memory.

Inside Macintosh

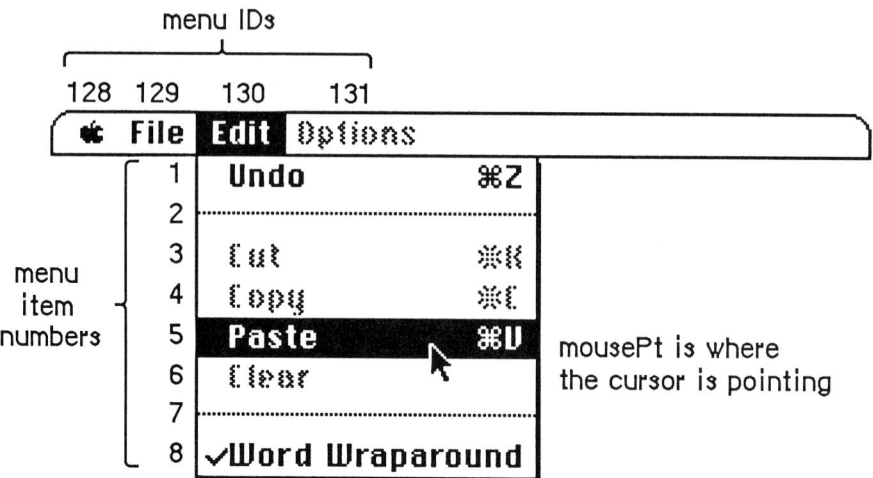

Figure 3. MenuSelect and MenuKey

___

Assembly-language note: If the global variable MBarEnable is nonzero, MenuSelect knows that every menu currently in the menu bar belongs to a desk accessory. (See chapter 14 for more information.)

You can store in the global variables MenuHook and MBarHook the addresses of routines that will be called during MenuSelect. Both variables are initialized to 0 by InitMenus. The routine whose address is in MenuHook (if any) will be called repeatedly (with no parameters) while the mouse button is down. The routine whose address is in MBarHook (if any) will be called after the title of the menu is highlighted and the menu rectangle is calculated, but before the menu is drawn. (The menu rectangle is the rectangle in which the menu will be drawn, in global coordinates.) The routine is passed a pointer to the menu rectangle on the stack. It should normally return 0 in register D0; returning 1 will abort MenuSelect.

___

```
FUNCTION MenuKey (ch: CHAR) : LONGINT;
```

MenuKey maps the given character to the associated menu and item for that character. When you get a key-down event with the Command key held down—or an auto-key event, if the command being invoked is repeatable—call MenuKey with the character that was typed. MenuKey highlights the appropriate menu title, and returns a long integer containing the menu ID in its high-order word and the menu item number in its low-order word, just as MenuSelect does (see Figure 3 above). After performing the chosen task, your application should call HiliteMenu(0) to remove the highlighting from the menu title.

If the given character isn't associated with any enabled menu item currently in the menu list, MenuKey returns 0 in the high-order word of the long integer, and the low-order word is undefined.

If the given character invokes a menu item in a menu belonging to a desk accessory, MenuKey (like MenuSelect) passes the menu ID and item number to the Desk Manager procedure SystemMenu for processing, and returns 0 to your application in the high-order word of the result.

> **Note:** There should never be more than one item in the menu list with the same keyboard equivalent, but if there is, MenuKey returns the first such item it encounters, scanning the menus from right to left and their items from top to bottom.

```
PROCEDURE HiliteMenu (menuID: INTEGER);
```

HiliteMenu highlights the title of the given menu, or does nothing if the title is already highlighted. Since only one menu title can be highlighted at a time, it unhighlights any previously highlighted menu title. If menuID is 0 (or isn't the ID of any menu in the menu list), HiliteMenu simply unhighlights whichever menu title is highlighted (if any).

After MenuSelect or MenuKey, your application should perform the chosen task and then call HiliteMenu(0) to unhighlight the chosen menu title.

> **Assembly-language note:** The global variable TheMenu contains the menu ID of the currently highlighted menu.

Controlling the Appearance of Items

```
PROCEDURE SetItem (theMenu: MenuHandle; item: INTEGER; itemString:
        Str255);
```

SetItem changes the text of the given menu item to itemString. It doesn't recognize the metacharacters used in AppendMenu; if you include them in itemString, they will appear in the text of the menu item. The attributes already in effect for this item—its character style, icon, and so on—remain in effect. ItemString may be blank but should not be the empty string.

> **Note:** It's good practice to store the text of itemString in a resource file instead of passing it directly.

Use SetItem to change between the two forms of a toggled command—for example, to change "Show Clipboard" to "Hide Clipboard" when the Clipboard is already showing.

> **Note:** To avoid confusing the user, don't capriciously change the text of menu items.

Inside Macintosh

```
PROCEDURE GetItem (theMenu: MenuHandle; item: INTEGER; VAR
        itemString: Str255);
```

GetItem returns the text of the given menu item in itemString. It doesn't place any metacharacters in the string. This procedure is useful for getting the name of a menu item that was installed with AddResMenu or InsertResMenu.

```
PROCEDURE DisableItem (theMenu: MenuHandle; item: INTEGER);
```

Given a menu item number in the item parameter, DisableItem disables that menu item; given 0 in the item parameter, it disables the entire menu.

Disabled menu items appear dimmed and are not highlighted when the cursor moves over them. MenuSelect and MenuKey return 0 in the high-order word of their result if the user attempts to invoke a disabled item. Use DisableItem to disable all menu choices that aren't appropriate at a given time (such as a Cut command when there's no text selection).

All menu items are initially enabled unless you specify otherwise (such as by using the "(" metacharacter in a call to AppendMenu).

When you disable an entire menu, call DrawMenuBar to update the menu bar. The title of a disabled menu and every item in it are dimmed.

```
PROCEDURE EnableItem (theMenu: MenuHandle; item: INTEGER);
```

Given a menu item number in the item parameter, EnableItem enables the item (which may have been disabled with the DisableItem procedure, or with the "(" meta-character in the AppendMenu string).

Given 0 in the item parameter, EnableItem enables the menu as a whole, but any items that were disabled separately (before the entire menu was disabled) remain so. When you enable an entire menu, call DrawMenuBar to update the menu bar.

The item or menu title will no longer appear dimmed and can be chosen like any other enabled item or menu.

```
PROCEDURE CheckItem (theMenu: MenuHandle; item: INTEGER; checked:
        BOOLEAN);
```

CheckItem places or removes a check mark at the left of the given menu item. After you call CheckItem with checked=TRUE, a check mark will appear each subsequent time the menu is pulled down. Calling CheckItem with checked=FALSE removes the check mark from the menu item (or, if it's marked with a different character, removes that mark).

Menu items are initially unmarked unless you specify otherwise (such as with the "!" metacharacter in a call to AppendMenu).

The Menu Manager

```
PROCEDURE SetItemMark (theMenu: MenuHandle; item: INTEGER;
        markChar: CHAR);
```

Assembly-language note: The macro you invoke to call SetItemMark from assembly language is named _SetItmMark.

SetItemMark marks the given menu item in a more general manner than CheckItem. It allows you to place any character in the system font, not just the check mark, to the left of the item. The character is passed in the markChar parameter.

Note: The Font Manager defines constants for the check mark and other special characters that can't normally be typed from the keyboard: the apple symbol, the Command key symbol, and a diamond symbol. See chapter 7 for more information.

To remove an item's mark, you can pass the following predefined constant in the markChar parameter:

```
CONST noMark = 0;
```

```
PROCEDURE GetItemMark (theMenu: MenuHandle; item: INTEGER; VAR
        markChar: CHAR);
```

Assembly-language note: The macro you invoke to call GetItemMark from assembly language is named _GetItmMark.

GetItemMark returns in markChar whatever character the given menu item is marked with, or the predefined constant noMark if no mark is present.

```
PROCEDURE SetItemIcon (theMenu: MenuHandle; item: INTEGER; icon:
        Byte);
```

Assembly-language note: The macro you invoke to call SetItemIcon from assembly language is named _SetItmIcon.

SetItemIcon associates the given menu item with an icon. It sets the item's icon number to the given value (an integer from 1 to 255). The Menu Manager adds 256 to the icon number to get the icon's resource ID, which it passes to the Resource Manager to get the corresponding icon.

Warning: If you call the Resource Manager directly to read or store menu icons, be sure to adjust your icon numbers accordingly.

Menu items initially have no icons unless you specify otherwise (such as with the "^" meta-character in a call to AppendMenu).

```
PROCEDURE GetItemIcon (theMenu: MenuHandle; item: INTEGER; VAR
        icon: Byte);
```

Assembly-language note: The macro you invoke to call GetItemIcon from assembly language is named _GetItmIcon.

GetItemIcon returns the icon number associated with the given menu item, as an integer from 1 to 255, or 0 if the item has not been associated with an icon. The icon number is 256 less than the icon's resource ID.

```
PROCEDURE SetItemStyle (theMenu: MenuHandle; item: INTEGER;
        chStyle: Style);
```

Assembly-language note: The macro you invoke to call SetItemStyle from assembly language is named _SetItmStyle.

SetItemStyle changes the character style of the given menu item to chStyle. For example:

```
SetItemStyle(thisMenu,1,[bold,italic])    {bold and italic}
```

Menu items are initially in the plain character style unless you specify otherwise (such as with the "<" meta-character in a call to AppendMenu).

```
PROCEDURE GetItemStyle (theMenu: MenuHandle; item: INTEGER; VAR
        chStyle: Style);
```

Assembly-language note: The macro you invoke to call GetItemStyle from assembly language is named _GetItmStyle.

GetItemStyle returns the character style of the given menu item in chStyle.

Miscellaneous Routines

```
PROCEDURE CalcMenuSize (theMenu: MenuHandle);
```

You can use CalcMenuSize to recalculate the horizontal and vertical dimensions of a menu whose contents have been changed (and store them in the appropriate fields of the menu record). CalcMenuSize is called internally by the Menu Manager after every routine that changes a menu.

```
FUNCTION CountMItems (theMenu: MenuHandle) : INTEGER;
```

CountMItems returns the number of menu items in the given menu.

```
FUNCTION GetMHandle (menuID: INTEGER) : MenuHandle;
```

Given the menu ID of a menu currently installed in the menu list, GetMHandle returns a handle to that menu; given any other menu ID, it returns NIL.

```
PROCEDURE FlashMenuBar (menuID: INTEGER);
```

If menuID is 0 (or isn't the ID of any menu in the menu list), FlashMenuBar inverts the entire menu bar; otherwise, it inverts the title of the given menu. You can call FlashMenuBar(0) twice to blink the menu bar.

```
PROCEDURE SetMenuFlash (count: INTEGER);
```

Assembly-language note: The macro you invoke to call SetMenuFlash from assembly language is named _SetMFlash.

When the mouse button is released over an enabled menu item, the item blinks briefly to confirm the choice. Normally, your application shouldn't be concerned with this blinking; the user sets it with the Control Panel desk accessory. If you're writing a desk accessory like the Control Panel, though, SetMenuFlash allows you to control the duration of the blinking. The count parameter is the number of times menu items will blink; it's initially 3 if the user hasn't changed it. A count of 0 disables blinking. Values greater than 3 can be annoyingly slow.

Note: Items in both standard and nonstandard menus blink when chosen. The appearance of the blinking for a nonstandard menu depends on the menu definition procedure, as described in "Defining Your Own Menus".

Assembly-language note: The current count is stored in the global variable MenuFlash.

Inside Macintosh

DEFINING YOUR OWN MENUS

The standard type of Macintosh menu is predefined for you. However, you may want to define your own type of menu—one with more graphics, or perhaps a nonlinear text arrangement. QuickDraw and the Menu Manager make it possible for you to do this.

To define your own type of menu, you write a menu definition procedure and store it in a resource file. The Menu Manager calls the menu definition procedure to perform basic operations such as drawing the menu.

A menu in a resource file contains the resource ID of its menu definition procedure. The routine you use to read in the menu is GetMenu (or GetNewMBar, which calls GetMenu). If you store the resource ID of your own menu definition procedure in a menu in a resource file, GetMenu will take care of reading the procedure into memory and storing a handle to it in the menuProc field of the menu record.

If you create your menus with NewMenu instead of storing them as resources, NewMenu stores a handle to the standard menu definition procedure in the menu record's menuProc field. You must replace this with a handle to your own menu definition procedure, and then call CalcMenuSize. If your menu definition procedure is in a resource file, you get the handle by calling the Resource Manager to read it from the resource file into memory.

The Menu Definition Procedure

The menu definition procedure is usually written in assembly language, but may be written in Pascal.

Assembly-language note: The procedure's entry point must be at the beginning.

You may choose any name you wish for the menu definition procedure. Here's how you would declare one named MyMenu:

```
PROCEDURE MyMenu (message: INTEGER; theMenu: MenuHandle; VAR menuRect:
        Rect; hitPt: Point; VAR whichItem: INTEGER);
```

The message parameter identifies the operation to be performed. It has one of the following values:

```
CONST mDrawMsg   = 0;   {draw the menu}
      mChooseMsg = 1;   {tell which item was chosen and highlight it}
      mSizeMsg   = 2;   {calculate the menu's dimensions}
```

The parameter theMenu indicates the menu that the operation will affect. MenuRect is the rectangle (in global coordinates) in which the menu is located; it's used when the message is mDrawMsg or mChooseMsg.

Note: MenuRect is declared as a VAR parameter not because its value is changed, but because of a Pascal feature that will cause an error when that parameter isn't used.

The message mDrawMsg tells the menu definition procedure to draw the menu inside menuRect. The current grafPort will be the Window Manager port. (For details on drawing, see chapter 6.) The standard menu definition procedure figures out how to draw the menu items by looking in the menu record at the data that defines them; this data is described in detail under "Formats of Resources for Menus" below. For menus of your own definition, you may set up the data defining the menu items any way you like, or even omit it altogether (in which case all the information necessary to draw the menu would be in the menu definition procedure itself). You should also check the enableFlags field of the menu record to see whether the menu is disabled (or whether any of the menu items are disabled, if you're using all the flags), and if so, draw it in gray.

Warning: Don't change the font from the system font for menu text. (The Window Manager port uses the system font.)

When the menu definition procedure receives the message mChooseMsg, the hitPt parameter is the mouse location (in global coordinates), and the whichItem parameter is the item number of the last item that was chosen from this menu (whichItem is initially set to 0). The procedure should determine whether the mouse location is in an enabled menu item, by checking whether hitPt is inside menuRect, whether the menu is enabled, and whether hitPt is in an enabled menu item:

- If the mouse location is in an enabled menu item, unhighlight whichItem and highlight the new item (unless the new item is the same as the whichItem), and return the item number of the new item in whichItem.

- If the mouse location isn't in an enabled item, unhighlight whichItem and return 0.

Note: When the Menu Manager needs to make a chosen menu item blink, it repeatedly calls the menu definition procedure with the message mChooseMsg, causing the item to be alternately highlighted and unhighlighted.

Finally, the message mSizeMsg tells the menu definition procedure to calculate the horizontal and vertical dimensions of the menu and store them in the menuWidth and menuHeight fields of the menu record.

FORMATS OF RESOURCES FOR MENUS

The resource type for a menu definition procedure is 'MDEF'. The resource data is simply the compiled or assembled code of the procedure.

Icons in menus must be stored in a resource file under the resource type 'ICON' with resource IDs from 257 to 511. Strings in resource files have the resource type 'STR'; if you use the SetItem procedure to change a menu item's text, you should store the alternate text as a string resource.

The formats of menus and menu bars in resource files are given below.

Inside Macintosh

Menus in a Resource File

The resource type for a menu is 'MENU'. The resource data for a menu has the format shown below. Once read into memory, this data is stored in a menu record (described earlier in the "Menu Records" section).

Number of bytes	Contents
2 bytes	Menu ID
2 bytes	0; placeholder for menu width
2 bytes	0; placeholder for menu height
2 bytes	Resource ID of menu definition procedure
2 bytes	0 (see comment below)
4 bytes	Same as enableFlags field of menu record
1 byte	Length of following title in bytes
n bytes	Characters of menu title

For each menu item:

1 byte	Length of following text in bytes
m bytes	Text of menu item
1 byte	Icon number, or 0 if no icon
1 byte	Keyboard equivalent, or 0 if none
1 byte	Character marking menu item, or 0 if none
1 byte	Character style of item's text
1 byte	0, indicating end of menu items

The four bytes beginning with the resource ID of the menu definition procedure serve as a placeholder for the handle to the procedure: When GetMenu is called to read the menu from the resource file, it also reads in the menu definition procedure if necessary, and replaces these four bytes with a handle to the procedure. The resource ID of the standard menu definition procedure is

```
CONST textMenuProc = 0;
```

The resource data for a nonstandard menu can define menu items in any way whatsoever, or not at all, depending on the requirements of its menu definition procedure. If the appearance of the items is basically the same as the standard, the resource data might be as shown above, but in fact everything following "For each menu item" can have any desired format or can be omitted altogether. Similarly, bits 1 to 31 of the enableFlags field may be set and used in any way desired by the menu definition procedure; bit 0 applies to the entire menu and must reflect whether it's enabled or disabled.

If your menu definition procedure does use the enableFlags field, menus of that type may contain no more than 31 items (1 per available bit); otherwise, the number of items they may contain is limited only by the amount of room on the screen.

Note: See chapter 6 for the exact format of the character style byte.

Menu Bars in a Resource File

The resource type for the contents of a menu bar is 'MBAR' and the resource data has the following format:

Number of bytes	Contents
2 bytes	Number of menus
For each menu:	
2 bytes	Resource ID of menu

SUMMARY OF THE MENU MANAGER

Constants

```
CONST  { Value indicating item has no mark }

    noMark = 0;

    { Messages to menu definition procedure }

    mDrawMsg    = 0;        {draw the menu}
    mChooseMsg  = 1;        {tell which item was chosen and highlight it}
    mSizeMsg    = 2;        {calculate the menu's dimensions}

    { Resource ID of standard menu definition procedure }

    textMenuProc = 0;
```

Data Types

```
TYPE MenuHandle = ^MenuPtr;
     MenuPtr    = ^MenuInfo;
     MenuInfo   = RECORD
                    menuID:      INTEGER;   {menu ID}
                    menuWidth:   INTEGER;   {menu width in pixels}
                    menuHeight:  INTEGER;   {menu height in pixels}
                    menuProc:    Handle;    {menu definition procedure}
                    enableFlags: LONGINT;   {tells if menu or items are}
                                            {enabled}
                    menuData:    Str255     {menu title (and other data)}
                  END;
```

Routines

Initialization and Allocation

```
PROCEDURE InitMenus;
FUNCTION  NewMenu       (menuID: INTEGER; menuTitle: Str255) : MenuHandle;
FUNCTION  GetMenu       (resourceID: INTEGER) : MenuHandle;
PROCEDURE DisposeMenu   (theMenu: MenuHandle);
```

Forming the Menus

```
PROCEDURE AppendMenu    (theMenu: MenuHandle; data: Str255);
PROCEDURE AddResMenu    (theMenu: MenuHandle; theType: ResType);
PROCEDURE InsertResMenu (theMenu: MenuHandle; theType: ResType;
                         afterItem: INTEGER);
```

The Menu Manager

Forming the Menu Bar

```
PROCEDURE InsertMenu    (theMenu: MenuHandle; beforeID: INTEGER);
PROCEDURE DrawMenuBar;
PROCEDURE DeleteMenu    (menuID: INTEGER);
PROCEDURE ClearMenuBar;
FUNCTION  GetNewMBar    (menuBarID: INTEGER) · Handle;
FUNCTION  GetMenuBar :  Handle;
PROCEDURE SetMenuBar    (menuList: Handle);
```

Choosing From a Menu

```
FUNCTION  MenuSelect    (startPt: Point) : LONGINT;
FUNCTION  MenuKey       (ch: CHAR) : LONGINT;
PROCEDURE HiliteMenu    (menuID: INTEGER);
```

Controlling the Appearance of Items

```
PROCEDURE SetItem       (theMenu: MenuHandle; item: INTEGER; itemString:
                          Str255);
PROCEDURE GetItem       (theMenu: MenuHandle; item: INTEGER; VAR
                          itemString: Str255);
PROCEDURE DisableItem   (theMenu: MenuHandle; item: INTEGER);
PROCEDURE EnableItem    (theMenu: MenuHandle; item: INTEGER);
PROCEDURE CheckItem     (theMenu: MenuHandle; item: INTEGER; checked:
                          BOOLEAN);
PROCEDURE SetItemMark   (theMenu: MenuHandle; item: INTEGER; markChar:
                          CHAR);
PROCEDURE GetItemMark   (theMenu: MenuHandle; item: INTEGER; VAR
                          markChar: CHAR);
PROCEDURE SetItemIcon   (theMenu: MenuHandle; item: INTEGER; icon: Byte);
PROCEDURE GetItemIcon   (theMenu: MenuHandle; item: INTEGER; VAR icon:
                          Byte);
PROCEDURE SetItemStyle  (theMenu: MenuHandle; item: INTEGER; chStyle:
                          Style);
PROCEDURE GetItemStyle  (theMenu: MenuHandle; item: INTEGER; VAR chStyle:
                          Style);
```

Miscellaneous Routines

```
PROCEDURE CalcMenuSize  (theMenu: MenuHandle);
FUNCTION  CountMItems   (theMenu: MenuHandle) : INTEGER;
FUNCTION  GetMHandle    (menuID: INTEGER) : MenuHandle;
PROCEDURE FlashMenuBar  (menuID: INTEGER);
PROCEDURE SetMenuFlash  (count: INTEGER);
```

Meta-Characters for AppendMenu

Meta-character	Usage
; or Return	Separates multiple items
^	Followed by an icon number, adds that icon to the item
!	Followed by a character, marks the item with that character
<	Followed by B, I, U, O, or S, sets the character style of the item
/	Followed by a character, associates a keyboard equivalent with the item
(	Disables the item

Menu Definition Procedure

```
PROCEDURE MyMenu (message: INTEGER; theMenu: MenuHandle; VAR menuRect:
                  Rect; hitPt: Point; VAR whichItem: INTEGER);
```

Assembly-Language Information

Constants

```
; Value indicating item has no mark

noMark          .EQU    0

; Messages to menu definition procedure

mDrawMsg        .EQU    0       ;draw the menu
mChooseMsg      .EQU    1       ;tell which item was chosen and highlight it
mSizeMsg        .EQU    2       ;calculate the menu's dimensions

; Resource ID of standard menu definition procedure

textMenuProc    .EQU    0
```

Menu Record Data Structure

menuID	Menu ID (word)
menuWidth	Menu width in pixels (word)
menuHeight	Menu height in pixels (word)
menuDefHandle	Handle to menu definition procedure
menuEnable	Enable flags (long)
menuData	Menu title (preceded by length byte) followed by data defining the items
menuBlkSize	Size in bytes of menu record except menuData field

Special Macro Names

Pascal name	Macro name
DisposeMenu	_DisposMenu
GetItemIcon	_GetItmIcon
GetItemMark	_GetItmMark
GetItemStyle	_GetItmStyle
GetMenu	_GetRMenu
SetItemIcon	_SetItmIcon
SetItemMark	_SetItmMark
SetItemStyle	_SetItmStyle
SetMenuFlash	_SetMFlash

Variables

MenuList	Handle to current menu list
MBarEnable	Nonzero if menu bar belongs to a desk accessory (word)
MenuHook	Address of routine called repeatedly during MenuSelect
MBarHook	Address of routine called by MenuSelect before menu is drawn (see below)
TheMenu	Menu ID of currently highlighted menu (word)
MenuFlash	Count for duration of menu item blinking (word)

MBarHook routine

On entry	stack: pointer to menu rectangle
On exit	D0: 0 to continue MenuSelect 1 to abort MenuSelect

Inside Macintosh

12 TEXTEDIT

- 373 About This Chapter
- 373 About TextEdit
- 374 Edit Records
- 374   The Destination and View Rectangles
- 375   The Selection Range
- 376   Justification
- 377   The TERec Data Type
- 380   The WordBreak Field
- 380   The ClikLoop Field
- 381 Using TextEdit
- 383 TextEdit Routines
- 383   Initialization and Allocation
- 383   Accessing the Text of an Edit Record
- 384   Insertion Point and Selection Range
- 385   Editing
- 387   Text Display and Scrolling
- 388   Scrap Handling
- 390   Advanced Routines
- 392 Summary of TextEdit

ABOUT THIS CHAPTER

TextEdit is the part of the Toolbox that handles basic text formatting and editing capabilities in a Macintosh application. This chapter describes the TextEdit routines and data types in detail.

You should already be familiar with:

- the basic concepts and structures behind QuickDraw, particularly points, rectangles, grafPorts, fonts, and character style
- the Toolbox Event Manager
- the Window Manager, particularly update and activate events

ABOUT TEXTEDIT

TextEdit is a set of routines and data types that provide the basic text editing and formatting capabilities needed in an application. These capabilities include:

- inserting new text
- deleting characters that are backspaced over
- translating mouse activity into text selection
- scrolling text within a window
- deleting selected text and possibly inserting it elsewhere, or copying text without deleting it

The TextEdit routines follow the Macintosh User Interface Guidelines; using them ensures that your application will present a consistent user interface. The Dialog Manager uses TextEdit for text editing in dialog boxes.

TextEdit supports these standard features:

- Selecting text by clicking and dragging with the mouse, double-clicking to select words. To TextEdit, a **word** is any series of printing characters, excluding spaces (ASCII code $20) but including nonbreaking spaces (ASCII code $CA).
- Extending or shortening the selection by Shift-clicking.
- Inverse highlighting of the current text selection, or display of a blinking vertical bar at the insertion point.
- **Word wraparound**, which prevents a word from being split between lines when text is drawn.
- Cutting (or copying) and pasting within an application via the Clipboard. TextEdit puts text you cut or copy into the **TextEdit scrap**.

Note: The TextEdit scrap is used only by TextEdit; it's not the same as the "desk scrap" used by the Scrap Manager. To support cutting and pasting between applications, or between applications and desk accessories, you must transfer information between the two scraps.

Inside Macintosh

Although TextEdit is useful for many standard text editing operations, there are some additional features that it doesn't support. TextEdit does *not* support:

- the use of more than one font or stylistic variation in a single block of text
- fully justified text (text aligned with both the left and right margins)
- "intelligent" cut and paste (adjusting spaces between words during cutting and pasting)
- tabs

TextEdit also provides "hooks" for implementing some features such as automatic scrolling or a more precise definition of a word.

EDIT RECORDS

To edit text on the screen, TextEdit needs to know where and how to display the text, where to store the text, and other information related to editing. This display, storage, and editing information is contained in an **edit record** that defines the complete editing environment. The data type of an edit record is called TERec.

You prepare to edit text by specifying a **destination rectangle** in which to draw the text and a **view rectangle** in which the text will be visible. TextEdit incorporates the rectangles and the drawing environment of the current grafPort into an edit record, and returns a handle of type TEHandle to the record:

```
TYPE  TEPtr    = ^TERec;
      TEHandle = ^TEPtr;
```

Most of the text editing routines require you to pass this handle as a parameter.

In addition to the two rectangles and a description of the drawing environment, the edit record also contains:

- a handle to the text to be edited
- a pointer to the grafPort in which the text is displayed
- the current **selection range**, which determines exactly which characters will be affected by the next editing operation
- the **justification** of the text, as left, right, or center

The special terms introduced here are described in detail below.

For most operations, you don't need to know the exact structure of an edit record; TextEdit routines access the record for you. However, to support some operations, such as automatic scrolling, you need to access the fields of the edit record directly. The structure of an edit record is given below.

The Destination and View Rectangles

The destination rectangle is the rectangle in which the text is drawn. The view rectangle is the rectangle within which the text is actually visible. In other words, the view of the text drawn in the destination rectangle is clipped to the view rectangle (see Figure 1).

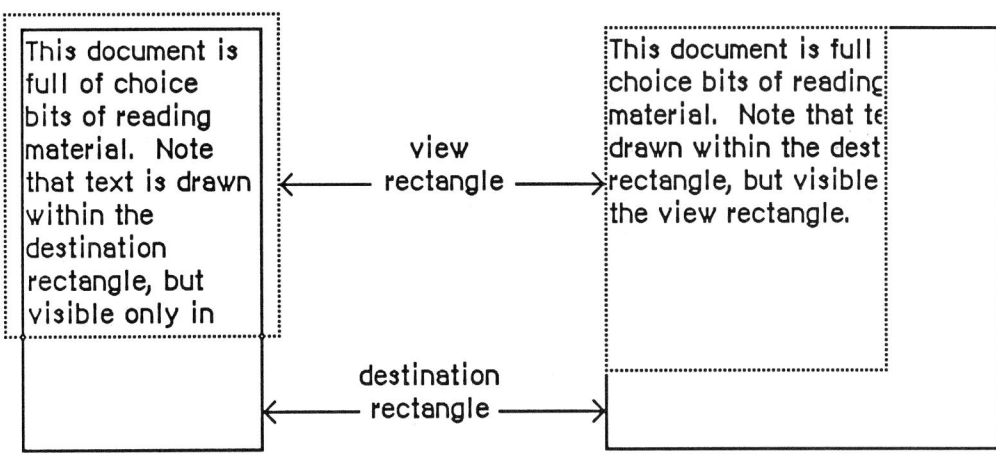

Figure 1. Destination and View Rectangles

You specify both rectangles in the local coordinates of the grafPort. To ensure that the first and last characters in each line are legible in a document window, you may want to inset the destination rectangle at least four pixels from the left and right edges of the grafPort's portRect (20 pixels from the right edge if there's a scroll bar or size box).

Edit operations may of course lengthen or shorten the text. If the text becomes too long to be enclosed by the destination rectangle, it's simply drawn beyond the bottom. In other words, you can think of the destination rectangle as bottomless—its sides determine the beginning and end of each line of text, and its top determines the position of the first line.

Normally, at the right edge of the destination rectangle, the text automatically wraps around to the left edge to begin a new line. A new line also begins where explicitly specified by a Return character in the text. Word wraparound ensures that no word is ever split between lines unless it's too long to fit entirely on one line, in which case it's split at the right edge of the destination rectangle.

The Selection Range

In the text editing environment, a **character position** is an index into the text, with position 0 corresponding to the first character. The edit record includes fields for character positions that specify the beginning and end of the current selection range, which is the series of characters where the next editing operation will occur. For example, the procedures that cut or copy from the text of an edit record do so to the current selection range.

The selection range, which is inversely highlighted when the window is active, extends from the beginning character position to the end character position. Figure 2 shows a selection range between positions 3 and 8, consisting of five characters (the character *at* position 8 isn't included). The end position of a selection range may be 1 greater than the position of the last character of the text, so that the selection range can include the last character.

If the selection range is empty—that is, its beginning and end positions are the same—that position is the text's **insertion point**, the position where characters will be inserted. By default, it's marked with a blinking caret. If, for example, the insertion point is as illustrated in Figure 2 and the inserted characters are "edit ", the text will read "the edit insertion point".

Inside Macintosh

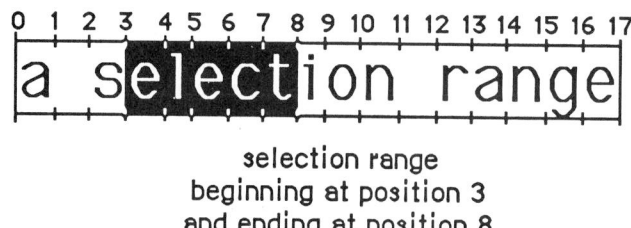

selection range
beginning at position 3
and ending at position 8

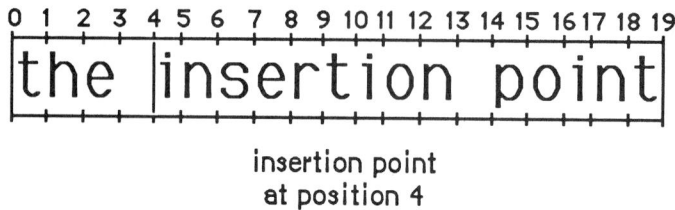

insertion point
at position 4

Figure 2. Selection Range and Insertion Point

Note: We use the word **caret** here generically, to mean a symbol indicating where something is to be inserted; the specific symbol is a vertical bar (|).

If you call a procedure to insert characters when there's a selection range of one or more characters rather than an insertion point, the editing procedure automatically deletes the selection range and replaces it with an insertion point before inserting the characters.

Justification

TextEdit allows you to specify the justification of the lines of text, that is, their horizontal placement with respect to the left and right edges of the destination rectangle. The different types of justification supported by TextEdit are illustrated in Figure 3.

- Left justification aligns the text with the left edge of the destination rectangle. This is the default type of justification.
- Center justification centers each line of text between the left and right edges of the destination rectangle.
- Right justification aligns the text with the right edge of the destination rectangle.

```
┌─────────────────┐  ┌─────────────────┐  ┌─────────────────┐
│This is an example│  │This is an example│  │This is an example│
│of left          │  │   of center     │  │         of right│
│justification. See│  │justification. See│  │justification. See│
│how the text is  │  │ how the text is │  │  how the text is│
│aligned with the │  │centered between │  │ aligned with the│
│left edge of the │  │ the edges of the│  │ right edge of the│
│rectangle.       │  │   rectangle.    │  │       rectangle.│
└─────────────────┘  └─────────────────┘  └─────────────────┘
```

Figure 3. Justification

Note: Trailing spaces on a line are ignored for justification. For example, "Fred" and "Fred " will be aligned identically. (Leading spaces are not ignored.)

TextEdit provides three predefined constants for setting the justification:

```
CONST teJustLeft   =  0;
      teJustCenter =  1;
      teJustRight  = -1;
```

The TERec Data Type

The structure of an edit record is given here. Some TextEdit features are available only if you access fields of the edit record directly.

```
TYPE TERec = RECORD
            destRect:    Rect;      {destination rectangle}
            viewRect:    Rect;      {view rectangle}
            selRect:     Rect;      {used from assembly language}
            lineHeight:  INTEGER;   {for line spacing}
            fontAscent:  INTEGER;   {caret/highlighting position}
            selPoint:    Point;     {used from assembly language}
            selStart:    INTEGER;   {start of selection range}
            selEnd:      INTEGER;   {end of selection range}
            active:      INTEGER;   {used internally}
            wordBreak:   ProcPtr;   {for word break routine}
            clikLoop:    ProcPtr;   {for click loop routine}
            clickTime:   LONGINT;   {used internally}
            clickLoc:    INTEGER;   {used internally}
            caretTime:   LONGINT;   {used internally}
            caretState:  INTEGER;   {used internally}
            just:        INTEGER;   {justification of text}
            teLength:    INTEGER;   {length of text}
            hText:       Handle;    {text to be edited}
            recalBack:   INTEGER;   {used internally}
            recalLines:  INTEGER;   {used internally}
            clikStuff:   INTEGER;   {used internally}
            crOnly:      INTEGER;   {if <0, new line at Return only}
            txFont:      INTEGER;   {text font}
            txFace:      Style;     {character style}
            txMode:      INTEGER;   {pen mode}
            txSize:      INTEGER;   {font size}
            inPort:      GrafPtr;   {grafPort}
            highHook:    ProcPtr;   {used from assembly language}
            caretHook:   ProcPtr;   {used from assembly language}
            nLines:      INTEGER;   {number of lines}
            lineStarts:  ARRAY[0..16000] OF INTEGER
                                    {positions of line starts}
       END;
```

Warning: Don't change any of the fields marked "used internally"—these exist solely for internal use among the TextEdit routines.

The destRect and viewRect fields specify the destination and view rectangles.

Inside Macintosh

The lineHeight and fontAscent fields have to do with the vertical spacing of the lines of text, and where the caret or highlighting of the selection range is drawn relative to the text. The fontAscent field specifies how far above the base line the pen is positioned to begin drawing the caret or highlighting. For single-spaced text, this is the ascent of the text in pixels (the height of the tallest characters in the font from the base line). The lineHeight field specifies the vertical distance from the ascent line of one line of text down to the ascent line of the next. For single-spaced text, this is the same as the font size, but in pixels. The values of the lineHeight and fontAscent fields for single-spaced text are shown in Figure 4. For more information on fonts, see chapter 7.

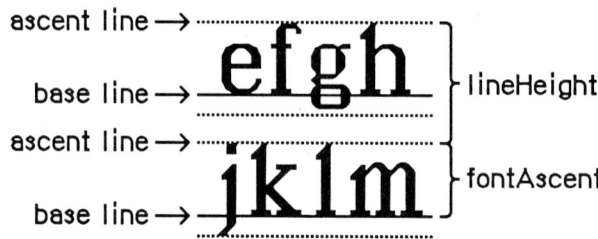

Figure 4. LineHeight and FontAscent

If you want to change the vertical spacing of the text, you should change both the lineHeight and fontAscent fields by the same amount, otherwise the placement of the caret or highlighting of the selection range may not look right. For example, to double the line spacing, add the value of lineHeight to both fields. (This doesn't change the size of the characters; it affects only the spacing between lines.) If you change the size of the text, you should also change these fields; you can get font measurements you'll need with the QuickDraw procedure GetFontInfo.

Assembly-language note: The selPoint field (whose assembly-language offset is named teSelPoint) contains the point selected with the mouse, in the local coordinates of the current grafPort. You'll need this for hit-testing if you use the routine pointed to by the global variable TEDoText (see "Advanced Routines" in the "TextEdit Routines" section).

The selStart and selEnd fields specify the character positions of the beginning and end of the selection range. Remember that character position 0 refers to the first character, and that the end of a selection range can be 1 greater than the position of the last character of the text.

The wordBreak field lets you change TextEdit's definition of a word, and the clikLoop field lets you implement automatic scrolling. These two fields are described in separate sections below.

The just field specifies the justification of the text. (See "Justification", above.)

The teLength field contains the number of characters in the text to be edited (the maximum length is 32K bytes). The hText field is a handle to the text. You can directly change the text of an edit record by changing these two fields.

The crOnly field specifies whether or not text wraps around at the right edge of the destination rectangle, as shown in Figure 5. If crOnly is positive, text does wrap around. If crOnly is negative, text does not wrap around at the edge of the destination rectangle, and new lines are specified explicitly by Return characters only. This is faster than word wraparound, and is useful in an application similar to a programming-language editor, where you may not want a single line of code to be split onto two lines.

```
┌─────────────────────────┐    ┌─────────────────────────┐
│ There's a Return        │    │ There's a Return charac │
│ character at the end    │    │ But not at the end of th│
│ of this line.           │    │                         │
│ But not at the end of   │    │                         │
│ this line. Or this line.│    │                         │
└─────────────────────────┘    └─────────────────────────┘
     new line at Return              new line at Return
   characters and edge of            characters only
    destination rectangle
```

Figure 5. New Lines

The txFont, txFace, txMode, and txSize fields specify the font, character style, pen mode, and font size, respectively, of all the text in the edit record. (See chapter 6 for details about these characteristics.) If you change one of these values, the entire text of this edit record will have the new characteristics when it's redrawn. If you change the txSize field, remember to change the lineHeight and fontAscent fields, too.

The inPort field contains a pointer to the grafPort associated with this edit record.

Assembly-language note: The highHook and caretHook fields—at the offsets teHiHook and teCarHook in assembly language—contain the addresses of routines that deal with text highlighting and the caret. These routines pass parameters in registers; the application must save and restore the registers.

If you store the address of a routine in teHiHook, that routine will be used instead of the QuickDraw procedure InvertRect whenever a selection range is to be highlighted. The routine can destroy the contents of registers A0, A1, D0, D1, and D2. On entry, A3 is a pointer to a locked edit record; the stack contains the rectangle enclosing the text being highlighted. For example, if you store the address of the following routine in teHiHook, selection ranges will be underlined instead of inverted:

```
UnderHigh
    MOVE.L      (SP),A0             ;get address of rectangle to be
                                    ; highlighted
    MOVE        bottom(A0),top(A0)  ;make the top coordinate equal to
    SUBQ        #1,top(A0)          ; the bottom coordinate minus 1
    _InverRect                      ;invert the resulting rectangle
    RTS
```

The routine whose address is stored in teCarHook acts exactly the same way as the teHiHook routine, but on the caret instead of the selection highlighting, allowing you to change the appearance of the caret. The routine is called with the stack containing the rectangle that encloses the caret.

The nLines field contains the number of lines in the text. The lineStarts array contains the character position of the first character in each line. It's declared to have 16001 elements to comply with Pascal range checking; it's actually a dynamic data structure having only as many elements as needed. You shouldn't change the elements of lineStarts.

Inside Macintosh

The WordBreak Field

The wordBreak field of an edit record lets you specify the record's word break routine—the routine that determines the "word" that's highlighted when the user double-clicks in the text, and the position at which text is wrapped around at the end of a line. The default routine breaks words at any character with an ASCII value of $20 or less (the space character or nonprinting control characters).

The word break routine must have two parameters and return a Boolean value. This is how you would declare one named MyWordBreak:

```
FUNCTION MyWordBreak (text: Ptr; charPos: INTEGER) : BOOLEAN;
```

The function should return TRUE to break a word at the character at position charPos in the specified text, or FALSE not to break there. From Pascal, you must call the SetWordBreak procedure to set the wordBreak field so that your routine will be used.

Assembly-language note: You can set this field to point to your own assembly-language word break routine. The registers must contain the following:

On entry	A0:	pointer to text
	D0:	character position (word)
On exit	Z (zero) condition code:	
	0 to break at specified character	
	1 not to break there	

The ClikLoop Field

The clikLoop field of an edit record lets you specify a routine that will be called repeatedly (by the TEClick procedure, described below) as long as the mouse button is held down within the text. You can use this to implement the automatic scrolling of text when the user is making a selection and drags the cursor out of the view rectangle.

The click loop routine has no parameters and returns a Boolean value. You could declare a click loop routine named MyClikLoop like this:

```
FUNCTION MyClikLoop : BOOLEAN;
```

The function should return TRUE. From Pascal, you must call the SetClikLoop procedure to set the clikLoop field so that TextEdit will call your routine.

Warning: Returning FALSE from your click loop routine tells the TEClick procedure that the mouse button has been released, which aborts TEClick.

Assembly-language note: Your routine should set register D0 to 1, and preserve register D2. (Returning 0 in register D0 aborts TEClick.)

An automatic scrolling routine might check the mouse location, and call a scrolling routine if the mouse location is outside the view rectangle. (The scrolling routine can be the same routine that the Control Manager function TrackControl calls.) The handle to the current edit record should be kept as a global variable so the scrolling routine can access it.

USING TEXTEDIT

Before using TextEdit, you must initialize QuickDraw, the Font Manager, and the Window Manager, in that order.

The first TextEdit routine to call is the initialization procedure TEInit. Call TENew to allocate an edit record; it returns a handle to the record. Most of the text editing routines require you to pass this handle as a parameter.

When you've finished working with the text of an edit record, you can get a handle to the text as a packed array of characters with the TEGetText function.

> **Note:** To convert text from an edit record to a Pascal string, you can use the Dialog Manager procedure GetIText, passing it the text handle from the edit record.

When you're completely done with an edit record and want to dispose of it, call TEDispose.

To make a blinking caret appear at the insertion point, call the TEIdle procedure as often as possible (at least once each time through the main event loop); if it's not called often enough, the caret will blink irregularly.

> **Note:** To change the cursor to an I-beam, you can call the Toolbox Utility function GetCursor and the QuickDraw procedure SetCursor. The resource ID for the I-beam cursor is defined in the Toolbox Utilities as the constant iBeamCursor.

When a mouse-down event occurs in the view rectangle (and the window is active) call the TEClick procedure. TEClick controls the placement and highlighting of the selection range, including supporting use of the Shift key to make extended selections.

Key-down, auto-key, and mouse events that pertain to text editing can be handled by several TextEdit procedures:

- TEKey inserts characters and deletes characters backspaced over.

- TECut transfers the selection range to the TextEdit scrap, removing the selection range from the text.

- TEPaste inserts the contents of the TextEdit scrap. By calling TECut, changing the insertion point, and then calling TEPaste, you can perform a "cut and paste" operation, moving text from one place to another.

- TECopy copies the selection range to the TextEdit scrap. By calling TECopy, changing the insertion point, and then calling TEPaste, you can make multiple copies of text.

- TEDelete removes the selection range (without transferring it to the scrap). You can use TEDelete to implement the Clear command.

- TEInsert inserts specified text. You can use this to combine two or more documents. TEDelete and TEInsert do not modify the scrap, so they're useful for implementing the Undo command.

After each editing procedure, TextEdit redraws the text if necessary from the insertion point to the end of the text. You never have to set the selection range or insertion point yourself; TEClick and the editing procedures leave it where it should be. If you want to modify the selection range directly, however—to highlight an initial default name or value, for example—you can use the TESetSelect procedure.

To implement cutting and pasting of text between different applications, or between applications and desk accessories, you need to transfer the text between the TextEdit scrap (which is a private scrap used only by TextEdit) and the Scrap Manager's desk scrap. Tou can do this using the functions TEFromScrap and TEToScrap. (See chapter 15 for more information about scrap handling.)

When an update event is reported for a text editing window, call TEUpdate—along with the Window Manager procedures BeginUpdate and EndUpdate—to redraw the text.

Note: After changing any fields of the edit record that affect the appearance of the text, you should call the Window Manager procedure InvalRect(hTE^^.viewRect) so that the text will be updated.

The procedures TEActivate and TEDeactivate must be called each time GetNextEvent reports an activate event for a text editing window. TEActivate simply highlights the selection range or displays a caret at the insertion point; TEDeactivate unhighlights the selection range or removes the caret.

To specify the justification of the text, you can use TESetJust. If you change the justification, be sure to call InvalRect so the text will be updated.

To scroll text within the view rectangle, you can use the TEScroll procedure.

The TESetText procedure lets you change the text being edited. For example, if your application has several separate pieces of text that must be edited one at a time, you don't have to allocate an edit record for each of them. Allocate a single edit record, and then use TESetText to change the text. (This is the method used in dialog boxes.)

Note: TESetText actually makes a copy of the text to be edited. Advanced programmers can save space by storing a handle to the text in the hText field of the edit record itself, then calling TECalText to recalculate the beginning of each line.

If you ever want to draw noneditable text in any given rectangle, you can use the TextBox procedure.

If you've written your own word break or click loop routine in Pascal, you must call the SetWordBreak or SetClikLoop procedure to install your routine so TextEdit will use it.

TextEdit

TEXTEDIT ROUTINES

Initialization and Allocation

```
PROCEDURE TEInit;
```

TEInit initializes TextEdit by allocating a handle for the TextEdit scrap. The scrap is initially empty. Call this procedure once and only once at the beginning of your program.

> **Note:** You should call TEInit even if your application doesn't use TextEdit, so that desk accessories and dialog and alert boxes will work correctly.

```
FUNCTION TENew (destRect,viewRect: Rect) : TEHandle;
```

TENew allocates a handle for text, creates and initializes an edit record, and returns a handle to the new edit record. DestRect and viewRect are the destination and view rectangles, respectively. Both rectangles are specified in the current grafPort's coordinates. The destination rectangle must always be at least as wide as the first character drawn (about 20 pixels is a good minimum width). The view rectangle must not be empty (for example, don't make its right edge less than its left edge if you don't want any text visible—specify a rectangle off the screen instead).

Call TENew once for every edit record you want allocated. The edit record incorporates the drawing environment of the grafPort, and is initialized for left-justified, single-spaced text with an insertion point at character position 0.

> **Note:** The caret won't appear until you call TEActivate.

```
PROCEDURE TEDispose (hTE: TEHandle);
```

TEDispose releases the memory allocated for the edit record and text specified by hTE. Call this procedure when you're completely through with an edit record.

Accessing the Text of an Edit Record

```
PROCEDURE TESetText (text: Ptr; length: LONGINT; hTE: TEHandle);
```

TESetText incorporates a copy of the specified text into the edit record specified by hTE. The text parameter points to the text, and the length parameter indicates the number of characters in the text. The selection range is set to an insertion point at the end of the text. TESetText doesn't affect the text drawn in the destination rectangle, so call InvalRect afterward if necessary. TESetText doesn't dispose of any text currently in the edit record.

```
FUNCTION TEGetText (hTE: TEHandle) : CharsHandle;
```

TEGetText returns a handle to the text of the specified edit record. The result is the same as the handle in the hText field of the edit record, but has the CharsHandle data type, which is defined as:

```
TYPE CharsHandle = ^CharsPtr;
     CharsPtr    = ^Chars;
     Chars       = PACKED ARRAY[0..32000] OF CHAR;
```

You can get the length of the text from the teLength field of the edit record.

Insertion Point and Selection Range

```
PROCEDURE TEIdle (hTE: TEHandle);
```

Call TEIdle repeatedly to make a blinking caret appear at the insertion point (if any) in the text specified by hTE. (The caret appears only when the window containing that text is active, of course.) TextEdit observes a minimum blink interval: No matter how often you call TEIdle, the time between blinks will never be less than the minimum interval.

> **Note:** The initial minimum blink interval setting is 32 ticks. The user can adjust this setting with the Control Panel desk accessory.

To provide a constant frequency of blinking, you should call TEIdle as often as possible—at least once each time through your main event loop. Call it more than once if your application does an unusually large amount of processing each time through the loop.

> **Note:** You actually need to call TEIdle only when the window containing the text is active.

```
PROCEDURE TEClick (pt: Point; extend: BOOLEAN; hTE: TEHandle);
```

TEClick controls the placement and highlighting of the selection range as determined by mouse events. Call TEClick whenever a mouse-down event occurs in the view rectangle of the edit record specified by hTE, and the window associated with that edit record is active. TEClick keeps control until the mouse button is released. Pt is the mouse location (in local coordinates) at the time the button was pressed, obtainable from the event record.

> **Note:** Use the QuickDraw procedure GlobalToLocal to convert the global coordinates of the mouse location given in the event record to the local coordinate system for pt.

Pass TRUE for the extend parameter if the Event Manager indicates that the Shift key was held down at the time of the click (to extend the selection).

TEClick unhighlights the old selection range unless the selection range is being extended. If the mouse moves, meaning that a drag is occurring, TEClick expands or shortens the selection range accordingly. In the case of a double-click, the word under the cursor becomes the selection range; dragging expands or shortens the selection a word at a time.

```
PROCEDURE TESetSelect (selStart,selEnd: LONGINT; hTE: TEHandle);
```

TESetSelect sets the selection range to the text between selStart and selEnd in the text specified by hTE. The old selection range is unhighlighted, and the new one is highlighted. If selStart equals selEnd, the selection range is an insertion point, and a caret is displayed.

SelEnd and selStart can range from 0 to 32767. If selEnd is anywhere beyond the last character of the text, the position just past the last character is used.

```
PROCEDURE TEActivate (hTE: TEHandle);
```

TEActivate highlights the selection range in the view rectangle of the edit record specified by hTE. If the selection range is an insertion point, it displays a caret there. This procedure should be called every time the Toolbox Event Manager function GetNextEvent reports that the window containing the edit record has become active.

```
PROCEDURE TEDeactivate (hTE: TEHandle);
```

TEDeactivate unhighlights the selection range in the view rectangle of the edit record specified by hTE. If the selection range is an insertion point, it removes the caret. This procedure should be called every time the Toolbox Event Manager function GetNextEvent reports that the window containing the edit record has become inactive.

Editing

```
PROCEDURE TEKey (key: CHAR; hTE: TEHandle);
```

TEKey replaces the selection range in the text specified by hTE with the character given by the key parameter, and leaves an insertion point just past the inserted character. If the selection range is an insertion point, TEKey just inserts the character there. If the key parameter contains a Backspace character, the selection range or the character immediately to the left of the insertion point is deleted. TEKey redraws the text as necessary. Call TEKey every time the Toolbox Event Manager function GetNextEvent reports a keyboard event that your application decides should be handled by TextEdit.

> **Note:** TEKey inserts every character passed in the key parameter, so it's up to your application to filter out all characters that aren't actual text (such as keys typed in conjunction with the Command key).

```
PROCEDURE TECut (hTE: TEHandle);
```

TECut removes the selection range from the text specified by hTE and places it in the TextEdit scrap. The text is redrawn as necessary. Anything previously in the scrap is deleted. (See Figure 6.) If the selection range is an insertion point, the scrap is emptied.

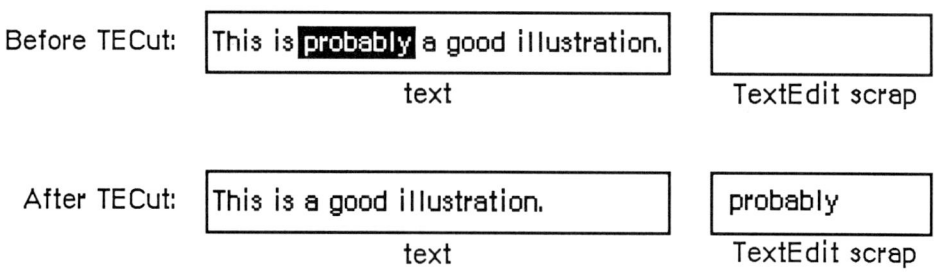

Figure 6. Cutting

```
PROCEDURE TECopy (hTE: TEHandle);
```

TECopy copies the selection range from the text specified by hTE into the TextEdit scrap. Anything previously in the scrap is deleted. The selection range is not deleted. If the selection range is an insertion point, the scrap is emptied.

```
PROCEDURE TEPaste (hTE: TEHandle);
```

TEPaste replaces the selection range in the text specified by hTE with the contents of the TextEdit scrap, and leaves an insertion point just past the inserted text. (See Figure 7.) The text is redrawn as necessary. If the scrap is empty, the selection range is deleted. If the selection range is an insertion point, TEPaste just inserts the scrap there.

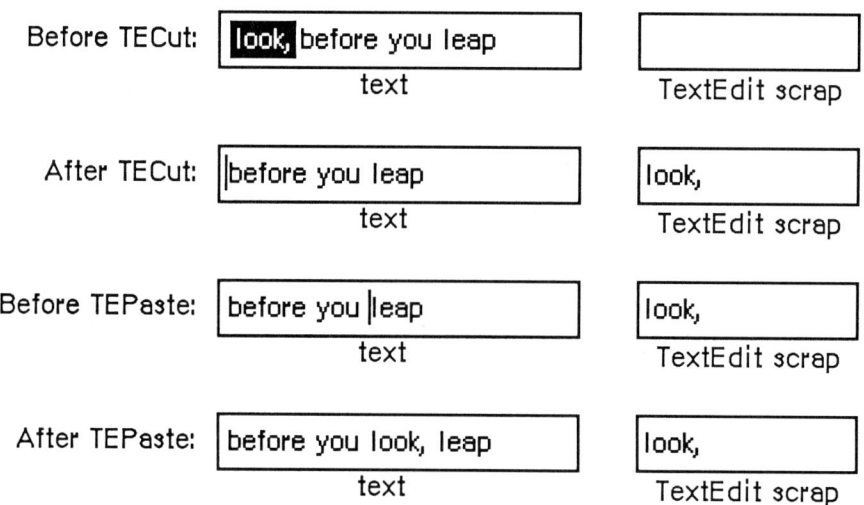

Figure 7. Cutting and Pasting

```
PROCEDURE TEDelete (hTE: TEHandle);
```

TEDelete removes the selection range from the text specified by hTE, and redraws the text as necessary. TEDelete is the same as TECut (above) except that it doesn't transfer the selection range to the scrap. If the selection range is an insertion point, nothing happens.

```
PROCEDURE TEInsert (text: Ptr; length: LONGINT; hTE: TEHandle);
```

TEInsert takes the specified text and inserts it just before the selection range into the text indicated by hTE, redrawing the text as necessary. The text parameter points to the text to be inserted, and the length parameter indicates the number of characters to be inserted. TEInsert doesn't affect either the current selection range or the scrap.

Text Display and Scrolling

```
PROCEDURE TESetJust (just: INTEGER, hTE: TEHandle);
```

TESetJust sets the justification of the text specified by hTE to just. TextEdit provides three predefined constants for setting justification:

```
CONST teJustLeft   =  0;
      teJustCenter =  1;
      teJustRight  = -1;
```

By default, text is left-justified. If you change the justification, call InvalRect after TESetJust, so the text will be redrawn with the new justification.

```
PROCEDURE TEUpdate (rUpdate: Rect; hTE: TEHandle);
```

TEUpdate draws the text specified by hTE within the rectangle specified by rUpdate (given in the coordinates of the current grafPort). Call TEUpdate every time the Toolbox Event Manager function GetNextEvent reports an update event for a text editing window—after you call the Window Manager procedure BeginUpdate, and before you call EndUpdate.

Normally you'll do the following when an update event occurs:

```
BeginUpdate(myWindow);
EraseRect(myWindow^.portRect);
TEUpdate(myWindow^.portRect,hTE);
EndUpdate(myWindow)
```

If you don't include the EraseRect call, the caret may sometimes remain visible when the window is deactivated.

Inside Macintosh

```
PROCEDURE TextBox (text: Ptr; length: LONGINT; box: Rect; just:
                   INTEGER);
```

TextBox draws the specified text in the rectangle indicated by the box parameter, with justification just. (See "Justification" under "Edit Records".) The text parameter points to the text, and the length parameter indicates the number of characters to draw. The rectangle is specified in local coordinates, and must be at least as wide as the first character drawn (a good rule of thumb is to make it at least 20 pixels wide). TextBox creates its own edit record, which it deletes when it's finished with it, so the text it draws cannot be edited.

For example:

```
str := 'String in a box';
SetRect(r,100,100,200,200);
TextBox(POINTER(ORD(@str)+1),LENGTH(str),r,teJustCenter);
FrameRect(r)
```

Because Pascal strings start with a length byte, you must advance the pointer one position past the beginning of the string to point to the start of the text.

```
PROCEDURE TEScroll (dh,dv: INTEGER; hTE: TEHandle);
```

TEScroll scrolls the text within the view rectangle of the specified edit record by the number of pixels specified in the dh and dv parameters. The edit record is specified by the hTE parameter. Positive dh and dv values move the text right and down, respectively, and negative values move the text left and up. For example,

```
TEScroll(0,-hTE^^.lineHeight,hTE)
```

scrolls the text up one line. Remember that you scroll text *up* when the user clicks in the scroll arrow pointing *down*. The destination rectangle is offset by the amount you scroll.

> **Note:** To implement automatic scrolling, you store the address of a routine in the clikLoop field of the edit record, as described above under "The TERec Data Type".

Scrap Handling

The TEFromScrap and TEToScrap functions return a result code of type OSErr (defined as INTEGER in the Operating System Utilities) indicating whether an error occurred. If no error occurred, they return the result code

```
CONST noErr = 0;   {no error}
```

Otherwise, they return an Operating System result code indicating an error. (See Appendix A in Volume III for a list of all result codes.)

TextEdit

```
FUNCTION TEFromScrap : OSErr;   [Not in ROM]
```

TEFromScrap copies the desk scrap to the TextEdit scrap. If no error occurs, it returns the result code noErr; otherwise, it returns an appropriate Operating System result code.

Assembly-language note: From assembly language, you can store a handle to the desk scrap in the global variable TEScrpHandle, and the size of the desk scrap in the global variable TEScrpLength; you can get these values with the Scrap Manager function InfoScrap.

```
FUNCTION TEToScrap : OSErr;   [Not in ROM]
```

TEToScrap copies the TextEdit scrap to the desk scrap. If no error occurs, it returns the result code noErr; otherwise, it returns an appropriate Operating System result code.

Warning: You must call the Scrap Manager function ZeroScrap to initialize the desk scrap or clear its previous contents before calling TEToScrap.

Assembly-language note: From assembly language, you can copy the TextEdit scrap to the desk scrap by calling the Scrap Manager function PutScrap; you can get the values you need from the global variables TEScrpHandle and TEScrpLength.

```
FUNCTION TEScrapHandle : Handle;   [Not in ROM]
```

TEScrapHandle returns a handle to the TextEdit scrap.

Assembly-language note: The global variable TEScrpHandle contains a handle to the TextEdit scrap.

```
FUNCTION TEGetScrapLen : LONGINT;   [Not in ROM]
```

TEGetScrapLen returns the size of the TextEdit scrap in bytes.

Assembly-language note: The global variable TEScrpLength contains the size of the TextEdit scrap in bytes.

TextEdit Routines I-389

Inside Macintosh

```
PROCEDURE TESetScrapLen (length: LONGINT);    [Not in ROM]
```

TESetScrapLen sets the size of the TextEdit scrap to the given number of bytes.

Assembly-language note: From assembly language, you can set the global variable TEScrpLength.

Advanced Routines

```
PROCEDURE SetWordBreak (wBrkProc: ProcPtr; hTE: TEHandle);   [Not in
            ROM]
```

SetWordBreak installs in the wordBreak field of the specified edit record a special routine that calls the word break routine pointed to by wBrkProc. The specified word break routine will be called instead of TextEdit's default routine, as described under "The WordBreak Field" in the "Edit Records" section.

Assembly-language note: From assembly language you don't need this procedure; just set the field of the edit record to point to your word break routine.

```
PROCEDURE SetClikLoop (clikProc: ProcPtr; hTE: TEHandle);   [Not in
            ROM]
```

SetClikLoop installs in the clikLoop field of the specified edit record a special routine that calls the click loop routine pointed to by clikProc. The specified click loop routine will be called repeatedly as long as the user holds down the mouse button within the text, as described above under "The ClikLoop Field" in the "Edit Records" section.

Assembly-language note: Like SetWordBreak, this procedure isn't necessary from assembly language; just set the field of the edit record to point to your click loop routine.

```
PROCEDURE TECalText (hTE: TEHandle);
```

TECalText recalculates the beginnings of all lines of text in the edit record specified by hTE, updating elements of the lineStarts array. Call TECalText if you've changed the destination rectangle, the hText field, or any other field that affects the number of characters per line.

Note: There are two ways to specify text to be edited. The easiest method is to use TESetText, which takes an existing edit record, creates a copy of the specified text, and stores a handle to the copy in the edit record. You can instead directly change the hText field of the edit record, and then call TECalText to recalculate the lineStarts array to match the new text. If you have a lot of text, you can use the latter method to save space.

Assembly-language note: The global variable TERecal contains the address of the routine called by TECalText to recalculate the line starts and set the first and last characters that need to be redrawn. The registers contain the following:

On entry	A3:	pointer to the locked edit record
	D7:	change in the length of the record (word)
On exit	D2:	line start of the line containing the first character to be redrawn (word)
	D3:	position of first character to be redrawn (word)
	D4:	position of last character to be redrawn (word)

Assembly-language note: The global variable TEDoText contains the address of a multi-purpose text editing routine that advanced programmers may find useful. It lets you display, highlight, and hit-test characters, and position the pen to draw the caret. "Hit-test" means decide where to place the insertion point when the user clicks the mouse button; the point selected with the mouse is in the teSelPoint field. The registers contain the following:

On entry	A3:	pointer to the locked edit record
	D3:	position of first character to be redrawn (word)
	D4:	position of last character to be redrawn (word)
	D7: (word)	0 to hit-test a character
		1 to highlight the selection range
		−1 to display the text
		−2 to position the pen to draw the caret
On exit	A0:	pointer to current grafPort
	D0:	if hit-testing, character position or −1 for none (word)

SUMMARY OF TEXTEDIT

Constants

```
CONST { Text justification }

    teJustLeft   = 0;
    teJustCenter = 1;
    teJustRight  = -1;
```

Data Types

```
TYPE TEHandle = ^TEPtr;
     TEPtr    = ^TERec;
     TERec = RECORD
                destRect:   Rect;     {destination rectangle}
                viewRect:   Rect;     {view rectangle}
                selRect:    Rect;     {used from assembly language}
                lineHeight: INTEGER;  {for line spacing}
                fontAscent: INTEGER;  {caret/highlighting position}
                selPoint:   Point;    {used from assembly language}
                selStart:   INTEGER;  {start of selection range}
                selEnd:     INTEGER;  {end of selection range}
                active:     INTEGER;  {used internally}
                wordBreak:  ProcPtr;  {for word break routine}
                clikLoop:   ProcPtr;  {for click loop routine}
                clickTime:  LONGINT;  {used internally}
                clickLoc:   INTEGER;  {used internally}
                caretTime:  LONGINT;  {used internally}
                caretState: INTEGER;  {used internally}
                just:       INTEGER;  {justification of text}
                teLength:   INTEGER;  {length of text}
                hText:      Handle;   {text to be edited}
                recalBack:  INTEGER;  {used internally}
                recalLines: INTEGER;  {used internally}
                clikStuff:  INTEGER;  {used internally}
                crOnly:     INTEGER;  {if <0, new line at Return only}
                txFont:     INTEGER;  {text font}
                txFace:     Style;    {character style}
                txMode:     INTEGER;  {pen mode}
                txSize:     INTEGER;  {font size}
                inPort:     GrafPtr;  {grafPort}
                highHook:   ProcPtr;  {used from assembly language}
                caretHook:  ProcPtr;  {used from assembly language}
                nLines:     INTEGER;  {number of lines}
                lineStarts: ARRAY[0..16000] OF INTEGER
                                      {positions of line starts}
             END;
```

```
CharsHandle = ^CharsPtr;
CharsPtr    = ^Chars;
Chars       = PACKED ARRAY[0..32000] OF CHAR;
```

Routines

Initialization and Allocation

```
PROCEDURE TEInit;
FUNCTION  TENew     (destRect,viewRect: Rect) : TEHandle;
PROCEDURE TEDispose (hTE: TEHandle);
```

Accessing the Text of an Edit Record

```
PROCEDURE TESetText (text: Ptr; length: LONGINT; hTE: TEHandle);
FUNCTION  TEGetText (hTE: TEHandle) : CharsHandle;
```

Insertion Point and Selection Range

```
PROCEDURE TEIdle       (hTE: TEHandle);
PROCEDURE TEClick      (pt: Point; extend: BOOLEAN; hTE: TEHandle);
PROCEDURE TESetSelect  (selStart,selEnd: LONGINT; hTE: TEHandle);
PROCEDURE TEActivate   (hTE: TEHandle);
PROCEDURE TEDeactivate (hTE: TEHandle);
```

Editing

```
PROCEDURE TEKey    (key: CHAR; hTE: TEHandle);
PROCEDURE TECut    (hTE: TEHandle);
PROCEDURE TECopy   (hTE: TEHandle);
PROCEDURE TEPaste  (hTE: TEHandle);
PROCEDURE TEDelete (hTE: TEHandle);
PROCEDURE TEInsert (text: Ptr; length: LONGINT; hTE: TEHandle);
```

Text Display and Scrolling

```
PROCEDURE TESetJust (just: INTEGER; hTE: TEHandle);
PROCEDURE TEUpdate  (rUpdate: Rect; hTE: TEHandle);
PROCEDURE TextBox   (text: Ptr; length: LONGINT; box: Rect; just:
                     INTEGER);
PROCEDURE TEScroll  (dh,dv: INTEGER; hTE: TEHandle);
```

Scrap Handling [Not in ROM]

```
FUNCTION   TEFromScrap   :   OSErr;
FUNCTION   TEToScrap     :   OSErr;
FUNCTION   TEScrapHandle :   Handle;
FUNCTION   TEGetScrapLen :   LONGINT;
PROCEDURE  TESetScrapLen :   (length: LONGINT);
```

Advanced Routines

```
PROCEDURE  SetWordBreak  (wBrkProc: ProcPtr; hTE: TEHandle);   [Not in ROM]
PROCEDURE  SetClikLoop   (clikProc: ProcPtr; hTE: TEHandle);   [Not in ROM]
PROCEDURE  TECalText     (hTE: TEHandle);
```

Word Break Routine

```
FUNCTION MyWordBreak (text: Ptr; charPos: INTEGER) : BOOLEAN;
```

Click Loop Routine

```
FUNCTION MyClikLoop : BOOLEAN;
```

Assembly-Language Information

Constants

```
; Text justification

teJustLeft     .EQU    0
teJustCenter   .EQU    1
teJustRight    .EQU    -1
```

Edit Record Data Structure

teDestRect	Destination rectangle (8 bytes)
teViewRect	View rectangle (8 bytes)
teSelRect	Selection rectangle (8 bytes)
teLineHite	For line spacing (word)
teAscent	Caret/highlighting position (word)
teSelPoint	Point selected with mouse (long)
teSelStart	Start of selection range (word)
teSelEnd	End of selection range (word)
teWordBreak	Address of word break routine (see below)
teClikProc	Address of click loop routine (see below)
teJust	Justification of text (word)

teLength	Length of text (word)
teTextH	Handle to text
teCROnly	If <0, new line at Return only (byte)
teFont	Text font (word)
teFace	Character style (word)
teMode	Pen mode (word)
teSize	Font size (word)
teGrafPort	Pointer to grafPort
teHiHook	Address of text highlighting routine (see below)
teCarHook	Address of routine to draw caret (see below)
teNLines	Number of lines (word)
teLines	Positions of line starts (teNLines*2 bytes)
teRecSize	Size in bytes of edit record except teLines field

Word break routine

On entry	A0:	pointer to text
	D0:	character position (word)
On exit	Z condition code:	0 to break at specified character
		1 not to break there

Click loop routine

On exit	D0:	1
	D2:	must be preserved

Text highlighting routine

On entry	A3:	pointer to locked edit record

Caret drawing routine

On entry	A3:	pointer to locked edit record

Variables

TEScrpHandle	Handle to TextEdit scrap
TEScrpLength	Size in bytes of TextEdit scrap (long)
TERecal	Address of routine to recalculate line starts (see below)
TEDoText	Address of multi-purpose routine (see below)

TERecal routine

On entry	A3:	pointer to locked edit record
	D7:	change in length of edit record (word)
On exit	D2:	line start of line containing first character to be redrawn (word)
	D3:	position of first character to be redrawn (word)
	D4:	position of last character to be redrawn (word)

Inside Macintosh

TEDoText routine

On entry	A3:	pointer to locked edit record
	D3:	position of first character to be redrawn (word)
	D4:	position of last character to be redrawn (word)
	D7:	(word) 0 to hit-test a character
		1 to highlight selection range
		−1 to display text
		−2 to position pen to draw caret
On exit	A0:	pointer to current grafPort
	D0:	if hit-testing, character position or −1 for none (word)

13 THE DIALOG MANAGER

399	About This Chapter
399	About the Dialog Manager
401	Dialog and Alert Windows
402	Dialogs, Alerts, and Resources
403	Item Lists in Memory
404	Item Types
405	Item Handle or Procedure Pointer
406	Display Rectangle
406	Item Numbers
407	Dialog Records
407	Dialog Pointers
408	The DialogRecord Data Type
409	Alerts
410	Using the Dialog Manager
411	Dialog Manager Routines
411	Initialization
412	Creating and Disposing of Dialogs
415	Handling Dialog Events
418	Invoking Alerts
421	Manipulating Items in Dialogs and Alerts
423	Modifying Templates in Memory
423	Dialog Templates in Memory
424	Alert Templates in Memory
425	Formats of Resources for Dialogs and Alerts
425	Dialog Templates in a Resource File
426	Alert Templates in a Resource File
427	Items Lists in a Resource File
429	Summary of the Dialog Manager

The Dialog Manager

ABOUT THIS CHAPTER

This chapter describes the Dialog Manager, the part of the Toolbox that allows you to implement dialog boxes and the alert mechanism, two means of communication between the application and the end user.

You should already be familiar with:

- resources, as discussed in chapter 5
- the basic concepts and structures behind QuickDraw, particularly rectangles, grafPorts, and pictures
- the Toolbox Event Manager, the Window Manager, and the Control Manager
- TextEdit, to understand editing text in dialog boxes

ABOUT THE DIALOG MANAGER

The Dialog Manager is a tool for handling dialogs and alerts in a way that's consistent with the Macintosh User Interface Guidelines.

A **dialog box** appears on the screen when a Macintosh application needs more information to carry out a command. As shown in Figure 1, it typically resembles a form on which the user checks boxes and fills in blanks.

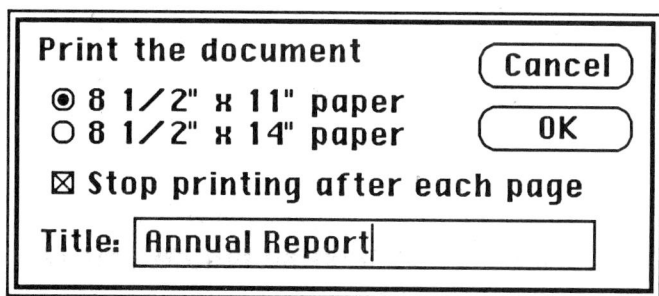

Figure 1. A Typical Dialog Box

By convention, a dialog box comes up slightly below the menu bar, is somewhat narrower than the screen, and is centered between the left and right edges of the screen. It may contain any or all of the following:

- informative or instructional text
- rectangles in which text may be entered (initially blank or containing default text that can be edited)
- controls of any kind
- graphics (icons or QuickDraw pictures)

Inside Macintosh

- anything else, as defined by the application

The user provides the necessary information in the dialog box, such as by entering text or clicking a check box. There's usually a button labeled "OK" to tell the application to accept the information provided and perform the command, and a button labeled "Cancel" to cancel the command as though it had never been given (retracting all actions since its invocation). Some dialog boxes may use a more descriptive word than "OK"; for simplicity, this chapter will still refer to the button as the "OK button". There may even be more than one button that will perform the command, each in a different way.

Most dialog boxes require the user to respond before doing anything else. Clicking a button to perform or cancel the command makes the box go away; clicking outside the dialog box only causes a beep from the Macintosh's speaker. This type is called a **modal** dialog box because it puts the user in the state or "mode" of being able to work only inside the dialog box. A modal dialog box usually has the same general appearance as shown in Figure 1 above. One of the buttons in the dialog box may be outlined boldly. Pressing the Return key or the Enter key has the same effect as clicking the outlined button or, if none, the OK button; the particular button whose effect occurs is called the dialog's **default button** and is the preferred ("safest") button to use in the current situation. If there's no boldly outlined or OK button, pressing Return or Enter will by convention have no effect.

Other dialog boxes do not require the user to respond before doing anything else; these are called **modeless** dialog boxes (see Figure 2). The user can, for example, do work in document windows on the desktop before clicking a button in the dialog box, and modeless dialog boxes can be set up to respond to the standard editing commands in the Edit menu. Clicking a button in a modeless dialog box will not make the box go away: The box will stay around so that the user can perform the command again. A Cancel button, if present, will simply stop the action currently being performed by the command; this would be useful for long printing or searching operations, for example.

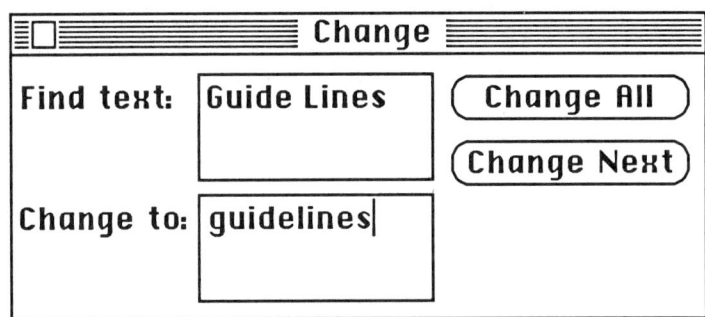

Figure 2. A Modeless Dialog Box

As shown in Figure 2, a modeless dialog box looks like a document window. It can be moved, made inactive and active again, or closed like any document window. When you're done with the command and want the box to go away, you can click its close box or choose Close from the File menu when it's the active window.

Dialog boxes may in fact require no response at all. For example, while an application is performing a time-consuming process, it can display a dialog box that contains only a message telling what it's doing; then, when the process is complete, it can simply remove the dialog box.

The Dialog Manager

The **alert** mechanism provides applications with a means of reporting errors or giving warnings. An **alert box** is similar to a modal dialog box, but it appears only when something has gone wrong or must be brought to the user's attention. Its conventional placement is slightly farther below the menu bar than a dialog box. To assist the user who isn't sure how to proceed when an alert box appears, the preferred button to use in the current situation is outlined boldly so it stands out from the other buttons in the alert box (see Figure 3). The outlined button is also the alert's default button; if the user presses the Return key or the Enter key, the effect is the same as clicking this button.

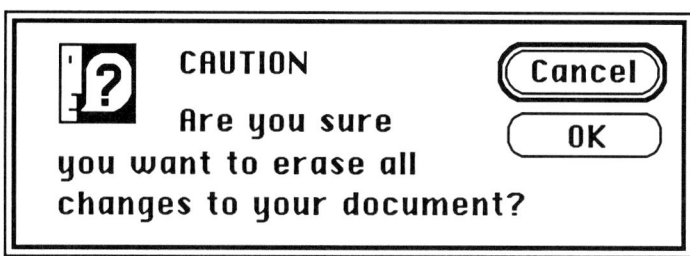

Figure 3. A Typical Alert Box

There are three standard kinds of alerts—Stop, Note, and Caution—each indicated by a particular icon in the top left corner of the alert box. Figure 3 illustrates a Caution alert. The icons identifying Stop and Note alerts are similar; instead of a question mark, they show an exclamation point and an asterisk, respectively. Other alerts can have anything in the the top left corner, including blank space if desired.

The alert mechanism also provides another type of signal: Sound from the Macintosh's speaker. The application can base its response on the number of consecutive times an alert occurs; the first time, it might simply beep, and thereafter it may present an alert box. The sound isn't limited to a single beep but may be any sequence of tones, and may occur either alone or along with an alert box. As an error is repeated, there can also be a change in which button is the default button (perhaps from OK to Cancel). You can specify different responses for up to four occurrences of the same alert.

With Dialog Manager routines, you can create dialog boxes or invoke alerts. The Dialog Manager gets most of the descriptive information about the dialogs and alerts from resources in a resource file. The Dialog Manager calls the Resource Manager to read what it needs from the resource file into memory as necessary. In some cases you can modify the information after it's been read into memory.

DIALOG AND ALERT WINDOWS

A dialog box appears in a **dialog window**. When you call a Dialog Manager routine to create a dialog, you supply the same information as when you create a window with a Window Manager routine. For example, you supply the window definition ID, which determines how the window looks and behaves, and a rectangle that becomes the portRect of the window's grafPort. You specify the window's plane (which, by convention, should initially be the frontmost) and whether the window is visible or invisible. The dialog window is created as specified.

Inside Macintosh

You can manipulate a dialog window just like any other window with Window Manager or QuickDraw routines, showing it, hiding it, moving it, changing its size or plane, or whatever—all, of course, in conformance with the Macintosh User Interface Guidelines. The Dialog Manager observes the clipping region of the dialog window's grafPort, so if you want clipping to occur, you can set this region with a QuickDraw routine.

Similarly, an alert box appears in an **alert window**. You don't have the same flexibility in defining and manipulating an alert window, however. The Dialog Manager chooses the window definition ID, so that all alert windows will have the standard appearance and behavior. The size and location of the box are supplied as part of the definition of the alert and are not easily changed. You don't specify the alert window's plane; it always comes up in front of all other windows. Since an alert box requires the user to respond before doing anything else, and the response makes the box go away, the application doesn't do any manipulation of the alert window.

Figure 4 illustrates a document window, dialog window, and alert window, all overlapping on the desktop.

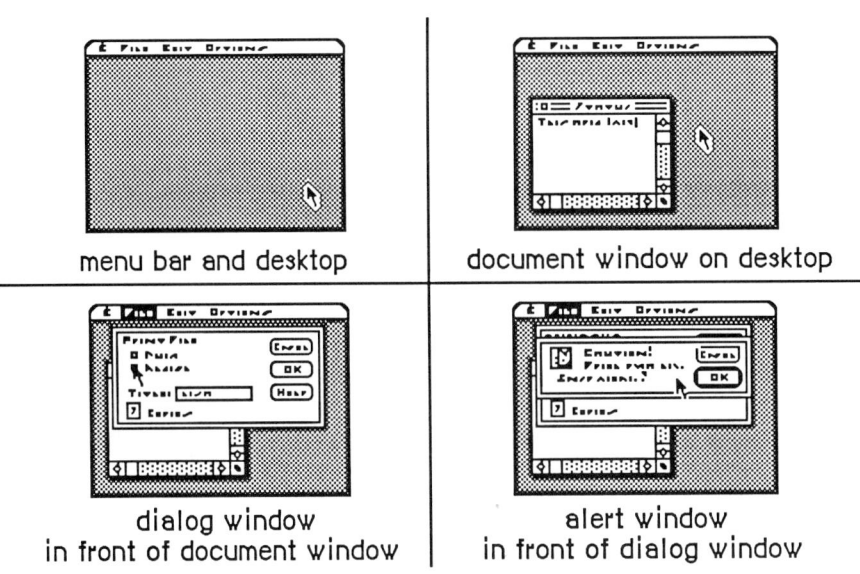

Figure 4. Dialog and Alert Windows

DIALOGS, ALERTS, AND RESOURCES

To create a dialog, the Dialog Manager needs the same information about the dialog window as the Window Manager needs when it creates a new window: The window definition ID along with other information specific to this window. The Dialog Manager also needs to know what items the dialog box contains. You can store the needed information as a resource in a resource file and pass the resource ID to a function that will create the dialog. This type of resource, which is called a **dialog template**, is analogous to a window template, and the function, GetNewDialog, is similar to the Window Manager function GetNewWindow. The Dialog Manager calls the Resource Manager to read the dialog template from the resource file. It then

The Dialog Manager

incorporates the information in the template into a dialog data structure in memory, called a **dialog record**.

Similarly, the data that the Dialog Manager needs to create an alert is stored in an **alert template** in a resource file. The various routines for invoking alerts require the resource ID of the alert template as a parameter.

The information about all the **items** (text, controls, or graphics) in a dialog or alert box is stored in an **item list** in a resource file. The resource ID of the item list is included in the dialog or alert template. The item list in turn contains the resource IDs of any icons or QuickDraw pictures in the dialog or alert box, and possibly the resource IDs of control templates for controls in the box. After calling the Resource Manager to read a dialog or alert template into memory, the Dialog Manager calls it again to read in the item list. It then makes a copy of the item list and uses that copy; for this reason, item lists should always be purgeable resources. Finally, the Dialog Manager calls the Resource Manager to read in any individual items as necessary.

If desired, the application can gain some additional flexibility by calling the Resource Manager directly to read templates, item lists, or items from a resource file. For example, you can read in a dialog or alert template directly and modify some of the information in it before calling the routine to create the dialog or alert. Or, as an alternative to using a dialog template, you can read in a dialog's item list directly and then pass a handle to it along with other information to a function that will create the dialog (NewDialog, analogous to the Window Manager function NewWindow).

> **Note:** The use of dialog templates is recommended wherever possible; like window templates, they isolate descriptive information from your application code for ease of modification or translation to other languages.

ITEM LISTS IN MEMORY

This section discusses the contents of an item list once it's been read into memory from a resource file and the Dialog Manager has set it up as necessary to be able to work with it.

An item list in memory contains the following information for each item:

- The type of item. This includes not only whether the item is a control, text, or whatever, but also whether the Dialog Manager should return to the application when the item is clicked.
- A handle to the item or, for special application-defined items, a pointer to a procedure that draws the item.
- A **display rectangle**, which determines the location of the item within the dialog or alert box.

These are discussed below along with **item numbers**, which identify particular items in the item list.

There's a Dialog Manager procedure that, given a pointer to a dialog record and an item number, sets or returns that item's type, handle (or procedure pointer), and display rectangle.

Inside Macintosh

Item Types

The item type is specified by a predefined constant or combination of constants, as listed below. Figure 5 illustrates some of these item types.

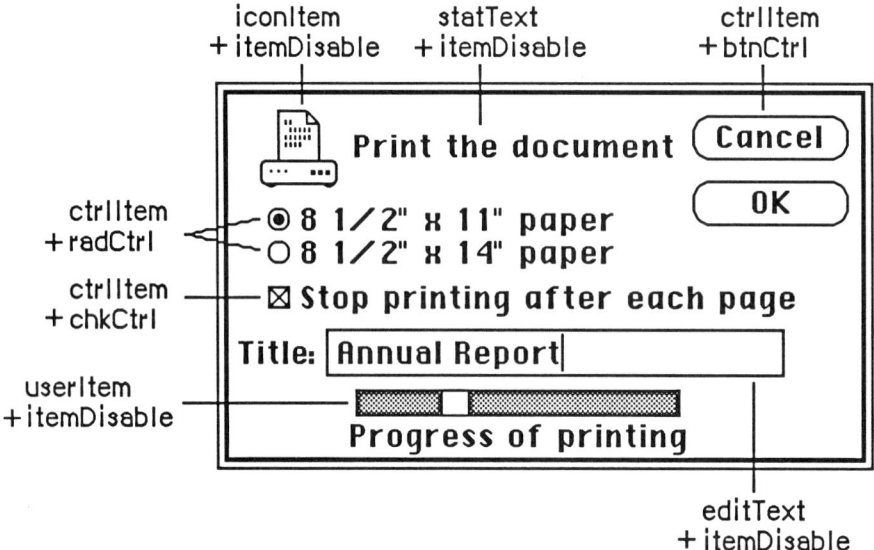

Figure 5. Item Types

Item type	Meaning
ctrlItem+btnCtrl	A standard button control.
ctrlItem+chkCtrl	A standard check box control.
ctrlItem+radCtrl	A standard radio button control.
ctrlItem+resCtrl	A control defined in a control template in a resource file.
statText	Static text; text that cannot be edited.
editText	(Dialogs only) Text that can be edited; the Dialog Manager accepts text typed by the user and allows editing.
iconItem	An icon.
picItem	A QuickDraw picture.
userItem	(Dialogs only) An application-defined item, such as a picture whose appearance changes.
itemDisable+<any of the above>	The item is **disabled** (the Dialog Manager doesn't report events involving this item).

The text of an editText item may initially be either default text or empty. Text entry and editing is handled in the conventional way, as in TextEdit—in fact, the Dialog Manager calls TextEdit to handle it:

- Clicking in the item displays a blinking vertical bar, indicating an insertion point where text may be entered.

The Dialog Manager

- Dragging over text in the item selects that text, and double-clicking selects a word; the selection is highlighted and then replaced by what the user types.
- Clicking or dragging while holding down the Shift key extends or shortens the current selection.
- The Backspace key deletes the current selection or the character preceding the insertion point.

The Tab key advances to the next editText item in the item list, wrapping around to the first if there aren't any more. In an alert box or a modal dialog box (regardless of whether it contains an editText item), the Return key or Enter key has the same effect as clicking the default button; for alerts, the default button is identified in the alert template, whereas for modal dialogs it's always the first item in the item list.

If itemDisable is specified for an item, the Dialog Manager doesn't let the application know about events involving that item. For example, you may not have to be informed every time the user types a character or clicks in an editText item, but may only need to look at the text when the OK button is clicked. In this case, the editText item would be disabled. Standard buttons and check boxes should always be enabled, so your application will know when they've been clicked.

Warning: Don't confuse disabling a control with making one "inactive" with the Control Manager procedure HiliteControl: When you want a control not to respond at all to being clicked, you make it inactive. An inactive control is highlighted to show that it's inactive, while disabling a control doesn't affect its appearance.

Item Handle or Procedure Pointer

The item list contains the following information for the various types of items:

Item type	Contents
any ctrlItem	A control handle
statText	A handle to the text
editText	A handle to the current text
iconItem	A handle to the icon
picItem	A picture handle
userItem	A procedure pointer

The procedure for a userItem draws the item; for example, if the item is a clock, it will draw the clock with the current time displayed. When this procedure is called, the current port will have been set by the Dialog Manager to the dialog window's grafPort. The procedure must have two parameters, a window pointer and an item number. For example, this is how it would be declared if it were named MyItem:

```
PROCEDURE MyItem (theWindow: WindowPtr; itemNo: INTEGER);
```

TheWindow is a pointer to the dialog window; in case the procedure draws in more than one dialog window, this parameter tells it which one to draw in. ItemNo is the item number; in case the procedure draws more than one item, this parameter tells it which one to draw.

Item Lists in Memory I-405

Display Rectangle

Each item in the item list is displayed within its display rectangle:

- For controls, the display rectangle becomes the control's enclosing rectangle.
- For an editText item, it becomes TextEdit's destination rectangle and view rectangle. Word wraparound occurs, and the text is clipped if there's more than will fit in the rectangle. In addition, the Dialog Manager uses the QuickDraw procedure FrameRect to draw a rectangle three pixels outside the display rectangle.
- StatText items are displayed in exactly the same way as editText items, except that a rectangle isn't drawn outside the display rectangle.
- Icons and QuickDraw pictures are scaled to fit the display rectangle. For pictures, the Window Manager calls the QuickDraw procedure DrawPicture and passes it the display rectangle.
- If the procedure for a userItem draws outside the item's display rectangle, the drawing is clipped to the display rectangle.

Note: Clicking anywhere within the display rectangle is considered a click in that item. If display rectangles overlap, a click in the overlapping area is considered a click in whichever item comes first in the item list.

By giving an item a display rectangle that's off the screen, you can make the item invisible. This might be useful, for example, if your application needs to display a number of dialog boxes that are similar except that one item is missing or different in some of them. You can use a single dialog box in which the item or items that aren't currently relevant are invisible. To remove an item or make one reappear, you just change its display rectangle (and call the Window Manager procedure InvalRect to accumulate the changed area into the dialog window's update region). The QuickDraw procedure OffsetRect is convenient for moving an item off the screen and then on again later. Note the following, however:

- You shouldn't make an editText item invisible, because it may cause strange things to happen. If one of several editText items is invisible, for example, pressing the Tab key may make the insertion point disappear. However, if you do make this type of item invisible, remember that the changed area includes the rectangle that's three pixels outside the item's display rectangle.
- The rectangle for a statText item must always be at least as wide as the first character of the text; a good rule of thumb is to make it at least 20 pixels wide.
- To change text in a statText item, it's easier to use the Dialog Manager procedure ParamText (as described later in the "Dialog Manager Routines" section).

Item Numbers

Each item in an item list is identified by an item number, which is simply the index of the item in the list (starting from 1). By convention, the first item in an alert's item list should be the OK button (or, if none, then one of the buttons that will perform the command) and the second item should be the Cancel button. The Dialog Manager provides predefined constants equal to the item numbers for OK and Cancel:

The Dialog Manager

```
CONST ok     = 1;
      cancel = 2;
```

In a modal dialog's item list, the first item is assumed to be the dialog's default button; if the user presses the Return key or Enter key, the Dialog Manager normally returns item number 1, just as when that item is actually clicked. To conform to the Macintosh User Interface Guidelines, the application should boldly outline the dialog's default button if it isn't the OK button. The best way to do this is with a userItem. To allow for changes in the default button's size or location, the userItem should identify which button to outline by its item number and then use that number to get the button's display rectangle. The following QuickDraw calls will outline the rectangle in the standard way:

```
PenSize(3,3);
InsetRect(displayRect,-4,-4);
FrameRoundRect(displayRect,16,16)
```

Warning: If the first item in a modal dialog's item list isn't an OK button and you don't boldly outline it, you should set up the dialog to ignore Return and Enter. To learn how to do this, see ModalDialog under "Handling Dialog Events" in the "Dialog Manager Routines" section.

DIALOG RECORDS

To create a dialog, you pass information to the Dialog Manager in a dialog template and in individual parameters, or only in parameters; in either case, the Dialog Manager incorporates the information into a dialog record. The dialog record contains the window record for the dialog window, a handle to the dialog's item list, and some additional fields. The Dialog Manager creates the dialog window by calling the Window Manager function NewWindow and then setting the window class in the window record to indicate that it's a dialog window. The routine that creates the dialog returns a pointer to the dialog record, which you use thereafter to refer to the dialog in Dialog Manager routines or even in Window Manager or QuickDraw routines (see "Dialog Pointers" below). The Dialog Manager provides routines for handling events in the dialog window and disposing of the dialog when you're done.

The data type for a dialog record is called DialogRecord. You can do all the necessary operations on a dialog without accessing the fields of the dialog record directly; for advanced programmers, however, the exact structure of a dialog record is given under "The DialogRecord Data Type" below.

Dialog Pointers

There are two types of dialog pointer, DialogPtr and DialogPeek, analogous to the window pointer types WindowPtr and WindowPeek. Most programmers will only need to use DialogPtr.

The Dialog Manager defines the following type of dialog pointer:

```
TYPE DialogPtr = WindowPtr;
```

Inside Macintosh

It can do this because the first field of a dialog record contains the window record for the dialog window. This type of pointer can be used to access fields of the window record or can be passed to Window Manager routines that expect window pointers as parameters. Since the WindowPtr data type is itself defined as GrafPtr, this type of dialog pointer can also be used to access fields of the dialog window's grafPort or passed to QuickDraw routines that expect pointers to grafPorts as parameters.

For programmers who want to access dialog record fields beyond the window record, the Dialog Manager also defines the following type of dialog pointer:

```
TYPE DialogPeek = ^DialogRecord;
```

Assembly-language note: From assembly language, of course, there's no type checking on pointers, and the two types of pointer are equal.

The DialogRecord Data Type

For those who want to know more about the data structure of a dialog record, the exact structure is given here.

```
TYPE DialogRecord =
        RECORD
            window:     WindowRecord;   {dialog window}
            items:      Handle;         {item list}
            textH:      TEHandle;       {current editText item}
            editField:  INTEGER;        {editText item number minus 1}
            editOpen:   INTEGER;        {used internally}
            aDefItem:   INTEGER         {default button item number}
        END;
```

The window field contains the window record for the dialog window. The items field contains a handle to the item list used for the dialog. (Remember that after reading an item list from a resource file, the Dialog Manager makes a copy of it and uses that copy.)

> **Note:** To get or change information about an item in a dialog, you pass the dialog pointer and the item number to a Dialog Manager procedure. You'll never access information directly through the handle to the item list.

The Dialog Manager uses the next three fields when there are one or more editText items in the dialog. If there's more than one such item, these fields apply to the one that currently is selected or displays the insertion point. The textH field contains the handle to the edit record used by TextEdit. EditField is 1 less than the item number of the current editText item, or –1 if there's no editText item in the dialog. The editOpen field is used internally by the Dialog Manager.

> **Note:** Actually, a single edit record is shared by all editText items; any changes you make to it will apply to all such items. See chapter 12 for details about what kinds of changes you can make.

The Dialog Manager

The aDefItem field is used for modal dialogs and alerts, which are treated internally as special modal dialogs. It contains the item number of the default button. The default button for a modal dialog is the first item in the item list, so this field contains 1 for modal dialogs. The default button for an alert is specified in the alert template; see the following section for more information.

ALERTS

When you call a Dialog Manager routine to invoke an alert, you pass it the resource ID of the alert template, which contains the following:

- A rectangle, given in global coordinates, which determines the alert window's size and location. It becomes the portRect of the window's grafPort. To allow for the menu bar and the border around the portRect, the top coordinate of the rectangle should be at least 25 points below the top of the screen.
- The resource ID of the item list for the alert.
- Information about exactly what should happen at each stage of the alert.

Every alert has four **stages**, corresponding to consecutive occurrences of the alert: The first three stages correspond to the first three occurrences, while the fourth stage includes the fourth occurrence and any beyond the fourth. (The Dialog Manager compares the current alert's resource ID to the last alert's resource ID to determine whether it's the same alert.) The actions for each stage are specified by the following three pieces of information:

- which is the default button—the OK button (or, if none, a button that will perform the command) or the Cancel button
- whether the alert box is to be drawn
- which of four sounds should be emitted at this stage of the alert

The alert sounds are determined by a **sound procedure** that emits one of up to four tones or sequences of tones. The sound procedure has one parameter, an integer from 0 to 3; it can emit any sound for each of these numbers, which identify the sounds in the alert template. For example, you might declare a sound procedure named MySound as follows:

```
PROCEDURE MySound (soundNo: INTEGER);
```

If you don't write your own sound procedure, the Dialog Manager uses the standard one: Sound number 0 represents no sound and sound numbers 1 through 3 represent the corresponding number of short beeps, each of the same pitch and duration. The volume of each beep depends on the current speaker volume setting, which the user can adjust with the Control Panel desk accessory. If the user has set the speaker volume to 0, the menu bar will blink in place of each beep.

For example, if the second stage of an alert is to cause a beep and no alert box, you can just specify the following for that stage in the alert template: Don't draw the alert box, and use sound number 1. If instead you want, say, two successive beeps of different pitch, you need to write a procedure that will emit that sound for a particular sound number, and specify that number in the alert template. The Macintosh Operating System includes routines for emitting sound; see chapter 8 of Volume II, and also the simple SysBeep procedure in chapter 13 of Volume II. (The standard sound procedure calls SysBeep.)

Inside Macintosh

> **Note:** When the Dialog Manager detects a click outside an alert box or a modal dialog box, it emits sound number 1; thus, for consistency with the Macintosh User Interface Guidelines, sound number 1 should always be a single beep.

Internally, alerts are treated as special modal dialogs. The alert routine creates the alert window by calling NewDialog. The Dialog Manager works from the dialog record created by NewDialog, just as when it operates on a dialog window, but it disposes of the window before returning to the application. Normally your application won't access the dialog record for an alert; however, there is a way that this can happen: For any alert, you can specify a procedure that will be executed repeatedly during the alert, and this procedure may access the dialog record. For details, see the alert routines under "Invoking Alerts" in the "Dialog Manager Routines" section.

USING THE DIALOG MANAGER

Before using the Dialog Manager, you must initialize QuickDraw, the Font Manager, the Window Manager, the Menu Manager, and TextEdit, in that order. The first Dialog Manager routine to call is InitDialogs, which initializes the Dialog Manager. If you want the font in your dialog and alert windows to be other than the system font, call SetDAFont to change the font.

Where appropriate in your program, call NewDialog or GetNewDialog to create any dialogs you need. Usually you'll call GetNewDialog, which takes descriptive information about the dialog from a dialog template in a resource file. You can instead pass the information in individual parameters to NewDialog. In either case, you can supply a pointer to the storage for the dialog record or let it be allocated by the Dialog Manager. When you no longer need a dialog, you'll usually call CloseDialog if you supplied the storage, or DisposDialog if not.

In most cases, you probably won't have to make any changes to the dialogs from the way they're defined in the resource file. However, if you should want to modify an item in a dialog, you can call GetDItem to get the information about the item and SetDItem to change it. In particular, SetDItem is the routine to use for installing a userItem. In some cases it may be appropriate to call some other Toolbox routine to change the item; for example, to change or move a control in a dialog, you would get its handle from GetDItem and then call the appropriate Control Manager routine. There are also two procedures specifically for accessing or setting the content of a text item in a dialog box: GetIText and SetIText.

To handle events in a modal dialog, just call the ModalDialog procedure after putting up the dialog box. If your application includes any modeless dialog boxes, you'll pass events to IsDialogEvent to learn whether they need to be handled as part of a dialog, and then usually call DialogSelect if so. Before calling DialogSelect, however, you should check whether the user has given the keyboard equivalent of a command, and you may want to check for other special cases, depending on your application. You can support the use of the standard editing commands in a modeless dialog's editText items with DlgCut, DlgCopy, DlgPaste, and DlgDelete.

A dialog box that contains editText items normally comes up with the insertion point in the first such item in its item list. You may instead want to bring up a dialog box with text selected in an editText item, or to cause an insertion point or text selection to reappear after the user has made an error in entering text. For example, the user who accidentally types nonnumeric input when a number is required can be given the opportunity to type the entry again. The SelIText procedure makes this possible.

For alerts, if you want other sounds besides the standard ones (up to three short beeps), write your own sound procedure and call ErrorSound to make it the current sound procedure. To

The Dialog Manager

invoke a particular alert, call one of the alert routines: StopAlert, NoteAlert, or CautionAlert for one of the standard kinds of alert, or Alert for an alert defined to have something other than a standard icon (or nothing at all) in its top left corner.

If you're going to invoke a dialog or alert when the resource file might not be accessible, first call CouldDialog or CouldAlert, which will make the dialog or alert template and related resources unpurgeable. You can later make them purgeable again by calling FreeDialog or FreeAlert.

Finally, you can substitute text in statText items with text that you specify in the ParamText procedure. This means, for example, that a document name supplied by the user can appear in an error message.

DIALOG MANAGER ROUTINES

Initialization

```
PROCEDURE InitDialogs (resumeProc: ProcPtr);
```

Call InitDialogs once before all other Dialog Manager routines, to initialize the Dialog Manager. InitDialogs does the following initialization:

- It saves the pointer passed in resumeProc, if any, for access by the System Error Handler in case a fatal system error occurs. ResumeProc can be a pointer to a resume procedure, as described in chapter 12 of Volume II, or NIL if no such procedure is desired.

Assembly-language note: InitDialogs stores the address of the resume procedure in a global variable named ResumeProc.

- It installs the standard sound procedure.
- It passes empty strings to ParamText.

```
PROCEDURE ErrorSound (soundProc: ProcPtr);
```

ErrorSound sets the sound procedure for alerts to the procedure pointed to by soundProc; if you don't call ErrorSound, the Dialog Manager uses the standard sound procedure. (For details, see the "Alerts" section.) If you pass NIL for soundProc, there will be no sound (or menu bar blinking) at all.

Assembly-language note: The address of the sound procedure being used is stored in the global variable DABeeper.

Inside Macintosh

```
PROCEDURE SetDAFont (fontNum: INTEGER);    [Not in ROM]
```

For subsequently created dialogs and alerts, SetDAFont causes the font of the dialog or alert window's grafPort to be set to the font having the specified font number. If you don't call this procedure, the system font is used. SetDAFont affects statText and editText items but not titles of controls, which are always in the system font.

Assembly-language note: Assembly-language programmers can simply set the global variable DlgFont to the desired font number.

Creating and Disposing of Dialogs

```
FUNCTION NewDialog (dStorage: Ptr; boundsRect: Rect; title:
        Str255; visible: BOOLEAN; procID: INTEGER; behind:
        WindowPtr; goAwayFlag: BOOLEAN; refCon: LONGINT; items:
        Handle) : DialogPtr;
```

NewDialog creates a dialog as specified by its parameters and returns a pointer to the new dialog. The first eight parameters (dStorage through refCon) are passed to the Window Manager function NewWindow, which creates the dialog window; the meanings of these parameters are summarized below. The items parameter is a handle to the dialog's item list. You can get the items handle by calling the Resource Manager to read the item list from the resource file into memory.

> **Note:** Advanced programmers can create their own item lists in memory rather than have them read from a resource file. The exact format is given later under "Formats of Resources for Dialogs and Alerts".

DStorage is analogous to the wStorage parameter of NewWindow; it's a pointer to the storage to use for the dialog record. If you pass NIL for dStorage, the dialog record will be allocated in the heap (which, in the case of modeless dialogs, may cause the heap to become fragmented).

BoundsRect, a rectangle given in global coordinates, determines the dialog window's size and location. It becomes the portRect of the window's grafPort. Remember that the top coordinate of this rectangle should be at least 25 points below the top of the screen for a modal dialog, to allow for the menu bar and the border around the portRect, and at least 40 points below the top of the screen for a modeless dialog, to allow for the menu bar and the window's title bar.

Title is the title of a modeless dialog box; pass the empty string for modal dialogs.

If the visible parameter is TRUE, the dialog window is drawn on the screen. If it's FALSE, the window is initially invisible and may later be shown with a call to the Window Manager procedure ShowWindow.

> **Note:** NewDialog generates an update event for the entire window contents, so the items aren't drawn immediately, with the exception of controls. The Dialog Manager calls the Control Manager to draw controls, and the Control Manager draws them immediately rather than via the standard update mechanism. Because of this, the Dialog Manager calls the Window Manager procedure ValidRect for the enclosing rectangle of each control, so the controls won't be drawn twice. If you find that the other items aren't being drawn

soon enough after the controls, try making the window invisible initially and then calling ShowWindow to show it.

ProcID is the window definition ID, which leads to the window definition function for this type of window. The window definition IDs for the standard types of dialog window are dBoxProc for the modal type and documentProc for the modeless type.

The behind parameter specifies the window behind which the dialog window is to be placed on the desktop. Pass POINTER(−1) to bring up the dialog window in front of all other windows.

GoAwayFlag applies to modeless dialog boxes; if it's TRUE, the dialog window has a close box in its title bar when the window is active.

RefCon is the dialog window's reference value, which the application may store into and access for any purpose.

NewDialog sets the font of the dialog window's grafPort to the system font or, if you previously called SetDAFont, to the specified font. It also sets the window class in the window record to dialogKind.

```
FUNCTION GetNewDialog (dialogID: INTEGER; dStorage: Ptr; behind:
        WindowPtr) : DialogPtr;
```

Like NewDialog (above), GetNewDialog creates a dialog as specified by its parameters and returns a pointer to the new dialog. Instead of having the parameters boundsRect, title, visible, procID, goAwayFlag, and refCon, GetNewDialog has a single dialogID parameter, where dialogID is the resource ID of a dialog template that supplies the same information as those parameters. The dialog template also contains the resource ID of the dialog's item list. After calling the Resource Manager to read the item list into memory (if it's not already in memory), GetNewDialog makes a copy of the item list and uses that copy; thus you may have multiple independent dialogs whose items have the same types, locations, and initial contents. The dStorage and behind parameters of GetNewDialog have the same meaning as in NewDialog.

> **Warning:** If either the dialog template resource or the item list resource can't be read, the function result is undefined.

> **Note:** GetNewDialog doesn't release the memory occupied by the resources.

```
PROCEDURE CloseDialog (theDialog: DialogPtr);
```

CloseDialog removes theDialog's window from the screen and deletes it from the window list, just as when the Window Manager procedure CloseWindow is called. It releases the memory occupied by the following:

- The data structures associated with the dialog window (such as the window's structure, content, and update regions).
- All the items in the dialog (except for pictures and icons, which might be shared resources), and any data structures associated with them. For example, it would dispose of the region occupied by the thumb of a scroll bar, or a similar region for some other control in the dialog.

Inside Macintosh

CloseDialog does *not* dispose of the dialog record or the item list. Figure 6 illustrates the effect of CloseDialog (and DisposDialog, described below).

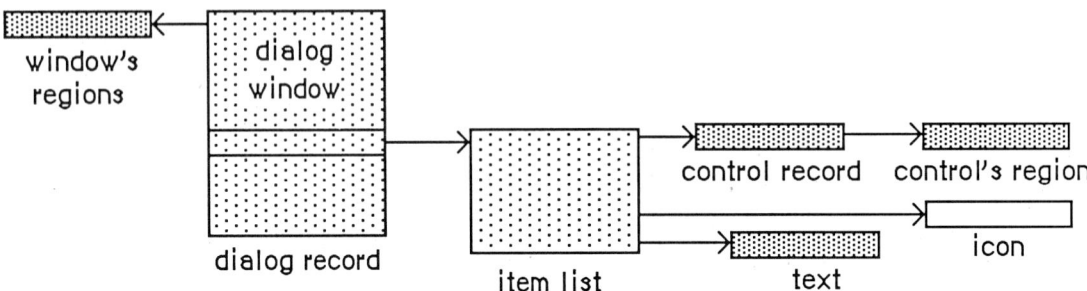

If you created the dialog with NewDialog:

If you created the dialog with GetNewDialog:

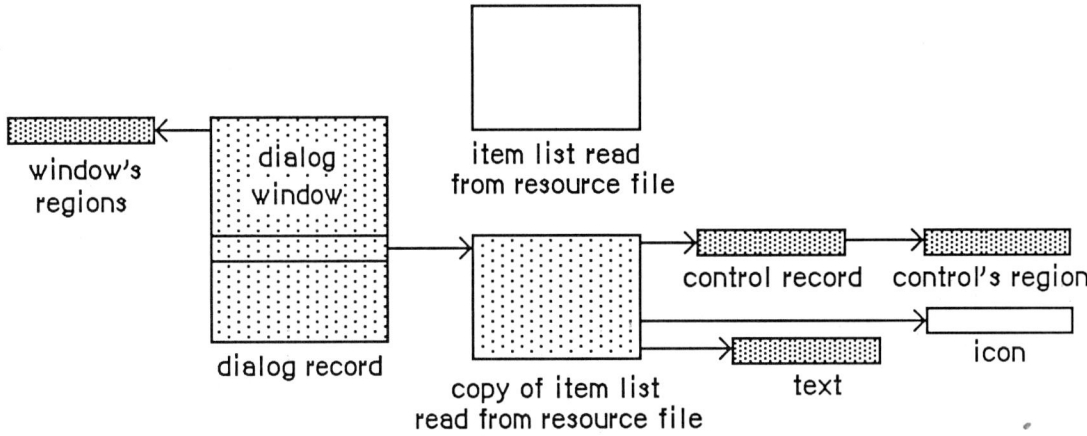

Figure 6. CloseDialog and DisposDialog

Call CloseDialog when you're done with a dialog if you supplied NewDialog or GetNewDialog with a pointer to the dialog storage (in the dStorage parameter) when you created the dialog.

Note: Even if you didn't supply a pointer to the dialog storage, you may want to call CloseDialog if you created the dialog with NewDialog. You would call CloseDialog if you wanted to keep the item list around (since, unlike GetNewDialog, NewDialog does not use a copy of the item list).

```
PROCEDURE DisposDialog (theDialog: DialogPtr);
```

DisposDialog calls CloseDialog (above) and then releases the memory occupied by the dialog's item list and dialog record. Call DisposDialog when you're done with a dialog if you let the dialog record be allocated in the heap when you created the dialog (by passing NIL as the dStorage parameter to NewDialog or GetNewDialog).

```
PROCEDURE CouldDialog (dialogID: INTEGER);
```

CouldDialog makes the dialog template having the given resource ID unpurgeable (reading it into memory if it's not already there). It does the same for the dialog window's definition function, the dialog's item list resource, and any items defined as resources. This is useful if the dialog box may come up when the resource file isn't accessible, such as during a disk copy.

> **Warning:** CouldDialog assumes your dialogs use the system font; if you've changed the font with SetDAFont, calling CouldDialog doesn't make the font unpurgeable.

```
PROCEDURE FreeDialog (dialogID: INTEGER);
```

Given the resource ID of a dialog template previously specified in a call to CouldDialog, FreeDialog undoes the effect of CouldDialog (by making the resources purgeable). It should be called when there's no longer a need to keep the resources in memory.

Handling Dialog Events

```
PROCEDURE ModalDialog (filterProc: ProcPtr; VAR itemHit:
        INTEGER);
```

Call ModalDialog after creating a modal dialog and bringing up its window in the frontmost plane. ModalDialog repeatedly gets and handles events in the dialog's window; after handling an event involving an enabled dialog item, it returns with the item number in itemHit. Normally you'll then do whatever is appropriate as a response to an event in that item.

ModalDialog gets each event by calling the Toolbox Event Manager function GetNextEvent. If the event is a mouse-down event outside the content region of the dialog window, ModalDialog emits sound number 1 (which should be a single beep) and gets the next event; otherwise, it filters and handles the event as described below.

> **Note:** Once before getting each event, ModalDialog calls SystemTask, a Desk Manager procedure that must be called regularly so that desk accessories will work properly.

The filterProc parameter determines how events are filtered. If it's NIL, the standard filterProc function is executed; this causes ModalDialog to return 1 in itemHit if the Return key or Enter key is pressed. If filterProc isn't NIL, ModalDialog filters events by executing the function it points to. Your filterProc function should have three parameters and return a Boolean value. For example, this is how it would be declared if it were named MyFilter:

```
FUNCTION MyFilter (theDialog: DialogPtr; VAR theEvent: EventRecord;
        VAR itemHit: INTEGER) : BOOLEAN;
```

A function result of FALSE tells ModalDialog to go ahead and handle the event, which either can be sent through unchanged or can be changed to simulate a different event. A function result of TRUE tells ModalDialog to return immediately rather than handle the event; in this case, the filterProc function sets itemHit to the item number that ModalDialog should return.

> **Note:** If you want it to be consistent with the standard filterProc function, your function should at least check whether the Return key or Enter key was pressed and, if so, return 1 in itemHit and a function result of TRUE.

You can use the filterProc function, for example, to treat a typed character in a special way (such as ignore it, or make it have the same effect as another character or as clicking a button); in this case, the function would test for a key-down event with that character. As another example, suppose the dialog box contains a userItem whose procedure draws a clock with the current time displayed. The filterProc function can call that procedure and return FALSE without altering the current event.

> **Note:** ModalDialog calls GetNextEvent with a mask that excludes disk-inserted events. To receive disk-inserted events, your filterProc function can call GetNextEvent (or EventAvail) with a mask that accepts only that type of event.

ModalDialog handles the events for which the filterProc function returns FALSE as follows:

- In response to an activate or update event for the dialog window, ModalDialog activates or updates the window.
- If the mouse button is pressed in an editText item, ModalDialog responds to the mouse activity as appropriate (displaying an insertion point or selecting text). If a key-down event occurs and there's an editText item, text entry and editing are handled in the standard way for such items (except that if the Command key is down, ModalDialog responds as though it's not). In either case, ModalDialog returns if the editText item is enabled or does nothing if it's disabled. If a key-down event occurs when there's no editText item, ModalDialog does nothing.
- If the mouse button is pressed in a control, ModalDialog calls the Control Manager function TrackControl. If the mouse button is released inside the control and the control is enabled, ModalDialog returns; otherwise, it does nothing.
- If the mouse button is pressed in any other enabled item in the dialog box, ModalDialog returns. If the mouse button is pressed in any other disabled item or in no item, or if any other event occurs, ModalDialog does nothing.

```
FUNCTION IsDialogEvent (theEvent: EventRecord) : BOOLEAN;
```

If your application includes any modeless dialogs, call IsDialogEvent after calling the Toolbox Event Manager function GetNextEvent.

> **Warning:** If your modeless dialog contains any editText items, you must call IsDialogEvent (and then DialogSelect) even if GetNextEvent returns FALSE; otherwise your dialog won't receive null events and the caret won't blink.

Pass the current event in theEvent. IsDialogEvent determines whether theEvent needs to be handled as part of a dialog. If theEvent is an activate or update event for a dialog window, a mouse-down event in the content region of an active dialog window, or any other type of event when a dialog window is active, IsDialogEvent returns TRUE; otherwise, it returns FALSE.

When FALSE is returned, just handle the event yourself like any other event that's not dialog-related. When TRUE is returned, you'll generally end up passing the event to DialogSelect for it to handle (as described below), but first you should do some additional checking:

- DialogSelect doesn't handle keyboard equivalents of commands. Check whether the event is a key-down event with the Command key held down and, if so, carry out the command if it's one that applies when a dialog window is active. (If the command doesn't so apply, do nothing.)

- In special cases, you may want to bypass DialogSelect or do some preprocessing before calling it. If so, check for those events and respond accordingly. You would need to do this, for example, if the dialog is to respond to disk-inserted events.

For cases other than these, pass the event to DialogSelect for it to handle.

```
FUNCTION DialogSelect (theEvent: EventRecord; VAR theDialog:
        DialogPtr; VAR itemHit: INTEGER) : BOOLEAN;
```

You'll normally call DialogSelect when IsDialogEvent returns TRUE, passing in theEvent an event that needs to be handled as part of a modeless dialog. DialogSelect handles the event as described below. If the event involves an enabled dialog item, DialogSelect returns a function result of TRUE with the dialog pointer in theDialog and the item number in itemHit; otherwise, it returns FALSE with theDialog and itemHit undefined. Normally when DialogSelect returns TRUE, you'll do whatever is appropriate as a response to the event, and when it returns FALSE you'll do nothing.

If the event is an activate or update event for a dialog window, DialogSelect activates or updates the window and returns FALSE.

If the event is a mouse-down event in an editText item, DialogSelect responds as appropriate (displaying a caret at the insertion point or selecting text). If it's a key-down or auto-key event and there's an editText item, text entry and editing are handled in the standard way. In either case, DialogSelect returns TRUE if the editText item is enabled or FALSE if it's disabled. If a key-down or auto-key event is passed when there's no editText item, DialogSelect returns FALSE.

> Note: For a keyboard event, DialogSelect doesn't check to see whether the Command key is held down; to handle keyboard equivalents of commands, you have to check for them before calling DialogSelect. Similarly, to treat a typed character in a special way (such as ignore it, or make it have the same effect as another character or as clicking a button), you need to check for a key-down event with that character before calling DialogSelect.

If the event is a mouse-down event in a control, DialogSelect calls the Control Manager function TrackControl. If the mouse button is released inside the control and the control is enabled, DialogSelect returns TRUE; otherwise, it returns FALSE.

If the event is a mouse-down event in any other enabled item, DialogSelect returns TRUE. If it's a mouse down event in any other disabled item or in no item, or if it's any other event, DialogSelect returns FALSE.

Inside Macintosh

> **Note:** If the event isn't one that DialogSelect specifically checks for (if it's a null event, for example), and there's an editText item in the dialog, DialogSelect calls the TextEdit procedure TEIdle to make the caret blink.

```
PROCEDURE DlgCut (theDialog: DialogPtr);   [Not in ROM]
```

DlgCut checks whether theDialog has any editText items and, if so, applies the TextEdit procedure TECut to the currently selected editText item. (If the dialog record's editField is 0 or greater, DlgCut passes the contents of the textH field to TECut.) You can call DlgCut to handle the editing command Cut when a modeless dialog window is active.

> **Assembly-language note:** Assembly-language programmers can just read the dialog record's fields and call TextEdit directly.

```
PROCEDURE DlgCopy (theDialog: DialogPtr);   [Not in ROM]
```

DlgCopy is the same as DlgCut (above) except that it calls TECopy, for handling the Copy command.

```
PROCEDURE DlgPaste (theDialog: DialogPtr);   [Not in ROM]
```

DlgPaste is the same as DlgCut (above) except that it calls TEPaste, for handling the Paste command.

```
PROCEDURE DlgDelete (theDialog: DialogPtr);   [Not in ROM]
```

DlgDelete is the same as DlgCut (above) except that it calls TEDelete, for handling the Clear command.

```
PROCEDURE DrawDialog (theDialog: DialogPtr);
```

DrawDialog draws the contents of the given dialog box. Since DialogSelect and ModalDialog handle dialog window updating, this procedure is useful only in unusual situations. You would call it, for example, to display a dialog box that doesn't require any response but merely tells the user what's going on during a time-consuming process.

Invoking Alerts

```
FUNCTION Alert (alertID: INTEGER; filterProc: ProcPtr) : INTEGER;
```

This function invokes the alert defined by the alert template that has the given resource ID. It calls the current sound procedure, if any, passing it the sound number specified in the alert template for this stage of the alert. If no alert box is to be drawn at this stage, Alert returns a

The Dialog Manager

function result of –1; otherwise, it creates and displays the alert window for this alert and draws the alert box.

Warning: If the alert template resource can't be read, the function result is undefined.

Note: Alert creates the alert window by calling NewDialog, and does the rest of its processing by calling ModalDialog.

Alert repeatedly gets and handles events in the alert window until an enabled item is clicked, at which time it returns the item number. Normally you'll then do whatever is appropriate in response to a click of that item.

Alert gets each event by calling the Toolbox Event Manager function GetNextEvent. If the event is a mouse-down event outside the content region of the alert window, Alert emits sound number 1 (which should be a single beep) and gets the next event; otherwise, it filters and handles the event as described below.

The filterProc parameter has the same meaning as in ModalDialog (see above). If it's NIL, the standard filterProc function is executed, which makes the Return key or the Enter key have the same effect as clicking the default button. If you specify your own filterProc function and want to retain this feature, you must include it in your function. You can find out what the current default button is by looking at the aDefItem field of the dialog record for the alert (via the dialog pointer passed to the function).

Alert handles the events for which the filterProc function returns FALSE as follows:

- If the mouse button is pressed in a control, Alert calls the Control Manager procedure TrackControl. If the mouse button is released inside the control and the control is enabled, Alert returns; otherwise, it does nothing.
- If the mouse button is pressed in any other enabled item, Alert simply returns. If it's pressed in any other disabled item or in no item, or if any other event occurs, Alert does nothing.

Before returning to the application with the item number, Alert removes the alert box from the screen. (It disposes of the alert window and its associated data structures, the item list, and the items.)

Note: When an alert is removed, if it was overlapping the default button of a previous alert, that button's bold outline won't be redrawn.

Note: The Alert function's removal of the alert box would not be the desired result if the user clicked a check box or radio button; however, normally alerts contain only static text, icons, pictures, and buttons that are supposed to make the alert box go away. If your alert contains other items besides these, consider whether it might be more appropriate as a dialog.

```
FUNCTION StopAlert (alertID: INTEGER; filterProc: ProcPtr) :
          INTEGER;
```

StopAlert is the same as the Alert function (above) except that before drawing the items of the alert in the alert box, it draws the Stop icon in the top left corner of the box (within the rectangle (10,20)(42,52)). The Stop icon has the following resource ID:

Inside Macintosh

```
CONST stopIcon = 0;
```

If the application's resource file doesn't include an icon with that ID number, the Dialog Manager uses the standard Stop icon in the system resource file (see Figure 7).

Figure 7. Standard Alert Icons

```
FUNCTION NoteAlert (alertID: INTEGER; filterProc: ProcPtr) :
        INTEGER;
```

NoteAlert is like StopAlert except that it draws the Note icon, which has the following resource ID:

```
CONST noteIcon = 1;
```

```
FUNCTION CautionAlert (alertID: INTEGER; filterProc: ProcPtr) :
        INTEGER;
```

CautionAlert is like StopAlert except that it draws the Caution icon, which has the following resource ID:

```
CONST cautionIcon = 2;
```

```
PROCEDURE CouldAlert (alertID: INTEGER);
```

CouldAlert makes the alert template having the given resource ID unpurgeable (reading it into memory if it's not already there). It does the same for the alert window's definition function, the alert's item list resource, and any items defined as resources. This is useful if the alert may occur when the resource file isn't accessible, such as during a disk copy.

> **Warning:** Like CouldDialog, CouldAlert assumes your alerts use the system font; if you've changed the font with SetDAFont, calling CouldAlert doesn't make the font unpurgeable.

```
PROCEDURE FreeAlert (alertID: INTEGER);
```

Given the resource ID of an alert template previously specified in a call to CouldAlert, FreeAlert undoes the effect of CouldAlert (by making the resources purgeable). It should be called when there's no longer a need to keep the resources in memory.

The Dialog Manager

Manipulating Items in Dialogs and Alerts

```
PROCEDURE ParamText (param0,param1,param2,param3: Str255);
```

ParamText provides a means of substituting text in statText items: param0 through param3 will replace the special strings '^0' through '^3' in all statText items in all subsequent dialog or alert boxes. Pass empty strings for parameters not used.

Assembly-language note: Assembly-language programmers may pass NIL for parameters not used or for strings that are not to be changed.

For example, if the text is defined as 'Cannot open document ^0' and docName is a string variable containing a document name that the user typed, you can call ParamText(docName,' ',' ',' ').

Note: All strings that may need to be translated to other languages should be stored in resource files.

Assembly-language note: The Dialog Manager stores handles to the four ParamText parameters in a global array named DAStrings.

```
PROCEDURE GetDItem (theDialog: DialogPtr; itemNo: INTEGER; VAR
        itemType: INTEGER; VAR item: Handle; VAR box: Rect);
```

GetDItem returns in its VAR parameters the following information about the item numbered itemNo in the given dialog's item list: In the itemType parameter, the item type; in the item parameter, a handle to the item (or, for item type userItem, the procedure pointer); and in the box parameter, the display rectangle for the item.

Suppose, for example, that you want to change the title of a control in a dialog box. You can get the item handle with GetDItem, coerce it to type ControlHandle, and call the Control Manager procedure SetCTitle to change the title. Similarly, to move the control or change its size, you would call MoveControl or SizeControl.

Note: To access the text of a statText or editText item, you can pass the handle returned by GetDItem to GetIText or SetIText (see below).

```
PROCEDURE SetDItem (theDialog: DialogPtr; itemNo: INTEGER;
        itemType: INTEGER; item: Handle; box: Rect);
```

SetDItem sets the item numbered itemNo in the given dialog's item list, as specified by the parameters (without drawing the item). The itemType parameter is the item type; the item parameter is a handle to the item (or, for item type userItem, the procedure pointer); and the box parameter is the display rectangle for the item.

Consider, for example, how to install an item of type userItem in a dialog: In the item list in the resource file, define an item in which the type is set to userItem and the display rectangle to

(0,0)(0,0). Specify that the dialog window be invisible (in either the dialog template or the NewDialog call). After creating the dialog, coerce the item's procedure pointer to type Handle; then call SetDItem, passing that handle and the display rectangle for the item. Finally, call the Window Manager procedure ShowWindow to display the dialog window.

> **Note:** Do not use SetDItem to change the text of a statText or editText item or to change or move a control. See the description of GetDItem above for more information.

```
PROCEDURE GetIText (item: Handle; VAR text: Str255);
```

Given a handle to a statText or editText item in a dialog box, as returned by GetDItem, GetIText returns the text of the item in the text parameter. (If the user typed more than 255 characters in an editText item, GetIText returns only the first 255.)

```
PROCEDURE SetIText (item: Handle; text: Str255);
```

Given a handle to a statText or editText item in a dialog box, as returned by GetDItem, SetIText sets the text of the item to the specified text and draws the item. For example, suppose the exact content of a dialog's text item cannot be determined until the application is running, but the display rectangle is defined in the resource file: Call GetDItem to get a handle to the item, and call SetIText with the desired text.

```
PROCEDURE SelIText (theDialog: DialogPtr; itemNo: INTEGER;
         strtSel,endSel: INTEGER);
```

Given a pointer to a dialog and the item number of an editText item in the dialog box, SelIText does the following:

- If the item contains text, SelIText sets the selection range to extend from character position strtSel up to but not including character position endSel. The selection range is inverted unless strtSel equals endSel, in which case a blinking vertical bar is displayed to indicate an insertion point at that position.
- If the item doesn't contain text, SelIText simply displays the insertion point.

For example, if the user makes an unacceptable entry in the editText item, the application can put up an alert box reporting the problem and then select the entire text of the item so it can be replaced by a new entry. (Without this procedure, the user would have to select the item before making the new entry.)

> **Note:** You can select the entire text by specifying 0 for strtSel and 32767 for endSel. For details about selection range and character position, see chapter 12.

```
FUNCTION GetAlrtStage : INTEGER;    [Not in ROM]
```

GetAlrtStage returns the stage of the last occurrence of an alert, as a number from 0 to 3.

The Dialog Manager

Assembly-language note: Assembly-language programmers can get this number by accessing the global variable ACount. In addition, the global variable ANumber contains the resource ID of the alert template of the last alert that occurred.

`PROCEDURE ResetAlrtStage;` [Not in ROM]

ResetAlrtStage resets the stage of the last occurrence of an alert so that the next occurrence of that same alert will be treated as its first stage. This is useful, for example, when you've used ParamText to change the text of an alert such that from the user's point of view it's a different alert.

Assembly-language note: Assembly-language programmers can set the global variable ACount to –1 for the same effect.

MODIFYING TEMPLATES IN MEMORY

When you call GetNewDialog or one of the routines that invokes an alert, the Dialog Manager calls the Resource Manager to read the dialog or alert template from the resource file and return a handle to it. If the template is already in memory, the Resource Manager just returns a handle to it. If you want, you can call the Resource Manager yourself to read the template into memory (and make it unpurgeable), and then make changes to it before calling the dialog or alert routine. When called by the Dialog Manager, the Resource Manager will return a handle to the template as you modified it.

To modify a template in memory, you need to know its exact structure and the data type of the handle through which it may be accessed. These are discussed below for dialogs and alerts.

Dialog Templates in Memory

The data structure of a dialog template is as follows:

```
TYPE DialogTemplate =
          RECORD
             boundsRect:   Rect;       {becomes window's portRect}
             procID:       INTEGER;    {window definiton ID}
             visible:      BOOLEAN;    {TRUE if visible}
             filler1:      BOOLEAN;    {not used}
             goAwayFlag:   BOOLEAN;    {TRUE if has go-away region}
             filler2:      BOOLEAN;    {not used}
             refCon:       LONGINT;    {window's reference value}
             itemsID:      INTEGER;    {resource ID of item list}
             title:        Str255      {window's title}
          END;
```

Inside Macintosh

The filler1 and filler2 fields are there because for historical reasons the goAwayFlag and refCon fields have to begin on a word boundary. The itemsID field contains the resource ID of the dialog's item list. The other fields are the same as the parameters of the same name in the NewDialog function; they provide information about the dialog window.

You access the dialog template by converting the handle returned by the Resource Manager to a template handle:

```
TYPE DialogTHndl = ^DialogTPtr;
     DialogTPtr  = ^DialogTemplate;
```

Alert Templates in Memory

The data structure of an alert template is as follows:

```
TYPE AlertTemplate =
            RECORD
              boundsRect: Rect;       {becomes window's portRect}
              itemsID:    INTEGER;    {resource ID of item list}
              stages:     StageList   {alert stage information}
            END;
```

BoundsRect is the rectangle that becomes the portRect of the window's grafPort. The itemsID field contains the resource ID of the item list for the alert.

The information in the stages field determines exactly what should happen at each stage of the alert. It's packed into a word that has the following structure:

```
TYPE StageList =
            PACKED RECORD
              boldItm4: 0..1;      {default button item number minus 1}
              boxDrwn4: BOOLEAN;   {TRUE if alert box to be drawn}
              sound4:   0..3       {sound number}
              boldItm3: 0..1;
              boxDrwn3: BOOLEAN;
              sound3:   0..3
              boldItm2: 0..1;
              boxDrwn2: BOOLEAN;
              sound2:   0..3
              boldItm1: 0..1;
              boxDrwn1: BOOLEAN;
              sound1:   0..3
            END;
```

Notice that the information is stored in reverse order—for the fourth stage first, and for the first stage last.

The boldItm field indicates which button should be the default button (and therefore boldly outlined in the alert box). If the first two items in the alert's item list are the OK button and the Cancel button, respectively, 0 will refer to the OK button and 1 to the Cancel button. The reason for this is that the value of boldItm plus 1 is interpreted as an item number, and normally items 1 and 2 are the OK and Cancel buttons, respectively. Whatever the item having the corresponding item number happens to be, a bold rounded-corner rectangle will be drawn outside its display rectangle.

> **Note:** When deciding where to place items in an alert box, be sure to allow room for any bold outlines that may be drawn.

The boxDrwn field is TRUE if the alert box is to be drawn.

The sound field specifies which sound should be emitted at this stage of the alert, with a number from 0 to 3 that's passed to the current sound procedure. You can call ErrorSound to specify your own sound procedure; if you don't, the standard sound procedure will be used (as described earlier in the "Alerts" section).

You access the alert template by converting the handle returned by the Resource Manager to a template handle:

```
TYPE  AlertTHndl = ^AlertTPtr;
      AlertTPtr  = ^AlertTemplate;
```

> **Assembly-language note:** Rather than offsets into the fields of the StageList data structure, there are masks for accessing the information stored for an alert stage in a stages word; they're listed in the summary at the end of this chapter.

FORMATS OF RESOURCES FOR DIALOGS AND ALERTS

Every dialog template, alert template, and item list must be stored in a resource file, as must any icons or QuickDraw pictures in item lists and any control templates for items of type ctrlItem+resCtrl. The exact formats of a dialog template, alert template, and item list in a resource file are given below. For icons and pictures, the resource type is 'ICON' or 'PICT' and the resource data is simply the icon or the picture. The format of a control template is discussed in chapter 10.

Dialog Templates in a Resource File

The resource type for a dialog template is 'DLOG', and the resource data has the same format as a dialog template in memory.

Inside Macintosh

Number of bytes	Contents
8 bytes	Same as boundsRect parameter to NewDialog
2 bytes	Same as procID parameter to NewDialog
1 byte	Same as visible parameter to NewDialog
1 byte	Ignored
1 byte	Same as goAwayFlag parameter to NewDialog
1 byte	Ignored
4 bytes	Same as refCon parameter to NewDialog
2 bytes	Resource ID of item list
n bytes	Same as title parameter to NewDialog (1-byte length in bytes, followed by the characters of the title)

Alert Templates in a Resource File

The resource type for an alert template is 'ALRT', and the resource data has the same format as an alert template in memory.

Number of bytes	Contents
8 bytes	Rectangle enclosing alert window
2 bytes	Resource ID of item list
2 bytes	Four stages

The resource data ends with a word of information about stages. As shown in the example in Figure 8, there are four bits of stage information for each of the four stages, from the four low-order bits for the first stage to the four high-order bits for the fourth stage. Each set of four bits is as follows:

Number of bits	Contents
1 bit	Item number minus 1 of default button; normally 0 is OK and 1 is Cancel
1 bit	1 if alert box is to be drawn, 0 if not
2 bits	Sound number (0 through 3)

Note: So that the disk won't be accessed just for an alert that beeps, you may want to set the resPreload attribute of the alert's template in the resource file. For more information, see chapter 5.

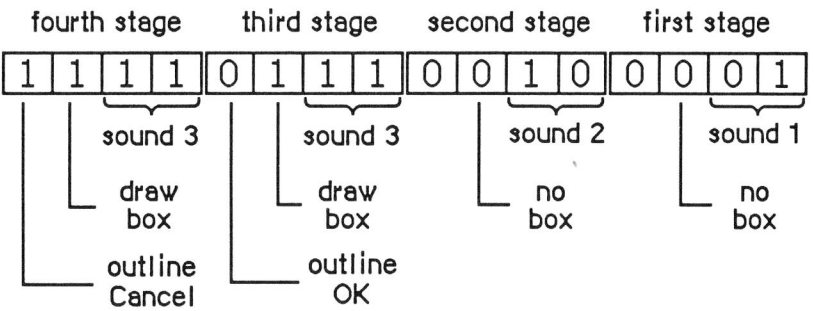

(value: hexadecimal F721)

Figure 8. Sample Stages Word

Item Lists in a Resource File

The resource type for an item list is 'DITL'. The resource data has the following format:

Number of bytes	Contents
2 bytes	Number of items in list minus 1
For each item:	
4 bytes	0 (placeholder for handle or procedure pointer)
8 bytes	Display rectangle (local coordinates)
1 byte	Item type
1 byte	Length of following data in bytes
n bytes (n is even)	If item type is: Content is:

       ctrlItem+resCtrl   Resource ID (length 2)
       any other ctrlItem   Title of the control
       statText, editText   The text
       iconItem, picItem   Resource ID (length 2)
       userItem   Empty (length 0)

As shown here, the first four bytes for each item serve as a placeholder for the item's handle or, for item type userItem, its procedure pointer; the handle or pointer is stored after the item list is read into memory. After the display rectangle and the item type, there's a byte that gives the length of the data that follows: For a text item, the data is the text itself; for an icon, picture, or control of type ctrlItem+resCtrl, it's the two-byte resource ID for the item; and for any other type of control, it's the title of the control. For userItems, no data is specified. When the data is text or a control title, the number of bytes it occupies must be even to ensure word alignment of the next item.

Note: The text in the item list can't be more than 240 characters long.

Inside Macintosh

Assembly-language note: Offsets into the fields of an item list are available as global constants; they're listed in the summary.

SUMMARY OF THE DIALOG MANAGER

Constants

```
CONST  { Item types }

       ctrlItem    = 4;    {add to following four constants}
       btnCtrl     = 0;    {standard button control}
       chkCtrl     = 1;    {standard check box control}
       radCtrl     = 2;    {standard radio button control}
       resCtrl     = 3;    {control defined in control template}
       statText    = 8;    {static text}
       editText    = 16;   {editable text (dialog only)}
       iconItem    = 32;   {icon}
       picItem     = 64;   {QuickDraw picture}
       userItem    = 0;    {application-defined item (dialog only)}
       itemDisable = 128;  {add to any of above to disable}

       { Item numbers of OK and Cancel buttons }

       ok     = 1;
       cancel = 2;

       { Resource IDs of alert icons }

       stopIcon    = 0;
       noteIcon    = 1;
       cautionIcon = 2;
```

Data Types

```
TYPE DialogPtr  = WindowPtr;
     DialogPeek = ^DialogRecord;

     DialogRecord =
            RECORD
               window:     WindowRecord; {dialog window}
               items:      Handle;       {item list}
               textH:      TEHandle;     {current editText item}
               editField:  INTEGER;      {editText item number minus 1}
               editOpen:   INTEGER;      {used internally}
               aDefItem:   INTEGER       {default button item number}
            END;

     DialogTHndl = ^DialogTPtr;
     DialogTPtr  = ^DialogTemplate;
```

```
DialogTemplate =
    RECORD
        boundsRect: Rect;       {becomes window's portRect}
        procID:     INTEGER;    {window definition ID}
        visible:    BOOLEAN;    {TRUE if visible}
        filler1:    BOOLEAN;    {not used}
        goAwayFlag: BOOLEAN;    {TRUE if has go-away region}
        filler2:    BOOLEAN;    {not used}
        refCon:     LONGINT;    {window's reference value}
        itemsID:    INTEGER;    {resource ID of item list}
        title:      Str255      {window's title}
    END;

AlertTHndl   = ^AlertTPtr;
AlertTPtr    = ^AlertTemplate;
AlertTemplate = RECORD
        boundsRect: Rect;       {becomes window's portRect}
        itemsID:    INTEGER;    {resource ID of item list}
        stages:     StageList   {alert stage information}
    END:

StageList = PACKED RECORD
        boldItm4: 0..1;     {default button item number minus 1}
        boxDrwn4: BOOLEAN;  {TRUE if alert box to be drawn}
        sound4:   0..3      {sound number}
        boldItm3: 0..1;
        boxDrwn3: BOOLEAN;
        sound3:   0..3
        boldItm2: 0..1;
        boxDrwn2: BOOLEAN;
        sound2:   0..3
        boldItm1: 0..1;
        boxDrwn1: BOOLEAN;
        sound1:   0..3
    END;
```

Routines

Initialization

```
PROCEDURE InitDialogs    (resumeProc: ProcPtr);
PROCEDURE ErrorSound     (soundProc: ProcPtr);
PROCEDURE SetDAFont      (fontNum: INTEGER);   [Not in ROM]
```

Creating and Disposing of Dialogs

```
FUNCTION  NewDialog      (dStorage: Ptr; boundsRect: Rect; title: Str255;
                          visible: BOOLEAN; procID: INTEGER; behind:
                          WindowPtr; goAwayFlag: BOOLEAN; refCon: LONGINT;
                          items: Handle) : DialogPtr;
```

```
FUNCTION    GetNewDialog     (dialogID: INTEGER; dStorage: Ptr; behind:
                              WindowPtr) : DialogPtr;
PROCEDURE   CloseDialog      (theDialog: DialogPtr);
PROCEDURE   DisposDialog     (theDialog: DialogPtr);
PROCEDURE   CouldDialog      (dialogID: INTEGER);
PROCEDURE   FreeDialog       (dialogID: INTEGER);
```

Handling Dialog Events

```
PROCEDURE   ModalDialog      (filterProc: ProcPtr; VAR itemHit: INTEGER);
FUNCTION    IsDialogEvent    (theEvent: EventRecord) : BOOLEAN;
FUNCTION    DialogSelect     (theEvent: EventRecord; VAR theDialog:
                              DialogPtr; VAR itemHit: INTEGER) : BOOLEAN;
PROCEDURE   DlgCut           (theDialog: DialogPtr);   [Not in ROM]
PROCEDURE   DlgCopy          (theDialog: DialogPtr);   [Not in ROM]
PROCEDURE   DlgPaste         (theDialog: DialogPtr);   [Not in ROM]
PROCEDURE   DlgDelete        (theDialog: DialogPtr);   [Not in ROM]
PROCEDURE   DrawDialog       (theDialog: DialogPtr);
```

Invoking Alerts

```
FUNCTION    Alert            (alertID: INTEGER; filterProc: ProcPtr) : INTEGER;
FUNCTION    StopAlert        (alertID: INTEGER; filterProc: ProcPtr) : INTEGER;
FUNCTION    NoteAlert        (alertID: INTEGER; filterProc: ProcPtr) : INTEGER;
FUNCTION    CautionAlert     (alertID: INTEGER; filterProc: ProcPtr) : INTEGER;
PROCEDURE   CouldAlert       (alertID: INTEGER);
PROCEDURE   FreeAlert        (alertID: INTEGER);
```

Manipulating Items in Dialogs and Alerts

```
PROCEDURE   ParamText        (param0,param1,param2,param3: Str255);
PROCEDURE   GetDItem         (theDialog: DialogPtr; itemNo: INTEGER; VAR
                              itemType: INTEGER; VAR item: Handle; VAR box:
                              Rect);
PROCEDURE   SetDItem         (theDialog: DialogPtr; itemNo: INTEGER;
                              itemType: INTEGER; item: Handle; box: Rect);
PROCEDURE   GetIText         (item: Handle; VAR text: Str255);
PROCEDURE   SetIText         (item: Handle; text: Str255);
PROCEDURE   SelIText         (theDialog: DialogPtr; itemNo: INTEGER;
                              strtSel,endSel: INTEGER);
FUNCTION    GetAlrtStage :   INTEGER;     [Not in ROM]
PROCEDURE   ResetAlrtStage;  [Not in ROM]
```

UserItem Procedure

```
PROCEDURE   MyItem (theWindow: WindowPtr; itemNo: INTEGER);
```

Inside Macintosh

Sound Procedure

```
PROCEDURE MySound (soundNo: INTEGER);
```

FilterProc Function for Modal Dialogs and Alerts

```
FUNCTION MyFilter (theDialog: DialogPtr; VAR theEvent: EventRecord;
                   VAR itemHit: INTEGER) : BOOLEAN;
```

Assembly-Language Information

Constants

```
; Item types

ctrlItem       .EQU    4       ;add to following four constants
btnCtrl        .EQU    0       ;standard button control
chkCtrl        .EQU    1       ;standard check box control
radCtrl        .EQU    2       ;standard radio button control
resCtrl        .EQU    3       ;control defined in control template
statText       .EQU    8       ;static text
editText       .EQU    16      ;editable text (dialog only)
iconItem       .EQU    32      ;icon
picItem        .EQU    64      ;QuickDraw picture
userItem       .EQU    0       ;application-defined item (dialog only)
itemDisable    .EQU    128     ;add to any of above to disable

; Item numbers of OK and Cancel buttons

okButton       .EQU    1
cancelButton   .EQU    2

; Resource IDs of alert icons

stopIcon       .EQU    0
noteIcon       .EQU    1
cautionIcon    .EQU    2

; Masks for stages word in alert template

volBits        .EQU    3       ;sound number
alBit          .EQU    4       ;whether to draw box
okDismissal    .EQU    8       ;item number of default button minus 1
```

Dialog Record Data Structure

dWindow	Dialog window
items	Handle to dialog's item list
teHandle	Handle to current editText item
editField	Item number of editText item minus 1 (word)
aDefItem	Item number of default button (word)
dWindLen	Size in bytes of dialog record

Dialog Template Data Structure

dBounds	Rectangle that becomes portRect of dialog window's grafPort (8 bytes)
dWindProc	Window definition ID (word)
dVisible	Nonzero if dialog window is visible (word)
dGoAway	Nonzero if dialog window has a go-away region (word)
dRefCon	Dialog window's reference value (long)
dItems	Resource ID of dialog's item list (word)
dTitle	Dialog window's title (preceded by length byte)

Alert Template Data Structure

aBounds	Rectangle that becomes portRect of alert window's grafPort (8 bytes)
aItems	Resource ID of alert's item list (word)
aStages	Stages word; information for alert stages

Item List Data Structure

dlgMaxIndex	Number of items minus 1 (word)
itmHndl	Handle or procedure pointer for this item
itmRect	Display rectangle for this item (8 bytes)
itmType	Item type for this item (byte)
itmData	Length byte followed by data for this item (data must be even number of bytes)

Variables

ResumeProc	Address of resume procedure
DAStrings	Handles to ParamText strings (16 bytes)
DABeeper	Address of current sound procedure
DlgFont	Font number for dialogs and alerts (word)
ACount	Stage number (0 through 3) of last alert (word)
ANumber	Resource ID of last alert (word)

14 THE DESK MANAGER

- 437 About This Chapter
- 437 About the Desk Manager
- 439 Using the Desk Manager
- 440 Desk Manager Routines
- 440   Opening and Closing Desk Accessories
- 441   Handling Events in Desk Accessories
- 442   Performing Periodic Actions
- 442   Advanced Routines
- 443 Writing Your Own Desk Accessories
- 445   The Driver Routines
- 448 Summary of the Desk Manager

The Desk Manager

ABOUT THIS CHAPTER

This chapter describes the Desk Manager, the part of the Toolbox that supports the use of desk accessories from an application; the Calculator, for example, is a standard desk accessory available to any application. You'll learn how to use the Desk Manager routines and how to write your own accessories.

You should already be familiar with:

- the basic concepts behind the Resource Manager and QuickDraw
- the Toolbox Event Manager, the Window Manager, the Menu Manager, and the Dialog Manager
- device drivers, as discussed in chapter 6 in Volume II, if you want to write your own desk accessories

ABOUT THE DESK MANAGER

The Desk Manager enables your application to support **desk accessories**, which are "mini-applications" that can be run at the same time as a Macintosh application. There are a number of standard desk accessories, such as the Calculator shown in Figure 1. You can also write your own desk accessories if you wish.

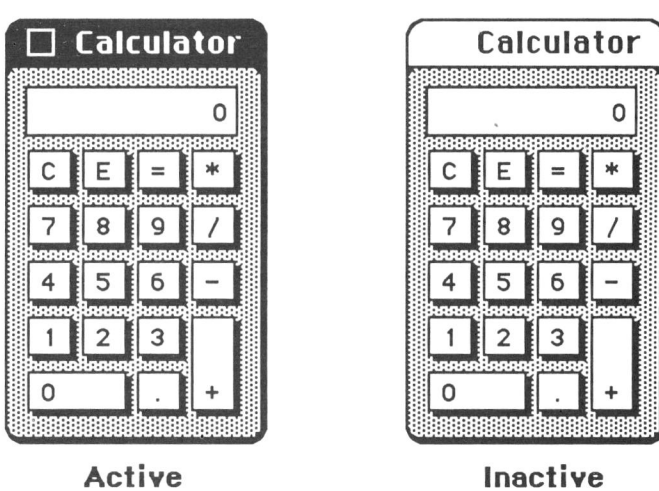

Figure 1. The Calculator Desk Accessory

The Macintosh user opens desk accessories by choosing them from the standard Apple menu (whose title is an apple symbol), which by convention is the first menu in the menu bar. When a desk accessory is chosen from this menu, it's usually displayed in a window on the desktop, and that window becomes the active window (see Figure 2).

About the Desk Manager I-437

Inside Macintosh

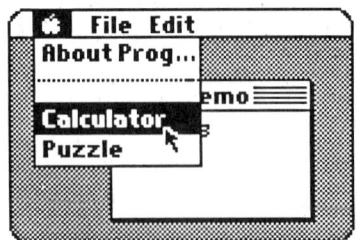
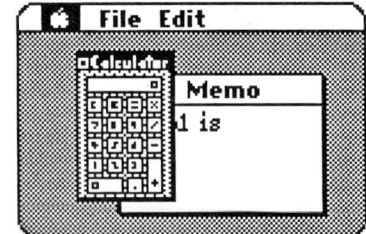

An accessory is chosen from the Apple menu.

The accessory's window appears as the active window.

Figure 2. Opening a Desk Accessory

After being opened, the accessory may be used as long as it's active. The user can activate other windows and then reactivate the desk accessory by clicking inside it. Whenever a standard desk accessory is active, it has a close box in its title bar. Clicking the close box (or choosing Close from the File menu) makes the accessory disappear, and the window that's then frontmost becomes active.

The window associated with a desk accessory is usually a rounded-corner window (as shown in Figure 1) or a standard document window, although it can be any type of window. It may even look and behave like a dialog window; the accessory can call on the Dialog Manager to create the window and then use Dialog Manager routines to operate on it. In any case, the window will be a system window, as indicated by the fact that its windowKind field contains a negative value.

The Desk Manager provides a mechanism that lets standard commands chosen from the Edit menu be applied to a desk accessory when it's active. Even if the commands aren't particularly useful for editing within the accessory, they may be useful for cutting and pasting between the accessory and the application or even another accessory. For example, the result of a calculation made with the Calculator can be copied and pasted into a document prepared in MacWrite.

A desk accessory may also have its own menu. When the accessory becomes active, the title of its menu is added to the menu bar and menu items may be chosen from it. Any of the application's menus or menu items that no longer apply are disabled. A desk accessory can even have an entire menu bar full of its own menus, which will completely replace the menus already in the menu bar. When an accessory that has its own menu or menus becomes inactive, the menu bar is restored to normal.

Although desk accessories are usually displayed in windows (one per accessory); it's possible for an accessory to have only a menu (or menus) and not a window. In this case, the menu includes a command to close the accessory. Also, a desk accessory that's displayed in a window may create any number of additional windows while it's open.

A desk accessory is actually a special type of device driver—special in that it may have its own windows and menus for interacting with the user. The value in the windowKind field of a desk accessory's window is a reference number that uniquely identifies the driver, returned by the Device Manager when the driver was opened. Desk accessories and other RAM drivers used by Macintosh applications are stored in resource files.

USING THE DESK MANAGER

To allow access to desk accessories, your application must do the following:

- Initialize TextEdit and the Dialog Manager, in case any desk accessories are displayed in windows created by the Dialog Manager (which uses TextEdit).

- Set up the Apple menu as the first menu in the menu bar. You can put the names of all currently available desk accessories in a menu by using the Menu Manager procedure AddResMenu.

- Set up an Edit menu that includes the standard commands Undo, Cut, Copy, Paste, and Clear (in that order, with a dividing line between Undo and Cut), even if your application itself doesn't support any of these commands.

Note: Applications should leave enough space in the menu bar for a desk accessory's menu to be added.

When the user chooses a desk accessory from the Apple menu, call the Menu Manager procedure GetItem to get the name of the desk accessory, and then the Desk Manager function OpenDeskAcc to open and display the accessory. When a system window is active and the user chooses Close from the File menu, close the desk accessory with the CloseDeskAcc procedure.

Warning: Most open desk accessories allocate nonrelocatable objects (such as windows) in the heap, resulting in fragmentation of heap space. Before beginning an operation that requires a large amount of memory, your application may want to close all open desk accessories (or allow the user to close some of them).

When the Toolbox Event Manager function GetNextEvent reports that a mouse-down event has occurred, your application should call the Window Manager function FindWindow to find out where the mouse button was pressed. If FindWindow returns the predefined constant inSysWindow, which means that the mouse button was pressed in a system window, call the Desk Manager procedure SystemClick. SystemClick handles mouse-down events in system windows, routing them to desk accessories where appropriate.

Note: The application needn't be concerned with exactly which desk accessories are currently open.

When the active window changes from an application window to a system window, the application should disable any of its menus or menu items that don't apply while an accessory is active, and it should enable the standard editing commands Undo, Cut, Copy, Paste, and Clear, in the Edit menu. An application should disable any editing commands it doesn't support when one of its own windows becomes active.

When a mouse-down event occurs in the menu bar, and the application determines that one of the five standard editing commands has been invoked, it should call SystemEdit. Only if SystemEdit returns FALSE should the application process the editing command itself; if the active window belongs to a desk accessory, SystemEdit passes the editing command on to that accessory and returns TRUE.

Keyboard equivalents of the standard editing commands are passed on to desk accessories by the Desk Manager, not by your application.

Inside Macintosh

Warning: The standard keyboard equivalents for the commands in the Edit menu must not be changed or assigned to other commands; the Desk Manager automatically interprets Command-Z, X, C, and V as Undo, Cut, Copy, and Paste, respectively.

Certain periodic actions may be defined for desk accessories. To see that they're performed, you need to call the SystemTask procedure at least once every time through your main event loop.

The two remaining Desk Manager routines—SystemEvent and SystemMenu—are never called by the application, but are described in this chapter because they reveal inner mechanisms of the Toolbox that may be of interest to advanced programmers.

DESK MANAGER ROUTINES

Opening and Closing Desk Accessories

```
FUNCTION OpenDeskAcc (theAcc: Str255) : INTEGER;
```

OpenDeskAcc opens the desk accessory having the given name and displays its window (if any) as the active window. The name is the accessory's resource name, which you get from the Apple menu by calling the Menu Manager procedure GetItem. OpenDeskAcc calls the Resource Manager to read the desk accessory from the resource file into the application heap.

You should ignore the value returned by OpenDeskAcc. If the desk accessory is successfully opened, the function result is its driver reference number. However, if the desk accessory can't be opened, the function result is undefined; the accessory will have taken care of informing the user of the problem (such as memory full) and won't display itself.

Warning: Early versions of some desk accessories may set the current grafPort to the accessory's port upon return from OpenDeskAcc. To be safe, you should bracket your call to OpenDeskAcc with calls to the QuickDraw procedures GetPort and SetPort, to save and restore the current port.

Note: Programmers concerned about the amount of available memory should be aware that an open desk accessory uses from 1K to 3K bytes of heap space in addition to the space needed for the accessory itself. The desk accessory is responsible for determining whether there is sufficient memory for it to run; this can be done by calling SizeResource followed by ResrvMem.

```
PROCEDURE CloseDeskAcc (refNum: INTEGER);
```

When a system window is active and the user chooses Close from the File menu, call CloseDeskAcc to close the desk accessory. RefNum is the driver reference number for the desk accessory, which you get from the windowKind field of its window.

The Desk Manager automatically closes a desk accessory if the user clicks its close box. Also, since the application heap is released when the application terminates, every desk accessory goes away at that time.

Handling Events in Desk Accessories

```
PROCEDURE SystemClick (theEvent: EventRecord; theWindow:
        WindowPtr);
```

When a mouse-down event occurs and the Window Manager function FindWindow reports that the mouse button was pressed in a system window, the application should call SystemClick with the event record and the window pointer. If the given window belongs to a desk accessory, SystemClick sees that the event gets handled properly.

SystemClick determines which part of the desk accessory's window the mouse button was pressed in, and responds accordingly (similar to the way your application responds to mouse activities in its own windows).

- If the mouse button was pressed in the content region of the window and the window was active, SystemClick sends the mouse-down event to the desk accessory, which processes it as appropriate.

- If the mouse button was pressed in the content region and the window was inactive, SystemClick makes it the active window.

- If the mouse button was pressed in the drag region, SystemClick calls the Window Manager procedure DragWindow to pull an outline of the window across the screen and move the window to a new location. If the window was inactive, DragWindow also makes it the active window (unless the Command key was pressed along with the mouse button).

- If the mouse button was pressed in the go-away region, SystemClick calls the Window Manager function TrackGoAway to determine whether the mouse is still inside the go-away region when the click is completed: If so, it tells the desk accessory to close itself; otherwise, it does nothing.

```
FUNCTION SystemEdit (editCmd: INTEGER) : BOOLEAN;
```

Assembly-language note: The macro you invoke to call SystemEdit from assembly language is named _SysEdit.

Call SystemEdit when there's a mouse-down event in the menu bar and the user chooses one of the five standard editing commands from the Edit menu. Pass one of the following as the value of the editCmd parameter:

editCmd	Editing command
0	Undo
2	Cut
3	Copy
4	Paste
5	Clear

Inside Macintosh

If your Edit menu contains these five commands in the standard arrangement (the order listed above, with a dividing line between Undo and Cut), you can simply call

```
SystemEdit(menuItem-1)
```

where menuItem is the menu item number.

If the active window doesn't belong to a desk accessory, SystemEdit returns FALSE; the application should then process the editing command as usual. If the active window does belong to a desk accessory, SystemEdit asks that accessory to process the command and returns TRUE; in this case, the application should ignore the command.

Note: It's up to the application to make sure desk accessories get their editing commands that are chosen from the Edit menu. In particular, make sure your application hasn't disabled the Edit menu or any of the five standard commands when a desk accessory is activated.

Performing Periodic Actions

```
PROCEDURE SystemTask;
```

For each open desk accessory (or other device driver performing periodic actions), SystemTask causes the accessory to perform the periodic action defined for it, if any such action has been defined and if the proper time period has passed since the action was last performed. For example, a clock accessory can be defined such that the second hand is to move once every second; the periodic action for the accessory will be to move the second hand to the next position, and SystemTask will alert the accessory every second to perform that action.

You should call SystemTask as often as possible, usually once every time through your main event loop. Call it more than once if your application does an unusually large amount of processing each time through the loop.

Note: SystemTask should be called at least every sixtieth of a second.

Advanced Routines

```
FUNCTION SystemEvent (theEvent: EventRecord) : BOOLEAN;
```

SystemEvent is called only by the Toolbox Event Manager function GetNextEvent when it receives an event, to determine whether the event should be handled by the application or by the system. If the given event should be handled by the application, SystemEvent returns FALSE; otherwise, it calls the appropriate system code to handle the event and returns TRUE.

In the case of a null or mouse-down event, SystemEvent does nothing but return FALSE. Notice that it responds this way to a mouse-down event even though the event may in fact have occurred in a system window (and therefore may have to be handled by the system). The reason for this is that the check for exactly where the event occurred (via the Window Manager function FindWindow) is made later by the application and so would be made twice if SystemEvent were also to do it. To avoid this duplication, SystemEvent passes the event on to the application and lets it make the sole call to FindWindow. Should FindWindow reveal that the mouse-down event did occur in a system window, the application can then call SystemClick, as described above, to get the system to handle it.

If the given event is a mouse-up or any keyboard event (including keyboard equivalents of commands), SystemEvent checks whether the active window belongs to a desk accessory and whether that accessory can handle this type of event. If so, it sends the event to the desk accessory and returns TRUE; otherwise, it returns FALSE.

If SystemEvent is passed an activate or update event, it checks whether the window the event occurred in is a system window belonging to a desk accessory and whether that accessory can handle this type of event. If so, it sends the event to the desk accessory and returns TRUE; otherwise, it returns FALSE.

> **Note:** It's unlikely that a desk accessory would *not* be set up to handle keyboard, activate, and update events, or that it *would* handle mouse-up events.

If the given event is a disk-inserted event, SystemEvent does some low-level processing (by calling the File Manager function MountVol) but passes the event on to the application by returning FALSE, in case the application wants to do further processing.
Finally, SystemEvent returns FALSE for network, dvice driver, and application-defined events.

> **Assembly-language note:** Advanced programmers can make SystemEvent always return FALSE by setting the global variable SEvtEnb (a byte) to 0.

```
PROCEDURE SystemMenu (menuResult: LONGINT);
```

SystemMenu is called only by the Menu Manager functions MenuSelect and MenuKey, when an item in a menu belonging to a desk accessory has been chosen. The menuResult parameter has the same format as the value returned by MenuSelect and MenuKey: the menu ID in the high-order word and the menu item number in the low-order word. (The menu ID will be negative.) SystemMenu directs the desk accessory to perform the appropriate action for the given menu item.

WRITING YOUR OWN DESK ACCESSORIES

To write your own desk accessory, you must create it as a device driver and include it in a resource file, as described in chapter 6 of Volume II. Standard or shared desk accessories are stored in the system resource file. Accessories specific to an application are rare; if there are any, they're stored in the application's resource file.

The resource type for a device driver is 'DRVR'. The resource ID for a desk accessory is the driver's unit number and must be between 12 and 31 inclusive.

> **Note:** A desk accessory will often have additional resources (such as pattern and string resources) that are associated with it. These resources *must* observe a special numbering convention, as described in chapter 5.

Inside Macintosh

The resource name should be whatever you want to appear in the Apple menu, but should also include a nonprinting character; by convention, the name should begin with a NUL character (ASCII code 0). The nonprinting character is needed to avoid conflict with file names that are the same as the names of desk accessories.

Device drivers are usually written in assembly language. The structure of a device driver is described in chapter 6 of Volume II. The rest of this section reviews some of that information and presents additional details pertaining specifically to device drivers that are desk accessories.

As shown in Figure 3, a device driver begins with a few words of flags and other data, followed by offsets to the routines that do the work of the driver, an optional title, and finally the routines themselves.

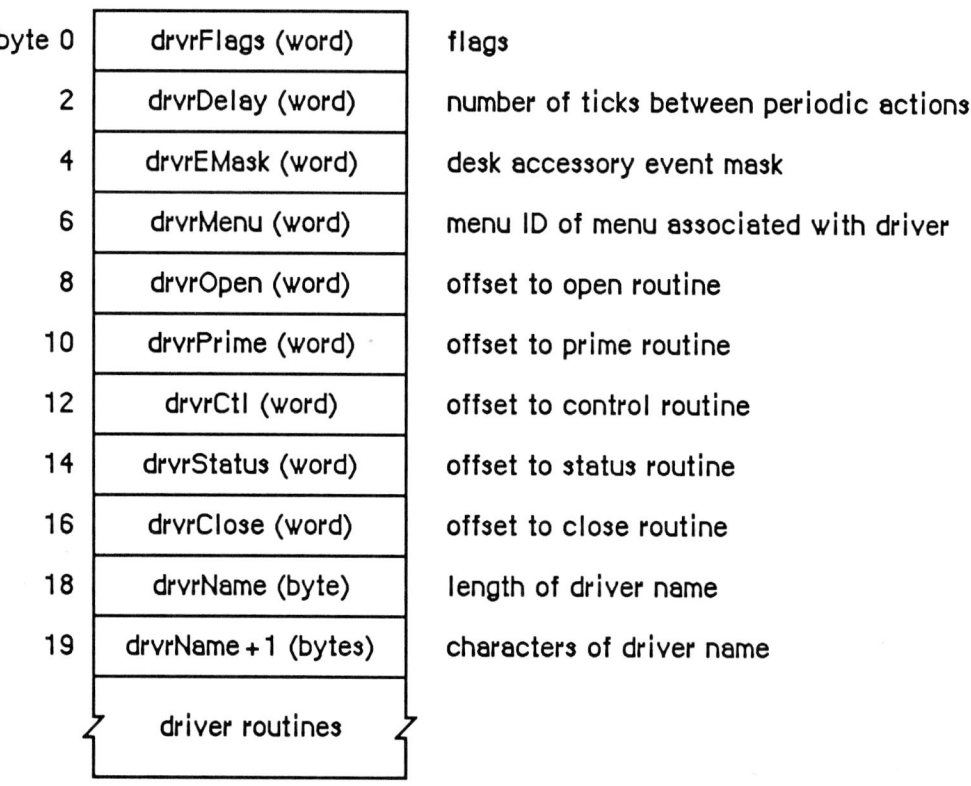

Figure 3. Desk Accessory Device Driver

One bit in the high-order byte of the drvrFlags word is frequently used by desk accessories:

```
dNeedTime   .EQU    5      ;set if driver needs time for performing a
                           ; periodic action
```

Desk accessories may need to perform predefined actions periodically. For example, a clock desk accessory may want to change the time it displays every second. If the dNeedTime flag is set, the desk accessory does need to perform a periodic action, and the drvrDelay word contains a tick count indicating how often the periodic action should occur. Whether the action actually occurs as frequently as specified depends on how often the application calls the Desk Manager procedure SystemTask. SystemTask calls the desk accessory's control routine (if the time indicated by drvrDelay has elapsed), and the control routine must perform whatever predefined action is desired.

> **Note:** A desk accessory cannot rely on SystemTask being called regularly or frequently by an application. If it needs precise timing it should install a task to be executed during the vertical retrace interrupt. There are, however, certain restrictions on tasks performed during interrupts, such as not being able to make calls to the Memory Manager. For more information on these restrictions, see chapter 11 of Volume II. Periodic actions performed in response to SystemTask calls are not performed via an interrupt and so don't have these restrictions.

The drvrEMask word contains an event mask specifying which events the desk accessory can handle. If the accessory has a window, the mask should include keyboard, activate, update, and mouse-down events, but must *not* include mouse-up events.

> **Note:** The accessory may not be interested in keyboard input, but it should still respond to key-down and auto-key events, at least with a beep.

When an event occurs, the Toolbox Event Manager calls SystemEvent. SystemEvent checks the drvrEMask word to determine whether the desk accessory can handle the type of event, and if so, calls the desk accessory's control routine. The control routine must perform whatever action is desired.

If the desk accessory has its own menu (or menus), the drvrMenu word contains the menu ID of the menu (or of any one of the menus); otherwise, it contains 0. The menu ID for a desk accessory menu must be negative, and it must be different from the menu ID stored in other desk accessories.

Following these four words are the offsets to the driver routines and, optionally, a title for the desk accessory (preceded by its length in bytes). You can use the title in the driver as the title of the accessory's window, or just as a way of identifying the driver in memory.

> **Note:** A practical size limit for desk accessories is about 8K bytes.

The Driver Routines

Of the five possible driver routines, only three need to exist for desk accessories: the open, close, and control routines. The other routines (prime and status) may be used if desired for a particular accessory.

The open routine opens the desk accessory:

- It creates the window to be displayed when the accessory is opened, if any, specifying that it be invisible (since OpenDeskAcc will display it). The window can be created with the Dialog Manager function GetNewDialog (or NewDialog) if desired; the accessory will look and respond like a dialog box, and subsequent operations may be performed on it with Dialog Manager routines. In any case, the open routine sets the windowKind field of the window record to the driver reference number for the desk accessory, which it gets from the device control entry. (The reference number will be negative.) It also stores the window pointer in the device control entry.

- If the driver has any private storage, it allocates the storage, stores a handle to it in the device control entry, and initializes any local variables. It might, for example, create a menu or menus for the accessory.

Inside Macintosh

If the open routine is unable to complete all of the above tasks (if it runs out of memory, for example), it must do the following:

- Open only the minimum of data structures needed to run the desk accessory.
- Modify the code of every routine (except the close routine) so that the routine just returns (or beeps) when called.
- Modify the code of the close routine so that it disposes of only the minimum data structures that were opened.
- Display an alert indicating failure, such as "The Note Pad is not available".

The close routine closes the desk accessory, disposing of its window (if any) and all the data structures associated with it and replacing the window pointer in the device control entry with NIL. If the driver has any private storage, the close routine also disposes of that storage.

Warning: A driver's private storage shouldn't be in the system heap, because the application heap is reinitialized when an application terminates, and the driver is lost before it can dispose of its storage.

The action taken by the control routine depends on information passed in the parameter block pointed to by register A0. A message is passed in the csCode parameter; this message is simply a number that tells the routine what action to take. There are nine such messages:

```
accEvent       .EQU    64      ;handle a given event
accRun         .EQU    65      ;take the periodic action, if any, for
                               ; this desk accessory
accCursor      .EQU    66      ;change cursor shape if appropriate;
                               ; generate null event if window was
                               ; created by Dialog Manager
accMenu        .EQU    67      ;handle a given menu item
accUndo        .EQU    68      ;handle the Undo command
accCut         .EQU    70      ;handle the Cut command
accCopy        .EQU    71      ;handle the Copy command
accPaste       .EQU    72      ;handle the Paste command
accClear       .EQU    73      ;handle the Clear command
```

Note: As described in chapter 6 of Volume II, the control routine may also receive the message goodBye in the csCode parameter telling it when the heap is about to be reinitialized.

Along with the accEvent message, the control routine receives in the csParam field a pointer to an event record. The control routine must respond by handling the given event in whatever way is appropriate for this desk accessory. SystemClick and SystemEvent call the control routine with this message to send the driver an event that it should handle—for example, an activate event that makes the desk accessory active or inactive. When a desk accessory becomes active, its control routine might install a menu in the menu bar. If the accessory becoming active has more than one menu, the control routine should respond as follows:

- Store the accessory's unique menu ID in the global variable MBarEnable. (This is the negative menu ID in the device driver and the device control entry.)
- Call the Menu Manager routines GetMenuBar to save the current menu list and ClearMenuBar to clear the menu bar.

The Desk Manager

- Install the accessory's own menus in the menu bar.

Then, when the desk accessory becomes inactive, the control routine should call SetMenuBar to restore the former menu list, call DrawMenuBar to draw the menu bar, and set MBarEnable to 0.

The accRun message tells the control routine to perform the periodic action for this desk accessory. For every open driver that has the dNeedTime flag set, the SystemTask procedure calls the control routine with this message if the proper time period has passed since the action was last performed.

The accCursor message makes it possible to change the shape of the cursor when it's inside an active desk accessory. SystemTask calls the control routine with this message as long as the desk accessory is active. The control routine should respond by checking whether the mouse location is in the desk accessory's window; if it is, it should set it to the standard arrow cursor (by calling the QuickDraw procedure InitCursor), just in case the application has changed the cursor and failed to reset it. Or, if desired, your accessory may give the cursor a special shape (by calling the QuickDraw procedure SetCursor).

If the desk accessory is displayed in a window created by the Dialog Manager, the control routine should respond to the accCursor message by generating a null event (storing the event code for a null event in an event record) and passing it to DialogSelect. This enables the Dialog Manager to blink the caret in editText items. In assembly language, the code might look like this:

```
CLR.L         -SP           ;event code for null event is 0
PEA           2(SP)         ;pass null event
CLR.L         -SP           ;pass NIL dialog pointer
CLR.L         -SP           ;pass NIL pointer
_DialogSelect               ;invoke DialogSelect
ADDQ.L        #4,SP         ;pop off result and null event
```

When the accMenu message is sent to the control routine, the following information is passed in the parameter block: csParam contains the menu ID of the desk accessory's menu and csParam+2 contains the menu item number. The control routine should take the appropriate action for when the given menu item is chosen from the menu, and then make the Menu Manager call HiliteMenu(0) to remove the highlighting from the menu bar.

Finally, the control routine should respond to one of the last five messages—accUndo through accClear—by processing the corresponding editing command in the desk accessory window if appropriate. SystemEdit calls the control routine with these messages. For information on cutting and pasting between a desk accessory and the application, or between two desk accessories, see chapter 15.

Warning: If the accessory opens a resource file, or otherwise changes which file is the current resource file, it should save and restore the previous current resource file, using the Resource Manager routines CurResFile and UseResFile. Similarly, the accessory should save and restore the port that was the current grafPort, using the QuickDraw routines GetPort and SetPort.

Writing Your Own Desk Accessories I-447

SUMMARY OF THE DESK MANAGER

Routines

Opening and Closing Desk Accessories

```
FUNCTION    OpenDeskAcc  (theAcc: Str255) : INTEGER;
PROCEDURE   CloseDeskAcc (refNum: INTEGER);
```

Handling Events in Desk Accessories

```
PROCEDURE   SystemClick  (theEvent: EventRecord; theWindow: WindowPtr);
FUNCTION    SystemEdit   (editCmd: INTEGER) : BOOLEAN;
```

Performing Periodic Actions

```
PROCEDURE   SystemTask;
```

Advanced Routines

```
FUNCTION    SystemEvent  (theEvent: EventRecord) : BOOLEAN;
PROCEDURE   SystemMenu   (menuResult: LONGINT);
```

Assembly-Language Information

Constants

```
; Desk accessory flag

dNeedTime       .EQU    5       ;set if driver needs time for performing a
                                ; periodic action

; Control routine messages

accEvent        .EQU    64      ;handle a given event
accRun          .EQU    65      ;take the periodic action, if any, for
                                ; this desk accessory
accCursor       .EQU    66      ;change cursor shape if appropriate;
                                ; generate null event if window was
                                ; created by Dialog Manager
accMenu         .EQU    67      ;handle a given menu item
accUndo         .EQU    68      ;handle the Undo command
```

```
accCut      .EQU    70    ;handle the Cut command
accCopy     .EQU    71    ;handle the Copy command
accPaste    .EQU    72    ;handle the Paste command
accClear    .EQU    73    ;handle the Clear command
```

Special Macro Names

Pascal name	Macro name
SystemEdit	_SysEdit

Variables

MBarEnable	Unique menu ID for active desk accessory, when menu bar belongs to the accessory (word)
SEvtEnb	0 if SystemEvent should return FALSE (byte)

15 THE SCRAP MANAGER

453 About This Chapter
453 About the Scrap Manager
454 Memory and the Desk Scrap
454 Desk Scrap Data Types
456 Using the Scrap Manager
457 Scrap Manager Routines
457   Getting Desk Scrap Information
458   Keeping the Desk Scrap on the Disk
458   Writing to the Desk Scrap
459   Reading from the Desk Scrap
461 Private Scraps
462 Format of the Desk Scrap
463 Summary of the Scrap Manager

ABOUT THIS CHAPTER

This chapter describes the Scrap Manager, the part of the Toolbox that supports cutting and pasting among applications and desk accessories.

You should already be familiar with:

- resources, as discussed in chapter 5
- QuickDraw pictures
- the Toolbox Event Manager

ABOUT THE SCRAP MANAGER

The Scrap Manager is a set of routines and data types that let Macintosh applications support cutting and pasting using the **desk scrap**. The desk scrap is the vehicle for transferring data between two applications, between an application and a desk accessory, or between two desk accessories; it can also be used for transferring data that's cut and pasted within an application.

From the user's point of view, all data that's cut or copied resides in the Clipboard. The Cut command deletes data from a document and places it in the Clipboard; the Copy command copies data into the Clipboard without deleting it from the document. The next Paste command—whether applied to the same document or another, in the same application or another—inserts the contents of the Clipboard at a specified place. An application that supports cutting and pasting may also provide a Clipboard window for displaying the current contents of the scrap; it may show the Clipboard window at all times or only when requested via the toggled command Show (or Hide) Clipboard.

> **Note:** The Scrap Manager was designed to transfer *small* amounts of data; attempts to transfer very large amounts of data may fail due to lack of memory.

The nature of the data to be transferred varies according to the application. For example, in a word processor or in the Calculator desk accessory, the data is text; in a graphics application it's a picture. The amount of information retained about the data being transferred also varies. Between two text applications, text can be cut and pasted without any loss of information; however, if the user of a graphics application cuts a picture consisting of text and then pastes it into a word processor document, the text in the picture may not be editable in the word processor, or it may be editable but not look exactly the same as in the graphics application. The Scrap Manager allows for a variety of data types and provides a mechanism whereby applications have some control over how much information is retained when data is transferred.

The desk scrap is usually stored in memory, but can be stored on the disk (in the **scrap file**) if there's not enough room for it in memory. The scrap may remain on the disk throughout the use of the application, but must be read back into memory when the application terminates, since the user may then remove that disk and insert another. The Scrap Manager provides routines for writing the desk scrap to the disk and for reading it back into memory. The routines that access the scrap keep track of whether it's in memory or on the disk.

Inside Macintosh

MEMORY AND THE DESK SCRAP

The desk scrap is initially located in the application heap; a handle to it is stored in low memory. When starting up an application, the Segment Loader temporarily moves the scrap out of the heap into the stack, reinitializes the heap, and puts the scrap back in the heap (see Figure 1). For a short time while it does this, two copies of the scrap exist in the memory allocated for the stack and the heap; for this reason, the desk scrap cannot be bigger than half that amount of memory.

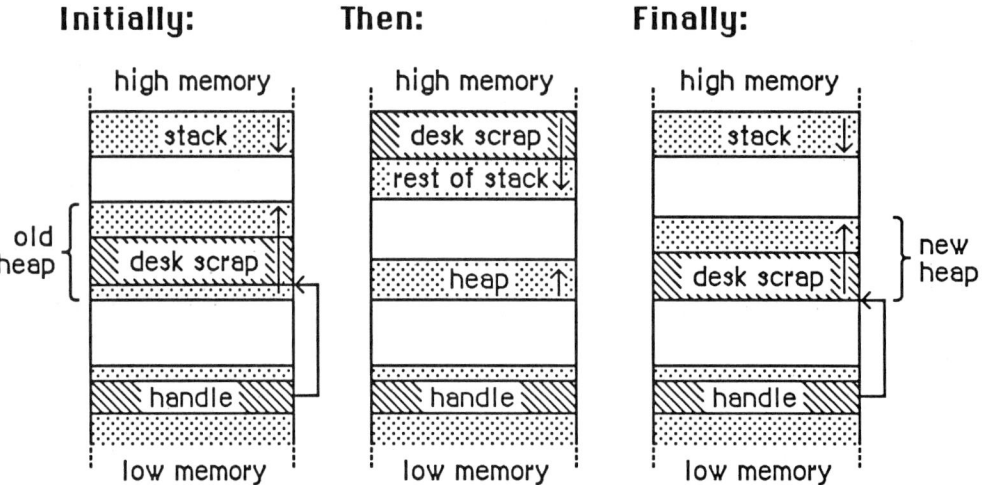

Figure 1. The Desk Scrap at Application Startup

The application can get the size of the desk scrap by calling a Scrap Manager function named InfoScrap. An application concerned about whether there's room for the desk scrap in memory could be set up so that a small initial segment of the application is loaded in just to check the scrap size. After a decision is made about whether to keep the scrap in memory or on the disk, the remaining segments of the application can be loaded in as needed.

There are certain disadvantages to keeping the desk scrap on the disk. The disk may be locked, it may not have enough room for the scrap, or it may be removed during use of the application. If the application can't write the scrap to the disk, it should put up an alert box informing the user, who may want to abort the operation at that point.

DESK SCRAP DATA TYPES

From the user's point of view there can be only one thing in the Clipboard at a time, but the application may store more than one version of the information in the scrap, each representing the same Clipboard contents in a different form. For example, text cut with a word processor may be stored in the desk scrap both as text and as a QuickDraw picture.

The Scrap Manager

Desk scrap data types, like resource types, are a sequence of four characters. As defined in the Resource Manager, their Pascal type is as follows:

```
TYPE ResType = PACKED ARRAY[1..4] OF CHAR;
```

Two standard types of data are defined:

- 'TEXT': a series of ASCII characters
- 'PICT': a QuickDraw picture, which is a saved sequence of drawing commands that can be played back with the DrawPicture command and may include picture comments (see chapter 6 for details)

Applications must write at least one of these standard types of data to the desk scrap and must be able to read *both* types. Most applications will prefer one of these types over the other; for example, a word processor prefers text while a graphics application prefers pictures. An application should write at least its preferred standard type of data to the desk scrap, and may write both types (to pass the most information possible on to the receiving application, which may prefer the other type).

An application reading the desk scrap will look for its preferred data type. If its preferred type isn't there, or if it's there but was written by an application having a different preferred type, the receiving application may or may not be able to convert the data to the type it needs. If not, some information may be lost in the transfer process. For example, a graphics application can easily convert text to a picture, but the reverse isn't true. Figure 2 illustrates the latter case: A picture consisting of text is cut from a graphics application, then pasted into a word processor document.

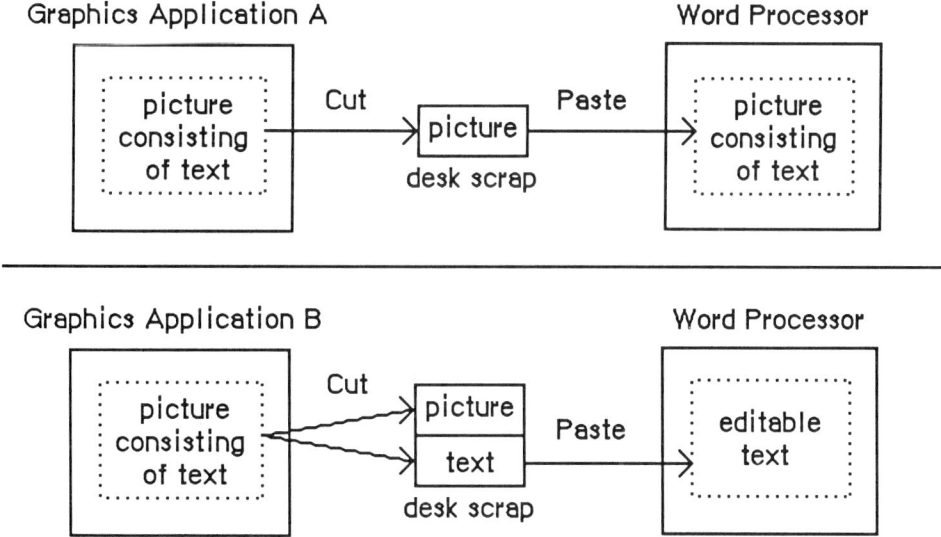

Figure 2. Inter-Application Cutting and Pasting

- If the graphics application writes only its preferred data type (picture) to the desk scrap—like application A in Figure 2—the text in the picture will not be editable in the word processor, because it will be seen as just a series of drawing commands and not as a sequence of characters.
- On the other hand, if the graphics application takes the trouble to recognize which characters have been drawn in the picture, and writes them out to the desk scrap both as a picture and

Inside Macintosh

as text—like application B in Figure 2—the word processor will be able to treat them as editable text. In this case, however, any part of the picture that isn't text will be lost.

In addition to the two standard data types, the desk scrap may also contain application-specific types of data. If several applications are to support the transfer of a private type of data, each one will write and read that type, but still must write at least one of the standard types and be able to read both standard types.

The order in which data is written to the desk scrap is important: The application should write out the different types in order of preference. For example, if it's a word processor that has a private type of data as its preferred type, but also can write text and pictures, it should write the data in that order.

Since the size of the desk scrap is limited, it may be too costly to write out both an application-specific data type and one (or both) of the standard types. Instead of creating your own type, if your data is graphic, you may be able to use the standard picture type and encode additional information in picture comments. (As described in chapter 6, picture comments may be stored in the definition of a picture with the QuickDraw procedure PicComment; they're passed by the DrawPicture procedure to a special routine set up by the application for that purpose.) Applications that are to process that information can do so, while others can ignore it.

USING THE SCRAP MANAGER

If you're concerned about memory use, call InfoScrap early in your program to find out the size of the desk scrap and decide whether there will be enough room in the heap for both the desk scrap and the application itself. If there won't be enough room for the scrap, call UnloadScrap to write the scrap from memory onto the disk.

InfoScrap also provides a handle to the desk scrap if it's in memory, its file name on the disk, and a count that changes when the contents of the desk scrap change. If your application supports display of the Clipboard, you can call InfoScrap each time through your main event loop to check this count: If the Clipboard window is visible, it needs to be updated whenever the count changes.

When a Cut or Copy command is given, you need to write the cut or copied data to the desk scrap. First call ZeroScrap to initialize the scrap or clear its previous contents, and then PutScrap to put the data into the scrap. (You can call PutScrap more than once, to put the data in the scrap in different forms.)

Call GetScrap when a Paste command is given, to access data of a particular type in the desk scrap and to get information about the data.

When the user gives a command that terminates the application, call LoadScrap to read the desk scrap back into memory if it's on the disk (in case the user ejects the disk).

> **Note:** ZeroScrap, PutScrap, and GetScrap all keep track of whether the scrap is in memory or on the disk, so you don't have to worry about it.

If your application uses TextEdit and the TextEdit scrap, you'll need to transfer data between the two scraps, as described in the section "Private Scraps", below.

The Scrap Manager

SCRAP MANAGER ROUTINES

Most of these routines return a result code indicating whether an error occurred. If no error occurred, they return the result code

```
CONST noErr = 0;    {no error}
```

If an error occurred at the Operating System level, an Operating System result code is returned; otherwise, a Scrap Manager result code is returned, as indicated in the routine descriptions. (See Appendix A in Volume III for a list of all result codes.)

Getting Desk Scrap Information

```
FUNCTION InfoScrap : PScrapStuff;
```

InfoScrap returns a pointer to information about the desk scrap. The PScrapStuff data type is defined as follows:

```
TYPE PScrapStuff = ^ScrapStuff;
     ScrapStuff  =
                 RECORD
                   scrapSize:    LONGINT;   {size of desk scrap}
                   scrapHandle:  Handle;    {handle to desk scrap}
                   scrapCount:   INTEGER;   {count changed by ZeroScrap}
                   scrapState:   INTEGER;   {tells where desk scrap is}
                   scrapName:    StringPtr  {scrap file name}
                 END;
```

ScrapSize is the size of the desk scrap in bytes. ScrapHandle is a handle to the scrap if it's in memory, or NIL if not.

ScrapCount is a count that changes every time ZeroScrap is called. You can use this count for testing whether the contents of the desk scrap have changed, since if ZeroScrap has been called, presumably PutScrap was also called. This may be useful if your application supports display of the Clipboard or has a private scrap (as described under "Private Scraps", below).

> **Warning:** Just check to see whether the value of the scrapCount field has changed; don't rely on exactly how it has changed.

ScrapState is positive if the desk scrap is in memory, 0 if it's on the disk, or negative if it hasn't been initialized by ZeroScrap.

> **Note:** ScrapState is actually 0 if the scrap *should* be on the disk; for instance, if the user deletes the Clipboard file and then cuts something, the scrap is really in memory, but ScrapState will be 0.

ScrapName is a pointer to the name of the scrap file, usually "Clipboard File".

Inside Macintosh

Note: InfoScrap assumes that the scrap file has a version number of 0 and is on the default volume. (Version numbers and volumes are described in chapter 4 of Volume II.)

Assembly-language note: The scrap information is available in global variables that have the same names as the Pascal fields.

Keeping the Desk Scrap on the Disk

```
FUNCTION UnloadScrap : LONGINT;
```

Assembly-language note: The macro you invoke to call UnloadScrap from assembly language is named _UnlodeScrap.

UnloadScrap writes the desk scrap from memory to the scrap file, and releases the memory it occupied. If the desk scrap is already on the disk, UnloadScrap does nothing. If no error occurs, UnloadScrap returns the result code noErr; otherwise, it returns an Operating System result code indicating an error.

```
FUNCTION LoadScrap : LONGINT;
```

Assembly-language note: The macro you invoke to call LoadScrap from assembly language is named _LodeScrap.

LoadScrap reads the desk scrap from the scrap file into memory. If the desk scrap is already in memory, it does nothing. If no error occurs, LoadScrap returns the result code noErr; otherwise, it returns an Operating System result code indicating an error.

Writing to the Desk Scrap

```
FUNCTION ZeroScrap : LONGINT;
```

If the scrap already exists (in memory or on the disk), ZeroScrap clears its contents; if not, the scrap is initialized in memory. You must call ZeroScrap before the first time you call PutScrap. If no error occurs, ZeroScrap returns the result code noErr; otherwise, it returns an Operating System result code indicating an error.

ZeroScrap also changes the scrapCount field of the record of information provided by InfoScrap.

The Scrap Manager

```
FUNCTION PutScrap (length: LONGINT; theType: ResType; source: Ptr)
          : LONGINT;
```

PutScrap writes the data pointed to by the source parameter to the desk scrap (in memory or on the disk). The length parameter indicates the number of bytes to write, and theType is the data type.

Warning: The specified type must be different from the type of any data already in the desk scrap. If you write data of a type already in the scrap, the new data will be appended to the scrap, and subsequent GetScrap calls will still return the old data.

If no error occurs, PutScrap returns the result code noErr; otherwise, it returns an Operating System result code indicating an error, or the following Scrap Manager result code:

```
CONST noScrapErr = -100;   {desk scrap isn't initialized}
```

Warning: Don't forget to call ZeroScrap to initialize the scrap or clear its previous contents.

Note: To copy the TextEdit scrap to the desk scrap, use the TextEdit function TEToScrap.

Reading from the Desk Scrap

```
FUNCTION GetScrap (hDest: Handle; theType: ResType; VAR offset:
          LONGINT) : LONGINT;
```

Given an existing handle in hDest, GetScrap reads the data of type theType from the desk scrap (whether in memory or on the disk), makes a copy of it in memory, and sets hDest to be a handle to the copy. Usually you'll pass in hDest a handle to a minimum-size block; GetScrap will resize the block and copy the scrap into it. If you pass NIL in hDest, GetScrap will not read in the data. This is useful if you want to be sure the data is there before allocating space for its handle, or if you just want to know the size of the data.

In the offset parameter, GetScrap returns the location of the data as an offset (in bytes) from the beginning of the desk scrap. If no error occurs, the function result is the length of the data in bytes; otherwise, it's either an appropriate Operating System result code (which will be negative) or the following Scrap Manager result code:

```
CONST noTypeErr = -102;   {no data of the requested type}
```

For example, given the declarations

```
VAR  pHndl: Handle;      {handle for 'PICT' type}
     tHndl: Handle;      {handle for 'TEXT' type}
     length: LONGINT;
     offset: LONGINT;
     frame: Rect;
```

Inside Macintosh

you can make the following calls:

```
pHndl := NewHandle(0);
length := GetScrap(pHndl,'PICT',offset);
IF length < 0
    THEN
        {error handling}
    ELSE DrawPicture(PicHandle(pHndl),frame)
```

If your application wants data in the form of a picture, and the scrap contains only text, you can convert the text into a picture by doing the following:

```
tHndl := NewHandle(0);
length := GetScrap(tHndl,'TEXT',offset);
IF length < 0
    THEN
        {error handling}
    ELSE
        BEGIN
        HLock(tHndl);
        pHndl := OpenPicture(thePort^.portRect);
        TextBox(tHndl^,length,thePort^.portRect,teJustLeft);
        ClosePicture;
        HUnlock(tHndl);
        END
```

The Memory Manager procedures HLock and HUnlock are used to lock and unlock blocks when handles are dereferenced (see chapter 1 of Volume II).

Note: To copy the desk scrap to the TextEdit scrap, use the TextEdit function TEFromScrap.

Your application should pass its preferred data type to GetScrap. If it doesn't prefer one data type over any other, it should try getting each of the types it can read, and use the type that returns the lowest offset. (A lower offset means that this data type was written before the others, and therefore was preferred by the application that wrote it.)

Note: If you're trying to read in a complicated picture, and there isn't enough room in memory for a copy of it, you can customize QuickDraw's picture retrieval so that DrawPicture will read the picture directly from the scrap file. (QuickDraw also lets you customize how pictures are saved so you can save them in a file; see chapter 6 for details about customizing.)

Note: When reading in a picture from the scrap, allow a buffer of about 3.5K bytes on the stack. (There's a convention that the application defining the picture won't call the QuickDraw procedure CopyBits for more than 3K, so 3.5K bytes should be large enough for any picture.)

PRIVATE SCRAPS

Instead of using the desk scrap for storing data that's cut and pasted within an application, advanced programmers may want to set up a private scrap for this purpose. In applications that use the standard 'TEXT' or 'PICT' data types, it's simpler to use the desk scrap, but if your application defines its own private type of data, or if it's likely that very large amounts of data will be cut and pasted, using a private scrap may result in faster cutting and pasting within the application.

The format of a private scrap can be whatever the application likes, since no other application will use it. For example, an application can simply maintain a pointer to data that's been cut or copied. The application must, however, be able to convert data between the format of its private scrap and the format of the desk scrap.

> **Note:** The TextEdit scrap is a private scrap for applications that use TextEdit. TextEdit provides routines for accessing this scrap; you'll need to transfer data between the TextEdit scrap and the desk scrap.

If you use a private scrap, you must be sure that the right data will always be pasted when the user gives a Paste command (the right data being whatever was most recently cut or copied in any application or desk accessory), and that the Clipboard, if visible, always shows the current data. You should copy the contents of the desk scrap to your private scrap at application startup and whenever a desk accessory is deactivated (call GetScrap to access the desk scrap). When the application is terminated or when a desk accessory is activated, you should copy the contents of the private scrap to the desk scrap: Call ZeroScrap to initialize the desk scrap or clear its previous contents, and PutScrap to write data to the desk scrap.

If transferring data between the two scraps means converting it, and possibly losing information, you can copy the scrap only when you actually need to, at the time something is cut or pasted. The desk scrap needn't be copied to the private scrap unless a Paste command is given before the first Cut or Copy command since the application started up or since a desk accessory that changed the scrap was deactivated. Until that point, you must keep the contents of the desk scrap intact, displaying it instead of the private scrap in the Clipboard window if that window is visible. Thereafter, you can ignore the desk scrap until a desk accessory is activated or the application is terminated; in either of these cases, you must copy the private scrap back to the desk scrap. Thus whatever was last cut or copied within the application will be pasted if a Paste command is given in a desk accessory or in the next application. If no Cut or Copy commands are given within the application, you never have to change the desk scrap.

To find out whether a desk accessory has changed the desk scrap, you can check the scrapCount field of the record returned by InfoScrap. Save the value of this field when one of your application's windows is deactivated and a system window is activated. Check each time through the main event loop to see whether its value has changed; if so, the contents of the desk scrap have changed.

If the application encounters problems in trying to copy one scrap to another, it should alert the user. The desk scrap may be too large to copy to the private scrap, in which case the user may want to leave the application or just proceed with an empty Clipboard. If the private scrap is too large to copy to the desk scrap, either because it's disk-based and too large to copy into memory or because it exceeds the maximum size allowed for the desk scrap, the user may want to stay in the application and cut or copy something smaller.

Inside Macintosh

FORMAT OF THE DESK SCRAP

In general, the desk scrap consists of a series of data items that have the following format:

Number of bytes	Contents
4 bytes	Type (a sequence of four characters)
4 bytes	Length of following data in bytes
n bytes	Data; n must be even (if the above length is odd, add an extra byte)

The standard types are 'TEXT' and 'PICT'. You may use any other four-character sequence for types specific to your application.

The format of the data for the 'TEXT' type is as follows:

Number of bytes	Contents
4 bytes	Number of characters in the text
n bytes	The characters in the text

The data for the 'PICT' type is a QuickDraw picture, which consists of the size of the picture in bytes, the picture frame, and the picture definition data (which may include picture comments). See chapter 6 for details.

SUMMARY OF THE SCRAP MANAGER

Constants

```
CONST { Scrap Manager result codes }

    noScrapErr = -100;   {desk scrap isn't initialized}
    noTypeErr  = -102;   {no data of the requested type}
```

Data Types

```
TYPE PScrapStuff = ^ScrapStuff;
     ScrapStuff  = RECORD
                     scrapSize:   LONGINT;   {size of desk scrap}
                     scrapHandle: Handle;    {handle to desk scrap}
                     scrapCount:  INTEGER;   {count changed by ZeroScrap}
                     scrapState:  INTEGER;   {tells where desk scrap is}
                     scrapName:   StringPtr  {scrap file name}
                   END;
```

Routines

Getting Desk Scrap Information

```
FUNCTION InfoScrap : PScrapStuff;
```

Keeping the Desk Scrap on the Disk

```
FUNCTION UnloadScrap : LONGINT;
FUNCTION LoadScrap   : LONGINT;
```

Writing to the Desk Scrap

```
FUNCTION ZeroScrap : LONGINT;
FUNCTION PutScrap  (length: LONGINT; theType: ResType; source: Ptr) :
                    LONGINT;
```

Reading from the Desk Scrap

```
FUNCTION GetScrap (hDest: Handle; theType: ResType; VAR offset: LONGINT)
                  : LONGINT;
```

Inside Macintosh

Assembly-Language Information

Constants

```
; Scrap Manager result codes

noScrapErr      .EQU    -100    ;desk scrap isn't initialized
noTypeErr       .EQU    -102    ;no data of the requested type
```

Special Macro Names

Pascal name	Macro name
LoadScrap	_LodeScrap
UnloadScrap	_UnlodeScrap

Variables

ScrapSize	Size in bytes of desk scrap (long)
ScrapHandle	Handle to desk scrap in memory
ScrapCount	Count changed by ZeroScrap (word)
ScrapState	Tells where desk scrap is (word)
ScrapName	Pointer to scrap file name (preceded by length byte)

16 TOOLBOX UTILITIES

467	About This Chapter
467	Toolbox Utility Routines
467	Fixed-Point Arithmetic
468	String Manipulation
468	Byte Manipulation
470	Bit Manipulation
471	Logical Operations
472	Other Operations on Long Integers
473	Graphics Utilities
475	Miscellaneous Utilities
476	Formats of Miscellaneous Resources
477	Summary of the Toolbox Utilities

ABOUT THIS CHAPTER

This chapter describes the Toolbox Utilities, a set of routines and data types in the Toolbox that perform generally useful operations such as fixed-point arithmetic, string manipulation, and logical operations on bits.

Depending on which Toolbox Utilities you're interested in using, you may need to be familiar with:

- resources, as described in chapter 5
- the basic concepts and structures behind QuickDraw

TOOLBOX UTILITY ROUTINES

Fixed-Point Arithmetic

Fixed-point numbers are described in chapter 3. Note that fixed-point values can be added and subtracted as long integers.

In addition to the following routines, the HiWord and LoWord functions (described under "Other Operations on Long Integers" below) are useful when you're working with fixed-point numbers.

```
FUNCTION FixRatio (numer,denom: INTEGER) : Fixed;
```

FixRatio returns the fixed-point quotient of numer and denom. Numer or denom may be any signed integer. The result is truncated. If denom is 0, FixRatio returns $7FFFFFFF if numer is positive or $80000001 if numer is negative.

```
FUNCTION FixMul (a,b: Fixed) : Fixed;
```

FixMul returns the signed fixed-point product of a and b. The result is computed MOD 65536, truncated, and signed according to the signs of a and b.

```
FUNCTION FixRound (x: Fixed) : INTEGER;
```

Given a positive fixed-point number, FixRound rounds it to the nearest integer and returns the result. If the value is halfway between two integers (.5), it's rounded up.

> **Note:** To round a negative fixed-point number, negate it, round, then negate it again.

Inside Macintosh

String Manipulation

```
FUNCTION NewString (theString: Str255) : StringHandle;
```

NewString allocates the specified string as a relocatable object in the heap and returns a handle to it.

> **Note:** NewString returns a handle to a string whose size is based on its actual length (not necessarily 255); if you're going to use Pascal string functions that could change the length of the string, you may want to call SetString or the Memory Manager procedure SetHandleSize first to set the string to the maximum size.

```
PROCEDURE SetString (h: StringHandle; theString: Str255);
```

SetString sets the string whose handle is passed in h to the string specified by theString.

```
FUNCTION GetString (stringID: INTEGER) : StringHandle;
```

GetString returns a handle to the string having the given resource ID, reading it from the resource file if necessary. It calls the Resource Manager function GetResource('STR ',stringID). If the resource can't be read, GetString returns NIL.

> **Note:** Like NewString, GetString returns a handle to a string whose size is based on its actual length.

> **Note:** If your application uses a large number of strings, storing them in a string list in the resource file will be more efficient. You can access strings in a string list with GetIndString, as described below.

```
PROCEDURE GetIndString (VAR theString: Str255; strListID:
        INTEGER; index: INTEGER);   [Not in ROM]
```

GetIndString returns in theString a string in the string list that has the resource ID strListID. It reads the string list from the resource file if necessary, by calling the Resource Manager function GetResource('STR#',strListID). It returns the string specified by the index parameter, which can range from 1 to the number of strings in the list. If the resource can't be read or the index is out of range, the empty string is returned.

Byte Manipulation

```
FUNCTION Munger (h: Handle; offset: LONGINT; ptr1: Ptr; len1:
        LONGINT; ptr2: Ptr; len2: LONGINT) : LONGINT;
```

Munger (which rhymes with "plunger") lets you manipulate bytes in the string of bytes (the "destination string") to which h is a handle. The operation starts at the specified byte offset in the destination string.

Note: Although the term "string" is used here, Munger does *not* assume it's manipulating a Pascal string; if you pass it a handle to a Pascal string, you must take into account the length byte.

The exact nature of the operation done by Munger depends on the values you pass it in two pointer/length parameter pairs. In general, (ptr1,len1) defines a target string to be replaced by the second string (ptr2,len2). If these four parameters are all positive and nonzero, Munger looks for the target string in the destination string, starting from the given offset and ending at the end of the string; it replaces the first occurrence it finds with the replacement string and returns the offset of the first byte past where the replacement occurred. Figure 1 illustrates this; the bytes represent ASCII characters as shown.

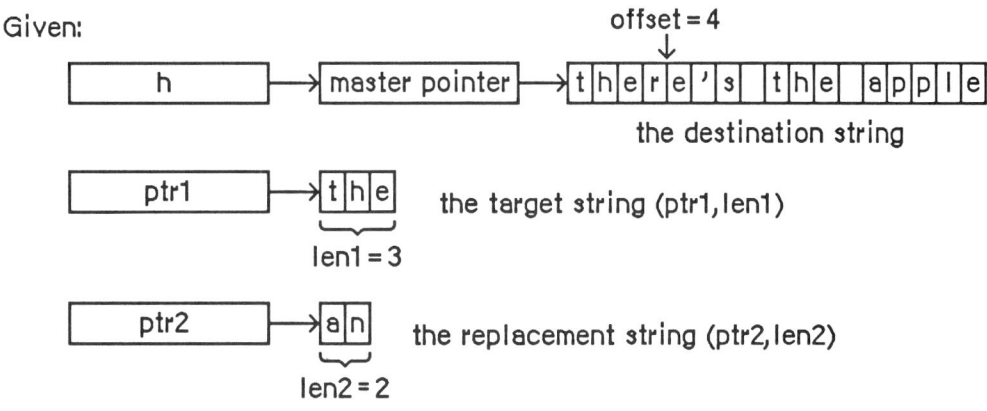

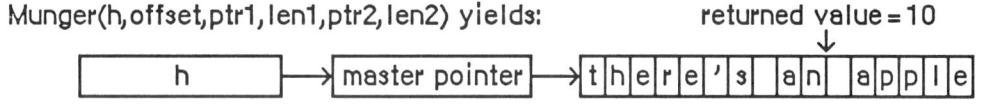

Figure 1. Munger Function

Different operations occur if either pointer is NIL or either length is 0:

- If ptr1 is NIL, the substring of length len1 starting at the given offset is replaced by the replacement string. If len1 is negative, the substring from the given offset to the end of the destination string is replaced by the replacement string. In either case, Munger returns the offset of the first byte past where the replacement occurred.

- If len1 is 0, (ptr2,len2) is simply inserted at the given offset; no text is replaced. Munger returns the offset of the first byte past where the insertion occurred.

- If ptr2 is NIL, Munger returns the offset at which the target string was found. The destination string isn't changed.

- If len2 is 0 (and ptr2 is *not* NIL), the target string is deleted rather than replaced (since the replacement string is empty). Munger returns the offset at which the deletion occurred.

If it can't find the target string in the destination string, Munger returns a negative value.

There's one case in which Munger performs a replacement even if it doesn't find all of the target string. If the substring from the offset to the end of the destination string matches the beginning of the target string, the portion found is replaced with the replacement string.

Inside Macintosh

Warning: Be careful not to specify an offset that's greater than the length of the destination string, or unpredictable results may occur.

Note: The destination string must be in a relocatable block that was allocated by the Memory Manager. Munger accesses the string's length by calling the Memory Manager routines GetHandleSize and SetHandleSize.

```
PROCEDURE PackBits (VAR srcPtr,dstPtr: Ptr; srcBytes: INTEGER);
```

PackBits compresses srcBytes bytes of data starting at srcPtr and stores the compressed data at dstPtr. The value of srcBytes should not be greater than 127. Bytes are compressed when there are three or more consecutive equal bytes. After the data is compressed, srcPtr is incremented by srcBytes and dstPtr is incremented by the number of bytes that the data was compressed to. In the worst case, the compressed data can be one byte longer than the original data.

PackBits is usually used to compress QuickDraw bit images; in this case, you should call it for one row at a time. (Because of the repeating patterns in QuickDraw images, there are more likely to be consecutive equal bytes there than in other data.) Use UnpackBits (below) to expand data compressed by PackBits.

```
PROCEDURE UnpackBits (VAR srcPtr,dstPtr: Ptr; dstBytes: INTEGER);
```

Given in srcPtr a pointer to data that was compressed by PackBits, UnpackBits expands the data and stores the result at dstPtr. DstBytes is the length that the expanded data will be; it should be the value that was passed to PackBits in the srcBytes parameter. After the data is expanded, srcPtr is incremented by the number of bytes that were expanded and dstPtr is incremented by dstBytes.

Bit Manipulation

Given a pointer and an offset, these routines can manipulate any specific bit. The pointer can point to an even or odd byte; the offset can be any positive long integer, starting at 0 for the high-order bit of the specified byte (see Figure 2).

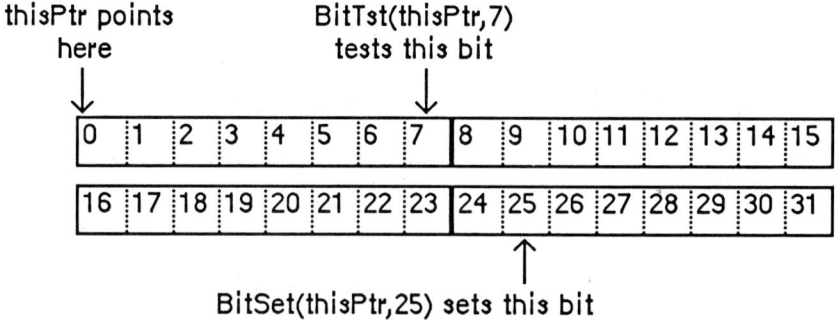

Figure 2. Bit Numbering for Utility Routines

Toolbox Utilities

Note: This bit numbering is the opposite of the MC68000 bit numbering to allow for greater generality. For example, you can directly access bit 1000 of a bit image given a pointer to the beginning of the bit image.

```
FUNCTION BitTst (bytePtr: Ptr; bitNum: LONGINT) : BOOLEAN;
```

BitTst tests whether a given bit is set and returns TRUE if so or FALSE if not. The bit is specified by bitNum, an offset from the high-order bit of the byte pointed to by bytePtr.

```
PROCEDURE BitSet (bytePtr: Ptr; bitNum: LONGINT);
```

BitSet sets the bit specified by bitNum, an offset from the high-order bit of the byte pointed to by bytePtr.

```
PROCEDURE BitClr (bytePtr: Ptr; bitNum: LONGINT);
```

BitSet clears the bit specified by bitNum, an offset from the high-order bit of the byte pointed to by bytePtr.

Logical Operations

```
FUNCTION BitAnd (value1,value2: LONGINT) : LONGINT;
```

BitAnd returns the result of the AND logical operation on the bits comprising the given long integers (value1 AND value2).

```
FUNCTION BitOr (value1,value2: LONGINT) : LONGINT;
```

BitOr returns the result of the OR logical operation on the bits comprising given long integers (value1 OR value2).

```
FUNCTION BitXor (value1,value2: LONGINT) : LONGINT;
```

BitXor returns the result of the XOR logical operation on the bits comprising the given long integers (value1 XOR value2).

```
FUNCTION BitNot (value: LONGINT) : LONGINT;
```

BitNot returns the result of the NOT logical operation on the bits comprising the given long integer (NOT value).

Inside Macintosh

```
FUNCTION BitShift (value: LONGINT; count: INTEGER) : LONGINT;
```

BitShift logically shifts the bits of the given long integer. The count parameter specifies the direction and extent of the shift, and is taken MOD 32. If count is positive, BitShift shifts that many positions to the left; if count is negative, it shifts to the right. Zeroes are shifted into empty positions at either end.

Other Operations on Long Integers

```
FUNCTION HiWord (x: LONGINT) : INTEGER;
```

HiWord returns the high-order word of the given long integer. One use of this function is to extract the integer part of a fixed-point number.

```
FUNCTION LoWord (x: LONGINT) : INTEGER;
```

LoWord returns the low-order word of the given long integer. One use of this function is to extract the fractional part of a fixed-point number.

> **Note:** If you're dealing with a long integer that contains two separate integer values, you can define a variant record instead of using HiWord and LoWord. For example, for fixed-point numbers, you could define the following type:
>
> ```
>     TYPE FixedAndInt =  RECORD CASE INTEGER OF
>                           1: (fixedView:  Fixed);
>                           2: (intView:    RECORD
>                                             whole: INTEGER;
>                                             part:  INTEGER
>                                           END;
>                         END;
> ```
>
> If you declare x to be of type FixedAndInt, you can access it as a fixed-point value with x.fixedView, or access the integer part with x.intView.whole and the fractional part with x.intView.part.

```
PROCEDURE LongMul (a,b: LONGINT; VAR dest: Int64Bit);
```

LongMul multiplies the given long integers and returns the signed result in dest, which has the following data type:

```
    TYPE Int64Bit = RECORD
                      hiLong: LONGINT;
                      loLong: LONGINT
                    END;
```

Toolbox Utilities

Graphics Utilities

```
PROCEDURE ScreenRes (VAR scrnHRes,scrnVRes: INTEGER);   [Not in ROM]
```

ScreenRes returns the resolution of the screen of the Macintosh being used. ScrnHRes and scrnVRes are the number of pixels per inch horizontally and vertically, respectively.

Assembly-language note: The number of pixels per inch horizontally is stored in the global variable ScrHRes, and the number of pixels per inch vertically is stored in ScrVRes.

```
FUNCTION GetIcon (iconID: INTEGER) : Handle;
```

GetIcon returns a handle to the icon having the given resource ID, reading it from the resource file if necessary. It calls the Resource Manager function GetResource('ICON',iconID). If the resource can't be read, GetIcon returns NIL.

```
PROCEDURE PlotIcon (theRect: Rect; theIcon: Handle);
```

PlotIcon draws the icon whose handle is theIcon in the rectangle theRect, which is in the local coordinates of the current grafPort. It calls the QuickDraw procedure CopyBits and uses the srcCopy transfer mode.

```
FUNCTION GetPattern (patID: INTEGER) : PatHandle;
```

GetPattern returns a handle to the pattern having the given resource ID, reading it from the resource file if necessary. It calls the Resource Manager function GetResource('PAT ',patID). If the resource can't be read, GetPattern returns NIL. The PatHandle data type is defined in the Toolbox Utilities as follows:

```
TYPE  PatPtr    = ^Pattern;
      PatHandle = ^PatPtr;
```

```
PROCEDURE GetIndPattern (VAR thePattern: Pattern; patListID:
          INTEGER; index: INTEGER);   [Not in ROM]
```

GetIndPattern returns in thePattern a pattern in the pattern list that has the resource ID patListID. It reads the pattern list from the resource file if necessary, by calling the Resource Manager function GetResource('PAT#',patListID). It returns the pattern specified by the index parameter, which can range from 1 to the number of patterns in the pattern list.

There's a pattern list in the system resource file that contains the standard Macintosh patterns used by MacPaint (see Figure 3). Its resource ID is:

```
CONST sysPatListID = 0;
```

Toolbox Utility Routines I-473

Inside Macintosh

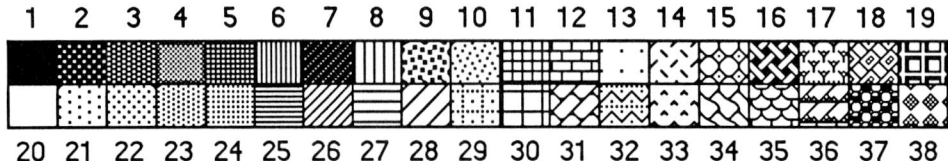

Figure 3. Standard Patterns

```
FUNCTION GetCursor (cursorID: INTEGER) : CursHandle;
```

GetCursor returns a handle to the cursor having the given resource ID, reading it from the resource file if necessary. It calls the Resource Manager function GetResource('CURS',cursorID). If the resource can't be read, GetCursor returns NIL. The CursHandle data type is defined in the Toolbox Utilities as follows:

```
TYPE  CursPtr    = ^Cursor;
      CursHandle = ^CursPtr;
```

The standard cursors shown in Figure 4 are defined in the system resource file. Their resource IDs are:

```
CONST iBeamCursor = 1;   {to select text}
      crossCursor = 2;   {to draw graphics}
      plusCursor  = 3;   {to select cells in structured documents}
      watchCursor = 4;   {to indicate a long wait}
```

  I   +   ✥   ⌚
iBeamCursor crossCursor plusCursor watchCursor

Figure 4. Standard Cursors

Note: You can set the cursor with the QuickDraw procedure SetCursor. The arrow cursor is defined in QuickDraw as a global variable named arrow.

```
PROCEDURE ShieldCursor (shieldRect: Rect; offsetPt: Point);
```

If the cursor and the given rectangle intersect, ShieldCursor hides the cursor. If they don't intersect, the cursor remains visible while the mouse isn't moving, but is hidden when the mouse moves.

Like the QuickDraw procedure HideCursor, ShieldCursor decrements the cursor level, and should be balanced by a call to ShowCursor.

The rectangle may be given in global or local coordinates:

- If they're global coordinates, pass (0,0) in offsetPt.

- If they're a grafPort's local coordinates, pass the top left corner of the grafPort's boundary rectangle in offsetPt. (Like the QuickDraw procedure LocalToGlobal, ShieldCursor will offset the coordinates of the rectangle by the coordinates of this point.)

```
FUNCTION GetPicture (picID: INTEGER) : PicHandle;
```

GetPicture returns a handle to the picture having the given resource ID, reading it from the resource file if necessary. It calls the Resource Manager function GetResource('PICT',picID). If the resource can't be read, GetPicture returns NIL. The PicHandle data type is defined in QuickDraw.

Miscellaneous Utilities

```
FUNCTION DeltaPoint (ptA,ptB: Point) : LONGINT;
```

DeltaPoint subtracts the coordinates of ptB from the coordinates of ptA. The high-order word of the result is the difference of the vertical coordinates and the low-order word is the difference of the horizontal coordinates.

> **Note:** The QuickDraw procedure SubPt also subtracts the coordinates of one point from another, but returns the result in a VAR parameter of type Point.

```
FUNCTION SlopeFromAngle (angle: INTEGER) : Fixed;
```

Given an angle, SlopeFromAngle returns the slope dh/dv of the line forming that angle with the y-axis (dh/dv is the horizontal change divided by the vertical change between any two points on the line). Figure 5 illustrates SlopeFromAngle (and AngleFromSlope, described below, which does the reverse). The angle is treated MOD 180, and is in degrees measured from 12 o'clock; positive degrees are measured clockwise, negative degrees are measured counterclockwise (for example, 90 degrees is at 3 o'clock and –90 degrees is at 9 o'clock). Positive y is down; positive x is to the right.

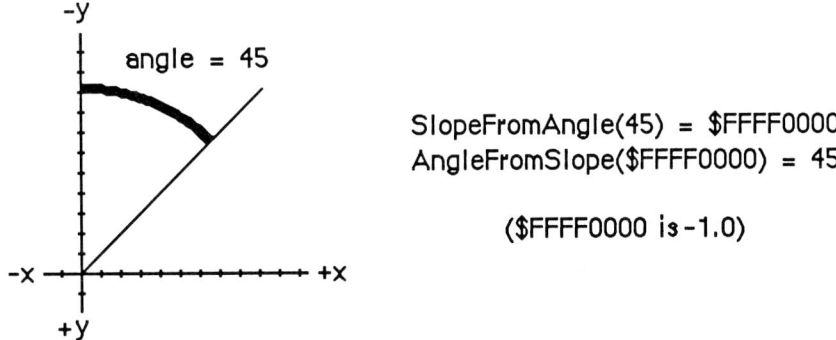

Figure 5. SlopeFromAngle and AngleFromSlope

```
FUNCTION AngleFromSlope (slope: Fixed) : INTEGER;
```

Given the slope dh/dv of a line (see SlopeFromAngle above), AngleFromSlope returns the angle formed by that line and the y-axis. The angle returned is between 1 and 180 (inclusive), in degrees measured clockwise from 12 o'clock.

AngleFromSlope is meant for use when speed is much more important than accuracy—its integer result is guaranteed to be within one degree of the correct answer, but not necessarily within half a degree. However, the equation

AngleFromSlope(SlopeFromAngle(x)) = x

is true for all x except 0 (although its reverse is not).

Note: SlopeFromAngle(0) is 0, and AngleFromSlope(0) is 180.

FORMATS OF MISCELLANEOUS RESOURCES

The following table shows the exact format of various resources. For more information about the contents of the graphics-related resources, see chapter 6.

Resource	Resource type	Number of bytes	Contents
Icon	'ICON'	128 bytes	The icon
Icon list	'ICN#'	n * 128 bytes	n icons
Pattern	'PAT '	8 bytes	The pattern
Pattern list	'PAT#'	2 bytes n * 8 bytes	Number of patterns n patterns
Cursor	'CURS'	32 bytes 32 bytes 4 bytes	The data The mask The hotSpot
Picture	'PICT'	2 bytes 8 bytes m bytes	Picture length (m+10) Picture frame Picture definition data
String	'STR '	m bytes	The string (1-byte length followed by the characters)
String list	'STR#'	2 bytes m bytes	Number of strings The strings

Note: Unlike a pattern list or a string list, an icon list doesn't start with the number of items in the list.

SUMMARY OF THE TOOLBOX UTILITIES

Constants

```
CONST  { Resource ID of standard pattern list }

       sysPatListID = 0;

       { Resource IDs of standard cursors }

       iBeamCursor  = 1;    {to select text}
       crossCursor  = 2;    {to draw graphics}
       plusCursor   = 3;    {to select cells in structured documents}
       watchCursor  = 4;    {to indicate a long wait}
```

Data Types

```
TYPE Int64Bit  =  RECORD
                    hiLong: LONGINT;
                    loLong: LONGINT
                  END;

     CursPtr    = ^Cursor;
     CursHandle = ^CursPtr;

     PatPtr     = ^Pattern;
     PatHandle  = ^PatPtr;
```

Routines

Fixed-Point Arithmetic

```
FUNCTION FixRatio (numer,denom: INTEGER) : Fixed;
FUNCTION FixMul   (a,b: Fixed) : Fixed;
FUNCTION FixRound (x: Fixed) : INTEGER;
```

String Manipulation

```
FUNCTION  NewString    (theString: Str255) : StringHandle;
PROCEDURE SetString    (h: StringHandle; theString: Str255);
FUNCTION  GetString    (stringID: INTEGER) : StringHandle;
PROCEDURE GetIndString (VAR theString: Str255; strListID: INTEGER;
                        index: INTEGER);   [Not in ROM]
```

Inside Macintosh

Byte Manipulation

```
FUNCTION   Munger     (h: Handle; offset: LONGINT; ptr1: Ptr; len1:
                       LONGINT; ptr2: Ptr; len2: LONGINT) : LONGINT;
PROCEDURE  PackBits   (VAR srcPtr,dstPtr: Ptr; srcBytes: INTEGER);
PROCEDURE  UnpackBits (VAR srcPtr,dstPtr: Ptr; dstBytes: INTEGER);
```

Bit Manipulation

```
FUNCTION   BitTst  (bytePtr: Ptr; bitNum: LONGINT) : BOOLEAN;
PROCEDURE  BitSet  (bytePtr: Ptr; bitNum: LONGINT);
PROCEDURE  BitClr  (bytePtr: Ptr; bitNum: LONGINT);
```

Logical Operations

```
FUNCTION BitAnd   (value1,value2: LONGINT) : LONGINT;
FUNCTION BitOr    (value1,value2: LONGINT) : LONGINT;
FUNCTION BitXor   (value1,value2: LONGINT) : LONGINT;
FUNCTION BitNot   (value: LONGINT) : LONGINT;
FUNCTION BitShift (value: LONGINT; count: INTEGER) : LONGINT;
```

Other Operations on Long Integers

```
FUNCTION   HiWord  (x: LONGINT) : INTEGER;
FUNCTION   LoWord  (x: LONGINT) : INTEGER;
PROCEDURE  LongMul (a,b: LONGINT; VAR dest: Int64Bit);
```

Graphics Utilities

```
PROCEDURE  ScreenRes     (VAR scrnHRes,scrnVRes: INTEGER);   [Not in ROM]
FUNCTION   GetIcon       (iconID: INTEGER) : Handle;
PROCEDURE  PlotIcon      (theRect: Rect; theIcon: Handle);
FUNCTION   GetPattern    (patID: INTEGER) : PatHandle;
PROCEDURE  GetIndPattern (VAR thePattern: Pattern; patListID: INTEGER;
                          index: INTEGER);   [Not in ROM]
FUNCTION   GetCursor     (cursorID: INTEGER) : CursHandle;
PROCEDURE  ShieldCursor  (shieldRect: Rect; offsetPt: Point);
FUNCTION   GetPicture    (picID: INTEGER) : PicHandle;
```

Miscellaneous Utilities

```
FUNCTION DeltaPoint     (ptA,ptB: Point) : LONGINT;
FUNCTION SlopeFromAngle (angle: INTEGER) : Fixed;
FUNCTION AngleFromSlope (slope: Fixed) : INTEGER;
```

Assembly-Language Information

Constants

```
; Resource ID of standard pattern list

sysPatListID      .EQU    0

; Resource IDs of standard cursors

iBeamCursor       .EQU    1       ;to select text
crossCursor       .EQU    2       ;to draw graphics
plusCursor        .EQU    3       ;to select cells in structured documents
watchCursor       .EQU    4       ;to indicate a long wait
```

Variables

ScrVRes	Pixels per inch vertically (word)
ScrHRes	Pixels per inch horizontally (word)

17 THE PACKAGE MANAGER

483   About This Chapter
483   About Packages
484   Package Manager Routines
485   Summary of the Package Manager

The Package Manager

ABOUT THIS CHAPTER

This chapter describes the Package Manager, which is the part of the Toolbox that provides access to **packages**. The Macintosh packages include one for presenting the standard user interface when a file is to be saved or opened, and others for doing more specialized operations such as floating-point arithmetic.

You should already be familiar with the Resource Manager.

ABOUT PACKAGES

Packages are sets of data types and routines that are stored as resources and brought into memory only when needed. They serve as extensions to the Toolbox and Operating System, for the most part performing less common operations.

The Macintosh packages, which are stored in the system resource file, include the following:

- The Standard File Package, for presenting the standard user interface when a file is to be saved or opened.
- The Disk Initialization Package, for initializing and naming new disks. This package is called by the Standard File Package; you'll only need to call it in nonstandard situations.
- The International Utilities Package, for accessing country-dependent information such as the formats for numbers, currency, dates, and times.
- The Binary-Decimal Conversion Package, for converting integers to decimal strings and vice versa.
- The Floating-Point Arithmetic Package, which supports extended-precision arithmetic according to IEEE Standard 754.
- The Transcendental Functions Package, which contains trigonometric, logarithmic, exponential, and financial functions, as well as a random number generator.

Packages have the resource type 'PACK' and the following resource IDs:

```
CONST dskInit = 2;     {Disk Initialization}
      stdFile = 3;     {Standard File}
      flPoint = 4;     {Floating-Point Arithmetic}
      trFunc  = 5;     {Transcendental Functions}
      intUtil = 6;     {International Utilities}
      bdConv  = 7;     {Binary-Decimal Conversion}
```

> **Assembly-language note:** Just as for the routines in ROM, you can invoke a package routine with a macro that has the same name as the routine preceded by an underscore. These macros, however, aren't trap macros themselves; instead, they expand to invoke the trap macro _PackN, where N is the resource ID of the package. The package determines which routine to execute from the **routine selector**, an integer that's passed to it in a word on the stack. For example, the routine selector for the Standard File Package procedure SFPutFile is 1, so invoking the macro _SFPutFile pushes 1 onto the stack and

Inside Macintosh

invokes _Pack3. The routines in the Floating-Point Arithmetic and Transcendental Functions packages also invoke a trap macro of the form _PackN, but the mechanism through which they're called is somewhat different, as explained in the chapter describing those packages.

PACKAGE MANAGER ROUTINES

There are two Package Manager routines that you can call directly from Pascal: one that lets you access a specified package and one that lets you access all packages. The latter will already have been called when your application starts up, so normally you won't ever have to call the Package Manager yourself. Its procedures are described below for advanced programmers who may want to use them in unusual situations.

```
PROCEDURE InitPack (packID: INTEGER);
```

InitPack enables you to use the package specified by packID, which is the package's resource ID. (It gets a handle that will be used later to read the package into memory.)

```
PROCEDURE InitAllPacks;
```

InitAllPacks enables you to use all Macintosh packages (as though InitPack were called for each one). It will already have been called when your application starts up.

SUMMARY OF THE PACKAGE MANAGER

Constants

```
CONST  { Resource IDs for packages }

       dskInit  = 2;      {Disk Initialization}
       stdFile  = 3;      {Standard File}
       flPoint  = 4;      {Floating-Point Arithmetic}
       trFunc   = 5;      {Transcendental Functions}
       intUtil  = 6;      {International Utilities}
       bdConv   = 7;      {Binary-Decimal Conversion}
```

Routines

```
PROCEDURE InitPack      (packID: INTEGER);
PROCEDURE InitAllPacks;
```

Assembly-Language Information

Constants

```
; Resource IDs for packages

dskInit    .EQU    2     ;Disk Initialization
stdFile    .EQU    3     ;Standard File
flPoint    .EQU    4     ;Floating-Point Arithmetic
trFunc     .EQU    5     ;Transcendental Functions
intUtil    .EQU    6     ;International Utilities
bdConv     .EQU    7     ;Binary-Decimal Conversion
```

Trap Macros for Packages

Disk Initialization	_Pack2	
Standard File	_Pack3	
Floating-Point Arithmetic	_Pack4	(synonym: _FP68K)
Transcendental Functions	_Pack5	(synonym: _Elems68K)
International Utilities	_Pack6	
Binary-Decimal Conversion	_Pack7	

18 THE BINARY-DECIMAL CONVERSION PACKAGE

489 About This Chapter
489 Binary-Decimal Conversion Package Routines
491 Summary of the Binary-Decimal Conversion Package

ABOUT THIS CHAPTER

This chapter describes the Binary-Decimal Conversion Package, which contains only two routines: One converts an integer from its internal (binary) form to a string that represents its decimal (base 10) value; the other converts a decimal string to the corresponding integer.

You should already be familiar with packages in general, as described in chapter 17.

BINARY-DECIMAL CONVERSION PACKAGE ROUTINES

The Binary-Decimal Conversion Package is automatically read into memory when one of its routines is called; it occupies a total of about 200 bytes. The routines are register-based, so the Pascal form of each is followed by a box containing information needed to use the routine from assembly language.

> **Assembly-language note:** The trap macro for the Binary-Decimal Conversion Package is _Pack7. The routine selectors are as follows:
>
> ```
> numToString   .EQU   0
> stringToNum   .EQU   1
> ```

```
PROCEDURE NumToString (theNum: LONGINT; VAR theString: Str255);
```

On entry	A0: pointer to theString (preceded by length byte)
	D0: theNum (long word)
On exit	A0: pointer to theString

NumToString converts theNum to a string that represents its decimal value, and returns the result in theString. If the value is negative, the string begins with a minus sign; otherwise, the sign is omitted. Leading zeroes are suppressed, except that the value 0 produces '0'. For example:

theNum	theString
12	'12'
−23	'−23'
0	'0'

Inside Macintosh

```
PROCEDURE StringToNum (theString: Str255; VAR theNum: LONGINT);
```

On entry	A0: pointer to theString (preceded by length byte)
On exit	D0: theNum (long word)

Given a string representing a decimal integer, StringToNum converts it to the corresponding integer and returns the result in theNum. The string may begin with a plus or minus sign. For example:

theString	theNum
'12'	12
'–23'	–23
'–0'	0
'055'	55

The magnitude of the integer is converted modulo 2^{32}, and the 32-bit result is negated if the string begins with a minus sign; integer overflow occurs if the magnitude is greater than $2^{31}-1$. (Negation is done by taking the two's complement—reversing the state of each bit and then adding 1.) For example:

theString	theNum
'2147483648' (magnitude is 2^{31})	–2147483648
'–2147483648'	–2147483648
'4294967295' (magnitude is $2^{32}-1$)	–1
'–4294967295'	1

StringToNum doesn't actually check whether the characters in the string are between '0' and '9'; instead, since the ASCII codes for '0' through '9' are $30 through $39, it just masks off the last four bits and uses them as a digit. For example, '2:' is converted to the number 30 because the ASCII code for ':' is $3A. Spaces are treated as zeroes, since the ASCII code for a space is $20. Given that the ASCII codes for 'C', 'A', and 'T' are $43, $41, and $54, respectively, consider the following examples:

theString	theNum
'CAT'	314
'+CAT'	314
'–CAT'	–314

The Binary-Decimal Conversion Package

SUMMARY OF THE BINARY-DECIMAL CONVERSION PACKAGE

Routines

```
PROCEDURE NumToString (theNum: LONGINT; VAR theString: Str255);
PROCEDURE StringToNum (theString: Str255; VAR theNum: LONGINT);
```

Assembly-Language Information

Constants

```
; Routine selectors

numToString     .EQU    0
stringToNum     .EQU    1
```

Routines

Name	On entry	On exit
NumToString	A0: ptr to theString (preceded by length byte) D0: theNum (long)	A0: ptr to theString
StringToNum	A0: ptr to theString (preceded by length byte)	D0: theNum (long)

Trap Macro Name

_Pack7

19 THE INTERNATIONAL UTILITIES PACKAGE

495   About This Chapter
495   International Resources
496   International Resource 0
500   International Resource 1
501   International String Comparison
503   Using the International Utilities Package
504   International Utilities Package Routines
508   Summary of the International Utilities Package

The International Utilities Package

ABOUT THIS CHAPTER

This chapter describes the International Utilities Package, which enables you to make your Macintosh application country-independent. Routines are provided for formatting dates and times and comparing strings in a way that's appropriate to the country where your application is being used. There's also a routine for testing whether to use the metric system of measurement. These routines access country-dependent information (stored in a resource file) that also tells how to format numbers and currency; you can access this information yourself for your own routines that may require it.

You should already be familiar with:

- resources, as discussed in chapter 5
- packages in general, as described in chapter 17

INTERNATIONAL RESOURCES

Country-dependent information is kept in the system resource file in two resources of type 'INTL', with the resource IDs 0 and 1:

- International resource 0 contains the formats for numbers, currency, and time, a short date format, and an indication of whether to use the metric system.
- International resource 1 contains a longer format for dates (spelling out the month and possibly the day of the week, with or without abbreviation) and a routine for localizing string comparison.

The system resource file released in each country contains the standard international resources for that country. Figure 1 illustrates the standard formats for the United States, Great Britain, Italy, Germany, and France.

The routines in the International Utilities Package use the information in these resources; for example, the routines for formatting dates and times yield strings that look like those shown in Figure 1. Routines in other packages, in desk accessories, and in ROM also access the international resources when necessary, as should your own routines if they need such information.

In some cases it may be appropriate to store either or both of the international resources in the application's or document's resource file, to override those in the system resource file. For example, suppose an application creates documents containing currency amounts and gets the currency format from international resource 0. Documents created by such an application should have their own copy of the international resource 0 that was used to create them, so that the unit of currency will be the same if the document is displayed on a Macintosh configured for another country.

Information about the exact components and structure of each international resource follows here; you can skip this if you intend only to call the formatting routines in the International Utilities Package and won't access the resources directly yourself.

Inside Macintosh

	United States	Great Britain	Italy	Germany	France
Numbers	1,234.56	1,234.56	1.234,56	1.234,56	1 234.56
List separator	;	,	;	;	;
Currency	$0.23	£0.23	L. 0,23	0,23 DM	0,23 F
	($0.45)	(£0.45)	L. -0,45	-0,45 DM	-0,45 F
	$345.00	£345	L. 345	325,00 DM	325 F
Time	9:05 AM	09:05	9:05	9.05 Uhr	9:05
	11:30 AM	11:30	11:30	11.30 Uhr	11:30
	11:20 PM	23:20	23:20	23.20 Uhr	23:20
	11:20:09 PM	23:20:00	23:20:09	23.20.09 Uhr	23:20:09
Short date	12/22/85	22/12/1985	22-12-1985	22.12.1985	22.12.85
	2/1/85	01/02/1985	1-02-1985	1.02.1985	1.02.85

		Unabbreviated	Abbreviated
Long date	United States	Wednesday, February 1, 1985	Wed, Feb 1, 1985
	Great Britain	Wednesday, February 1, 1985	Wed, Feb 1, 1985
	Italy	mercoledì 1 Febbraio 1985	mer 1 Feb 1985
	Germany	Mittwoch, 1. Februar 1985	Mit, 1. Feb 1985
	France	Mercredi 1 fevrier 1985	Mer 1 fev 1985

Figure 1. Standard International Formats

International Resource 0

The International Utilities Package contains the following data types for accessing international resource 0:

```
TYPE Intl0Hndl = ^Intl0Ptr;
     Intl0Ptr  = ^Intl0Rec;
```

The International Utilities Package

```
Intl0Rec   =
  PACKED RECORD
    decimalPt:      CHAR;      {decimal point character}
    thousSep:       CHAR;      {thousands separator}
    listSep:        CHAR;      {list separator}
    currSym1:       CHAR;      {currency symbol}
    currSym2:       CHAR;
    currSym3:       CHAR;
    currFmt:        Byte;      {currency format}
    dateOrder:      Byte;      {order of short date elements}
    shrtDateFmt:    Byte;      {short date format}
    dateSep:        CHAR;      {date separator}
    timeCycle:      Byte;      {0 if 24-hour cycle, 255 if 12-hour}
    timeFmt:        Byte;      {time format}
    mornStr:        PACKED ARRAY[1..4] OF CHAR;
                               {trailing string for first 12-hour cycle}
    eveStr:         PACKED ARRAY[1..4] OF CHAR;
                               {trailing string for last 12-hour cycle}
    timeSep:        CHAR;      {time separator}
    time1Suff:      CHAR;      {trailing string for 24-hour cycle}
    time2Suff:      CHAR;
    time3Suff:      CHAR;
    time4Suff:      CHAR;
    time5Suff:      CHAR;
    time6Suff:      CHAR;
    time7Suff:      CHAR;
    time8Suff:      CHAR;
    metricSys:      Byte;      {255 if metric, 0 if not}
    intl0Vers:      INTEGER    {version information}
  END;
```

Note: A NUL character (ASCII code 0) in a field of type CHAR means there's no such character. The currency symbol and the trailing string for the 24-hour cycle are separated into individual CHAR fields because of Pascal packing conventions. All strings include any required spaces.

The decimalPt, thousSep, and listSep fields define the number format. The **thousands separator** is the character that separates every three digits to the left of the decimal point. The **list separator** is the character that separates numbers, as when a list of numbers is entered by the user; it must be different from the decimal point character. If it's the same as the thousands separator, the user must not include the latter in entered numbers.

CurrSym1 through currSym3 define the currency symbol (only one character for the United States and Great Britain, but two for France and three for Italy and Germany). CurrFmt determines the rest of the currency format, as shown in Figure 2. The decimal point character and thousands separator for currency are the same as in the number format.

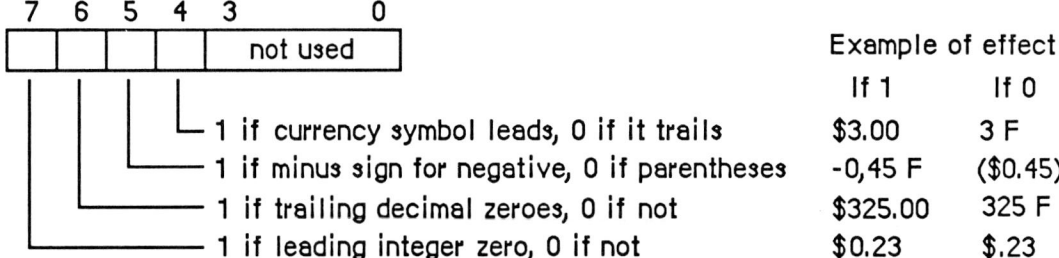

Figure 2. CurrFmt Field

The following predefined constants are masks that can be used to set or test the bits in the currFmt field:

```
CONST currSymLead   = 16;   {set if currency symbol leads}
      currNegSym    = 32;   {set if minus sign for negative}
      currTrailingZ = 64;   {set if trailing decimal zeroes}
      currLeadingZ  = 128;  {set if leading integer zero}
```

Note: You can also apply the currency format's leading- and trailing-zero indicators to the number format if desired.

The dateOrder, shrtDateFmt, and dateSep fields define the short date format. DateOrder indicates the order of the day, month, and year, with one of the following values:

```
CONST mdy = 0;   {month day year}
      dmy = 1;   {day month year}
      ymd = 2;   {year month day}
```

ShrtDateFmt determines whether to show leading zeroes in day and month numbers and whether to show the century, as illustrated in Figure 3. DateSep is the character that separates the different parts of the date.

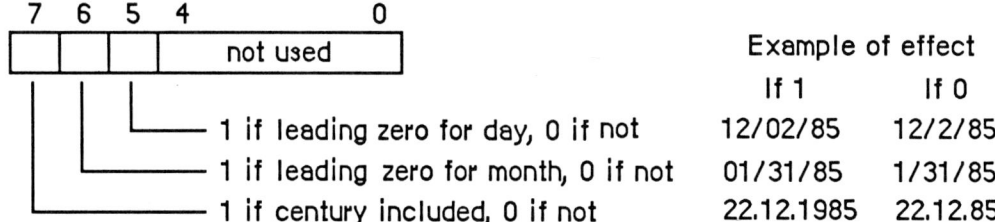

Figure 3. ShrtDateFmt Field

To set or test the bits in the shrtDateFmt field, you can use the following predefined constants as masks:

```
CONST dayLdingZ = 32;   {set if leading zero for day}
      mntLdingZ = 64;   {set if leading zero for month}
      century   = 128;  {set if century included}
```

The International Utilities Package

The next several fields define the time format: the cycle (12 or 24 hours); whether to show leading zeroes (timeFmt, as shown in Figure 4); a string to follow the time (two for 12-hour cycle, one for 24-hour); and the time separator character.

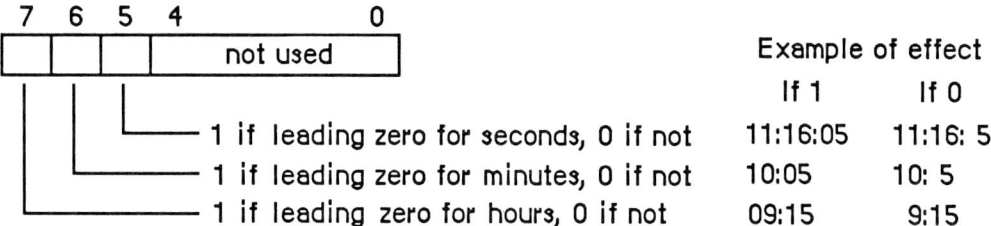

Figure 4. TimeFmt Field

The following masks are available for setting or testing bits in the timeFmt field:

```
CONST secLeadingZ = 32;   {set if leading zero for seconds}
      minLeadingZ = 64;   {set if leading zero for minutes}
      hrLeadingZ  = 128;  {set it leading zero for hours}
```

MetricSys indicates whether to use the metric system. The last field, intl0Vers, contains a version number in its low-order byte and one of the following constants in its high-order byte:

```
CONST verUS          = 0;
      verFrance      = 1;
      verBritain     = 2;
      verGermany     = 3;
      verItaly       = 4;
      verNetherlands = 5;
      verBelgiumLux  = 6;
      verSweden      = 7;
      verSpain       = 8;
      verDenmark     = 9;
      verPortugal    = 10;
      verFrCanada    = 11;
      verNorway      = 12;
      verIsrael      = 13;
      verJapan       = 14;
      verAustralia   = 15;
      verArabia      = 16;
      verFinland     = 17;
      verFrSwiss     = 18;
      verGrSwiss     = 19;
      verGreece      = 20;
      verIceland     = 21;
      verMalta       = 22;
      verCyprus      = 23;
      verTurkey      = 24;
      verYugoslavia  = 25;
```

International Resources I-499

Inside Macintosh

International Resource 1

The International Utilities Package contains the following data types for accessing international resource 1:

```
TYPE Intl1Hndl = ^Intl1Ptr;
     Intl1Ptr  = ^Intl1Rec;
     Intl1Rec  =
            PACKED RECORD
                days:         ARRAY[1..7] OF STRING[15];  {day names}
                months:       ARRAY[1..12] OF STRING[15]; {month names}
                suppressDay:  Byte;       {0 for day name, 255 for none}
                lngDateFmt:   Byte;       {order of long date elements}
                dayLeading0:  Byte;       {255 for leading 0 in day number}
                abbrLen:      Byte;       {length for abbreviating names}
                st0:          PACKED ARRAY[1..4] OF CHAR; {strings }
                st1:          PACKED ARRAY[1..4] OF CHAR; { for }
                st2:          PACKED ARRAY[1..4] OF CHAR; { long }
                st3:          PACKED ARRAY[1..4] OF CHAR; { date }
                st4:          PACKED ARRAY[1..4] OF CHAR; { format}
                intl1Vers:    INTEGER;    {version information}
                localRtn:     INTEGER     {routine for localizing string }
                                          { comparison; actually may be }
                                          { longer than one integer}
            END;
```

All fields except the last two determine the long date format. The day names in the days array are ordered from Sunday to Saturday. (The month names are of course ordered from January to December.) As shown below, the lngDateFmt field determines the order of the various parts of the date. St0 through st4 are strings (usually punctuation) that appear in the date.

lngDateFmt	Long date format								
0	st0	day name	st1	day	st2	month	st3	year	st4
255	st0	day name	st1	month	st2	day	st3	year	st4

See Figure 5 for examples of how the International Utilities Package formats dates based on these fields. The examples assume that the suppressDay and dayLeading0 fields contain 0. A suppressDay value of 255 causes the day name and st1 to be omitted, and a dayLeading value of 255 causes a 0 to appear before day numbers less than 10.

lngDateFmt	st0	st1	st2	st3	st4	Sample result
0	''	', '	'. '	' '	''	Mittwoch, 2. Februar 1985
255	''	', '	' '	', '	''	Wednesday, February 1, 1985

Figure 5. Long Date Formats

AbbrLen is the number of characters to which month and day names should be abbreviated when abbreviation is desired.

The intl1Vers field contains version information with the same format as the intl0Vers field of international resource 0.

LocalRtn contains a routine that localizes the built-in character ordering (as described below under "International String Comparison").

INTERNATIONAL STRING COMPARISON

The International Utilities Package lets you compare strings in a way that accounts for diacritical marks and other special characters. The sort order built into the package may be localized through a routine stored in international resource 1.

The sort order is determined by a ranking of the entire Macintosh character set. The ranking can be thought of as a two-dimensional table. Each row of the table is a class of characters such as all A's (uppercase and lowercase, with and without diacritical marks). The characters are ordered within each row, but this ordering is secondary to the order of the rows themselves. For example, given that the rows for letters are ordered alphabetically, the following are all true under this scheme:

	'A'	<	'a'
and	'Ab'	<	'ab'
but	'Ac'	>	'ab'

Even though 'A' < 'a' within the A row, 'Ac' > 'ab' because the order 'c' > 'b' takes precedence over the secondary ordering of the 'a' and the 'A'. In effect, the secondary ordering is ignored unless the comparison based on the primary ordering yields equality.

> **Note:** The Pascal relational operators are used here for convenience only. String comparison in Pascal yields very different results, since it simply follows the ordering of the characters' ASCII codes.

When the strings being compared are of different lengths, each character in the longer string that doesn't correspond to a character in the shorter one compares "greater"; thus 'a' < 'ab'. This takes precedence over secondary ordering, so 'a' < 'Ab' even though 'A' < 'a'.

Besides letting you compare strings as described above, the International Utilities Package includes a routine that compares strings for equality without regard for secondary ordering. The effect on comparing letters, for example, is that diacritical marks are ignored and uppercase and lowercase are not distinguished.

Figure 6 shows the two-dimensional ordering of the character set (from least to greatest as you read from top to bottom or left to right). The numbers on the left are ASCII codes corresponding to each row; ellipses (...) designate sequences of rows of just one character. Some codes do not correspond to rows (such as $61 through $7A, because lowercase letters are included in with their uppercase equivalents). See chapter 8 for a table showing all the characters and their ASCII codes.

Characters combining two letters, as in the $AE row, are called **ligatures**. As shown in Figure 7, they're actually expanded to the corresponding two letters, in the following sense:

- Primary ordering: The ligature is equal to the two-character sequence.
- Secondary ordering: The ligature is greater than the two-character sequence.

Inside Macintosh

```
$00    ASCII NUL
...
$1F    ASCII US
$20    space    nonbreaking space
$21    !
$22    "    «  »  "  "
$23    #
$24    $
$25    %
$26    &
$27    '    '  '
$28    (
...
$40    @
$41    A  À  Ä  Ã  Å  a  á  à  â  ä  ã  å
$42    B  b
$43    C  Ç  c  ç
$45    E  É  e  é  è  ê  ë
$49    I  í  i  í  ì  î  ï
$4E    N  Ñ  n  ñ
$4F    O  Ö  Õ  Ø  o  ó  ò  ô  ö  õ  ø
$55    U  Ü  u  ú  ù  û  ü
$59    Y  y  ÿ
$5B    [
$5C    \
$5D    ]
$5E    ^
$5F    _
$60    `
$7B    {
$7C    |
$7D    }
$7E    ~
$7F    ASCII DEL
$A0    †
...
$AD    ≠
$AE    Æ  æ  Œ  œ    (see remarks about ligatures)
$B0    ∞
...
$BD    Ω
$C0    ¿
...
$C9    …
$D0    –
$D1    —
$D6    ÷
$D7    ◊
```

letters not shown are like "B b"

Figure 6. International Character Ordering

I-502 *International String Comparison*

Ligatures are ordered somewhat differently in Germany to accommodate umlauted characters (see Figure 7). This is accomplished by means of the routine in international resource 1 for localizing the built-in character ordering. In the system resource file for Germany, this routine expands umlauted characters to the corresponding two letters (for example, "AE" for A-umlaut). The secondary ordering places the umlauted character between the two-character sequence and the ligature, if any. Likewise, the German double-s character expands to "ss".

Built-in ordering:

AE Æ ae æ

OE Œ oe œ

German ordering:

AE Ä Æ ae ä æ

OE Ö Œ oe ö œ

ss ß

UE Ü ue ü

Figure 7. Ordering for Special Characters

In the system resource file for Great Britain, the localization routine in international resource 1 orders the pound currency sign between double quote and the pound weight sign (see Figure 8). For the United States, France, and Italy, the localization routine does nothing.

```
$22    "   «  »  "  "
$A3    £
$23    #
```

Figure 8. Special Ordering for Great Britain

Assembly-language note: The null localization routine consists of an RTS instruction.

USING THE INTERNATIONAL UTILITIES PACKAGE

The International Utilities Package is automatically read into memory from the system resource file when one of its routines is called. When a routine needs to access an international resource, it asks the Resource Manager to read the resource into memory. Together, the package and its resources occupy about 2K bytes.

As described in chapter 13 of Volume II, you can get the date and time as a long integer from the GetDateTime procedure. If you need a string corresponding to the date or time, you can pass this long integer to the IUDateString or IUTimeString procedure in the International Utilities Package. These procedures determine the local format from the international resources read into memory by the Resource Manager (that is, resource type 'INTL' and resource ID 0 or 1). In some situations,

Inside Macintosh

you may need the format information to come instead from an international resource that you specify by its handle; if so, you can use IUDatePString or IUTimePString. This is useful, for example, if you want to use an international resource in a document's resource file after you've closed that file.

Applications that use measurements, such as on a ruler for setting margins and tabs, can call IUMetric to find out whether to use the metric system. This function simply returns the value of the corresponding field in international resource 0. To access any other fields in an international resource—say, the currency format in international resource 0—call IUGetIntl to get a handle to the resource. If you change any of the fields and want to write the changed resource to a resource file, the IUSetIntl procedure lets you do this.

To sort strings, you can use IUCompString or, if you're not dealing with Pascal strings, the more general IUMagString. These routines compare two strings and give their exact relationship, whether equal, less than, or greater than. Subtleties like diacritical marks and case differences are taken into consideration, as described above under "International String Comparison". If you need to know only whether two strings are equal, and want to ignore the subtleties, use IUEqualString (or the more general IUMagIDString) instead.

> **Note:** The Operating System Utility function EqualString also compares two Pascal strings for equality. It's less sophisticated than IUEqualString in that it follows ASCII order more strictly; for details, see chapter 13 of Volume II.

INTERNATIONAL UTILITIES PACKAGE ROUTINES

Assembly-language note: The trap macro for the International Utilities Package is _Pack6. The routine selectors are as follows:

```
iuDateString      .EQU   0
iuTimeString      .EQU   2
iuMetric          .EQU   4
iuGetIntl         .EQU   6
iuSetIntl         .EQU   8
iuMagString       .EQU   10
iuMagIDString     .EQU   12
iuDatePString     .EQU   14
iuTimePString     .EQU   16
```

```
PROCEDURE IUDateString (dateTime: LONGINT; form: DateForm; VAR
        result: Str255);
```

Given a date and time as returned by the Operating System Utility procedure GetDateTime, IUDateString returns in the result parameter a string that represents the corresponding date. The form parameter has the following data type:

```
TYPE DateForm = (shortDate,longDate,abbrevDate);
```

The International Utilities Package

ShortDate requests the short date format, longDate the long date, and abbrevDate the abbreviated long date. IUDateString determines the exact format from international resource 0 for the short date or 1 for the long date. See Figure 1 above for examples of the standard formats.

If the abbreviated long date is requested and the abbreviation length in international resource 1 is greater than the actual length of the name being abbreviated, IUDateString fills the abbreviation with NUL characters (ASCII code 0); the abbreviation length should not be greater than 15, the maximum name length.

```
PROCEDURE IUDatePString (dateTime: LONGINT; form: DateForm; VAR
         result: Str255; intlParam: Handle);
```

IUDatePString is the same as IUDateString except that it determines the exact format of the date from the resource whose handle is passed in intlParam, overriding the resource that would otherwise be used.

```
PROCEDURE IUTimeString (dateTime: LONGINT; wantSeconds: BOOLEAN;
         VAR result: Str255);
```

Given a date and time as returned by the Operating System Utility procedure GetDateTime, IUTimeString returns in the result parameter a string that represents the corresponding time of day. If wantSeconds is TRUE, seconds are included in the time; otherwise, only the hour and minute are included. IUTimeString determines the time format from international resource 0. See Figure 1 for examples of the standard formats.

```
PROCEDURE IUTimePString (dateTime: LONGINT; wantSeconds: BOOLEAN;
         VAR result: Str255; intlParam: Handle);
```

IUTimePString is the same as IUTimeString except that it determines the time format from the resource whose handle is passed in intlParam, overriding the resource that would otherwise be used.

```
FUNCTION IUMetric : BOOLEAN;
```

If international resource 0 specifies that the metric system is to be used, IUMetric returns TRUE; otherwise, it returns FALSE.

```
FUNCTION IUGetIntl (theID: INTEGER) : Handle;
```

IUGetIntl returns a handle to the international resource numbered theID (0 or 1). It calls the Resource Manager function GetResource('INTL',theID). For example, if you want to access individual fields of international resource 0, you can do the following:

```
VAR myHndl: Handle;
    int0: Intl0Hndl;
    . . .
myHndl := IUGetIntl(0);
int0 := Intl0Hndl(myHndl)
```

International Utilities Package Routines I-505

Inside Macintosh

```
PROCEDURE IUSetIntl (refNum: INTEGER; theID: INTEGER; intlParam:
            Handle);
```

In the resource file having the reference number refNum, IUSetIntl sets the international resource numbered theID (0 or 1) to the data specified by intlParam. The data may be either an existing resource or data that hasn't yet been written to a resource file. IUSetIntl adds the resource to the specified file or replaces the resource if it's already there.

```
FUNCTION IUCompString (aStr,bStr: Str255) : INTEGER;    [Not in ROM]
```

IUCompString compares aStr and bStr as described above under "International String Comparison", taking both primary and secondary ordering into consideration. It returns one of the values listed below.

		Example	
Result	Meaning	aStr	bStr
−1	aStr is less than bStr	'Ab'	'ab'
0	aStr equals bStr	'Ab'	'Ab'
1	aStr is greater than bStr	'Ac'	'ab'

Assembly-language note: IUCompString was created for the convenience of Pascal programmers; there's no trap for it. It eventually calls IUMagString, which is what you should use from assembly language.

```
FUNCTION IUMagString (aPtr,bPtr: Ptr; aLen,bLen: INTEGER) :
            INTEGER;
```

IUMagString is the same as IUCompString (above) except that instead of comparing two Pascal strings, it compares the string defined by aPtr and aLen to the string defined by bPtr and bLen. The pointer points to the first character of the string (any byte in memory, not necessarily word-aligned), and the length specifies the number of characters in the string.

```
FUNCTION IUEqualString (aStr,bStr: Str255) : INTEGER;   [Not in ROM]
```

IUEqualString compares aStr and bStr for equality without regard for secondary ordering, as described above under "International String Comparison". If the strings are equal, it returns 0; otherwise, it returns 1. For example, if the strings are 'Rose' and 'rose', IUEqualString considers them equal and returns 0.

Note: See also EqualString in chapter 13 of Volume II.

The International Utilities Package

Assembly-language note: IUEqualString was created for the convenience of Pascal programmers; there's no trap for it. It eventually calls IUMagIDString, which is what you should use from assembly language.

```
FUNCTION IUMagIDString (aPtr,bPtr: Ptr; aLen,bLen: INTEGER) :
         INTEGER;
```

IUMagIDString is the same as IUEqualString (above) except that instead of comparing two Pascal strings, it compares the string defined by aPtr and aLen to the string defined by bPtr and bLen. The pointer points to the first character of the string (any byte in memory, not necessarily word-aligned), and the length specifies the number of characters in the string.

SUMMARY OF THE INTERNATIONAL UTILITIES PACKAGE

Constants

```
CONST  { Masks for currency format }

       currSymLead    = 16;   {set if currency symbol leads}
       currNegSym     = 32;   {set if minus sign for negative}
       currTrailingZ  = 64;   {set if trailing decimal zeroes}
       currLeadingZ   = 128;  {set if leading integer zero}

       { Order of short date elements }

       mdy = 0;       {month day year}
       dmy = 1;       {day month year}
       ymd = 2;       {year month day}

       { Masks for short date format }

       dayLdingZ = 32;   {set if leading zero for day}
       mntLdingZ = 64;   {set if leading zero for month}
       century   = 128;  {set if century included}

       { Masks for time format }

       secLeadingZ = 32;   {set if leading zero for seconds}
       minLeadingZ = 64;   {set if leading zero for minutes}
       hrLeadingZ  = 128;  {set if leading zero for hours}

       { High-order byte of version information }

       verUS           = 0;
       verFrance       = 1;
       verBritain      = 2;
       verGermany      = 3;
       verItaly        = 4;
       verNetherlands  = 5;
       verBelgiumLux   = 6;
       verSweden       = 7;
       verSpain        = 8;
       verDenmark      = 9;
       verPortugal     = 10;
       verFrCanada     = 11;
       verNorway       = 12;
       verIsrael       = 13;
       verJapan        = 14;
       verAustralia    = 15;
       verArabia       = 16;
       verFinland      = 17;
```

```
        verFrSwiss       = 18;
        verGrSwiss       = 19;
        verGreece        = 20;
        verIceland       = 21;
        verMalta         = 22;
        verCyprus        = 23;
        verTurkey        = 24;
        verYugoslavia    = 25;
```

Data Types

```
TYPE Intl0Hndl = ^Intl0Ptr;
     Intl0Ptr  = ^Intl0Rec;
     Intl0Rec  =
        PACKED RECORD
           decimalPt:    CHAR;   {decimal point character}
           thousSep:     CHAR;   {thousands separator}
           listSep:      CHAR;   {list separator}
           currSym1:     CHAR;   {currency symbol}
           currSym2:     CHAR;
           currSym3:     CHAR;
           currFmt:      Byte;   {currency format}
           dateOrder:    Byte;   {order of short date elements}
           shrtDateFmt:  Byte;   {short date format}
           dateSep:      CHAR;   {date separator}
           timeCycle:    Byte;   {0 if 24-hour cycle, 255 if 12-hour}
           timeFmt:      Byte;   {time format}
           mornStr:      PACKED ARRAY[1..4] OF CHAR;
                                 {trailing string for first 12-hour cycle}
           eveStr:       PACKED ARRAY[1..4] OF CHAR;
                                 {trailing string for last 12-hour cycle}
           timeSep:      CHAR;   {time separator}
           time1Suff:    CHAR;   {trailing string for 24-hour cycle}
           time2Suff:    CHAR;
           time3Suff:    CHAR;
           time4Suff:    CHAR;
           time5Suff:    CHAR;
           time6Suff:    CHAR;
           time7Suff:    CHAR;
           time8Suff:    CHAR;
           metricSys:    Byte;   {255 if metric, 0 if not}
           intl0Vers:    INTEGER {version information}
        END;
```

```
Intl1Hndl = ^Intl1Ptr;
Intl1Ptr  = ^Intl1Rec;
Intl1Rec  =
      PACKED RECORD
        days:         ARRAY[1..7] OF STRING[15];   {day names}
        months:       ARRAY[1..12] OF STRING[15];  {month names}
        suppressDay:  Byte;  {0 for day name, 255 for none}
        lngDateFmt:   Byte;  {order of long date elements}
        dayLeading0:  Byte;  {255 for leading 0 in day number}
        abbrLen:      Byte;  {length for abbreviating names}
        st0:          PACKED ARRAY[1..4] OF CHAR;  {strings }
        st1:          PACKED ARRAY[1..4] OF CHAR;  { for }
        st2:          PACKED ARRAY[1..4] OF CHAR;  { long }
        st3:          PACKED ARRAY[1..4] OF CHAR;  { date }
        st4:          PACKED ARRAY[1..4] OF CHAR;  { format}
        intl1Vers:    INTEGER; {version information}
        localRtn:     INTEGER  {routine for localizing string }
                              { comparison; actually may be }
                              { longer than one integer}
      END;

DateForm = (shortDate,longDate,abbrevDate);
```

Routines

```
PROCEDURE IUDateString  (dateTime: LONGINT; form: DateForm; VAR result:
                         Str255);
PROCEDURE IUDatePString (dateTime: LONGINT; form: DateForm; VAR result:
                         Str255; intlParam: Handle);
PROCEDURE IUTimeString  (dateTime: LONGINT; wantSeconds: BOOLEAN; VAR
                         result: Str255);
PROCEDURE IUTimePString (dateTime: LONGINT; wantSeconds: BOOLEAN; VAR
                         result: Str255; intlParam: Handle);
FUNCTION  IUMetric    :  BOOLEAN;
FUNCTION  IUGetIntl     (theID: INTEGER) : Handle;
PROCEDURE IUSetIntl     (refNum: INTEGER; theID: INTEGER; intlParam:
                         Handle);
FUNCTION  IUCompString  (aStr,bStr: Str255) : INTEGER;   [Not in ROM]
FUNCTION  IUMagString   (aPtr,bPtr: Ptr; aLen,bLen: INTEGER) : INTEGER;
FUNCTION  IUEqualString (aStr,bStr: Str255) : INTEGER;   [Not in ROM]
FUNCTION  IUMagIDString (aPtr,bPtr: Ptr; aLen,bLen: INTEGER) : INTEGER;
```

Assembly-Language Information

Constants

```
; Masks for currency format

currSymLead     .EQU    16      ;set if currency symbol leads
currNegSym      .EQU    32      ;set if minus sign for negative
currTrailingZ   .EQU    64      ;set if trailing decimal zeroes
currLeadingZ    .EQU    128     ;set if leading integer zero

; Order of short date elements

mdy             .EQU    0       ;month day year
dmy             .EQU    1       ;day month year
ymd             .EQU    2       ;year month day

; Masks for short date format

dayLdingZ       .EQU    32      ;set if leading zero for day
mntLdingZ       .EQU    64      ;set if leading zero for month
century         .EQU    128     ;set if century included

; Masks for time format

secLeadingZ     .EQU    32      ;set if leading zero for seconds
minLeadingZ     .EQU    64      ;set if leading zero for minutes
hrLeadingZ      .EQU    128     ;set if leading zero for hours

; High-order byte of version information

verUS           .EQU    0
verFrance       .EQU    1
verBritain      .EQU    2
verGermany      .EQU    3
verItaly        .EQU    4
verNetherlands  .EQU    5
verBelgiumLux   .EQU    6
verSweden       .EQU    7
verSpain        .EQU    8
verDenmark      .EQU    9
verPortugal     .EQU    10
verFrCanada     .EQU    11
verNorway       .EQU    12
verIsrael       .EQU    13
verJapan        .EQU    14
verAustralia    .EQU    15
verArabia       .EQU    16
verFinland      .EQU    17
verFrSwiss      .EQU    18
verGrSwiss      .EQU    19
```

Inside Macintosh

```
verGreece       .EQU    20
verIceland      .EQU    21
verMalta        .EQU    22
verCyprus       .EQU    23
verTurkey       .EQU    24
verYugoslavia   .EQU    25

; Date form for IUDateString and IUDatePString

shortDate       .EQU    0       ;short form of date
longDate        .EQU    1       ;long form of date
abbrevDate      .EQU    2       ;abbreviated long form

; Routine selectors

iuDateString    .EQU    0
iuTimeString    .EQU    2
iuMetric        .EQU    4
iuGetIntl       .EQU    6
iuSetIntl       .EQU    8
iuMagString     .EQU    10
iuMagIDString   .EQU    12
iuDatePString   .EQU    14
iuTimePString   .EQU    16
```

International Resource 0 Data Structure

decimalPt	Decimal point character (byte)
thousSep	Thousands separator (byte)
listSep	List separator (byte)
currSym	Currency symbol (3 bytes)
currFmt	Currency format (byte)
dateOrder	Order of short date elements (byte)
shrtDateFmt	Short date format (byte)
dateSep	Date separator (byte)
timeCycle	0 if 24-hour cycle, 255 if 12-hour (byte)
timeFmt	Time format (byte)
mornStr	Trailing string for first 12-hour cycle (long)
eveStr	Trailing string for last 12-hour cycle (long)
timeSep	Time separator (byte)
timeSuff	Trailing string for 24-hour cycle (8 bytes)
metricSys	255 if metric, 0 if not (byte)
intl0Vers	Version information (word)

International Resource 1 Data Structure

days	Day names (112 bytes)
months	Month names (192 bytes)
suppressDay	0 for day name, 255 for none (byte)
lngDateFmt	Order of long date elements (byte)

dayLeading0	255 for leading 0 in day number (byte)
abbrLen	Length for abbreviating names (byte)
st0	Strings for long date format (longs)
st1	
st2	
st3	
st4	
intl1Vers	Version information (word)
localRtn	Comparison localization routine

Trap Macro Name

Pack6

20 THE STANDARD FILE PACKAGE

517 About This Chapter
517 About the Standard File Package
518 Using the Standard File Package
519 Standard File Package Routines
527 Summary of the Standard File Package

The Standard File Package

ABOUT THIS CHAPTER

This chapter describes the Standard File Package, which provides the standard user interface for specifying a file to be opened or saved. The Standard File Package allows the file to be on a disk in any drive connected to the Macintosh, and lets a currently inserted disk be ejected so that another can be inserted.

You should already be familiar with:

- the basic concepts and structures behind QuickDraw, particularly points and rectangles
- the Toolbox Event Manager
- the Dialog Manager, especially the ModalDialog procedure
- packages in general, as described in chapter 17

ABOUT THE STANDARD FILE PACKAGE

Standard Macintosh applications should have a File menu from which the user can save and open documents, via the Save, Save As, and Open commands. In response to these commands, the application can call the Standard File Package to find out the document name and let the user switch disks if desired. As described below, a dialog box is presented for this purpose.

When the user chooses Save As, or Save when the document is untitled, the application needs a name for the document. The corresponding dialog box lets the user enter the document name and click a button labeled "Save" (or just click "Cancel" to abort the command). By convention, the dialog box comes up displaying the current document name, if any, so the user can edit it.

In response to an Open command, the application needs to know which document to open. The corresponding dialog box displays the names of all documents that might be opened; the user opens one by clicking it and then clicking a button labeled "Open", or simply by double-clicking on the document name. If there are more names than can be shown at once, the user can scroll through them using a vertical scroll bar, or type a character on the keyboard to cause the list to scroll to the first name beginning with that character.

Both of these dialog boxes let the user:

- access a disk in an external drive connected to the Macintosh
- eject a disk from either drive and insert another
- initialize and name an inserted disk that's uninitialized
- switch from one drive to another

On the right in the dialog box, separated from the rest of the box by a dotted line, there's a disk name with one or two buttons below it; Figure 1 shows what this looks like when an external drive is connected to the Macintosh but currently has no disk in it. Notice that the Drive button is inactive (dimmed). After the user inserts a disk in the external drive (and, if necessary, initializes and names it), the Drive button becomes active. If there's no external drive, the Drive button isn't displayed at all.

Inside Macintosh

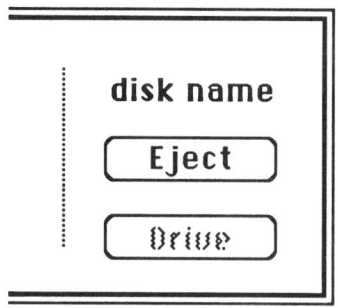

Figure 1. Partial Dialog Box

The disk name displayed in the dialog box is the name of the current disk, initially the disk from which the application was started. The user can click Eject to eject the current disk and insert another, which then becomes the current disk. If there's an external drive, clicking the Drive button changes the current disk from the one in the external drive to the one in the internal drive or vice versa. The Drive button is inactive whenever there's only one disk inserted.

> **Note:** Clicking the Drive button actually cycles through all volumes in drives currently connected to the Macintosh. (Volumes and drives are discussed in chapter 4 of Volume II.)

If an uninitialized or otherwise unreadable disk is inserted, the Standard File Package calls the Disk Initialization Package to provide the standard user interface for initializing and naming a disk.

USING THE STANDARD FILE PACKAGE

The Standard File Package and the resources it uses are automatically read into memory when one of its routines is called. It in turn reads the Disk Initialization Package into memory if a disk is ejected (in case an uninitialized disk is inserted next); together these packages occupy about 8.5K to 10K bytes, depending on the number of files on the disk.

Call SFPutFile when your application is to save to a file and needs to get the name of the file from the user. Standard applications should do this when the user chooses Save As from the File menu, or Save when the document is untitled. SFPutFile displays a dialog box allowing the user to enter a file name.

Similarly, SFGetFile is useful whenever your application is to open a file and needs to know which one, such as when the user chooses the Open command from a standard application's File menu. SFGetFile displays a dialog box with a list of file names to choose from.

You pass these routines a reply record, as shown below, and they fill it with information about the user's reply.

The Standard File Package

```
TYPE SFReply =    RECORD
                    good:     BOOLEAN;       {FALSE if ignore command}
                    copy:     BOOLEAN;       {not used}
                    fType:    OSType;        {file type or not used}
                    vRefNum:  INTEGER;       {volume reference number}
                    version:  INTEGER;       {file's version number}
                    fName:    STRING[63]     {file name}
                  END;
```

The first field of this record determines whether the file operation should take place or the command should be ignored (because the user clicked the Cancel button in the dialog box). The fType field is used by SFGetFile to store the file's type. The vRefNum, version, and fName fields identify the file chosen by the user; the application passes their values on to the File Manager routine that does the actual file operation. VRefNum contains the volume reference number of the volume containing the file. The version field always contains 0; the use of nonzero version numbers is *not* supported by this package. For more information on files, volumes, and file operations, see chapter 4 of Volume II.

Assembly-language note: Before calling a Standard File Package routine, if you set the global variable SFSaveDisk to the negative of a volume reference number, Standard File will use that volume and display its name in the dialog box. (Note that since the volume reference number is negative, you set SFSaveDisk to a positive value.)

Both SFPutFile and SFGetFile allow you to use a nonstandard dialog box; two additional routines, SFPPutFile and SFPGetFile, provide an even more convenient and powerful way of doing this.

STANDARD FILE PACKAGE ROUTINES

Assembly-language note: The trap macro for the Standard File Package is _Pack3. The routine selectors are as follows:

```
sfPutFile     .EQU    1
sfGetFile     .EQU    2
sfPPutFile    .EQU    3
sfPGetFile    .EQU    4
```

```
PROCEDURE SFPutFile (where: Point; prompt: Str255; origName:
        Str255; dlgHook: ProcPtr; VAR reply: SFReply);
```

SFPutFile displays a dialog box allowing the user to specify a file to which data will be written (as during a Save or Save As command). It then repeatedly gets and handles events until the user either confirms the command after entering an appropriate file name or aborts the command by

Inside Macintosh

clicking Cancel in the dialog. It reports the user's reply by filling the fields of the reply record specified by the reply parameter, as described above; the fType field of this record isn't used.

The general appearance of the standard SFPutFile dialog box is shown in Figure 2. The where parameter specifies the location of the top left corner of the dialog box in global coordinates. The prompt parameter is a line of text to be displayed as a statText item in the dialog box, where shown in Figure 2. The origName parameter contains text that appears as an enabled, selected editText item; for the standard document-saving commands, it should be the current name of the document, or the empty string (to display an insertion point) if the document hasn't been named yet.

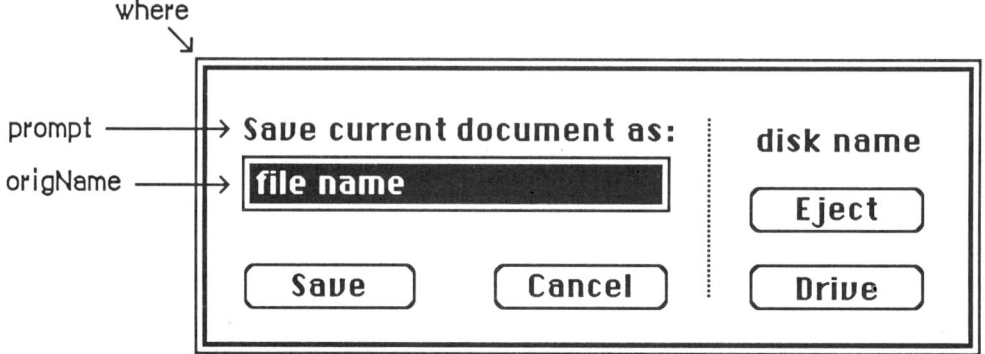

Figure 2. Standard SFPutFile Dialog

If you want to use the standard SFPutFile dialog box, pass NIL for dlgHook; otherwise, see the information for advanced programmers below.

SFPutFile repeatedly calls the Dialog Manager procedure ModalDialog. When an event involving an enabled dialog item occurs, ModalDialog handles the event and returns the item number, and SFPutFile responds as follows:

- If the Eject or Drive button is clicked, or a disk is inserted, SFPutFile responds as described above under "About the Standard File Package".

- Text entered into the editText item is stored in the fName field of the reply record. (SFPutFile keeps track of whether there's currently any text in the item, and makes the Save button inactive if not.)

- If the Save button is clicked, SFPutFile determines whether the file name in the fName field of the reply record is appropriate. If so, it returns control to the application with the first field of the reply record set to TRUE; otherwise, it responds accordingly, as described below.

- If the Cancel button in the dialog is clicked, SFPutFile returns control to the application with the first field of the reply record set to FALSE.

Note: Notice that disk insertion is one of the user actions listed above, even though ModalDialog normally ignores disk-inserted events. The reason this works is that SFPutFile calls ModalDialog with a filterProc function that lets it receive disk-inserted events.

I-520 Standard File Package Routines

The Standard File Package

The situations that may cause an entered name to be inappropriate, and SFPutFile's response to each, are as follows:

- If a file with the specified name already exists on the disk and is different from what was passed in the origName parameter, the alert in Figure 3 is displayed. If the user clicks Yes, the file name is appropriate.

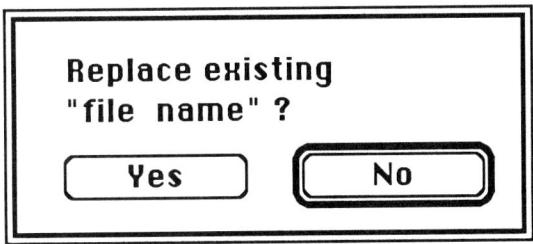

Figure 3. Alert for Existing File

- If the disk to which the file should be written is locked, the alert in Figure 4 is displayed. If a system error occurs, a similar alert is displayed, with the message "A system error occurred; please try again" (this is unrelated to the fatal system errors reported by the System Error Handler).

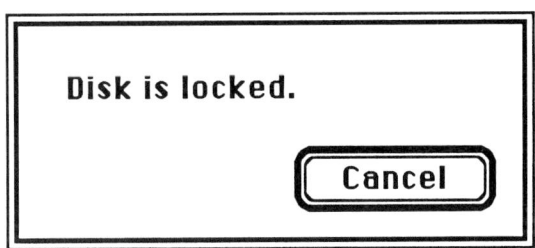

Figure 4. Alert for Locked Disk

Note: The user may specify a disk name (preceding the file name and separated from it by a colon). If the disk isn't currently in a drive, an alert similar to the one in Figure 4 is displayed. The ability to specify a disk name is supported for historical reasons only; users should not be encouraged to do it.

After the user clicks No or Cancel in response to one of these alerts, SFPutFile dismisses the alert box and continues handling events (so a different name may be entered).

Advanced programmers: You can create your own dialog box rather than use the standard SFPutFile dialog. However, future compatibility is *not* guaranteed if you don't use the standard SFPutFile dialog. To create a nonstandard dialog, you must provide your own dialog template and store it in your application's resource file with the same resource ID that the standard template has in the system resource file:

```
CONST putDlgID = -3999;   {SFPutFile dialog template ID}
```

Note: The SFPPutFile procedure, described below, lets you use any resource ID for your nonstandard dialog box.

Your dialog template must specify that the dialog window be invisible, and your dialog must contain all the standard items, as listed below. The appearance and location of these items in your dialog may be different. You can make an item "invisible" by giving it a display rectangle that's off the screen. The display rectangle for each item in the standard dialog box is given below. The rectangle for the standard dialog box itself is (0,0)(304,104).

Item number	Item	Standard display rectangle
1	Save button	(12,74)(82,92)
2	Cancel button	(114,74)(184,92)
3	Prompt string (statText)	(12,12)(184,28)
4	UserItem for disk name	(209,16)(295,34)
5	Eject button	(217,43)(287,61)
6	Drive button	(217,74)(287,92)
7	EditText item for file name	(14,34)(182,50)
8	UserItem for dotted line	(200,16)(201,88)

Note: Remember that the display rectangle for any "invisible" text item must be at least about 20 pixels wide.

If your dialog has additional items beyond the standard ones, or if you want to handle any of the standard items in a nonstandard manner, you must write your own dlgHook function and point to it with dlgHook. Your dlgHook function should have two parameters and return an integer value. For example, this is how it would be declared if it were named MyDlg:

```
FUNCTION MyDlg (item: INTEGER; theDialog: DialogPtr) : INTEGER;
```

Immediately after calling ModalDialog, SFPutFile calls your dlgHook function, passing it the item number returned by ModalDialog and a pointer to the dialog record describing your dialog box. Using these two parameters, your dlgHook function should determine how to handle the event. There are predefined constants for the item numbers of standard enabled items, as follows:

```
CONST putSave    = 1;    {Save button}
      putCancel  = 2;    {Cancel button}
      putEject   = 5;    {Eject button}
      putDrive   = 6;    {Drive button}
      putName    = 7;    {editText item for file name}
```

ModalDialog returns the "fake" item number 100 when it receives a null event. Note that since it calls GetNextEvent with a mask that excludes disk-inserted events, ModalDialog sees them as null events, too.

After handling the event (or, perhaps, after ignoring it) the dlgHook function must return an item number to SFPutFile. If the item number is one of those listed above, SFPutFile responds in the standard way; otherwise, it does nothing.

Note: For advanced programmers who want to change the appearance of the alerts displayed when an inappropriate file name is entered, the resource IDs of those alerts in the system resource file are listed below.

The Standard File Package

Alert	Resource ID
Disk not found	–3994
System error	–3995
Existing file	–3996
Locked disk	–3997

```
PROCEDURE SFPPutFile (where: Point; prompt: Str255; origName:
        Str255; dlgHook: ProcPtr; VAR reply: SFReply; dlgID:
        INTEGER; filterProc: ProcPtr);
```

SFPPutFile is an alternative to SFPutFile for advanced programmers who want to use a nonstandard dialog box. It's the same as SFPutFile except for the two additional parameters dlgID and filterProc.

DlgID is the resource ID of the dialog template to be used instead of the standard one (so you can use whatever ID you wish rather than the same one as the standard).

The filterProc parameter determines how ModalDialog will filter events when called by SFPPutFile. If filterProc is NIL, ModalDialog does the standard filtering that it does when called by SFPutFile; otherwise, filterProc should point to a function for ModalDialog to execute *after* doing the standard filtering. The function must be the same as one you would pass directly to ModalDialog in its filterProc parameter. (See chapter 13 for more information.)

```
PROCEDURE SFGetFile (where: Point; prompt: Str255; fileFilter:
        ProcPtr; numTypes: INTEGER; typeList: SFTypeList;
        dlgHook: ProcPtr; VAR reply: SFReply);
```

SFGetFile displays a dialog box listing the names of a specific group of files from which the user can select one to be opened (as during an Open command). It then repeatedly gets and handles events until the user either confirms the command after choosing a file name or aborts the command by clicking Cancel in the dialog. It reports the user's reply by filling the fields of the reply record specified by the reply parameter, as described above under "Using the Standard File Package".

The general appearance of the standard SFGetFile dialog box is shown in Figure 5. File names are sorted in order of the ASCII codes of their characters, ignoring diacritical marks and mapping lowercase characters to their uppercase equivalents. If there are more file names than can be displayed at one time, the scroll bar is active; otherwise, the scroll bar is inactive.

The where parameter specifies the location of the top left corner of the dialog box in global coordinates. The prompt parameter is ignored; it's there for historical purposes only.

The fileFilter, numTypes, and typeList parameters determine which files appear in the dialog box. SFGetFile first looks at numTypes and typeList to determine what types of files to display, then it executes the function pointed to by fileFilter (if any) to do additional filtering on which files to display. File types are discussed in chapter 1 of Volume III. For example, if the application is concerned only with pictures, you won't want to display the names of any text files.

Inside Macintosh

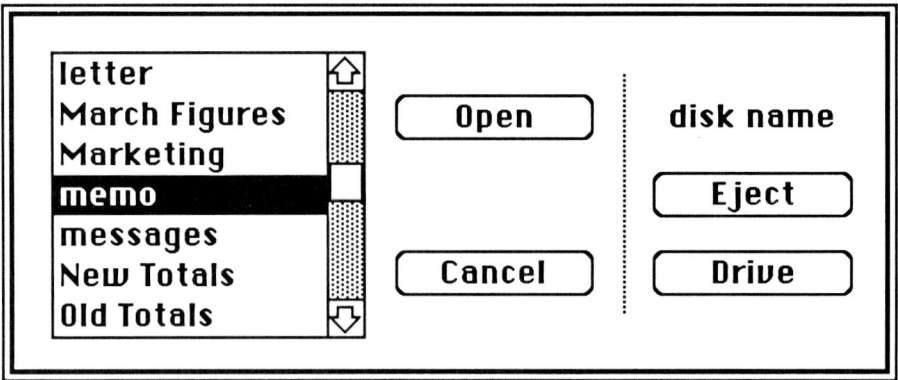

Figure 5. Standard SFGetFile Dialog

Pass −1 for numTypes to display all types of files; otherwise, pass the number of file types (up to 4) that you want to display, and pass the types themselves in typeList. The SFTypeList data type is defined as follows:

```
TYPE SFTypeList = ARRAY[0..3] OF OSType;
```

Assembly-language note: If you need to specify more than four types, pass a pointer to an array with the desired number of entries.

If fileFilter isn't NIL, SFGetFile executes the function it points to for each file, to determine whether the file should be displayed. The fileFilter function has one parameter and returns a Boolean value. For example:

```
FUNCTION MyFileFilter (paramBlock: ParmBlkPtr) : BOOLEAN;
```

SFGetFile passes this function the file information it gets by calling the File Manager procedure GetFileInfo (see chapter 4 of Volume II for details). The function selects which files should appear in the dialog by returning FALSE for every file that should be shown and TRUE for every file that shouldn't be shown.

> **Note:** As described in chapter 4 of Volume II, a flag can be set that tells the Finder not to display a particular file's icon on the desktop; this has no effect on whether SFGetFile will list the file name.

If you want to use the standard SFGetFile dialog box, pass NIL for dlgHook; otherwise, see the information for advanced programmers below.

Like SFPutFile, SFGetFile repeatedly calls the Dialog Manager procedure ModalDialog. When an event involving an enabled dialog item occurs, ModalDialog handles the event and returns the item number, and SFGetFile responds as follows:

- If the Eject or Drive button is clicked, or a disk is inserted, SFGetFile responds as described above under "About the Standard File Package".

The Standard File Package

- If clicking or dragging occurs in the scroll bar, the contents of the dialog box are redrawn accordingly.
- If a file name is clicked, it's selected and stored in the fName field of the reply record. (SFGetFile keeps track of whether a file name is currently selected, and makes the Open button inactive if not.)
- If the Open button is clicked, SFGetFile returns control to the application with the first field of the reply record set to TRUE.
- If a file name is double-clicked, SFGetFile responds as if the user clicked the file name and then the Open button.
- If the Cancel button in the dialog is clicked, SFGetFile returns control to the application with the first field of the reply record set to FALSE.

If a character key is pressed, SFGetFile selects the first file name starting with the character typed, scrolling the list of names if necessary to show the selection. If no file name starts with the character, SFGetFile selects the first file name starting with a character whose ASCII code is greater than the character typed.

Advanced programmers: You can create your own dialog box rather than use the standard SFGetFile dialog. However, future compatibility is *not* guaranteed if you don't use the standard SFGetFile dialog. To create a nonstandard dialog, you must provide your own dialog template and store it in your application's resource file with the same resource ID that the standard template has in the system resource file:

```
CONST getDlgID = -4000;   {SFGetFile dialog template ID}
```

Note: The SFPGetFile procedure, described below, lets you use any resource ID for your nonstandard dialog box.

Your dialog template must specify that the dialog window be invisible, and your dialog must contain all the standard items, as listed below. The appearance and location of these items in your dialog may be different. You can make an item "invisible" by giving it a display rectangle that's off the screen. The display rectangle for each item in the standard dialog box is given below. The rectangle for the standard dialog box itself is (0,0)(348,136).

Item number	Item	Standard display rectangle
1	Open button	(152,28)(232,46)
2	Invisible button	(1152,59)(1232,77)
3	Cancel button	(152,90)(232,108)
4	UserItem for disk name	(248,28)(344,46)
5	Eject button	(256,59)(336,77)
6	Drive button	(256,90)(336,108)
7	UserItem for file name list	(12,11)(125,125)
8	UserItem for scroll bar	(124,11)(140,125)
9	UserItem for dotted line	(244,20)(245,116)
10	Invisible text (statText)	(1044,20)(1145,116)

Inside Macintosh

If your dialog has additional items beyond the standard ones, or if you want to handle any of the standard items in a nonstandard manner, you must write your own dlgHook function and point to it with dlgHook. Your dlgHook function should have two parameters and return an integer value. For example, this is how it would be declared if it were named MyDlg:

```
FUNCTION MyDlg (item: INTEGER; theDialog: DialogPtr) : INTEGER;
```

Immediately after calling ModalDialog, SFGetFile calls your dlgHook function, passing it the item number returned by ModalDialog and a pointer to the dialog record describing your dialog box. Using these two parameters, your dlgHook function should determine how to handle the event. There are predefined constants for the item numbers of standard enabled items, as follows:

```
CONST   getOpen     = 1;     {Open button}
        getCancel   = 3;     {Cancel button}
        getEject    = 5;     {Eject button}
        getDrive    = 6;     {Drive button}
        getNmList   = 7;     {userItem for file name list}
        getScroll   = 8;     {userItem for scroll bar}
```

ModalDialog also returns "fake" item numbers in the following situations, which are detected by its filterProc function:

- When it receives a null event, it returns 100. Note that since it calls GetNextEvent with a mask that excludes disk-inserted events, ModalDialog sees them as null events, too.
- When a key-down event occurs, it returns 1000 plus the ASCII code of the character.

After handling the event (or, perhaps, after ignoring it) your dlgHook function must return an item number to SFGetFile. If the item number is one of those listed above, SFGetFile responds in the standard way; otherwise, it does nothing.

```
PROCEDURE SFPGetFile (where: Point; prompt: Str255; fileFilter:
        ProcPtr; numTypes: INTEGER; typeList: SFTypeList;
        dlgHook: ProcPtr; VAR reply: SFReply; dlgID: INTEGER;
        filterProc: ProcPtr);
```

SFPGetFile is an alternative to SFGetFile for advanced programmers who want to use a nonstandard dialog box. It's the same as SFGetFile except for the two additional parameters dlgID and filterProc.

DlgID is the resource ID of the dialog template to be used instead of the standard one (so you can use whatever ID you wish rather than the same one as the standard).

The filterProc parameter determines how ModalDialog will filter events when called by SFPGetFile. If filterProc is NIL, ModalDialog does the standard filtering that it does when called by SFGetFile; otherwise, filterProc should point to a function for ModalDialog to execute *after* doing the standard filtering. The function must be the same as one you would pass directly to ModalDialog in its filterProc parameter. (See chapter 13 for more information.) Note that the standard filtering will detect key-down events only if the dialog template ID is the standard one.

SUMMARY OF THE STANDARD FILE PACKAGE

Constants

```
CONST  { SFPutFile dialog template ID }

       putDlgID = -3999;

       { Item numbers of enabled items in SFPutFile dialog }

       putSave   = 1;    {Save button}
       putCancel = 2;    {Cancel button}
       putEject  = 5;    {Eject button}
       putDrive  = 6;    {Drive button}
       putName   = 7;    {editText item for file name}

       { SFGetFile dialog template ID }

       getDlgID = -4000;

       { Item numbers of enabled items in SFGetFile dialog }

       getOpen    = 1;   {Open button}
       getCancel  = 3;   {Cancel button}
       getEject   = 5;   {Eject button}
       getDrive   = 6;   {Drive button}
       getNmList  = 7;   {userItem for file name list}
       getScroll  = 8;   {userItem for scroll bar}
```

Data Types

```
TYPE  SFReply = RECORD
                  good:    BOOLEAN;      {FALSE if ignore command}
                  copy:    BOOLEAN;      {not used}
                  fType:   OSType;       {file type or not used}
                  vRefNum: INTEGER;      {volume reference number}
                  version: INTEGER;      {file's version number}
                  fName:   STRING[63]    {file name}
                END;

      SFTypeList = ARRAY[0..3] OF OSType;
```

Routines

```
PROCEDURE SFPutFile   (where: Point; prompt: Str255; origName: Str255;
                       dlgHook: ProcPtr; VAR reply: SFReply);
PROCEDURE SFPPutFile  (where: Point; prompt: Str255; origName: Str255;
                       dlgHook: ProcPtr; VAR reply: SFReply; dlgID:
                       INTEGER; filterProc: ProcPtr);
PROCEDURE SFGetFile   (where: Point; prompt: Str255; fileFilter: ProcPtr;
                       numTypes: INTEGER; typeList: SFTypeList; dlgHook:
                       ProcPtr; VAR reply: SFReply);
PROCEDURE SFPGetFile  (where: Point; prompt: Str255; fileFilter: ProcPtr;
                       numTypes: INTEGER; typeList: SFTypeList; dlgHook:
                       ProcPtr; VAR reply: SFReply; dlgID: INTEGER;
                       filterProc: ProcPtr);
```

DlgHook Function

```
FUNCTION MyDlg (item: INTEGER; theDialog: DialogPtr) : INTEGER;
```

FileFilter Function

```
FUNCTION MyFileFilter (paramBlock: ParmBlkPtr) : BOOLEAN;
```

Standard SFPutFile Items

Item number	Item	Standard display rectangle
1	Save button	(12,74)(82,92)
2	Cancel button	(114,74)(184,92)
3	Prompt string (statText)	(12,12)(184,28)
4	UserItem for disk name	(209,16)(295,34)
5	Eject button	(217,43)(287,61)
6	Drive button	(217,74)(287,92)
7	EditText item for file name	(14,34)(182,50)
8	UserItem for dotted line	(200,16)(201,88)

The Standard File Package

Resource IDs of SFPutFile Alerts

Alert	Resource ID
Disk not found	–3994
System error	–3995
Existing file	–3996
Locked disk	–3997

Standard SFGetFile Items

Item number	Item	Standard display rectangle
1	Open button	(152,28)(232,46)
2	Invisible button	(1152,59)(1232,77)
3	Cancel button	(152,90)(232,108)
4	UserItem for disk name	(248,28)(344,46)
5	Eject button	(256,59)(336,77)
6	Drive button	(256,90)(336,108)
7	UserItem for file name list	(12,11)(125,125)
8	UserItem for scroll bar	(124,11)(140,125)
9	UserItem for dotted line	(244,20)(245,116)
10	Invisible text (statText)	(1044,20)(1145,116)

Assembly-Language Information

Constants

```
; SFPutFile dialog template ID

putDlgID     .EQU    -3999

; Item numbers of enabled items in SFPutFile dialog

putSave      .EQU    1    ;Save button
putCancel    .EQU    2    ;Cancel button
putEject     .EQU    5    ;Eject button
putDrive     .EQU    6    ;Drive button
putName      .EQU    7    ;editText item for file name

; SFGetFile dialog template ID

getDlgID     .EQU    -4000
```

Summary of the Standard File Package I-529

Inside Macintosh

```
; Item numbers of enabled items in SFGetFile dialog

getOpen     .EQU    1       ;Open button
getCancel   .EQU    3       ;Cancel button
getEject    .EQU    5       ;Eject button
getDrive    .EQU    6       ;Drive button
getNmList   .EQU    7       ;userItem for file name list
getScroll   .EQU    8       ;userItem for scroll bar

; Routine selectors

sfPutFile   .EQU    1
sfGetFile   .EQU    2
sfPPutFile  .EQU    3
sfPGetFile  .EQU    4
```

Reply Record Data Structure

rGood	0 if ignore command (byte)
rType	File type (long)
rVolume	Volume reference number (word)
rVersion	File's version number (word)
rName	File name (length byte followed by up to 63 characters)

Trap Macro Name

_Pack3

Variables

SFSaveDisk   Negative of volume reference number used by Standard File Package (word)

INDEX

A

ABByte data type II-276
ABCallType data type II-274
ABProtoType data type II-274
ABRecHandle data type II-274
ABRecPtr data type II-274
ABusRecord data type II-274
  ALAP parameters II-276
  ATP parameters II-287
  DDP parameters II-281
  NBP parameters II-298
ABusVars global variable II-328
access path II-83
access path buffer II-84
ACount global variable I-423
action procedure I-316, 324, 328
  in control definition function I-332
activate event I-244, 279
  event message I-252
active
  control I-313
  window I-46, 270, 284
AddPt procedure I-193
AddrBlock data type II-281
AddResMenu procedure I-353
AddResource procedure I-124
AddResponse function II-318
address mark II-211
ALAP   See AppleTalk Link Access Protocol
ALAP frame II-264
ALAP protocol type II-264
alert I-401, 409
  guidelines I-68
alert box I-401
Alert function I-418
alert stages I-409
alert template I-403, 424
  resource format I-426
alert window I-402
AlertTemplate data type I-424
AlertTHndl data type I-425
AlertTPtr data type I-425
alias II-266
Allocate function
  high-level II-94
  low-level II-113
allocated block II-10
allocation block II-79
amplitude of a wave II-223
AngleFromSlope function I-476
ANumber global variable I-423
ApFontID global variable I-219

AppendMenu procedure I-352
AppFile data type II-58
Apple menu I-54
AppleTalk address II-265
AppleTalk Link Access Protocol II-263
  assembly language II-306
  data reception II-325
  Pascal II-276
AppleTalk Manager I-13; II-261, 271
  assembly language II-304
  Pascal II-273
AppleTalk Transaction Protocol II-266, 267
  assembly language II-312
  Pascal II-287
application font I-219
application heap I-74; II-9
  limit II-17, 29
application parameters II-20
application space II-20
application window I-270
ApplicZone function II-32
ApplLimit global variable II-19, 21, 29
ApplScratch global variable I-85
ApplZone global variable II-19, 21, 32
AppParmHandle global variable II-57
arrow cursor I-163, 167
arrow global variable I-147, 163
ascent of a font I-228
  in TextEdit I-378
ASCII codes I-247
assembly language I-83
asynchronous communication II-245
asynchronous execution
  AppleTalk Manager II-273
  Device Manager II-180
  File Manager II-97
at-least-once transaction II-266
ATP   See AppleTalk Transaction Protocol
ATPAddRsp function II-295
ATPCloseSocket function II-291
ATPGetRequest function II-293
ATPLoad function II-290
ATPOpenSocket function II-290
ATPReqCancel function II-293
ATPRequest function II-292
ATPResponse function II-296
ATPRspCancel function II-296
ATPSndRequest function II-291
ATPSndRsp function II-294
ATPUnload function II-290
AttachPH function II-308
auto-key event I-244, 246
auto-key rate I-246; II-371

I-531

Inside Macintosh

auto-key threshold I-246; II-371
auto-pop bit I-89
automatic scrolling I-48
  in TextEdit I-380

B

BackColor procedure I-174
background procedure II-153
BackPat procedure I-167
base line I-227
baud rate II-246, 251, 254
BDSElement data type II-288
BDSPtr data type II-288
BDSType data type II-288
BeginUpdate procedure I-292
Binary-Decimal Conversion Package I-12, 487
bit image I-143
bit manipulation I-470
bit map
  AppleTalk Manager II-268
    printing II-164
    QuickDraw I-144
BitAnd function I-471
BitClr procedure I-471
BitMap data type I-144
BitMapType data type II-287
BitNot function I-471
BitOr function I-471
Bits16 data type I-146
BitSet procedure I-471
BitShift function I-472
BitTst function I-471
BitXor function I-471
black global variable I-162
block (file) *See* allocation block
block (memory) I-73; II-10
block contents II-10
block device II-175
block header II-10
  structure II-24
block map II-122
BlockMove procedure II-44
boot blocks *See* system startup information
boundary rectangle I-144
break II-246
bridge II-265
BringToFront procedure I-286
broadcast service II-264
BufPtr global variable II-19, 21
BufTgDate global variable II-212
BufTgFBkNum global variable II-212
BufTgFFlag global variable II-212
BufTgFNum global variable II-212

bundle II-85; III-11
  resource format III-12
Button function I-259
button type of control I-311, 404
Byte data type I-78

C

CalcMenuSize procedure I-361
CalcVBehind procedure I-297
CalcVis procedure I-297
CalcVisBehind procedure I-297
caret I-376, 379
caret-blink time I-260; II-371
CaretTime global variable I-260
CautionAlert function I-420
Chain procedure II-59
ChangedResource procedure I-123
character codes I-246
character device II-175
character image I-227
character keys I-33, 246
character offset I-228
character origin I-228
character position I-375
character rectangle I-228
character set I-247
character style I-151
  of menu items I-348, 360
character width I-173, 228
Chars data type I-384
CharsHandle data type I-384
CharsPtr data type I-384
CharWidth function I-173
check box I-312, 404
check mark in a menu I-347, 358
CheckItem procedure I-358
CheckUpdate function I-296
ClearMenuBar procedure I-354
click *See* mouse-down event
click loop routine I-380
ClipAbove procedure I-296
Clipboard I-58 *See also* scrap
clipping region of a grafPort I-149
ClipRect procedure I-167
clipRgn of a grafPort I-149
clock chip II-369
  hardware III-36
close box *See* go-away region
Close command I-56
Close function, high-level
  Device Manager II-178
  File Manager II-94

Close function, low-level
  Device Manager II-184
  File Manager II-114
close routine
  of a desk accessory I-446
  of a driver II-187, 193
CloseATPSkt function II-316
closed device driver II-176
closed file II-83
CloseDeskAcc procedure I-440
CloseDialog procedure I-413
CloseDriver function II-178
ClosePgon procedure I-190
ClosePicture procedure I-189
ClosePoly procedure I-190
ClosePort procedure I-164
CloseResFile procedure I-115
CloseRgn procedure I-182
CloseSkt function II-312
CloseWindow procedure I-283
ClrAppFiles procedure II-58
CmpString function II-377
color drawing I-158, 173
ColorBit procedure I-174
Command-key equivalent *See* keyboard equivalent
Command-period II-154
Command-Shift-number I-258
commands I-51, 341
compaction, heap I-74; II-12, 39
CompactMem function II-39
completion routine
  Device Manager II-180, 181
  File Manager II-97, 99
  Sound Driver II-231
ConfirmName function II-323
content region of a window I-271
control I-65, 311
  defining your own I-328
  in a dialog/alert I-404
control definition function I-314, 328
control definition ID I-315, 328
Control function
  high-level II-179
  low-level II-186
control information II-176
control list I-274, 317
Control Manager I-11, 309
  routines I-319
control record I-316
control routine
  of a desk accessory I-446
  of a driver II-187, 194
control template I-315
  resource format I-332
ControlHandle data type I-317
ControlPtr data type I-317

ControlRecord data type I-317
coordinate plane I-138
CopyBits procedure I-188
CopyRgn procedure I-183
CouldAlert procedure I-420
CouldDialog procedure I-415
CountAppFiles procedure II-57
CountMItems function I-361
CountResources function I-118
CountTypes function I-117
Create function
  high-level II-90
  low-level II-107
CreateResFile procedure I-114
creator of a file III-9
CrsrThresh global variable II-372
CurActivate global variable I-280
CurApName global variable II-58
CurApRefNum global variable II-58
CurDeactive global variable I-280
CurJTOffset global variable II-62
CurMap global variable I-117
CurPageOption global variable II-60
CurPitch global variable II-226, 232
current heap zone II-10, 31
current resource file I-105, 116
CurrentA5 global variable I-95; II-19, 21, 386
CurResFile function I-116
CursHandle data type I-474
cursor I-146
  QuickDraw routines I-167
  standard cursors I-147, 474
  utility routines I-474
Cursor data type I-146
cursor level I-167
CursPtr data type I-474
CurStackBase global variable II-19, 21, 358
cut and paste I-59
  intelligent I-63
  in TextEdit I-385

D

DABeeper global variable I-411
DAStrings global array I-421
data bits II-245
data buffer II-83, 176
data fork I-105; II-81
data mark II-211
datagram II-265
  loss recovery II-268
Datagram Delivery Protocol II-265
  assembly language II-308
  Pascal II-281
date operations II-377

Inside Macintosh

Date2Secs procedure II-379
DateForm data type I-504
date/time record II-377
DateTimeRec data type II-378
DCtlEntry data type II-190
DCtlHandle data type II-190
DCtlPtr data type II-190
DDP *See* Datagram Delivery Protocol
DDPCloseSocket function II-282
DDPOpenSocket function II-282
DDPRdCancel function II-284
DDPRead function II-283
DDPWrite function II-283
default button
   in an alert I-69, 401, 424
   in a dialog I-67, 400, 407
default volume II-80
   getting *See* GetVol function
   setting *See* SetVol function
DefltStack global variable II-17
DefVCBPtr global variable II-126
Delay procedure II-384
Delete function
   high-level II-97
   low-level II-119
DeleteMenu procedure I-354
DeltaPoint function I-475
Dequeue function II-383
dereferencing a handle II-14
descent of a font I-228
desk accessory I-437
   writing your own I-443
Desk Manager I-12, 435
   routines I-440
desk scrap I-453
   data types I-454
   format I-462
   routines I-457
DeskHook global variable I-282, 288
DeskPattern global variable I-282
desktop I-32, 269
Desktop file III-10
destination rectangle I-374
DetachPH function II-308
DetachResource procedure I-120
device II-175
device control entry II-189
device driver I-13; II-175
   for a desk accessory I-443
   structure II-187
   writing your own II-193
device driver event I-244
Device Manager I-13; II-173

Device Manager routines II-177
   device control entry access II-190
   high-level II-178
   low-level II-180
   for writing drivers II-194
dial I-312
dialog box I-66, 399
Dialog Manager I-12, 397
   routines I-411
dialog pointer I-407
dialog record I-403, 407
dialog template I-402, 403
   resource format I-425
dialog window I-401
DialogPeek data type I-408
DialogPtr data type I-407
DialogRecord data type I-408
DialogSelect function I-417
DialogTemplate data type I-423
DialogTHndl data type I-424
DialogTPtr data type I-424
DIBadMount function II-396
DiffRgn procedure I-184
DIFormat function II-398
DILoad procedure II-396
dimmed
   control I-313
   menu item I-342, 343
   menu title I-342
disabled
   dialog/alert item I-405
   menu I-342, 358
   menu item I-349, 358
DisableItem procedure I-358
discontinuous selection I-40
Disk Driver I-13; II-209
   Device Manager calls II-213
   routines II-214
Disk Initialization Package I-13; II-393
   routines II-396
disk-inserted event I-244
   event message I-252
   responding to I-257
disk interface III-33
disk-switch dialog II-80
DiskEject function II-214
dispatch table *See* trap dispatch table
display rectangle I-406
DisposControl procedure I-321
DisposDialog procedure I-415
DisposeControl procedure I-321
DisposeMenu procedure I-352
DisposeRgn procedure I-182
DisposeWindow procedure I-284
DisposHandle procedure I-76, 80; II-33
DisposMenu procedure I-352

Index

DisposPtr procedure I-75, 79; II-36
DisposRgn procedure I-182
DisposWindow procedure I-284
DIUnload procedure II-396
DIVerify function II-398
DIZero function II-399
dkGray global variable I-162
DlgCopy procedure I-418
DlgCut procedure I-418
DlgDelete procedure I-418
DlgFont global variable I-412
DlgHook function
   SFGetFile I-526
   SFPutFile I-522
DlgPaste procedure I-418
document window I-269
double-click I-37, 255
double-click time I-260; II-371
DoubleTime global variable I-260
draft printing II-151, 153
drag region of a window I-271, 289
DragControl procedure I-325
DragGrayRgn function I-294
DragHook global variable
   Control Manager I-324, 326
   Window Manager I-288, 289, 290, 295
DragPattern global variable
   Control Manager I-324, 326
   Window Manager I-295
DragTheRgn function I-295
DragWindow procedure I-289
DrawChar procedure I-172
DrawControls procedure I-322
DrawDialog procedure I-418
DrawGrowIcon procedure I-287
drawing I-155
   color I-158, 173
DrawMenuBar procedure I-354
DrawNew procedure I-296
DrawPicture procedure I-190
DrawString procedure I-172
DrawText procedure I-172
drive number II-80
drive queue II-127
driver *See* device driver
driver I/O queue II-180, 191
driver name II-176
driver reference number II-176
DriveStatus function II-215
DrvQEl data type II-127
DrvQHdr global variable II-128
DrvSts data type II-215
DSAlertRect global variable II-362
DSAlertTab global variable II-359, 362
DSErrCode global variable II-362

E

Edit menu I-58
   and desk accessories I-441, 447
edit record I-374
Eject function
   high-level II-90
   low-level II-107
Elems68K *See* Transcendental Functions Package
empty handle I-76; II-14, 40
EmptyHandle procedure II-40
EmptyRect function I-176
EmptyRgn function I-186
enabled
   dialog/alert item I-405
   menu I-358
   menu item I-358
EnableItem procedure I-358
end-of-file II-81
end-of-message flag II-270
EndUpdate procedure I-293
Enqueue procedure II-382
entity name II-265, 298
EntityName data type II-298
Environs procedure II-385
EntityPtr data type II-298
equal-tempered scale II-237
EqualPt function I-193
EqualRect function I-176
EqualRgn function I-185
EqualString function II-377
EraseArc procedure I-180
EraseOval procedure I-178
ErasePoly procedure I-192
EraseRect procedure I-177
EraseRgn procedure I-186
EraseRoundRect procedure I-179
error number *See* result code
ErrorSound procedure I-411
event I-243
   priority I-245
event code I-249
Event Manager, Operating System I-13; II-65
   routines II-68
Event Manager, Toolbox I-11, 241
   routines I-257
event mask I-253
event message I-249
event queue I-243
   structure II-70
event record I-249
event types I-244
EventAvail function I-259
EventQueue global variable II-71
EventRecord data type I-249
EvQEl data type II-71

I-535

Inside Macintosh

exactly-once transaction II-266
example program I-13
exception II-195
exception vector III-17
ExitToShell procedure II-59
exponential functions II-407
extended selection I-39
  in TextEdit I-384
external file system II-128
external reference I-95
ExtStsDT global variable II-199

F

FCBSPtr global variable II-127
Fetch function II-194
FFSynthPtr data type II-228
FFSynthRec data type II-228
file II-79, 81
file control block II-126
file-control-block buffer II-126
file creator III-9
file directory II-79, 122
file icon II-85; III-10
file I/O queue II-97, 124
File Manager I-13; II-77
File Manager routines
  high-level II-88
  low-level II-97
  for queue access II-125, 126, 128
File menu I-55
file name II-81
file number II-122
file reference III-10
  resource format III-12
file tags II-212
file tags buffer II-212
file type III-9
fileFilter function I-524
FillArc procedure I-181
FillOval procedure I-178
FillPoly procedure I-192
FillRect procedure I-177
FillRgn procedure I-187
FillRoundRect procedure I-179
filterProc function I-415
financial functions II-407
FindControl function I-323
Finder information II-55
Finder interface II-55, 84; III-7
FinderName global variable II-59
FindWindow function I-287
FInfo data type II-84
FInitQueue procedure II-103
Fixed data type I-79

fixed-point
  arithmetic I-467
  numbers I-79
fixed-width font I-228
FixMul function I-467
FixRatio function I-467
FixRound function I-467
FlashMenuBar procedure I-361
Floating-Point Arithmetic Package I-13; II-403
FlushEvents procedure II-69
FlushFile function II-114
FlushVol function
  high-level II-89
  low-level II-105
FMInput data type I-224
FMOutPtr data type I-227
FMOutput data type I-227
FMSwapFont function I-223
folder II-85
font I-60, 151, 217
  characters I-220
  format I-227
  resource format I-234
  resource ID I-234
font characterization table I-225
font height I-228
Font Manager I-11, 215
  communication with QuickDraw I-224
  routines I-222
Font menu I-60, 353
font number I-217, 219
font record I-230
font rectangle I-228
font scaling I-220
font size I-153, 217
FontInfo data type I-173
FontRec data type I-231
FontSize menu I-61
ForeColor procedure I-173
fork I-105; II-81
four-tone record II-227
four-tone synthesizer II-223, 226
FP68K *See* Floating-Point Arithmetic Package
frame
  ALAP II-264
  picture I-158
  serial communication II-246
  stack I-96; II-17
  window I-271
frame check sequence II-265
frame header II-264
frame pointer (stack) I-96
frame trailer II-264
FrameArc procedure I-180
FrameOval procedure I-177
FramePoly procedure I-192

FrameRect procedure I-176
FrameRgn procedure I-186
FrameRoundRect procedure I-178
framing error II-246
free-form synthesizer II-223, 228
free memory block II-10
FreeAlert procedure I-420
FreeDialog procedure I-415
FreeMem function II-38
FreeWave data type II-228
frequency of a wave II-223
FrontWindow function I-286
FScaleDisable global variable I-222
FSClose function II-94
FSDelete function II-97
FSOpen function II-91
FSQHdr global variable II-125
FSRead function
 Device Manager II-178
 File Manager II-92
FSWrite function
 Device Manager II-179
 File Manager II-92
FTSndRecPtr data type II-227
FTSoundRec data type II-227
FTSynthPtr data type II-227
FTSynthRec data type II-227
full-duplex communication II-245

G

GetAlrtStage function I-422
GetAppFiles procedure II-58
GetApplLimit function II-29
GetAppParms procedure II-58
GetCaretTime function I-260
GetClip procedure I-167
GetCRefCon function I-327
GetCTitle procedure I-321
GetCtlAction function I-328
GetCtlMax function I-327
GetCtlMin function I-327
GetCtlValue function I-326
GetCursor function I-474
GetDateTime procedure II-378
GetDblTime function I-260
GetDCtlEntry function II-190
GetDItem procedure I-421
GetDrvQHdr function II-128
GetEOF function
 high-level II-93
 low-level II-112
GetEvQHdr function II-71

GetFileInfo function
 high-level II-95
 low-level II-115
GetFInfo function II-95
GetFName procedure I-223
GetFNum procedure I-223
GetFontInfo procedure I-173
GetFontName procedure I-223
GetFPos function
 high-level II-92
 low-level II-111
GetFSQHdr function II-125
GetHandleSize function II-33
GetIcon function I-473
GetIndPattern procedure I-473
GetIndResource function I-118
GetIndString procedure I-468
GetIndType procedure I-117
GetItem procedure I-358
GetItemIcon procedure I-360
GetItemMark procedure I-359
GetItemStyle procedure I-360
GetIText procedure I-422
GetItmIcon procedure I-360
GetItmMark procedure I-359
GetItmStyle procedure I-360
GetKeys procedure I-259
GetMaxCtl function I-327
GetMenu function I-351
GetMenuBar function I-355
GetMHandle function I-361
GetMinCtl function I-327
GetMouse procedure I-259
GetNamedResource function I-119
GetNewControl function I-321
GetNewDialog function I-413
GetNewMBar function I-354
GetNewWindow function I-283
GetNextEvent function I-257
GetNodeAddress function II-303
GetOSEvent function II-69
GetPattern function I-473
GetPen procedure I-169
GetPenState procedure I-169
GetPicture function I-475
GetPixel function I-195
GetPort procedure I-165
GetPtrSize function II-37
GetRequest function II-317
GetResAttrs function I-121
GetResFileAttrs function I-127
GetResInfo procedure I-121
GetResource function I-119
GetRMenu function I-351
GetScrap function I-469
GetSoundVol procedure II-232

Inside Macintosh

GetString function   I-468
GetSysPPtr function   II-381
GetTime procedure   II-380
GetTrapAddress function   II-384
GetVBLQHdr function   II-352
GetVCBQHdr function   II-126
GetVInfo function   II-89
GetVol function
  high-level   II-89
  low-level   II-104
GetVolInfo function
  high-level   II-89
  low-level   II-104
GetVRefNum function   II-89
GetWindowPic function   I-293
GetWMgrPort procedure   I-282
GetWRefCon function   I-293
GetWTitle procedure   I-284
GetZone function   II-31
GhostWindow global variable   I-287
global coordinates   I-155
global variables
  list   III-227
  QuickDraw   I-138, 162
GlobalToLocal procedure   I-193
go-away region of a window   I-271, 288
GrafDevice procedure   I-165
grafPort   I-147
  routines   I-162
GrafPort data type   I-148
GrafPtr data type   I-148
GrafVerb data type   I-198
gray global variable   I-162
GrayRgn global variable   I-282, 296
grow image of a window   I-289
grow region of a window   I-272, 289
grow zone function   II-14, 42
GrowWindow function   I-289
GZRootHnd global variable   II-43
GZSaveHnd function   II-43

H

HandAndHand function   II-375
handle   I-75, 78; II-12
  dereferencing   II-14
  empty   II-40
  manipulation   II-374
Handle data type   I-78
HandleZone function   II-34
HandToHand function   II-374
hardware   III-15
hardware overrun error   II-246

heap   I-12, 23; II-9, 17
  compaction   I-74; II-12, 39
  creating on the stack   II-45
  zone   II-9, 22
HeapEnd global variable   II-19, 21
HideControl procedure   I-322
HideCursor procedure   I-168
HidePen procedure   I-168
HideWindow procedure   I-283
highlighted   I-31
  control   I-313
  menu title   I-357
  window   I-270
HiliteControl procedure   I-322
HiliteMenu procedure   I-357
HiliteWindow procedure   I-286
HiWord function   I-472
HLock procedure   II-41
HNoPurge procedure   II-42
HomeResFile function   I-117
horizontal blanking interval   III-18
hotSpot of a cursor   I-146
HPurge procedure   II-41
HUnlock procedure   II-41

I

icon   I-32
  in a dialog/alert   I-404
  for a file   II-85; III-10
  in a menu   I-347, 359
  utility routines   I-473
icon list   III-11
  resource format   I-476; III-12
icon number   I-347
image width   I-228
inactive
  control   I-313
  window   I-46, 270
indicator of a dial   I-312
InfoScrap function   I-457
InitAllPacks procedure   I-484
InitApplZone procedure   II-28
InitCursor procedure   I-167
InitDialogs procedure   I-411
InitFonts procedure   I-222
InitGraf procedure   I-162
InitMenus procedure   I-351
InitPack procedure   I-484
InitPort procedure   I-164
InitQueue procedure   II-103
InitResources function   I-114
InitUtil function   II-380
InitWindows procedure   I-281
InitZone procedure   II-29

input driver II-246
insertion point I-41, 375
InsertMenu procedure I-353
InsertResMenu procedure I-353
InsetRect procedure I-175
InsetRgn procedure I-184
Int64Bit data type I-472
interface routine I-95
international resources I-495
International Utilities Package I-12, 493
   routines I-504
internet II-265
internet address II-265, 314
interrupt II-195
   level-1 (VIA) II-197; III-38
   level-2 (SCC) II-198
   level-3 II-196
   vertical retrace II-349
interrupt handler II-195
   writing your own II-200
interrupt priority level II-196
interrupt vector II-196
Intl0Hndl data type I-496
Intl0Ptr data type I-496
Intl0Rec data type I-497
Intl1Hndl data type I-500
Intl1Ptr data type I-500
Intl1Rec data type I-500
InvalRect procedure I-291
InvalRgn procedure I-291
InverRect procedure I-177
InverRgn procedure I-186
InverRoundRect procedure I-179
InvertArc procedure I-181
InvertOval procedure I-178
InvertPoly procedure I-192
InvertRect procedure I-177
InvertRgn procedure I-186
InvertRoundRect procedure I-179
invisible
   control I-316
   dialog/alert item I-406
   file icon II-85
   window I-274
IODone function II-195
I/O queue *See* driver I/O queue or file I/O queue
I/O request II-97, 180
IsATPOpen function II-304
IsDialogEvent function I-416
IsMPPOpen function II-304
item
   dialog/alert I-403
   menu I-341
item list I-403
   resource format I-427

item number
   dialog/alert I-406
   menu I-350
item type I-404
IUCompString function I-506
IUDatePString procedure I-505
IUDateString procedure I-504
IUEqualString function I-506
IUGetIntl function I-505
IUMagIDString function I-507
IUMagString function I-506
IUMetric function I-505
IUSetIntl procedure I-506
IUTimePString procedure I-505
IUTimeString procedure I-505
IWM III-17
IWM global variable III-34

J

JFetch global variable II-194
JIODone global variable II-195
job dialog II-149
job subrecord II-150
journal code I-262
JournalFlag global variable I-261
journaling mechanism I-261
JournalRef global variable I-261
JStash global variable II-195
jump table II-60
jump vector II-194
just-tempered scale II-237
justification I-376
   setting I-387

K

kerning I-152, 228
key codes I-250
key-down event I-244
   responding to I-256
key-up event I-244, 254
keyboard I-33
   hardware III-29
keyboard configuration I-248
keyboard equivalent I-343
   meta-character I-348
   responding to I-356
   standard equivalents I-53
keyboard event I-244, 246
   event message I-250
   responding to I-256
keyboard touch *See* auto-key threshold
KeyMap data type I-260

keypad I-35
   hardware III-29
KeyRepThresh global variable I-246
KeyThresh global variable I-246
KillControls procedure I-321
KillIO function
   high-level II-179
   low-level II-187
KillPicture procedure I-190
KillPoly procedure I-191

L

LAPAdrBlock data type II-276
LAPCloseProtocol function II-277
LAPOpenProtocol function II-277
LAPRdCancel function II-279
LAPRead function II-278
LAPWrite function II-277
Launch procedure II-60
leading I-228
ligatures I-501
line height I-378
Line procedure I-171
LineTo procedure I-170
list separator I-497
Lo3Bytes global variable I-85; II-25
LoadNBP function II-324
LoadResource procedure I-119
LoadScrap function I-458
LoadSeg procedure II-60
local coordinates I-153
local ID III-10
LocalToGlobal procedure I-193
location table I-231
lock bit II-25
locked block I-76; II-10
locked file II-84
locked volume II-80
locking a block I-76; II-41
LodeScrap function I-458
logarithmic functions II-407
logical block II-119
logical end-of-file II-81
logical operations I-471
logical size of a block II-22
LongMul procedure I-472
LookupName function II-323
LoWord function I-472
ltGray global variable I-162
Lvl1DT global variable II-197
Lvl2DT global variable II-198

M

magnitude of a wave II-223
main event loop I-16
main segment II-55
MapPoly procedure I-197
MapPt procedure I-196
MapRect procedure I-196
MapRgn procedure I-196
mark
   in a file II-82
   in a menu I-347, 359
mark state II-245
master directory block II-120
master pointer I-75; II-12
   allocation II-22, 31
   structure II-25
MaxApplZone procedure II-30
MaxMem function II-38
MBarEnable global variable I-356, 446
MBarHook global variable I-356
MemError function II-44
memory block I-73; II-10
memory management II-7
   introduction I-71
Memory Manager I-12; II-7
   routines II-27
memory organization II-19
MemTop global variable II-19, 21, 44
menu I-341
   defining your own I-362
   guidelines I-51
   resource format I-364
   standard menus I-54, 342
menu bar I-341
   resource format I-365
menu definition procedure I-344, 362
menu ID I-344
menu item I-341
   blinking I-361; II-371
menu item number I-350
menu list I-345
Menu Manager I-12, 339
   routines I-351
menu record I-344
menu title I-341
MenuFlash global variable I-361
MenuHandle data type I-345
MenuHook global variable I-356
MenuInfo data type I-345
MenuKey function I-356
MenuList global variable I-346
MenuPtr data type I-345
MenuSelect function I-355

meta-characters
   AppleTalk Manager II-266, 320
   Menu Manager I-346
MinStack global variable II-17
MinusOne global variable I-85
missing symbol I-152, 220, 230
modal dialog box I-67, 400, 415
ModalDialog procedure I-415
modeless dialog box I-67, 400, 416
modes I-28
modifier flags I-252
modifier keys I-34, 246
   flags in event record I-252
MoreMasters procedure II-31
mounted volume II-79
MountVol function II-103
mouse I-36
   hardware III-25
mouse-down event I-244
   responding to I-255
mouse scaling II-372
mouse-scaling threshold II-372
mouse-up event I-244
   responding to I-255
Move procedure I-170
MoveControl procedure I-325
MoveHHi procedure II-44
MovePortTo procedure I-166
MoveTo procedure I-170
MoveWindow procedure I-289
MPP II-271
MPPClose function II-275
MPPOpen function II-275
Munger function I-468

N

Name-Binding Protocol II-266
   assembly language II-319
   Pascal II-298
name lookup II-266
names directory II-266
names information socket II-266
names table II-266, 321
NBP *See* Name-Binding Protocol
NBP tuple II-266
NBPConfirm function II-301
NBPExtract function II-300
NBPLoad function II-301
NBPLookup function II-300
NBPRegister function II-299
NBPRemove function II-301
NBPUnload function II-301
network event I-244; II-275
network number II-265

network-visible entity II-265
New command I-56
NewControl function I-319
NewDialog function I-412
NewHandle function I-76, 80; II-32
newline character II-84
newline mode II-84
NewMenu function I-351
NewPtr function I-75, 79; II-36
NewRgn function I-181
NewString function I-468
NewWindow function I-282
node II-263
node ID II-263
nonbreaking space I-246
nonrelocatable block I-75; II-10
   allocating II-36
   releasing II-36
NoteAlert function I-420
null event I-245
NumToString procedure I-489

O

ObscureCursor procedure I-168
off-line volume II-80
OffLine function II-106
OffsetPoly procedure I-191
OffsetRect procedure I-174
OffsetRgn procedure I-183
offset/width table I-231
OfsetRgn procedure I-183
OldContent global variable I-296
OldStructure global variable I-296
on-line volume II-80
OneOne global variable I-85
Open command I-56
open device driver II-176
open file II-83
Open function, high-level
   Device Manager II-178
   File Manager II-91
Open function, low-level
   Device Manager II-184
   File Manager II-108
open permission II-83
open routine
   of a desk accessory I-445
   of a driver II-187, 193
OpenATPSkt function II-315
OpenDeskAcc function I-440
OpenDriver function II-178
OpenPicture function I-189
OpenPoly function I-190
OpenPort procedure I-163

OpenResFile function I-115
OpenRF function
  high-level II-91
  low-level II-109
OpenRgn procedure I-181
OpenSkt function II-311
Operating System I-9
  queues II-372
Operating System Event Manager I-13; II-65
  routines II-68
Operating System Utilities I-13; II-367
  routines II-374
OSErr data type II-373
OSEventAvail function II-70
OSType data type II-373
output driver II-246
overrun error *See* hardware overrun error
    or software overrun error
owned resources I-109

P

Pack2 *See* Disk Initialization Package
Pack3 *See* Standard File Package
Pack4 *See* Floating-Point Arithmetic Package
Pack5 *See* Transcendental Functions Package
Pack6 *See* International Utilities Package
Pack7 *See* Binary-Decimal Conversion Package
Package Manager I-12, 481
packages I-12, 483
PackBits procedure I-470
page rectangle II-150
Page Setup command I-57
PaintArc procedure I-180
PaintBehind procedure I-297
PaintOne procedure I-296
PaintOval procedure I-178
PaintPoly procedure I-192
PaintRect procedure I-177
PaintRgn procedure I-186
PaintRoundRect procedure I-179
PaintWhite global variable I-297
palette I-32
pane I-49
panel I-50
paper rectangle II-150
ParamBlkType data type II-98, 181
ParamBlockRec data type II-98, 181
  driver I/O queue entry II-191
  file I/O queue entry II-124
parameter block I-93; II-97, 180
parameter RAM II-369
  default values II-370
  routines II-380
ParamText procedure I-421

parity bit II-245
parity error II-246
ParmBlkPtr data type II-98, 181
part code I-315, 330
path reference number II-83
PatHandle data type I-473
PatPtr data type I-473
pattern I-145, 473
Pattern data type I-146
pattern list I-473
  resource format I-476
pattern transfer mode I-157
PBAllocate function II-113
PBClose function
  Device Manager II-184
  File Manager II-114
PBControl function II-186
PBCreate function II-107
PBDelete function II-119
PBEject function II-107
PBFlushFile function II-114
PBFlushVol function II-105
PBGetEOF function II-112
PBGetFInfo function II-115
PBGetFPos function II-111
PBGetVInfo function II-104
PBGetVol function II-104
PBKillIO function II-187
PBMountVol function II-103
PBOffLine function II-106
PBOpen function
  Device Manager II-184
  File Manager II-108
PBOpenRF function II-109
PBRead function
  Device Manager II-185
  File Manager II-110
PBRename function II-118
PBRstFLock function II-117
PBSetEOF function II-112
PBSetFInfo function II-116
PBSetFLock function II-116
PBSetFPos function II-111
PBSetFVers function II-117
PBSetVol function II-105
PBStatus function II-186
PBUnmountVol function II-106
PBWrite function
  Device Manager II-185
  File Manager II-110
pen characteristics I-150
PenMode procedure I-169
PenNormal procedure I-170
PenPat procedure I-170
PenSize procedure I-169
PenState data type I-169

period of a wave II-223
phase of a wave cycle II-223
physical end-of-file II-81
physical size of a block II-23
PicComment procedure I-189
PicHandle data type I-159
PicPtr data type I-159
picture I-158
   QuickDraw routines I-189
   utility routine I-475
picture comments I-159
Picture data type I-159
picture frame I-158
PinRect function I-293
pixel I-139, 143
PlotIcon procedure I-473
point (coordinate plane) I-139
   routines I-193
point (font size) I-61, 153, 217
Point data type I-139
pointer (to memory) I-75, 78; II-11
   manipulation II-374
   type coercion I-79
pointer (on screen) I-36, 37 See also cursor
polygon I-159
   routines I-190
Polygon data type I-159
PolyHandle data type I-160
PolyPtr data type I-160
portBits of a grafPort I-148
PortBUse global variable II-305
portRect of a grafPort I-149
PortSize procedure I-165
post an event I-243
PostEvent function II-68
PrClose procedure II-157
PrCloseDoc procedure II-160
PrClosePage procedure II-160
PrCtlCall procedure II-163
PrDrvrClose procedure II-163
PrDrvrDCE function II-163
PrDrvrOpen procedure II-163
PrDrvrVers function II-163
PrError function II-161
prime routine of a driver II-187, 193
Print command I-57
print dialogs II-148
print record II-148
PrintDefault procedure II-158
Printer Driver I-13; II-147, 162
printer information subrecord II-150
printer resource file II-147
PrintErr global variable II-161
printing grafPort II-147
Printing Manager I-13; II-145
   routines II-157

printing methods II-153
   low-level II-164
private scraps I-461
PrJobDialog function II-158
PrJobMerge procedure II-159
processor priority II-196
ProcPtr data type I-78
PrOpen procedure II-157
PrOpenDoc function II-159
PrOpenPage procedure II-159
proportional font I-228
protocol II-263
protocol handler II-264
   writing your own II-324, 326
protocol handler table II-264
PrPicFile procedure II-160
PrSetError procedure II-161
PrStlDialog function II-158
PrValidate function II-158
PScrapStuff data type I-457
Pt2Rect procedure I-175
PtInRect function I-175
PtInRgn function I-185
Ptr data type I-78
PtrAndHand function II-376
PtrToHand function II-375
PtrToXHand function II-375
PtrZone function II-38
PtToAngle procedure I-175
purge bit II-25
purge warning procedure II-23
purgeable block I-76; II-10, 41
PurgeMem procedure II-40
purging a block I-76; II-14, 40
PutScrap function I-459

Q

QDProcs data type I-197
QDProcsPtr data type I-197
QElem data type II-373
QElemPtr data type II-373
QHdr data type II-372
QHdrPtr data type II-373
QTypes data type II-373
queue II-373
   drive II-127
   driver I/O II-180, 191
   file I/O II-97, 124
   manipulation II-382
   vertical retrace II-350, 352
   volume-control-block II-125
QuickDraw I-11, 135
   communication with Font Manager I-224
   routines I-162

Inside Macintosh

Quit command I-57

R

radio button I-312, 404
RAM III-17
RAM Serial Driver I-13; II-246
   advanced Control calls II-254
   Device Manager calls II-248
   routines II-249
RAMBase global variable I-87
RAMSDClose procedure II-250
RAMSDOpen function II-249
Random function I-194
random number generator I-194; II-407
randSeed global variable I-163, 194
Read function, high-level
   Device Manager II-178
   File Manager II-92
Read function, low-level
   Device Manager II-185
   File Manager II-110
ReadDateTime function II-378
ReadPacket function II-327
ReadRest function II-327
read/write permission II-83
RealFont function I-223
reallocating a block I-76; II-14
ReallocHandle procedure II-35
RecoverHandle function II-35
Rect data type I-141
rectangle I-140
   routines I-174
RectInRgn function I-185
RectRgn procedure I-183
reference number of a resource file I-105
reference value
   control I-316
   window I-274
region I-141
   routines I-181
Region data type I-142
register-based routines I-90, 93
register-saving conventions I-94
RegisterName function II-322
relative handle II-24
release timer II-270
ReleaseResource procedure I-120
relocatable block I-75; II-10
   allocating II-32
   releasing II-33
RelRspCB function II-319
RelTCB function II-319
RemoveName function II-324

Rename function
   high-level II-96
   low-level II-118
ResErr global variable I-116
ResError function I-116
ResErrProc global variable I-116
ResetAlrtStage procedure I-423
ResLoad global variable I-118
resource I-103
   within a resource I-127
resource attributes I-111
   getting I-121
   setting I-122
resource data I-106
resource file I-105
   attributes I-126
   current I-105, 116
   format I-128
resource fork I-105; II-81
resource header I-128
resource ID I-108
   of fonts I-234
   of owned resources I-109
Resource Manager I-9, 101
   routines I-113
resource map I-106
resource name I-110
resource reference I-110
   format I-130
resource specification I-103, 107
resource type I-103
   list I-107
response BDS II-288, 314
ResrvMem procedure II-39
Restart procedure II-385
RestoreA5 procedure II-386
ResType data type I-107
result code I-116; II-27, 374
   assembly language I-94
   list III-205
resume procedure I-411; II-358
ResumeProc global variable I-411
RetransType data type II-298
retry count II-266
retry interval II-266
Revert to Saved command I-57
RgnHandle data type I-142
RgnPtr data type I-142
RmveResource procedure I-124
RndSeed global variable I-195
ROM III-18
ROM Serial Driver I-13; II-246
   Device Manager calls II-248
   routines II-250
ROMBase global variable I-87; II-383; III-18
ROMFont0 global variable I-233

routine selector I-483
routing table II-265
Routing Table Maintenance Protocol II-265
row width I-143
RsrcZoneInit procedure I-114
RstFilLock function
   high-level II-96
   low-level II-117
RstFLock function II-96
RTMP II-265
RTMP socket II-265
RTMP stub II-265

S

sample program I-13
SANE II-405
Save As command I-57
Save command I-57
SaveOld procedure I-296
SaveUpdate global variable I-297
SaveVisRgn global variable I-293
ScalePt procedure I-195
scaling factors I-218
SCC III-22
SCC interrupts II-198
SCCRd global variable II-199; III-25
SCCWr global variable II-199; III-25
scrap
   between applications I-453
   in TextEdit I-373, 388
scrap file I-453
Scrap Manager I-12, 451
   routines I-457
ScrapCount global variable I-457
ScrapHandle global variable I-457
ScrapName global variable I-457
ScrapSize global variable I-457
ScrapState global variable I-457
ScrapStuff data type I-457
Scratch8 global variable I-85
Scratch20 global variable I-85
ScrDmpEnb global variable I-258
screen buffer III-18, 19
screenBits global variable I-145, 163
ScreenRes procedure I-473
ScrHRes global variable I-473
ScrnBase global variable II-19, 21
scroll bar I-47, 312
   updating I-291
ScrollRect procedure I-187
ScrVRes global variable I-473
SdVolume global variable II-232
Secs2Date procedure II-380
sector II-211

SectRect function I-175
SectRgn procedure I-184
segment II-55
Segment Loader I-12; II-53
   routines II-57
selection range I-375
SelectWindow procedure I-284
SelIText procedure I-422
SendBehind procedure I-286
SendRequest function II-316
SendResponse function II-317
sequence number of a datagram II-266
SerClrBrk function II-253
SerGetBuf function II-253
SerHShake function II-251
serial communication II-245
   hardware III-22
Serial Communications Controller III-22
serial data II-245
Serial Drivers I-13; II-243
   advanced Control calls II-254
   Device Manager calls II-248
   routines II-249
SerReset function II-250
SerSetBrk function II-252
SerSetBuf function II-251
SerShk data type II-252
SerStaRec data type II-253
SerStatus function II-253
SetAppBase procedure II-28
SetApplBase procedure II-28
SetApplLimit procedure II-30
SetClikLoop procedure I-390
SetClip procedure I-166
SetCRefCon procedure I-327
SetCTitle procedure I-321
SetCtlAction procedure I-328
SetCtlMax procedure I-327
SetCtlMin procedure I-326
SetCtlValue procedure I-326
SetCursor procedure I-167
SetDAFont procedure I-412
SetDateTime function II-379
SetDItem procedure I-421
SetEmptyRgn procedure I-183
SetEOF function
   high-level II-93
   low-level II-112
SetEventMask procedure II-70
SetFileInfo function
   high-level II-95
   low-level II-116
SetFilLock function
   high-level II-95
   low-level II-116
SetFilType function II-117

Inside Macintosh

SetFInfo function II-95
SetFLock function II-95
SetFontLock procedure I-223
SetFPos function
  high-level II-93
  low-level II-111
SetGrowZone procedure II-42
SetHandleSize procedure II-34
SetItem procedure I-357
SetItemIcon procedure I-359
SetItemMark procedure I-359
SetItemStyle procedure I-360
SetIText procedure I-422
SetItmIcon procedure I-359
SetItmMark procedure I-359
SetItmStyle procedure I-360
SetMaxCtl procedure I-327
SetMenuBar procedure I-355
SetMenuFlash procedure I-361
SetMFlash procedure I-361
SetMinCtl procedure I-326
SetOrigin procedure I-166
SetPBits procedure I-165
SetPenState procedure I-169
SetPort procedure I-165
SetPortBits procedure I-165
SetPt procedure I-193
SetPtrSize procedure II-37
SetRecRgn procedure I-183
SetRect procedure I-174
SetRectRgn procedure I-183
SetResAttrs procedure I-122
SetResFileAttrs procedure I-127
SetResInfo procedure I-122
SetResLoad procedure I-118
SetResPurge procedure I-126
SetSoundVol procedure II-233
SetStdProcs procedure I-198
SetString procedure I-468
SetTagBuffer function II-214
SetTime procedure II-380
SetTrapAddress procedure II-384
SetUpA5 procedure II-386
SetVol function
  high-level II-89
  low-level II-105
SetWindowPic procedure I-293
SetWordBreak procedure I-390
SetWRefCon procedure I-293
SetWTitle procedure I-284
SetZone procedure II-31
SEvtEnb global variable I-443
SFGetFile procedure I-523
SFPGetFile procedure I-526
SFPPutFile procedure I-523
SFPutFile procedure I-519

SFReply data type I-519
SFSaveDisk global variable I-519
SFTypeList data type I-523
ShieldCursor procedure I-474
ShowControl procedure I-322
ShowCursor procedure I-168
ShowHide procedure I-285
ShowPen procedure I-168
ShowWindow procedure I-285
signature III-9
SignedByte data type I-78
size
  of parameters I-90
  of variables I-85
size box I-287 *See also* grow region
size correction II-24
Size data type II-18
SizeControl procedure I-326
SizeResource function I-121
SizeRsrc function I-121
SizeWindow procedure I-290
SlopeFromAngle function I-475
socket II-265
socket client II-265
socket listener II-265
  writing your own II-324, 329
socket number II-265
socket table II-265
software overrun error II-246
sound buffer II-233; III-18, 21
Sound Driver I-13; II-221
  hardware II-233
  routines II-231
sound generator II-223; III-20
sound procedure I-409, 411, 425
SoundBase global variable III-21
SoundDone function II-232
SoundLevel global variable II-234
SoundPtr global variable II-227
source transfer mode I-157
space state II-246
SpaceExtra procedure I-172
SPAlarm global variable *See* parameter RAM
SPATalkA global variable *See* parameter RAM
SPATalkB global variable *See* parameter RAM
SPClikCaret global variable *See* parameter RAM
SPConfig global variable II-305
speaker volume II-232, 371
SPFont global variable *See* parameter RAM
SPKbd global variable *See* parameter RAM
split bar I-49
SPMisc2 global variable *See* parameter RAM
spool printing II-151, 153
SPortSel data type II-249
SPPortA global variable *See* parameter RAM
SPPortB global variable *See* parameter RAM

SPPrint global variable *See* parameter RAM
SPValid global variable *See* parameter RAM
SPVolCtl global variable *See* parameter RAM
square-wave synthesizer II-223, 225
stack I-73; II-17
stack-based routines I-90
stack frame I-96; II-17
StageList data type I-424
stages of an alert I-409
Standard File Package I-12, 515
   routines I-519
start bit II-245
StartSound procedure II-231
Stash function II-195
Status function
   high-level II-179
   low-level II-186
status information II-176
status routine of a driver II-187, 194
StdArc procedure I-199
StdBits procedure I-199
StdComment procedure I-199
StdGetPic procedure I-200
StdLine procedure I-198
StdOval procedure I-199
StdPoly procedure I-199
StdPutPic procedure I-200
StdRect procedure I-198
StdRgn procedure I-199
StdRRect procedure I-198
StdText procedure I-198
StdTxMeas function I-199
StillDown function I-259
stop bit II-245
StopAlert function I-419
StopSound procedure II-232
Str32 data type II-298
Str255 data type I-78
string comparison I-501, 506; II-376
string list I-468
   resource format I-476
string manipulation I-468
StringHandle data type I-78
StringPtr data type I-78
StringToNum procedure I-490
StringWidth function I-173
structure region of a window I-271
StuffHex procedure I-195
style *See* character style
Style data type I-152
style dialog II-149
Style menu I-61
StyleItem data type I-152
SubPt procedure I-193
SWSynthPtr data type II-225
SWSynthRec data type II-225

synchronous execution
   AppleTalk Manager II-273
   Device Manager II-180
   File Manager II-97
synthesizer buffer II-225
SysBeep procedure II-385
SysEdit function I-441
SysError procedure II-362
SysEvtMask global variable II-70
SysMap global variable I-114
SysMapHndl global variable I-114
SysParam global variable II-369
SysParmType data type II-370
SysPPtr data type II-370
SysResName global variable I-114
system error alert II-357
system error alert table II-357, 359
System Error Handler I-13; II-18, 355
   routine II-362
system error ID II-357
system event mask I-254; II-70
system font I-219
system font size I-219
system heap I-74; II-9
system resource I-103
system resource file I-103
system startup information II-120
system traps III-215
system window I-270, 438
SystemClick procedure I-441
SystemEdit function I-441
SystemEvent function I-442
SystemMenu procedure I-443
SystemTask procedure I-442, 444; II-189
SystemZone function II-32
SysZone global variable II-19, 21, 32

T

tag byte II-24
TEActivate procedure I-385
TECalText procedure I-390
TEClick procedure I-384
TECopy procedure I-386
TECut procedure I-385
TEDeactivate procedure I-385
TEDelete procedure I-387
TEDispose procedure I-383
TEDoText global variable I-391
TEFromScrap function I-389
TEGetScrapLen function I-389
TEGetText function I-384
TEHandle data type I-374
TEIdle procedure I-384
TEInit procedure I-383

Inside Macintosh

TEInsert procedure I-387
TEKey procedure I-385
TENew function I-383
TEPaste procedure I-386
TEPtr data type I-374
TERec data type I-377
TERecal global variable I-391
TEScrapHandle function I-389
TEScroll procedure I-388
TEScrpHandle global variable I-389
TEScrpLength global variable I-389
TESetJust procedure I-387
TESetScrapLen procedure I-390
TESetSelect procedure I-385
TESetText procedure I-383
TestControl function I-325
TEToScrap function I-389
TEUpdate procedure I-387
text characteristics I-151
text in a dialog/alert I-404, 408
text streaming II-165
TextBox procedure I-388
TextEdit I-12, 371
   routines I-383
   scrap I-373, 388
TextFace procedure I-171
TextFont procedure I-171
TextMode procedure I-171
TextSize procedure I-171
TextWidth function I-173
TheMenu global variable I-357
thePort global variable I-162, 165
TheZone global variable II-31
thousands separator I-497
THPrint data type II-149
thumb I-312
THz data type II-22
tick I-246
TickCount function I-260
Ticks global variable I-260; II-198
Time global variable II-198, 369, 378
time operations II-377
ToExtFS global variable II-128
toggled command I-53, 357
Tone data type II-225
Tones data type II-225
Toolbox I-9
Toolbox Event Manager I-11, 241
   routines I-257
Toolbox Utilities I-12, 465
   routines I-467
ToolScratch global variable I-85
TopMapHndl global variable I-115
TopMem function II-44
TPPrint data type II-149
TPPrPort data type II-147

TPrInfo data type II-150
TPrint data type II-149
TPrJob data type II-151
TPrPort data type II-147
TPrStatus data type II-161
TPrSt1 data type II-152
TPrXInfo data type II-152
track on a disk II-211
TrackControl function I-323
TrackGoAway function I-288
transaction II-266
transaction ID II-266
transaction release II-270
transaction request II-266
transaction response II-266
Transcendental Functions Package I-13; II-403, 407
transfer mode I-156
trap dispatch table I-87
   routines II-383
trap dispatcher I-89
trap macro I-88, 90
   list III-215
trap number I-89, 384
trap word I-88
TRel *See* transaction release
TReq *See* transaction request
TResp *See* transaction response
trigonometric functions II-407
type coercion I-79
type size *See* font size

U

Undo command I-59
unimplemented instruction I-88
UnionRect procedure I-175
UnionRgn procedure I-184
UniqueID function I-121
unit number II-191
unit table II-191
UnloadNBP function II-324
UnloadScrap function I-458
UnloadSeg procedure II-59
unlocked block I-76; II-10
unlocking a block I-76; II-41
UnlodeScrap function I-458
unmounted volume II-79
UnmountVol function
   high-level II-90
   low-level II-106
UnpackBits procedure I-470
unpurgeable block I-76; II-10, 42
update event I-244, 278
   event message I-252

update region of a window I-272
   maintenance I-291
UpdateResFile procedure I-125
UprString procedure II-377
use type II-305
user bytes II-266
user interface guidelines I-23
User Interface Toolbox I-9
UseResFile procedure I-117
userItem in a dialog I-404, 405
   installing I-421
UTableBase global variable II-192
Utilities, Operating System I-13; II-307
   routines II-374
Utilities, Toolbox I-12, 465
   routines I-467

V

validity status II-370
ValidRect procedure I-292
ValidRgn procedure I-292
variation code
   control I-328
   window I-298
VBL interrupt *See* vertical blanking interrupt
VBL task II-350
VBLQueue global variable II-352
VBLTask data type II-350
VCB data type II-125
VCBQHdr global variable II-126
vector II-196
vector table II-196
Versatile Interface Adapter III-39
version data III-10
version number of a file II-81
vertical blanking interrupt II-349; III-18
vertical blanking interval III-18
vertical retrace interrupt I-13; II-349
Vertical Retrace Manager I-13; II-347
   routines II-351
vertical retrace queue II-350, 352
VHSelect data type I-139
VIA III-39
VIA global variable I-198; III-39
VIA interrupts II-197; III-38, 41
video interface III-18
view rectangle I-374
VInstall function II-351
visible
   control I-316
   window I-274
visRgn of a grafPort I-149
volume (on a disk) II-79
volume (speaker) II-232, 371

volume allocation block map II-122
volume attributes II-121
volume buffer II-79
volume control block II-125
volume-control-block queue II-125
volume index II-102
volume information II-121
volume name II-79
volume reference number II-79
VRemove function II-351

W

WaitMouseUp function I-259
Wave data type II-227
waveform II-223
waveform description II-224
wavelength II-223
WavePtr data type II-227
white global variable I-162
window I-44, 269
   closing I-45, 283
   defining your own I-297
   moving I-46, 289
   opening I-45, 282
   resource format I-302
   sizing I-47, 289
   splitting I-49
window class I-274, 276
window definition function I-272, 298
window definition ID I-273, 298
window frame I-271
window list I-274, 277
Window Manager I-11, 267
   routines I-281
Window Manager port I-271, 282
window pointer I-275
window record I-274, 276
window template I-274
   resource format I-302
WindowList global variable I-255, 277
WindowPeek data type I-275
WindowPtr data type I-275
WindowRecord data type I-276
WMgrPort global variable I-282
word I-42
   in TextEdit I-373
word break routine I-380
word wraparound I-373
write data structure II-306
Write function, high-level
   Device Manager II-179
   File Manager II-92

Write function, low-level
   Device Manager II-185
   File Manager II-110
WriteDDP function II-312
WriteLAP function II-307
WriteParam function II-382
WriteResource procedure I-125

X

XorRgn procedure I-185

Y

Z

ZeroScrap function I-458
zone
   AppleTalk Manager II-266
   Memory Manager *See* heap zone
Zone data type II-22
zone header II-22
zone pointer II-22
zone record II-22
zone trailer II-22